WOMEN AND THE LAW
IN THE ROMAN EMPIRE

It is widely recognized that Roman law is an important source of information about women in the Roman world, and can present a more rounded and accurate picture than literary sources.

This sourcebook exploits fully the rich legal material of the imperial period – from Augustus (31 BCE–14 CE) to the end of the western Roman Empire (476 CE), incorporating both pagan and Christian eras, and explaining the rights women held under Roman law, the restrictions to which they were subject, and legal regulations on marriage, divorce and widowhood.

The main focus is on the major legal texts (the *Digest*, the *Institutes* of Gaius, the *Code of Justinian*, the *Theodosian Code*), but a significant number of non-legal documentary sources are included. These are particularly important as they illustrate how the law worked in practice, and how this practice (particularly in the provinces) could differ from the letter of the law.

Accessible English translations are enhanced by clear, concise background material, which includes useful explanation of historical and geographical context, and a helpful glossary of Roman legal and administrative terms adds to the volume. Comprehensive and user-friendly, this will be a core text for students and an essential reference guide for more advanced scholars.

Judith Evans Grubbs is Professor of Classical Studies at Sweet Briar College, where she has taught since 1987. She is also the author of *Law and Family in Late Antiquity: The Emperor Constantine's Legislation on Marriage* (1995), and articles on women and the family in imperial Roman law.

WOMEN AND THE LAW IN THE ROMAN EMPIRE

A sourcebook on marriage, divorce
and widowhood

Judith Evans Grubbs

London and New York

First published 2002
by Routledge
11 New Fetter Lane, London EC4P 4EE

Simultaneously published in the USA and Canada
by Routledge
29 West 35th Street, New York, NY 10001

Routledge is an imprint of the Taylor & Francis Group

Typeset in Garamond by Taylor & Francis Books Ltd
Printed and bound in Great Britain by MPG Books Ltd, Bodmin

British Library Cataloguing in Publication Data
A catalogue record for this book is available from the British Library

Library of Congress Cataloging in Publication Data
A catalog record for this book has been requested

ISBN 0–415–15240–2 (hbk)
ISBN 0–415–15241–0 (pbk)

CONTENTS

CONTENTS

CONTENTS

PREFACE

A sourcebook on women and the law in the Roman Empire: marriage, divorce, and widowhood

"In many parts of our law the condition of women is below that of men," stated the third-century legal writer Papinian (D.1.5.9). Examination of the sources for Roman law under the Empire bears out the basic truth of his statement, while also revealing that women in the Roman classical period enjoyed greater property rights and freedom to divorce than did their American and European counterparts before the twentieth century.

This book presents, in English translation, sources from the Roman imperial period which illustrate the rights women held under Roman law, the restrictions to which they were subject, and legal regulations on marriage, divorce, and widowhood. It is intended as an aid for the study of women in antiquity, Roman imperial law, and Roman social history in general. It is what is known as a "sourcebook," a collection of ancient sources translated from the original languages with introductory material and commentary. *Women and the Law in the Roman Empire* covers the Roman imperial period, from the reign of the first emperor Augustus (31 B.C.E.–14 C.E.) to the end of the Roman Empire in the west (476 C.E.). It draws heavily on the major legal texts (the *Digest*, the *Institutes* of Gaius, the *Code of Justinian*, and the *Theodosian Code*, all written in Latin, the language of Roman jurists), and also on non-legal documentary sources in Greek and Latin that illustrate women's interaction with Roman imperial law.

Today it is widely recognized that Roman legal and documentary sources are an important source of information about women in the Roman world, and can present a more well-rounded and accurate picture of women's lives than classical literature, which is often tendentious and bound by the conventions of genre. Much of this rich source material is still unexploited, however; sometimes it is not even available in a reliable or accessible English translation. Many books on "women in antiquity" either ignore the legal sources or present them sketchily and inaccurately, providing little in the way of context. On the other hand, the work now being done on the Roman family makes extensive use of classical Roman law, but in general focuses on the city of Rome, or at most, the elite classes of Italy and the Latin-speaking western Empire. Moreover, the law of the *later* Roman Empire (284–476

xi

C.E.) has only recently begun to receive attention even from scholars of the Roman family, who concentrate on the "classical" period of Roman law and culture – the first century B.C.E. to the early third century C.E.

Several different types of sources appear in this book. Most important, of course, are the Roman legal sources that lay out the norms and regulations of the law: in particular, for the classical period, the *Digest* and the *Institutes* of Gaius, and for the later period, the *Theodosian Code*. The nature and limitations of these sources are discussed in Part I of the Introduction. Also included are documents illustrating how these regulations worked in "real life" and how actual practice, particularly in the provinces, differed from the norms of Roman law. These "documentary" sources comprise documents written on papyrus, a paper-like material made from the stalk of the papyrus reed plant, and documents inscribed on stone or bronze. Unlike the legal sources, which have been transmitted to us (albeit in incomplete form) via the manuscript tradition, documentary papyri and inscriptions were found in the ground, either in proper excavations or in a more haphazard way. Of these, the papyri are almost all written in Greek, and almost all found in Egypt; a few are in Latin (generally for those few Roman citizens living in Egypt before 212), and a few were discovered elsewhere in the Middle East, for instance the Babatha archive in the "Cave of Letters" on the Dead Sea (see Chapter 5, Part II.B.2), or documents from the Roman outpost of Dura Europus on the Euphrates. Papyri in other languages (Syriac, Coptic, and Aramaic) are not included in this book. Inscriptions on stone or bronze survive in Latin (from Italy or the western provinces) or Greek (from the provinces of the eastern Mediterranean). Most extant inscriptions are either funerary or honorific; those appearing in this sourcebook are included because they illustrate Roman law. A few texts of actual laws are also known from inscriptions, usually on bronze, which have been found in Italy and the provinces. For instance, the Flavian Municipal Law is known from several sites in Spain (see Chapter 1, Part III.A.3).

Also preserved via the manuscript tradition are selections from Latin and Greek literature found in this sourcebook. I include far fewer examples of literary than of the legal or documentary sources, for several reasons. In general, I have included "literary" sources only when they directly mention or illustrate Roman law and its workings in ordinary life. Works of classical literature are in general more likely to be accessible in English translation than are legal or documentary sources, and most of the many books that have already been published on women in antiquity focus on literary sources. I have, however, made an effort to include Christian sources relevant to Roman law because these are usually not included in books devoted to women in antiquity, and are often little known.

Something should be said about the limits I have imposed on this work, in terms of time, space, and topic. My chronological and spatial limits coincide with the traditional historical view of the "Roman Empire" as a political and geographical whole. The time limits are admittedly arbitrary: 31 B.C.E. is the year in which Octavian (the future emperor Augustus) defeated Mark Antony and Cleopatra at the Battle of Actium and thus became the first sole ruler of territory which at that time extended from the Hispanic peninsula in the west to the Euphrates in the east and from France in the north to the Sahara in the south. The Empire at its height in the second century included even more territory, having added Britain and lands west of the Rhine and south of the Danube (as well as modern Rumania, north of the Danube). By the mid-fifth century parts of the western Empire in Europe and North Africa had fallen under the control of Germanic peoples, and in 476 the last Roman emperor in the west, Romulus Augustulus, was deposed. At that point the Roman Empire as we think of it today can be said to have ended, although the Byzantine Empire continued in the eastern Mediterranean for another millenium, and Roman law continued to shape the legal traditions of east and (for a time) west.

These time limits are not hard and fast: even before 31 B.C.E., Roman power extended over almost the same amount of territory, and the accession of Octavian/Augustus did not have immediate consequences for the legal systems of regions where few of the inhabitants were Roman citizens, and which continued by and large to follow their local law and custom until (and indeed, in many respects, even after) the grant of universal citizenship by the emperor Caracalla in 212. Moreover, already in the fourth century, the administration of the Empire was devolving into eastern and western halves, with two imperial capitals (Rome and Constantinople), each with their own Senate, and usually at least two reigning emperors with their own legal staffs. However, the publication of the *Theodosian Code* in 438 (see Part I.B of the Introduction) did bring legal unity to east and west, albeit very briefly. In 476, the promulgation of post-Theodosian "new" Roman laws (*novellae*) in the west ended, and although the new Germanic nations did use Roman law for their Roman inhabitants, and were influenced by Roman legislation in their own law-making, I believe a case can be made for ending a treatment of "Roman imperial law" in 476. Nevertheless, it must be recognized that Roman law, and Roman administration, did continue, *mutatis mutandis*, in the "Byzantine" (our word, not theirs) eastern Empire for centuries. Indeed, our knowledge of "classical" Roman law is almost entirely dependent on the project of the sixth-century Roman/Byzantine emperor Justinian, which resulted in the publication of the *Digest*, the Justinianic *Code*, and the *Institutes* of Justinian (see Part I.A. of the Introduction).

My self-imposed chronological limits do mean that two voluminous and extremely valuable sources of Roman law are omitted: at the one end, the many speeches of the late Republican orator and statesman Cicero, at the other end, the original legislation of Justinian promulgated in his *"novellae."* Considerations of space, and, in particular, the limitations of my own expertise, have necessitated this.

I hope that this sourcebook will serve as a complement and companion to the works of Jane Gardner and Antti Arjava, who have provided clear and thorough accounts of the position of women in Roman law of the classical and late antique period respectively. Their books are narratives which include excerpts from ancient sources to illustrate specific points. This book, on the other hand, centers on the ancient sources themselves, providing extended translations of examples from the sources for the topics they discuss. It is certainly not the first "sourcebook" on women and family life in the Roman Empire; the past twenty years have seen many books that collect and translate ancient sources focusing on women, beginning with Mary Lefkowitz and Maureen Fant's *Women's Life in Greece and Rome* (first published in 1982, with a second edition ten years later), and including also Jane Gardner and Thomas Wiedemann's sourcebook on *The Roman Household* in 1991. More recently, there is the excellent collection of texts (mostly from papyri) on *Women and Society in Greek and Roman Egypt*, edited by Jane Rowlandson and published in 1998. All of these books include selections from legal sources, and there is inevitably some overlap between them and this sourcebook. The difference is that my book focuses on the legal evidence, and restricts its coverage to the Roman imperial period. I have also tried to include texts which have been published within the past fifteen years (such as documents from the Babatha archive or the *lex Irnitana* from Spain) or which are from regions of the Empire outside Italy or Egypt, and which therefore have not received as much attention in previous source-books. Although I have tried not to duplicate selections found in earlier books, in some cases the material is so important or so unique that it had to be included. Needless to say, I have greatly benefited from these and other sourcebooks as models of an ever-growing genre.

This book is intended primarily for students and teachers (undergraduate and graduate) in the fields of women's studies, classics, ancient and medieval history, and history of the family. There will be much less here for specialists in Roman law, who will already be familiar with most of the material covered, and will find the commentary rather over-simplified. My focus in this book is on the sources, and I do not attempt to provide thorough analysis or detailed legal and historical context; however, the footnotes contain details which may be of interest to some. I have also (with a few important exceptions) restricted bibliographic items to those written in English, particularly during the last twenty years, although there is a voluminous bibliography of works on Roman law and on women in the Empire published in European languages. For more detailed coverage, readers should go to the fine works of Gardner and Arjava, as well as the many other scholars who are cited in the notes and bibliography.

ABBREVIATIONS

Legal texts

Cod. Just.   *Corpus Iuris Civilis, ii. Codex Iustinianus*, ed. P. Krueger (Zurich: Weidmann, 14th edn., 1967)

Cod. Theod.   *Theodosiani Libri XVI cum Constitutionibus Sirmondianis et Leges Novellae ad Theodosianum Pertinentes*, ed. Th. Mommsen and P. Meyer (Berlin: Weidmann, 1904)

D.   *The Digest of Justinian*, Latin text, ed. Th. Mommsen (Berlin: Weidmann, 1868); repr. with English trans., ed. A. Watson (Philadelphia: University of Pennsylvania Press, 1985)

FIRA   *Fontes Iuris Romani Antejustiniani* (Florence: Barbera, 2nd edn); *I. Leges*, ed. S. Riccobono (1968); *II. Auctores*, ed. J. Baviera (1968); *III. Negotia*, ed. V. Arangio-Ruiz (1969)

Frag. Vat.   *Fragmenta Vaticana*, in *FIRA* II, 463–540

Rules of Ulpian   *Regulae Ulpiani* (*Tituli ex corpore Ulpiani*), in *FIRA* II, 261–301

Sent. Pauli   *Sententiae Pauli*, in *FIRA* II, 319–417

Epigraphic and papyrological collections

BL   *Berichtigungsliste der Griechischen Papyruskunden aus Aegypten*

CIL   *Corpus Inscriptionum Latinarum*, ed. Th. Mommsen

CPL   *Corpus Papyrorum Latinarum*, ed. R. Cavenaile (Wiesbaden, 1958)

ILS   *Inscriptiones Latinae Selectae*, ed. H. Dessau (Berlin, 1892)

M.Chr.   *Grundzüge und Chrestomathie der Papyruskunde II. Juristischer Teil*, L. Mitteis and U. Wilcken, (Leipzig and Berlin, 1912)

P.Oxy.   *The Oxyrhynchus Papyri*, Egypt Exploration Society (London)

SB   *Sammelbuch Griechischer Urkunden aus Aegypten*

Complete references for the abbreviations of papyrus collections not listed here can be found in the *Checklist of Editions of Greek and Latin Papyri, Ostraca and Tablets*, ed. J.F. Oates, W.H.Willis, R.S Bagnall, and K.S. Worp (BASP Supplement, 4th edn., 1992), on-line at http://scriptorium.lib.duke.edu/papyrus/texts/clist.html

Journal abbreviations:

BASP	*Bulletin of the American Society of Papyrologists*
EMC/CV	*Echoes du Monde Classique/Classical Views*
JRS	*Journal of Roman Studies*
PBSR	*Papers of the British School at Rome*
RHDFE	*Revue historique de droit françois et étranger*
RIDA	*Revue internationale des droits de l'antiquité*
TAPA	*Transactions of the American Philological Association*
ZPE	*Zeitschrift für Papyrologie und Epigraphik*
ZSSRRA	*Zeitschrift der Savigny-Stiftung für Rechtsgeschichte. Romanistische Abteilung*

GLOSSARY OF LATIN
LEGAL TERMS

arrhae sponsaliciae   in late antiquity, sureties exchanged by a betrothed couple to ensure that the marriage took place [see Chapter 2, II.C].

bona materna   "maternal goods," property inherited by children from their mother.

bonorum possessio   possession obtained by succeeding to a deceased person's property.

calumnia   vexatious prosecution or the bringing of a false charge.

clarissima femina   "most splendid woman," a title indicating senatorial status [see Introduction, Part II and Chapter 1, VI.A].

coemptio   a mock sale of herself by means of *mancipatio* that a woman had to undergo before entering a *manus*-marriage or before making a will [see Chapter 1, II.B].

concubinatus   a non-legal but long-term sexual relationship, usually between an unmarried man and a woman of lower status with whom *iustum matrimonium* was either legally impossible or socially inappropriate [see Chapter 3, I.B.5].

contubernium   a quasi-marital union, entered into by those who were unable to make a legal marriage, particularly slaves [see Chapter 3, I.B].

conubium   the legal ability to enter into legitimate marriage (*iustum matrimonium*)

curator minorum   "caretaker of minors," who assisted fatherless young men and women under twenty-five but over the age of puberty, replacing the *tutor impuberum*, the guardian of children below puberty.

dikaion teknon   the Greek term for the *ius liberorum*.

donatio ante nuptias   pre-nuptial gifts [see Chapter 2, II.C].

Edictum Perpetuum   the Praetor's Edict, published at the beginning of his year in office by the urban praetor of Rome, in which he stated what legal remedies he would make available for particular situations. Under Hadrian, the Praetor's Edict was put into a fixed form.

epitropos (1) the Greek name for a guardian of fatherless minors [see Chapter 5, II.B.1]; (2) the word used in Judaea and Arabia to describe a woman's guardian, elsewhere called *kyrios* [see Chapter 1, III.C].

equites "equestrians," a man of high rank, below senators but above other *honestiores* [see Introduction, Part II].

familia "household" or "family;" the word has several connotations, but generally denotes all members of a household under the power of a *paterfamilias*, including slaves [see Chapter 1, I.B].

filiafamilias (masc. *filiusfamilias*) "daughter (son) of a family;" a child who was under the power of a *paterfamilias*. Even adult children were *filiifamilias* unless they had been emancipated from *patria potestas*.

honestiores the "more honorable;" men and women of higher status, who could expect better treatment under the law [see Introduction, Part II].

humiliores the "more lowly;" men and women of low status, who could expect harsher penalties and treatment under the law [see Introduction, Part II].

infamia legal infamy, a state which carried certain legal disabilities such as the inability to represent someone else in court or to appoint a legal representative for oneself, or to be a witness in court. *Infamia* was a penalty for a number of offenses under Roman law. Practitioners of certain professions considered particularly shameful (prostitution, pimping, appearing as a gladiator) were also *infames* (infamous).

ingenua (masc. *ingenuus*) freeborn, i.e., born to a free mother.

iniuria "outrage" or "insult" against another person, punishable by law.

iudicium publicum trial by jury, in particular a trial held before one of the permanent jury courts (*quaestiones perpetuae*) which dealt with the crimes of adultery, forgery, murder, violence, and treason.

ius (trium) liberorum "right of (three) children," granted by the Augustan marriage laws to women who had borne three children; it enabled them to conduct their legal affairs without a *tutor mulierum* [see Chapter One, III.D].

ius vitae necisque "right of life and death" which legally a *paterfamilias* wielded over his direct descendants [see Chapter 1, II.A].

iustum matrimonium legal marriage, marriage made in accordance with Roman law. Also called *iustae nuptiae* [see Chapter 2, I.A].

kyrios the name for a woman's guardian in some Greek-speaking parts of the Empire, analogous to the Roman *tutor mulierum* [see Chapter 1, III.C].

lex Aelia Sentia "Aelian–Sentian law," enacted in 4 C.E., said that slaves could not be legally freed until they were at least 30 years of age and that slaveowners had to be at least 20 to manumit their slaves [see Introduction, Part II].

lex generalis   "general law;" in the late Empire, refers to legislation which applied to all subjects throughout the Empire [see Introduction, I.B].

lex Julia de adulteriis   "Julian law on adulteries," part of the marriage legislation of Augustus enacted in 18 B.C.E. [see Chapter 2, I.B]

lex Julia de maritandis ordinibus   "Julian law on the marriages of the social orders," enacted by Augustus in 18 B.C.E. [see Chapter 2, I.B].

lex Julia et Titia   "Julian and Titian law" enacted in the first century B.C.E., which gave provincial governors the right to appoint guardians.

libellus   petition directed to the emperor or a provincial or local official.

liberta (masc. *libertus*): a former slave.

mancipatio   an ancient way of conveying property in which the seller transferred ownership to the buyer "by means of bronze and scales" (*per aes et librum*) in the presence of five witnesses.

manus   literally, "hand," the legal authority a husband had over his wife in early Roman society. *Manus*-marriage was virtually obsolete by the time of Augustus [see Chapter 1, II.B].

munera   "duties" owed by men and women of wealthy families to their communities, usually involving expenditure on public works or entertainment [see Chapter 1, VI.C].

nomen   the Roman family name. Children born in legitimate marriage took their father's *nomen*; *libertae* and *liberti* took their patron's *nomen*. (Married women retained their father's *nomen*.)

parapherna   Greek word meaning "things in addition to the dowry," items a bride brought to a marriage in addition to her dowry.

paterfamilas   "father of the family," the oldest male ascendant who had *patria potestas* over all his male and female children and his sons' children.

patria potestas   "paternal power," the legal authority a *paterfamilias* had over all his children and sons' children, including ownership of any property they held and the *ius vitae necisque* [Chapter 1, II.A].

patronus (fem. *patrona*)   (1) the former owner of a freed slave (*libertalus*), who had certain rights over the property and activities of his or her *libertalus*; (2) the patron of a town or *collegium*, who was expected to provide financial and political support.

peculium   the "allowance" given by a *paterfamilias* to those under his *potestas*, particularly sons (but sometimes also daughters) and slaves.

peregrina (masc. *peregrinus*)   a foreigner; someone who does not have Roman citizenship.

postulare   to make a legal request, that is, to ask the praetor or other magistrate to appoint a judge to hear one's case (in civil law) or to accept an accusation (in criminal law).

procurator   representative appointed by a woman (or man) to represent her (or him) in court or in business dealings.

publicum iudicium see *iudicium publicum* above.

pupilla (masc. *pupillus*) a minor (for girls, under age twelve, for boys, under fourteen) whose *paterfamilias* was dead; they needed the assistance of a *tutor impuberum* [see Chapter 1, II.C and Chapter 5, II.A].

querela inofficiosi testamenti "complaint of undutiful will," which could be brought against a will by a legitimate child who had been left less than one-fourth (or less than his or her share of one-fourth, if there was more than one child) of a parent's property by will.

repudium notice of divorce sent by one spouse to the other [see Chapter 4].

res mancipi certain kinds of property whose ownership had to be transferred by the form of sale called *mancipatio*, including certain animals, urban and rural estates in Italy, and slaves [see Chapter 1, III.A–B].

rescriptum (pl. *rescripta*) imperial response to a petition from a private subject (*subscriptio*) or from an imperial official; a rescript.

senatusconsultum (pl. *senatusconsulta*): a decree of the Roman Senate.

senatusconsultum Claudianum (1) senatorial decree of 49 C.E. legalizing marriage between a man and his brother's daughter [see Chapter 3, I.A.2]; (2) senatorial decree of 52 C.E. penalizing unions between a free woman and someone else's slave [see Chapter 3, I.B.2].

senatusconsultum Plancianum senatorial decree passed in the early second century to regulate cases where a divorced woman claimed to be pregnant by her ex-husband [see Chapter 4, I.E.2].

senatusconsultum Tertullianum senatorial decree passed under Hadrian, which granted a woman with the *ius liberorum* the right to inherit from her children who died intestate (i.e. without a will).

senatusconsultum Velleianum decree of the mid-first century C.E. which discouraged women from guaranteeing the debts of others and said that such a guarantee would not be enforceable in court [Chapter 1, IV.D].

stipulatio an oral contract, binding in Roman law, in which the stipulating party requested a verbal promise from the other party.

stuprum illicit sex, punishable under the *lex Julia de adulteriis*. This included adultery (sexual relations between a married woman and someone other than her husband), as well as sexual relations with an unmarried woman or virgin of respectable status.

subscriptio (pl. *subscriptiones*) the emperor's reply to a petition from a private subject, so called because the emperor would write *"subscripsi"* ("I have subscribed") in his response below the original petition.

sui heredes a person's heirs if he or she died intestate (i.e. without a will). All a *paterfamilias'* children, male or female, were *sui heredes*, unless he had emancipated them from *patria potestas*.

sui iuris legally independent. Women (and men) whose *paterfamilias* was dead were *sui iuris*, and could own and inherit property in their own right.

tutela   guardianship. This could either be *tutela impuberum* (guardian-ship of a fatherless minor) or *tutela mulierum* (guardianship of a woman).

tutor impuberum   the guardian of a fatherless minor (*pupilla/us*), who would be responsible for administering the minor's property until he or she reached puberty (considered to be twelve for girls, fourteen for boys).

tutor legitimus   a guardian who was the closest male agnate (relative on the father's side), often a paternal uncle. If the person (woman or *pupillus*) whose tutor he was died without a will, he would stand to inherit, and therefore had a vested interest in the guardianship [Chapter 1, III.A.1].

tutor mulierum   the guardian of a woman over twelve whose *paterfa-milias* was dead; she needed his authorization in order to carry out certain legal and business activities [see Chapter 1, Part III].

Administrative offices

boule   Greek name for the town council (*curia* in Latin).

curia   the local town council, on which *decurions* (*curiales*, pl.) served.

decurion   town councilor, member of the *honestiores* (s.v. above); in late antiquity known as *curialis*.

epistrategos   regional magistrate in Roman Egypt, representing a level of authority between the *strategos* and the prefect.

exegetes   municipal official in Roman Egypt.

praetor   in the Republic and early Empire, the Roman magistrate respon-sible for administering justice in Rome. At the beginning of his year in office, he published an edict setting out what legal remedies he would offer (s.v. above, *Edictum Perpetuum*).

praetorian prefect   in the late Empire, the most important imperial offi-cial (besides the emperor), responsible for publishing and enforcing the emperors' laws and for receiving petitions and hearing legal cases. There were four praetorian prefects, one for Gaul, one for Italy, one for Illyricum, and one for the Orient (east).

prefect (of Egypt)   the governor of the province of Egypt, of equestrian rank.

prefect (of the city)   in the late Empire, there were two urban prefects, one in Rome and one in Constantinople. They were responsible for criminal justice and maintaining law and order in the city.

quaestor   in the late Empire, the official responsible for drafting the laws

strategos   magistrate in the province of Egypt, with authority over a *nome* (district).

vir clarissimus (v.c.)   "most splendid man," indicating a man of senatorial status. The feminine equivalent was *clarissima femina* (c.f.)

Monetary units

denarius   a Roman silver coin, worth four sesterces.

drachma   the standard unit of currency in Roman Egypt, equivalent to one sestertius.

sestertius (pl. *sestertii*)   "sesterce," a silver coin, the standard unit of currency in much of the Empire. Senators were required to have a net worth of 1,000,000 sesterces; equestrians had to have a net worth of 400,000 sesterces.

ACKNOWLEDGEMENTS

This book has been more than five years in the making, and has been helped along by many individuals and institutions. The idea for a sourcebook on women and the law in the Roman Empire first occurred to me while I was a Jessie Ball Dupont Fellow at the National Humanities Center in 1993–4, completing my book on Constantine's marriage legislation and beginning a project on the rescripts in the *Code of Justinian*. Though I was then working on quite different projects, the work I did at the NHC certainly contributed to the completion of this book. I am especially grateful to the National Endowment for the Humanities, for its generosity granting me a Fellowship for College Teachers, which made it possible for me to take a leave from teaching in fall 1997 to work on this sourcebook. Finally, a sabbatical leave in 2000 provided by Sweet Briar College enabled me to complete a draft of almost all of the book.

This book includes not only selections from Roman law, but also from epigraphical and papyrological sources, areas of classical studies in which I have little expertise and experience. Fortunately I was able to take a few steps toward remedying these deficiencies by attending two summer programs. The first was an NEH Summer Seminar held in 1995 at the American Academy in Rome on "Death and Commemoration in ancient Rome" led by John Bodel and Richard Saller, and the second was the International Summer School in Papyrology held at Christ Church College, Oxford in July 1997, under the direction of Dirk Obbink. I would like to express my appreciation to the NEH and to Sweet Briar College's Faculty Grants Committee for making my participation in these programs possible.

Most importantly, I have benefited from the advice and suggestions of colleagues who read various pieces of this book in draft, answered my queries, and corrected errors in my interpretation of the sources. My greatest debt is to Antti Arjava and Susan Treggiari, who both read multiple drafts of all the chapters, and helped me to narrow the focus and refine the organization of the whole book. Tolly Boatwright read a very early draft of Chapter 1, and offered her considerable expertise in matters epigraphical. Tom

McGinn read the final draft of the Introduction and Chapter 1; his knowledge and understanding of Roman law are truly amazing. Ann Hanson read a draft of Chapter 5 and the papyrological selections in Chapters 1, 2, and 4, which she improved immeasurably by her advice and corrections. Needless to say, any errors and misunderstandings that remain (and undoubtedly there are some) are mine alone. Thanks also to Jane Rowlandson, who allowed me to see a pre-publication diskette of the sourcebook she edited, *Women and Society in Greek and Roman Egypt* (Cambridge University Press, 1998), a book which has been extremely helpful to me both for information on women and marriage in Roman Egypt and as a model for this book.

I want also to acknowledge all my Sweet Briar students, past and present, who have read parts of this book as course selections in classes on the Roman Empire, the Roman family, and gender and sexuality in the Roman world. My inspiration for writing this sourcebook arose from teaching, when I realized that there were no reliable translations with commentary on women in Roman law which were available and appropriate for such courses. In particular, I want to express my thanks to the six students who took my Honors Seminar on "Women and the Law in the Roman Empire" in fall 1995: Katherine Carr, Laura Lamb, Laura Myers, Rebecca Moats, Katherine Rinehart, and Laurel Shay. All of these women have long since graduated and gone on to careers outside of classics, but they too contributed to the making of this book.

Finally, I want to thank Richard Stoneman of Routledge and his editorial staff for their patience in waiting for me to complete this book and their promptness (in such contrast to my tardiness!) in bringing it forth. Thanks especially to Catherine Bousfield, Lauren Dallinger, and Carol Baker for all their hard work.

Amherst, Virginia
January 2, 2002

INTRODUCTION
Historical and legal background

I The legal sources

The sources of Roman law include several different kinds of legal text: constitutions of Roman emperors (both general laws and responses to individual cases), and writings of legal experts called jurists. Virtually all the texts found in Roman legal sources were written in Latin, the language of Roman law and administration. The selections in this book cover the period from the reign of Augustus (31 B.C.E.–14 C.E.) to the fall of the last Roman emperor in the western Empire in 476 C.E., spanning in legal terms both the "classical" and "late antique" periods of Roman law. The "classical" period is generally defined as running from the early first century B.C.E. to 235 C.E.; the "late antique" is often seen as extending from the early fourth through the sixth centuries. The last two-thirds of the third century occupy a liminal area, both historically and legally. This period is usually considered the beginning of late antiquity, a time of intense social and political change, but the law of the later third century adhered to classical principles despite a rapid turnover in emperors and almost continual military crises.[1] In distributing the sources in this book, I have therefore included the imperial rescripts of the post-Severan emperors in the sections on "classical" law, and have begun "late antique" source material with the reign of Constantine (307–337).

A The sources of classical law

The most important source for our knowledge of "classical" Roman law is the *Digest* of Justinian, comprising fifty books of selections from the voluminous commentaries of the most influential jurists.[2] The *Digest* was compiled under the sixth-century emperor Justinian (reigned 527–565), much later than the jurists whose work it collects. Justinian instructed his team of legal scholars to read through thousands of pages of classical legal texts and distill them into a much shorter work, preserving only what was still valid and useful (hence the title "*Digest*"). The fifty books of the *Digest* are divided into "titles," denoting the topics treated in the particular book. Within each title is a varying number of excerpts from different juristic works. Justinian's compilers carefully noted which jurist and which work by that jurist were being cited, thus enabling modern scholars to reconstruct (to a limited extent) the content of the original works, which are now lost. Most of the jurists whose works are excerpted in the *Digest* wrote in the second or early third centuries C.E. The most famous and influential was Ulpian, from Phoenicia (Syria), who wrote in the early third century. Other important jurists are Modestinus and Paulus, both also writing in the early third century, and Julian (writing under the emperor Hadrian in the early second century). It should be remembered, however, that the Justinianic compilers took their excerpts out of their original contexts, which were much longer works. The final shape of the *Digest* is due to the sixth-century lawyers, not to the jurists whose works are quoted.[3]

Unlike the emperors and the Senate, jurists were not makers of law, but rather interpreters of it. However, passages from the jurists preserved in the *Digest* often discuss, and sometimes quote verbatim, imperial enactments and also laws passed by the Roman Senate (*senatusconsulta*). Nor were jurists always in agreement with each other on points of law: though most evidence of disagreement among legal authorities was omitted by Justinian's compilers, who were harmonizing and condensing the hundreds of volumes of juristic writings, it is still possible to find evidence for such differences of opinion and interpretation in the *Digest*.

Though the *Digest* is the major source for our knowledge of classical Roman law, a sourcebook of this size and scope can only include a small selection of the entire fifty books. Selections from the *Digest* in this sourcebook are indicated by "D.," followed by the number of the book, title, and number within the title from which the excerpt is taken. After the *Digest* book, title, and selection numbers, in parentheses, is the name of the jurist from whose work the excerpt was taken. Some of the *Digest*'s fifty books are much better represented here than others: for instance, Book 23, which deals exclusively with marriage, is quoted extensively in Chapter 2, Part I.

Other Roman legal texts from the "classical" period have been preserved outside of the *Digest*. The most important is the *Institutes* of Gaius, a handbook dating to the second century C.E. which has survived virtually complete.[4] Gaius' *Institutes* are particularly valuable in providing information about aspects of classical law no longer valid in Justinian's day, which were therefore not included in the Justinianic corpus. For instance, almost all our knowledge of the legal guardianship of women (*tutela mulierum*) derives from Gaius's *Institutes* (see Chapter 1, Part III.A). Later handbooks setting forth the law of the late classical period (the end of the third century C.E.) have also survived: the *Rules of Ulpian* (*Regulae Ulpiani*, also called *Epitome Ulpiani* or *Tituli ex Corpore Ulpiani*), and the "Opinions of Paul" (*Sententiae Pauli*). Though attributed to the third-century jurists Ulpian and Paulus respectively, these handbooks were composed after their lifetimes, in

the early decades of the fourth century. Another interesting legal compilation, also apparently of the fourth century, is the so-called *Vatican Fragments*
(*Fragmenta Vaticana*), which contains excerpts from juristic commentaries as
well as some imperial rescripts.[5]

In addition to the *Digest*, the emperor Justinian was responsible for
compiling another important source for Roman private law of the second
and third centuries C.E., the Codex Justinianus or *Code of Justinian*.[6]
Whereas the *Digest* contains extracts from jurists' commentaries, the *Code*
is a collection of legal enactments by Roman emperors from Hadrian
(reigned 117–138) up to Justinian, under whose auspices the *Code* was
published in 534. Beginning with the reign of Constantine (307–337),
these imperial enactments are usually in the form of general laws, often
edicts or letters addressed to an imperial official and intended to have
general publication and application throughout the Empire. But the legislation of the emperors of the second and third centuries is usually in the
form of rescripts (*subscriptiones,* or more generally, *rescripta*): replies given by
the emperor to petitions from individuals, mostly private subjects, who
had written to the emperor for information or assistance on particular
points of law. Rescripts were probably not the work of the emperors themselves, but were composed by the imperial secretary *a libellis* ("for
petitions") and signed (subscribed) by the emperor. They were posted in a
public place (the forum, or other meeting area) in the city where the
emperor was residing at the time he answered the petition. The petitioner had to make sure that the emperor and his bureau *a libellis* actually
received the petition – not an easy undertaking for ordinary subjects, especially in areas not regularly visited by the emperor – and also to wait for
the reply to be posted and then copy down its contents before returning
home to make use of the information or imperial ruling that the rescript
contained.

Almost all of the approximately 2500 rescripts in the *Code of Justinian*
date between 193 and 305; more than half are from the reign of Diocletian
(282–305). The recipients of imperial rescripts represent a much broader
spectrum of the population of the Roman Empire. About a fifth of all the
rescripts are addressed to women (a quarter for the reign of Diocletian) – a
far greater representation of women than in any literary source of Greco-
Roman antiquity. Many of the people who wrote to the emperors were from
the provinces of the Empire rather than Rome; almost all the rescripts from
Diocletian's reign emanate from the eastern chancellery, and so are addressed
to recipients in Greece or Asia Minor or the Middle East. Unfortunately, the
petitions (called *libelli*) to which the rescripts reply were not preserved, but
their contents can often be inferred from the responses.[7]

Imperial rescripts are cited in this sourcebook to illustrate points of law
known through the jurists, and to show which issues or questions about
Roman law were of particular concern to ordinary women (and men) in the

Empire. Like the *Digest*, the *Code of Justinian* is divided into books (there are only twelve books of the *Code*, however), and titles and numbers within books. Citations from the *Code of Justinian* in this sourcebook appear as "Cod. Just." plus the book number, the title number, and the number of the rescript under that title. Most rescripts are dated, either by date of subscribing by the emperor or date of posting, and I have also included these dates.

B Sources of late Roman law

Very little general legislation (as opposed to rescripts, sent to individuals) of emperors before the fourth century C.E. is actually extant. Even the famous legislation on marriage and adultery of Augustus (see Chapter 2, Part I.B) is known only from snippets in the *Digest* and from Roman historians rather than in its original form. This changes in the late antique period of Roman law. For the period from Constantine onward, we have a much fuller record of emperors' enactments than for the preceding three centuries. Though rescripts continued to be issued to private petitioners, few survive from after the reign of Diocletian. On the other hand, another form of legal enactment becomes much more common: *leges generales* ("general laws"), which applied to all subjects (not just to those individuals to whom rescripts were sent) and were intended for public distribution throughout the Empire. *Leges generales* include both imperial edicts and letters (*epistulae*) sent to government officials, particularly the praetorian prefects, the most important imperial officials after the emperor, who were supposed to relay their contents to their subordinates or to the public.[8]

After the death of the emperor Julian in 363 (the last of the Constantinian dynasty), the Empire was almost always ruled by at least two emperors simultaneously, the essential division being between the Greek-speaking eastern half, whose imperial seat was Constantinople, and the Latin-speaking western half, whose emperor(s) resided in Trier or Milan, or (in the fifth century) Ravenna or Rome. Each emperor would have his own consistory and would make his own laws. In the fourth century, particularly under the emperor Theodosius I, laws made by one emperor would be received by his colleague(s), but after Theodosius' death in 395, the imperial split became more pronounced and emperors did not always accept each other's laws. It is sometimes possible to detect the working out of contrasting policies in east and west, for instance in regard to the situation of illegitimate children (see Chapter 3, Part II.B) or divorce (see Chapter 4, Part II).[9]

The laws of emperors from Constantine to Theodosius II (ruled 408–450) were collected and published in 438 by Theodosius II in the Codex Theodosianus, or *Theodosian Code*.[10] Theodosius' compilers actually did not retain the full text of the laws they were collecting (which were very long), but made excerpts, deleting the rhetorical prefaces and other verbiage, but keeping what they considered the gist of the original laws. We also have the

4

complete texts of many laws enacted after the publication of the *Code*, known as the post-Theodosian *novellae* ("new laws"), up until the fall of the last emperor in the west in 476. For the sixth-century eastern Empire, we have, in addition to his collections of earlier Roman law, many *novellae* of Justinian (which are not included in this sourcebook).

Late Roman legislation may seem totally unlike "classical" law. In part, this is due to a change in the nature of our sources.[11] In what we have preserved of classical law in the *Digest*, the emperor's voice is mediated through the explanations of professional lawyers; in the pre-Constantinian rescripts of the *Code of Justinian*, the emperor (or his secretary for petitions) is responding to concerns and questions from below. In the edicts and general laws of the *Theodosian Code* and post-Theodosian *novellae*, the emperor is addressing his subjects directly and bluntly. Late Roman laws also tended to be verbose (though much of their original wordiness was deleted by the compilers of the Theodosian Code) and were designed to impress, or even to frighten, the emperors' subjects into compliance. The emperors state in no uncertain terms what Roman subjects must do and not do, and threaten horrific punishments for those who disobey. The overall effect of reading late antique laws is to be nearly overwhelmed by a combination of verbal obfuscation and moral exhortation that contrasts sharply with the calm deliberations of the jurists or the short, to-the-point responses of the rescripts.

The wording of late Roman legislation is highly rhetorical, sometimes to the point where it is difficult to know what the emperor (or his *quaestor*, the official who actually drafted the laws) is really saying. Often the laws have to be deconstructed to determine what they mean and what issues or events lie behind them. Furthermore, as public pronouncements of what the emperor stood for and what he desired for his Empire, late antique laws had a strong propaganda purpose. Penalties for criminal offenses (which become a more important aspect of late Roman law than previously) are explicitly stated in the laws, rather than being left to the discretion of individual judges, as they were before. But these often-horrific penalties also serve as propaganda, setting forth the ideals of the ruler, and we should not assume that such penalties were always carried out.

Late Roman law also reflects a change in imperial ideology and administration, from a generally "hands-off" attitude toward the private lives of its subjects, particularly in the provinces, to an emphasis on what we would today call "micromanagement": the number of provinces was greatly increased, the size of provinces correspondingly decreased, and the number of positions in imperial administration for running the empire increased enormously.[12] At the same time, imperial ideology projected the emperor as concerned with the lives and welfare of all his subjects, including those who were not wealthy and influential, and imperial enactments take on a strongly moralistic flavor. This has often been linked with the rise of Christianity (most emperors of this period were Christians), but moralistic fervor is not unique to Christians, as can be seen from Diocletian's edict against close-kin marriage, or in earlier imperial rescripts setting forth Roman *mores*.[13]

Unlike the Justinianic *Code*, which was intended as a working document of current law, and therefore omitted references to laws no longer valid in the sixth century, the *Theodosian Code* was supposed to collect all general laws enacted by legitimate emperors (legislation of rulers later branded "usurpers" was supposed to be omitted) from Constantine through Theodosius. This gives the *Theodosian Code* a historical dimension absent in the later Justinianic compilation: even laws overturned or substantially modified by later emperors were included, so we can see how legal policy developed over a century and a half. Laws in the *Theodosian Code* were arranged in sixteen books, each comprised of a number of "titles" (headings) for different topics. Under each title, excerpts of the laws relevant to that topic would be arranged in chronological order, the principle being that the latest law in the title (whether of an eastern or western emperor) would express the current legal stance as of 438. The historical importance of Theodosius II's decision to include laws no longer relevant in his day cannot be underestimated; it is only because of his scholarly and traditionalist interests that we have so much legislation of earlier emperors like Constantine, whose laws underwent considerable alteration in the century after his death.[14]

Translations from the *Theodosian Code* in this sourcebook are indicated by "Cod. Theod.," the book number, the title number, and the number of the rescript, along with the date of promulgation or posting. Sometimes a law preserved in the *Theodosian Code* also appears in the *Code of Justinian*, though often in abbreviated or otherwise altered form. Where a law appears in both codes, I have translated the *Theodosian Code* version, which is closer to the original text (though still having undergone abbreviation and editing), and have noted the corresponding Justinianic text in a footnote. It has some-times been difficult to render a translation of a late Roman law which remains faithful to the rhetorical spirit and colorful verbosity of the original but is still intelligible to modern readers. While I have often broken up the sometimes incredibly long sentences and added connectives and punctuation where they did not originally exist (and, like Theodosius' compilers, I have occasionally simply omitted long-winded passages that were not directly relevant to the law's intent), I have retained much of the ornateness and opacity of the original laws. Because the late Roman laws are more difficult to understand and are less familiar to most classicists, I have also provided more footnotes and explanatory material than for the classical material, while trying to let the sources speak for themselves as much as possible.

II Roman social structure and the legal system

The social structure of the Roman Empire has been described as a pyramid, with the very narrow tip being the wealthiest aristocracy, the middle part being the more prosperous upper classes of the cities of the Empire, and the broadest part being the vast majority of inhabitants of the Empire who existed at subsistence level.[15] Roman society was always very conscious of social status and rank. Not only honors, but legal privileges and penalties were allotted according to the individual's status in society.

Until the second century C.E., the main factor determining legal status was citizenship. Roman citizens could expect better treatment under the law, and non-citizens were liable to penalties, such as corporal punishment and execution, that citizens usually did not suffer. Even humble citizens had important rights that non-citizens (*peregrini*) did not have – they could not be beaten or abused by officials, and if convicted of a capital crime would generally be subject to exile rather than outright execution. But by the second century, as more and more people in the Empire acquired citizenship and as the Empire became less and less focused on Rome and Italy, Roman citizenship as a criterion for legal status began to lose importance. Then, in 212, the emperor Antoninus (Caracalla) granted Roman citizenship to all free inhabitants of the Empire, which ultimately led to devaluation of its worth.[16]

Even before 212, the legal dichotomy of citizen/non-citizen was being replaced, or supplemented, by a distinction based on rank, at least in some areas of the law. In terms of rank, the two basic groups were the "more honorable" (*honestiores*) and the "more lowly" (*humiliores*). The *honestiores* were those of higher status, who received public honor and legal privileges: members of the Senate and their children and grandchildren, *equites* (equestrians), decurions (town councillors), and military veterans. All others were *humiliores*, or classed with *humiliores* in terms of legal treatment. By the reign of Hadrian (117–138), the *honestiores/humiliores* distinction was enshrined in law.[17]

Highest in the Roman social order, at the top of the *honestiores*, were senators and their families. By the end of the first century, the offices that led to membership in the Senate were no longer elected in the popular assemblies, but were chosen by the Senate (with the Emperor's approval) or by the Emperor. Membership in the imperial Senate was not hereditary, in that sons of senators did not automatically become senators, but they were encouraged to attend meetings and hold offices on the traditional *cursus honorum*, and preference in choosing senators would generally be given to those from a senatorial family. There were about 600 senators in the Empire (Augustus had reduced the numbers considerably, but there were still about twice as many as there had been before the first century B.C.E.), many of whom originated not from Rome or Italy, but from all over the Empire, though mostly from the west (especially Italy, Spain, and North Africa). Members of the Senate, their wives, children, and their sons' children held the honorary title of *clarissimus* (for males) or *clarissima* (for females).[18]

As part of his policy to restore Rome, Augustus made rules concerning membership in the Senate. Senators had to have a net worth of at least one million sesterces. Some senators, of course, had many times that much,[19] but emperors were known to give gifts to senators or to their sons who had fallen below that census. By the second century if not before, they were required to have at least one-third of their property in Italy. In 18 B.C.E., Augustus also enacted legislation which placed restrictions on the marriages and social behavior of senators. By this legislation, senators (and their children and grandchildren of both sexes) could not marry ex-slaves, actors or children of actors, or those prohibited to all freeborn people. Other legislation passed by the Senate forbade senators and their children and grandchildren to perform in public.[20] Emperors could and did use the powers of censor to remove from the Senate those considered unfit in some way.

In the third century, the power and influence of the Senate (never as important as it had been in the late Republic) declined, as imperial priorities shifted to defense of the frontiers and shoring up of a collapsing economy, and emperors, who for the first time were not themselves of senatorial rank, gave preference to equestrians and military men. In the late Empire, however, senatorial numbers and prestige again increased, beginning with the social reforms of Constantine and his inauguration in 330 of a new capital in the east, Constantinople. The number of senators expanded to about 2000, and senatorial ranks were divided into *illustres* (the highest of the high), *spectabiles*, and simple *clarissimi*.[21] The new social structure again had ramifications for marriage law, as had been the case at the beginning of the Empire with Augustus' reforms.[22]

Next in the Roman status hierarchy was the equestrian order. Equestrians (*equites*) had to have a net worth of at least 400,000 sesterces. Many had much more; some who were worth over a million sesterces preferred to remain equestrians rather than to become senators by holding offices which led to membership in the Senate (among these were some sons of senators who "opted out" of politics and remained equestrians).[23] The background and wealth of equestrians varied more widely than did that of senators, and there were many more of them. In the Empire, there were administrative, and certainly military, positions reserved for *equites* – the most important being the prefect of Egypt (governor) and the praetorian prefect, head of the praetorian guard and often the Emperor's right-hand man. Thus there was little real difference between senators and the upper echelon of equestrians – they could be equally wealthy and both were involved in imperial administration (indeed, often the same family would include both senators and equestrians). In addition to the census requirement of 400,000 sesterces, equestrians had to meet certain requirements to ensure their respectability: they and their parents and grandparents had to be of free birth, and, like senators, they were barred from performing on stage or in the amphitheater. Unlike senators, they could marry freedwomen.

Also included among the *honestiores* were decurions (called *curiales* in late antiquity), members of municipal senates (town councils). Most towns had an "order" of 100 decurions (though smaller towns might have fewer). They, and their families, formed the upper rank of the towns of the Empire. Some decurions were wealthier and more powerful than others. There was not a universal census requirement as there was for senators and equestrians, but individual towns and cities presumably had requirements.[24] Only those of free birth could become decurions; freedmen could not, but their sons could. Decurions were responsible for the upkeep of their cities – including constructing and maintaining public buildings like theaters, temples, and civic buildings.[25] In fact, they were ultimately responsible for ensuring that the taxes owed to the imperial treasury were paid (though collection was in the hands of the imperial procurators, often equestrians): if the people of their municipality did not provide the full amount of taxes owed to the imperial government, decurions would have to make up the difference.

Until the third century, the honor attached to being a decurion and to those who benefited their cities, and the general prosperity of the Empire, meant that in spite of these drawbacks there were still many men willing to hold such a position. But in the later Empire, being a decurion became more and more onerous because of increased demands made by the imperial government and a tight economic situation. The spirit of pride and desire to benefit their city by gifts and building projects suffered as more and more decurions tried to escape their obligations. At this point emperors began trying to make decurial status hereditary, so that the children of decurions had to follow in their fathers' footsteps, whether they wanted to or not; others who had enough property were forced to become decurions.[26]

Women could not hold office, either as senators or as local magistrates such as decurions. They could, however, wield influence, particularly in their home towns or provinces, by serving as priestesses of public cults. Often the women of prominent and wealthy local families held religious office, and participated in public benefaction (euergetism) by endowing building projects or financing festivals. Elite and wealthy women were sometimes honored as patronesses of towns or of *collegia* (trade associations), to which they had contributed money, and if they held high rank, this would be indicated on inscriptions honoring them for their generosity.[27]

The basis of wealth in ancient society was land. The Empire's wealthiest families would have property in many different parts of the Empire (imperial senators were required to own land in Italy), especially the west – North Africa, Sicily, Gaul and Spain, and perhaps Asia Minor. Senators and equestrians of moderate wealth would have local estates in the country (their family seat) and perhaps one or two other properties elsewhere. Decurions generally owned property in and around their town.[28] Women in the Roman Empire, though barred from imperial and municipal offices, did own property in their own right (generally via family inheritance), and are found in legal and documentary sources as owners, purchasers, leasers and renters of land.

Though the biggest difference in terms of wealth and privilege was between the *honestiores* and *humiliores*, there were status distinctions within the *humiliores* also. *Humiliores* as a group were not defined as closely as *honestiores*, and comprised a much wider economic and social range. They included freeborn people (*ingenui*) below the status of decurions, and freedpeople (*libertini*), who had been born slaves but subsequently freed. Slaves, while technically not *humiliores*, were subject to the same − or worse − legal treatment, and so are generally grouped with *humiliores*.

Ingenui (feminine form *ingenuae*) were "freeborn," that is, born of a free mother, as normally it was the mother's status that determined the status of the child.[29] Virtually all *honestiores* were *ingenui* (senators and decurions had to be of free birth, though they could be descended from former slaves), but the *humiliores* also included many *ingenui*. Many were the children of former slaves; to be freeborn, it was only necessary that one's mother have been freed by the time of one's birth. Augustus' marriage legislation laws barred all *ingenui* from marrying prostitutes and pimps. Other than that, the legal situation of non-elite *ingenui* might not differ much from that of former slaves, except that the freeborn did not owe duties to a patron (former master). Freeborn *humiliores* might be peasants, tenant farmers, or (along with many former slaves) the lower-class inhabitants of towns and cities.

Slaves frequently appear in Roman legal sources and in documentary evidence, but almost always as property to be sold, bought or inherited. There has been considerable debate over the sources of the slave supply in the Empire.[30] In the Republic, slaves came into Italy in large numbers by way of Roman conquest, particularly from Greece, Asia Minor, and Gaul. By the early Empire, the number of slaves acquired each year by conquest had decreased, but the slave population continued to be enhanced by defeated rebel peoples (especially Jews after the revolts of 66–72 and under Hadrian) and by "barbarians" from outside the borders of the Empire who had either been defeated in war or purchased from traders. Slaves in the imperial period were frequently acquired by breeding and by the rescue and rearing of newborn infants abandoned ("exposed") or even sold by parents unable or unwilling to bring them up.[31]

Slave labor on a large-scale basis was only found in Italy and Sicily, a legacy of the large estates of the Republic. In many parts of the Empire, other sources of agricultural labor supply, such as free tenant farmers (*coloni*) or serfs, were more common than enslaved people, who were more likely to be employed in domestic chores within households. Even families of fairly modest wealth would have one or two slaves; only the very wealthy, senatorial families, and the imperial household, would have hundreds of slaves. It used to be thought that slavery declined in the later Empire, and that enslaved workers were largely replaced by *coloni*, whose legal status became closer to that of actual slaves. But scholars now recognize that different kinds of labor were used all along, even on the same lands, and indeed there is plenty of evidence in the legal sources for the continuation of the institution of slavery in late antiquity.[32]

The circumstances and conditions of slavery varied enormously. Whereas legally slaves were at the bottom of the social scale, some might be better off, or have better chances of improving their life or their children's lives, than the freeborn poor. Domestic slaves had the best chance of being manumitted and joining the large freed population. They also might be given an allowance (*peculium*) by their owner, which they might be able to use to purchase their freedom, or be allowed to keep after manumission. Legally slaves could not marry, but some managed to have a family life, and even to maintain ties with children and partners in slavery after manumission.[33]

Manumission of a slave by his or her master or mistress was quite possible, either during the owner's lifetime or (more often) in his or her will. A large number of slaves was freed, and those still in slavery could always look to successful freedmen as models. However, the vast majority of slaves in the Empire were never manumitted.[34] Moreover, as part of his extensive social legislation, Augustus placed restrictions on the circumstances under which slaves could be freed. The *lex Fufia Caninia* of 2 B.C.E. limited the number of slaves an owner could free in his or her will: those with ten slaves or fewer could free up to half their slaves; those with between eleven and thirty slaves could free up to a third; and those with between thirty-one and a hundred slaves could free up to a fourth.[35] The *lex Aelia Sentia* of 4 C.E. said that for a slave to be legally manumitted, he or she had to be at least thirty years of age, and the manumittor at least twenty. There were exceptions to this rule, however: a master could free one of his slavewomen in order to marry her, or could free his blood relatives (perhaps his own children by a slave), even if master or slave did not meet the age requirements, as long as this was done before a tribunal (*consilium*) specially constituted for that purpose.[36] It was not illegal or unusual for a man to free his slavewoman and marry her (unless he was a member of the senatorial aristocracy and so forbidden to marry ex-slaves; see above). On the other hand, for a slave mistress to free her male slave in order to marry him was generally not approved socially and was illegal in the later Empire.[37]

The situation of former slaves who had not been freed under the rules of the *lex Aelia Sentia* was addressed by a later *lex Junia*. Under this law, such freedmen and freedwomen, called Junian Latins, did not have Roman citizenship (unlike those who had been manumitted under the law by Roman citizens) and occupied a sort of legal limbo. They lived in freedom and could own property and marry (as could legally manumitted freedpeople), but they could neither inherit nor leave property to their children, and when they died their property reverted to their former master (patron), as did a slave's *peculium*. Any children that Junian Latins had after being freed informally would be freeborn (those born while their mother was still in slavery would be slaves) but illegitimate. However, Junians could convert their status to that of Roman citizens by the procedure of *anniculi probatio* ("evidence of a one-year old child") if they went before the urban praetor or a provincial governor with a child they had borne who had attained the age of one year. The number of Junian freedmen is unknown, but they may have comprised a large percentage of the former slave population in the early Empire and, to judge from late Roman laws, this continued to be the case in late antiquity.[38]

Rank carried legal privileges. Ancient society was much more concerned with honor than modern western society – and honor was what one had in the eyes of others, due to birth and social status. More credence and respect was given to *honestiores* as a matter of course; in a legal dispute with an *honestior*, a *humilior* could not hope to prevail unless, perhaps, he had a very powerful patron. *Honestiores* were rarely subject to capital punishment; even for serious crimes they were likely to be exiled instead. One of the most obvious differences in the legal treatment of *honestiores* and *humiliores* can be seen in the criminal penalties to which the two groups were subject. In general, *honestiores* were punished by monetary penalties, or, in the case of serious crimes, exile. Exile came in two forms, depending on the seriousness of the offense: *relegatio* involved banishment for a period of time but not confiscation of property; *deportatio*, the severer form, entailed not only physical banishment but also loss of citizenship and confiscation of property by the imperial treasury. Also, *honestiores* were not supposed to be liable to torture, except in cases where they were suspected of treason against the emperor. (This rule was not always followed, however, and the lower end of the *honestiores* were vulnerable to treatment from which they were supposed to be exempted.) *Humiliores*, on the other hand, who generally had neither the financial resources nor the honorable standing in the community of *honestiores*, received corporal punishment: beating, if the offense was not serious, or condemnation to the mines, or, for serious crimes, a degrading form of the death penalty such as burning, crucifixion or condemnation to animals in the arena.[39] Under the Empire, slaves were subject to the same legal treatment as *humiliores*, or indeed, to worse treatment. Torture of slaves to extract evidence was standard legal procedure; this included not only slaves who were themselves accused of crimes, but also in some cases those whose owners had been accused.[40]

Status was almost as critical a factor in determining one's place in society as gender. Though women were subject to some legal restrictions with regard to their public activities, and their actions were subject to the approval of some man (father, *tutor*, or husband), women of the elite had privileges not available to men who were below them legally.[41] In studying the legal position of women in the Roman Empire, the importance of social status must always be kept in mind.

12

III Timetable of important events and laws

753 B.C.E.   Traditional founding date of Rome

508 B.C.E.   Last king of Rome overthrown. Beginning of the Republic.

450 B.C.E.   Publication of the Twelve Tables, Rome's first written law code.

169 B.C.E.   *Lex Voconia* (Voconian Law) stating that in families with the highest property rating (i.e., the very wealthiest), women could not be made heirs. This was considered unfair and ways were found to get round it.

40 B.C.E.   *Lex Falcidia* (Falcidian Law) stating that at least one-fourth of an estate had to be left to the heir or heirs; otherwise they could sue for "undutiful will."

31 B.C.E.   Octavian (Augustus) defeats Mark Antony and Cleopatra at the Battle of Actium, marking the beginning of one-man rule over Empire.

18 B.C.E.   Augustus introduces the *lex Julia de maritandis ordinibus* (Julian law on regulating the marriages of the social orders). The *lex Julia de adulteriis* (Julian law on adultery) probably dates from this year also [Chapter 2, Part I.B].

2 B.C.E.   *Lex Fufia Caninia* limits the number of slaves a slaveowner could free in his or her will [Introduction, Part II].

4 C.E.   *Lex Aelia Sentia* sets limits on the circumstances in which slaves could be legally freed [Introduction, Part II].

At some point, either under Augustus or Tiberius (probably either 17 B.C.E or 19 C.E.), the *lex Junia* (Junian Law) regulated the situation of slaves who had been freed without following the rules set out in the *lex Aelia Sentia* [Introduction, Part II].

9 C.E.   Additional legislation on marriage, modifying the laws of 18 B.C.: the *lex Papia–Poppaea* (Papian–Poppaean Law) [Chapter 2, Part I.B].

41–54   *Lex Claudia* abolished *tutela legitima* for all citizen women except freedwomen [Chapter 1, Part III.A].

46   *Senatusconsultum Velleianum* stated women cannot provide surety or take on financial obligations for anyone else [Chapter One, Part IV.D].

49   A *senatusconsultum Claudianum* legalized marriage of a man with his brother's daughter [Chapter 3, Part I.A].

52   Another *senatusconsultum Claudianum* penalized a free woman who entered into an informal union (*contubernium*) with someone's else slave [Chapter 3, Part I.B].

13

early 2nd c.	*Senatusconsultum Plancianum* laid down procedure to follow when a divorced woman claims she is pregnant by her ex-husband [Chapter 4, Part I.E].
117–138	*Senatusconsultum* gave women the right to make wills without going through complicated procedure of *coemptio fiduciaria*.
	Senatusconsultum Tertullianum enables a mother who has *ius liberorum* to succeed to a child who died without making a will [Chapter 5, Introduction].
	Floruit of jurist Julian, who put the Praetor's Edict into final form.
*c.*160	The Roman jurist Gaius writes his *Institutes*.
175–180	Law of Marcus Aurelius and Commodus bans marriage between a guardian (*tutor*) and his ward (*pupilla*) [Chapter 3, Part I.C].
178	*Senatusconsultum Orphitianum* gives a woman's children first claim as her heirs if she died intestate [Chapter 5, Introduction].
193–235	Floruit of jurists Papinian, Ulpian, Modestinus, and Paulus.
202–3	Law of Septimius Severus and Caracalla relaxed the ban on gifts between husband and wife [Chapter 2, Part I.E].
212	Edict of Caracalla (*Constitutio Antoniniana*) granted Roman citizenship to all free inhabitants of the Roman Empire.
284–305	Publication of two collections of imperial rescripts (*Codex Gregorianus* and *Codex Hermogenianus*) under emperor Diocletian.
	Probable date of *Sent. Pauli* and *Rules of Ulpian*.
295	Edict of Diocletian against close-kin marriage [Chapter 3, Part I.A]
320	Constantine repealed Augustan penalties on the unmarried [Chapter 2, Part II.A].
330	Foundation by Constantine of Constantinople (modern Istanbul).
331	Constantine restricted unilateral divorce [Chapter 4, Part II].
380	Theodosius I made Nicene Christianity the Roman state religion.
390	Theodosius I allowed mothers who vow not to remarry to serve as their children's guardian [Chapter 5, Part II.A].
438	Publication of the *Theodosian Code* under Theodosius II.
476	End of Roman emperors in the west.

527–565   Justinian emperor in the east, attempts to reconquer west.
Compilation and publication of Justinianic corpus of
Roman law (*Digest*, *Code of Justinian*, *Institutes* of Justinian,
Novels).

1

THE STATUS OF WOMEN IN
ROMAN LAW

I Definitions

The final book of the *Digest* included several excerpts from the classical jurists that defined
terms relevant to women and their role in the family.[1]

A Gender and inclusiveness

Latin is a gendered language. All nouns have a grammatical "gender," either masculine, feminine, or neuter, according to their endings. Adjectives also usually have at least two sets of
endings, one for masculine and feminine and another for neuter, and they often have three.
But in general, a noun's gender had nothing to do with any "masculine" or "feminine" or
"neuter" qualities; the gender system goes back to Latin's Indo-European origins.

There were, of course, some nouns denoting human beings whose grammatical gender also
described their sexual gender: e.g., *vir* (= man) was masculine; *femina* (woman) was feminine.
Sometimes, the same root would have different endings depending on whether it denoted a
male or female person: *filius* was a son; *filia* a daughter. A general rule was that if a mixed
group of males and females was being referred to, the masculine noun or adjective would be
used to cover both males and females: " ... because the masculine sex always contains the
feminine sex" [D.32.62 (Julian)]. Roman legal writers noted this inclusive use of masculine
nouns or pronouns in law, to make it clear that women as well as men were covered by its
provisions. However, as Jane Gardner and Richard Saller have recently pointed out, the
generalizing use of the masculine tends to obscure the presence of women as property owners
and actors in Roman society [Gardner 1995; Saller 1999; cf. Treggiari 1979, 185–6]:

D.50.16.1 (Ulpian): This expression "if anyone" embraces males as well as
females.

D.50.16.152 (Gaius): There is no doubt that in the name "man" (*homo*), the
feminine as well as the masculine is included.

D.50.16.195 pr. (Ulpian): An expression of language in terms of the
masculine sex is generally extended to both sexes.

D.50.16.163.1 (Paulus): In the name "boy" (*puer*) a girl is also meant: for
they even call women who have recently given birth "boy-bearers" (*puer-
peras*), and in Greek *paidion* is used for both in common.

Sometimes there could be doubt about whether female persons were included in a masculine
term, and this could have important consequences. For instance, in the law of inheritance:

D.50.16.84 (Paulus): In the name "son" (*filius*) we understand all children.

D.50.16.116 (Javolenus): "Whatever other son or (son) of my son shall be my heir": Labeo (said) it does not seem to include a daughter, Proculus (said) the opposite. Labeo seems to me to follow the literal meaning of the words, Proculus the mind of the testator. He replied: I do not doubt that the opinion of Labeo is not true.

Proculus and (following him) Javolenus upheld the more generous interpretation of the father's will, that by "son" (*filius*) he meant all his children, female as well as male. Labeo on the other hand did not want to take the Latin *filius* inclusively. Another case where jurists expressed uncertainty about the inclusiveness of a father's use of the masculine term occurs at D. 50.16.122 (Pomponius), where a father had appointed guardians for his *filius* in his will. Clearly, a prudent parent would want to be explicit.

However, when feminine forms of nouns and adjectives were used, they referred exclusively to females, not to males [Gardner 1995, 379]:

D.31.45 pr. (Pomponius): If it has been written thus: "I give a hundred *aurei* (gold coins) to my daughters (*filiabus*)," does it appear to be a legacy to children of both the masculine and feminine gender? For if it had been written thus: "I give these men as guardians to my sons (*filiis*)," the response has been that the guardians had been given also to daughters. But the reverse should not be accepted, that males are included also in the name of "daughters": for it is a very bad model for males to be included in a feminine word.

Similar problems of interpretation could arise when speaking of slaves or former slaves. Were all slaves, male and female, meant when a testator referred to his *servi* (the masculine plural form of the word "slave")?

D.50.16.40.1 (Ulpian): The name "slave" also refers to a slavegirl.

D.50.16.101.3 (Modestinus): Certain people think that when slaves (*servi*) are left as a legacy, slavegirls (*ancillae*) ought (to be included) as if the common name includes both sexes.

D.50.16.172 (Ulpian): It has been agreed that in the name "freedman" (*libertus*), a freedwoman (*liberta*) is also included.

D.50.16.52 (Ulpian): In the name "patron" (*patronus*), a patroness (*patrona*) is also included.[2]

B Women in the family

The Romans did not have a Latin word corresponding exactly to the English "family." *Familia*, the word translated below as "family," really has a meaning closer to "household." In one sense, the Roman *familia* comprised all those under the legal power (*potestas*) of the male head, the *paterfamilias*. This included slaves belonging to the *paterfamilias* as well as his children. Often, in fact, the word *familia* denoted only the slave members of a household. It could also refer to an estate rather than a collection of people. Sometimes *familia* had a sense closer (but not identical) to that of the modern "family" – that is, those connected by kinship – but this was not its primary meaning; "*domus*" (house) was more likely to be used in that case [Dixon 1992, 1–3; Saller 1994, 74–101].

In the following passage,[3] the early third-century jurist Ulpian sets out the various meanings *familia* could have:

D.50.16.195.1 (Ulpian): Let us see how the name "family" (*familia*) is to be taken. And indeed it has been taken in various ways: for it is used in regard to both things and persons. In regard to things, as for instance, in the law of the Twelve Tables, with these words: "Let the nearest agnate have the *familia*."[4] However, the meaning of *familia* refers to persons thus, when the law is speaking about patron and freedman: "From that family," it says, "into that family," and here it is agreed that the law is speaking about individual persons. **2:** ... Strictly speaking, we call a *familia* several persons, who are subjected under the power of one person, either by nature or by law, as for instance, the father of the family (*paterfamilias*), the mother of the family (*materfamilias*), the son of the family (*filiusfamilias*), the daughter of the family (*filiafamilias*) and those who follow them in succession, as for instance, grandsons and granddaughters and so on. However, he who has dominion in the home is called *paterfamilias*, and he is called by this name correctly, even though he does not have a son; for we are describing not only the person, but also the legal status. In fact, we call even a fatherless male ward (*pupillus*) a *paterfamilias*. And when the *paterfamilias* dies, all persons (*capita*, literally, "heads") that were subject to him begin to have their individual families: for individuals succeed to the name of fathers of the family. And it will happen likewise in the case of he who has been emancipated: for even this one, having been made legally independent (*sui iuris*), has his own family.... **3:** We are also accustomed to call a body of slaves a *familia* ... **4:** Likewise, (a group) of several persons, who come forth from the blood of the same original progenitor, is called a *familia* – just as we speak of the Julian *familia* – as if from a certain source of remembrance. **5:** However, a woman is both the beginning (*caput*, "head") and the end (*finis*) of her family.

If a woman's *paterfamilias* died or emancipated her, she became legally independent (though she still needed a *tutor mulierum*; see Part III below), but she could never become a *paterfamilias* herself because she could never have legal power (*potestas*) over anyone other than herself. Even her own children were not under her *potestas*, but that of her husband (their *paterfamilias*), and therefore they were part of his *familia*, not hers:

D.50.16.196 (Gaius): The leader (*princeps*) of the family himself is included in the name "family" (*familia*). **1:** It is obvious that women's children are not in their (the women's) *familia*, since those who are born follow the *familia* of their father.

D.50.16.51 (Gaius): In the name "parent" (*parens*) not only father, but even grandfather and great-grandfather and finally all elders are included; but also mother and grandmother and great-grandmother.

18

THE STATUS OF WOMEN IN ROMAN LAW

D.50.16.220 pr (Callistratus): In the name of "children" (*liberi*), grandchildren and great-grandchildren and others who are descended from them are included: for the law of the Twelve Tables includes all of these under the name of "one's own" (*sui*).

D.50.16.136 (Ulpian): In the name "son-in-law" it is clear that the husbands of both a granddaughter and a great-granddaughter born from one's son as well as from one's daughter are included, and the husbands of other female (descendants).

Likewise, "daughter-in-law" extended to a grandson's or great-grandson's wife [D.50.16.50 (Ulpian)], and "father-in-law" and "mother-in-law" included the grandparents of one's spouse [D.50.16.146 (Terentius Clemens)].

A woman might also be described according to marital and sexual status:

D.50.16.13 pr. (Ulpian): In the name "woman" (*mulier*) a virgin ready for a man (*virgo viripotens*) is also included.

D.50.16.242.3 (Javolenus): Labeo says that not only that woman who had at one time been married is called "widow" (*vidua*), but also that woman who had not (ever) had a man: since she has been called *vidua* in the same way as a senseless (*vecors*) person would be one without feeling (*cors*) or an insane (*vesanius*) person would be one without sanity (*sanitas*). Similarly a widow is said to be without "twoness"(*duitas*).

The term *materfamilias* ("mother of the family") had an interesting array of meanings. In early Roman usage, *materfamilias* described a wife whose marriage brought her *in manu*, that is, under her husband's legal power [Part II.B]. However, by Ulpian's day (early third century), *manus*-marriage was obsolete, and *materfamilias* referred to a respectable matron, whether married or not [Treggiari 1991a, 34–5, 279–80; Gardner 1995, 384–8]. The defining factor was a woman's behavior, specifically her observance of social propriety and concern for her sexual honor [McGinn 1998, 147–56; Saller 1999].

D.50.16.46.1 (Ulpian): We ought to understand that a "mother of the family" (*materfamilias*) is she who has not lived dishonorably: for behavior (*mores*) distinguish and separate "mothers of the family" from other women. Therefore there will be no difference, whether she is married or a widow or divorcée, freeborn or freedwoman: for neither marriage nor birth make a "mother of the family," but rather good behavior (*boni mores*).

D.48.5.11 pr (Papinian): Moreover, *materfamilias* means not only a married woman, but also an unmarried one (*vidua*; cf. D.50.16.242.3).

D.43.30.3.6 (Ulpian): ... When you hear "*materfamilias*," understand a woman of well-known reputation (*auctoritas*).

This idea of *materfamilias* was implicit in the adultery law of the emperor Augustus [Chapter 2, Part I.B], which made women of respectable standing, whether married or not, liable to the penalties laid down for illicit sexual behavior (*stuprum*). Augustus could be said

19

to have created "a status to which it should have been the ambition of every free woman to aspire" [McGinn 1998, 156] – that of *materfamilias*.

II Forms of legal power: *potestas, manus* and *tutela impuberum*

In ancient Rome, virtually all free Roman women were under one of the following three types of legal authority: *patria potestas* ("paternal power"), *manus* (subordination to a husband's legal power), or *tutela* ("guardianship"), for those not under *potestas* or *manus*. (Slavewomen, like slavemen, would be under the control of their master or mistress.) By the reign of Augustus, *manus* had practically disappeared, and Augustus himself weakened *tutela mulierum* by granting freedom from *tutela* to freeborn women with three children and freedwomen with four [see Chapter 2, Part I.B]. *Patria potestas*, however, survived until the end of antiquity, though weakened by late imperial legislation [see Arjava 1998].

A Patria potestas *("paternal power")*

Patria potestas was the all-inclusive legal authority of the *paterfamilias*, the male head of the family, over all his children, male and female, and over his sons' children. Male children were as much subject to paternal power as female. The *paterfamilias* was the oldest male ascendant; thus, if a man's sons had children, he would be the *paterfamilias* of his sons and his grandchildren by his sons (his daughters' children would come under the *potestas* of their fathers, the daughters' husbands). A man became a *paterfamilias* himself when all his male ascendants (i.e., paternal grandfather and father) had died. A woman never became a *paterfamilias*; she did not exercise *potestas* over any other person, though if her *paterfamilias* was dead (and if she was not married in a *manus*-marriage, see Part B below), she would be *sui iuris*, i.e, legally independent [see D.50.16.195.1–5 in Part I.B].

The legal authority of the *paterfamilias* over his children was quite extensive. He had the "right of life and death" (*ius vitae necisque*) over them, and theoretically could put even an adult child to death. In fact, there are very few attested cases of a *paterfamilias* executing his adult child, and by the imperial period it seems a *paterfamilias* would utilize his "right of life and death," if at all, only in deciding whether or not to rear a newborn child [Harris 1986; Saller 1994, 114–17].

Far more relevant to Romans of the imperial period than the theoretical *ius vitae necisque* was the father's control over all his children's possessions. Children under *patria potestas* could not own property. Everything given or bequeathed to them legally belonged to their *paterfamilias*. Only when the *paterfamilias* was dead (or had emancipated them; see Part C below) could his children, both male and female, own property in their own names. If a *paterfamilias* died without a will, all his children, male and female, were his heirs in equal shares, as was his wife if she had come under his *manus* upon marriage (if he made a will, however, he might apportion his estate less equally). The *paterfamilias*' consent was also required in order for his children's legal transactions, including their marriages, to be valid [Saller 1994, 118–32; see also Chapter 2, Parts I.C.3 and II.B on consent to marriage].

Roman jurists describe *patria potestas* from the point of view of men like themselves – free male citizens:

Gaius, *Institutes* I.48: Concerning the law of persons another division follows. For certain persons are legally independent (*sui iuris*), certain are subject to someone else's law. **49:** But again, of those persons, who are subject to someone else's law, some are in power (*potestas*), some in marital subordination (*manus*), some in ownership (*mancipium*) ... **55:** Likewise in our power (*potestas*) are our children whom we have begotten in legitimate marriage (*iustae nuptiae*). This law belongs to Roman citizens; for there are almost no other men, who have such a power over their children as we have.

D.1.6.4 (Ulpian): For of Roman citizens, some are fathers of families (*patres familiarum*), some are sons of families (*filii familiarum*), some are mothers of families (*matres familiarum*[5]), some are daughters of families (*filiae familiarum*). Fathers of families are those who are under their own legal power (*potestas*) whether they have reached puberty or are still below puberty; similarly mothers of families; sons and daughters of families are those who are in someone else's power. For whoever is born from me and my wife is in my power; likewise whoever is born from my son and his wife, that is my grandson and granddaughter, are equally in my power, and my great-grandson and great-granddaughter and so on with the rest.

Women did not have *patria potestas* and could never be *patresfamilias* [see Part I.B above]. And though mothers had considerable responsibility and socially approved authority over their children [Dixon 1988], they could never have *potestas* as fathers could, and could not serve as their child's guardian (*tutor*) after their husband's death [see Chapter 5, Part II]. Nor could they legally adopt children, since this involved placing the adoptee under the *potestas* of the adopter. However, by the third century C.E., if not earlier, a woman could receive special imperial permission to "adopt" a child (though without acquiring *potestas* over it) if her own children were dead [Cod. Just. 8.47.5 (dated 291); Gardner 1998, 155–65].

B Manus (*marital subordination*)

In early Roman law, most women entered their husband's legal control when they married. This marital power was called *manus* (literally, "hand") rather than *potestas*. While not as extensive as the *paterfamilias*' powers over his children, the husband's authority over a wife under his legal power (*in manu*) were similar. A wife *in manu* could not own property; any possessions she had when she married would henceforth belong to her husband (or to his *paterfamilias*, if he was still alive). She would inherit equally with her husband's children under intestate succession. However, a husband did *not* have the "right of life and death" over his wife.[6]

By the time of Augustus, "*manus*-marriage" had mostly disappeared [Looper-Friedman 1987].[7] Instead, almost all Roman women entered a form of marriage in which the wife remained under her father's *potestas*, though she would leave her family's home and live with her husband. Her children were in the *potestas* of their father (her husband), but she was still under *patria potestas* until her *paterfamilias* died, at which point she became *sui iuris*. The change in marriage form did not mean any more real legal independence for women, except that she might become *sui iuris* sooner, since fathers would probably die before husbands. Marriage without *manus* served the interests of a woman's natal family, because if she remained under her father's power, her property still legally belonged to him (just as his male children's property did).

Because *manus*-marriage had disappeared hundreds of years before the Justinianic legal corpus was compiled, our only description of it in the legal sources is found in the *Institutes* of Gaius, written in the second century:

Gaius, *Institutes* I.109: But indeed, both males and females are accustomed to be in *potestas*; however, only women come into *manus*. **110:** Accordingly, in the past they used to come into *manus* in three ways: by *usus*, *farreum* and *coemptio*. 111: She who remained married for a year continuously would come into *manus* by *usus*; indeed, since she was taken by *usus* by means of yearly possession, she would cross over into her husband's *familia* and would obtain the place of a daughter. Thus by the law of the Twelve Tables it was provided that, if a woman was not willing to come into her husband's *manus* in this way, she was to be away every year for a period of three nights, and in this way would interrupt the *usus* of each year. But this whole law has partly been abolished by legal enactments and partly has fallen into oblivion by its very disuse. 112: They come into *manus* by *farreum* through a certain kind of sacrifice, which is made to Jupiter Farreus; in which bread made of emmer grain (*farreus*) is employed, wherefore it is also called "sharing of emmer bread" (*confarreatio*); many things besides this are done and occur for the purpose of establishing this legal relationship, with certain solemn words and ten witnesses being present. This law is still in use in our own times: for the greater priests, that is, the priests of Jupiter, of Mars, and of Quirinus, and likewise the kings of sacred rites, are not chosen unless they were born from *farreate* marriage: for not even they are able to have their priesthood without *confarreatio*. 113: But they come into *manus* by *coemptio* through mancipation (*mancipatio*), that is, through a kind of imaginary sale. For after summoning not fewer than five Roman (male) citizens and also a scale-holder, the man "buys" the woman, and she comes into his *manus*.[8]

A passage in the Roman historian Tacitus suggests that by the reign of Tiberius (14–37 C.E.), *confarreatio* was considered a cumbersome and undesirable procedure, and that it was difficult to find candidates for the position of flamen Dialis (a priesthood of Jupiter), whose parents were supposed to have been married by *confarreatio*:

Tacitus, *Annales* IV.16 (written early 2nd c.)

Around the same time, the emperor (Tiberius) made a pronouncement about choosing a flamen Dialis in place of the late Servus Maluginensis, and at the same time about approving a new law. For (he said), by the ancient custom, three patricians born from parents married by *confarreatio* were nominated together, from whom one would be chosen. But there was not, as there once had been, a plentiful supply (of candidates), because the custom of marriage by *confarreatio* had been abandoned or retained only among a few. He adduced several reasons for this situation, the foremost being the indifference of men and women; added to that the difficulties of the ceremony which were deliberately avoided, and the fact that the man who obtained that priesthood would escape from paternal law and the woman (his wife) would enter the *manus* of the flamen. Thus (the rule) should be amended by a decree of the Senate or a law, just as Augustus had turned certain practices from their uncouth antiquity to present-day usage. Therefore, after deliberating the religious practices, it was decided to depart in no way from the custom of the flamens; but a law was passed by which the flaminica Dialis (would be) in the power (*potestas*) of her husband in regard to religious rites, but otherwise would act by the law common to (other) women. And the son of Maluginensis was appointed in place of his father.

By Gaius' time *manus*-marriage by *usus* was obsolete, and marriage by *confarreatio* was probably entered into by only a few members of the elite, whose families customarily held the high priesthoods at Rome which required priests to be the children of *confarreatio* marriage.[9] All references to *manus*-marriage in the jurists were deleted by the sixth-century editors of the *Digest*.

C Tutela impuberum *(guardianship of minors)*

Patria potestas lasted throughout the *paterfamilias'* life. Upon his death, his children, both male and female, would become legally independent (*sui iuris*), and his male children would have *patria potestas* over their own children. Those who had not yet reached puberty (considered to be age fourteen for boys, twelve for girls) when their father died would be placed under *tutela impuberum* ("guardianship of those below puberty"). The guardian, called a tutor, of an underage ward (*pupillus* or *pupilla*) would be appointed by the father in his will, or, if no appointment had been made, guardianship would go to the nearest male relative on the father's side (agnate), usually the paternal uncle. In the absence of eligible agnates, application would be made to the authorities, usually by the children's mother, for appointment of a tutor. Under Roman law, a woman could not serve as tutor, though mothers sometimes got around this rule [see Chapter 5, Part II]. A tutor did not usually live with his ward, nor was he a substitute parent. Fatherless children generally lived with their mother, but she did not have *potestas* over them or control their property. The original purpose of *tutela impuberum* was to safeguard the child's property in the interests of the agnate relatives until the child was mature enough to manage the property. By the time of Augustus, there was a feeling that guardians should be concerned with their wards' welfare as well as their property, and this belief in the tutor's moral responsibility intensified in the later Empire [Schulz 1951, 162–80, 190–7; Saller 1994, 181–203].

Sometimes a *paterfamilias* "emancipated" his children from *patria potestas* during his lifetime; he would then be in the position of their tutor, though with more authority over them than had other tutors. To judge from the legal sources, by the fourth century it was not uncommon for fathers to emancipate their children from paternal power if they had reached maturity.[10]

When they reached puberty, fatherless male children became, in classical Roman law, free of legal authority. Females over twelve would go from *tutela impuberum* to *tutela mulierum* [see Part III]. But Roman law realized that young people in their teens were still vulnerable to attempts by the unscrupulous to defraud them, and another type of guardianship developed, the *cura minorum* ("care of minors") for those who had reached puberty but were still under the legal age of twenty-five. A curator's responsibilities were fewer than a tutor's, and in the earlier Empire appointment of a curator was optional (whereas a tutor was required). By the reign of Septimius Severus (193–211), however, curators were common, and by the fourth century they were required for both male and female minors under twenty-five, though those who demonstrated good behavior could request release from guardianship earlier [cf. Cod. Theod. 2.17.1.1 (324), in Part IV.B].

III *Tutela mulierum* (the guardianship of women)

Under classical Roman law a woman whose *paterfamilias* was dead and who had not entered *manus*-marriage was required to have a "guardian." If she was still below the age of twelve when her father died, she would have a *tutor impuberum* (see Part II.C), but aged twelve she would come under *tutela mulierum* – the "guardianship of women." (Vestal Virgins, who were free from *tutela mulierum* were an exception.) A woman would continue to be under *tutela mulierum* after she married, unless she had entered her husband's *manus*, a form of marriage which had become rare by the time of Augustus [see Part II.B].

It appears that the original purpose of *tutela mulierum* was to safeguard a woman's paternal inheritance in the interests of her father's relatives, who would be her heirs when she died. Until the first century C.E., a woman's tutor was usually her closest male agnate (relative on her father's side), probably her paternal uncle. Such a tutor was called a *tutor legitimus*. If a woman's *paterfamilias* emancipated her from paternal power, he became a *tutor legitimus* to her. A freedwoman (*liberta*) also had a *tutor legitimus*: her former master (patron) [Dixon 1984; Gardner 1986a, 14–22; 166–8; Schulz 1951, 180–90].

Tutela is usually translated as "guardianship," but a *tutor mulierum* was not a legal guardian of the sort envisioned when we use the word today. He did not live with the woman, nor did he have any real control over her or her property. Certain legal and business activities that she might undertake, such as making a will, selling certain types of property (called *res mancipi*; see Part A below at Gaius II.80–5), or manumitting her slaves, required his consent. The tutor's authority was certainly not as extensive as that of a *paterfamilias* (or that of a *tutor impuberum*): he did not own the woman's property, and his consent was not needed for her to enter marriage without *manus* (though it was needed for her to constitute a dowry, which involved property). A tutor was not a personal watchdog, and did not control the woman's private behavior. As the jurist Gaius remarked (*Institutes* I.190, Part A below), many women were quite capable of running their affairs without a tutor.

Augustus, as part of his promotion of marriage and procreation, granted women who served the state by child-bearing the *ius (trium) liberorum*, "the right of (three) children" [see Part III.D]. This released freeborn women who had borne three children and freedwomen who had borne four from the need for a tutor. Women with the *ius liberorum* could conduct all their legal and business affairs without a tutor. The emperor Claudius abolished the *tutor legitimus* for most women, which meant they no longer had to have a close agnate relative as tutor, but could have someone with no personal interest in their financial or legal affairs. (The exceptions were emancipated daughters, whose father continued to be *tutor legitimus*, and freedwomen, whose patron was still *tutor legitimus*.) For instance, a woman might have as tutor one of her freedmen, who could be expected to be loyal and obedient. Thus by the mid-first century, *tutela mulierum* did not impose real restrictions on most women's freedom of legal and commercial action. Moreover, at least by Gaius' time, a tutor (except a *tutor legitimus*) could be forced by the urban praetor to authorize a woman's action even if he did not want to, and women could arrange to change tutors.

A Roman husband was not usually his wife's tutor. The emperors Marcus Aurelius and Commodus prohibited a tutor from marrying his ward, but do not seem to have forbidden a husband to act as his wife's tutor after the marriage took place.[11] Roman law frowned on a man being his wife's tutor, for it was believed that this would create a conflict of interest and lead to the corruption of marital affection – though spouses themselves may have felt differently [Arjava 1996, 140–1]. In the eastern provinces, husbands were usually their wives' guardians [see Part III.B].

A *Legal sources on* tutela mulierum

Because *tutela mulierum* had disappeared two centuries before Justinian (527–565), the compilers of the Justinianic corpus of Roman law omitted all reference to it in the *Digest*, the *Code of Justinian*, and Justinian's *Institutes*. Nor is there any mention of *tutela mulierum* in the *Theodosian Code*. Our understanding of *tutela mulierum* in the classical period depends on the

Institutes of Gaius, of the second century, and the *Rules of Ulpian* (*Regulae Ulpiani*, probably of the early fourth century).

1 The Institutes *of Gaius on* tutela mulierum

***Institutes* I.144:**Therefore it has been permitted to parents to give guardians (*tutores*) to their children whom they have in their power: to male children below puberty, but to female children both below and above puberty, even when they have married. For the ancients wanted women, even if they are of full age, to be in guardianship (*tutela*) on account of their lightmindedness.

See Part IV.C for more on the "lightmindedness" of women.

I.145: And so if anyone has given a tutor to his son and daughter in his will and they have both arrived at puberty, the son of course stops having a tutor, but the daughter remains nevertheless in *tutela*: only according to the Julian and Papian–Poppaean law are women freed from *tutela* by means of the *ius liberorum*. We are speaking, however, of women other than the Vestal Virgins, whom indeed the ancients wished to be free (of guardianship) out of honor for their priesthood: thus it was decreed even by a law of the Twelve Tables.

The "Julian and Papian–Poppaean law" refers to the Augustan laws on marriage enacted in 18 B.C.E. and 9 C.E. [see Chapter 2, Part I.B].

I.148: A tutor is able to be given (by a man in his will) to a wife married with *manus*, just as to a daughter, and likewise to a daughter-in-law who married with *manus* to a son, just as to a granddaughter.

Gaius goes on to say (*Inst.* I.151–3) that a man can, in his will, give his wife in a *manus*-marriage the ability to choose her own tutor after his death. This seems to have been true only for the appointing of a *tutor mulierum* for a wife married in a *manus*-marriage; a father could not in his will give a daughter the ability to choose her own *tutor*. By the imperial period, very few women were in a *manus*-marriage. Most would be assigned a tutor in their father's will or have one chosen for them after his death.

I.155: For those (fatherless children; see Part II.C above) to whom a tutor was not given by will, by a law of the Twelve Tables their agnate relations are tutors, who are called legitimate (*legitimi*) tutors.

The *tutor legitimus* was a male on the agnate (paternal) side of the family, who would probably be the next in line to inherit if the person in *tutela* died without a will. In the mid-first century, the emperor Claudius abolished agnate *tutela* for women. After that, only fatherless children below puberty (male and female) would have an agnate relative as a *tutor legitimus*:

25

I.157: Indeed in the past, so far as pertains to the law of the Twelve Tables, even women had agnate tutors. But afterwards, the Claudian law was enacted, which, as pertains to women, removed the *tutela* of agnates. And so indeed a male minor has his grown brother or uncle as a tutor, but a woman is not able to have such a tutor.

Since agnates had first claim on a woman's estate if she died without a will, a *tutor legitimus* had a direct interest in a woman's financial affairs. And since a woman needed her tutor's authorization to make a valid will, a *tutor legitimus* who did not want her to leave her property away from her agnates (for instance, by making her own children heirs) could prevent her making a will. Claudius' law therefore provided a significant benefit. Presumably a woman could have an agnate relative as her tutor, but he would not have the authority of a *tutor legitimus*; for instance, he could be replaced by another tutor if the woman requested [see below], whereas a *tutor legitimus* could not. Only daughters freed from *patria potestas*, whose fathers became *tutor legitimus* to them, and freedwomen, whose former owners (patrons) were *tutor legitimus*, were not affected by the Claudian law [see below on freedwomen and *tutela*].

A woman could also change her tutor (if her current tutor approved) by making a "mock sale" (*coemptio*) of herself and then having herself freed by the man she wanted as tutor. She might undergo the same process of *coemptio* if she wanted to enter into a marriage with *manus* (Part II.B) and until the reign of Hadrian (117–138), she had to undergo *coemptio* before she could make a will:

I.115: ... if anyone wishes to get rid of the tutors she has and find another, she makes a "mock sale" (*coemptio*) with their authorization. Then, having been transferred back again from the other party in the sale to the man whom she wants and having been mancipated by him, she begins to have as her tutor the man by whom she was manumitted, who is called a fiduciary tutor (*tutor fiduciarius*) ...

Moreover, a woman had the right to request a different tutor if for some reason her current tutor could not (or would not) authorize her activities:

I.173: Besides, it has been permitted to women by a decree of the Senate to request another tutor in place of one who is absent, and when this is requested, the first one ceases to be tutor. It does not make any difference how far away that (first) tutor is.
I.174: But an exception is made, so that a freedwoman is not permitted to request another tutor in place of her absent patron.

Roman citizen women living in the provinces also had to have a *tutor mulierum*, as, apparently, did women in provincial *municipia* which had been granted Latin rights [see on the *lex Irnitana*, Part III.A.3 below]. Other non-citizen women were not subject to the Roman *tutela mulierum*, but similar institutions existed in at least some other provinces [see Part III.B].

I.183: All these things are observed in a similar way at Rome and in the provinces, so that of course in the provinces a tutor ought to be requested from the governor of the province.

I.185: If someone has no tutor at all, one is given to her, in the city of Rome, according to the Atilian law, by the urban praetor and the majority of the tribunes of the plebs, who is called an Atilian tutor. In the provinces, however, (a tutor is given) by the governors of the provinces according to the Julian and Titian law.[12]

I.193: Among foreigners (*peregrini*), women are not in *tutela* in the same way as among us. However, they often are in a sort of *tutela*: as, for instance, the law of the Bithynians orders that if a woman undertakes any contract, her husband or adult son must give his authority.

After the mid-first century, the only women really restricted by *tutela mulierum* were freedwomen. The tutor of a freedwoman (*liberta*) was her former owner, her *patronus*, and he (like the now-abolished agnate tutors of freeborn women) was *tutor legitimus* and had inheritance rights in regard to his freedwoman's property [see Gardner 1998, 64–7]. This type of *tutor legitimus* was *not* abolished by Claudius or by later emperors.

The need to get her patron-tutor's authorization for legal and business transactions could put the *liberta* in a bind, for instance if her original patron died and his role was inherited by his under-age son.

I.179: Of course the son of a patron, even if he is below puberty, will nevertheless be made the tutor of (his father's) freedwoman, though in no act is he able to be a legal agent, since he himself is not permitted to act at all without his tutor's authority.

The law did at times step in and enable a freedwoman to change her tutor if the action she wanted to undertake was perceived to be socially desirable, such as inheriting wealth or, especially, getting married:

I.176: But at times indeed it is permitted to request a tutor in place of an absent patron, for example for the purpose of entering on an inheritance.

I.177: The Senate decided the same thing in the case of the minor son of a patron.

I.178: For also by the Julian law *de maritandis ordinibus* she who is in the *tutela legitima* of a minor is permitted to request (another) tutor from the urban praetor for the sake of constituting a dowry.

I.180: Likewise if a woman is in the *tutela legitima* of a madman or a mute person, she is permitted by a decree of the Senate to request (another) tutor for the sake of constituting a dowry.

The Julian law *de maritandis ordinibus* ("on the marrying of the social orders") was passed in 18 B.C.E. to promote marriage and procreation [see Chapter 2, Part I.B]. Though the lack of a dowry did not in itself invalidate a marriage under Roman law (as, for instance, it did in Athenian Greek law), it might suggest that the woman was a concubine rather than a legitimate wife – particularly if, as in the case of the freedwoman, she was of low birth.

In some cases, even freedwomen did not have a *tutor legitimus*:

I.195: However, a freedwoman is able to have a tutor of another kind, for instance if she was manumitted by a woman; then indeed she ought to request a tutor according to the Atilian law, or in a province according to the Julian and Titian law: for she cannot be in the *tutela* of a female patron.

I.195c: Similarly, a freedwoman is able to request a tutor according to the same laws, if her patron has died and has left no child of the male sex in the household.

> Freedwomen were discriminated against in other ways:

I.194: Moreover, freeborn women are freed from *tutela* by the right of three children (*ius trium liberorum*), but freedwomen [only if they have] four, if they are in the *tutela legitima* of their patron or his sons. Certainly the others, who have tutors of another kind, such as Atilian or *fiduciarii*, are freed by the law of three children.

> The four children would have to be those born after she had been released from slavery–an additional disadvantage.
> What did the *tutor mulierum* actually do? His authorization was needed for certain acts by a woman to be valid. She needed his consent to make a will (though he need not know or approve of its contents), or to sell or give away certain types of property that were classified as *res mancipi* ("property subject to mancipation"), which included certain animals (cattle, horses, mules, asses), urban and rural estates in Italy, and slaves. His authorization was also required if a woman wanted to manumit (emancipate) her slaves or to engage in litigation [see Part IV.E].

II.80: Now, we must be warned that neither a woman nor a *pupillus* (fatherless minor, who would have a *tutor impuberum*) is able to alienate *res mancipi* without a tutor's authorization. However, it is possible for a woman to alienate something that is not *res mancipi*, but not possible for a *pupillus* to do so.

II.81: And therefore whenever a woman has given a loan to someone without her tutor's authorization, because she makes it the recipient's, she contracts an obligation, since of course money is not *res mancipi*.

> In other words, she is herself responsible for having made the loan, which did not require her tutor's authorization (unlike the *pupillus* who cannot make a valid loan without his tutor's authorization).

II.83: And, on the contrary, all property, whether or not it is *res mancipi*, can be paid over to women and to *pupilli* without a tutor's authorization, since it has been allowed for them to improve their own condition even without their tutor's authorization.

II.85: Moreover, it is possible for a debt to be paid properly to a woman without her tutor's authority: for he who has paid the debt, is freed from an obligation, since, as we just said, women are able to discharge property that is not *res mancipi* even without a tutor's authorization. However, this is the case if she actually receives the money, but if she doesn't receive (money) but says that she has it and without her tutor's authorization she wishes to free her debtor through a formal discharge from debt, she is not able to.

II.118: Further, it must be observed that if a woman who is in *tutela* makes a will, she ought to do it with her *tutor's* authorization: otherwise it will be made ineffectively according to the civil law.

Gaius goes on to say (*Inst.* II.119–21) that even in cases where a will was not made properly, the appointed heirs were still enabled to inherit under both the Praetor's Edict and a ruling of Antoninus Pius, and this applied to the wills of women as well as men. As to whether it also applied to cases where a woman had made a will without her tutor's authorization, Gaius seems unsure, though he implies that it did, except for those women who still had a *tutor legitimus*, that is, *libertae* and daughters emancipated from *patria potestas*:

II.122: But of course we are talking about those women, who are not in the *tutela legitima* of parents or patrons, but who have tutors of another kind, tutors who are forced to give their authorization even against their will. Otherwise it is clear that if a will is made without his authorization a parent or a patron is not removed (as heir to the woman's property).

Yet, though Gaius duly explains the technicalities of *tutela mulierum*, he does not really understand the need for it in his own day:

I.190: However, almost no reason of value appears to recommend that women of full age be in *tutela*. For the reason which is commonly believed, that since they are very often deceived due to their lightmindedness, it was right for them to be ruled by the authority of tutors, seems to be specious rather than true. Indeed, women who are of full age transact business deals for themselves, and in certain cases the tutor interposes his authority for the sake of legal form; often he is even forced by the praetor to give his authority against his will.

2 Selections from the Rules of Ulpian 11

11.1: Guardians (*tutores*) are appointed for both males and females, but for males only as long as they are below puberty, on account of the weakness of their age; however, for females both below puberty and above, both on account of the weakness of their sex (*sexus infirmitas*) and on account of their ignorance of legal affairs.

On the "weakness" of the female sex, see Part IV.C below.

11.20: According to the Julian law *de maritandis ordinibus* a tutor is given by the urban praetor to that woman or unmarried girl who ought to marry according to that very law, for the purpose of giving and declaring and promising a dowry, if she has a minor as her *tutor legitimus*. But afterwards the Senate decided, that tutors should be given also in the provinces in a similar way by their governors for the same purpose.

11.25: The tutors of minor males and females both transact their business affairs and give their authorization, but women's guardians only give their authorization.

11.27: The guardian's authorization is required for women in these matters: if they are acting legally or in a statutory court[13], if they put themselves under an obligation, if they are undertaking civil business, if they are allowing their freedwoman to live in an unofficial union (*contubernium*) with someone else's slave, or if they alienate property that is *res mancipi*.

On the *contubernium* of a freedwoman with someone else's slave, which was regulated by a *senatusconsultum Claudianum*, see Chapter 3, Part I.B.2.

3 The Flavian Municipal Law (lex Irnitana)

Almost all our knowledge of the actual texts of laws derives from sources like the *Institutes* of Gaius or the jurists preserved in the *Digest*, or imperial constitutions found in the *Code of Justinian* and the *Theodosian Code* [see Introduction to this book, Part I]. But a few legal texts are known directly from documentary sources, that is, inscriptions or papyri. An important example is the so-called "Flavian Municipal Law," known from several inscriptions found at the sites of towns in Spain. The most recently discovered and most complete version of the Flavian law, engraved on six bronze tablets, was found at the ancient Muncipium Flavium Irnitanum (Irni). This *lex Irnitana* is not completely preserved, but some missing parts can be filled in from another text of the Flavian law found at Malaga [Gonzalez 1986; Lintott 1993, 140–5].

The Flavian Municipal Law was apparently a constitution given to non-Roman towns (*municipia*) in Spain who had been granted Latin rights by the emperor Vespasian (reigned 69–79). The law set forth legal regulations to be followed by *municipes* (citizens of a *municipium*), most of whom were at this time not Roman citizens. In *municipia* with Latin rights, those who held a local magistracy, such as the *duoviri* (the two chief officials of the town), would receive Roman citizenship upon leaving office, along with their wives, parents, children, and their sons' children. Of particular interest is the fact that even those *municipes* who were not Roman citizens were assumed already to have certain Roman legal institutions, most notably *patria potestas* and *manus*, and were expected to follow Roman law in their dealings with each other at Irni [Gonzalez 1986, 148–9; Gardner 1993, 188–90].

Among the Roman institutions assumed for the *municipes* of Irni was *tutela*, guardianship, both that of fatherless minors (*tutela impuberum*) and *tutela mulierum*. Both minors under a *tutor impuberum* (called *pupilli*) and women under a *tutor mulierum* needed their tutor's consent to emancipate their slaves, and Chapter 28 of the law specifies that only then are manumissions by those under guardianship valid. This obviously meant that a procedure needed to be in place for appointing tutors, and we see from Chapter 29 that in *municipia*, the *duovir* played the role of the praetor in Rome and of the governor in Egypt [see Gaius, *Inst.* I.183 above, and cf. Part III.C for Egypt].

The Latin text of the *lex Irnitana* used here is that of Gonzalez 1986. Texts of other versions of the Flavian Municipal Law, from Malaga and from Salpensa, Spain, are found in *FIRA* III, 202–19. It was engraved in 91 C.E. (as appears from a "postscript" to the law, a rescript of the emperor Domitian regarding the validity of marriages at Irni).[14] The Flavian law itself dates to about a decade before then.

Lex Irnitana 28–9 Irni (Spain), *c*.80–90

Chapter 28. About manumitting slaves in the presence of the duoviri.

If any citizen of the municipium of Flavian Irni, who is a Latin, has manumitted his or her own male or female slave from slavery to liberty in the presence of the duoviri of this municipium (chosen) for making law or has ordered (the slave) to be free – as long as no fatherless minor (*pupillus*) or unmarried girl (*virgo*) or woman manumits anyone or orders him or her to be free without the authorization of a tutor – whatever male has thus been manumitted and ordered to be free, is to be free, and whatever female has been thus manumitted and ordered to be free, is to be free, just as any Latin freedmen with the fullest rights are or will be free. (This is the case) provided that anyone who is less than twenty years old only manumits, if that number of decurions, by which under this law decrees are made and validated, has agreed that the reason for manumission is legitimate.[15]

Chapter 29. About the giving of tutors.

Whoever does not have a tutor or whose tutor is uncertain, if he or she is a citizen of the municipium of Flavian Irni, and is not a *pupillus* or *pupilla*, and has requested a duovir for making law of that municipium to give him or her a tutor, and has nominated the one whom he or she wishes to be given, then he (the duovir), who has been so requested, whether he has one or more colleagues in office, according to the opinion of all his colleagues, who is (sic) at that time in that municipium or within its boundaries, after a hearing has been held, shall give as tutor the one who was nominated if it seems best to him. But if he or she, in whose name the request is thus made, is a *pupillus* or *pupilla*, or if he, who has been so requested, does not have a colleague, or no colleague of his is in that municipium or within its boundaries, then he, who has been so requested, after a hearing has been held, within the next ten days from a decree of the decurions, which has been passed when no less than two-thirds of the decurions are present, shall give to him or her that tutor who was nominated, provided that the *tutela* does not pass from the legitimate tutor.[16] Whoever has been given as tutor under this statute, provided that the *tutela* does not pass from the legitimate tutor, shall be as much legitimate tutor as if he were a Roman citizen and nearest agnate to a Roman citizen.

B Tutela mulierum *in non-legal sources*

Though nowhere in the Latin-speaking west preserves documentation comparable in quantity or variety to that found in the papyri of Roman Egypt [cf. Part C below], some documentary evidence for women's transactions involving tutors does survive from the towns around the Bay of Naples destroyed by the eruption of the volcano Vesuvius in 79 C.E. Two very fragmentary wax tablets from Herculaneum record the assignment of tutors to women by a duovir [Arangio-Ruiz 1956; Modrzejewski 1974, 271–2]. They appear to follow the same pattern as the documents assigning tutors to Roman citizen women in Egypt in Part III.C [P.Oxy. XII.1466; SB III.6223; other examples can be found at Modrzejewski 1974, 265–71].

They show that in municipalities, the duovir was responsible for the granting of tutors, as in the Spanish municipia which received the Flavian Municipal Law [see Part III.A.3], and that assignment of tutors was carried out in accordance with the Julian and Titian law, as in the provinces, rather than the Atilian law, as at Rome [Arangio-Ruiz 1956; Modrzejewski 1974, 287–8; cf. Gaius *Inst*. I.185 in Part III.A.1]. Another tablet from Herculaneum records that a woman, Calatoria Themis, provided bail for appearing in court on the authority of her tutor, who was her former slave (for freedmen as tutors, see inscriptions below).[17]

Wax tablets have also been found at Murecine, near Pompeii, though they were written at Puteoli (Pozzuoli). These Murecine tablets record business dealings of a group of moneylenders, the Sulpicii, all either freedmen or the sons of freedmen. Among the 170 tablets found (which date between 26 and 61 C.E.) are a few in which women figure as borrowers or creditors – generally, with their tutors authorizing the transaction. The women include a non-Roman citizen, Euplia from the Greek island of Melos, who appears as borrower in several transactions, also accompanied by her tutor. "What does emerge clearly from the tablets is that the *tutela* system, in the first half of the first century AD, is actively functioning in the daily commerical transactions of townsfolk around the Bay of Naples, without seeming to offer any particular hindrance to women's dealings" [Gardner 1999, 27]. Other references to *tutela mulierum* are found on Latin inscriptions from Rome, both epitaphs and inscriptions recording transactions, as the following selections will show.

It was customary for wealthier Romans, who owned slaves and set up imposing funeral monuments, to include their freedmen and freedwomen (and the descendants of their freedmen and freedwomen) in their tombs. Former slaves took the family name (*nomen*) of their former owner upon manumission, and could therefore perpetuate the cult of the bearers of the *nomen* – which is clearly what their former owners intended for them to do. In these inscriptions, women commemorate their tutor along with family members and former slaves.

In the following epitaph from Rome, Furfania Saturnina identifies her tutor as the freedman of her husband, and names him in her dedication among other former slaves.[18] Furfania herself is freeborn, as her filiation indicates.[19] M. Valerius Hesychus was clearly below Furfania Saturnina socially, and as her husband's *libertus* could be expected to be a "rubber-stamp" for any transactions requiring a tutor's authorization.

CIL VI.2650, 1st–early 2nd c. C.E.

Furfania Saturnina, daughter of Lucius, made (this tomb) for herself and for her son, A. Manneius Celsus son of A(ulus),[20] of the tribe Collina, a soldier of the Seventh Praetorian Cohort, and for M. Valerius Ismarus her husband, and for M. Valerius Semnus, her home-born slave,[21] and for M. Valerius Hesychus, freedman of Ismarus, her tutor, and for Saturnina Veneria, her home-born slave, and for her freedwoman Epicharis and for Secunda Veneria her home-born slave and for her freedmen and freedwomen and their descendants. [added later?] To Natalis Veneria her home-born slave.

The next epitaph, also from Rome, probably illustrates a similar situation. Ostoria Acte and her tutor have the same *nomen*. Conceivably she is his freedwoman, rather than the other way around (recall that a *liberta's* former owner would be *tutor legitimus* to her; see Part A above), but in that case we would expect her to call him *patronus* as well as tutor. His inclusion in her family tomb along with her freedmen and freedwomen slaves suggests that he is also her former slave.

CIL VI.7468, 1st–2nd c. C.E.?

To the Spirits of the Dead

To Isidorus who is also called Hermias Lintiarius, Ostoria Acte (set this tomb up) for her well-deserving husband and for herself and for her son, T. Calestrius Herminus, and for her tutor, M. Ostorius Lamyrus, and for her freedmen and freedwomen and their descendants of either sex.

The next inscription is not from a tombstone, but records the donation of land outside Rome by a woman named Julia Monime.[22] The donation was effected by the ancient procedure of mancipation (*mancipatio*) [see further at CIL VI.10247 in Part III.D below], a form of conveyance used when the item being transferred from one owner to another was *res mancipi* ("property subject to mancipation"): urban or rural land in Italy, slaves, certain beasts of burden, and "rustic praedial servitudes," that is, access through rural properties such as right of way, the right to drive cattle, the right to draw water. As both Gaius [*Institutes* II.80] and the *Rules of Ulpian* [11.27] tell us, women needed the authorization of their tutor in order to alienate *res mancipi*.

It is not clear who the "associates" (*socii*) of Julia Monime are, but perhaps they are joint owners with her of the land in question. The recipients of the gift are a *collegium*, a club devoted to the cult of the Italic rustic god Silvanus. Evidently the land donated by Julia Monime was already being used by the *collegium*, since a building for the cult of Silvanus already existed. The *collegium* was primarily a funerary association, which assured proper burial and commemoration for those not included in the funerary monuments of the wealthy [Hopkins 1983, 211–17]. The *schola* is the place where the group met, and the *curator* mentioned is presumably the group's manager.

The inscription is on a marble cippus (small stone pillar, either a gravestone or a boundary-marker) found in 1773 on the outskirts of Rome. At the top of the inscription were relief carvings of a dog, a boy wearing a *pallium* (a sort of cloak), a tree trunk, and another dog. The text contains several grammatical errors, and the stone is broken off at the bottom, so the inscription becomes fragmentary near the end. (In my translations of inscriptions, ... indicates where letters have been lost; words within [ ] are possible restorations.)

CIL VI.10231 = ILS 7313, 2nd–3rd c.

The place, or field, which is on the Via Appia between the second and third milestone for those going away from Rome, on the right side, in the land of Curtianus Talarchianus on the estates of Julia Monime and her associates, the place in which has been built a *schola* beneath a porticus, consecrated to Silvanus and to his *collegium*, the members of the fellowship received by mancipation, free of burden, and the curator and the whole people of this *collegium* (received) from Julia Monime and her associates for one sestertius coin for the sake of donation, with the tutor of Julia Monime, C. Memius Orion (giving his consent). And to this place the right of way, the right of driving cattle, going around, making sacrifice, feeding and banqueting thus shall be permitted as long as that *collegius* (sic) shall stand. But if it should be done otherwise, that which pertains to the *collegium* of Silvanus, this sanctified place shall be restored ... [to Julia Monime and her associates?] without any argument. These things ... have been [stipulated?].

There are surprisingly few references to a woman's tutor in Roman literary sources, which supports the assumption that the role of the *tutor mulierum* was insignificant in most women's everyday lives. One of the few surviving references is found in the *Apology* of the North African intellectual and writer Apuleius of Madaura, best known for his novel, the

Metamorphoses (also called *The Golden Ass*).[23] The *Apology* is a very long defense speech given by Apuleius when he was on trial before the governor in the province of Africa Proconsularis. All the parties are Roman citizens and Apuleius makes frequent reference to Roman laws in his speech.

Apuleius' accusers had charged him with using magical means to inveigle his wife, Pudentilla, into marrying him. This was a serious charge; conviction under the *lex Cornelia de sicariis et veneficis* (which dealt with murder, poisoning and magic) would carry the death penalty. Pudentilla was a wealthy widow probably a good ten years (or more) older than Apuleius, and his opponents not surprisingly suspected him of being a gold-digger [see further Chapter 2, Parts I.D.2 and E.2 and Chapter 5, Part I.B]. One of the criticisms made against Apuleius was that he had purchased some property for himself with money given him by Pudentilla. Apuleius counters by saying that Pudentilla bought it herself, and he calls as witness her tutor, who had to authorize the purchase that Pudentilla made. It is not clear where this estate was located; since Pudentillla needed her tutor's authorization to buy it, it was presumably *res mancipi*. [24]

Apuleius, *Apologia* 101.4–5, 158/9 C.E.

You have said that I bought a very attractive estate in my own name with a large amount of my wife's money. I say that it was a trifling little property worth 60,000 sesterces, and that it was not I, but Pudentilla who bought it in her own name, that Pudentilla's name is in the records, and that the tax for this little property was paid in Pudentilla's name. The public treasurer to whom it was paid out, the excellent Corvinius Celer, is present (in the court); and indeed my wife's guardian (*tutor auctor*) is here, a most important and venerable man, to be named by me with all honor – Cassius Longinus. Ask him, Maximus,[25] whose purchase he authorized, and for what tiny little price a wealthy woman bought her own little property.

C The guardianship of women in the Roman East

Gaius tells us that non-Roman women in the provinces, while not subject to the same *tutela* as Roman women, nevertheless "often are in a sort of *tutela*" [*Institutes* I.193; see III.A]. His statement is borne out by evidence from non-legal, non-literary sources: inscriptions from Asia Minor and Greece and documents on papyri and other material from Egypt and the Near East.

In the ancient Greek cities on either side of the Aegean, the institution of such a guardian, called a *kyrios* ("lord"), went back many centuries. Before she was married, a woman's *kyrios* was her father; after marriage, her husband was *kyrios* (whereas the husband of a Roman woman would not be her *tutor*). If her husband died, her son or another male relative would take over the role of *kyrios*. Many inscriptions commemorating public actions by women, including sales, gifts to cities or associations, and legal transactions, state that the woman was acting "with *kyrios*" (adding the name of the *kyrios*), implying that his consent was necessary for the action to be valid [van Bremen 1996, 217–25].

Women in Roman Egypt also had *kyrioi*, the custom having been brought to Egypt by Greek settlers in the wake of Alexander's conquest. Again, the *kyrios* was usually a husband or a close male relative such as her father, brother, or son. The approval of the *kyrios* was required in certain types of written agreements and in legal proceedings, including some which did not require a *tutor*'s approval under Roman law [Taubenschlag 1955, 170–8; 1959, 353–77; Arjava 1996, 118–23; Arjava 1997].

Guardians are also mentioned in documents from the Jewish communities of the Roman provinces of Judaea and Arabia that are written in Greek (but not those written in Aramaic or

Nabatean). In these documents the guardian is called an *epitropos*, the word used for the guardian of a fatherless orphan in Egypt and the Aegean, and also for the guardian of a minor in the Jewish documents. Normally a woman's *epitropos* was her husband, unless he was himself a party to the transaction [Cotton 1997]. The presence of a woman's *epitropos* is noted in legal proceedings and marriage contracts of the Babatha archive [P.Yadin 14 and 20; see further Chapter 2, Part III.B and Chapter 5, Part II.B.2], and also appears in a recently published marriage contract from Judaea [Cotton 1994].

No *kyrios* (or *epitropos*) is mentioned in legal documents found at the Roman military outpost of Dura Europos on the Euphrates River in which women are active participants. This led the editors of the Dura documents to suggest that unlike women elsewhere in the Roman East, women at Dura were free of male guardianship [Welles, Fink and Gilliam 1959, 12 and 151]. However, a recently published parchment document from the Middle Euphrates area, not far from Dura, mentions a woman who claimed to have the *ius liberorum*, the "right of children" which freed mothers of three children from guardianship [P.Euphr. 15; on the *ius liberorum*, see III.D] . This suggests the existence of the Roman *tutela mulierum* in this area the first half of the third century, when the Dura and Middle Euphrates documents are dated.[26]

We can conclude that the institution of lifelong guardianship of women was known throughout the eastern half of the Roman Empire, where the guardian was usually the husband or a close male relative. The consent of the guardian was necessary to validate certain legal and financial activities to which women were parties, though the actions which required a guardian seem to have varied somewhat according to region. This guardianship was similar in many respects to the Roman *tutela mulierum*, except that the Roman *tutor* was not usually the husband nor, after Claudius' abolition of agnate *tutela*, was he necessarily a relative. The fact that after the mid-first century, a Roman woman's *tutor* often was not a family member and might be someone in a dependent relationship to her, such as her former slave, suggests that Roman women may have had more independence of action than their eastern sisters. Nevertheless, as recent studies have pointed out, male control or influence over women's actions could come from other sources, particularly within the family, whether or not such males were actually designated as "guardian" [van Bremen 1996; Beaucamp 1992; see Part III.E].

In addition to many documents in which women are mentioned as acting with (or without) a guardian in various transactions, we also have from Egypt a number of requests to officials from women, both Roman citizens and non-citizens, asking that a particular guardian be appointed for them.

The following petition from the town of Oxyrhynchus is dated before the Edict of Caracalla granted Roman citizenship to virtually all free inhabitants of the Empire.[27] It is in Greek, and from a woman who is not a Roman citizen and who needs a *kyrios* in order to borrow money. If a woman in Egypt who was not a Roman citizen did not have a *kyrios* (perhaps because she was a widow without grown male children) and wanted to transact a matter requiring a *kyrios'* approval, she would request a *kyrios* for that one transaction. Though the body of the petition was written by someone else (probably a professional scribe), Tabesammon, who explicitly says that she is literate, signed it herself.

Petitions for assignment of a *kyrios* were sent to a regional official, the *strategos* of the nome (district) where the woman lived, or his deputy, the "royal scribe" (*basilikos grammateus*). In the absence of both these officials, Tabesammon has addressed her request to a municipal official, the *exegetes*.

P.Oxy. I.56, 211 C.E.[28]

To Maximus, priest, *exegetes* in office, town councillor, from Tabesammon, daughter of Ammonios also known as Cassius, from the city of Oxyrhynchus, her mother being Diophantis, a citizen.[29] Borrowing for my essential needs money at interest to the sum of six thousand drachmas, upon the security of a vineyard belonging to me near the village of Sinarou and all things appertaining to it, knowing letters, I request of you – due to the fact that the acting *strategos*, the royal scribe, is not present – that Amoitas son of Ploution, his mother being Demetrous, from the afore-mentioned city of Oxyrhynchus, who is present and consents, be registered as my *kyrios* for this transaction only. I have paid the established tax for this request.[30]

Year 20 of the Emperors Caesars Lucius Septimius Severus Pius Pertinax Arabicus Adiabenicus Parthicus Maximus and Marcus Aurelius Antoninus Pius the Augusti [and Publius Septimius Geta][31] the Caesar Augustus, Phaophi 30.

(in another hand) I, Tabesammon daughter of Ammonios, have presented this.

(in a third hand) I, Amoitas son of Ploution, [consent].

Roman citizen women living in Egypt, like Roman women elsewhere, were supposed to have a *tutor* (called a *kyrios* in Egypt) on a permanent basis, unless they were still under *patria potestas* or had been released from the need for a *tutor* by the *ius liberorum*. The Julian and Titian law (*lex Iulia et Titia*), enacted in the mid-first century B.C.E., gave provincial governors the power to appoint guardians [Gaius, *Inst* I.185, in III.A; *Rules of Ulpian* 11.18]. Several petitions from Roman citizen women requesting as *kyrios* a man of their own choosing survive from second- and third-century Egypt [Modrzejewski 1974].

In the following petition (also from Oxyrhynchus) on papyrus to the prefect (governor) of Egypt, Aurelia Arsinoe asks that Aurelius Herminus be appointed as her *kyrios*. The petition is dated 21 May, 245, some years after the Edict of Caracalla, and so both Aurelia Arsinoe and the man she requests as *kyrios* are Roman citizens.[32] Like most women (and men) in antiquity, she was illiterate; someone else signs for her "since she does not know letters" – a standard phrase found on many documents from Roman Egypt.[33]

The prefect of Egypt probably received thousands of petitions each year, both while he was in residence at Alexandria and when he was conducting his assizes (*conventus*) elsewhere in the province [Lewis 1983, 185–95]. These petitions were pasted together in long papyrus rolls and kept in the prefect's office. This papyrus is not the original, but a copy made in the prefect's office, presumably for Aurelia Arsinoe to keep for herself. It preserves the petition, which was written in Latin, a Greek translation, and the prefect's subscription – that is, his response and official signature, written below the petition. It also records the number of the sheet and of the papyrus roll in which the original was pasted for storage in the prefect's archives. The text is fragmentary, but can be reconstructed from similar documents (e.g., P.Oxy. IV.720, written two years later to the same prefect; P.Oxy. XXXIV.2710; and SB III.6223, below).[34]

P.Oxy. XII.1466, 245 C.E.

[in Latin] To Valerius Firmus, prefect of Egypt, from Aurelia Arsinoe. I ask, lord [that you give to me as guardian, according to the Julian and Titian law and the decree of the Senate,[35] Aurelius] Erminus.

(in Greek) Year 2 Pachon 26. Sheet 94, Roll 1.[36]

(in Greek) Translation of the Latin:

(in Greek, in another hand)

To Valerius Firmus, prefect of Egypt from [Aurelia Arsinoe. I ask, lord, to give to me] as registered guardian according to the Julian and [Titian] law [according to the decree of the Senate, Aurelios Herminos. It was presented?] on the twelfth day before the Kalends of June in the consulship of Emperor [Philip Augustus and Titianus].

I, Aurelia Arsinoe, daughter of Sarapion [have presented this, asking that Aurelius Hermin]os be registered as my guardian.

I, Aurelius Tima[genes ... wrote this on her behalf] since she does not know letters. I, Aurelius Herminos son of Dionysios [consent to the request. Year 2, Pachon 26?]

(in Greek, perhaps in another hand) Unless you have the right to another guardian,[37] [I give you as guardian] the one whom [you request].

The preceding examples were on papyri. A different medium, the wax tablet, was used for the following document, which recorded the assignment of a guardian by the prefect of Egypt.[38] This was a diptych, with two wooden leaves (A and B) fastened together to form four pages (two exterior and two interior; the interior had a wax surface on which to write). The fourth page (the exterior of B) had the names in Latin of seven witnesses, all Roman citizen males (including C. Terentius Sarapammon, who had requested the tutor), and (in a different hand) the beginning of the same text as on the interior pages, which continued on the first page (the exterior of A). "Double documents" such as this are rare in Roman Egypt, almost all in Latin and from official Roman circles, but are found elsewhere in the Middle East, such as the Babatha archive from the "Cave of Letters" on the Dead Sea [see Lewis 1989, 6–10].

SB III.6223 (inner text only), 198 C.E.

(On the two interior pages:)

(in Latin) Q. Aemilius Saturninus, prefect of Egypt, with C. Terentius Sarapammon bringing the request,[39] gave as tutor to Mevia Dionysarion, according to the Julian and Titian law and the decree of the Senate, M. Julius Alexander, provided that *tutela* does not pass from a legitimate tutor.[40] D. E. R. E. E. B. T. S. S. [41]

Transacted at Alexandria in Egypt on the ninth day before the Kalends of October in the consulship of Saturninus and Gallus, in the seventh year of the Emperors Caesars L. Septimius Severus Pius Pertinax Arabicus Adiabenicus Parthicus Maximus and M. Aurelius Antoninus the Augusti, in the month Thot on day 26.[42]

(in another hand, in Greek) I, Mevia Dionysarion, have requested as registered (guardian) Julius Alexander, as above. I, Gaius Julius Heraklas, have written on her behalf as she does not know letters.

The outer leaves of the diptych (see above) have the same text as the inner leaves, and the names of seven witnesses.

D The ius liberorum

According to Gaius, freeborn women who had three children, and freedwomen who had four, were freed from *tutela mulierum* by the *ius (trium) liberorum*, the "right of (three) children" [*Institutes*. I.145 and I.194, Part III.A.1 above]. It is unclear if the children had to survive to a certain age in order for a woman to qualify for the *ius liberorum*, or if those who died shortly after birth also counted. If in fact all live births counted, then many, perhaps most, adult freeborn women would have been eligible for the *ius liberorum*.[43] It was much more difficult for freedwomen to obtain the *ius liberorum*. Not only did they have to have four rather than three children, but all four had to be born after their mother had been freed, and many women would not be freed until after their child-bearing years had mostly passed.[44]

Many women, however, may not have known about this imperial privilege or have been in a position to take advantage of it. Only Roman citizen women were eligible for the *ius liberorum*, as Augustus' marriage legislation was aimed only at Roman citizens. After the Edict of Caracalla in 212, the "right of children" became much more widespread, and the number of women in the papyri who claim that they have it increases, though a disproportionate number are from the well-to-do and influential class of *bouletai* (town councilors) [Sheridan 1996; cf. Sijpesteijn 1965; Beaucamp 1992, 193–267].

After the emperor Claudius abolished *tutela legitima* for freeborn women, *tutela mulierum* ceased to be a very restrictive institution for most women (again, freedwomen were at a disadvantage), leading one scholar to suggest that the *ius liberorum* then became "honorific rather than a practical advantage" [Dixon 1988, 89–91]. Certainly women who held the *ius liberorum* were proud of that fact; it is mentioned on their tombstones, and in Egypt Roman citizen women mention that they have the *ius liberorum* even in situations for which a tutor's consent would not have been required. We should not discount the importance of an imperially granted honor for women in the highly honor-conscious society of the Roman Empire. And despite the legal ability of women to participate in a number of business and legal actions, there was still a distrust of "womanly weakness" and the alleged "lightmindedness" of females in the popular mind [Part IV.C]. The *ius liberorum* gave a woman some clout when she acted in public and demonstrated that by fulfilling her child-bearing duty to the state, she had earned an imperial privilege.

Moreover, the *ius liberorum* carried other, more practical benefits for both women and men, particularly in regard to inheritance rights [Treggiari 1991a, 66–75]. The *senatusconsultum Tertullianum*, under the emperor Hadrian, granted women with the *ius liberorum* inheritance rights to their children who died without a will; previously the children's agnate relatives would have succeeded upon intestacy [See Chapter 5, Introduction]. Spouses with the *ius liberorum* were not subject to the Augustan legislation's restrictions on how much they could leave each other by will [see Chapter 2, Part I.B]. The emperor even sometimes granted the *ius liberorum* to those without children, as Trajan did for Pliny the Younger and Suetonius, thereby freeing them from the inheritance restrictions placed on childless people by the Augustan legislation [Pliny, *Epistles* X.2; X.94–5; cf. CIL VI.1877 and XI.6354 below].

As with *manus*-marriage and *tutela mulierum*, we are mainly dependent upon Gaius for our knowledge of the *ius liberorum* in classical law. Explicit mentions of the *ius liberorum* in the classical legal sources in the Justinianic corpus were deleted by Justinian's editors, though some rescripts and excerpts from jurists' commentaries on the Augustan legislation do refer more generally to privileges for those with children [e.g., Cod. Just. 5.37.12 in Part III.E; Cod. Just. 10.52.5 in Part VI.C]. That is because the *ius liberorum* itself was abolished in the fifth century [see Chapter 2, Part II.A]. However, there are references to the *ius liberorum* in non-literary sources. Papyri from Roman Egypt include many examples of women acting with the *ius liberorum*, called the *dikaion teknon* in Greek [Sijpesteijn 1965; P.Mich. XV, Appendix II; Sheridan 1996]. And among the documents recently discovered on the Middle Euphrates is a parchment in Greek dated 235 recording some sort of legal act (which was not carried out) by a widow with the *ius liberorum*.[45]

Presumably women who qualified for the *ius liberorum* had to submit proof of their child-bearing to the authorities so that their right to act without a tutor would be officially registered. However, only one such application for the *ius liberorum* actually survives, from mid-third century Oxyrhynchus. Aurelia Thaisous (who also goes by the Greek name Lolliane) asks the prefect to keep her application for the *ius liberorum* on file in his office.[46] Literacy was not required for release from guardianship, but few women in Roman Egypt could read, let alone write, and Thaisous' claim to literacy is meant to show that "she is particularly capable of acting on her own behalf" [Sheridan 1998, 199].

Another document, of four years later, records a business transation of the same Aurelia Thaisous [P.Oxy. XII.1475; see Pestman 1994, 245]. There she is explicitly said to be acting without a guardian by virtue of the *ius liberorum*.

P.Oxy. XII.1467, 263 C.E.

... [There have long been laws], most eminent prefect, which give power to women who have been adorned with the right of three children to have control over their own affairs and to act without a *kyrios* in the transactions that they undertake, and much more so to women who know letters. And therefore I myself, having been blessed with the honor of a goodly number of children and also being literate and especially being able to write with ease, with exceptional assurance address your greatness through this petition of mine in regard to being able to carry out without hindrance those transactions which I undertake henceforth. I ask that you keep this (petition) without verifying it beforehand[47] in your eminence's office, in order that I may be aided (by you) and acknowledge always my gratitude to you. Farewell.

I, Aurelia Thaisous, also known as Lolliane, have sent this for handing-in. Year 10, Epeiph 2?[48]

(reply from the prefect's office) Your petition will be kept in the office.

Though few documents recording legal and economic transactions survive from the Roman west, the *ius liberorum* is attested on several Latin inscriptions, mostly from Rome itself. This indicates that even if obtaining a tutor's authorization for legal acts was a formality for most freeborn women, the right to act without a tutor was still considered important.

A marble tablet, dug up in 1554 in a vineyard but now lost, recorded the donation by Statia Irene to Marcus Licinius Timotheus (also spelled Licinnius and Timoteus) of land outside Rome on which a funeral monument had been built.[49] The donation was made by the legal procedure of *mancipatio*, as was the similar donation by Julia Monime (in the presence of her tutor) to the *collegium* of Silvanus (translated in Part III.B above). No doubt it is because this transaction normally required a tutor's authorization that Statia Irene's possession of the *ius liberorum* is stated four times in this inscription, the last three times with the initials *i.l.h.* (*ius liberorum habens* = "having the *ius liberorum*").

Mancipatio is described by Gaius as an "imaginary sale" requiring five adult male Roman citizen witnesses and a scale-holder [Gaius, *Inst.* I.119–22; Schulz 1951, 344–8]. The person receiving the mancipated item struck the scales with a piece of bronze (here perhaps represented by the sestertius coin) and declared that he had bought the item "by bronze and bronze scales." Only one witness is mentioned in this inscription (and none in the inscription recording Julia Monime's donation). By the mid-third century, *mancipatio* was beginning to fall out of use, and the procedure may not always have been strictly followed.[50]

Statia Irene and Licinius Timotheus conclude their transaction with a stipulation (*stipulatio*), a verbal contract in which the stipulating party requested a verbal promise from the other party, who would reply "I solemnly promise" (*spondeo*) [Crook 1967, 207–8]. By the mid-third century, written documents were being used to supplement and provide evidence for the existence of oral contracts [see Gardner 1993, 182–6] . Here the verbal agreement is recorded in writing, on the stone inscription and also on a document (mentioned at the end of the inscription) which Statia Irene signed and sealed on the day of the transaction (31 July, 252).

CIL VI.10247, 252 C.E.

Statia Irene, having the *ius liberorum*, has given to M. Licinius Timotheus for the sake of donation and mancipation, for one sestertius coin, the monument which is on the Via Triumphalis between the second and third milestone for those going away from the city on the left side, on Cinna's hill, and is on the land of Aurelius Primianus, the baker[51] of the priests, men of senatorial status,[52] and is called (the land) of the Terentiani, next to the monument of the late Claudius Proculus and whatever other neighbors there are and where and whatever people it borders on; with Claudius Dativus holding the scales (and) Cornelius Victor as witness; and she has yielded to vacant possession of the above-mentioned monument.[53] And the right of way, access, going around, drawing of water, wreathing and feeding or bringing in the bones of a dead person, dead females or dead males, to that monument shall be permitted.[54]

This above-mentioned monument you, Statia Irene, *i.l.h.*, have given to me, Licinnius Timotheus, by manicipation for one sestertius coin, (and) that about this matter evil intent is absent and will be absent from you (and) your heir and from all those to whom this matter will pertain, (and) that these things were thus correctly given and done and performed, Licinius Timoteus has stipulated (and) Statia Irene, *i.l.h.*, has solemnly promised.

Transacted on the day before the Kalends of August in the consulship of the emperors, our lords, Gallus Augustus for the second time and Volusianus Augustus.

In the same consulship on the same day, I, Statia Irene, *i.l.h.*, have consented, subscribed, and given my seal to the donation of the above-mentioned monument just as has been written above. Transacted.

Because the *ius liberorum* was an honor as well as a legal benefit, it is sometimes mentioned on inscriptions commemorating women who held it. The following inscription was set up by the town council (decurions) of Pisaurum (on the Adriatic coast of Italy) to honor their town's patron, Abeiana Balbina. It was not uncommon, especially in the third and fourth centuries, for communities to seek support and patronage from a prominent individual, who would look out for their interests by interceding for them with the imperial or provincial government, building or restoring public buildings in the town, and giving out largesse. Almost all known municipal patrons are men; out of over 1200 known patrons of civic communities from the western Empire, only about twenty are women, all from Italy or North Africa. Female patrons are first attested in the Severan period, and their appearance has been linked to the public prominence of the imperial women of this dynasty [Nicols 1989, 122–3]. *Patronae* are always of very high status, usually of senatorial or high equestrian rank [Nicols 1989, 118; Kajava 1990, 28–9]. Their status and family connections made them attractive patrons to towns and to other municipal organizations [see also Part VI.C].

Abeiana Balbina was a priestess of the imperial cult (*flaminica*), and her husband had been a *quinquennalis*, the highest municipal magistracy, one of the two chief decurions elected every five years to take the census [Dyson 1992, 204–5]. They had been granted the *ius liberorum commune* (elsewhere called the *ius liberorum communium*). This enabled them to inherit fully from each other by will, a privilege not available to couples without children [see Chapter 2, Part I.B]. The name of the emperor who granted the *ius liberorum* has been obliterated, indicating that he suffered a *damnatio memoriae* (official condemnation of memory) after his death. He was probably Commodus, son of Marcus Aurelius, who was assassinated at the end of 192.

CIL XI.6354 = ILS 6655, late 2nd c.

To Abeiana Balbina, daughter of Gaius, a *flaminica* of Pisaurum and Ariminum, *patrona* of the town of the Pitinatian Pisaurensians. To her, in the year when her husband Petinus Aper was *quinquennalis*, the common people of the city of the Pisaurum (set this up) on account of their meritorious actions. To her the emperor [the name has been obliterated] granted the common right of children (*ius commune liberorum*). Place given by decree of the decurions (*L.d.d.d.*)[55]

In the following epitaph from Rome, the freedman Persicus commemorates his wife Cornelia Zosima, also an ex-slave, and their freeborn son, C. Cornelius Persicus.[56] Persicus had held important posts as an *apparitor* (public servant), positions which could lead to social advancement for an ambitious freedman. His son had gained equestrian status (the "public horse"), and his wife, Cornelia Zosima, had been granted the *ius quattuor liberorum* – the "right of four children" rather than "three" because she was a freedwoman [Gaius, *Inst.* I.194; Part III.A]. The expression "by the favor of Caesar" (*beneficio Caesaris*) indicates that Cornelia Zosima, like Abeiana Balbina, had received the *ius liberorum* as a personal benefit from the Emperor, an interesting example of an imperial grant of the *ius liberorum* to a former slave [cf. Arjava 1996, 78].

CIL VI.1877 (ILS 1910), late 1st c. C.E.

The freedman Persicus, who was manumitted by a *consilium* before the Caesar Domitian acting in a procuratorial capacity during his (Domitian's) second consulship,[57] was employed in two companies of public servants for the consuls, the company of summoners and the company of lictors, (and set this up) for his son C. Cornelius Persicus, who had the public horse, (and) for Cornelia Zosima, his (the son's) mother, who had the right of four children by the favor of Caesar, and for his and their freedmen and freedwomen and their descendants.

The following semi-literate inscription was found on marble tablet at Rome, erected by the wife of an imperial freedman as a tomb monument for herself, her husband, and two of her children, whose nomenclature indicates that they were freeborn but illegitimate (presumably born while their father was still a slave; see above for a similar situation). Women did not require a tutor's authorization to set up a gravestone, and it appears that the only reason Septimia Dionisias mentions her possession of the *ius liberorum* is because she is proud of it, as she is also of her frugality in saving enough to afford this funerary monument. She may have been a former slave herself (in which case she would had to have borne four children rather than three) or the descendant of freedmen. The fact that she herself has *liberti* who are given burial rights in her tomb is a further indication of the social success of which she is so proud.

The Latin of the inscription contains a number of grammatical and spelling errors and is not fully intelligible (note, for instance, the variations in spelling of the *nomen*: Dionisias herself has the correct form Septimia; her son Venerius is Setimius, and her daughter's name,

41

originally spelled Setimia, was corrected by squeezing the "p" in above the line). The inscription apparently dates to the third century [Weaver 1972, 24, note 2].

CIL VI.10246, 3rd c.

Septimia Dionisias, having the *ius liberorum*, in this little Peladian place of confinement[58] with a little building and a monument which I built from the ground out of my own frugality for me and my husband, Titus the freedman of Augustus and for my children, Setimius Venerius and Septimia Efesia, and I order that it not go out of my name; but if anyone has broken the law of my passing (*preteriti mei*) he shall bear in the name of punishment (a fine of) 50,000 denarii.[59] (For my) freedmen and freedwomen (and) their descendants.

A number of Greek inscriptions commemorating women in Greece and Asia Minor mention that the women held the *dikaion teknon* [see Spawforth 1985, 192, 207–8, 234; van Bremen 1996, 226–8]. These were women of the local elites, many of whom had received Roman citizenship even before the universal grant of Caracalla. The following inscription from Ephesus was inscribed on a sarcophagus, and records a legal transaction in which Claudia Antonia Tatiane grants her brother[60] and his wife right of burial in her *heroon* (burial shrine). As with Statia Irene above, possession of the *ius liberorum* is mentioned in order to give validation to the transaction and demonstrate the woman's right to act on her own. Claudia Antonia Tatiane and her brother were Roman citizens and of equestrian status, as his title (*kratistos*, "most excellent") indicates. She is known from other inscriptions for her benefactions [van Bremen 1996, 227]. The sarcophagus on which this Greek inscription was written may have been that of Aemilius Aristides and his wife.[61]

SEG IV.544, 204 C.E.

Claudia Antonia Tatiane greetings to the most excellent Aemilius Aristides. I grant to you, my lord brother, [the ... sarcophagus] in my heroon in Ephesus before the [Magnesian] Gate, in which to bury your wife. I have written this letter through my slave Dionysios, which I also myself have subscribed, in the consulship of Fabius Chilo for the second time and An[nius Libo ... you have the power to keep it] or to put it away into whatever archives you wish, even without my being present. Cl. Antonia Tatiane, having the right of children, I have ordered [... it to happen ... just as] it has been written above, and I bid you farewell, my lord.

And it was put into the archives on the tenth day before the Kalends of December in the consulship of Fabius Chilo [and Annius Libo].

The next inscription, written in Latin, is an epitaph for a Christian woman, set up by her husband, a Christian priest (*presbyter*). It was found at Nicopolis in the province of Moesia (Bulgaria), near Aurelia Marcellina's hometown of Oescus.[62] The use of the Christian *chi rho* symbol, which appears in art and inscriptions only after the victory of Constantine over Maxentius, indicates that the epitaph is later than 312, though probably before 400. Thus even in the fourth century, among Christians, the *ius liberorum* was an honor worth noting on a woman's tomb [see Evans Grubbs 1995, 81]

CIL III.755, 4th c.

[chi rho symbol]
To the good memory of Aurelia Marcellina from Oescus, a most dutiful woman, who had the *ius liberorum*, formerly the daughter of Marcellinus, ex-prefect of the legion Tertia Gallica, at Danaba (near) Damascus, who lived fifty years. The priest Turranius Leontius made this while alive as a memorial for his well-deserving wife and for himself.

E Tutela mulierum *in late antiquity*

Tutela mulierum disappears from Roman legal sources in the early fourth century. The latest references appear in the *Rules of Ulpian* [Part III.A] and in a fragmentary collection of legal sources now known as the *Vatican Fragments* (*Fragmenta Vaticana*), which includes selections from classical jurists and imperial rescripts. Both the *Rules of Ulpian* and the *Vatican Fragments* probably date to around 320 [Robinson 1997, 64–5]. The last clearly dated legal evidence for *tutela mulierum* is an imperial rescript of 293, preserved in the *Vatican Fragments* but not in the *Code of Justinian*:

Frag. Vat. 325, 9 November, 293

The deified Diocletian and Constantius to Aurelia Panthea:

The plaintiff ought to follow the forum[63] of the defendant, and indeed, a woman is not prohibited from appointing a procurator without her tutor's authorization. Therefore if you have a legal action, you ought to go to law legally rather than make any claims contrary to those (legal rules) which have been established according to your status. Posted on the fifth day before the Ides of November at Heraclea in the fifth and fourth consulships respectively of the emperors.

The subject of Aurelia Panthea's legal claim is not known, but the rescript is in keeping with earlier law. A woman did not need her tutor's authorization to appoint a representative (*procurator*[64]) to act for her in court. Given ancient attitudes about the impropriety of women appearing in court [see Part V], many women would have appointed such a representative rather than appear to act inappropriately.

Tutela mulierum is mentioned elsewhere in the *Vatican Fragments*, including several excerpts from the works of jurists. The following fragment was taken from the fifteenth book of *Responses* of a jurist whose name is not preserved, perhaps Papinian or Paulus:

Frag. Vat. 327: Also a woman, even without her tutor's authorization, is able to appoint a procurator.

Note again the reference to a woman's appointing a procurator to represent her; a *tutor mulierum* did not act as a legal advocate.

The first passage below (Frag. Vat. 1) appears also at D.18.1.27 in a context relating to the guardianship of under-age children (*tutela impuberum*), where it is attributed to the jurist Paulus. Justinian's compilers may have adapted a text that originally referred to *tutela mulierum* so that it applied to *tutela impuberum*, since by Justinian's day the guardianship of women was no longer a reality [Schulz 1951, 184]. The second passage (Frag. Vat. 45) is said to be from the *Handbooks* (*Manuales*) of Paulus:

Frag. Vat. 1: Someone who knowingly buys *res mancipi* (from a woman) without her tutor's authorization or with the authorization of a false tutor who he knew was not (her real tutor), appears not to have bought in good faith; so the ancient legal authorities also think and so Sabinus and Cassius write. [the rest of the passage is here omitted]

Frag. Vat. 45: Though the usufruct of an estate is not *(res) mancipi*, nevertheless a woman is not able to alienate it without her tutor's authorization, since she is not able to do it other than by legally surrendering and legal surrender is not able to be done without a tutor's authorization. The same is true in regard to praedial urban servitudes.[65]

The *Vatican Fragments* are from a compilation probably made during the reign of the emperor Constantine. Though considerable legislation of Constantine relating to women is known from the two major collections of imperial legislation, the *Theodosian Code* and the *Code of Justinian*, it includes no clear reference to the guardianship of women. A fragment of a Constantinian edict has in the past been interpreted as repealing the law of Claudius that had abolished the *tutela legitima* of a woman's agnate relatives almost three centuries earlier [see Part III.A]:

Cod. Theod. 3.17.2, 31 December, 326
Constantine Augustus and the Caesar to the people:

A paternal uncle related by blood is not to refuse *tutela legitima* over women. Given on the day before the Kalends of January in the seventh consulship of the Augustus himself and the consulship of the Caesar.

But in the fifth century, the eastern emperor Leo interpreted Constantine's law as referring to *tutela pupillarum*, the guardianship of fatherless minor women, rather than *tutela mulierum* [Cod. Just. 5.30.3, 472]. Scholars who have written recently on women in late Roman law agree with Leo [Beaucamp 1992, 261; Evans Grubbs 1995, 327; Arjava 1996, 116–17].

In contrast with the lack of legal references to *tutela mulierum*, late Roman legal sources have a good deal to say about the guardianship of fatherless minors, both those below puberty (who had a *tutor impuberum*) and those above puberty but below twenty-five, the age of majority (who had a *curator minorum*). By this period it was obligatory for both males and females under twenty-five whose father was dead to have either a tutor or a curator [see Part II.C]. The increased importance of the curator no doubt contributed to the decline of *tutela mulierum*, since the curator made the *tutor mulierum* for women under twenty-five appear unnecessary.

Even women who had earned the *ius liberorum*, which gave them the right to conduct their affairs without a *tutor mulierum* [see Part III.D], had to have a curator if they had not yet attained the legal age of twenty-five:

Cod. Just. 5.37.12, 5 October, 241
Emperor Gordian Augustus to Octaviana:

Only if you have attained legal age should you go to law about those matters which you allege have been done by the tutor in regard to fraudulent administration or have been conducted negligently by the curators of those to whom you have succeeded. For you are not unaware that an abundance of children does not provide much support to women in regard to managing their own affairs, if they are below legal age. Posted on the third day before the Nones of October in the second consulship of Gordian Augustus and the consulship of Pompeianus.

Octaviana had inherited the estate of a minor whose property had been mismanaged by his guardians, and she wished to bring charges against these guardians [see Chapter 5, Part II on accusations against guardians]. But the emperor tells her that she cannot act for herself if she is still under twenty-five. Her "abundance of children" (*fecunditatem liberorum*) refers to possession of the *ius liberorum*, which would have freed her from a *tutor mulierum* but not from a *curator minorum* [Arjava 1996, 115]. Other rescripts rule that a minor (male or female) may appoint a procurator to handle his or her legal affairs, with the approval of the *curator minorum* or *tutor impuberum* [cf. Frag. Vat. 326 and Cod. Just. 3.6.2 (294)].

By the mid-third century the *curator minorum* seems to have superseded the *tutor mulierum* for women below the age of twenty-five.[66] (A law of Constantine allowed young women at age eighteen to petition for the *venia aetatis*, the "indulgence of legal age", which would release them from the need for a curator; see Part IV.B). By the time they turned twenty-five and were free of a curator's supervision, most women would be married, and many would be eligible for the *ius liberorum* by having had three children [Arjava 1997, 29].

In earlier Roman law, a woman's husband was not also her tutor; on the contrary, the original purpose of *tutela mulierum* had been to safeguard the woman's property for her natal family against its possible depredation by non-relatives, including her husband. This purpose had been long forgotten, and Claudius' abolition of agnate *tutela*, along with second-century legislation favoring the transmission of a mother's estate to her children, meant that a woman's natal family no longer could control her disposition of property.

Some later imperial legal sources recognize the husband as representing his wife in public situations, particularly in court. A rescript of Marcus Aurelius and Lucius Verus allows a woman Sextilia to be represented through her husband in litigation over a financial matter, assuming that she formally appoints him her procurator [Cod. Just. 2.12.2, 161]. Eighty years later, Gordian told a petitioner that the fact that his opponent, a married woman under twenty-five, appointed her husband as procurator without her curator's consent does not provide grounds for overturning the court's decision in her favor [Cod. Just. 2.12.14, 241]. This is particularly remarkable in view of the same emperor's reply to another minor woman that her possession of the *ius liberorum* did not enable her to go to court without her curator's permission [Cod. Just. 5.37.12, see above]. Generally, minors of either sex could not act legally without the authorization of their tutor or curator.

In the early fourth century, Constantine ruled that a husband could represent his wife in court as her procurator, even if she had not formally appointed him by mandate [Cod. Just. 2.12.21, 315; see Part IV.B]. In two other laws he assumed that husbands acted legally for their wives [Cod. Theod. 3.5.3, 330; cf. 3.1.3 of the emperor Julian]. This was in line with social practice in the eastern Mediterranean, where the husband was generally his wife's *kyrios*. This does not mean that Constantine actually made the husband his wife's tutor, or was directly influenced by eastern legal systems.[67] Rather, he granted de facto recognition to a social practice which already existed, probably in the west as well as the east, where the husband was considered to represent his wife in public [Beaucamp 1992, 264–6; Evans Grubbs 1995, 326–8].

The classical Roman *tutela mulierum* may never have been actually abolished by law. (At any rate, no such law survives, though this could be due to the incomplete preservation of legal sources like the *Theodosian Code*.) Instead, it faded into desuetude by the end of the fourth century. The *ius liberorum* lasted longer, but this was because of its importance in inheritance matters, not *tutela*: women with the *ius liberorum* had improved succession rights to the property of their intestate children, and couples with the *ius commune liberorum* could inherit from each other by will.[68] By the end of the fourth century, the *ius liberorum* was no longer associated with freedom from *tutela mulierum*, because *tutela mulierum* itself was no longer a living legal concept.

The same evolution appears in the papyri from Egypt, where considerable documentary evidence survives. After an exhaustive study of the evidence for guardianship in late antique Egypt, Joelle Beaucamp came to the following conclusions [Beaucamp 1992, 193–267; cf. Arjava 1996, 112–56]:

1 There are only four documents from the fourth through sixth centuries in which women are said to be acting with a *kyrios*. In all four, the *kyrios* is the woman's husband. (This was common practice also in earlier Roman Egypt, unlike the situation in Roman law.)

2 There are almost sixty cases from the same period where women are explicitly said to be acting *without* a *kyrios*. Up until the later fourth century they are said to be acting without *kyrios* because they have the *ius liberorum* (*dikaion teknon*). The last reference to the *dikaion teknon* is in 389. After this, it appears that the reason the women act without *kyrios* is because they have no husband; in almost all cases, they are clearly widows. Sometimes women who do not have a *kyrios* are accompanied by a male *synestos* ("associate") in their legal transactions [see P.Oxy. X.1273 in Chapter 2, Part III.A.4 for an example]. Apparently women themselves could serve as *synestos*: in a divorce agreement of 391 a woman is accompanied by her mother as *synestos* [P.Stras. III.142; see Chapter 4, Part III.A.5].

3 Thus in late antique Egypt the husband's role took over and eclipsed that of *kyrios*, and the only way to escape guardianship by a husband-*kyrios* was via widowhood. Beaucamp sees this as a strengthening of marital control over women: a woman needed her husband's authorization, or at least his consent, for all legal acts which directly affected her property, especially selling land or houses and manumitting slaves.

Though this evolution of the concept of guardianship and of the husband's role was not due to any imperial legislative enactment, the authority granted the husband in his wife's affairs parallels the development in late Roman law, as seen in the legislation of Constantine mentioned above. Whether this means that women, specifically married women, were more subject to "control" than in the earlier Empire, is debatable. Rather, law and practice coincide in recognizing the nuclear family as the essential unit in property transmission, and a woman's husband and children as those most concerned regarding the fate of her property. There was no sudden transformation in late antiquity; these trends go back at least to the Principate, with the abolition of agnatic *tutela* and the recognition of mother–child inheritance rights. Only the innate conservatism of Roman law kept *tutela mulierum* in second- and third-century legal manuals like Gaius' *Institutes* and the *Rules of Ulpian*.

IV Legal stereotypes of women's abilities and behavior

The Romans, like the Greeks before them, held many traditional ideas about women's behavior and the role women should play in society. These views are reflected in the writings of the jurists, even when, at times, the jurists themselves do not agree with them. Imperial pronouncements of the third, fourth, and fifth centuries also endorse popular ideas of woman's "weakness" and legal inadequacy. Such stereotypes helped to explain the restrictions on women's legal and public activities [for which see Parts V and VI], which were often at odds with the realities of women's activities and evident competence.

A Legal assistance for women

Roman legal writers believed that women (and *pupilli*, fatherless minors) should receive assistance in legal matters and their ignorance of the law could be excused. Though some scholars have believed such references in classical jurists to be Justinianic interpolations, this is unlikely. Indeed, late Roman law may even have been less inclined to grant women the benefit of ignorance of the law [Beaucamp 1990, 87–92].

D.1.16.9.5 (Ulpian): He (a provincial governor) should in general also grant advocates to those requesting them: to women or *pupilli* or those weak in other respects, or to those who are not in their right mind, if someone else requests on their behalf; or if there is no one who requests (on their behalf), he should of his own accord give them (an advocate).

D.2.13.1.5 (Ulpian): Aid will be given to those who, having made a mistake on account of their age or rusticity,[69] or on account of their sex, have not given formal notice (of their intention to bring a legal action).

The jurist Paulus is less certain that women deserve extra legal help:

D.2.8.8.2 (Paulus): [the first sentence is here omitted] ... Help must be given to the minor under twenty-five years, and perhaps also to a woman on account of her inexperience (*imperitia*).

D.22.6.9 pr. (Paulus): The rule is that ignorance of the law does hurt a person, but ignorance of fact does not. Let us see therefore, in what types (of situation) this can hold true, having mentioned in advance that minors under twenty-five are allowed to be ignorant of the law. This is also said in regard to women in certain cases, on account of the weakness of their sex; and so wherever there is not a delict, but ignorance of the law, they are not harmed.[70]

One instance where her ignorance of the law would not hurt her was when a woman informed on herself to the imperial treasury; those who were ignorant due to "rusticity" were also excused [D.49.14.2.7 (Callistratus); cf. D.2.13.1.5 above]. On female "weakness," see Part IV.C below.

D.50.17.110.4 (Paulus): Aid must be given to women when they are being defended in court, not so that they more easily practice legal chicanery.

Sometimes women may have claimed the benefit of ignorance of the law when it did not apply. Thus one female petitioner was sternly informed:

Cod. Just. 6.9.6, 29 April, 294

Emperors Diocletian and Maximian and the Caesars to Frontina:
It is clear in the development of the Perpetual Edict on recognizing *bonorum possessio*[71] that ignorance of the law does not benefit women. Given

at Sirmium on the third day before the Kalends of May in the consulship of the Caesars.

Late imperial law continued to recognize that women (and minors) deserved special help, while stating clearly that women were not to take advantage of this leniency for their own financial gain:

Cod. Theod. 3.5.3 (first sentence only), 28 April, 330
Emperor Constantine Augustus to Valerian, acting Vicar of the prefect:

Though in matters of profit it is not customary to come to the aid of women who are ignorant of the law, the statutes of former emperors declare that this does not hold true in regard to (women) not yet of the age of majority ... [the rest of the law is omitted here][72]

Given on the fourth day before the Kalends of May in the consulship of Gallicanus and Symmachus.

Cod. Theod. 2.16.3, 6 March, 414
Emperors Honorius and Theodosius Augusti to Julianus Secundus, proconsul of Africa:

It is agreed by numerous authorities that consideration is (to be given) to women and minors in those situations, in which they have been either negligent or ignorant. Given at Ravenna on the day before the Nones of March in the consulship of Constantius and Constans.[73]

Cod. Just. 1.18.13, 1 July, 472
Emperors Leo and Anthemius Augusti to Erythrius, praetorian prefect:

In order that women not be allowed indiscriminately to retract all their contracts in those matters where they have been negligent or ignorant, we have decided that if through ignorance of the law they should suffer some loss about the law or their property, aid is to be given to them only in those cases, in which the authority of the laws that they neglected favors them. Given on the Kalends of July in the consulship of Marcianus.[74]

B Women's modesty and the need for protection

Imperial legal sources frequently invoke the notions of female "modesty" (*pudor*) and sexual chastity (*pudicitia*), and sometimes their "sense of shame" (*verecundia*). Concern with preserving women's modesty and good reputation is behind laws which restrict women's right of public action and laws which seek to protect women from dishonor. Like the idea of womanly weakness, concern with female modesty appears often in non-legal writers, and made its way into Roman law through popular ideas of gender roles [Evans Grubbs 1995, 321–30; Gardner 1993, 101–7]. Stress on feminine chastity and sense of modesty is particularly marked in late Roman law, reaching its culmination with the sixth-century emperor Justinian [Beaucamp 1990, 17–23].

For instance, the Praetor's Edict[75] stated that women could not bring a prosecution on behalf of another person [see Part V.A]. According to Ulpian :

D.3.1.1.5 (Ulpian): [see Part V.A for the beginning of the passage] ... And indeed there is a reason for prohibiting them: so that women not get themselves mixed up in other people's lawsuits contrary to the modesty suitable for their sex, (and) so that women not discharge men's duties.

Only in certain circumstances could women initiate legal action on behalf of others, and even then only with respect for their modesty. For example, female relatives could bring an accusation of "untrustworthy guardian" [see Chapter 5, Part II.A.2]

D.26.10.1.7 (Ulpian): [see Chapter 5, Part II.A.2 for the beginning of the passage] ... And if there is any other woman, whose well-considered sense of duty (*pietas*) the praetor has understood to be that of a woman who does not go beyond the sense of shame for her sex (*sexus verecundia*), but, induced by her sense of duty, is not able to keep to herself the injury done to the minor, he will allow her to bring an accusation.

Several laws of Constantine restrict and protect women from face-to-face involvement in public proceedings. They express a view found in some ancient literary sources but not before stated in such strong terms in Roman law, that respectable women should lead a secluded and modest life away from the public eye. This combination of restriction and protection of women's public activities is not found again in Roman law until Justinian [Arjava 1996, 243–6; Beaucamp 1990, 136–8; Clark 1993, 56–62; Evans Grubbs 1995, 326–9].

Cod. Just. 2.12.21, 12 March, 315
Emperor Constantine Augustus to the Council of the province of Africa:
    A husband shall have the free capacity of interceding in his wife's affairs without a mandate (but) with the usual giving of security and other observances, so that women not rush irreverently into scorn of their matronly modesty (*matronalis pudor*) on the pretext of prosecuting a lawsuit, and so that they not be compelled to be present at the gatherings of men or at trials ...[76]
    Posted at Hadrumetum on the fourth day before the Ides of March in the fourth consulship of Constantine Augustus and the fourth consulship of Licinius.

Cod. Theod. 1.22.1, 11 January, 316
Emperor Constantine Augustus to Domitius Celsus, Vicar (of the province of Africa):
    Let no judge determine with any command that an official should be sent to that home in which resides a *materfamilias* in order to drag her out into public, since it is certain that the financial obligations of a woman who keeps herself within her home out of consideration for her sex can be safeguarded for the public needs by the division and sale of her home or some other property.[77] So if anyone hereafter believes that a *materfamilias* is to be dragged into public, (he shall be considered) among the most greatest

criminals without any hope of reprieve, (and) he shall be struck by a capital penalty, or rather, by exquisite torments of destruction.

Given at Trier on the third day before the Ides of January in the consulship of Sabinus and Rufinus.[78]

By the fourth century, men and women under the legal age of twenty-five whose *paterfamilias* was dead were required to have either a tutor or a curator [see Part III.E. above]. In a law of 324, Constantine allowed minors who had displayed *honestas morum* ("honorable character") to request the *venia aetatis* ("indulgence of age"), which would enable them to manage their own properties before they turned twenty-five. Young men could request the *venia aetatis* when they turned twenty, women when they turned eighteen (because, according to the law, they matured more quickly). To receive this privilege, they had to provide proof of age and have their character vouched for by men of rank and reputation, apparently in a public assembly. But the emperor made a concession to young women: they did not have to appear in public:

Cod. Theod. 2.17.1.1, 9 April, 324

Emperor Constantine Augustus to Verinus, urban prefect:

[the beginning of the law is omitted here] ... (1) We have decreed that women also, whose age (of maturity) precedes (that of) men by two years due to early puberty, after an interval of time has been observed also in this case, are able to earn the right of legal age after they have turned eighteen; but (only) those whom an honorable character, an intelligent mind, and a steady reputation commend. But on account of (their) modesty and sense of shame (*propter pudorem ac verecundiam*), we do not force them to be pointed out by witnesses in a public gathering, but we allow them, after receiving the *venia aetatis*, only to prove their age by means of documents or witnesses, having sent a representative (*procurator*), so that in all business matters they too shall have the same right as we have ordered that men have ... [the rest of the law is omitted here]

Given at Thessalonika on the fifth day before the Ides of April, posted at Rome on the third day before the Kalends of June in the second [third] consulship of the Caesars Crispus and Constantine.[79]

A law of Constantine's son Constantius called for separation of the sexes in prison cells, evidently out of concern for sexual propriety:

Cod. Theod. 9.3.3, 5 April, 340

Emperor Constantius Augustus to Acindynus, praetorian prefect:

Since one closed chamber of a prison includes criminals mixed up together, we ordain by this law that, even if the nature of their penalty must be associated by this mixing together, however, it shall be ordered that separate guarded enclosures hold the different sexes.

Given on the Nones of April in the consulship of Acindynus and Proculus.[80]

C "Womanly weakness"

Because the original purpose of *tutela mulierum* [see Introduction to Part III] had been forgotten by Gaius' time, he and other legal writers looked for another reason for a woman's need to have her legal actions authorized by an unrelated male. They turned to traditional, popular ideas about the weakness and "lightmindedness" of women, and their need for supervision, ideas which also appear in literature of the late Republic and early Empire.[81]

1 "Womanly weakness" in Roman legal sources

Legal references to womanly weakness go back at least to the early third century C.E., and Joelle Beaucamp has shown that they cannot all be due to post-classical interpolations, as used to be supposed [Beaucamp 1976; 1990, 11–15]. The concept of "womanly weakness" may have been alien to Roman law originally, but it was useful for explaining legal constraints on women's public actions [Clark 1993, 56–62; Crook 1986a; Dixon 1984; Gardner 1993, 85–109; Marshall 1989, 51–4].

Gaius, *Institutes* I.144: [See III.A.1 for the beginning of this passage.] ... For the ancients wanted women, even if they are of full age, to be in *tutela* because of their lightmindedness (*animi levitas*).

Later, however, Gaius expresses skepticism about the traditional explanation:

I.190: However, almost no reason of value appears to recommend that women of full age be in *tutela*. For the reason which is commonly believed, that since they are very often deceived due to their lightmindedness, it was right for them to be ruled by the authority of tutors, seems to be specious rather than true ... [see Part III.A.1 for the rest of this passage]

But the concept of "womanly weakness" persisted in legal texts of the third and fourth centuries. The *Rules of Ulpian*, dating to the early fourth century, repeats Gaius' explanation for *tutela mulierum* but not his reservations about the necessity for it:

Rules of Ulpian 11.1: Guardians are appointed for both males and females, but for males only as long as they are below puberty, on account of the weakness of their age; however, for females both below puberty and above, both on account of their weakness of their sex (*sexus infirmitas*) and their ignorance of legal affairs [see also Part III.A.2].

Women's alleged "weakness" was cited by jurists and emperors as the reason for the different legal treatment of men and women. Thus their weakness explained why in some circumstances women were allowed ignorance of the law [D.22.6.9 pr; Part IV.A], why women were not allowed to be informers [D.49.14.18 pr; Part V.A], and why mothers could not serve as guardians of their fatherless children [Chapter 5, Part II.A.3]. Women's *infirmitas* was even used to explain why the obligation to serve as a decurion (town councillor) was transmitted through the paternal rather than the maternal line:

Cod. Theod. 12.1.137.1, 9 August, 393

Emperors Theodosius, Arcadius and Honorius Augusti to Rufinus, praetorian prefect:

[the beginning of the law is omitted here] ... (1) Of course, no one shall be bound (to curial service) by the bonds of maternal blood alone, since the weakness of women never renders them liable for discharging this sort of duties, from which it shall be considered immune. Given at Constantinople on the fifth day before the Ides of August in the third consulship of Theodosius Augustus and the consulship of Abundantius.[82]

Several fourth-century laws mention the possibility of different, more lenient penalties for women in certain cases. For instance, Constantine called for distinctions in penalties for counterfeiting according not only to status but also to sex.[83] On the other hand, he was so strongly opposed to abduction that he decreed the same penalty for those assisting an abduction regardless of sex [see Cod. Theod. 9.24.1 in Chapter 3, Part II.C]. As we have them, these laws do not explicitly mention "womanly weakness" as the reason for the difference in punishments, but in a law of 397, the eastern emperor Arcadius cited the "weakness of their sex" (*sexus infirmitas*) as the reason for different penalties for daughters and sons of conspirators against the state. Sons were to be deprived of their inheritance rights from both their fathers (whose property had been confiscated) and their mothers. The law continues:

Cod. Theod. 9.14.3.2, 4 September, 397

Emperors Arcadius and Honorius Augusti to Eutychianus, praetorian prefect:

[the beginning of the law is omitted here] ... However, to their daughters, however many there are, we wish to fall only the Falcidian portion[84] from their mother's property, whether she has died testate or intestate, so that they may have the sustenance in the manner of an ungrateful daughter rather than the benefit and name of heir in full. For the sentence ought to be gentler in regard to those who, we trust, will be less daring due to the weakness of their sex ... [the rest of the law is omitted here]

Given on the day before the Nones of September at Ancyra in the consulship of Caesarius and Atticus.[85]

Not all late antique emperors made special concessions to feminine "weakness." In 424, a law of Theodosius II set a statute of limitations of thirty years for making claims to property in the hands of another, and explicitly denied that exception could be made due to "frailty of sex" [Cod. Theod. 4.14.1.2].

2 "Womanly weakness" in the papyri

In papyri from Roman Egypt, women themselves invoke "womanly weakness" in their petitions to authorities. In particular, widows and unmarried women whose fathers were dead could claim to have been taken advantage of by unscrupulous males because of their vulnerability and lack of protection. It is tempting to suspect that, in Ulpian's words [D.16.1.2.2–3; in Part IV.D], women sometimes claimed legal assistance out of *calliditas* (cleverness, cunning) rather than *infirmitas* (weakness, vulnerability). Evidently, claiming to be weak and liable to deception by others due to one's sex was a useful rhetorical device for attracting sympathy from officials.[86]

The following papyrus documents from the city of Oxyrhynchus, all in Greek, illustrate the types of situation in which women might claim "womanly weakness" as a reason for receiving aid or special treatment.

In the agreement below, Demetria (accompanied by her *kyrios*; see III.C), authorizes her grandson to serve as her legal representative in a legal dispute, claiming she cannot go to court herself because of "womanly weakness."[87] This Greek document dates from around the time that the *senatusconsultum Velleianum* was enacted [Part IV.D]. Demetria was not a Roman citizen (she calls herself "citizen," but this refers to Alexandrian citizenship[88]) and so would not have been affected by the Senate's decree. But the fact that both the Roman Senate and a provincial woman give feminine "weakness" as a reason for women to avoid legal obligations suggests it was a standard excuse, which it was thought to be to a woman's advantage to cite.

Demetria was probably fairly elderly, since her grandson is old enough to be her representative. "Weakness" (*astheneia*), whether feminine or not, may have been a standard reason to appoint a legal representative: in a very similar agreement dated eighty years later, one man appoints another to represent him at an investigation against him to be held at the governor's assizes [P.Oxy. IV.726; cf. P.Oxy. VIII.1120 from a "weak widow"]. Demetria's "weakness" does not prevent her from engaging in a legal dispute with a man, but does enable her to avoid appearing in person against him in court!

Demetria's *kyrios*, also a relative, does not represent her in court; he merely gives his approval when she appoints her grandson as her representative. Perhaps her grandson had some legal training, or had the time and financial means to undertake what could be a lengthy suit involving expense and travel.

P.Oxy. II.261, 55 C.E.

Second year of Nero Claudius Caesar Augustus Germanicus Imperator, ___ of the month Neos Sebastos,[89] in the city of Oxyrhynchus of the Thebaid.

Demetria daughter of Chaeremon, a citizen woman, with her *kyrios*, Theon son of Antiochos, of the Auximetoreian tribe and the Zeneian deme,[90] the husband of her granddaughter Demetria, a citizen woman, makes an agreement with her grandson Chaeremon son of Chaeremon, the brother of her granddaugher Demetria, of the Maronian deme, in the street,[91] about those matters which Demetria, the one making the agreement, is disputing with Epimachos son of Polydeukes, or (those matters which) Epimachos himself also is disputing with her. Not being able to be in attendance in court on account of womanly weakness, (Demetria agrees) that she has appointed the afore-mentioned grandson Chaeremon as her legal representative, before every authority and every court, just as would be possible for Demetria herself, the one who has made the appointment, if she were present. For she consents to this appointment. The agreement is valid.

In the following papyrus, a young woman petitions the prefect (governor of Egypt) for help in recovering property inherited from her mother which she claims her maternal uncles appropriated.[92] It appears that Aurelia Didyme's mother, a widow, and her brothers lived in one household, each having inherited one-third of the property from their father (Aurelia Didyme's grandfather). When Aurelia Didyme's mother died, her brothers took over her share and refused to let Didyme have her mother's third, which was hers by right as her mother's heir. The complaint that a wicked guardian, usually an uncle, has cheated fatherless minors of their rightful inheritance is quite frequent in the papyri; often, as here, the minor is a female, sometimes petitioning on behalf of her siblings as well as herself.[93] In her petition, Aurelia Didyme does not say that her uncles were her guardians (she appears to have no other kin to assist her). She emphasizes instead her orphan state and the weakness of her female nature, which have caused her uncles to take advantage of her.

P.Oxy. XXXIV.2713, *c.*297 C.E.

To Aristios Optatus, the most eminent prefect of Egypt from Aurelia Didyme, daughter of Didymos from the splendid and most splendid city of the Oxyrhynchites. It is difficult to be wronged by strangers, but most difficult (to be wronged) by those who are also relatives. Dioskoros, my grandfather on my mother's side, had in all[94] three children, Theon and Dioskoros and Ploutarche, my mother, and he died leaving them as his heirs. But, after some intervening time, my mother paid her debt,[95] with me being a minor and an orphan. You know quite well, my lord governor, that the race of women is easily despised on account of the weakness of our nature. For all the things left to us from the inheritance falling (on us), since we were one household and one family, were in the same house in which they were there co-resident[96] – I mean, of course, slaves and building-sites[97] and household goods and movables were undivided. But in the meantime, my mother's brothers from the same mother, in collusion with each other for the purpose of defrauding me, with empty and vain foolishness took possession of the rest as they wished, each (taking possession) of what he wanted of the slaves and all the other things, thinking nothing of me but, so to speak, even thrusting me out from the third part of the inheritance that fell to me. Now, at least, I have recovered, with the aid of your vigilant fortune, and am beginning to recognize that I can go back to no one else other than you, the benefactor and guardian of me and of everyone. (And so) I have hastened to implore you that, having considered me in my loss, you order, whenever it seems best to you, my maternal uncles to be compelled to restore to me the shares belonging to me, that fell to me from succession to my mother, along with the profits from the slaves and house-rents and all the rest, and having recovered my mother's property by your good faith and noble character, I will acknowledge gratitude to your fortune forever. Farewell.

[in a second hand]Aurelia Didyme, have sent this for handing in.

I, Aurelius Thoneis, have written on her behalf because she does not know letters.

In the following petition to the prefect, a widow (whose full name has been lost) claims to have been cheated by the men she hired to help her run her estate while her adult sons were away in the army.[98] She was clearly wealthy and of high status. She describes herself in the petition's opening as *lamprotate* ("most splendid"), a word often considered the Greek equivalent of the Latin *clarissima*, denoting senatorial rank [see Part VI.A]. It is unlikely, however, that this petitioner was of senatorial status, and the term *lamprotate* seems to have been used more loosely at this period to indicate high social standing [Arjava 1991].

Petitions in later Roman Egypt become more fulsome and elaborate, and here the petitioner artfully combines the pitiableness of her vulnerability as a woman without menfolk with pointed reference to her wealth and status. No *kyrios* is mentioned; a woman did not need to have a *kyrios'* approval to send a petition. However, Aurelia Gl——— may not have had a *kyrios* at all, since by the fourth century the *kyrios'* role was being taken over by the husband and widows do not appear to have *kyrioi* [see Part III.E]. (For another widow who claimed to have been taken advantage of by an unscrupulous man after her husband's death, see Aurelia Artemis in Chapter 5, Part II.C).

P.Oxy. I.71, 303 C.E.

To Clodius Culcianus, the most eminent prefect of Egypt, from Aurelia Gl ..., most illustrious, living in the city of the Arsinoites.

You come to the aid of all, lord governor, and you render to all their own, especially to women on account of the weakness of their nature. For this reason I too approach your greatness, being very hopeful of receiving aid from you. Since I have very many [estates] around the Arsinoite nome itself, and pay a considerable amount of public taxes – I refer to payments for public purposes and military supplies – and as I happen to be a weak woman and a widow, with my children in the army and away in foreign parts, I took on as an aid to myself and for the management of my affairs, first a certain Secundus, and then also Tyrannus, thinking that they would keep good faith with me. But they turned out to be crooked and robbed me, and taking away from me the possessions which came into their hands, they never brought to me the customary accounts, perhaps recognizing their error in the things which they did, having snatched away from me also two cows[99] from those which I have ... of the same estates of mine ... having contempt for my inexperience. Therefore ... your auspicious visit, I flee to your feet, my lord, seeking ... if it seems good to your excellence ... to me your most powerful subscription[100] ... [the rest is too fragmentary to read]

D *The* senatusconsultum Velleianum

Related to the notion that women were somehow "weaker" and in greater need of protection than men was the belief that certain types of transactions and responsibilities were "men's business" and should not be engaged in by women. Both ideas form the rationale for the *senatusconsultum Velleianum* ("Velleian decree of the Senate") of the mid-first century. This law attempted to discourage the practice of women "interceding" on behalf of another person. In a legal context, the Latin word *intercedere* means "to intervene, interpose oneself between a debtor and a creditor, that is, to undertake a debt on someone's behalf (i.e, in the commonest case to guarantee someone's debt, to be a guarantor or surety)" [Crook 1986a, 86]. Undertaking the defense of someone else in court was also considered a form of interceding [see below, Part V.A].

Imperial bans on women's "interceding" on behalf of their husbands had already been enacted by Augustus and Claudius, evidently ineffectively. It is relevant that both those emperors had undercut the power of *tutela mulierum*, Augustus by granting the *ius liberorum* (which freed women with three children from *tutela*), and Claudius by abolishing the *tutela legitima* of agnate kin [See Part III]. The date of the *s.c. Velleianum* is uncertain, but it was during the reign of either the emperor Claudius (41–54) or Nero (54–68).

Release from a restrictive tutor, though beneficial to women who owned property and engaged in legal and financial transactions, might also have made them, and their property, more vulnerable to the designs of the unscrupulous, including their own husbands. The *s.c. Velleianum* can be seen as an attempt to remedy this situation: since women were not supposed to "intercede" on behalf of others, a transaction in which they had done so could be invalidated on the basis of the Senate's decree.[101] Indeed, Roman legal writers describe the Senate's decree as an aid to women, not as a restriction.

The first title of the sixteenth book of the *Digest* is devoted entirely to the *senatusconsultum Velleianum*, indicating that it was still relevant to the society of sixth-century Byzantium. All the jurists whose commentaries on the *senatusconsultum* are cited in the *Digest* were writing in the third century, about 150 years after the law's passage. The reason they give for the ruling decision, that it was to protect "weak" women, may not have been the Senate's original concern.[102] In the absence of earlier sources, we cannot know.

D.16.1.1 (Paulus): By the *senatus consultum Velleianum* it has been most fully expressed that women are not to intercede on anyone else's behalf. For just as women have by custom been deprived of civic responsibilities and (such responsibilities if undertaken by women) are in general not legally valid,[103] so much the more should they be deprived of that responsibility in which not only their efforts and their service alone are involved, but also the risk of their family property. Moreover, it seemed right that a woman be aided in such a way that an action be given against the old debtor or against the man who had made the woman financially responsible on his own behalf. For he, rather than the creditor, deceived the woman.

D.16.1.2 pr (Ulpian): And indeed first in the time of the deified Augustus, and soon thereafter in the time of Claudius, it had been prohibited by their edicts that women intercede on behalf of their own husbands. 1: Afterwards, a decree was made, by which aid was very fully given to all women. These are the words of this decree of the Senate:

"In regard to the speech which the consuls Marcus Silanus and Velleus Tutor made concerning what ought to be done about the obligations of women who become answerable for debts on behalf of others, they (the Senate) decided the following about this matter:

Though the law which pertains to providing guarantees and giving loans on behalf of others for whom women have interceded seems to have been stated before in this way: that there should not be an action for recovery of the debt by them (the creditors on whose behalf the women provided guarantees), nor should a legal action be given against the women, since it is not right that they discharge men's duties and be bound by obligations of this kind; (however) the Senate thought that those to whom there will be legal recourse on this matter[104] would act correctly and properly if they give their attention to preserving the will of the Senate in this matter."

The Senate did not forbid women to guarantee the debts of others, but said that women ought not to take on such a responsibility and that therefore creditors who attempted to recover a debt from a woman guarantor should be denied an action against the woman in court. Moreover, it appears that women who did not want the benefit of the law could renounce their right to use the exception that the Senate's decree offered [Beaucamp 1990, 67–8].

Juristic commentary on the *senatus consultum Velleianum* discusses the circumstances in which a woman can claim the benefit of the law and so be released from responsibility for the debts of another person which she had guaranteed. In some cases she was not protected by the *s.c. Velleianum*:

D.16.1.21 (Callistratus): If a woman has interceded on behalf of another, but that which was received was turned to her profit, the exception of the Senate's decree does not apply, because she does not become poorer. 1: Likewise if she has acted generously, for instance so that her father, who was condemned in court, not be distressed on account of payment (of his debts), she will not be protected by the decree of the Senate. For the Senate comes to the aid of women's burdens.[105]

Roman jurists were aware that women themselves might abuse the law. Thus Ulpian, writing over a century after the decree was passed, stresses that it was intended to assist "weak" women, not women who cleverly took advantage of the law in order to cheat creditors:

D.16.1.2.2 (Ulpian): Therefore let us examine the words of the Senate's decree, first having praised the foresight of the most splendid order (the Senate) because it brought aid to women who, on account of the weakness of their sex, had been overcome and thwarted by many incidents of this kind. 3: But it helped them in this way only if they were not engaged in cunning; indeed, the deified (Antoninus) Pius and (Septimius) Severus have issued rescripts to this effect. For it assists those who have been deceived, not those practicing deceit, and there is also such a rescript of Severus in Greek: "The decree of the Senate does not help women who have used deception." For the weakness of women, not their cunning, deserved help.

The Senate's decree was rather vaguely worded and evidently created some confusion about the circumstances under which women could claim the law's protection and not be liable for another's debts. There are twenty rescripts (replies from the emperors to individual petitioners) dated between 212 and 294 under the title "Regarding the *s.c. Velleianum*" in the *Code of Justinian*, ten of them addressed to women, and all attempting to clarify the situations in which the Senate's decree did and did not apply. A few examples follow:

Cod. Just. 4.29.2, 11 August, 213
The Emperor Antoninus (Caracalla) Augustus to Nepotiana:

In vain did you attempt to use the legal exception of the Senate's decree which was made concerning women's interceding, since you yourself are the principal debtor. For the exception of the Senate's decree is given to a woman when she herself owes nothing originally, but has interceded on behalf of another debtor with his creditor. If, however, women have obligated themselves to others on behalf of their own creditor or have allowed

57

themselves or their own debtor to be made over (for their own debt), they do not have the aid of the Senate's decree. Posted on the third day before the Ides of August in the fourth consulship of the Emperor Antoninus and the consulship of Balbinus.

Cod. Just. 4.29.5, 18 June, 223
The Emperor Alexander Augustus to Popilia:

If your property was pledged by your husband (for a debt) without your consent, it is not under legal obligation. Or if you, with the knowledge of his (female) creditor, consented to the obligation, you are able to use the Senate's decree. But if you allowed your husband to obligate your property as if it were his own, you wanted to deceive the person giving him the loan and therefore you are not aided by the decree of the Senate, which was looking out for women's weakness, not their cunning. Given on the fifteenth day before the Kalends of July in the consulship of Julianus and Crispinus.

Cod. Just. 4.29.12, 21 February, 258
The Emperors Valerian and Gallienus Augusti to Sepiduca:

If, wishing to give your daughter a dowry, you pledged your property to your son-in-law, you are mistaken in supposing that the benefit of the Senate's decree applies to you. For legal experts thought this reason should be removed from the benefit of the law.[106] Posted on the ninth day before the Kalends of March in the consulship of Tuscus and Bassus.

Like the desire to help a condemned father pay his debts [see D.16.1.21 above], the wish to give a daughter a dowry stems from familial generosity, not financial obligation. Thus the *senatusconsultum Velleianum* does not apply.

Sometimes the *s.c. Velleianum* could afford protection for a woman, who might otherwise be obligated for the debts or contracts of family members:

Cod. Just. 4.12.1, 12 April, 287
Emperors Diocletian and Maximian Augusti to Asclepiodota:

In vain do you dispute about whether contracts made with your husband have legal standing or not, since it should be sufficient for you, if you did not have any contract in your own name, that you cannot be called into court on behalf of your husband. Because not even if you had interceded on his behalf willingly, could anything be accomplished at law by you on account of the *senatusconsultum*. Given on the day before the Ides of April in the consulship of Diocletian for the third time and Maximian.

Cod. Just. 4.12.4, 23 August, 301
Emperors Diocletian and Maximian Augusti and the Caesars to Philotera:

Since you relate that in fact you were brought to court as representative of the person of your son (*ex persona filii*), because you apparently contributed something on behalf of his debts, you are not at all prevented from using your legal defenses in the presence of the man who has legal cognizance over this matter, so that he shall not allow you to be pressed for the payment of someone else's debts. Given on the tenth day before the Kalends of September in the consulship of Titianus and Nepotianus.

In the late fourth century, the emperor Theodosius repeated the classical prohibition on women "intervening" on behalf of others. This is an excerpt from a long law, which may have referred to a particular case involving inheritance claims in which a woman was taking an active role:

Cod. Theod. 2.12.5, 28 September, 393

Theodosius, Arcadius and Honorius Augusti to Rufinus, praetorian prefect:

In no way are women able to act (legally) beyond what is fitting for them, or to intervene on behalf of other persons. Given at Constantinople on the fourth day before the Kalends of October in the third consulship of Theodosius and the consulship of Abundantius.[107]

The rescripts translated above were all written after 212, when the Edict of Caracalla granted Roman citizenship to virtually all free inhabitants of the Empire. Thus their recipients were Roman citizens, and could be expected to know of and respect Roman legal rules, including the *s.c. Velleianum*. One would expect that before 212, provincials who were not Roman citizens would not care about the Senate's decree. But one provincial woman was worried enough about its ramifications to approach the emperors for clarification.

In 199–200, Septimius Severus and his son Caracalla were in Egypt. A number of imperial decisions addressed to or concerning those living in Egypt are known from that year, reflecting the importance of an imperial visit to a province: locals would take advantage of the emperor's proximity to send petitions or even bring legal actions before his court. Among the imperial decisions dating to 199–200 are thirteen short responses found on a single sheet of papyrus, with the heading "In Alexandria. Copy of the *apokrimata* posted in the stoa of the gymnasium in the eighth year, 18 Phamenoth,"[108] with the emperors' names and titles written in a different hand. Then follow the thirteen decisions, each addressed to a specific recipient or recipients.[109] What exactly *apokrimata* were is a matter of debate, but clearly the decisions were made by the emperors while in Egypt and responded to the concerns of provincials, not necessarily only those who were residents of Egypt but also perhaps those from neighboring provinces who traveled to Alexandria to get an imperial ruling.[110] The original responses may have been in Latin, of which the papyrus gives a Greek translation.[111]

The fifth *apokrima* is addressed to a woman, the beginning of whose name is lost; it ended in –*thalge*.[112] But from what does remain of the name, and from the name of her father (Ambrelos) and son (Abdomanchos), it appears that the recipient was of Arabic origin [Westerman-Schiller 1954, 18].

P.Col. VI.123, lines 18–20, 200 C.E.

To [Ma]thalge daughter of Ambrelos, through her son Abdomanchos:

Women are not prevented from borrowing money and from making payments on behalf of others.

In keeping with Greco-Roman ideas of feminine modesty [see Part IV.B], (Ma)halge approached the emperors through her son rather than appearing herself.[113] She is evidently not a Roman citizen; no traces of a *nomen* appear, and it would be surprising to find a woman of Semitic origin with Roman citizenship at this date. Her question suggests knowledge of the *s.c. Velleianum* and concern that something she wants to do might not be valid [Gaudemet 1959 (1979), 212–13]. It is surprising that a non-Roman woman in pre-212 Egypt would be worried about the legality of borrowing money and paying on others' behalf: such activities were allowable under Greco-Egyptian law. Perhaps the custom in her homeland (if she was not from Egypt) was more restrictive [Schiller in Schiller-Westerman 1954, 64]. In the second century, Babatha, a Jewish resident of the newly created Roman province of Arabia, had utilized the Roman legal system to take action against her son's guardians [Chapter 5, Part II.B.2].

In any case, the imperial reply is in keeping with Roman law: such activities are not forbidden [Schiller in Schiller-Westerman 1954, 64–5]. A woman could borrow money on her own account and then use it to pay someone else's debt. What she was not supposed to do was pledge herself as surety for the debt of another person. In her case, the *s.c. Velleianum* did not apply and (Ma)thalge could use the money she had borrowed as she saw fit.

V Women in court: restrictions and rights

Under Roman law women were able to lay charges and appear in court, but there were restrictions on the circumstances in which they could act both in civil and criminal law. And if they were under *tutela mulierum*, they could not initiate legal action without their tutor's authorization [*Rules of Ulpian* 11.27, in Part III.A]. (They could, however, appoint a procurator to represent them without their tutor's permission; see Frag. Vat. 325, Part III.E.) The main feature of these restrictions is that underlying virtually all restrictions on women in Roman law: women could not represent others, only themselves [see Thomas 1992, 126–37].

According to Jane Gardner, the origins of these restrictions lay in the highly patriarchal nature of early Roman society, where the male head of household (*paterfamilias*) not only had legal power (*potestas*) over his dependants, but also was responsible for representing their interests in the outside world. Law, like politics, was transacted between *patresfamilias*, and women, who never had *potestas*, could not be players in the legal or political world [Gardner 1993, 85–109]. Jurists of the imperial period, however, explained the restrictions on women's public roles as due to women's "weakness" or to the moral impropriety of a woman appearing in an active role in public [Part IV.C.1].

A Restrictions on women's right to act legally

1 Prohibition on bringing a request on others' behalf

Under the Praetor's Edict, a woman could bring a request (*postulare*) for a judicial hearing in a civil case only on her own behalf, not on behalf of others.[114] The *Digest* passages in this section were all taken from commentaries by classical jurists discussing the restrictions set forth in the Praetor's Edict.

In his sixth book on the Praetor's Edict, Ulpian began by noting [D.3.1.1.3–4] that deaf persons and youths below the age of seventeen could not even represent themselves in court, though they could have an advocate appointed for them. (It was also considered preferable for women to appoint representatives, even when they could bring charges themselves; see below.) In the rest of the passage, not translated here, Ulpian notes that those disqualified from bringing a request on behalf of others include a man blind in both eyes ("because he cannot see and revere the magistracy's insignia"), a man "who has allowed womanly treatment on his body" (i.e., has been the passive partner in homosexual relations), a man condemned on a capital charge, a man convicted of *calumnia* (see below), and a man who hires himself out to fight wild beasts (in the arena).[115]

D.3.1.1.5 (Ulpian): In the second section, an edict is published in regard to those who are not to bring a request on behalf of others. In this edict the praetor made particular mention of sex and misfortune, and likewise he marked with disgrace persons conspicuous due to shameful behavior. In regard to sex: he prohibits women from bringing a request on behalf of others. And indeed there is a reason for prohibiting them: so that women not get themselves mixed up in other people's lawsuits contrary to the modesty suitable for their sex, (and) so that women not discharge men's duties. But the origin (of the prohibition) was introduced by Carfania, a very wicked woman, who, by bringing requests without shame and disturbing the magistrate, provided the reason for the edict ... [the rest of the passage is omitted]

We hear about the notorious "Carfania" (elsewhere called "Afrania" or "Carfinia") in literary sources also, where she is the quintessential example of the litigious female. The Roman moralist Valerius Maximus, writing under the emperor Tiberius, also mentions Carfania, along with Maesia of Sentinum (on whom see below) and Hortensia, daughter of the orator Hortensius. This passage is from his *Memorable Deeds and Sayings (Facta et Dicta Memorabilia)*, in a chapter entitled: "Those women who pled causes before magistrates on their own or others' behalf" [see Shackleton Bailey 2000 for the Latin text]:

Valerius Maximus VIII.3.2 (written *c*.30 C.E.)
Nor should I be silent even about those women whose nature and matron's sense of shame[116] did not avail to restrain (them) so that they would be silent in the forum and in legal cases. [The case of Maesia of Sentinum follows, for which see Part V.D below.]

(2) But Carfania, the wife of the senator Licinius Buccio, quick to engage in lawsuits, always made speeches on her own behalf before the Praetor, not because she lacked advocates, but because she abounded in impudence. And so by her unusual barking in the forum in continually harassing the tribunals, she ended up being the most notorious example of female *calumnia*[117] to the point where the name of Carfania is thrown at women of shameless habits as a reproach. She prolonged her life to the consulship of Gaius Caesar for the second time and Publius Servilius (48 B.C.E.); for it should be handed down for tradition when such a monstrosity was extinguished rather than when it arose.

Neither Ulpian nor Valerius Maximus says that Carfania was acting legally on behalf of someone else, but only that she was behaving in an improper and unfeminine fashion by continually undertaking legal action on her own behalf [Gardner 1993, 101–5; Marshall 1989, 43–7]. It is unlikely that she was the real reason for the ban on women acting on behalf of others [Gardner 1986a, 263].

D.3.3.54 pr. (Paulus): Neither a woman nor a soldier nor a man who is going to be absent on government business or who is held back by permanent illness or is about to undertake a magistracy or, against his will, is unable to undergo a trial, is understood to be a suitable (legal) defender.

D.47.23.6 (Ulpian): The right to bring "popular actions"[118] is not given to a woman or a fatherless minor (*pupillus*), except when the matter pertains to them.

Women were also prohibited from defending others in court. This was associated by the jurists with the general ban on women's interceding for another, as set forth in the first-century *s.c. Velleianum* [see Part IV.D]:

D.16.1.2.5 (Ulpian): But also if a woman should be someone's defender, she is doubtless interceding. For she undertakes someone else's obligation onto herself, since indeed she undergoes condemnation in consequence of this act (that is, if she loses). Therefore it is not permitted to a woman to defend her husband or her son or her father.

If his wife suffered insult or outrage,[119] a man could bring an action for *iniuria* to himself, since, according to ancient ideas of honor and reputation, an insult to a married woman was an insult to her husband. But such defense of honor was peculiarly masculine, so for a wife to bring an action for *iniuria* done to her insulted husband was inappropriate and unfeminine [Gardner 1995, 388–9]:

D.47.10.2 (Paulus): But if outrage (*iniuria*) has been done to her husband, a wife does not act, since it is right for wives to be defended by their husbands, but not for husbands to be defended by their wives.

If a woman did act legally for her husband, and he lost the case, he had grounds for appeal, as we see from this imperial reply:

Cod. Just. 2.12.4, 4 January, 207
Emperors Septimius Severus and Caracalla Augusti to Saturninus:
  Since you say that judgment was made against you in your absence, it is fair that the defense of your case be restored to you. Nor will you be hindered by the fact that your wife was present at the trial or even acquiesced in the judgment, since someone else's affairs are not otherwise able to be transacted through women, except when legal actions have been mandated to them in regard to their own property or their own profit. Posted on the day before the Nones of January in the consulship of Aper and Maximus.

Widowed mothers who wanted to represent their fatherless children were told in imperial rescripts that this was beyond their responsibilities [Cod. Just. 2.12.18 and 9.1.5, in Chapter 5, Part II.A.3]. However, exception might be made when a mother acted out of the Roman sense of duty (*pietas*) to appeal a judgment already made against her child [D.49.5.1, in Chapter 5, Part II.A.2]. And sometimes defending someone else could be construed as self-defense:

D.16.1.3 (Paulus): But if she is defending a man who, if condemned, would have redress against her, such as when she defends the seller of an inheritance that was sold to her or the person who gives security for her, she does not appear to be interceding.

2 Prohibition on bringing criminal charges

Women were also among those restricted from bringing accusations on criminal charges such as murder, adultery, or forgery. Most such restrictions were either temporary, because of the person's age or occupation, or because his lifestyle or actions had made him ineligible to bring a prosecution. But women were subject to a blanket prohibition, simply on the basis of their sex.[120] The following passages are from the jurist Macer's commentary on *iudicia publica*, trials held before one of the standing jury-courts that tried certain crimes:[121]

D.48.2.8 (Macer): We will understand who is able to bring a criminal accusation, if we know who is not able. And so some are prohibited from bringing an accusation on account of sex or age, like the woman or the *pupillus*; others on account of their oath of allegiance, like those who perform military service; others on account of their magistracy or power, in which capacity they are not able to be called to court without damage (to their authority); others on account of their own wrong-doing, like infamous persons;[122] and others on account of their shameful way of earning money, like those who have their names subscribed to two judgments against two defendants or have received money for the purpose of bringing an accusation or not bringing one; others because of their own legal position, like freedmen (who cannot bring a accusation) against their patrons.

D.48.2.11 pr. (Macer): However, all these, if they are pursuing their own injury or avenging the death of their relatives, are not excluded from bringing an accusation. [See further below on this exception.]

Though under Augustus' adultery law, husbands were positively required to bring adultery charges against a wife they knew was unfaithful or risk prosecution for pimping [see Chapter 2, Part I.B], wives did not have the right to charge their husbands with adultery. Legally, adultery was an offense committed against a married woman's husband, and a woman who brought charges against her adulterous husband would *ipso facto* be acting on behalf of someone else (her husband's lover's husband) [Beaucamp 1990, 43]. Thus a woman Cassia was told by the emperors Septimius Severus and Caracalla:

Cod. Just. 9.9.1, 20 July, 197
Emperors Severus and Antoninus Augusti to Cassia:
The Julian law (on adultery) declares that women do not have the right of accusation in a criminal court (*publicum iudicium*), though they wish to complain about the violation of their own marriage. Though (the law) had offered the ability to accuse (a wife) to men by the right of the husband, it did not offer the same privilege to women. Posted on the thirteenth day before the Kalends of August in the consulship of Lateranus and Rufinus.

Sometimes the emperor's replies take on an admonishing tone, as in this rescript to a woman who wanted to bring a criminal charge of forgery (*falsum*) [see also Cod. Just. 9.1.5 in Chapter 5, Part II.A.2]:

Cod. Just. 9.22.19, 8 March, 294
Emperors Diocletian and Maximian Augusti and the Caesars to Cosmia:

Even if the business pertained to you, you should have deliberated with yourself again and again, so that you would not bring a disgraceful accusation, by striving to charge that the deed which you had signed was forged. (1) But since it has not been allowed to women to bring an accusation in someone else's forgery case, (and) you, moreover, claim that you had previously given these same estates to someone else, you are asking for the ability to bring an accusation against the form of the law. Subscribed[123] on the eighth day before the Ides of March in the consulship of the Caesars.

In the following rescript to a certain Agricolanus (whose official position, if any, is unknown), the fourth-century emperor Constantine restates in strong terms the classical prohibition on women bringing criminal prosecutions except in matters involving injury to themselves or their family. As Constantine admits, sometimes women were allowed to bring charges despite the general prohibition. In another law, Constantine explicitly granted husbands the right to act in court on their wife's behalf without a mandate [Cod. Just. 2.12.21, in Part IV.B]. His law of 326 on abduction marriage, however, exaggerated and distorted earlier law when it claimed that women had been completely excluded "from making legal complaints and from giving testimony and from all judicial matters" [Cod. Theod. 9.24.1; in Chapter 3, Part II.C].

Cod. Theod. 9.1.3, 9 February, 322
Emperor Constantine Augustus to Agricolanus:

Since it is clear and manifest law that women do not have the capacity to bring a criminal charge except for certain reasons, that is, if they are prosecuting outrage (*iniuria*) to themselves or their family, it is necessary that the statutes of ancient times be observed. For it is not right that the capacity to bring an accusation be permitted to women indiscriminately. Yet sometimes in public trials in the past either a trial or the authority of an accuser was granted (to women). Defenders of cases must also be warned not to take up rashly, because of regard for personal gain, (the cases of) women who perhaps rush into illegal action, heedless of their sex.

Posted on the fifth day before the Ides of February in the consulship of Probianus and Julianus.

3 Prohibition on being an informer to the fiscus

Women were also not allowed to be informers (*delatores*) to the imperial treasury (*fiscus*). This would entail bringing an accusation that another person had defrauded the *fiscus* by not reporting that he (or she) had received something under a will (legacies were taxable, unless the legatee was a close relative of the deceased).[124] Informers received a share of the legacy that they had reported, and many people informed on their fellow-citizens for personal gain

64

or revenge. The official position on informers was ambivalent; the state welcomed the revenues from confiscated legacies, but emperors deplored the motives that led people to be informers, and informing was considered underhanded and not honorable. This passage is from Marcian's commentary "on informers" (*de delatoribus*):

D.49.14.18 (Marcian): Women are not able to be informers on account of the weakness of their sex, and thus imperial constitutions have ordered. 1: Likewise men of senatorial status are not able to be informers. 2: Likewise condemned men are not able to be informers, as the deified brothers (Marcus Aurelius and Lucius Verus) ruled in a rescript, and he who, after being beaten with rods, had been sentenced to hard labor. 3: Likewise by the constitutions of the emperors those who have been sent to the mines are forbidden to be informers. [4 is omitted.] 5: Veterans also, by imperial constitutions, are forbidden to be informers, particularly on account of the honor and importance of having been in the military. 6: Likewise soldiers on account of the military service they perform are forbidden to be informers. [the rest of D.49.14.18 is here omitted]

The list of those who may not be informers to the *fiscus* includes both those whose honor is so high (senators, soldiers, veterans) that their reputation will be damaged if they receive money for the sordid activity of informing on others, and those whose honor is extremely low because they have been condemned to degrading penalties. Where do women fit in? The reason Marcian gives, "because of the weakness of their sex," simply repeats the old cliché of "womanly weakness" found elsewhere in Roman law, which even some jurists like Gaius thought made little sense [Part IV.C]. The ban on women informers is really due to traditional Roman ideas about honor and female behavior: it was considered improper and immodest for a woman to be so bold and interested in material gain that she would inform on another for a financial reward.

B Right to act legally on behalf of oneself or one's family

Women could act legally, however, in regard to a matter pertaining to their own property or person. Indeed, the papyri show plenty of evidence for women appearing in court on behalf of themselves or family members, though often represented by a male relative or professional advocate [Anagnostou-Canas 1984; Beaucamp 1992, 21–8]. The parameters within which women could act legally are set out in the jurists and clarified in imperial replies to petitioners:

1 Right to act legally in civil cases

Sent. Pauli I.ii.2: A woman is not prohibited from undertaking the work of a legal representative[125] in regard to her own affair.

A married woman who was legally independent [*sui iuris*; see Part II] could bring charges for insult (*iniuria*) to herself. However, in such a case her husband could bring charges for *iniuria* to himself, because insult to a married woman was considered to be insult to her husband also [cf. D.47.10.2, Part V.A.1]. This and the following passage are from Paulus' commentaries on the Praetor's Edict:

D.47.10.18.2 (Paulus): If a married woman under paternal power has received an injury and both her husband and father bring a charge of *iniuria*, Pomponius correctly thinks that the defendant is to be condemned to pay to the father as much as he would be condemned to pay if she were an unmarried woman,[126] but to the husband, he is to be condemned to pay as much as he would if she were not in anyone's legal power, because each one's injury has its own proper value. And therefore, if a married woman is in no one's power, she is no less able to bring legal action for *iniuria* (committed against herself), because her husband may also act in his own name.

> Exceptions to the prohibition on women acting legally on behalf of others were made in the case of family members, particularly in cases where there was no male relative competent to do so. For instance, widowed mothers could bring charges of "untrustworthy guardianship" against their children's guardians or go to court on behalf of their children [see Chapter 5, Part II].

D.3.3.41 (Paulus): It is permitted for women to act sometimes on behalf of their parents, when there is a legal hearing, if by chance illness or age impedes their parents, or they do not have anyone (else) who can act for them.

2 Right to bring criminal charges

Even in regard to the major offenses subject to criminal trials (*iudicia publica*; cf. V.A.2 above) a woman could approach the authorities to make an accusation, provided that she or a close relative was the victim:

D.48.2.1 (Pomponius): It has not been permitted for a woman to make someone a defendant in a criminal court (*iudicium publicum*), unless of course they are avenging the death of their parents, children, or of their patron or patroness and their (the patrons') son, daughter, grandson, or granddaughter.
D.48.2.2 pr. (Papinian): In certain cases, the right of public accusation has been conceded to women, as for example, if they are avenging the death of those men or women against whom they do not (have to) testify against their will by the law of criminal (proceedings). And the Senate decided likewise in the Cornelian law on wills; but it has been permitted to women to speak in a criminal court also concerning the will of a slave owned by their father or mother.

Cod. Just. 9.20.5, 7 May, 259
Emperors Valerian and Gallienus Augusti and Valerian the Caesar to Juliana:
    If an adversary is detaining your brother, you ought to request a hearing (*postulare*) against him under the Fabian law,[127] after approaching the governor of the province. Posted on the Nones of May in the consulship of Aemilianus and Bassus.

Cases are known in which women did take legal action concerning the death of a family member [cf. Part V.C below]. For instance, the woman known as Turia avenged her parents' murder, which had occurred shortly before her wedding day. We hear about "Turia" in the eulogy given by her husband at her funeral, which was later engraved on a marble inscription at Rome.[128] Note, however, that her husband says the duty fell on her *because* her male kin were unavailable to take action themselves.

Laudatio Turiae I.3–5, late 1st c. B.C.E.

You were suddenly orphaned before our wedding day when both of your parents were killed together in the deserted countryside. Through your efforts most of all, since I was away in Macedonia and your sister's husband Cluvius was in the province of Africa, your parents' death did not remain unavenged.

Emperors sometimes received requests for clarification on whether a woman could bring murder charges. Though the imperial replies reiterated the classical rule that women could prosecute in cases involving injury (including murder) to themselves or family members, it is clear that the emperors thought this right should be used rarely, and with great caution:

Cod. Just. 9.1.4, 16 June, 222

Emperor Alexander Augustus to Dionysius:

Your wife should approach the governor of the province if she thinks the murder of her (male) cousin should be avenged. Posted on the sixteenth day before the Kalends of July in the consulship of Alexander Augustus.

Cod. Just. 9.46.2, 27 June, 224

Emperor Alexander Augustus to Apollonia:

A mother is among those persons who are able to avenge their own son's death without fear of the penalty for *calumnia*, and this benefit of the Senate's decree has been preserved also in other criminal trials. [The rest of the rescript is omitted.] Posted on the sixth day before the Kalends of July in the consulship of Julianus and Crispinus.

Cod. Just. 9.1.9, 2 March, 239

Emperor Gordian Augustus to Severianus:

A competent judge is not unaware that a woman who chooses to pursue revenge (for the) murder of a son, should not be admitted rashly to bring an accusation, until she has proven that she is the mother. Posted on the sixth day before the Nones of March in the consulship of Gordian Augustus and Aviola.

Cod. Just. 9.1.12, 27 April, 293

Emperors Diocletian and Maximian Augusti and the Caesars to Corinthia:

A woman is not permitted to bring an accusation concerning a crime which has been (put) among *publica iudicia* except for certain reasons, that is, if she is pursuing outrage (*iniuria*) to herself or her family, (and) according to the ancient statues only concerning those (reasons) for which it has been specially allowed, and not by demanding an (imperial) rescript from the Emperor. (1) Therefore the governor of the province, after being approached (by you), will first investigate whether the crime is such, that a woman is not prohibited from entering an accusation about it. Subscribed on the fifth day before the Kalends of May in the consulship of the Augusti.

Particularly awkward was the case where a mother wished to accuse her own son of planning her death, since this involved a violation of familial *pietas* as much as a woman's right to prosecute:

Cod. Just. 9.1.14, 14 February, 294
Emperors Diocletian and Maximian Augusti and the Caesars to Aelia:
You are able to undertake an accusation against your son on account of the plot which you claim was prepared against your life, if your sense of duty (*pietas*) and the natural reason of your mind do not revoke your intention. Subscribed on the sixteenth day before the Kalends of March in the consulship of the Caesars.

3 Right to bring an action over a family member's freedom

If someone was thought to be held in slavery unjustly, it was possible to bring a legal action *de liberali causa* ("concerning freedom") to force the slaveholder to release the enslaved person. Slaves themselves could not bring this action; they had to find an advocate (*adsertor*) who would act for them. Usually women were not allowed to bring a case *de liberali causa*, since they were not supposed to undertake legal action on behalf of others. However, in one of his commentaries on the Praetor's Edict, Ulpian notes an exception:

D.40.12.3.2 (Ulpian): But when there is no other (male) person of this sort, who would litigate on his behalf, then it is necessary that the ability to approach the praetor and give information about this be given even to a mother or to daughters or sisters or other women who are related, or even to a wife, so that, when the case has been heard, help may be given to (the enslaved person) even if he is unwilling.

Related to the action *de liberali causa* was an action to force someone who was unjustly holding another in captivity to "exhibit" (*exhibere*) the wrongly held person.

D.43.29.3.8 (Ulpian): The Praetor says: "You are to exhibit." "To exhibit" is to bring forth into public and offer people the ability to see and touch: strictly speaking, "to exhibit" is to have outside of a concealed place. 9: This injunction (*interdictum*[129]) is available to all: for no one should be prohibited from favoring freedom. [10 is omitted here.] 11: But even if a woman or a *pupillus* should wish this injunction, being anxious on behalf of a kinsman or a parent or a relation by marriage, it must be said that the injunction must be given to them. For they are even able to bring an accusation against someone in a criminal trial (*publicum iudicium*) as long as they are avenging their own or their family's injuries.

4 Right to bring an action for the public welfare

Women were also allowed to bring a public legal action when the state was believed to be in danger; for instance, if they wanted to accuse someone of treason (*maiestas*) against the emperor or the Roman people. Here Papinian refers to a famous example of a woman's information leading to suppression of a plot against the government, when a woman named Fulvia (not Julia, as Papinian reports) informed Cicero about the conspiracy led by the disaffected aristocrat, Catiline, in 63 B.C.E.:

D.48.4.8 (Papinian): In criminal inquiries of treason even women are heard. In fact, a woman, Julia (sic), uncovered the conspiracy of Sergius Catiline and provided the consul Marcus Tullius (Cicero) with evidence.

A public accusation was also open to women who had information about the government distribution of free grain to the people of Rome, which was under the supervision of the prefect of the grain dole (*praefectus annonae*). Protecting the food supply to Rome was so essential to public order that people normally not able to bring a public action are allowed, even encouraged to do so. This passage is from the jurist Marcian's first book on *iudicia publica*:

D.48.2.13 (Marcian): The deified (Septimius) Severus and Antoninus (Caracalla) said in a rescript that a woman bringing information pertaining to the grain dole is to be heard by the prefect of the grain dole for the public good. Those branded with legal infamy (*infamia*) also are allowed to bring an accusation without any doubt. Soldiers also, who are not able to bring others' lawsuits to court, (since) they are on guard on behalf of peace, even more should be allowed to bring this type of accusation. Slaves who bring an accusation also are heard.

The same rescript referred to by Marcian is quoted by another jurist, from which it is clear that the emperors were replying to a female petitioner:

D.48.12.3.1 (Papirius Justus): [the beginning of the passage is omitted] Likewise (the emperors)[130] replied in a rescript in these words: "Though it is not customary for women to employ this sort of denunciation, however, since you have promised that you will show things which pertain to the benefit of the grain supply, you are able to inform the prefect of the grain supply."

C A sister seeks to avenge her brother's murder

In 1988, a previously unknown group of twenty-one documents of the mid-third century came to light. The exact provenance of the documents is not known, but they are from the

Middle Euphrates area, in the same region as Dura Europos (for which see Chapters Two and Four). Two of the new documents are in Syriac, the rest in Greek. Nine are written on parchment, the traditional writing material of the region, and twelve are on papyrus. They date from 232 to 256, a time when the Roman imperial power was solidifying its control over a volatile frontier region.

Five of the new documents are petitions to provincial and local officials, two of them addressed to the governor of the recently formed province of Coele Syria.[131] All the petitions were written in Greek on papyrus, and bear many similarities to petitions from Roman Egypt. One is to the centurion in charge of public order in the region from a woman, Bathsabbatha ("daughter of the God of the Sabbath"[132]), who claimed that her brother was murdered and, apparently, that his body had been taken away. She had recovered his body but not his property (which evidently belonged to her as his heir), which was in the possession of another woman, Iabathnanaia, whom Bathsabbatha wants to charge with murder. The relationship of Iabathnanaia to the deceased is not stated, but perhaps she was his widow (and therefore in a position to take control of his property). Having already presented witnesses (both military men, in this frontier zone) to back up her claim, Bathsabbatha now seeks the centurion's subscription (endorsement), which would enable her to bring an accusation against Iabathnanaia to provincial authorities.[133] The case would have to go before the governor, for his delegates and subordinates did not have jurisdiction in a murder case [D.1.21.1 (Papinian)]. Bathsabbatha received the centurion's subscription, but we do not know how the case turned out.

P.Euphr. 5, 27 May, 243 C.E.

To Julius Marinus, centurion for maintaining order in Sphorakene, from Bathsabbatha daughter of Arsinoe,[134] from the village of Magdala of Sphorakene.

My lord, while you were in Appadana I brought before you Aurelius Abilaas, a soldier of the sixteenth legion Flavia Firma, and Barsemaias, a veteran, trustworthy men who gave evidence to you that Nisraiabos my deceased brother, who had been snatched away by some evil-doers, had been recovered by me.[135] Iabathnanaia holds his possessions, which belong to me, and I am ready to bring an accusation against her in regard to his murder. And so for this reason, I ask that you give your subscription to this petition of mine, so that I can use it as testimony.

[in another hand, in Latin] I received this at Appadana on the sixth day before the Kalends of June in the consulship of Ariannus and Pappus.[136]

D Women as defendants or witnesses

Though their right to initiate legal action was restricted, women could certainly be made defendants in civil or criminal cases, and many examples are known from legal and literary sources [see Marshall 1990b]. In such cases also, it was considered more fitting for a woman to be represented by a male, but it was possible for a woman to defend herself in court. Valerius Maximus cites the example of Maesia of Sentinum [see Part V.A above for another example from Valerius Maximus]. The date and circumstances of Maesia's trial are not known, but it appears to have been a criminal trial, perhaps in the aftermath of the Social War of the early first century B.C.E. [Marshall 1990b].

70

Valerius Maximus VIII.1 (written *c*.30 C.E.)
Maesia of Sentinum, a defendant, pled her own case with the Praetor Lucius Titius convening the court and a very great gathering of the people being present. She pursued all the manners and points of her defense not only diligently but also bravely, and she was acquitted on the first *actio* and by almost all votes.[137] They called her Androgyne, because she bore a manly spirit under the appearance of a woman.

An exception to the general rule that women could be made defendants in court involved very young girls under paternal power, whose *paterfamilias* would have represented them:

D.2.4.22 (Gaius): Nor has it been permitted to call into court prepubescent girls, who have been placed under someone else's legal power.

Women could also be witnesses in cases initiated by others.[138] Ulpian and Paul both infer that in general women could give evidence in court from the fact that in particular cases they could not:

D.22.5.18 (Paulus): From the fact that the Julian law on adulteries[139] prohibits a woman condemned (for adultery) from giving testimony, it is also deduced that (all other) women have the right of giving testimony in court.

D.28.1.20.6 (Ulpian): Indeed, a woman will not be able to witness a will,[140] but as an argument that in other cases a woman can be a witness, there is the Julian law on adulteries, which forbids a woman convicted of adultery from being produced as a witness or giving testimony.

VI Women in public life: restrictions and responsibilities

At no time in Roman history could women themselves serve as senators or hold political magistracies on the imperial, provincial or local level.[141] But women of high status – those from senatorial and equestrian families and those in the municipal elites of the Empire – played an important role in imperial society because of their wealth and family connections. For this reason the law was interested in them, and regulated their rank and their munificent activities. The sources translated in this section, along with dozens of laudatory inscriptions set up by communities to honor elite women, demonstrate that women were in fact expected to play a role in public life, albeit to a much more limited extent than their fathers, brothers, and husbands. However, it should be stressed that this role, and the honor paid to these women, was contingent on their membership in wealthy, elite families. Just as women's role in legal matters was restricted to matters involving themselves or close family members [Part V], so their role in civic life was restricted to acting as part of, or on behalf of, their family [van Bremen 1996].

A *The importance of status*

Roman society was always highly status-conscious, so it is not surprising that many legal enactments and juristic writings deal with the subject of status. The highest status was held by members of senatorial families. Though membership in the Senate was not automatically inherited, the wives, children, and grandchildren (by their sons) of senators did possess senatorial status. This endowed them with greater *dignitas* (status, prestige) than other citizens, and made them subject to certain privileges and restrictions (such as the ban on marriage with former slaves; see Chapter 3, Part I.B). By the end of the second century, many senators came from the provinces rather than Italy.

Men of senatorial status held the title of *clarissimi* ("most splendid"). By the second century the wives and daughters of senators were given the title *clarissima femina* ("most splendid woman"). This title, usually abbreviated "c.f.," appears beginning in the second century on Latin inscriptions which commemorate senatorial women.[142]

D.50.16.100 (Ulpian): We ought to accept as "respectable persons" *clarissimi* persons of both sexes, and likewise those who enjoy senatorial distinctions.

D.1.5.9 (Papinian): In many sections of our law the condition of women is lower than that of males.

D.1.9.1 (Ulpian): No one doubts that a man of consular rank (*vir consularis*) is certainly to be placed before a woman of consular rank (*consularis femina*). But whether a man of prefectorial rank (*vir praefectorius*) is to be placed before a woman of consular rank must be determined. I would think that he is, because there is greater status (*dignitas*) in the male sex. Moreover, we say that the wives of consular men are consular women. Saturninus adds mothers (of consular men) also, but this has neither been noted anywhere nor ever accepted.

A *vir consularis* was one who had reached the consulship, the highest senatorial office. A *vir praefectorius* is presumably one who had held one of the top prefectures, e.g., the praetorian prefecture or the governorship of a province such as Egypt. He would be an equestrian, but still one of the top men in the Empire. Only a few women are known to have borne the title *consularis femina*, which was more prestigious than *clarissima femina* [Chastagnol 1979].

It was clearly a great honor to be a *clarissima*, and women who had at one time enjoyed that title were anxious to retain it even if they married a non-senatorial man:

D.1.9.12 (Ulpian): Women previously married to a man of consular rank are accustomed to request from the emperor, though very rarely, that if they have married again to a man of lesser status they may nevertheless remain of consular status: as I know the emperor Antoninus (Caracalla) granted to his own cousin Julia Mamaea.

D.1.9.8 (Ulpian): Women married to *clarissimi* persons are included in the term "*clarissimae* persons." The daughters of senators are not included in the name "*clarissimae* women" except those who have been allotted *clarissimi* men (as husbands); for husbands impart clarissimate status to women, but parents (only impart status) until they (daughters) have been joined in marriage with a plebeian. Therefore a woman will be *clarissima* for as long as she is married to a senator or *clarissimus* or, (as long as) having separated from him, she has not married another man of lower status (*dignitas*).

This rule, whose date is uncertain,[143] caused some concern to the daughters or former wives of senatorial men, who wished to retain their title even after marrying someone outside the senatorial order:

Cod. Just. 12.1.1, 222–235

Emperor Alexander Augustus to Severiana:

If, as you claim, your grandfather had consular rank and your father had been a praetor, and you married men of senatorial status (*clarissimi*), not of private status, you retain your family's splendor (*claritas*).

Though only one woman, Severiana, is addressed in this rescript, the use of the second person plural in all the verbs indicates that more than one person was petitioning the emperor. Severiana evidently was writing on behalf of her sister(s) as well as of herself.

Cod. Just. 5.4.10, 286–293

Emperors Diocletian and Maximian Augusti to Paulina:

Since you say that you were not born from a senator father but took the name of *clarissima femina* because of a marriage contracted with a senator, if you afterwards were allotted a husband of the second rank (i.e. an equestrian) as a husband, you have given up the senatorial distinction which was bestowed on you as a benefit from your husband and have been reduced to your former status.

Despite the ruling, it appears that in the third century some *clarissimae* who married equestrians were able to retain their senatorial status, including several Christian women [Chastagnol 1979; cf. Evans Grubbs 1995, 79]. This may be because the rule was abrogated under Alexander Severus or slightly later [Chastagnol 1982, 258–9; Raepsaet-Charlier 1993, 158–9] or frequently waived in the case of senators' daughters. Paulina, to whom this rescript applies the rule, was not a *clarissima* by birth, and so did not receive the exemption that some senators' daughters evidently did [Chastagnol 1982].

A person's *forum* was the place where he or she would be tried in court. *Clarissimi* had the privilege of having Rome (or, in the late Empire, Constantinople) as their *forum*, rather than a provincial court. Senators' wives would have that privilege, but lose it if they remarried a non-senator. The following law repeats the principle found in third-century rescripts that women follow their *clarissimus* husband's status, but lose it if they remarry:

Cod. Just. 12.1.13, 10 November, 392

Emperors Valentinian (II), Theodosius (I) and Arcadius Augusti to Marcianus, Count of the Orient:

We raise up women by the honor of their husbands, we ennoble them by their family and we determine their legal forum and change their legal residence (*domicilium*) on the basis of their (the husbands') person. If, however, they have later been allotted a husband of a lesser rank, deprived of their former status (*dignitas*), they shall follow the condition of their later husband.

Given at Constantinople on the fourth day before the Ides of November in the second consulship of Arcadius Augustus and the consulship of Rufinus.[144]

B Prohibitions on holding public office

Just as women were banned from representing others in court [Part V.A], they also could not themselves serve as judges in court cases or hold public office, both of which *ipso facto* involved representing others. As the jurist Paulus (writing in the third century) realized, the real reason for this restriction was that it had been instituted by Romans in the long-ago past, and respect for the "customs of the ancestors" (*mos maiorum*) was so great that it over-rode contemporary social realities. This is from one of his books on the Praetor's Edict:

D.5.1.12.2 (Paulus): However, not all people are able to be appointed as judges (*iudices*) by those who have the right to appoint judges; for some are prevented by law from being judges, some by nature, and some by custom. By nature: like the deaf-mute, and the man who is permanently mad, and the minor, because they lack judgment. The man who has been removed from the Senate is prevented by law. Women and slaves are prevented by custom, not because they do not have judgment, but because it has been accepted that they do not discharge civil duties.

Restrictions on women's public and legal activities are neatly summed up by Ulpian in this passage:

D.50.17.2 (Ulpian): Women are removed from all civil or public functions and therefore are neither able to be judges nor to undertake a magistracy nor to bring a prosecution nor to intervene on behalf of another nor to be procurators. 1: Likewise, (a male) who has not reached puberty ought to stay away from all civil functions.

In general, women were not legally banned from any business occupation, with the apparent exception of banking:

D.2.13.12 (Callistratus): Women seem to be removed from the service of banking, since that is man's work.

This ban was probably a result of the *senatusconsultum Velleianum*, which advised women not to provide surety for others' debts [Part IV.D; Gardner 1993, 99–100]. It applied only to the formal profession of banking; women could – and frequently did – act as go-betweens in business deals, and lend and borrow money, as seen in many imperial rescripts and papyri [Arjava 1996, 249]. A woman is even attested in the position of tax-farmer, responsible for collecting revenues for the imperial treasury [D.49.14.47 pr; Gardner 1986a, 236].

C Wealthy women and munera

Prohibitions on holding office, however, did not exclude wealthy women of high rank from contributing financially to their communities. There were only about 600 senators in the early Empire, so the number of *clarissimae* was always quite small. But many more women in the Empire had equestrian status (the next highest rank below senators) or were members of municipal aristocracies. As members of wealthy and high-ranking families, they shared not only the privileges (apart from office-holding) but also the responsibilities associated in antiquity with the upper classes of cities. They participated in the social institution known as euergetism, which was widespread in the eastern Mediterranean during the Hellenistic and Roman periods, and in the west (particularly Italy and North Africa) from the early Empire through the mid-third century.

Euergetism (from the Greek meaning "good-deed-doing") was the practice of public benefaction by local elite families for the maintenance of the cities of the Empire. Men often performed these benefactions while holding municipal office, and indeed the ability and willingness to use their own resources for the public good were essential prerequisites to holding office in the cities of the Empire. The obligations (which might or might not be financial) of those who held public office were known as *honores*, and carried prestige. In addition, however, those with wealth and social rank were liable to perform *munera* (duties), which did not in themselves carry any prestige [Millar 1983; Sirks 1989]. Both *honores* and *munera* might involve public benefaction, such as paying for the erection of new public buildings and the repair of old ones, sponsorship of public games and entertainments, and the distribution of largesse to citizens on holidays and special occasions.

In return for these services by the wealthy elite, cities would honor their benefactors with statues and honorific inscriptions praising their munificence and their excellent qualities.

Women of wealthy, office-holding families were also subject to *munera*, the responsibility to pay for and put on performances, such as gladiatorial shows or theatrical groups, or other public entertainment. Legal rulings specify who was responsible for *munera* and under what conditions those who were unwilling or unable to fulfill their public responsibilities might be exempted. There were some *munera*, perhaps those involving physical exertion, which women did not have to take on, though it is not clear what these were [see Arjava 1996, 251; Beaucamp 1990, 32–4; van Bremen 1996, 48–9]:

D.50.4.3.3 (Ulpian): Their very sex prevents women from undertaking *munera* of a physical nature (*corporalia*).

It was customary for men running for public office to promise to undertake or pay for a show or other public benefit if elected. The following passage is from one of Ulpian's books on the duties of provincial governors. Its reference to the promises of female candidates for office presumably refers to situations in the Greek east, particularly the cities of Asia Minor, where women did hold some magistracies, unlike in the west [see van Bremen 1996].

D.50.12.6.2 (Ulpian): It should be understood that not only males, but also females, ought to fulfill any promises they have made because of public office (*honores*). And this is supported by a rescript of our emperor and his deified father (Caracalla and Septimius Severus).

The following case, from a book of *Responsa* ("replies") by the third-century jurist Modestinus, records a promise in Greek by a woman, Septicia. It must be from the eastern Empire, probably one of the cities of Asia Minor:

D.50.12.10 (Modestinus): Septicia promised a contest to her native land, under this condition, that the principal (of the sum she gave for the foundation of the contests) would remain with her and she herself would pay the monthly interest of half an *as*[145] for the prizes of the contestants. The promise was made in these words: [the following paragraph is in Greek, in Septicia's own words].

"Seeking honor,[146] I dedicate a contest to be held every fourth year, (using the interest) from 30,000 (*denarii*), myself holding the money of the capital and giving sufficient surety to the *dekaprotoi* (the chief magistrates of the city) for the purpose of paying the interest on the 30,000 in the customary way, with my husband as judge of the contests and presiding officer, and in turn the children that will be born from me. The interest will go to the prizes of the theatrical players, according to what the Council (Boule) decides for each contest."

I (Modestinus) ask, whether Septicia's children (*filii*) can suffer insult (*iniuria*) from not presiding themselves over the contest according to the words and condition of her promise. Herennius Modestinus replied, in the event that the exhibition of the contest was legal, the form given to (Septicia's) promise must be preserved.

Septicia endowed a quadrennial theatrical contest for her (unnamed) city, with strings attached: she kept control of the principal and disbursed the interest for the prizes, and her husband and children were to preside over the contest. Apparently after the death of Septicia and her husband, the city tried to take the presidency out of the hands of her children, who then brought suit for *iniuria*.[147] The jurist Modestinus ruled that according to the terms of the endowment, the donor's children should preside.

It is unusual to find in the *Digest* explicit mention of a provincial woman, and the verbatim quotation (in Greek) of her promise of *munera*. But there is extensive epigraphical evidence from the cities of the Empire, especially those in the provinces of Asia Minor, to show that many women did undertake these financial burdens. Honorary inscriptions recording the dedication of statues or other honors on munificent women tell us about those who took on such duties willingly [Boatwright 1991; van Bremen 1983 and 1996; Forbis 1990; Kajava 1990; Nicols 1989; Rogers 1992]. Often they held provincial or imperial priesthoods; in the Greek east, they might also hold certain magistracies (see above). The following inscriptions are just a small sample of the dedicatory inscriptions honoring munificent women in the towns and cities of the Empire (cf. the inscription honoring Senbreidase of Xanthos in Chapter 5, Part II.B.3).[148]

This decree from the Aegean island of Syros honors Berneike after her death for her office-holding and benefactions, noting at the same time her fulfillment of traditional womanly ideals. Her role as *archeine* presumably resembled that of the male *archon*, and so would have involved leading public celebrations at the beginning of the year, presiding over sacrifices, and providing public feasts and hand-outs [van Bremen 1996, 130–1].

Pleket #25 (*IG* XII.5.655), 2nd–3rd c.

The Council and People decided; the opinion of the chief magistrates: Since Berneike daughter of Nikomachos, wife of Aristokles son of Isidoros, has led a good and seemly way of life in all respects, and after she became *archeine* she generously from her own resources discharged her duties to gods and men on behalf of the fatherland, and after she was made priestess of the heavenly gods Demeter and Kore and served as priest of the holiest of the gods and of the city in a chaste and worthy way, she died, having also borne and brought up children. (They decided) both to praise the life which the woman had lived, and to crown her with a golden crown, with which it is customary for us to crown good women. And the one making this proposal to us shall proclaim publicly at the woman's funeral that, "The People of Syros crown Berneike daughter of Nikomachos with a gold crown because of her virtue and good-will towards it (Syros)."

Like Berneike, Aurelia Leite of Paros was praised by her city for traditional womanly virtues as well for as her generosity and wisdom. The reference to Augusti and Caesars dates the following dedication to the period of the tetrarchy, between 293–305. Note that as a Roman citizen (whose ancestors probably received citizenship under the Edict of Caracalla,), Aurelia Leite has a Roman *nomen* (Aurelia) as well as a Greek name (Leite).

Pleket #31 (IG XII.5.292), *c*.300

The most remarkable and best in every respect Aurelia Leite daughter of Theodotus, wife of Marcus Aurelius Faustus the first man of the city, high-priest from his ancestors for life of the Augusti and the Caesars, and Kabarnos (priest of Demeter) and gymnasiarch. When she was gymnasiarch she constructed and restored the gymnasium which was worn out from the passage of time. The most magnificent city of Paros, her fatherland, taking honor rather than giving it in exchange for her many great deeds, concerning which it often voted resolutions, erected a marble statue of the wisdom-loving, husband-loving, children-loving and fatherland-loving woman. (in verse) The glorious Faustus fully honored Leite, his wisdom-bearing wife who bore the best of children.

Though euergetism was most firmly rooted in the Greek cities of the eastern Empire, the practice of local elites performing acts of civic generosity also took hold in the communities of the west. Here Junia Rustica (whose name indicates she holds the Roman citizenship) in the small town of Cartima in southern Spain, who holds a priesthood of the imperial cult, is honored in a Latin inscription for her munificence. Such priesthoods, and the promotion of the local elites who performed benefactions, contributed to the "Romanization" of provinces like Baetica in Spain [Mackie 1990, 184–5]. In this case, Junia Rustica also paid for her own statue and statues of her son and husband, all of which had been decreed by the town council.

CIL II.1956 (ILS 5512), later 1st c. C.E.

Junia Rustica, daughter of Decimus, first and perpetual priestess in the town of Cartima, rebuilt the public porticos, which were broken by age, gave the land for the baths, maintained the public revenues, placed a bronze image of Mars in the forum, gave from her own money and dedicated porticos for the baths on her own land with a swimming-pool and an image of Cupid, after having given a feast and having produced public shows. (She also) had made with her own money and gave statues that had been decreed by the town council of Cartima to herself and to her son Gaius Fabius Junianus, after having remitted the expense, and likewise a statue to her husband Gaius Fabius Fabianus.

The honoring of local women for undertaking public benefactions was not limited to the provinces, of course; see, e.g., the dedication to Abeiana Balbina (priestess, patron, and holder of the *ius liberorum*) in Part III.D.

It was important for the purpose of assessing *munera* on wealthy men and women to know in what city they owed *munera*. Normally, one performed *munera* in the city of one's birth (*origo*). Women, however, often moved away from their place of origin when they married and took up their residence (*domicilium*) in their husband's home. A woman who married a citizen of another city performed *munera* there:[149]

D.50.1.38.3 (Papirius Justus): The same emperors (Marcus Aurelius and Lucius Verus) decided in a rescript that a woman seems to be the resident of the same city as her husband for as long as she has been married, and is not forced to perform *munera* in that place whence she takes her origin.

D.50.1.22.1 (Paulus): A widowed woman retains the residence (*domicilium*) of her departed husband, by the example of a woman who has been made a *clarissima* person through her husband; but both (residence and status) are changed if another marriage occurs.

D.50.1.32 (Modestinus): She who has been betrothed does not change her own *domicilium* before the marriage is contracted.

D.50.1.37.2 (Callistratus): It should be known that women, who have given themselves in marriage which is not legitimate, should not perform *munera* in that place where their husbands are, but where they themselves originated. The deified brothers (Marcus Aurelius and Lucius Verus) decided that in a rescript.

An example of such an illegitimate marriage would be that between a senatorial woman and a freedman [see Chapter 3, Part I.B]. It is the exception to the rule stated above, that married women perform *munera* in their husband's city.

Women were also liable for *munera* on property they had inherited from their father, in whatever place that paternal property happened to be:

Cod. Just. 10.64.1, 244–249

Emperor Philip Augustus to Claudius:

Malchea, who was born in one place but married in another, can be compelled to (perform) *honores* or *munera* which are connected with persons and which her sex is capable of, not at her own place of origin but at her husband's residence, if her husband is not staying in the city of Rome. This has been often stated in rescripts. But it is necessary that women undertake the *munera* inherited from their father in those places in which they possess property.

Cod. Just. 10.42.9, 293–305

Emperors Diocletian and Maximian Augusti and the Caesars to Marcia:

Women also ought to undertake the *munera* they have inherited from their fathers.

This reply was probably part of the same original rescript as:

Cod. Just. 10.52.5, 293–305
Emperors Diocletian and Maximian Augusti and the Caesars to Marcia:
Our deified parents decided, on the example of males,[150] that women who have five surviving children are excused from personal *munera*, which are imposed on women according to the condition of their sex.

A law of Constantine relieved senatorial women of some inherited *munera*: if their father had been elected praetor but had died before carrying out the obligations incumbent on praetors in late antiquity (which mainly consisted of paying for gladiatorial contests and the like), women who had no brothers did not have to undertake their dead father's *munera*. (Clearly, if they did have brothers, the brothers were expected to undertake the *munera*.) Constantine's law is no longer extant; we know of it from a later law of Valentinian[151] which apparently rescinds it:

Cod. Theod. 6.4.17, 19 January, 370
Emperors Valentinian and Valens Augusti to Olybrius, urban prefect:
We have learned that our divine parent Constantine decreed that in the case when a father acknowledges all his senatorial *munera* when alive, and then died after being nominated praetor, and his survivors appear to be daughters, with no masculine offspring surviving at all, the women have no (necessity of) carrying out (his financial obligations as praetor). Therefore, since[152] it happens that not only males are heirs to their father, but also females come to succeed by the law of inheritance, you should in no way excuse these same women from (the obligations of) the praetorship as well as the gifts, if they have become of full age or adults.[153] But you will take care to compel them also to sustain their paternal obligations according to the hereditary portion of individual persons. Though it seems unjust and dishonorable for women to advance to the purple stripe and the (senatorial) insignia, however they will be able to acknowledge the (obligations of) the car***narian praetorship according to the glebal tax on their paternal property.[154]
Given on the fourteenth day before the Kalends of February in the consulship of the emperors.

Senatorial daughters as well as sons are responsible for carrying out their deceased father's *munera*, assuming that the daughters have at least reached the age of puberty. The law can be traced to the policy of Diocletian and his co-rulers, that women are responsible for the *munera* they have inherited from their office-holding fathers. Senatorial women are to pay for their status by performing *munera*, but are not to enjoy its perks (the broad purple stripe of a senator's toga and other insignia), which would be "unjust and dishonorable"!
Another law of the same emperors assigns liability for patrimonial *munera* to the daughters of *navicularii*, the corporation responsible for the transport of grain and other essential supplies by ship to Rome and Constantinople [Sirks 1989, 109–11]. Such women were bound by their inherited responsibilities even if their husbands had obligations elsewhere:

Cod. Theod. 13.5.12, 14 May, 369

The same Augusti to Demetrianus, prefect of the grain supply (*annona*) of Africa:

If any *navicularius* has been able to obtain transferal of legal forum by the indulgence of Our Eternity, he shall be deprived of the enjoyment of his granted request.[155] But concerning the persons of women the statutes of ancient (emperors) shall be kept, that, in whatever forums it is decreed by ancient disposition that they have been enrolled, there they are to recognize the duty of their ship-master's burden. For just as it is fitting for the same women to follow the forums of their husbands in lawsuits and private legal cases, so in public obligations they ought to preserve the procedure of their birth-place (*origo*).

Given at Trier on the day before the Ides of May in the consulship of Valentinian, noble boy,[156] and of Victor.

A woman's *munera* are based on those of her father (which she inherits along with his property) or of her husband (when she changes her domicile to reside with him). Legal sources generally discuss women mainly in terms of their family roles – daughter, wife, mother. A woman acting publicly outside of those roles, as advocate, magistrate, or judge, was not only a social but a legal anomaly. We turn now to legal sources treating women in their family roles – marriage, divorce, and motherhood.

2

MARRIAGE IN ROMAN LAW AND SOCIETY

I Marriage and its consequences in classical Roman law

Marriage was one of the fundamental institutions of Roman society, as it joined not only two individuals but two families. Only from legal marriage (*iustum matrimonium* or *iustae nuptiae*) could legitimate children, who would be their father's heirs, be born. Thus it was important to define what constituted a legitimate marriage and what did not. Most of the juristic passages in this chapter are taken from Book 23 of the *Digest* (on marriage and dowry) or Book 24 (on gifts between husband and wife).

A The purpose and nature of marriage

1 What is marriage?

The Romans considered marriage a partnership, whose primary purpose was to have legitimate descendants to whom property, status, and family qualities could be handed down through the generations. Marriage and procreation were not only socially useful, they were in accordance with natural law:

D.23.2.1 (Modestinus): Marriage is the joining of male and female and a partnership for all of life, a sharing of divine and human law.
D.1.1.1.3 (Ulpian): Natural law (*ius naturale*) is that which nature has taught all animals: for that law is not unique to the human race, but to all animals which arise on the earth or in the sea; and also common to the birds. From this follows the joining of male and female, which we call marriage, from this follows the procreation of children, and their upbringing: for indeed we see also the other animals, even the wild beasts, are thought to have experience of that law.
D.50.16.220.3 (Callistratus): In addition, nature also teaches us that dutiful parents, who take wives with the intention and desire of procreating children, hold by the name of "children" all who descend from us: for we are not able to call our grandchildren by a sweeter name than "children." For this reason indeed we conceive and bring up sons and daughters, so that from the offspring of our male or female (children) we may leave for ourselves a lasting memorial for all time.

Two aspects of marriage were of particular concern to Roman law and are amply documented in the *Digest* and other legal sources: consent to the marriage by all parties involved [Part I.C.3 below], and the partners' legal eligibility for marriage with each other [see Chapter 3].

Rules of Ulpian **5.2**: Legitimate marriage (*iustum matrimonium*) occurs, if the right to marry (*conubium*) exists between those who are contracting marriage, and the male is as mature as the female is capable (sc., of intercourse), and they both consent, if they are legally independent, or their parents also consent if they are in (paternal) power. **3.** *Conubium* is the ability to take a wife by law.

Children born in *iustum matrimonium* received their father's family name (*nomen*) and were his legal heirs. They also came under his paternal power (*patria potestas*) until he died or emancipated them – a power which, at least in theory, was all-encompassing and life-long [see Chapter 1, Part II.A].

2 What makes a marriage valid?

Cohabitation and sexual intercourse did not make a marriage, according to the jurists, nor did their absence necessarily imply the absence of marriage:

D.50.17.30 (Ulpian): Sleeping together does not make marriage, but consent does.[1]

D.24.1.32.13 (Ulpian): Indeed, if a woman and her husband have lived apart for a long time, but kept the honor of marriage on both sides, which we know sometimes ensues even among consular persons, I think that gifts (between them) are not valid, just as if the marriage has lasted. For sexual intercourse does not make a marriage, but the marital frame of mind (*affectio maritalis*) does.

Gifts between husband and wife during the marriage were not valid in Roman law [Part I.E]. Thus it was important to determine whether a marriage still existed, and the juristic criterion was whether the couple thought of themselves as being married, even if they lived apart – that is, whether they maintained *affectio maritalis* toward each other.[2] "Consular persons" are those who had reached the consulship [see Chapter 1, Part VI.A]. Ulpian may be referring to cases where a provincial governor or other high-ranking official was abroad on government service, and his wife stayed home.

Roman law did not require the performance of any ceremony, religious or secular, for validation of a marriage. There were ceremonies connected with betrothal and weddings, but there is no mention of them in the legal sources – both because they were not relevant to the legal validity of a marriage, and because the late Roman compilers of classical law would have deleted any reference to pagan rituals. It was not even strictly necessary that a husband be present at his own marriage, as long as there was a *deductio in domum*, an escorting of the bride into the husband's home. This could lead to a woman becoming a widow before her marriage had been consummated:

D.23.2.5 (Pomponius): It is agreed that a woman is able to be married to an absent man by means of a letter from him or through his messenger, if she is led into his home. However, it is not possible for a woman who is absent to be led in marriage by a husband by letter or by her own messenger. For there needs to be an escorting into the husband's home, not the wife's, as if into the marital domicile.

D.23.2.6 (Ulpian): Lastly, Cinna writes: It has been replied that the man who took a wife who was absent, and then perished next to the Tiber river as he was returning from dinner, must be mourned by his wife.[3]

The jurist Gaius pointed out that a marriage, like a mortgage (*hypotheca*), depended for validity on the consent of both parties, not on written documentation:

D.20.1.4 (Gaius): [the beginning of the passage is omitted here] For written documents are made about these things (mortgages), in order that through them (documents) what has been done can be proved more easily. Even without these, however, what has been done is valid, if there is (unwritten) evidence to prove it.[4] Just as also a marriage exists, though testimonies (to it) have not been put in writing.

However, there were people in the Empire who thought, following their local customs, that a marriage's validity required written documentation. Thus third-century emperors responded to subjects like Fortunatus, who was worried about the legitimacy of his children [see Gardner 1986b; Watson 1974a]:

Cod. Just. 5.4.9, 276–282
Emperor Probus Augustus to Fortunatus:
    If, with the knowledge of neighbors or others, you had a wife at home "for the sake of producing children,"[5] and a daughter was begotten from this marriage, though neither marriage tablets nor records pertaining to your daughter's birth were made, nevertheless the truth of the marriage and of the daughter begotten (in it) has its own value.

Cod. Just. 5.4.13, 292–305
Emperors Diocletian and Maximian Augusti and the Caesars to Onesimus:
    Documents that were made without marriage (taking place) are not suitable for proof of marriage if the truth of the matter is otherwise. Nor is a marriage that was lawfully contracted without the introduction of documents invalid, since, even if written documentation has been omitted, other indications of marriage are not invalid.

B The Augustan marriage legislation

The first emperor Augustus (31 B.C.E.–14 C.E.) enacted several laws whose purpose was to promote marriage and child-bearing among Roman citizens, and to repress adultery and extra-marital sex. His legislation endured for several hundred years (with modifications by later emperors), and directly affected all Roman citizens, especially the upper classes, at whom it was aimed. The legislation comprised three laws: the *lex Julia de maritandis ordinibus* (Julian law on the regulating the marriages of the social orders) of 18 B.C.E.; the *lex Julia de adulteriis* (Julian law on adultery), probably also of 18 B.C.E.; and the *lex Papia–Poppaea* (Papian–Poppaean law) of 9 C.E. The last law, twenty-seven years later, was passed in response to unhappiness on the part of the elite (see below), and modified certain provisions of the *lex Julia de maritandis ordinibus*. It is not possible to tell which provisions of the Augustan marriage legislation belonged to the original law of 18 B.C.E. and which to the law of 9 C.E. In imperial juristic commentaries and in marriage contracts from Roman Egypt, the legislation is referred to generally as the *"lex Julia et Papia–Poppaea."* Briefly summarized, the main features of the Augustan legislation were [see further Treggiari 1991a, 37–80; McGinn 1998, 70–104]:

1   All male citizens between the ages of twenty-five and sixty and all female citizens between twenty and fifty were to be married.[6] Widows were to marry within two (or perhaps three; see Suetonius, *Deified Augustus* 34, below) years of their husband's death, divorcées within eighteen months. Those who had not married by that time were penalized financially: they could not receive inheritances or legacies from those to whom they were not related within six degrees of relationship (which would include second cousins and great-uncles/aunts). Those married but childless could receive only half of any such legacies, and childless married couples could only inherit one-tenth of each other's property. Those who were married and had children were rewarded with certain privileges, in particular the *ius (trium) liberorum*, the "right of (three) children." Men had priority in receiving government appointments and, if they had the *ius liberorum*, were released from the duty of serving as legal guardian. Women who obtained the *ius liberorum* were freed from the need for a *tutor* for legal and business transactions [see Chapter 1, Part III.D]. Spouses with the *ius liberorum* could leave more than one-tenth of their property to each other by will.

2   Marriage between members of the senatorial order (senators, their children, and their sons' children) and former slaves were prohibited. Any such unions which did take place were not considered legitimate marriage (*iustum matrimonium*) and couples in such a relationship were considered not in compliance with the Augustan law. Also prohibited were marriages between those of senatorial rank and actors, and marriage between all freeborn people (including senators) and prostitutes, pimps, condemned adulteresses or those caught in the act of adultery [see further Chapter 3, Part I.B.4].

3   Adultery, defined as sexual relations between a married woman and a man other than her husband, became a criminal offense to be tried in standing courts. Conviction led to relegation to an island and confiscation of property (for a woman, half her dowry and a third of her other property; for her male lover, half his property). *Stuprum* (denoting illicit, non-marital sexual relations in general) with an unmarried woman of respectable status, was also punishable under the adultery law. This was the first time sexual offenses had been punished as public crimes; in the Republic, chastisement of adulterous wives had been the role of the *paterfamilias* and the family council, not the state. Husbands were required to divorce adulterous wives or risk being prosecuted themselves for *lenocinium* (pimping). Divorce for adultery required the presence of seven witnesses to be fully ratified [Treggiari 1991a, 454–7; Evans Grubbs 1995, 203–16; McGinn 1998, 140–247].

In 320, the emperor Constantine repealed the inheritance penalties on the unmarried [Part II.A], and in the early fifth century, the restrictions on inheritance between childless spouses were lifted. Most of the prohibitions on marriage between those of different rank were lifted by Justinian in the mid-sixth century. The adultery legislation continued in force throughout antiquity, with some changes under Constantine. Because Augustus' legislation underwent modification and abrogation over the next 550 years, the text of the original laws survives only in excerpts and paraphrases by later writers, some of which appear in this and the next chapter.

According to imperial literary sources, public reaction to Augustus' legislation was not favorable. The elite saw the laws as government intrusion into their private affairs. The restrictions on the right of the unmarried to inherit from those beyond the sixth degree of relationship may seem mild today, when virtually all inheritance is between close family members. This was in fact the case for most of Roman society too [Champlin 1991, 126–30]. Among the Roman elite, however, the giving and receiving of sometimes quite sizable legacies to and from other aristocrats was customary, and marked esteem and friendship beyond immediate family [Wallace-Hadrill 1981; Hopkins 1983, 235–47]. Augustus' legislation would have disrupted this practice.

Following are accounts of Augustus's legislation and of reaction to it by the elite, senators and equestrians. These accounts were all written more than a century after the legislation was passed but evidently reflect dissatisfaction during Augustus' reign.

Cassius Dio, a Roman senator and historian from Bithynia (northern Turkey), writing in Greek in the early third century, briefly summarized the marriage legislation of 18 B.C.E.:

Cassius Dio, *Roman History* 54.16.1–2 (18 B.C.E.): Upon the unmarried men and the women without husbands he imposed rather heavy penalties, and conversely, he set up prizes for marriage and child-bearing. And since there were many more males than females among the well-born, he permitted those who wished, except for Senators, to take freedwomen (as wives), ordering that their offspring be legitimate.[7]

Dio recounts how Augustus responded to a group of *equites* (equestrians, see Introduction, Part II) who were complaining about his legislation during celebratory games in Rome in 9 C.E., the year the *lex Papia–Poppaea* was passed:

56.1 (9 C.E.): And since the *equites* (*hippeis*), were there (at the games) asking very zealously that the law about those who weren't marrying or having children be relaxed, he (Augustus) gathered together into the forum in separate groups those of them without wives on the one hand, and those who had married and had children on the other. And seeing that the latter were much fewer than the former, he grieved and lectured to them in the following way ... [The speech, not included here, exhorted the *equites* to do their duty to state and family by marrying and procreating.]

56.10: ... Then after this he increased further the honors for those who had children, and he separated by a distinction in penalties those who had married from those who were without wives, and gave in addition to both (of the latter groups) a year for those who obeyed him within that time to be guiltless (and therefore not be penalized). To certain women, contrary to the Voconian law, according to which it was not possible for any of them to inherit an estate of more than 100,000 (sesterces), he allowed the ability to do this.[8] And to the always-virgins (Vestal Virgins) he granted all the things which the women who had borne children had. And subsequent to this was passed the Papian–Poppaean law by Marcus Papius Mutilus and Quintus Poppaeus Secundus, who were consuls then for part of the year. And it happened that both of them did not have children, and moreover did not

85

even have wives. And from this very fact the necessity for the law was seen clearly.

The biographer Suetonius, writing in the early second century, also mentions Augustus' legislation and the negative reaction it encountered:

Suetonius, *The Deified Augustus* 34: He (Augustus) renewed laws and decreed some laws anew, as for instance a luxury-law, and a law about adulteries and chastity (*pudicitia*), a law about bribery, a law about the marriages of the orders. When he had amended this last one somewhat more severely than the others, he was not able to carry it through in the face of the uproar of those refusing (to accept it) except after part of the penalties had been removed or lightened and a three-year exemption had been given[9] and the rewards had been increased. Thus also when the *equites* were obstinately demanding its (the law's) abolition at a public show, he summoned the children of Germanicus[10] and held them up as an example, receiving some in his own lap and some in their father's lap, showing with his hand and face that they should not regard it as a burden to imitate the young man's example. And also, when he perceived that the force of the law was being frustrated by the immaturity of the betrothed girls and the frequent change (of spouses), he shortened the time for having fiancées and imposed a limit on divorce.

The last sentence refers to two ways men reluctant to marry were avoiding fulfilling the intention of the law: they were marrying in order to receive a legacy and then divorcing soon afterwards, or were betrothing themselves to girls well under the legal marriage age of twelve (before Augustus' later tightening of the law, being betrothed had been considered compliance). Cassius Dio tells us that Augustus put a limit of two years on betrothals, which meant the betrothed girl had to be at least ten [*Roman History* 54.16.7]. Men who still had not married after two years would be subject to the penalties. The reference to Augustus' "limit on divorce" is unclear, but may refer to a requirement for more evidence for divorce when one partner unilaterally repudiated the other [Treggiari 1991a, 453–4, 457].

Legacies and inheritances left to those who did not marry and have children fell either to other heirs or legatees who were in compliance or, if there were none, to the state treasury. To guard against the unmarried and childless inheriting illegally, the government encouraged third parties to report information they had about such bequests; informers were rewarded with a share of the illegal legacy. Obviously this encouraged the relaying of information, and thus arose the dreaded scourge of the *delatores* (informers) in Roman society, according to Suetonius' contemporary, the historian Tacitus:

Tacitus, *Annales* III.25: Then (20 C.E.) there was a proposal (before the Senate) concerning mitigating the Papian–Poppaean (law), which the elder Augustus had decreed after the Julian proposals for increasing the penalties on the unmarried and increasing the treasury. But marriages and the bringing up of children did not increase for that reason, as childlessness was very prevalent. But the multitude of those who were at risk increased, since every home was turned upside down by the statements of informers, so that just as before this (Rome) had been oppressed by disgraceful behavior, so now it was oppressed by laws.

Tacitus then has a digression on the development of Roman law and the increasing corruption and civil disorder arising from law, which he traces down to Augustus' reign. The informers became such a problem that Augustus' successor Tiberius, like many modern leaders faced with an intractable social problem, appointed an official commission to look into the matter:

Annales III.28: ... In his sixth consulship (28 B.C.E.) Caesar Augustus, secure in power, abolished the measures which he had ordered during his triumvirate and gave the laws which we use under peace and *princeps* (emperor). Harsher bonds (arose) from this, guards were imposed and induced by the rewards of the Papian–Poppaean law so that, if there was default from the privileges of parents, then the people (i.e. the state), as if the parent of all, would keep the ownerless properties (which had been bequeathed illegally). But they (the "guards," i.e., informers) penetrated deeper and seized hold of the city and Italy and wherever there were citizens, and the positions of many were destroyed. And terror would have spread over all had not Tiberius chosen by lot five men of consular rank, five of praetorian rank, and as many from the rest of the Senate for the purpose of establishing a remedy, at the hands of whom many fetters of the law were loosed, and they (the Commission) brought a slight relief for the immediate present.

Only the protests of male members of the upper classes are mentioned; there is no record of any female demonstration against the Augustan laws. Probably the legislation had less impact on women, because all women (with the exception of the Vestal Virgins) had always been expected to marry and have children and had little or no choice in marrying at least once. Widows and divorcées were more affected, since under the Julian law they were expected to remarry within a short amount of time, which ran counter to the tradition of the *univira*, the "one-man woman," who never remarried after her first marriage ended [see Chapter 5, Part I.B]. The Papian–Poppaean law did in fact mitigate the Julian law's demands for remarriage of widows and divorcées by extending the time by which they had to remarry (see above).

The actual effect of Augustus' legislation on the Roman birth-rate is unknown; no demographic data exists for Roman Italy, and statements by ancient writers are biased and not based on statistics. The *ius liberorum* was sometimes granted as a special mark of favor to those who did not actually have children: Trajan gave the *ius liberorum* to Pliny the Younger, and, at Pliny's request, to Suetonius (Pliny, *Epistles* X.2 and X.94–5; cf. *Epistles*. II.13 for another friend for whom Pliny obtained the *ius liberorum*), so it was not always necessary to comply with the laws in order to reap the benefits. Perhaps, as Tacitus suggests, one of Augustus' motives was to increase the treasury with the confiscated legacies left to those who were ineligible. But there was another reason why the legislation remained in force until the fourth century: Augustus and his successors were promoting an imperial ideology that stressed marriage and child-bearing as the foundation for the state. This ideology was promoted in imperial art (such as the *Ara Pacis*) and on coins, and probably had as much impact on Romans as the penalties and privileges of the laws.

C Preliminaries to marriage: age, betrothal, and consent

1 Age

Girls had to be at least twelve years old to be legally married, though they could be betrothed at an earlier age:

D.23.1.14 (Modestinus): In contracting a betrothal the age of the contracting parties has not been defined as it has in the case of marriage. Therefore even from the earliest age a betrothal can be made, as long as it is understood by each party that this is happening, that is, as long as they are not younger than age seven.

D.23.2.4 (Pomponius): A girl married when she was less than twelve years old will be a legitimate wife at the time when she has completed her twelfth year at her husband's home.

Usually Roman women married in their mid- to late teens, with the elite marrying earlier, perhaps in their early teens [Shaw 1987a; cf. Hopkins 1964]. There was no legal age of marriage for men in the classical period, but few males would marry before twenty, and most seem to have married in their mid- to late twenties, with the elite again marrying a few years earlier [Saller 1987].

2 Betrothal

In the case of first marriage for a young woman (who might be as young as twelve), the choice of spouse and arrangements for the marriage would be in the hands of her parents. They (primarily the father) would investigate the possibilities for suitable husbands and undertake negotiations with the families of potential spouses. It was assumed that parents, with greater experience of the world and society, were much better able to make this important decision than the young woman herself, who (if she had been properly brought up) would have little direct knowledge of the opposite sex.

Among the elite (about whom we have the most information), marriage was usually preceded by betrothal (*sponsalia*), which might last for two or more years. The match was usually arranged by negotiation between the males involved (fathers of marriageable children and often the prospective groom), sometimes acting through intermediaries [Noy 1990; Treggiari 1991a, 124–45].

D.23.1.1 (Florentinus): Betrothal is the proposal and counter-promising of future marriage.

D.23.1.4 (Ulpian): Bare consent suffices to constitute betrothal. In fact, it is agreed that an absent person can be betrothed to an absent person, and this happens every day.

D.23.1.18 (Ulpian): In constituting a betrothal it makes little difference whether this is done through oneself (either face-to-face or through an intermediary or a letter) or through someone else. Most often matches are arranged with third parties serving as intermediaries.

3 Consent

It was essential for both betrothal and marriage to be valid that all parties consent to it: the bride, the groom, and those who had *patria potestas* over them. (A mother's consent, while not legally required, was clearly advisable.) Although apparently straightforward, the issue of consent to marriage was complex and nuanced, and clearly depended on family inter-relationships that were beyond the scope of the law. A woman, even one still under *patria potestas*, had to consent to her betrothal and marriage. But "consent" could be broadly interpreted, and the absence of active objection could be construed as tacit consent [see Treggiari 1982]:

D. 23.2.2 (Paulus): Marriage is not able to occur unless all consent, that is, those who join together and those in whose power they are.

D. 23.1.11 (Julian): Betrothal, like marriage, occurs by the consent of those contracting it: and just as in marriage, it is necessary for a daughter under paternal power to consent to her betrothal.

D.23.1.12 (Ulpian): But she who does not fight against her father's will is understood to consent. Moreover, the liberty to dissent from her father is only allowed to the daughter if her father chooses for her a shameful fiancé or one of unworthy habits.

Young men would probably have had more say in their marriage arrangements, not only because they were male, but because they would be older. The jurists stress the necessity for a son under paternal power to consent to the marriage which his *paterfamilias* would have arranged. But if a son actually entered the marriage even under duress, he too was understood to have consented:

D. 23.1.13 (Paulus): Betrothal is not able to take place in the name of a son under paternal power if he objects.

D. 23.2.21 (Terentius Clemens): A son under paternal power is not forced to take a wife.

D. 23.2.22 (Celsus): If, when his father forces him, he does take as wife a woman whom he would not marry of his own free will, he has nevertheless contracted marriage, which is not contracted between those who are unwilling. He appears to have preferred this course.

In reality, both sons and daughters would have been subject to considerable parental pressure to accept the spouse chosen for them. However, a son, being older and perhaps with greater knowledge of what the law said, would be able to avoid an unwanted marriage more easily than a daughter.

Ideally, the *paterfamilias* would be responsible for arranging the marriages of children under his power, and therefore his consent would be obvious. But there were times when he might be away from home for an extended period of time and unable to arrange matters personally. Sometimes children under power, particularly sons (who might be in their twenties) or daughters who had already been married once before, would arrange their own marriage, perhaps with their mother's participation, as happened in the late Republic with the third marriage of Cicero's daughter Tullia [Treggiari 1991a, 127–34]. An absent father might not even be aware of his child's marriage arrangements until presented with a *fait accompli*. But in this case, *his* lack of active objection implied tacit consent:

D.23.1.7.1 (Paulus): Even in betrothal consent must be demanded of those whose (consent) is desired in marriage. Julian writes, however, that the father is always understood to consent to his daughter's (betrothal), unless he clearly objects.

What was the legal status of a union that not only took place without the *paterfamilias'* consent, but to which he later openly stated his lack of consent? This is not clear from the classical legal sources, and scholars today are of different opinions.[11]

The following statement, from a legal manual of the late third or early fourth century, reveals the tension between the idea that marriage was a public good to be encouraged and the legal authority vested in the *paterfamilias*:[12]

Sent. Pauli **II.xix.2:** The marriages of those who are in their father's power are not lawfully contracted without his agreement, but once contracted, they are not dissolved. For consideration of the public benefit is set before the convenience of private individuals.

Sometimes a father might actually refuse to arrange or allow his children's marriages. Such obstruction ran counter to the intent of Augustus' marriage legislation [see Part I.B], which said that Roman officials could force fathers to provide for their children's marriages. Later, Septimius Severus and Caracalla gave the same authority to provincial governors [Treggiari 1991a, 65]:

D.23.2.19 (Marcian): In the thirty-fifth chapter of the Julian law (on the marrying of the social orders), those who unjustly prohibit the children they have in power from taking wives or marrying, or who refuse to give a dowry according to the constitution of the deified Severus and Antoninus, are forced through the provincial governors to place their children in marriage and give a dowry. Moreover, he who does not seek a marriage seems to be prohibiting it.

If the *paterfamilias* were dead, his children would no longer be under *patria potestas*, but would be legally independent and need no one's consent to their marriage. Neither a mother nor a legal guardian (whether a *tutor mulierum*, a *tutor impuberum*, or a *curator minorum*; see Chapter 1, Part II.C and III.E) had the legal power a father had. Nevertheless, a mother and guardians did play a role in marriage arrangements, particularly if a young woman were still in her early teens or even younger. Disputes could arise where no one had *potestas*, as happened in the following case, referred to Septimius Severus and Caracalla [see Part II.B for an imperial decision of the early fifth century]:

Cod. Just. 5.4.1, 7 May, 199
Emperors Severus and Antoninus to Potitus:

When a girl's marriage is being sought and there is no agreement between her *tutor* and her mother and relatives concerning the choice of a future husband, the official judgment of the governor of the province is necessary. Given on the Nones of May in the consulship of Anullinus and Fronto.

The young woman in the case above was probably still under twelve (and therefore had a *tutor impuberum*). The same emperors had a different opinion with regard to a woman above puberty but below the age of majority of twenty-five, who would have a *curator* rather than a *tutor* [see Chapter 1, Part III.E]:

D.23.2.20 (Paulus): ... And thus Severus and Antoninus replied in a rescript in these words: "The administration of the affairs of a female ward (*pupilla*) pertains to the curator's duty. However, the ward can marry by her own choice."[13]

Sometimes, however, it was unclear whether the *paterfamilias* was really dead, if he were away for a long period of time.[14] He might have been captured by barbarians and taken across the frontier (always a possibility, particularly in the third century). A Roman in captivity outside the Empire was legally considered a slave, and lost legal power over his children until he returned to Roman territory [Buckland 1908, 291–8; Treggiari 1991a, 174].

D.23.2.10 (Paulus): If the father is so far away that it is not known where he is or whether he is alive, there is rightly some doubt about what should be done. And if a three-year period has passed after there has very clearly been no knowledge of where the father lives or if he survives, his children of either sex are not prohibited from contracting legal marriage.

D.23.2.11 (Julian): If the son of a man who is among the enemy or away has taken a wife before (the end of) a three-year period of captivity or absence on the part of his father, or if his daughter has married, I think that the marriage is correctly contracted, as long as the son takes such a woman as wife, or the daughter marries such a man, as it is certain their father would not repudiate as a match.

D Dowry

It was customary in Roman marriages for the bride to bring a dowry, which could include land as well as money and movable property. However, the dowry was not usually (at least among the Roman elite, about whom we know) intended to serve as a daughter's inheritance from her father; she could expect to receive more upon his death, and he might also give her a *peculium* (funds granted by a *paterfamilias* to his children for their own use) during his lifetime [Saller 1984; Saller 1994, 204–24].

1 Dotal pacts and the purpose of dowry

Since property was involved, dowry agreements were often made in writing, even when there was no marriage contract per se. The pact would usually be made before the marriage took place and the contracting parties would be the *paterfamilias* of each party. If his father were dead, the groom would be the contracting party. Women no longer under paternal power needed the agreement of their *tutor* to make a dowry pact, since transfer of property was involved [see Chapter 1, Part III.A].

In particular, pacts addressed the question of the return of the dowry if the marriage ended in divorce or by the death of one of the partners. There were general rules about the return of dowry after a marriage ended [see below], but contracting parties could stipulate other arrangements in a dotal pact, and as long as the pact did not break a law, it would be upheld in court. No pacts from Roman Italy survive, but juristic discussions in the *Digest* provide an idea of what a dotal pact might include:

D.23.4.12.1 (Paulus): Some of the arranged pacts which are accustomed to be introduced before or after the wedding suit the wish (of the parties involved), as for instance that a woman is to support herself with the promised dowry and the dowry is not to be requested from her as long as she is married, or that she is to offer a certain sum of money to her husband and is to be supported by him, and others similar to these. Others relate to law, such as when a dowry is to be claimed (or) how it is to be returned; in these (agreements) the wish of those contracting is not always preserved. But if it has been agreed that the dowry is not to be claimed at all, the woman will be undowered.
D.23.4.1 pr. (Javolenus): It is permitted to make a pact after the wedding, even if nothing has been agreed beforehand.
***Sent. Pauli* II.xxi[b].1:** Dowry either precedes or follows the marriage, and therefore it is possible to give it either before or after the wedding. But if it has been given before the marriage, there is an expectation of its (the marriage's) advent.

While a private transaction, dowry also had a public importance:

D. 23.3.2 (Paulus): It is in the interest of the state that women have their dowries secure, on account of which they are able to marry.

D.24.3.1 (Pomponius): An action for dowry is always and everywhere of special importance; for it is in the public interest that dowries be preserved undiminished for women, since it is especially necessary that women have dowries for the purpose of procreating offspring and replenishing the state with children.

2 Providing a dowry

Most often the dowry would be provided by the bride's father, if still alive, or by the bride herself, if she were no longer under *patria potestas* and had her own property. Mothers and other relatives, and even benevolent friends from outside the family might also contribute to a dowry. Dowry contributed by the bride's father or a male ascendant was called "profectitious dowry;" that contributed by others was "adventitious" [Treggari 1991a, 350–1].

D.23.3.41 pr. (Paulus): In promising a dowry, all are obligated, of whatever sex and status they are.
D.23.3.44 pr. (Julian): If a father had promised dowry in the name of his daughter and had emancipated her (from paternal power) before the

wedding, the promise is not annulled. For even when the father died before the wedding, nevertheless his heirs will remain obligated to his promise.

If the union was not *iustum matrimonium*, there was, legally speaking, no dowry [see Chapter 3 on non-legal unions]. Therefore a father who promised his daughter a dowry was not obligated to provide it if she made an illegal marriage:

D.23.3.3 (Ulpian): The name of dowry is not given to those marriages which are not able (by law) to exist. Nor can there be a dowry without marriage. Therefore, wherever the name of (legitimate) marriage does not exist, there is no dowry.

But if her marriage subsequently became valid, he then had to pay the dowry [see Part I.C. on the importance of age and consent].

D.23.3.68 (Papinian): The promise of a dowry will not be less valid because the father was initially unaware that there had been a marriage, if afterwards he consented, since every promise of dowry accepts the unstated condition of a future marriage. For even if a girl less than twelve years has been led as wife (into her husband's home) as if she were older, (the dowry) will first be requested at the time when she has begun to be older than twelve at the same man's house. [the rest of the passage is here deleted]

Contributing toward a relative's dowry, or the dowry of the daughter of a friend or dependent, was a mark of *pietas* (dutifulness born from family feeling), and also a sign of wealth and noblesse oblige. In a long funeral oration (*laudatio*) of the Augustan period which was inscribed on a large marble tablet, a husband praised his wife's many deeds of generosity and valor during and after the Roman civil wars. Unfortunately, the wife's name has not been preserved. She used to be identified by scholars with Turia, a woman who, according to the writer Valerius Maximus (2.1.4), saved her husband's life during the civil wars, as the wife praised on the inscription also did, but this identification is no longer held [Wistrand 1976; Horsfall 1983]. The inscription, though fragmentary, still offers a peerless testimony of marital devotion and provides interesting details about the lives of a wealthy couple of the second half of the first century B.C.E.[15]

Among her other good deeds, "Turia," along with her sister, undertook to provide dowries to needy family members and social connections (*necessarii*, who could be relatives or clients, or others connected with the family):

Laudatio Turiae I.42 and 46–8, Rome, late 1st c. B.C.E.

42: With a sense of family duty (*pietas*), you demonstrated your [generosi]ty not only to very many social connections but also especially to your family (*familia*) … 46–8: In order that the same women might be able to obtain a match worthy of your family, you provided dowries which, though agreed upon by you, C. Cluvius (her sister's husband) and I by common intent undertook (to pay); and approving your generosity, in order that you not be penalized from your own patrimony, we supplied our own family property and gave our own estates for their dowries.

Likewise, the wealthy senator Pliny the Younger contributed 100,000 sesterces to the dowry of Calvina, his relative by marriage (*adfinis*), whose father had died in debt.[16] Calvina was her father's heir; note Pliny's assumption that as a woman, she would have found a debt-burdened estate particularly difficult.[17] His gift is a sizable sum; 100,000 sesterces was the census required of a town councilor in Pliny's hometown of Comum.

Pliny, *Epistles* II.4, late 1st–early 2nd c.

Gaius Pliny to his own Calvina: If your father had owed money to many people, or to any one person other than myself, it would perhaps have to be doubted, whether you would enter upon an inheritance which would be burdensome even for a man. But I, led by the duty of kinship, remain as sole creditor, having discharged the debts to all who were, so to speak, somewhat persistent rather than obnoxious, and while he was alive, I contributed 100,000 sesterces towards your dowry when you got married, besides that sum which your father designated, as it were, from my account (for it had to be paid out from my account).[18] Therefore you have a great guarantee of my benevolence, relying on which, you ought to embrace the reputation and modest demeanor (*pudor*) of the deceased. In addition to this, so that I not encourage you more by words than by deeds, I will order that whatever your father owed me is to be considered received from you.... [the rest of the letter is not translated here]

Pliny also gave a friend 50,000 sesterces to help with his daughter's dowry. Here the daughter was still under *patria potestas*, and so the money was a gift to the father, not to the woman herself [Gardner 1998, 86]:

Pliny, *Epistles* VI.32, late 1st–early 2nd c.

Gaius Pliny to his own Quintilian: Although you yourself are most moderate, and have brought up your daughter in such a way as befitted a daughter of yours (and) a granddaughter of Tutilius; however, since she is about to be married to the most honorable man, Nonius Celer, on whom the matter of public duties places a certain need for splendor, she ought to have use of clothing (and) attendants in accordance with her husband's position. Of course, status is not increased by these things, but it is adorned and equipped. Furthermore, I know that you are most fortunate in regard to intellect, but modest in resources. And so I claim a part of your burden for myself, and, like a second father, I confer upon our daughter 50,000 sesterces. I would offer more, except that I believe that you are able to be prevailed upon by your sense of shame (*verecundia*) not to refuse (my offer) only because of the modest amount of my little gift. Farewell.

The size of the dowry would depend on the social and economic standing of both parties. It was important, as Pliny points out, that a wife have the resources appropriate to her husband's position, and a future husband clearly had an interest in receiving a sizable dowry [Treggiari 1991a, 340–8]. On the other hand, if a woman offered a dowry disproportionately higher than her family's wealth, it might suggest that her family was overly-anxious to marry her off, and was hoping to entice prospective bridegrooms. Dowries were not the crippling expense for the wife's family that they were to become in some later European societies, but providing a suitable dowry at the right time might still present difficulties to Roman families [Treggiari 1991a, 346–8, modifying Saller 1994, 204–24 and Saller 1984].

A man who accepted a smaller dowry than might be expected could be seen as gracious and generous. So, at least, suggests the second-century North African writer and intellectual Apuleius. Apuleius was accused in court of having literally bewitched his wife Pudentilla (a long-time widow about ten years older than Apuleius) into marrying him; we have his defense speech (*Apologia*), but not the speeches of his opponents [see also Chapter 1, Part III.B; Chapter 5, Part I.B; and Parts I.D.3 and I.E.2 below]. According to Apuleius, whereas he happily accepted a small dowry (relative to his wife's overall wealth), one of his opponents, Herennius Rufinus (father-in-law of one of Pudentilla's sons by her first marriage) had over-endowed his daughter because she had (allegedly) lost her virginity to a former fiancé and was therefore "damaged goods." Pudentilla's dowry came to about 7 percent of her entire property, equivalent to a year's income on her estate [Saller 1994, 216–17].

In court, Apuleius presented the marriage contract (*tabulae nuptiales*) which stated the terms of the dowry, including provisions for its eventual return to Pudentilla's sons. He challenged another opponent, Sicinius Aemilianus (brother of Pudentilla's first husband), to read the agreement:

Apuleius, *Apologia* 92, 158/9 C.E.

These things, as I say, I will show from the contract itself. There may be a chance that Aemilianus may not even believe the mere 300,000 sesterces written in the contract and the right of recovery of (the dowry) that is given to the sons of Pudentilla. Take that contract in your own hands, give them to your instigator Rufinus; let him read them; let him be ashamed of his swollen pride and his ambitious begging. Since indeed, he himself, though needy and destitute, endowed his daughter with 400,000 sesterces – which he had received on loan! But Pudentilla, a wealthy woman, was content with 300,000 sesterces of dowry, and she has a husband who is content with the empty name of this tiny little dowry – though he has often spurned many huge dowries in the past – who reckons up nothing else except his own wife and, in a wife's concord and mutual love, sets aside all household goods and all wealth. [The rest of the passage is omitted here.]

Apuleius goes on to say that the most valuable dowry a bride could bring was her virginity – something which could be offered by neither Pudentilla, a middle-aged widow with two grown sons, nor (according to Apuleius' slur on her reputation) the sexually experienced daughter of Rufinus!

3 The dowry during marriage

During the marriage, the dowry belonged to the husband, and he could invest it or use the income from it. Dowry was intended to offset the expenses of maintaining the wife, the "burdens" of marriage [Saller 1984; 1994, 207–11].

D.23.3.1 (Paulus): The purpose of a dowry is perpetual, and, by the wish of the person who gives it, it is established so as to be always in the husband's keeping.

D.23.3.7 pr-1 (Ulpian): Equity suggests that the profit from the dowry ought to pertain to the husband; for since he undertakes the burdens of the marriage, it is right that he also receive the profits. If the profits have been acquired while the marriage is in existence, they will not be (part) of the dowry. But if they have been acquired before the wedding, they are converted into dowry. Unless by chance something (else) has been agreed between future husband and his intended wife: for then the profits are not returned, as if a gift had been made.

Sent. Pauli II.xxii.1: While the marriage is in existence, the fruits gathered from a dotal estate accrue to the husband's gain, and indeed are prorated for the year in which the divorce has occurred.

But though the husband possessed the dowry during the marriage, if the marriage ended by divorce or by the husband's death, the wife (or her *paterfamilias*, if still alive) could bring a legal action to have her dowry returned to her [see Chapter 4, Part I.C.] Therefore a husband would be unwise to spend or otherwise alienate his wife's dowry, and the wife was considered to have a very legitimate interest in the disposition of the dowry during the marriage. Indeed, despite the fact that legally the dowry belonged to the husband during marriage, the general popular view considered it the wife's property. This feeling is expressed by the jurist Tryphoninus in the early third century: "Although the dowry is among the husband's possessions, however, it is the woman's ... " [D.23.3.75; cf. D.2.8.15.3 (Macer)]. This led to the "paradox that while the husband was legally owner of the dowry, his ownership was hedged about by social expectation and, slowly, by legal limitations" [Dixon 1992, 51–2].

For instance, Augustus' adultery law restricted the husband's right to sell or give away the dowry, presumably because this would create tension in an extant marriage and cause legal problems if the marriage ended in divorce:

Gaius, *Institutes* II.62: Sometimes it happens that he who is the master (*dominus*) does not have the power of alienating a thing, and he who is not master can alienate it. 63: For a husband is prohibited by the Julian law (on adultery) from alienating dotal property if his wife is unwilling, though it is his, having either been mancipated to him for the sake of dowry or lawfully ceded or taken by usucaption. But indeed, whether this law pertains only to Italian lands or also to provincial lands, is a matter of doubt.

Moreover, the dowry was considered separately from the husband's own property in assessing his financial worth:

D.50.1.21.4 (Paulus): The same man responded that while a marriage is in existence, the dowry is among the husband's goods; but if fortunes above a certain amount should be called upon for performing municipal obligations (*munera*[19]), the dowry ought not to be figured in the amount.

Because of the possibility that the marriage would break up and the husband would have to return the dowry intact, a detailed list of the dotal property might be made before the marriage took place. Sometimes a precise monetary value would be placed on the property, which the husband was committed to repay:

D.23.3.10 pr. (Ulpian): Generally it is in the man's interest that the items (brought as dowry) not be valued for this reason, so that the risk to the items not pertain to him, especially if he has received animals as part of the dowry or clothing, which the woman uses. For it will turn out, if there has been valuation and the wife wears the things out, that nevertheless the husband is responsible for their valued amount. Therefore, whenever items are given as part of the dowry without valuation, they become both better and worse for the woman.

D.23.3.42 (Gaius): Things given as dowry, which exist by weight, number, or measure, are at the husband's risk, since they are given for this purpose, that the husband sell them at his own free-will and when the marriage is dissolved, either he or his heir is to restore other things of the same kind and quality.

Apuleius, who characterized the 300,000 sesterces dowry of his wife Pudentilla as almost ridiculously small [Part I.D.2], notes that he received it, so to speak, on trust, since it would all go to Pudentilla's children after her death:

Apuleius, *Apologia* 91, 158/9 C.E.
[the beginning of the passage is here omitted] Now first of all, (you will see) that the dowry of a very wealthy woman was modest, nor was it given, but really only entrusted, and besides this the marriage was made on this condition, that if she departed this life without having any children from me, all the dowry would remain with her sons Pontianus and Pudens, but if she died with only one boy or girl surviving (from her marriage with Apuleius), then the dowry would be divided so that part would go to the later child, the rest to the earlier ones.

4 Recovery of dowry after marriage

If a wife died before her husband, he kept any dowry that had been given by anyone other than her father or a male ascendant ("adventitious dowry"). Dowry contributed by the wife's father ("profectitious dowry") would be returned to him, unless other arrangements had been made in the dotal pact:

D. 23.3.6 pr. (Pomponius): Assistance has been given by law to a father, so that if he has lost his daughter, it grants to him for comfort that the dowry which came from him is returned to him, in order that he not feel the loss of both his deceased daughter and his money.

However, the wife's father would probably have predeceased her, given ancient mortality probabilities. In such cases, the dotal agreement might stipulate that the husband keep the dowry, if there were children of the marriage he had to support [Saller 1994, 208–9].

In certain circumstances, the dowry might be returned to the wife even while the couple were still married [Gardner 1986a, 108–9; cf. D.24.3.20 (Paulus)]:

D.23.3.73.1 (Paulus): While the marriage is still in existence, the dowry is able to be returned to the wife, who will not waste it, on account of these reasons: in order that she may support herself and her children; in order that she might buy a suitable estate; in order that she might offer sustenance to a parent in exile or in relegation on an island; or in order that she might sustain a needy husband, brother, or sister.

Confiscation of her dowry by the state was among the penalties for a woman convicted of a serious crime, such as treason, murder, or magic [D.48.20.3 (Ulpian)]. Women convicted of adultery under the Augustan law lost half of their dowry and a third of the rest of their property [see Part I.B]. But when the father of an innocent woman was condemned and his property was confiscated, the state did not take the daughter's dowry, even if it had come from her father:

D.48.20.8.4 (Macer): If a father who has given a dowry on behalf of his daughter is condemned, the imperial fisc does not have a right to that dowry, even if the daughter should afterwards die during the marriage,
D.48.20.8.9 (Callistratus): unless the father will be proven to have provided for his children out of fear of condemnation.

This concern for the dowry of the offspring of a condemned man can be seen in the recently published decree of the Senate concerning the punishment of Gnaeus Calpurnius Piso (governor of Syria under Tiberius and enemy of Tiberius' adopted son Germanicus, whose death he was suspected of bringing about). The Senate's decree called for the confiscation of Piso's property, but returned almost all of it to his sons, stipulating that a million sesterces was to be set aside for the dowry of his granddaughter, along with another four million sesterces for her *peculium*.[20]

E Gifts between spouses and a married woman's property

Unless a woman had come under her husband's legal power in a *manus*-marriage, which was very uncommon by the early Empire [see Chapter 1, Part II.B.], during the marriage she kept control over her own property (other than her dowry, which was in her husband's keeping; cf. Part I.D).

1 The ban on gifts between husband and wife

Because of the Roman legal disapproval of mixing of spousal property, there was even a ban on gifts between spouses [see Treggiari 1991a, 365–79]:

D.24.1.1 (Ulpian): It has been accepted among us by custom that gifts between husband and wife are not valid. Moreover, it has been accepted for this reason, that they not be reciprocally despoiled from love for each other, by not acting with restraint in their gifts, but (by acting) with immoderate good-nature towards each other.

D.24.1.2 (Paulus): (and) so that they not be remiss in their zeal for bringing up children. Sextus Caecilius added another reason as well, because it would often occur, that marriages would be torn apart, if the one who was able to give did not, and so in this way it would come about that marriages would be up for sale.

D.24.1.3 pr. (Ulpian): This reason also has been taken from the speech of our emperor Antoninus (Caracalla) Augustus, for he spoke thus: "Our ancestors prohibited gifts between husband and wife, valuing honorable love by feelings alone, and also considering the reputation of couples, so that they not appear to be united in marital harmony for a price, nor should the better partner fall into poverty and the worse partner become richer."

Pre-nuptial gifts were allowable, and were to become an important part of marriage arrangements in the later Empire [see Part II.C below]:

D.24.1.27 (Modestinus): A gift made before the wedding between those who are about to come together in marriage is valid by law, even if the wedding has followed on the same day.

A spouse could also make a gift to the other to take effect only after the giver's death. This was known as a gift *mortis causa* ("on account of death"):

D.24.1.9.2 (Ulpian): Gifts between husband and wife "on account of death" have been accepted,

D.24.1.10 (Gaius): because the occurrence of the gift happens at that time when they cease to be husband and wife.

D.24.1.11 pr. (Ulpian): But meanwhile the items do not immediately belong to the person to whom they were given, but not until the time when death has followed. Therefore in the meantime ownership remains with the person who gave.

Some types of gifts between spouses were allowed, even during marriage, particularly if the gift had not actually enriched the other spouse materially:

D.24.1.18 (Pomponius): If a husband has used the slaves or clothing of his wife or a wife has used the slaves or clothing of her husband, or has lived for free in the other's house, the gift is valid.

D.24.1.21 pr. (Ulpian): If someone had paid out on his wife's behalf the tolls which it is usual to pay on a journey, would there be a demand for repayment (by her) as if she had been made richer by this, or would this not be a gift? And I rather think that this is not forbidden, especially if she set out (on the journey) for his sake ...

D.24.1.28.2 (Paulus): If the husband's slaves have offered services to his wife or vice versa, it has been decided preferably that no account should be had of these (services). And clearly the law of prohibited gift-giving must not be handled harshly or as if between enemies, but as between those joined by the greatest affection and fearing only poverty.

D.24.1.31.8 (Pomponius): If a man had given his wife an extravagant gift on the Kalends of March or on her birthday, it is a gift (and therefore not valid). 9: But if (he had covered) expenses which she made in order to maintain herself in a more honorable way, the opposite (is the case). For a woman does not seem to have been made richer, if she has spent money given to her on victuals or on perfumes or on food for her slave-household.

However, the ban on gifts between spouses came to be considered overly strict, and was relaxed by later imperial rulings. Antoninus (Caracalla) allowed a wife to make her husband a gift of money if it enabled him to pursue a political career:

D.24.1.40 (Ulpian): That which was brought by a wife to her husband for the purpose of acquiring office is valid to the extent that it was necessary for fulfilling the office;

D.24.1.41 (Licinnius Rufus): for the emperor Antoninus also decided, that a wife could give a gift for her husband's advancement.

D.24.1.42 (Gaius): Recently from the indulgence of the emperor Antoninus another reason for a gift has been accepted, which we call "for the sake of honor;" as, for instance, if a wife makes a gift to her husband who is seeking the senatorial stripe or in order that he become a member of the equestrian order or for the sake of (giving) games.[21]

In 206 Caracalla ruled that such gifts were valid if the giver died without revoking the gift (see D.24.1.3 above for more of Caracalla's speech):

D.24.1.32 pr. (Ulpian): Although this was the status of gifts between husband and wife, as we earlier related, our emperor Antoninus Augustus, before the death of his father the deified (Septimius) Severus, in a speech held in the Senate during the consulship of Fulvius Aemilianus and Nummius Albinus, proposed that there should be some relaxation from the rigor of the law. [D.24.1.32.1 is omitted.] 2: The speech says that "It is allowable for the person who gave a gift to regret it; but for the heir to seize (what had been intended as a gift), perhaps against the final wish of the person who gave it, is a hard and greedy act." [D.24.1.32.3–28 are omitted here.]

Despite these relaxations of the rule, and the fact that the ban on gifts ran counter to the practice of many couples, the general rule that gifts between spouses were invalid persisted until Justinian's day [Arjava 1996, 136–7].

2 Women's property within marriage

In addition to a dowry, a woman no longer under paternal power might come into the marriage with property of her own, most likely what she had inherited from her father. Unless she had entered into her husband's *manus*, she kept this property during the marriage, as well as any property she later acquired. In fact, married women had more property rights in ancient Rome than they had in Britain or the United States until the twentieth century.

It was advisable for a woman who brought non-dotal property into a marriage to be sure that it was kept separate from the dowry and from her husband's own property. This could be done by drawing up a document at the time of marriage listing such property. The following passage from the early third-century jurist Ulpian comes right after a passage discussing whether Roman law should consider Greek *parapherna* as the husband's property [see Arjava 1996, 137–9]. *Parapherna* (literally "things in addition to the dowry") comprised personal items like clothing and household utensils [see the marriage contracts from Egypt in Part III]. Ulpian concluded that *Greek parapherna* can be considered the husband's property, but not the non-property items brought by a *Roman* to marriage, about which he says:

D.23.3.9.3 (Ulpian): Clearly if an account-book of the things (brought to the marriage by the wife) is given to the husband, as we see commonly happens at Rome – for a woman is accustomed to compile into an account-book the things which she is accustomed to have for her use in her husband's home but does not give toward the dowry, and to offer that account-book to her husband for him to sign, as if he has received the things, and his wife keeps the things which are contained in the account-book, just as his signed word (attests) that she had brought them into his home. Let us see therefore whether these things become the husband's. And I don't think so, not because they are not handed over to him (for what difference does it make, whether they are brought into his home with his consent or are handed over to him?), but because I don't think this was intended between husband and wife, that ownership be transferred to him, but rather (it was intended) that it be certain that they were brought into his house, so that this not be denied, if and when a separation should take place. And generally the husband binds himself to custody of these things, unless they have been entrusted to the woman. [the rest of the passage is omitted here]

Because women generally did not have as many opportunities for personal enrichment as men had, it was assumed that anything a wife owned whose provenance was unaccounted for had been given to her by her husband. The rationale for this is based on Roman ideas of reputation and honor: it would be most inappropriate for a wife to receive money or gifts (apart from inherited wealth) from a man other than her husband. Without the assumption that such property had come from her husband, people might think she had received it as a gift from a lover or in return for sexual favors [Gardner 1986a, 73–4]:

D.24.1.51 (Pomponius): Quintus Mucius (Scaevola)[22] says, when there is a controversy regarding the source of something that has come into a woman's possession, it is both more likely and more honorable for something whose origin cannot be shown to be considered to have come to her from her husband or from someone who is in his power. Moreover, Quintus Mucius seems to have approved of this for the sake of avoiding (an inquiry into the question of) shameful gain concerning the woman.

This assumption, even if it were made to protect a woman's reputation, could result in her losing some of her property after her husband's death or upon divorce. Perhaps this is why women who brought non-dotal property into a marriage were careful to have a record of it drawn up!

Despite the detailed rules about separation of spousal property and the invalidity of gifts, in reality there was a good deal of sharing of resources. A husband might administer his wife's property along with his own, perhaps even serving as her *tutor*, though this was not the usual Roman practice [Chapter 1, Part III.A]; the wife, in managing household affairs, might well supervise her husband's slaves; and among the lower classes, married couples operated businesses jointly [Treggiari 1991a, 374–8; Gardner 1998, 233–4]. The law did place limits on this sharing of resources; see, for example, the *s.c. Velleianum*, which forbade a wife to serve as guarantor for her husband's debt [Chapter 1, Part IV.D].

"Turia" handed over her property to her husband to administer:

Laudatio Turiae I.37–9, late 1st c. B.C.E.

We preserved all your patrimony received from your parents with shared diligence; for you had no concern for acquiring that which you handed over completely to me. We divided our duties so that I bore the guardianship (*tutela*) of your fortune, (and) you sustained the care of mine.[23]

"Turia" and her husband were childless [see Chapter 4, Part I.A], and their mutual trust was evidently well-founded. But if one spouse died and the other remarried, children of the first marriage might be concerned that their surviving parent would give the new spouse property which otherwise would go to her children. That was certainly the fear that the sons of Apuleius' wife Pudentilla had when she announced her desire to marry again. (For more on the family conflicts caused by a mother's remarrying, see Chapter 5, Part I.B.)

Apuleius, *Apologia* 71, 158/9 C.E.

[The beginning of the passage is omitted.] For Pontianus, after he had received his mother's letter, immediately hurried from Rome, fearing that if she had taken some greedy husband, she would take with her to her husband's home all her property, as often happens. This anxiety vexed his mind considerably, (since) all hopes of wealth for him and his brother had been placed in their mother's resources. [the rest of the passage is omitted]

II Marriage and its consequences in late Roman law

In the fourth and fifth centuries, Roman marriage law takes on quite a different appearance from the "classical" law of the first three centuries. The late antique laws are *leges generales*, often in the form of edicts, setting forth imperial policy to be applied universally. Unlike juristic texts, late Roman laws come from the emperors' consistory directly; unlike the imperial rescripts of the second and third centuries, late Roman laws are intended to apply to all subjects and, though they may be in response to inquiries and cases presented to the emperor by his subordinates, they are not individual responses [see further Introduction, Part I.B].

Yet the changes in format and tone of late antique legislation should not obscure some basic continuities in Roman marriage law. Marriage in late antiquity continued to be a transaction conducted between families, and the purpose of marriage continued to be the production of legitimate children to whom family wealth and status could be transmitted. The same concerns are evident as in classical law: observation of the proper preliminaries in making a marriage: the need for paternal consent; regulation of the transfer of property that comes with the joining of two people in marriage; and, especially, the prohibition and penalization of unions that run counter to moral and social propriety because of kinship or status disparity [on which see Chapter 3]. There are new developments, however: the centuries-old legislation of Augustus penalizing the unmarried and childless is rescinded by Constantine, betrothal agreements become legally binding, prenuptial gifts from bridegroom to bride and sureties to guarantee that the marriage takes place become subject to regulation, and the range of prohibited unions widens considerably.

A Repeal of the Augustan penalties on celibacy

In 320, the emperor Constantine repealed the penalties on the unmarried and childless enacted by Augustus more than 300 years earlier [Chapter 2, Part I.B]. Constantine's motives for enacting this law have been much discussed. Given the early date of the law, it is likely that he intended mainly to benefit the upper classes of Rome (especially the senatorial aristocracy), who had always hated the restrictions of the Augustan law, rather than Christian adherents of asceticism (self-denial and sexual abstinence), who were still very rare in the western Empire in 320. Christian ascetics would also have benefited, however, and this law may have contributed to the growing popularity of asceticism in the fourth century [see Evans Grubbs 1995, 103–39].

Cod. Theod. 8.16.1, 31 January, 320
Emperor Constantine Augustus to the People:

Those who were considered celibate under the ancient law are to be freed from the threatening terrors of the laws and are to live in such a way as though they were among the number of married (and) were supported by the bond of matrimony, and all are to have an equal condition of taking whatever each one deserves. Moreover, no one is to be considered childless: the penalties proposed for this name shall not harm him. (1) We determine this matter also in regard to women and we release from everyone indiscriminately the commands of the law which were placed on their necks like yokes.

(2) But the usurpation of this benefit will not lie open to husbands and wives between themselves, whose false blandishments very often are scarcely even contained by the opposing rigor of the law; but the ancient authority of the laws shall remain among those persons.

Given at Serdica on the day before the Kalends of February (Jan. 31); posted at Rome on the Kalends of April (April 1) in the sixth consulship of Constantine Augustus and the consulship of Constantine Caesar.[24]

Although Constantine removed the restrictions on the right of celibate and childless men and women to inherit from those outside their circle of close relatives, he did not repeal another provision of the Augustan law which said that childless couples could not inherit more than 10 percent of each other's property. His refusal to do so, and his disparaging reference to the "false blandishments" spouses might use on each other, adhere to traditional

103

Roman concerns that spouses would be mercenary or over-indulgent toward each other (cf. the ban on gifts between spouses during the marriage in Part I.E). The restrictions on the right of childless spouses to inherit from each other's will were not repealed until the early fifth century, but individuals could petition the emperor for the *ius liberorum* ("right of children"), which would enable spouses to inherit from each other by will.[25]

In the eastern Empire, the nine-year-old emperor Theodosius II abolished the provision of the Augustan legislation (here called the "Papian law") which had limited those without the *ius liberorum* to taking only 10 percent of each other's property by will. Both of the following excerpts[26] bear the same date and are addressed to the same official, indicating that they were originally part of the same law, which was later divided in two by the compilers of the *Theodosian Code* [cf. Cod. Theod. 3.5.4. and 5 in Part II.B].

Cod. Theod. 8.17.2 and 3, 4 September, 410

Emperors Honorius and Theodosius (II) Augusti to Isidorus, prefect of the city (of Constantinople):

(8.17.2) We decree by this law for perpetuity that the policy of (inheritance of) 10 percent between husband and wife according to the Papian law is ended, and, though they have no children, they can inherit in full from their wills, unless by chance another law has reduced what can be left behind. Therefore, after this, husband and wife may leave to each other just as much as their surviving love has required.

(8.17.3) No one shall seek the *ius liberorum* from us after this, because by this law we have conveyed it to everyone.

Given on the day before the Nones of September in the consulship of Varanes, *v.c.*[27]

Eighteen years later, however, Theodosius II reiterated the traditional Roman rule that spouses did not inherit from each other by intestate succession when they had surviving kin.[28] But it was not until the publication of the *Theodosian Code* in 438 that Theodosius' legislation of 410 became law in the western Empire (which was ruled by Theodosius' uncle Honorius from 394 until 423 and then by his nephew Valentinian III until 455). Even then, it appears that some childless couples did not realize they could make each other heir by will. In 446, a law of Valentinian III specially addressed the case of a certain Leonius, a man of high rank who had petitioned the emperor to allow him to inherit in full from his wife Jucunda. The couple had made a properly witnessed joint will to this effect, and had previously petitioned for the grant of the *ius liberorum*, but Leonius was still unsure of his right to inherit.[29] Despite the repeal of the Augustan legislation and the tendency of spouses even in the classical period to pool resources [see Part I.E] and despite the fact that husbands in late antiquity took on more of the functions of the classical tutor [Chapter 1, Part III.E], the legal idea that husbands and wives were not kin to each other and did not have mutual inheritance rights continued throughout antiquity.[30]

B Paternal power and consent to marriage

Betrothal had always been an important part of elite Roman marriage arrangements. In classical law, betrothal pacts were not legally actionable; either side could break off an engagement without penalty as long as he (or she) notified the other party that the engagement was off before making a pact with someone else. There is very little pre-Constantinian imperial law on betrothal precisely because it was not a binding legal contract.[31] Late Roman

104

law placed more importance on betrothal agreements. Breaking a betrothal became a serious matter, subject to possible financial penalties, the need for the consent of a woman's father to her marriage was stressed, and the exchange of pre-nuptial gifts and sureties between the betrothed couple was regulated [see Evans Grubbs 1995, 140–202].

A law of Constantine dated 332 set a sort of "statute of limitations" on betrothals. The original law was split into two by the compilers of the *Theodosian Code* 100 years later, but as both excerpts bear the same date and place of issue and both are addressed to the same official, it is clear that they originally belonged to the same law [cf. Cod. Theod. 8.17.2–3 in Part II.A]. One excerpt addresses the specific case of a woman betrothed to a soldier: if the man responsible for her marriage (father, other relative, or guardian) married her to someone else before the end of two years, he (the man responsible) was penalized by temporary exile (relegation). As it stands in the *Theodosian Code*, the law does not appear to have penalized broken engagements to those other than soldiers.[32] On the other hand, any betrothal, including those with soldiers, that had lasted for more than two years without marriage taking place could be broken with impunity.

This legislation indicates that Constantine considered betrothal a more serious contract than had been the case in earlier imperial law. The same attitude is found in his legislation on pre-nuptial gifts [Part II.C]. Note that the guardian (*tutor* or *curator*, on which see Chapter 1, Parts II.A and III.E) of a fatherless girl is here considered as responsible for her betrothal as her father would be if he were alive; see below on Cod. Theod. 3.5.12.

Cod. Theod. 3.5.4 and 5, 12 April, 332

Emperor Constantine Augustus to Pacatianus, praetorian prefect:

(3.5.4) If a man who has made a contract with a girl for his own marriage should omit to accomplish the marriage within two years, and after the end of this time period has passed, the girl should later enter into a union with another man, she shall suffer no legal damage, because she did not allow her vows to be mocked any longer by delaying the marriage.

(3.5.5) It shall not be permitted for a girl's father or *tutor* or *curator* or any relative of hers when he has previously betrothed her to a soldier, to hand her over to another in marriage. If (he does this) within two years (of betrothing her to the soldier), he shall be relegated to an island as one convicted of perfidy. But if he who betrothed her has joined her to another after a two-year period has elapsed since the (first) betrothal pact was made, it shall be considered the (soldier) fiancé's fault rather than the girl's, nor shall the man who handed the girl over to another husband after the two-year period be at all liable.

Given at Marcianopolis on the day before the Ides of April in the consulship of Pacatianus and Hilarianus.[33]

Classical law had required that the *paterfamilias* of each partner consent to their marriage, and indeed a woman's marriage would normally be arranged by her parents, particularly in the case of a teenage girl marrying for the first time [see Part I.C]. This was still the case in late Roman law [Arjava 1996, 29–37].

The following laws stress the importance of paternal consent for daughters under twenty-five, even those who had been emancipated from *patria potestas*. In classical law, an emancipated daughter would have been legally independent (*sui iuris*) and her father would have been her *tutor legitimus*. Legally, she would not have needed his consent to marry, but would have needed it in order to make a dowry for her husband [see Part I.C and Chapter 1,

Part III.A]. Thus, though the late antique laws requiring paternal consent to marriage even for emancipated daughters under twenty-five do indeed impose a new restriction, in reality women in the earlier Empire whose fathers were still alive would have been unlikely to marry without paternal consent, even if they had been emancipated, at least for their first marriage.[34] The laws reflect the frequency of emancipation of adult children in late antiquity [Arjava 1998] and the increased significance of twenty-five as the age of majority [see Chapter 1, Part III.E]. As emancipation of grown children increased, the significance of emancipation in its classical sense (as a release from paternal power) decreased. The rule that a woman needed her father's consent to marry persisted, but now the view was that paternal consent was essential for all women below twenty-five, whether or not they were emancipated. On the other hand, women over twenty-five, even if still under *patria potestas*, may no longer have needed their father's permission to marry [Beaucamp 1990, 246–50].

Of course, given ancient mortality rates, many young woman of marriageable age (usually their late teens in this period; see Shaw 1987a) would not have a *paterfamilias* still living [Saller 1994]. By the later fourth century, *tutela mulierum* was basically obsolete, but all women and men under twenty-five whose fathers were dead were subject to a *curator*, who was responsible for overseeing their property and financial matters; girls below age twelve and boys below puberty would have a *tutor impuberum* rather than a *curator* [see Chapter 1, Part III.E]. But without the decisive voice of a girl's *paterfamilias*, conflict over choice of her marriage partner could easily arise between various relatives, especially the girl's mother, and the girl herself. The following laws anticipate such conflicts. The first two call for a judicial hearing if the issue cannot be resolved within the family; note that the same decision was given in a similar case in a rescript of Septimius Severus and Caracalla almost 200 years earlier [Cod. Just. 5.4.1, in Part I.C.3 above]. The third says that a betrothal pact made by a girl's father is still binding even after his death, and explicitly denies her guardian the right to overturn the paternal decision. This was contrary to classical law, and created a new restriction on a young woman's choice of husband, since even if her father had betrothed her many years before she could legally marry, she would still be bound by his decision after his death.[35]

It is likely that all three of these laws were prompted by particular situations where family conflicts over choice of marriage partner had become so intense that legal recourse was sought. Only elite families, where a great deal of money and property would be at stake, would have bothered to approach the emperor or a judge about such a matter. Indeed, the first law, of the western emperor Valentinian, is addressed to the Senate of Rome, and was probably prompted by a request from the Senate for guidance in a particular case.

Cod. Theod. 3.7.1, 16 July, 371
Emperors Valentinian, Valens, and Gratian Augusti to the Senate:

Widows less than twenty-five years old, even if they enjoy the freedom of emancipation, are not to enter upon a second marriage without their father's agreement or in opposition to him. Therefore the go-betweens and marriage-brokers shall cease, the secret messengers and corrupt reporters of information! No one is to purchase noble marriages, no one is to cause a disturbance, but a marriage alliance is to be deliberated publicly, and a multitude of suitors is to be summoned.

(1) But if in the choice of alliance, the woman's will opposes the opinion of her close relatives, it is certainly pleasing, as has been ordained in the marriage arrangements of women minors whose fathers are dead, that in weighing the issue the authority also of a judicial hearing be added, so that if suitors are equal in birth and morals, he shall be judged preferable whom

the woman, deliberating with herself, shall have approved. (2) But lest by chance those who are nearest in line to succeed to the widows hinder even honorable marriages, if there should be suspicion of such a thing happening, we wish that the authority and judgment rest on those to whom the advantage of the inheritance cannot fall even if a fatal lot should intervene.[36]

Given on the seventeenth day before the Kalends of August in the second consulship of Gratian Augustus and the consulship of Probus.[37]

Cod. Just. 5.4.20, 408–409

Emperors Honorius and Theodosius (II) Augusti to Theodorus, praetorian prefect:

In the joining in marriage of daughters placed in the sacred rites,[38] the father's decision shall be awaited: if the girl should be legally independent and determined to be less than twenty-five years old, the consent of (the girl) herself is also to be ascertained. If she has been bereft of a father's aid, the judgment of her mother and kinsmen and also of the minor herself is to be inquired about. (I) But if, orphaned of both parents, she is placed under the protection of a *curator* and perhaps a contest between honorable competitors for marriage should arise, so that it is asked to whom above all the girl should be joined, if the girl because of concern for her sense of shame[39] has not wished to bring forth her own will, it shall be permitted for a judge in the presence of the kinsmen to determine to whom the young woman is better joined.[40]

Cod. Theod. 3.5.12, 3 November, 422

Emperors Honorius and Theodosius (II) Augusti to Marinianus, praetorian prefect:

(After other matters) If a father has initiated a pact concerning his daughter's marriage and has not been able to fulfill his promises, having been destroyed by the lot of humans, that which will be shown to have been completed by the father shall remain firm and established between the betrothed couple, and nothing which will be shown to have been transacted with the protector[41] who is concerned with what is advantageous to the minor (girl) is permitted to have any influence. For it is very unjust that the decision of a *tutor* or *curator* who has perhaps been bribed should be admitted against the paternal will, since often even the counsel of the woman herself may be found to work against what is advantageous to her. (And other matters)[42]

Given at Ravenna on the third day before the Nones of November in the consulship of our lords the Augusti Honorius for the thirteenth time and Theodosius for the tenth time.[43]

According to the two laws of Honorius, young women were too modest to say how they feel, or too naive and inexperienced to know what was best for them. We do not know how often young women (emancipated or not) would go against their father's wishes for their marriages, nor do we know of specific cases where a daughter preferred a different husband to that chosen by her father. We do hear, however, of women in late antiquity who refused to marry at all (or, more often, to remarry after widowhood), because they preferred a life of Christian celibacy [Clark 1979; 1981; Cloke 1995].[44]

For instance, Macrina, of a wealthy Christian family in Cappadocia (Asia Minor) and the sister of Basil of Caesarea and Gregory of Nyssa, did not object when her father chose a husband (a relative) for her after she turned twelve years old. But when the young man died before the marriage took place, she refused another match. Her insistence that her betrothal amounted to an actual marriage and therefore that she could not remarry (since her spouse was still alive in God) has been taken as evidence of a more serious view of betrothal in late antiquity, but this case was probably exceptional [Evans Grubbs 1995, 172–3].

This passage is from Gregory of Nyssa's *Life* of his sister, written (in Greek) after her death in about 380. Macrina was born about 327, so the events recorded here would have taken place about 340.[45]

Gregory of Nyssa, *Life of Macrina* 5

The girl was not ignorant of what had seemed best to her father. But when what had been decided upon for her was broken off by the young man's death, calling her father's decision a marriage – as if what had been decided had (actually) happened – she resolved to remain on her own from then on, and her decision was more steadfast than her age. For often when her parents introduced conversations about marriage to her, because there were many who wanted to be her suitors on account of the fame of her beauty, she would say that it was strange and unlawful not to be content with the marriage confirmed for her by her father once and for all, but even to force her to look to another, when there is one marriage in nature just as there is one birth and one death. For she declared confidently that the man united (with her) according to her parents' decision was not dead, but that she decided that he, who was "living with God" on account of the hope of the resurrection, was out of town and not dead, and that it was strange for her not to keep faith with her bridegroom who was away from home. With such words rejecting those who were trying to persuade her, she thought that one thing would be a safeguard of her good decision, never to separate from her own mother not even for a little bit of time [the rest of the passage is omitted here] ...

Macrina lived in domestic monasticism with her mother and other female relatives for more than thirty years. She was fortunate to have family support (including financial) for her decision not to marry. Cappadocia and Pontus (in north-central Turkey), where Macrina lived, had long been predominantly Christian. In general, the Greek eastern half of the Empire became "Christianized" earlier than the west, where there was more family opposition to young women refusing marriage. Families were reluctant to forgo the possibility of heirs to family estates, especially among the senatorial aristocracy.

In his work *On Virgins* (*de Virginibus*), written about 377 C.E., Ambrose, the Christian bishop of Milan, a former imperial official (he had been governor of Liguria in Italy before being made bishop) and member of the senatorial elite, urged young women who wished to preserve their virginity to defy pressure from relatives to marry. Note, however, that he is speaking of women whose fathers are dead and who therefore have some say in their future – not even a powerful bishop would encourage rebellion from the *paterfamilias*. Ambrose closes with a cautionary tale to show relatives who try to thwart a young woman's vocation of virginity what the cost of their opposition may be.[46]

Ambrose, *On Virgins* (*de Virginibus*) I.10–11

I.10 (58): ... For I have learned that many virgins wish (to remain such), and are forbidden by their mothers, and what is more serious, by *widows*, with whom my talk is now concerned. For to be sure, if your daughters wanted to marry a man, they would be able by law to choose whom they wished. Therefore are those who are permitted to choose a man not permitted to choose God?

I.11 (62): Indeed (it is) good if the zeal of her relatives[47] breathes breezes of modesty, as it were, on a virgin. But it is more glorious, if the fire of her tender age should hasten itself of its own will even without the nourishment of the old. Relatives will deny a dowry, but you have a rich spouse (and) content with his treasure, you shall not seek the profits of a paternal inheritance. By how much does chaste poverty surpass dotal gains!

I.11 (65): In our memory a girl formerly noble in the world, now more noble in God, when she was being urged to marriage by her relatives and kinsmen, fled to the holy altar.... (the girl addresses her relatives): "What is distressing you, kinsmen? Why do you worry your mind with still seeking a marriage? Now already I have one prepared. Are you offering a spouse? I have found a better one. Exaggerate (suitors') wealth as much as you like, boast of their nobility, proclaim their power: I have him with whom no one can compare himself – rich in the world, powerful in rule, noble in heaven. If you have such a one, I do not refuse your choice. But if you do not find (such a one), you are not providing for me, relatives, but you are begrudging me. (66) The rest were silent, but one (spoke) too hastily: "What if your father were alive," he said, "would he allow you to remain unmarried?" Then she (replied), with rather great devoutness, but a somewhat more moderate sense of family duty: "And indeed perhaps he died so that no one would be able to present an impediment." But he[48] showed by his own premature death that her response about her father (was) an oracle about himself. And so the others, who were seeking to prevent her, began to be favorable, each fearing the same thing for themselves. Nor did her virginity bring her the loss of the property owed her, but even the profit of her chastity. You have, girls, the reward of devotion – relatives, beware the example of opposition.

Gregory and Ambrose provide anecdotal evidence of young women resisting the pressure of relatives to marry – in order to maintain their virginity. Christian teachings emphasizing the superiority of sexual celibacy could be used by some women to subvert the traditional societal expectations of marriage and childbearing, even in the face of family opposition [Clark 1979; 1981; Cloke 1995]. But once the possibility of remaining unmarried and embracing a life of Christian celibacy was established and endorsed by church leaders, some parents tried to make their daughters remain virgins, perhaps from true religious motivations, perhaps in order to avoid paying a dowry. We hear of this abuse of the option offered to women by Christian asceticism already in the third quarter of the fourth century, in the writings of Basil, bishop of Caesarea in central Asia Minor [Basil, *Epistle* 199.18]. And by the mid-fifth century, the problem of parents forcing their daughters into a life of holy virginity was real enough to attract the attention of the short-reigned (457–461) western emperor Majorian.

Majorian attacked what he saw as abusive marriage strategies on the part of Roman families in a long law dealing with various issues involving marriage, remarriage, and Christian celibate women [see Part II.C and Chapter 5, Part I.B for other excerpts from this law]. Majorian had two concerns about the practice of families forcing daughters to take the veil: he felt that the fecundity of young women was needed to help the Roman state (which was rapidly disintegrating in the west[49]); and he feared that rather than restraining young women's sexual urges, enforced celibacy would push them into undesirable and illegal unions.

Novel 6 (preface) of Majorian, 26 October, 458

Emperors Leo and Majorian Augusti to Basilius, praetorian prefect:

Having taken up the rudder of imperial rule, we ought to think about how our republic is to be preserved and to advance, in arms, in laws and in the wholesome reverence of religion. It will most greatly benefit under this improvement: if the desirable good stock of noble women grows, increased by the procreation of children, if the dutiful bonds of kinship between parents and children are not changed by any vicious plots, and an unwilling mind does not undertake the true veneration of God.... For who would bear that parents, by these plans to condemn rather than to consecrate, should consign their daughters – whom they hate – to the constraint of perpetual virginity when they are still minors? And that, lest their youthful minds have the freedom to wish for something else, they place the sacred veil upon the heads of unwilling girls, when observance of this kind, taking up philosophy with a pious mind, is undertaken not by the command of one who forces, but by willing and mature deliberation? For indeed, the allurements of human desire, towards which the ardor of young age is particularly impelled, must be avoided and overcome with great attentions, so that, after the heat of youth has been calmed, virginity dedicated to God shall deserve to arrive at old age and the palm of celestial service without any defect of penitence. For what good does it do if virginal desire, repressed by paternal power, conceives deep within a deceitful desire for marriage and, having been restrained from legitimate union, it is drawn to illicit allurements?

Majorian's solution [Novel 6.1–3] was to forbid the consecration of Christian virgins until they had reached the age of forty, by which time they would be safely past the ardor of youthful desire.[50] Majorian added that if a woman had been prevented from marrying and forced to remain a virgin, she could, upon the death of her parents, marry (if she was still under forty) and inherit an equal share with her siblings, even if her parents had disinherited her: "Seeing that she must be thought worthy of such a reward and of succession (to her parents), since, having undertaken the procreation of children, she is striving to rescue the noble stock of her family from annihilation" [Novel 6.3].

C Pre-nuptial gifts, arrhae sponsaliciae, and dowry

Often pre-nuptial arrangements in the Roman world had included the giving of gifts from one party to the other. Unlike gifts exchanged between spouses once a marriage had taken place, which were legally invalid [Part I.E], gifts before marriage were legal. Gifts that were given specifically in order to form a marriage alliance could be reclaimed by the giver if the marriage did not take place, unless the giver was him/herself responsible for breaking off the match. Other types of pre-nuptial gifts, such as tokens of affection to the betrothed, could not, however, be reclaimed. This distinction between which gifts could and could not be reclaimed on the basis of the giver's intention could lead to confusion, and third-century imperial rescripts (replies from the emperors to petitions) indicate that many people in the Empire were unsure whether they could bring a legal action to reclaim gifts they had given if the engagement were broken off. Late Roman laws on pre-nuptial gifts can be seen as an attempt to regulate the exchange of gifts in order to avoid legal disputes [Evans Grubbs 1995, 156–9].[51]

Legislation on pre-nuptial gifts begins with Constantine, who enacted two laws regulating the fate of gifts given by a betrothed person to his or her future spouse, in the event that the couple did not marry after all. In the first law, addressed to the urban prefect of Rome, the rule is that whoever is responsible for breaking a betrothal has to give back any gifts he or she received and forfeits any he or she gave. Note especially paragraph (2), which refuses to recognize any reasons for breaking off the betrothal once it had been made – any objections to the prospective spouse should have been brought up in advance [Evans Grubbs 1995, 159–64].

Cod. Theod. 3.5.2, 16/27 Oct., 319

Emperor Constantine Augustus to Maximus, urban prefect:

Because the opinion of the ancients is displeasing, which decreed that gifts to a fiancée were valid even when marriage did not follow, we order that those things that are customarily done by law between betrothed persons with the intent of bestowing gifts be regulated according to the following conditions: whether they appear to be under paternal power or in any way under their own legal authority and they bestow something, on their own account or with the mutual consent of their parents, as if for the sake of a future marriage, if by his own will the man should be unwilling to receive his wife (in marriage), that which had been given by him is not to be taken back once it has been handed over and, if anything still remains in the possession of the giver, it is to be transferred to his fiancée without attempts at evasion.

(1) But if it should be revealed that the cause of the marriage not being contracted is the betrothed woman (*sponsa*) or (the person) in whose power she is, then (the gifts) are to be returned in full to the betrothed man (*sponsus*) or to his heirs.

(2) The same should be observed if the gift was made on the part of the fiancée to her fiancé. Nor should the reasons (for breaking off the match) be inquired into further, lest by chance character or birth be alleged, or anything else which anyone thinks is not suitable for himself or herself be brought forth as an objection, since all these things should have been foreseen long before the betrothals were contracted. Therefore only the desire (to break off the betrothal) is to be looked into, and a change of mind (on the part of the person breaking the betrothal) is to be sufficient for the return or retrieval of the things given, since, after all pretexts have been discarded,

nothing more ought to be established except to make clear who said that contracting the marriage was displeasing.

(3) And since it can happen that one partner dies before the marriage is contracted with the desire (to marry) still unimpaired, we have considered it fitting that if the person to whom a gift had been made died before the marriage day, those things which were either given under the name of betrothal gifts or bestowed under any description, are to be returned to the giver. And if the giver dies before the wedding, the gift immediately becomes invalid and the things given are to be returned to his or her heirs without any difficulty.

[The fourth paragraph says that the heirs who can retrieve the gifts are restricted to parents and children by a former marriage; if there aren't any parents or children surviving the deceased, the person to whom the betrothal gifts were given may keep them.]

Given on the seventeenth day before the Kalends of November, posted at Rome on the sixth day before the afore-mentioned Kalends, in the fifth consulship of Constantine Augustus and the consulship of Licinius Caesar.[52]

Seventeen years later, Constantine enacted new regulations for the return of betrothal gifts if a marriage did not take place because one of the partners died, modifying the policy set forth in paragraph (3) of Cod. Theod. 3.5.2 (above). Here the disposition of the gifts rests on whether or not a kiss has been exchanged by the couple (presumably during the betrothal ceremony, unless the "kiss" is a euphemism for more intimate relations). Note the remark that betrothed women "rarely" give betrothal gifts – and the emperor's insistence that whatever a woman has given is to be returned to her or her heirs, whether or not a kiss has been exchanged [see Evans Grubbs 1995, 170–1]. This law took nine months to get from Constantinople (Istanbul, Turkey), where Constantine was, to its recipient in Spain!

Cod. Theod. 3.5.6, 15 July, 334/18 April, 335

Emperor Constantine Aug. to Tiberianus, the Vicar of Spain:

If it should happen, after gifts have been given by a betrothed man to his fiancée and a kiss has been exchanged, that either he or she dies before the wedding, we order that half of the things given belong to the survivor, (and) half to the heirs of the deceased man or woman, whatever degree of relationship they are and by whatever right they have succeeded, so that the gift appear to be half-valid and half-cancelled. But if a kiss has not been exchanged, whether it is the betrothed man or woman who has died, the entire gift is invalidated and returned to the betrothed man who gave it or to his heirs.

(1) But if the betrothed woman has given anything to her fiancé under the name of betrothal gifts – which rarely occurs – if it should happen that he or she dies before the wedding, whether or not a kiss has been exchanged, the whole gift is invalidated and possession of the things given is transferred to the betrothed woman who gave it or to her successors.

Given on the Ides of July at Constantinople. Received on the fourteenth day before the Kalends of May at Hispalis in the consulship of Nepotianus and Facundus.[53]

The fourth century also saw the introduction into Roman law of another purpose of pre-nuptial gifts: as the exchange of sureties (*arrhae*) to guarantee that the marriage would take place. These sureties, called *arrhae sponsaliciae*, would have to be returned if the marriage did not occur, with a penalty of four times the amount originally given (later reduced to double the original amount). The origin of *arrhae sponsaliciae* has been much debated; some scholars have thought the practice had its beginnings in eastern law and custom, but the evidence is very weak [Evans Grubbs 1995, 174–82]. Although the first mention of the term *arrhae sponsaliciae* in Roman law is in 380 (see below), it is likely that earlier fourth-century legislation, now lost, had already dealt with the idea of such sureties. The idea is already adumbrated in Constantine's law of 319 [Cod. Theod. 3.5.2, above]. But whereas in Constantine's law all pre-nuptial gifts were to be returned in full if a marriage did not take place, later *arrhae sponsaliciae* made up only part of the total pre-nuptial gifts given [Arjava 1996, 55–9].

The earliest extant law explicitly to address *arrhae sponsaliciae* was a long constitution of the emperor Theodosius I in 380.[54] Pieces of this law survive in the *Theodosian* and the *Justinianic Codes*; like many laws, it was broken up into separate parts by the codes' compilers. This law refers to the "fourfold" penalty for breaking a betrothal as an "old law;" there must have been earlier legislation, perhaps of Constantine, which called for such a penalty. However, this earlier legislation has not been preserved.

Cod. Theod. 3.5.11, 17 June, 380

Emperors Gratian, Valentinian (II) and Theodosius (I) Augusti to Eutropius, praetorian prefect:

We remit the penalty of fourfold from the father, mother, *tutor* or whatever (relative) of a girl when betrothal gifts have been given before her tenth year.

(1) But a father or any other person who is concerned with the affairs of a girl in her tenth year or beyond, (but) before twelve years old, that is up to the limits of her eleventh year, if he has believed that the pledges that were undertaken should be retained, ceasing from his good faith as the time of marriage approaches, he shall be liable for the fourfold penalty.

(2) There is a different rule for a widow, however, who is not supported by the aid of her age, namely that she, if she does not complete the marriage, shall be held to the quadruple penalty according to the old law.

(3) Moreover, if she has fulfilled her twelfth year, whoever is making the agreement about her marriage, if indeed her father puts himself under obligation, or her mother or *curator* or other relatives, the girl shall be liable.

(4) But an action on the grounds of fairness and justness for the full amount of those pledges which she returned out of her own property according to the penalty of the law, shall be reserved for her against her mother, *tutor*, *curator*, or any relative, if she has shown that she had been forced by them to consent to accepting the *arrhae*.

Given at Thessalonica on the fifteenth day before the Kalends of June in the fifth consulship of Gratian and the first consulship of Theodosius.[55]

It is interesting that different rules for penalizing broken betrothals operate depending on the girl's age: if she is under ten, there is no penalty. Twelve was still the minimum legal age of marriage in late antiquity, so any betrothal made with a girl under ten years old would have had to last more than two years. Constantine, in his law of 332 [Cod. Theod. 3.5.4 and

5, Part II.B], had said that women betrothed for more than two years could marry someone else with impunity. Evidently two years was considered a reasonable limit for betrothals to last. Note also the possibility raised in the last paragraph of the law, that a girl over twelve might be coerced into a betrothal (that is, into accepting *arrhae sponsaliciae*). If she can claim to have been forced by her mother, guardian, or other relative (except her *father*, whose word is binding; cf. the laws in Part II.B), she can sue them for the amount of the fourfold penalty that she has to pay if she breaks the betrothal. In Theodosius' law, the mother has a role equal to that of a guardian or other relative (except the father), whereas mothers were not even mentioned in Constantine's law [Cod. Theod. 3.5.5], which had given guardians the same responsibility as a father.

Another part of the law of 380 said that if either of the betrothed couple died before the marriage, *arrhae sponsaliciae* were to be returned, unless the giver had given cause for not celebrating the marriage.[56] This modified Constantine's last ruling [Cod. Theod. 3.5.6, above] on pre-nuptial gifts (not called *arrhae sponsaliciae*), which had made the fate of the gifts dependent on whether or not a kiss had been exchanged.

Late Roman legislation on the dowry brought to a marriage by the wife tends to be overshadowed by the large number of laws relating to pre-nuptial gifts and *arrhae sponsaliciae*, but dowry was still a matter of interest to Roman law-givers. The following law of the western emperor Honorius says that if the husband dies during the marriage, his widow is to receive back her entire dowry. There is no longer a distinction between adventitious dowry (contributed by those other than the wife's father), which would have been kept by the husband's heirs, and profectitious dowry (contributed by the wife's father), which would have returned to him or his daughter [see Part I.D.4]. Honorius' law also notes that a husband would sometimes return his wife's dowry to her during the marriage, which was illegal, since it would then appear to be a gift given during the marriage [see Part I.E]. There was classical precedent for this, however [see D.23.3.73.1 in Part I.D.4].

Cod. Theod. 3.13.3, 3 November, 422

Emperors Honorius and Theodosius (II) Augusti to Marinianus, praetorian prefect:

(After other matters) If, while a marriage is stable, a husband has been consumed by a fatal lot, the dowry which is said to have been given or promised from the resources of his wife reverts to the woman, and the heir of the dead man shall dare to claim nothing from it for himself, because her husband's death has made it return to the woman.

(1) And if by chance, while a marriage is stable, the dowry has been restored to the wife by the husband – which is not able to stand in law, since it is perceived that she obtains it like a gift – when the same wife has died it shall be given back to the husband by her heirs with its income from the day on which the dowry was restored (to the wife), in such a way that ownership of the (dowry) shall not be able to be alienated by the husband from the children born from the same woman. (And other matters)

Given at Ravenna on the third day before the Nones of November in the thirteenth consulship of Honorius Augustus and the tenth consulship of Theodosius Augustus.[57]

In classical Roman law, dowry was not necessary for a marriage to be valid, but it provided a safeguard for the wife, and demonstrated to outside parties that a union was legitimate marriage and not concubinage [Part I.D]. In the fifth century there were attempts by western emperors to make dowry a requisite of *iustum matrimonium*, but this was resisted by the more classically-oriented legislation of the eastern Empire.[58] This eastern law[59] of Theodosius II responded to and refuted a law recently enacted in the west that had described "natural" (i.e. illegitimate) children as those "begotten without an honorable celebration of marriage" [Cod. Theod. 4.6.7; in Chapter 3, Part II.B.3]. It reaffirms the classical idea that a valid marriage rested on the *consent* of both parties, as long as there were no legal impediments [Wolff 1950, 291–2; cf. Novel 12 of Theodosius II, in Chapter 4, Part II].

Cod. Theod. 3.7.3, 20 February, 428

Emperors Theodosius (II) and Valentinian (III) Augusti to Hierius, praetorian prefect:

If instruments of pre-nuptial gifts or dowry have been lacking, (or) a procession or other celebration of marriage should also be omitted, let no one think that for this reason legal validity is lacking, if the marriage has otherwise been begun in a correct way, nor that the rights of legitimate (heirs) can be taken away from children born from that (marriage). Since no law impedes, between persons equal in honor (there is) marriage (*consortium*), which is confirmed by the consent of the parties themselves and by the belief of friends. (And other matters)

Given at Constantinople on the tenth day before the Kalends of March in the consulship of Felix and Taurus.[60]

Theodosius II's law of 428 suggests that by the fifth century, pre-nuptial gifts (*donatio ante nuptias*) and dowry (*dos*) tended to be considered in tandem, with the *donatio ante nuptias* being the bridegroom's contribution and the *dos* being the bride's [Arjava 1996, 56–60]. This tendency appears in several later laws, which assume (or require) that the two contributions be equal and be governed by the same rules.

The following law, also of Theodosius II, ruled that if a husband died during the marriage, his wife was to pass on the pre-nuptial gift he had given her to their children, and likewise, if the wife died first, her husband was to pass on her dowry to their children in common. Even if the spouse who died had still been under paternal power, his or her *paterfamilias* did not get the pre-nuptial gift or dowry, but it was transmitted instead to the couple's children. This is part of a trend in late Roman law to safeguard the inheritance that children received from their mother (called *bona materna*, "maternal goods") from exploitation by their father, particularly if he remarried [Arjava 1996, 98–105]. Theodosius is reiterating a law of his grandfather, Theodosius I [Cod. Theod. 3.8.2, in Chapter 5, Part I.B], that a woman was to preserve the pre-nuptial gift she had received from her husband for her children by him and could have only the usufruct of it, and is expanding it to apply to men also. This law also notes that wives often converted the pre-nuptial gift they received from their husbands into dowry, an interesting detail.

Novel 14 of Theodosius II, 7 September, 439

Emperors Theodosius (II) and Valentinian (III) Augusti to Florentius, praetorian prefect:

It is the duty of the imperial majesty to look out for even those who have not yet been born, and to provide, in the contracts of parents, the fruit owed to nature for future children also.

(1) Past laws have ordered that when a marriage has been dissolved by the

husband's death and there are children in common, the woman preserve, under certain conditions, the pre-nuptial gift and other properties which devolved to her in certain ways from the person of her husband, for these same children.

(2) The divine grandfather of Our Gentleness with humane mind had also urged that men too, when the marriage has been dissolved by the wife's death and there are children, observe these things, under the same conditions, in regard to the dowry and other properties devolving to him (sic) from the person of the wife.[61]

(3) We felicitously decree by the bonds of law, that these things are to be observed by men. For, in general, in whatever situation constitutions before this law have decreed that the wife preserve for their common children those things which devolved upon her from her husband's property when a marriage has been dissolved by the husband's death, in those same situations we decree also that the husband preserve for their common children those things which devolved upon him from his wife's property, when the marriage was dissolved by the wife's death. Nor do we want it to make any difference, if someone else has believed he should offer a pre-nuptial gift on behalf of the husband or a dowry on behalf of the woman. We order these things to be observed even if the properties given before marriage should be converted into dowry, as usually happens.

(4) Furthermore, even if the marriage has been dissolved by a notice of divorce (*repudium*) by the woman's fault, the husband will retain the gift in full, not in part as in the case of the other dowry.[62]

[Paragraphs 5–7, omitted here, are concerned with the fate of properties which one deceased spouse has left to the other, and refer to the rule laid down by Theodosius I, that a remarried widow was to preserve what she had inherited from her first husband for her children by him [see Chapter 5, Part I.B].]

(8) Moreover, we confirm what is contained in earlier laws, that a father not acquire the pre-nuptial gift from a daughter who is in his power, nor the dowry from a son, with this addition, that if they have died while still in their father's power and there are children, these same properties are to be transmitted to their children by the right of inheritance, not to the father by the right of *peculium* nor, of course, to the grandfather through his grandchildren, dearest and most beloved parent Florentius.[63]

(9) And so your illustrious and magnificent authority shall see that this most salubriously promulgated law come to the notice of all peoples by the posting of edicts.

Given at Constantinople on the seventh day before the Ides of September in the seventeenth consulship of our lord Theodosius Augustus and the consulship of Festus, *v.c.*[64]

Another law of Theodosius II addressed the question of the husband's power over non-dotal property that a wife brought into the marriage, specifically the personal items called by the Greek inhabitants of the Empire *parapherna*. This had also been discussed by the third-century jurist Ulpian [see Part I.E.2]. Theodosius, a promoter of "classical" law, was willing to abide by the opinions of earlier law-givers, even though he thought it was preferable for a wife to allow her husband to manage all her property.

Cod. Just. 5.14.8, 9 January, 450

Emperors Theodosius (II) and Valentinianus (III) Augusti to Hormisdas, praetorian prefect:

By this law we decree, that if his wife forbids it, a husband has no right of sharing in the possessions his wife has in addition to the dowry, (possessions) which the Greeks call *parapherna*, nor may he impose any constraint upon her. For though it would be good for a woman, who entrusts her very self to her husband, to allow her property also to be guided under his control, however, since it is fitting that the founders of the laws be supporters of equity, in no way, as was said (above), do we wish a husband to be involved in the *parapherna* if his wife forbids it.

Subscribed (by the emperor) on the fifth day before the Ides of January in the year after the consulship of Protogenis and Asterius.[65]

In the western Empire, legal attitudes were less attached to classical precedents, and probably more in tune with contemporary mores. Thus the western emperor Valentinian III (cousin of Theodosius II and like him, a grandson of Theodosius I) professed himself shocked that a widowed mother could bring a legal claim against her own children for expenses incurred on her property during the marriage. He pointed out that it was impossible to determine who had owned what in a marriage where the spouses had an "equality of living in common" and shared resources, and was contemptuous of the uses to which wives put their wealth, which he thought went mainly for "feminine adornment."

The first paragraph of Valentinian's law fulsomely thanks the Senate (of Rome, not Constantinople, which had its own Senate) for asking certain imperial officials[66] to bring the matter to the emperor's attention. No doubt the senatorial aristocracy, who would be those most likely to inherit substantial wealth and property from both parents, were particularly concerned about preserving patrimonies.[67]

Novel 14 of Valentinian III, 11 September, 444

Our lords the Emperors Theodosius (II) and Valentinian (III) Augusti to Albinus, praetorian prefect for the second time:

We joyfully acknowledge the most magnificent Senate, mindful of its own authority, whose counsel always runs counter to wicked matters. Hence it is that (the Senate) recently enjoined upon illustrious and sublime men, whom the utility of public necessity demanded be recalled to the most sacred imperial retinue, that (a law) be suggested to us, so that a usurpation abhorrent to all honorable intercourse no longer have force.

(1) For we learn that certain women, after their husband's death, have denuded their own children by proposing a dishonorable legal action, since they sought from them (their children) the profits of their own patrimony; (profits) which, while the marriage is in existence, it is agreed are considered consumed in that equality of living in common, and whose tangled and

117

confused computation we do not believe can be discerned with regard to the credibility of truth. And since we know that it happens rather frequently that matronly adornment demands the greater part of the expenses, and since men, after their wife's death, never believe that anything of this kind should be brought against their common children, it is hard that such things are allowed only to female license.

(2) And so, dearest and most loving parent Albinus, your illustrious and lofty greatness shall know that with this edictal law we have decided that the partner surviving from a conjugal joining is not to think that heirs of the deceased should be struck with a lawsuit over this reclaiming of expenses. Indeed, we wish both wives and husbands to be held by this condition. For whether dowry has intervened or whether it was not offered, all dispute over this reclaiming and accounting is to be silent.

(3) Moreover, your greatness shall make this law, which is to benefit the utility and concord of the human race, arrive at the notice of all by means of edicts posted throughout the provinces.

Given at Ravenna on the third day before the Ides of September in the sixteenth consulship of our lord Theodosius Augustus and the consulship of Albinus, *v.c.*

Several years later, Valentinian III dealt with the disposition of pre-nuptial gifts and dowry when there were no children from a marriage, applying the same policy to both. This introduces a change to the ruling of Valentinian's uncle, Honorius, that a widow was to receive back all of her dowry [Cod. Theod. 3.13.3, above]. The following is an excerpt from Valentinian's Novel 35, a very long law which also legislated on *bona materna*, divorce, and the conducting of lawsuits.[68]

Novel 35.8–9 of Valentinian III, 15 April, 452

(8) We have considered it opportune, on the occasion of this law, to decree about succession these things which were not clearly expressed in earlier decisions. Therefore, if a man should die without children, with his wife surviving him, the woman shall restore half of the betrothal gift which she received to the father or mother of the deceased and shall keep the remaining portion for herself. If the persons of whom we speak are lacking, everything she received in return for her modesty[69] shall go to her gain, since it ought not to be diminished when such dear and devout names are not extant.[70]

(9) There will be a similar condition concerning the dowry. The authority of the present oracle decrees that in the event of the wife's death, the husband is to return to the father or mother of the deceased woman half of the dowry he received, if it was contributed to the husband with no intervening conditions and is able to be to his gain. But the wife's side ought to give back (to the widowed husband) as much as the husband had brought (to the wife) in betrothal gifts, so that there be an equal condition of giving and receiving, lest an acceptable future marriage be a source of gain to one, but a detriment to the other.[71]

By the mid-fifth century, the size of the pre-nuptial gift offered by prospective husbands had become so important a part of the marriage negotiations that parents of marriageable girls were trying to extort as much as they could out of eager suitors. So, at least, was the opinion of the western emperor Majorian, who ruled in 458 that dowries must equal pre-nuptial gifts in size. Elsewhere in the same long *novella*, Majorian had condemned parents who forced their nubile daughters into a life of Christian celibacy; the law as a whole reveals cynical mistrust of the marital politics of the Roman elite of his day [see Part I.B and Chapter 5, Part I.B for other excerpts from this law].

Majorian also decreed that unions made without dowry were not valid marriages. Earlier in the fifth century, the eastern emperor Theodosius II had explicitly stated that lack of dowry or pre-nuptial gifts did not invalidate an otherwise legal marriage [Cod. Theod. 3.7.3, above]; his law was probably a response to a declaration by the western emperor Valentinian III that children born from unions "without honorable celebration of matrimony" would be considered illegitimate [Cod. Theod. 4.6.7, in Chapter 3, Part II.B.4]. There appears to have been a difference between eastern and western legal attitudes on this point, with western rulers requiring some sort of external evidence of marriage while eastern law upheld the classical Roman policy that neither dowry nor ceremony was necessary for a valid marriage.

Novel 6.9–10 of Majorian, 26 October, 458

(9) What is advantageous for children is of concern to us, and we wish that they be begotten more numerously for the increase of the Roman name and do not allow benefits for those who have been begotten to be lost. Therefore, as a necessary consequence, we have considered that precautions must be taken so that an equal condition on both sides constrain the male and female who are to be joined by the nuptial bond; that is, that a future wife should know that she will never bring less under the title of dowry than she demands as pre-nuptial munificence. And girls and the parents of girls, or whatever persons are about to marry, shall know that both parties who have been joined without a dowry are to be branded with the stains of infamy, with the result that it shall not be judged a marriage nor shall legitimate children be born from them.

(10) Of course, we must resist the greediness of some people, who exhaust the resources of their sons-in-law either for themselves or for their daughters or for certain persons whom they have suborned, before they make any settlement concerning a marriage pact. They arrange by secret fraud for many things to be conferred upon them by heedless young men aroused by the desire of future marriage, which they refund to their daughters after the solemnity of marriage vows has ensued,[72] or perhaps, by a greater love of perfidy, they think (the gifts) have been acquired for themselves. Wherefore we order that none of this clever and frivolous scheme shall have effect, so that after the sham of such a contract has been voided, a son-in-law who is legally independent may afterwards assert his claim and confidently seek back, by publicly stated legal action, whatever he was compelled to give over through a specious contract that is henceforth illegal.

By the later fifth century, both eastern and western emperors felt that the husband's contribution to the marriage (the pre-nuptial gift) and the wife's (the dowry) ought to be equal, while realizing that this was not always the case. The eastern emperor Leo addressed the same situation as Valentinian III's law of 452 [Novel 35.8–9, above], but reached a somewhat different solution. Leo's law evidently held for all cases when one spouse predeceased the other, whether or not there were children (who are not mentioned). The law suggests that mothers could also make valid betrothal pacts on behalf of their sons or daughters (though presumably only widowed mothers; if the father were still alive and had *potestas* over his child, it would certainly be his responsibility).

Cod. Just. 5.14.9, 18 August, 468

Emperors Leo and Anthemius Augusti to Nicostratus, praetorian prefect:

We decree that after the death of whichever person, whether the husband or the wife, the husband acquires as much from the dowry as the wife does from the pre-nuptial gift – the same portion, not the amount of money (that he or she originally contributed).

(1) For example, if the husband has contributed a thousand *solidi* before the marriage as the gift, the woman will be permitted to offer a dowry of lesser or greater amount. However, the following must be observed: that as great a portion as the wife stipulates to go to her profit from the pre-nuptial gift, if it should happen that her husband dies first, so great a portion – not the amount of money – shall the husband stipulate (goes to him) from the dowry if, while the marriage is intact, the woman has fallen to her fate first. (2) And if a pact has followed against the prohibition, we give notice that it is ineffectual and invalid, so that no enforcement can proceed from it.

(3) We think the same (rule) is maintained, whether the father has given the pre-nuptial gift to the bride on behalf of his son or the mother (has given the gift), or the one who will marry, after he has become legally independent (has given it), or anyone else (has given it) on his behalf. (4) Also in a similar way, whether the father has given the dowry or promised it to the man about to marry on behalf of his daughter, or the mother (has given it), or (the daughter) herself, that is, after she has become legally independent, on her own behalf, or anyone else on her behalf – since also, if another offers the dowry on her behalf, she herself seems to offer it on her own behalf.

(5) Which indeed is so true, that she herself may seek back for her own gain the dowry offered by another on her behalf, unless by chance he who offered it immediately (that is, at the time of offering or of promising) stipulated or made an agreement that the afore-mentioned dowry would be returned to him.

Given on the fifteenth day before the Kalends of September in the second consulship of Anthemius Augustus.

In the law below, Leo returned to the subject of *arrhae sponsaliciae*, the sureties given by each party before marriage to guarantee that it would take place [see Cod. Theod. 3.5.11, above]. This was part of a much longer law, which also discussed whether women could claim ignorance of the law [see Chapter 1, Part IV.A].[73]

By Leo's day the fourfold penalty for breaking a betrothal had been reduced to double the original amount of *arrhae*. Like Theodosius I's law of 380 on *arrhae sponsaliciae* [Cod. Theod. 3.5.11], Leo's law sets different liabilities for women who broke betrothals depending on their age, but whereas for Theodosius I, the age of liability was twelve, for Leo it is twenty-five, the age of majority in late antiquity [see Chapter 1, Parts II.C and III.E and cf. Cod. Theod. 3.7.1 and Cod. Just. 5.4.20 in Part I.A].

This law also mentions several causes for which a betrothal could be broken without penalty (that is, merely by giving back the *arrhae* received from the other party): if it was learned after the engagement was made that the other party was of shameful character or different religious persuasion, or (in the case of a male) impotent.

Cod. Just. 5.1.5, 1 July, 472

Emperors Leo and Anthemius Augusti Erythrius, praetorian prefect:

A woman who has become legally independent shall be held to the double penalty for *arrhae sponsaliciae* (made) in her name, that is, for that which she received and just so much else and no more, if, after the completion of her twenty-fifth year or after having been granted the "indulgence of age" as confirmed in a competent court,[74] she has received *arrhae* of this kind. However, (she shall be held) to the onefold penalty, that is, only as much as she received, if she is of lesser age, whether she is a virgin or a widow, or whether she received these *arrhae* through herself or through a *tutor* or *curator* or another person.

(1) But it has been agreed that a father or mother, who of course are of legal age, whether they undertook the *arrhae* on behalf of their daughter together or separately, are held just as much to the double penalty; moreover, (so is) a grandfather or great-grandfather on behalf of his granddaughter or great-granddaughter.[75]

(2) We think these (rules) are to be thus followed, if the future marriage is not prohibited from existing on account of the person or status or other cause forbidden by laws or general constitutions. For then we warn that by no means, seeing as (the broken betrothal) is without cause, does it follow that these *arrhae*, when they have been offered, can be merely returned (onefold).[76]

(3) We add this only to this, that even if the intended marriages were not prohibited by law, but after the (exchange of) *arrhae sponsaliciae*, the betrothed woman refused marriage with her fiancé on account of his shameless or unchaste behavior, or a difference of religion or religious sect, or for the reason that he would not have been able to have intercourse like a man, from which the hope of offspring arises, or on account of any other just excuse, if indeed it has been proven that the woman or her parents knew this before the *arrhae sponsaliciae* were given, they ought to accept their loss.

(4) But if they undertook the *arrhae sponsaliciae* in ignorance of these things or, after the *arrhae* had been given, a just cause for repentance arose,

having returned only these same (*arrhae*), they shall be kept free (from any penalty) beyond the onefold penalty of the other...[77]

III Marriage contracts from Egypt and the Near East

Roman law did not require documentation to make a marriage valid, though often contracts were drawn up stating the terms of the dowry [see Part I.D]. In some provinces, marriage contracts were a custom long pre-dating Roman rule. Most surviving marriage contracts are from Egypt, but a few also survive from the eastern provinces of Judaea and Arabia and from the military outpost of Dura Europos on the Euphrates.[78]

A Marriage contracts from Roman Egypt

When Egypt came under Greek control after the conquest of Alexander the Great in 332/1 B.C.E., the Greeks found an ancient culture with long-established marriage customs. Marriage agreements from Ptolemaic Egypt (from the later fourth century until the defeat of Cleopatra at Actium in 31 B.C.E.) written in Demotic (the Egyptian language) demonstrate that native marriage practices continued.[79] Greeks living in Egypt maintained their own culture and customs, but there was inevitably mutual influence between the two cultures in regard to marriage practices. Greek marriage contracts in Egypt go back to the last quarter of the fourth century B.C.E.; indeed, the earliest dated papyrus from Ptolemaic Egypt is a marriage contract [P.Eleph. 1, 311/310 B.C.E.; see Pestman 1994, 67–9]. The marriage law of the old Greek city-states, especially Athens, influenced that of Greco-Roman Egypt, but there were also significant differences. In classical Greece and in Egypt throughout the Greek and Roman periods, the purpose of marriage was the production of legitimate children – just as it was in Roman law and society. But whereas the essential component of legal Roman marriage was the consent of all parties, in Greek marriage it was *ekdosis*, the "giving over" of the bride to the groom. In classical Greece this was the prerogative of the bride's father only, but in Greco-Roman Egypt we find both parents giving their daughter together, or the mother alone giving her daughter [P.Oxy. X.1273, below], or even the bride "giving" herself without any parent [P.Oxy. XLIX.3500, below]. By the Roman period, *ekdosis*, though still a component of marriage, was more of a formality than a reality and found mainly in contracts from Oxyrhynchus [Modrzejewski 1993 (1981), 57–60; cf. Wolff 1939, 7–34].

In other contracts, there is no mention of *ekdosis*, but the husband simply acknowledges (*homologei*) that he has received the dowry from the wife or her father. In both types of contract (*ekdosis* and *homologia*), it was usual to list the respective duties of husband and wife, in particular, the husband's obligation to provide support, food and clothing for his wife; sometimes the wife's obligation to behave properly and remain faithfully at home is also mentioned. There would also be provision made in case of divorce (in particular, for return of the dowry, also sometimes for support of children of the marriage, who would usually remain with their father). But the most salient feature of the marriage agreement was a careful enumeration of the dowry brought by the wife.

Dowry was always a very important component of marriage in Ptolemaic and Roman Egypt, as in Roman society. There were several different terms denoting the property brought by a wife to the marriage, indicating different types of property. The dowry proper was usually called *pherne* (as opposed to *proix*, in classical Greece) and consisted of money and movable goods, not property or slaves. In the Roman period immovable property (land) and slaves are sometimes part of the dowry, under the influence of Roman custom; this kind of dowry may be called *proix* or *prosphora* rather than *pherne*. We also find the *parapherna*, "things in addition to the dowry," comprising personal items belinging to the wife, such as clothing and household utensils [cf. Part I.E.2]. Dowries varied widely in monetary value, depending on the resources of the bride's family, and the descriptions in the marriage contracts of dowry and other bridal appurtenances provide interesting evidence of the social and economic status of the couples involved.[80]

The dowry served not only as the wife's contribution to the expenses of the marriage, but also to enforce the respective duties of husband and wife. In contracts of the Ptolemaic and early Roman periods, a wife who did not respect the "moral clause" of the marriage contract, which laid down her responsibilities, would forfeit the dowry upon divorce; a husband who did not respect the "moral clause" or who, when a divorce was requested by the wife, failed to return the dowry within a set period of time (usually sixty days after the divorce), would have to pay an additional 50 percent of the original dowry amount [cf. P.Oxy. II.281 in Chapter 4, Part III.A.2]. In later contracts, the husband has only to return the dowry, immediately if he was the one who instigated the divorce, within sixty days if it was at the wife's initiative [Modrzejewski 1993 (1981), 65–7; Katzoff 1995a; Rowlandson 1996, 152–71].

Not all marriages had written documentation. As in Roman law, it was perfectly possible for a couple to contract an "unwritten" marriage, which was as legally valid as a "written" marriage. Sometimes unwritten marriages would later be converted into "written" ones by the drawing up of a contract after the couple had been married for some time.[81]

In many regards, such as the ideology of marriage as a union for the purpose of bearing legitimate children and the importance of dowry, marriage in Roman Egypt resembled marriage in Italy and elsewhere in the Roman west. But in other respects, there were significant differences, the most obvious being attitudes toward marriage between close relatives. In Roman law, and in Roman society, close-kin marriages, particularly brother–sister unions, but also marriage between a woman and her maternal uncle, were illegal and morally repugnant [see Chapter 3, Part I.A]. But elsewhere in the Empire, particularly in the eastern provinces, attitudes were different. There is considerable evidence for the practice of close-kin marriage in the first two and a half centuries of Roman rule in Egypt, though the origins of this practice and reasons for it are matters of debate. Before the Edict of Caracalla in 212 granted Roman citizenship to all free provincials (and thus made all provincials subject to Roman private law), unions between close kin, especially siblings, comprised about 20 percent of all marriages in Roman Egypt [Bagnall and Frier 1994, 127–34; Hopkins 1980]. These were not Roman citizens, however. Roman citizens in Egypt were subject to the Roman law of marriage, including the Augustan marriage legislation [Part I.B above], as we know from regulations in the *Gnomon of the Idiologos*.[82] Even after all provincials received Roman citizenship in 212, it appears there was for several decades an imperial amnesty for those already in incestuous marriages at the time of Caracalla's decree.[83] Only in the late third century do we find emperors actively taking steps to eradicate close-kin unions.[84]

Sibling marriage produced the same kind of documentation as other marriages. An agreement from the reign of Domitian records the marriage of a brother and sister, who had already been living together in an unwritten marriage. The agreement contains all the usual features of a marriage contract: the husband's acknowledgment that he has received a dowry, his obligation to provide support for his wife, and provisions for divorce, and is followed by a division of property among her children by the couple's mother to take effect after her death.[85] Sibling unions might also end in divorce; in a divorce agreement from Tebtunis dated 138, we learn that the husband squandered his sister-wife's dowry [P.Kron. 52; see Rowlandson 1998, 130–1].

The following selections, arranged chronologically, are chosen out of more than a hundred surviving contracts to illustrate the different types of marriage contract found in Egypt under Roman rule.[86]

1 A synkhoresis *from Alexandria*

Alexandria was one of the largest cities of the Mediterranean world and the center of Roman government for the province of Egypt, but almost no papyri have survived there. Alexandrian papyri that do survive were actually found elsewhere, such as a large and interesting group of papyri preserved in mummy cartonnage at a site further south, Abusir el Melik (ancient Bousiris). Dating from the reign of Augustus (within two decades of Egypt's becoming a Roman province), these papyri belonged to the archive of a certain Protarchos, who from 25/4 B.C.E. to 5/4 B.C.E. was head of an Alexandrian tribunal with whom legal documents in the form of a *synkhoresis* (agreement, acknowledgement) were registered.[87]

The Protarchos archive includes eight marriage contracts, all written in Greek.[88] They represent Greek, not native Egyptian or Roman practice. Although differing in their particulars according to the couple's personal circumstances, all eight follow the same format and have very similar, often identical, wording (some papyri are fragmentary and so are missing some parts):

1 Address to Protarchos, from the parties to the marriage.
2 Description of bride's dowry (clothes, jewelry, and money).
3 Husband's obligations and the penalty he faces if he fails to meet them (almost always forfeiture of dowry plus one-half of original dowry amount).
4 Wife's obligations and her penalty (always loss of dowry) if she fails to meet them.
5 Couple's intention to file another contract (*syngraphe*) with officials called the *hierothytai* within five working days (this clause does not appear in all the *synkhoreseis*).
6 Request that the contract be filed; date of contract.

In the marriage contract below, as in other official documents of Roman Egypt, the woman, Isidora, is accompanied by a guardian (*kyrios*), in this case her brother.[89] After the marriage, her *kyrios* would be her husband, except for transactions (such as divorce) in which he was involved in some other way [Chapter 1, Part III.C]. Here the bride, rather than being "given" in marriage by her parents, "comes together" with the groom in mutual acknowledgment of their marriage. In fact, most of the *synkhoreseis* from Alexandria make no mention of *ekdosis* [Modrzejewski 1993 (1981), 61–2; Katzoff 1995a, 39].

BGU IV.1050, 12–11 B.C.E.

To Protarchos, from Isidora daughter of Herakleides son of Dionysios, with her *kyrios*, her brother Bakhios, son of Herakleides son of Dionysios from the deme of Isis. Isidora and Dionysios acknowledge that they have come together with each other in marriage. And Dionysios also acknowledges that he has received from Isidora by hand from her house a dowry of women's clothes valued at 100 drachmas[90] of silver, a pair of gold earrings of two quarters weight (of a gold didrachmon) and sixty drachmas of coined Ptolemaic silver.

(They marry on the understanding that) Dionysios, taking the aforementioned dowry, supports and clothes Isidora as befits a married woman, according to his means, and that he not mistreat her or abuse her or throw her out or bring another woman into (the house) or (if he does), he pays back in full the dowry plus 50 percent, there being the right (to Isidora) to exact payment from the same Dionysios and from all his possessions as if by a court judgment. And (on the understanding that) Isidora does not sleep away or be away for a day from Dionysios' house without Dionysios' approval, or damage the home, or be with another man, or (if she does), after being judged guilty of having done so, she is deprived of her dowry.[91]

(They acknowledge) that they will also deposit a contract about the marriage at the office of the *hierothytai* within five working days from the day when they announce this to each other, in which will be written both the dowry and the other customary things and the things concerning the death of either one of the spouses, as it is decided (by them) in common at the right time.[92] We ask (that this document be registered).

2 Abstract of an alimentary contract from Tebtunis

A different type of marriage agreement is found in the early Roman period at Tebtunis in the Fayum. These are known as "alimentary" or "maintenance" contracts (*syngraphai trophitides*), between the husband (or his parents) and the wife. Abstracts of five such agreements are preserved in a roll of abstracts of contracts prepared by the record office (*grapheion*) of Tebtunis in the year 42 C.E. Thus what we have is not the original contract, but an abbreviated version of it. The abstracts are in Greek, whereas the original alimentary contract would have been written in Demotic, the native Egyptian language. The alimentary contract itself is a later development of an originally Egyptian marriage arrangement, also called an "alimentary contract," but differing from the Roman-period agreements.[93]

In the Tebtunis alimentary contracts, the husband declares that he is making over to his wife a certain amount of money and all the property he owns or will own during the marriage. The wife's contribution to the marriage is then described: the dowry (*pherne*), always in money, and the *parapherna*, personal items given in addition to the *pherne*. Then come the names, ages, and physical descriptions of the parties to the marriage, and the name, age and description of the *hypographeus* (subscriber to the contract) who signs for each party. The dowry given here is rather low compared to other marriage contracts from Tebtunis of the same period [see Hopkins 1980, 342].

Unlike many other marriage contracts (except those which put into written form unions previously existing as "unwritten marriages"), the alimentary contracts usually are between couples who have already been married for some time. That is why the couple is considerably older (often in their thirties or forties) than the parties in other types of marriage contracts.[94]

P.Mich. II.121.recto III.i, 42 C.E.

Alimentary contract of eleven gold-pieces of money and deed of cession and conveyance in regard to my portion of my maternal inheritance of a house and courtyard and all the things appertaining to it in Tebtunis of the Polemon district now, and (in regard to) the possessions I will acquire from now on, allotments and slaves and movable property and household goods, in any way whatever.

The dowry given is sixty silver drachmas and the *parapherna*, without valuation, is a pair of gold earrings of three quarters (weight) and a gold crescent necklace of one and a half (quarters weight) and silver armlets of eight drachmas of uncoined bullion (weight) and a bronze basin and two bronze water-jars and tin utensils of two minas weight.

This is the contract which Patunis son of Kronion and Soueris, about 40 years old, with a scar on his left cheek, made with his wife Thatres daughter of Nikomedes(?), her mother being Thomenis daughter of Olios(?), about 26 years old, with a scar in the middle of her forehead below the hair. The subscriber (for Patunis) was Ptolemaios son of Chairemon, about 75 years old, with a scar above the left elbow, and for the other (Thatres), Herakleides son of Horion, about 60 years old with a scar on his left ankle. The rest in conformity (with the general format of such contracts).

3 A Latin marriage contract

Almost all marriage contracts found in Egypt from the Roman imperial period are in Greek, but several Latin documents relating to marriage do exist, all unfortunately very fragmentary. This Latin marriage contract, on papyrus, was written in duplicate, which was an unusual practice for documents from Egypt (but cf. the wax tablet diptych, also in Latin, requesting a guardian in Chapter 1, Part III.C), though more common in the Near East (see below on P.Yadin 18). It appears that one copy of the text was written above the other; then the upper (inner) text was rolled up and fastened shut (sealed or sewn up). That way the lower (outer) text could still be read, and if the outer text were damaged or there were doubts about its validity, the inner text could be unfastened and read.[95]

Three fragments of the document survive; two were published as P.Mich. VII.434 (= FIRA III.17); the third was later published as P.Ryl. IV.612. The text of what was probably the inner script (P.Ryl. IV.612) differs slightly from the text of the outer script (P.Mich. VII.434), but they can be used to supplement each other. Even with the supplements, much of the text is still missing.[96]

The provenance and date of the contract are not given in the document. The full name of the bride's father is not preserved, but only his cognomen Nomissianus. A certain Gaius Antistius Nomissianus is known from another papyrus dated 141 [P.Phil. 11], to have owned land in the village of Philadelphia, which is also the location of the dotal land mentioned in this contract. If this Nomissianus is identical to the father of Zenarion, the marriage contract may also come from Philadelphia, and can be dated to sometime in the early to mid-second century.[97] The *tria nomina* (three names) of the groom, Marcus Petronius Servillius, indicate that he was a Roman citizen, as was the bride's father (assuming he is Gaius Antistius Nomissianus). As with other Latin documents relating to marriage found in Egypt [P.S.I. 730; P.Mich. VII.442, 444], the agreement was witnessed and signed by seven Roman citizens.

The contract shows an interesting combination of Greek and Roman elements. The marriage is said to be in accordance with Augustus' marriage legislation, applicable only to Roman citizens [see Part I.B]. The dowry consists of jewelry and clothing (as in Greek contracts), but also landed property and a slave (uncommon in Greek contracts). Many of the dowry items are Greek words written in Latin letters. Like Greek brides in Egypt, Zenarion also had *parapherna*. The groom too contributes property, an early instance of the pre-nuptial gift that becomes standard in late Roman law [see Part II.C].

P.Mich. VII.434 + P.Ryl. IV.612, 2nd c.

[C. Antistiu]s Nomissianus gave in marriage his own daughter Zenarion, a virgin,[98] according to the Julian law which [was] passed concerning the Marrying of the Orders for the sake of [procreating children],[99] M. Petronius Servillius [took her as wife], and he (Nomissianus) declared to him (in the name of) dowry and gave all the things [which are written below on behalf of the same] above-mentioned (daughter): near the village of Philadelphia, two and three-quarters iugera of katoikic land[100] from her father's estate in the place Cor ... [the rest of the place name is missing] , and [in] the same village ... three and a half (iugera) of sandy (land) from her father's estate ... half part of a vineyard, and among gold items, a very long earring of two and a half quarters weight and necklaces (or rings?[101]) of one and a half quarters weight, (which altogether) make four quarters, silver bracelets (?) one pair, seven staters in weight; and in clothing whose value has been appraised: a tunic and a little cloak and a cloak from Scyros worth 180 Augustan drachmas and a *heratianon*[102] and a striped garment; and a bronze Venus[103] and a small bronze jar worth forty-eight Augustan drachmas, and a mirror and a chest ... and two oil flasks and another small jar seven minas and a quarter in weight, and a little wooden box, a chair, a perfume jar, a basket; and a slavewoman, Herais, from her father's estate; and as *parapherna*, a tunic and a little worn-out cloak. And likewise M. Petronius Servillius himself said that he had brought [his] own (contribution) in the village of Philadelphia two iugera of grain-land in the place ... [the rest is missing]

[On the back were the signatures of seven witnesses, all but the last in Greek.]

4 A mother gives her daughter in marriage

In 212, the Edict of Caracalla bestowed Roman citizenship on all free inhabitants of the Empire. In theory, this meant that all marriages had to be according to Roman law, but by and large provincials continued to follow their traditional marriage customs. In this Greek contract from the mid-third century, the participants all bear the *nomen* (family name) Aurelia (feminine form) or Aurelius (masculine form), indicating that they or their forefathers received citizenship from Caracalla, whose *nomen* was Aurelius. (This does not imply any blood relationship among Aurelii; after 212, almost everyone whose family had not received the citizenship earlier was called Aurelius/a.)

Aurelia Tauseiris is given in marriage by her mother Aurelia Thaesis, presumably a widow.[104] Neither one is said to have a *kyrios*, but Thaesis is accompanied by a man called a *synestos*, who assists her in the transaction and signs the contract for her, since (like most women in Roman Egypt) she is illiterate [see Chapter 1, Part III.E on use of a *synestos* by women without a *kyrios*]. The dowry (*pherne*), consisting of jewelry and clothing, is all assigned a monetary value and if the marriage ends by divorce, Aurelius Arsinoos must repay the full value which the dowry had at the time of the wedding. This was a shrewd move on Aurelia Thaesis' part; as Roman jurists warned, it was not in the husband's best interest for non-monetary items in the dowry, especially clothing, to be given a monetary value, since he would be responsible for any wear or loss during the marriage [D.23.3.10 pr; Gardner 1986a, 102; see Part I.D].

P.Oxy. X.1273, 260 C.E.

For good fortune. Aurelia Thaesis daughter of Eudaimon, her mother being Herais, from the city of Oxyrhynchus, with Aurelius Theon, also called Neoptianus and however he is called, assisting (*synestos*), gave her own daughter Aurelia Tauseiris in marriage to a husband, Aurelius Arsinoos son of Tryphon, his mother being Demetria, from the same city. To him also the same giver (Aurelia Thaesis), on behalf of the same daughter of hers who is being married, provides as dowry of common gold on the Oxyrhynchite standard: a neckpiece called a *maniakes* with a stone, of thirteen quarters weight excluding the stone; a brooch having five stones with a gold setting, of four quarters weight excluding the stones; a pair of earrings having ten pearls, of three quarters weight excluding the pearls; a little ring of half a quarter weight. And in clothing whose value has been appraised: a silvery hooded Dalmatic cape,[105] worth 260 drachmas of coined silver, a white fringed single-cloth little chiton[106] worth 160 drachmas of coined silver, a blue-green Dalmatic cape worth 100 drachmas, another Dalmatic cape, white with purple border, worth 100 drachmas, so that the whole dowry is worth one mina, four quarters and a half of common gold, and the value of the clothing is 620 drachmas, the sum total to which nothing has been added. And the bridegroom, Aurelius Arsinoos, having been asked about the afore-mentioned dowry by the giver, Aurelia Thaesis, agreed that he had received the full amount in regard to the afore-mentioned weight and value.

Therefore let the married couple live with each other blamelessly, guarding the rights of marriage, and let the husband ... provide to the wife all the necessities according to his ability. But if – and may it not happen – there should be a separation of the couple arising from disagreement, the husband shall give back to the giver (Aurelia Thaesis, the mother), if she is still alive, or if not, to the bride, the afore-mentioned dowry in full within 60 days from the time the request is made, the gold according to the reckoning of the weight of each item, but in regard to the clothing whose value has been appraised, those on the bride's side will have a choice either to have them at the value they will have at that time, and take the balance in silver, or to take the afore-mentioned appraised value itself, and the groom will have responsibility for wear and tear and loss of all items.

And if at the time of separation the bride should be pregnant, the groom shall give to her 40 drachmas for the expenses of childbirth. Concerning the request for return of the afore-mentioned dowry, those on the bride's side will have the right of execution on the groom and all his possessions.[107]

This contract, having been written in duplicate so that each party can have a single copy, is legally valid. And whenever they choose, both or one of them will make it public at the record-office, without the need for the participation of the other nor any other consent, because they agree henceforth to its future publication. And, having asked each other about whether these things were done correctly and well, they agreed (that they were).

In the seventh year of the Emperors and Caesars, Publius Licinnius Valerianus and Publius Licinnius Valerianus Gallienus, Germanici, greatest, pious, (and) fortunate, and Publius Licinnius Cornelius Saloninus Valerianus the most notable Caesar, Augusti, the 2nd of Mecheir.[108]

[in a 2nd hand] I, Aurelia Thaesis, have given my daughter in marriage to the above-mentioned Arsinoos and I have brought to him the afore-mentioned dowry as is set forth above and having been asked, I agreed. I, Aurelius Theon, also called Nepotianus, assisted her and I wrote on her behalf since she does not know letters.

[in a 3rd hand] I, Aurelius Arsinoos, have had the afore-mentioned dowry and if – may it not happen – there should be a separation, I will give it back as stated above and having been asked, I agreed.

5 The marriage of two embalmers

The date of this fragmentary contract in Greek from Oxyrhynchus is unknown, but it is from the same period as the previous one or earlier.[109] (The fact that all participants are Aurelii indicates a date after 212; see above.) The bride and groom are embalmers, involved in the preservation of mummies, and the contract was made in the presence of two other embalmers. The bride gives herself in marriage, which is unusual.[110] There does not seem to be a dowry, perhaps due to the humble socio-economic status of the couple.[111] The end of the contract, unfortunately lost, made provisions for divorce.

P.Oxy. XLIX.3500, 3rd c.

For good fortune. Aurelia Kyrilla daughter of Isidoros, her mother being Sinthonis, from the city of Oxyrhynchus, has given herself to Aurelius Pasigonis son of Paeis(?), his mother being Taues, from the same city, both being embalmers.

Therefore let the married couple live with each other, guarding the rights of marriage. And let the [husband] also provide to his wife all the necessities according to his ability.

They established this agreement with each other in the presence of the Aurelii Diogas son of Diogenes and Sarapion son of Paulinus, both of the same kind,[112] on condition that if on the one hand Kyrilla without any reasonable cause ... [the rest is lost]

Far fewer marriage contracts survive from the later imperial period than from the early Empire. Whereas we have dozens of marriage agreements from the first and second centuries, fewer than a dozen are known from the third century, three from the fourth century, and two from the fifth.[113]

In a lacunose agreement dated 304 from Hermopolis [P.Vind.Bosw. 5], Aurelia Ammonia states that she has given her daughter in marriage "according to the the the Papion-Pappaeon (sic) law."[114] The daughter (whose name does not survive) is said to be "present and consenting" to the union, the only explicit mention of the bride's consent in any of the late contracts [Beaucamp 1992, 116]. The groom is accompanied by his *curator*, the guardian for fatherless children under twenty-five. The dowry, given by the bride's mother, comprises items of clothing, linen, "female implements," and two slaves. This is one of the last references to the Augustan marriage legislation (which had come to be known collectively as the "Papian–Poppaean laws"), abolished by Constantine fifteen years later [see Parts I.B. and II.A].[115]

6 A husband moves in with his wife and her father

The only marriage contract to survive more or less intact from the fourth century presents a type of marital arrangement unusual in Roman Egypt, though it is known from later Byzantine documents [Montevecchi 1936, 18; Beaucamp 1992, 108]. In the following Greek contract between Aurelius Asep and Aurelius Aron, Aron not only marries his daughter Apia to Asep, but also agrees to receive him into his home, as Asep is said to be "destitute" (*gymnieuonta*).[116] Aron does this "by persuasion," suggesting that he may not have been entirely happy about the marriage of his daughter to a pauper. He and his daughter are far from wealthy themselves; note the small dowry (here called *doryphion*, "wedding-gift"). However, if Asep leaves Aron and his daughter, he must pay a fine; one wonders how he would be expected to have the money. Aron is getting not just a son-in-law, but a bound laborer!

Because both parties are illiterate, a priest (*papas*) writes on their behalf – an interesting early reference to the participation of a Christian cleric in marriage arrangements [see Evans Grubbs 1995, 152].[117]

P.Ross.Georg. III.28, 24 February, 358

In the consulship of our lord Constantius the eternal Augustus on the ... Mecheir. This is a copy.

The Aurelii, Asep son of Ol ..., his mother being Termouthis, from the village of Taurinon of the Arsinoite nome, and Aron, son of Kounias from the settlement Psetra of the same nome, have made an agreement concerning the coming together of Aurelius Asep with Apia, the daughter of Aron, for the partnership of marriage. But Aron, by persuasion, has received Asep, who is destitute, from the time of the current first indiction[118] and Aron has offered to his own daughter for the purpose of wedding-gift three hooded Dalmatic cape and one mantle (*pallium*). Henceforth, therefore, let the married couple live together. But indeed, also a face-cloth and ... and an earring.[119]

As Asep does not have the power (*exousia*) to leave Sophia (Apia) after this, the one who transgresses after this will give to the one who remains in the name of penalty and intrigue[120] and insulting treatment, ten gold coins; nor again (does he have the power) to leave her father, Aron, because it has been thus agreed and settled by persuasion. And having been asked (if they consented to this agreement), they agreed (that they did).

I, Aurelius Asep, the above-mentioned, have agreed to all the things that have been written as is set out above.

I, Aurelius Aron, son of Kounias, have agreed to all the things that have been written as is set out above.

I, Aurelius Ammonios, priest, have written on their behalf as they are illiterate.

The only other surviving fourth-century contract, dated 363, is very lacunose, but appears to be more conventional. The groom, Aurelius Leontios, acknowledges to Flavius Tiambos, a veteran, that he has received a dowry (whose contents are enumerated) on behalf of Tiambos' daughter Mamoukia. The respective duties of the couple are set out: he is to provide all necessities and clothing to her; she is to keep herself blameless and without accusation in her way of life (the so-called "moral clause," cf. BGU IV.1050 above). There follow provisions for the immediate return of the dowry to Mamoukia or her father in the event of a separation (cf. P.Oxy. X.1273 above), but the rest is too fragmentary to read.[121] One Greek marriage contract is known from the late fifth century, from Oxyrhynchus, but it is very fragmentary (and beyond the chronological limits of this book).[122]

In addition to the handful of Greek marriage contracts from this period found in Egypt, there is also a *ketubah* (Jewish marriage contract) from Antinoopolis, dated 417. It is in Aramaic and Greek, but written in Hebrew characters. It shows the traditions both of the *ketubat* of Palestinian Judaism and of Greco-Egyptian contracts. Samuel declares he is taking Metra to wife, and Metra's duties as wife are laid out (as in the Greek *synkhoresis* from Alexandria above and in later Byzantine contracts). The dowry items (given by Metra's mother) are described, followed by the bride-gift given by Samuel (which is transliterated from the Greek term *hedna*). The dowry items indicate that the social class of the couple was quite modest.[123]

B Marriage agreement from the "Cave of Letters"

In addition to the fifth-century *ketubah* from Egypt, mentioned above, nine marriage contracts between Jews are known from the provinces of Judaea and Arabia, all dating to the late first or early second centuries. Five of these are in Greek, and four are in Aramaic.[124] The Greek contracts show many resemblances to marriage contracts from Roman Egypt, and show a fusion of Greek and Jewish elements (whereas the Aramaic documents are traditional Jewish *ketubat*). The families in these Greek documents are not secular, "hellenized" Jews, but have adapted their contracts to the norms of the multicultural society in which they live [see Cotton 1994]. It is probable also that they recorded their marriages in Greek so that the documents would be valid in Roman provincial courts.[125]

Two of the Jewish marriage contracts in Greek [P.Yadin 18 and 37] and one of the Aramaic *ketubat* [P.Yadin 10] are from the cache of documents now known as the "Babatha archive." The "Babatha archive" comprises the personal papers of a Jewish woman, Babatha, who lived in the village of Maoza in the new Roman province of Arabia (modern Jordan), which until 106 C.E. had been the kingdom of Nabatea. The papers were found in a cave along the Dead Sea now known as the "Cave of Letters," where they had evidently been hidden in 132 by local residents caught up in the Bar-Kokhba revolt led by the Jewish leader Shim'on Bar Kosiba (several letters written by Bar Kosiba were found in the same cave, though not among Babatha's papers). Babatha never returned to reclaim her documents, and scholars have concluded that she died in the revolt.[126]

In Babatha's archive were thirty-five documents in three languages, Greek, Aramaic, and Nabatean, ranging in date from 93 (thirteen years before Nabatea became a Roman province under the emperor Trajan) to 132, the year the Bar-Kokhba revolt began. They shed valuable light on the life and legal affairs of a provincial woman in the early second century [see Chapter 5, Part II.B.2 for more on the Babatha archive].

Many of the papyri in the Babatha archive, including the marriage contract below, were what are called "double documents." The text would be written twice on the same papyrus, with one copy written above the other. The upper (inner) portion of the papyrus, with the first copy, was rolled up and fastened with string to protect the text and prevent tampering with it. The second copy, on the lower (outer) portion, would be accessible, and its veracity could be checked, if necessary, by comparison with the upper text [see Lewis 1989, 6–10]. "Double documents" are rare in Egypt (but cf. the Latin marriage contract, Part A.3 above), but evidently more common further east, as they are found also at Dura Europos (see below) and among the recently published texts from the Middle Euphrates [Bowersock 1991, 337–8].

The marriage agreement below, written in Greek, was made between the groom, Judah also called Cimber, and the bride's father, Judah son of Eleazar (also called Khthousion), who was Babatha's second husband.[127] The bride, Shelamzion, is thus Babatha's stepdaughter, and presumably that is why her marriage document was found among Babatha's papers. None of the parties are Roman citizens; the groom bears a Roman name, Cimber, but that is not an indication of Roman citizen status.[128] All are Jews living either in the province of Arabia (where the marriage took place, at Maoza) or the neighboring province of Judaea (where Ein-gedi, the hometown of both parties, was located). This contract has engendered much scholarly debate since its publication in 1987, centering around the question of how "Jewish" a document it actually is. Its original editor has described it as a "remarkable blend of Roman, Greek, and Jewish elements" [Katzoff, in Lewis, Katzoff and Greenfield 1987, 236], but his identification of "Jewish" elements in it have been challenged.[129] The document shares a number of features with marriage contracts from Roman Egypt, some of which are noted below. It cannot be described as a *ketubah*, unlike the Aramaic *ketubat* found in the Judaean desert (above). This does not mean that the participants were not practicing Jews, or that they did not know about or use the Jewish type of marriage agreement; indeed, not many years before Judah son of Khthousion, father of the bride, had given his second wife Babatha a traditional *ketubah* written in Aramaic which was also found in the Cave of Letters.[130]

Shelamzion brings jewelry and clothing as *prosphora*, which is given a monetary value of 200 denarii; her new husband adds another 300 denarii to make up a dowry (here called *proix*) of 500 denarii total. This addition to the dowry by the husband may be a "Jewish" feature of the marriage document, or may be an early appearance of the husband's pre-nuptial gift (called *hedna* in documents from Egypt) which becomes a regular part of marriage agreements in the fourth century.[131] In any case, the total dowry comes to a significant amount, indicating that both families were quite well-off [Lewis 1989, 77].

P.Yadin 18 (outer text only), 5 April, 128

In the consulship of Publius Metilius Nepo for the second time and of Marcus Annius Libo, [on the nones of April], on the fifteenth of the month Xandikos [of the twenty-third year] according to the numbering of the new province of Arabia, in Maoza around Zoara. [Judah] son of Eleazar also called Khthousion, gave Shelamzion, his own daughter, a virgin, to Judah called Cimber, son of Ananias son of Somalas, both from the village of Ein-gedi of Judaea, residing here, for Shelamzion to be wedded wife to Judah Cimber for the partnership of marriage according to the laws. She brings to him for the purpose of wedding-gift (*prosphora*) female finery in silver and gold and clothing valued by mutual agreement, as they both say, to be worth 200 denarii of silver. The groom, Judah called Cimber, acknowledged that he has taken this assessment from her by hand, immediately from Judah her father, and that he owes (it) to the same Shelamzion, his wife, together with another 300 denarii which he acknowledged that he gave to her in addition to all the items of her wedding-gift written above, for the purpose of her dowry (*proix*) in accordance with the purpose of support and clothing for both her and (their) future children by the Hellenic custom,[132] on the guarantee of the same Judah Cimber and at his risk and (on the security) of all the possessions which he has in his same homeland and here and of all those which he will possess anywhere lawfully. (And he acknowledged) that he will make the payment due in whatever way Shelamzion, his wife, chooses, or whoever is acting through [her] or on her behalf chooses. Judah, called Cimber, will exchange for [his] wife Shelamzion this contract in guaranteed silver as is appropriate, whenever she asks him, from his own money with no dispute.[133] But if he doesn't, he will pay to her double all the denarii written above, there being to her lawfully the right to exact payment [from] her husband Judah Cimber and from his possessions, in whatever way Shelamzion, or whoever is acting through her or on her behalf, chooses that the payment due be made.[134]

The question was asked in good faith and it was acknowledged in reply that these things were thus done well.[135]

[There follow, in Aramaic, the signatures of Judah son of Eleazar Khthousion and Judah Cimber. Cimber guarantees Shelamzion's dowry of 500 silver denarii.]

I, Theenas son of Simon, the scribe,[136] wrote this.

[The signatures of Judah son of Eleazar and Judah Cimber, and of five witnesses, are written on the back of the document in Aramaic.]

C Marriage contract from Dura Europos

Another part of the ancient Near East where documents of the Roman period have been found is Dura Europos, a Roman military outpost (now in Syria) on the Euphrates very near the frontier between the Roman Empire and the Persian Empire. Extensive excavations have yielded over a hundred papyri, one wax tablet, and several dozen documents on parchment, a material often used in this part of the world, but rare further west (cf. Chapter 1, Part V.C. on the recently published documents from the Middle Euphrates). Dura was a multi-cultural society where several different ethnic groups (Greeks, Jews, Persians and Romans) mingled and several different languages (Greek, Aramaic, Palmyrene, Iranian, Syriac, and Latin) were used. There was also considerable religious diversity: not only are there temples to eastern gods, but also a synagogue (well-known for its paintings) and even a Christian house-church [Millar 1993, 467–71].

Dura was originally a Macedonian foundation and had been part of the Seleucid empire during the Hellenistic period. It then came under Parthian (Persian) control until the 160s, when the Romans took it. Roman domination lasted less than a century, however; Dura was destroyed by the Persians in the 250s and abandoned. Inscriptions from the first century C.E. indicate that the inhabitants practiced marriage between uncle and niece and even between half-siblings, evidently influenced by Persian custom.[137] After Caracalla's grant of Roman citizenship in 212, such marriage practices should have stopped, but probably did not; more than three centuries later, Justinian and Justin II both had to grant amnesties to inhabitants of the region who continued to live in incestuous unions [Corcoran 2000, 10–11].

The Dura documents include one marriage contract on papyrus, in Greek and dated 232 (using the Roman dating system by consuls). The marriage did not actually take place at Dura, but at a place called Qatna, where the groom, who served in the Roman army, was stationed (by this time, soldiers could legally marry; see Chapter 3, Part I.C.4). The bride is a widow, and gives herself in marriage; there is no mention of a *kyrios* [cf. Chapter 1, Part III.C]. Her mother and brother are present; evidently her father is dead. Both bride and groom are Roman citizens and have the nomen Aurelius/a; probably they (or their parents) received citizenship under the Edict of Caracalla twenty years earlier.

The bride's dowry, consisting of clothing, jewelry, and housewares, is listed and valued, along with apparently an almost equivalent amount in silver. The groom is said to owe 175 denarii, to make a total dowry (*proix*) of 750 denarii of silver.[138] This addition to the dowry on the groom's part is similar to the arrangement in P.Yadin 18 [Part B], though there the groom contributed significantly more than the bride. The couple appears to have been "moderately affluent," according to the document's editors [Welles, Fink and Gilliam 1959,

156]. Provisions are made for return of the items contributed by Marcellina in the case of divorce, but the fragmentary nature of the text does not allow us to know the details.

Like the documents from the Cave of Letters, all the legal documents from Dura were "double documents," with the text written twice on the same sheet. The copy of the text written above, called the "inner text," was then sewn or otherwise sealed shut. The outer text, written below, also contained the signatures of participants and witnesses to the transaction, and would be open for easy access. The inner text of the marriage contract is almost entirely lost, but much remains of the outer text, though it, too, is very fragmentary. The papyrus on which it was written was folded fourteen times after being sewn shut, and then doubled over. This would have made it into a very small packet, which was perhaps worn around the neck of one of the partners.[139]

P.Dura 30 (outer text only), 1 October, 232

(first hand) In the consulship of Virius Lupus and Marius Maximus, on the Kalends of October, of the month Hyperberetaios at the first of the month, in Qatna in the winter quarters of the Twelfth Cohort of ... Palestinii, Severiana Alexandriana.

Good Fortune.[140]

On the present day Aurelius Alexander, soldier of the cohort written above, of the century of Papius, and Aurelia Marcellina, daughter of Marcellinus, living in Qatna, there being present with her..., her mother, and Agrippinus, her brother, have acknowledged and drawn up (a contract) for each other on the present day that Marcellina has given herself from widowhood for the partnership of marriage ... to Alexander and that they will remain with each other for all [time] ... bringing[141] ... from her possessions ... in clothing and goods, having been valued with suitable men as mediators,[142] the items written below:

a new white mantle (*pallium*), valued at 1[2]5 denarii; another new white mantle, valued at fifty denarii; a new ... tunic, valued at forty denarii; a new undyed Dalmatic cape, valued at thirty denarii; a [scarlet] Dalmatic cape and new purple hood, valued at seventy-five denarii; another new white Dalmatic cape, valued at fifty denarii; a new purple ..., valued at twenty-five denarii; silken garments with diagonal stripes, new, valued at fifty denarii; ceramic and [bronze] ware, valued at twenty-five denarii; earrings and finger-rings ... valued at fifty denarii; ... 565 denarii of silver brought by her,

which ... Alexander acknowledged that he has received and has ... for himself among his possessions the items ... and that he is content with the things coming to himself and [several words are missing] ... to owe 175 denarii ... dowry (*proix*) (to the value of) 750 denarii of silver. There is an agreement between them that if Alexander should wish to get rid of Marcellina ... because of ... [several words are missing] the things belonging ... [several lines are missing] he will give back the ... denarii which he received ... [several words are missing] ... it has been agreed between them, happened, if any ... each ...

(another hand) I, Faustinus Avianus, veteran, having been asked, wrote [on behalf of Aurelia] Marcellina daughter of Marcellinus, who is illiterate and who agrees with the things written above.

(another hand) I, [Aurelius] Alexander [agree with the things] written above … [the rest is too fragmentary to read].

[On the other side are the signatures of five witnesses.]

3

PROHIBITED AND
NON-LEGAL UNIONS

I Prohibited and non-marital unions in classical law

The main criteria for a valid marriage in Roman law were the consent of both parties (and the *paterfamilias* of each) and the absence of any legal prohibitions on marriage between the two people involved [see Chapter 2, Part I.A.2]. In both the classical and late antique periods, the major prohibitions on marriage derived from kinship and status.

A *Prohibitions based on kinship*

Unlike some Mediterranean peoples (cf. for instance Roman Egypt, see Chapter 2, Part III), the Romans had an incest taboo. Roman law placed restrictions on marriage between very close kin, including those related by adoption. In general, marriage between those related within three degrees was prohibited (for an exception, see Part I.A.2 below).[1]

1 *Parent–child and sibling marriage*

Gaius, *Institutes* I.59: Indeed, marriage cannot be contracted between those persons who have the position of parents and children, nor is there a right of marriage (*conubium*) between them: as for instance, between a father and a daughter or between a mother and a son or between a grandfather and a granddaughter or between a grandmother and a grandson. And if such persons have joined themselves to each other, they are said to have contracted an unholy and incestuous marriage. And this is true to the extent that, though they have begun to be in the position of parents or children to each other through adoption, they are not able to be joined to each other in marriage, so much so that even if the tie of adoption has been dissolved, the same rule remains. And so I will not be able to marry a woman who has begun to be in the position of daughter or granddaughter to me through adoption, though I have emancipated her.

D.23.2.54 (Scaevola): And it makes no difference whether the kinship arises from legitimate marriage or not: for a man is forbidden to marry even an illegitimate sister.

Marriage between step-siblings was allowed, as was marriage between an adopted child and his or her adoptive sibling, provided that at least one of the two had been formally emancipated from paternal power [see Chapter 1, Part II.C.] and therefore was no longer legally related to the other:

D.23.2.34.2 (Papinian): Marriage can be contracted between step-siblings, even if they have a common brother conceived from the new marriage of their parents.

Gaius, *Institutes* I.61: Clearly marriage is prohibited between brother and sister, whether they have been born from the same father and mother or from one or the other of them. But if someone has begun to be a sister to me through adoption, indeed for as long as the adoption holds, clearly there cannot be marriage between her and me. However, when the adoption has been dissolved through emancipation, I will be able to marry her. But also if I have been emancipated, there will be no impediment to marriage.

However, marriage between an adopted child and a member of an older generation (either a direct ascendant or an ascendant's sibling) remained illegal even if the child were emancipated from paternal power:

D.23.2.14 (Paulus): If an adopted son is emancipated, he cannot marry the woman who was the wife of his adoptive father, since she has the position of step-mother. 1: Likewise, if someone has adopted a son, not even after emancipation of the son will he be able to marry the man's wife, who is in the position of a daughter-in-law, since she was once his daughter-in-law.

Gaius, *Institutes* I.63: [the beginning of the passage is omitted] ... Likewise, (it is not permitted to marry) her who was once my mother-in-law or my daughter-in-law or my step-daughter or my step-mother.... [the rest of the passage is omitted]

2 Uncle–niece and aunt–nephew marriage

D.23.217.2 (Gaius): We are prohibited from marrying a paternal aunt and a maternal aunt, and likewise a paternal great-aunt and a maternal great-aunt, though a paternal great-aunt and a maternal aunt are in the fourth degree of kinship. And so moreover, we are prohibited from marrying a paternal aunt and paternal great aunt, even if they have been joined to us through adoption.

Originally, all uncle–niece marriage had been banned also. But an exception to the rule was made to accommodate the emperor Claudius, who wished to marry his brother Germanicus' daughter Agrippina. Claudius' marriage was quite controversial, and is mentioned by the jurist Gaius and the historians Tacitus and Suetonius, both writing in the early second century. Tacitus and Suetonius say that Claudius, incited by Agrippina's feminine blandishments, forced the Senate to pass a decree legalizing marriage between an uncle and his brother's daughter, but the ban on marriage with a sister's daughter remained:

Gaius, *Institutes* I.62:
It is permitted to marry the daughter of a brother. This first came into use when the deified emperor Claudius had married Agrippina, his brother's daughter. However, it is not permitted to marry the daughter of a sister. And these things are shown thus by imperial constitutions.

Tacitus, *Annales* XII.6–7 (excerpts[2])

[The senator Lucius Vitellius, a partisan of Claudius, is justifying the marriage]: " ... Indeed, marriages with our brothers' daughters are new to us; but among other peoples they are customary and are not prohibited by any law, and marriages with second cousins,[3] which were for a long time unknown (among Romans) have become frequent as time has passed. Just as it is useful for custom to be adjusted, so even this (new custom) will be among those which are quickly adopted."

XII.7: ... Claudius ... entered the Senate and requested a decree by which marriages between uncles and their brothers' daughters would be established as legitimate for the future. However, no one was found desirous of such a marriage except one man, the Roman knight Alledius Severus, who, most said, was impelled by Agrippina's favor.[4]

The ban on marriage between a man and his sister's daughter continued even after Claudius's law [see below, D.23.2.57a], and in late antiquity the ban on paternal uncle–niece marriage was reintroduced [see Part II.A].

3 *Former slaves and incestuous marriage*

Under Roman law, slaves could not have legal marriages, and were not recognized as having a family. However, they did have quasi-marital non-legal relationships called *contubernia* [see Part I.B.1]. Former slaves could legally marry, but their natal family relationships were still not recognized by law, since they had been born slaves. However, freedmen and women were expected to observe the restrictions on unions between close kin:

D.23.2.14.2 (Paulus):
Even servile relationships by blood must be observed in this law (of incest). Therefore a manumitted man may not take his own mother as wife, and it is just as much a law regarding a sister and a sister's daughter. The same must be said for the opposite situation, that a father shall not be able to take his daughter as wife, if they have been manumitted from slavery, even if there should be doubt that he is her father. Wherefore a natural father is not able to take as wife even an illegitimate daughter, since in contracting marriage natural law and modesty (*pudor*) must be considered: it is against modesty, moreover, to take one's own daughter as wife. **3:** Moreover, the same (rule) must be observed in servile relationships by marriage as has been decided in the case of servile relationships by blood, for

example, that I shall not be able to marry a woman who has been in *contubernium* relationship with my father, as if (she were) my step-mother, and on the other hand, it is not possible for a father to marry a woman who has been in a *contubernium* relationship with his son, as if (she were) his daughter-in-law. For since servile cognate relationship is understood, why should not affine relationship also be understood? But in doubtful cases the more certain and more modest thing is to refrain from marriage of this sort.

D.23.2.8 (Pomponius): A freedman is not able to marry his freedwoman mother or sister, since this law has been introduced by custom, not by legislation.

D.23.2.56 (Ulpian): Also if someone has taken his sister's daughter as a concubine, even if she is a freedwoman, he is committing incest.

4 Legal consequences of incestuous marriage

Marriage to someone related within the prohibited degrees of kinship was invalid, and had none of the legal consequences of marriage. Incestuous unions were also punishable under the Augustan adultery law [see Chapter 2, Part I.B], particularly if the participants knew they were doing wrong:

D.23.2.68 (Paulus): Someone commits incest by the law of peoples (*ius gentium*) if he has taken a wife from a degree of ascendants or descendants. Moreover, whoever has married a woman who is a collateral relative whom he is forbidden (to marry), or a woman related by marriage whom there is some impediment to marrying, is punished, more lightly if in fact he has done this openly, but more seriously if he has committed this (incest) secretly. The reason for this difference is the following: concerning marriage which is not decently contracted in the collateral line, those openly offending are excused from the greater penalty as having made a mistake, but those committing (incest) secretly are punished as being disobedient.

Gaius, *Institutes* I.64: Therefore if someone has contracted an unholy and incestuous marriage, he appears to have neither wife nor children. And thus those who are born from this sexual union seem indeed to have a mother, but certainly not a father, nor for this reason are they in his power, (but) they are such as those whom their mother has conceived promiscuously. For also those (children) are understood not to have a father, when he (his identity) is uncertain, whence they are accustomed to be called "spurious" children, either from the Greek word, as if conceived "from scattered seed" or as if children without a father (*sine patre*).

D.23.2.52 (Paulus): Incestuous marriages do not have a dowry, and therefore everything which has been received (as dowry) is to be taken away, even if it is under the name of profits.

Participants in an incestuous marriage who were unaware that they were breaking the law could be pardoned because of their ignorance. This was especially true of women, particularly if they were very young and could be assumed to have no choice in the marriage. Two cases where women in incestuous relationships were pardoned are known:

D.48.5.39 (Papinian): In fact, the brother emperors remitted the charge of incest against Claudia on account of her age, but they ordered that the illegal union be broken up, though in other cases the crime of adultery which is committed in puberty is not excused because of age. For it has been said above that women also, who make a mistake in regard to the law, are not held by the crime of incest, though they can have no excuse when adultery has been committed.

The "brother emperors" are Marcus Aurelius and Lucius Verus (ruled jointly 161–9), who also made another decision regarding an incestuous marriage in reply to a petition from a woman called Flavia Tertulla:

D.23.2.57a (Marcian): The emperors the deified Marcus and Lucius wrote the following in a rescript to Flavia Tertulla, through her freedman, a measurer: "We are moved by the length of time in which you, ignorant of the law, were in a marriage with your maternal uncle, and by the fact that you were placed in marriage by your grandmother, and by the number of your children. And therefore, since all these things are in accord, we confirm the status of your children acquired within this marriage, which was contracted forty years ago, just as if they had been conceived legitimately."

Flavia Tertulla's names (*nomen* plus *cognomen*) indicate that she had the Roman citizenship and therefore was subject to Roman marriage law, but do not tell us anything about where she lived or her ethnicity. She may have been a provincial whose family had at some point obtained Roman citizenship, who lived in a region where uncle–niece marriage was customary and still legal under local law (such as Egypt or the Greek Aegean). Her case arose in the joint reign of Marcus Aurelius and Lucius Verus (161–9), fifty years before the emperor Caracalla bestowed Roman citizenship throughout the Empire. Flavia Tertulla had not known that her marriage ran counter to imperial law, and it is possible that her grandmother and uncle had not known either. Most Romans in Italy and heavily Romanized western provinces probably were aware of the prohibition on marriage between close kin related by blood, including siblings. They were perhaps more likely to have problems in regard to marriages with those related not by blood, but by some other relationship, such as in-laws or stepchildren (see above).

5 Diocletian's edict against close-kin marriage

In 212, the *Constitutio Antoniniana* of the emperor Caracalla granted Roman citizenship to virtually all free inhabitants of the Empire. All citizens had to abide by the Roman law of marriage, and to observe Roman marriage prohibitions. But in areas where close-kin marriage was firmly entrenched, it could not easily be eradicated by imperial law.

On 1 May, 295, the emperors Diocletian and Maximian, along with their Caesars (junior emperors) Galerius and Constantius, promulgated a strongly worded edict against close-kin marriages of all kinds. The law was enacted at Damascus, in Syria, and may have been prompted by reports of incestuous marriages in that region of the Empire, where marriages between uncles and nieces and between siblings (especially half-siblings) had a long tradition. This edict, which was meant to have general application, differs in form and in tone from rescripts such as the one to Flavia Tertulla quoted above, which was sent to an individual in response to a petition. In the later Empire, general laws such as this edict become the most common form of legislative enactment [see Introduction, Part I.B]. Late antique edicts, like this one, are often long, verbose, and highly rhetorical, and threaten heavy penalties for offenders.

Note especially the moralistic flavor: close-kin marriages are represented as an abomination to the gods, whose divine favor is needed for the safety of the Empire. Emphasis is placed on the importance of respecting the Roman virtue of *pietas*, which means "sense of duty, especially to one's family." This edict was preserved in a fourth-century legal collection known as the "Collation of Mosaic and Roman Laws," compiled by a Christian or a Jew who wanted to show the compatibility of secular Roman law with the law of Moses.[5] Moralistic outrage and concern to act in a pious and god-fearing manner are more usually associated with the laws of the Christian, late Roman emperors. But the edict against close-kin marriage was not enacted by Christian emperors; on the contrary, Diocletian and his Caesar Galerius (who, according to one scholar, was the instigator of this law[6]) were well-known as persecutors of Christians, and the last, "Great" persecution took place in 303–6, under the same rulers as had enacted this edict eight years earlier. Moral fervor and piousness are hallmarks of late Roman law, pagan and Christian alike.

Nor was this the only Diocletianic legislation on the topic of incestuous marriages. Several years prior to this edict, a rescript of Diocletian and Maximian to an imperial official and preserved in the same collection, had said that those who had contracted incestuous marriages "by error" were not to be punished if they broke up after the issuing of the rescript [*Collatio* VI.5.i.; see Corcoran 1996, 125]. And another rescript, not found in current editions of the *Code of Justinian* but evidently emanating from the same emperors, forbids the children of incestuous unions to obtain positions as judge, advocate, or procurator in a legal case [Corcoran 2000].

Mosaicarum et Romanarum Legum Collatio VI.4, 1 May, 295

Example of an edict of Diocletian and Maximian Augusti and Constantius and Maximianus (Galerius), most noble Caesars:

Since those matters, which have been established by Roman laws in a chaste and holy manner, seem to our pious and religious minds to be especially venerable and in need of preserving, we do not believe it is necessary to dissemble about those acts which have been committed wickedly and unchastely (*inceste*) by certain people in the past. Since (these acts) must be repressed or indeed punished, the discipline of our times urges us to rise up. For thus there is no doubt that even the immortal gods themselves will be favorable and gentle to the Roman name, as they always have been, if they have seen that all people living under our rule lead a wholly pious and religious and peaceful and chaste life in all respects.

(2) In this matter we have decided that this also should be provided for as much as possible: when marriages have been joined in a religious and legitimate way according to the discipline of the ancient law, that, with religion having been safeguarded, there begin to be deliberation as much for the honorableness of those who pursue the joining of marriages, as also for those who are born thereafter as a result, and that even posterity itself be purified

by the honorableness of being born. For it has especially pleased our sense of duty (*pietas*), that the sacred names of kinship maintain among one's own loved ones the dutiful (*pia*) and religious affection (*caritas*) owed to blood relationship. For it is wicked to believe those things, which it is agreed have been committed by very many in the past, when in the promiscuous manner of cattle or wild beasts they have rushed into illicit marriages at the instigation of accursed lust, without any respect for modesty or sense of duty (*pietas*).

(3) But whatever (acts) appear to have been committed before this time from illicit marriages by the custom of barbaric enormity, either because of the inexperience of those who transgressed or by virtue of ignorance of the law, though they should be most severely punished, however, by the consideration of our clemency we wish to tend to indulgence. Accordingly, however, those people who have polluted themselves in illicit and incestuous marriages before this time shall know that they have obtained our indulgence to this extent, that after such nefarious crimes they should be thankful that even their life has been allowed them. Let them know, moreover, that the children they have borne from so wicked a union are not legitimate. For thus it will happen that no one in the future shall dare to obey unrestrained desires, since they also shall know that the previous committers of this kind of crime were liberated by pardon in such a way that they are prohibited from the succession of the children whom they illicitly bore, which was denied by Roman laws according to antiquity. And we would have wished indeed that nothing of this kind had been committed before this, which had to be forgiven by clemency or corrected by the laws.

(4) But after this we wish that religion and sanctity in joining in marriages be preserved by each person, so that they should recall that they are concerned with Roman discipline and laws and they should know that only those marriages are licit, which have been allowed by Roman law.

(5) Moreover, we have included in this edict of ours those persons, from those related by blood (*cognati*) as well as those related by marriage (*adfines*), with whom it is not allowed to contract marriage:

with a daughter, granddaughter, great-granddaughter, likewise a mother, grandmother, great-grandmother, and a sister on the father's side or on the mother's side, and the daughter of a sister and the granddaughter from her.

And likewise from those related by marriage (*adfines*): a step-daughter, a step-mother, a mother-in-law, a daughter-in-law, and the others which are forbidden by the ancient law, from whom we wish all to abstain.

(6) For our laws protect nothing except what is sacred and venerable, and thus the Roman majesty has arrived at so great a magnitude by the favor of all the divinities, since it has bound all its laws by wise religion and by the observation of modesty (*pudor*).

(7) Therefore we wish in this edict of ours that it become plainly known to all, that the pardon of past events, which seems to have been indulged by

our clemency contrary to discipline, pertains only to those crimes, which appear to have been committed up to the third day before the Kalends of January in the consulship of Tuscus and Anullinus.[7]

(8) However, if any crimes are discovered to have been committed contrary to the honor of the Roman name and the sanctity of the laws after the above-mentioned day, they shall be struck with a worthy severity. Nor, indeed, should anyone who does not hesitate to rush into so obvious a crime even after our edict think that he can obtain pardon in so nefarious a wicked deed.

Given at Damascus on the Kalends of May in the consulship of Tuscus and Anullinus.[8]

For all its rhetoric, the law of 295 simply repeats the classical Roman legal attitude toward incestuous marriages. Note that nothing is said about marriage between a man and his *brother's* daughter, which had been legalized in the first century under the emperor Claudius (see above). In fact, marriage between paternal uncle and niece was not prohibited until 342 [Cod. Theod. 3.12.1, in Part II.A]. Moreover, though dire punishments threaten those who do not obey the law, the specific penalty is not actually stated. Those who have been pardoned for illicit unions in the past are told they are lucky to have been allowed to live, which implies that the penalty for continuing in incestuous marriage is death. But it is possible that exile with confiscation of goods (*deportatio*), considered a "capital" penalty, would have been applied instead, at least in the case of *honestiores*.[9]

B Non-marital unions based on social status

Roman law refused to recognize some unions as legitimate marriage because of the legal status of one or both partners. Such unions could still exist and might even last longer than a legal marriage. However, the partners did not enjoy the rights of married persons.

1 Slave unions and slave-free unions

Marriage between slaves or between a slave and a free person was a legal impossibility, though relationships between free persons and slaves certainly occurred in real life. If monogamous and long-lasting, such a union would be called *contubernium*, as would a union between two slaves. Such quasi-marital relationships are often attested in funerary inscriptions from the city of Rome [Weaver 1972, 1986; Rawson 1974; Treggiari 1981b; Flory 1978; 1984].

Rules of Ulpian 5.5: There is no right of legal marriage (*conubium*) with slaves. **Sent. Pauli II.xix.6:** Between slaves and free people marriage (*matrimonium*) is not able to be contracted, but *contubernium* can be.

Children born to such unions were not legitimate and followed the legal status of their mother: if she was a slave, they were slaves and belonged to her master. If she had been freed before giving birth, her children were freeborn [Weaver 1986; 1991]:

Gaius, *Institutes* I.82: It also follows from these (rules) that by the law of nations (*ius gentium*) a slave is born from a slavewoman and a free man, and on the other hand, a free person is born from a free woman and a slave man.

Gaius, *Institutes* I.89: It also has been decided that if a slavewoman has conceived from a Roman citizen and then has given birth after being manumitted, (the child) who is born is born free; this (has been decided) by natural reason. For those who are conceived illegitimately take the status (they have) at the time they are born. And so if they are born from a free woman, they become free. Nor does it matter from whom their mother conceived them, since she was a slave. But those, who are legitimately conceived, take the status (they have) at the time of conception.

Though these rules sound relatively simple, the reality could be quite complicated. In a society which did not require written documentation for the validity of legal transactions [see Chapter 2, Part I.A], freedpeople might not be able to prove that they had been manumitted, and it might not be clear whether the child of a freedwoman had been born after the mother's manumission (in which case the child was freeborn) or before (in which case, the child would have been slaveborn). An actual case of such confusion is known from the wax tablets unearthed at the town of Herculaneum (destroyed by the eruption of Vesuvius in 79 C.E.). Petronia Justa, the daughter of a freedwoman, was in dispute with her deceased mother's former mistress, Calatoria Themis, who claimed that Justa had been born before her mother was manumitted, and had later been manumitted by Calatoria Themis herself.[10]

If both partners in a slave *contubernium* were legally manumitted[11] and wished to continue in a marital relationship, the union automatically became legal marriage. Funerary epitaphs erected by former slaves show the efforts many ex-slaves made to preserve and commemorate their unions and, if possible, free their slaveborn children from slavery [Rawson 1966; Bradley 1987, 47–52]. Children born thereafter were freeborn and legitimate. Those born before the union became marriage were, however, illegitimate, and if their mother had been a slave at their birth, they remained slaves of her former master.

If a slave *contubernium* were converted into a legal marriage, any non-legal "dowry" brought by the slavewoman might become legal also:

D.23.3.39 pr. (Ulpian): If a slavewoman gave (something) to a slaveman as a dowry, then, if they both arrive at freedom with the union still intact, and if their *peculium* has not been taken from them[12] and they have remained in the same union, the matter is so regulated that, if anything remained from the material goods given as if for the purpose of dowry during their time in slavery, this seems to have been tacitly converted into (legal) dowry, so that a valuation of it is owed to the woman.

On the other hand, it was possible that one partner might mistakenly think she or he was legally married when in fact the other partner's status precluded *iustum matrimonium*. Thus the emperor Caracalla replied to a woman named Hostilia, who was the victim of a case of mistaken identity:

Cod. Just. 5.18.3, 26 August, 215
Emperor Antoninus (Caracalla) Augustus to Hostilia:
If, in ignorance of Eros' status, you married[13] him as if a free man and gave him a dowry, and he afterwards was judged a slave, you will get your dowry back out of his *peculium*, along with anything else it appears that he

144

owed you. Moreover, your children are understood to be illegitimate free-born, as they were born from a free mother but an "uncertain" father. Posted on the sixth day before the Kalends of September in the second consulship of Laetus and the consulship of Cerealis.

Hostilia had married a man named Eros,[14] thinking he was free. But later it was revealed that he was a slave of someone else, who no doubt had reclaimed ownership. Hostilia had brought a "dowry" to what she assumed was a legal marriage, and when the union was broken up by Eros' return to slavery, she wanted to bring an action for its return. Legally, of course, it was not a dowry [see D.23.3.3 in Chapter 2, Part I.D], but since Hostilia was not at fault, the emperor ruled that she could recover what she had brought to the marriage (including the "dowry"), out of the funds that were customarily given to slaves by their masters (*peculium*). The same situation, where a free woman has unwittingly married a slave and given him a dowry, is mentioned by Ulpian in the *Digest* [24.22.13], where the woman's right to recover her dowry out of the slave's *peculium* is said to be "conceded as a privilege" to her.

Because children normally followed their mother's status in a non-legal marriage, the children she had with Eros are freeborn rather than slaves. But because slave family relationships were not legally recognized, Eros could not be considered the father, and the children were legally fatherless.

2 *The* senatusconsultum Claudianum

A union between a free man and a slavewoman was not penalized, except that it did not have the status of legal marriage and their children were slaves and illegitimate.[15] But a quasi-marital union between a free woman and a slaveman was more problematical. In part this was because of long-standing Roman ideas about gender and status hierarchy, which disapproved of relationships where the woman was socially superior to her partner [cf. Part I.B.3 below on *patrona*–freedman marriages]. But there was another, more practical, factor: whereas the children of a slavewoman by a free man would belong to her master (who would then benefit by the increase to his slave supply), the children engendered by a slaveman in union with a free woman would not belong to his master, but would be her own, freeborn, illegitimate children. This could deprive his owner of the possibility of slave offspring, and therefore be considered a financial loss.

In 52 C.E., Pallas, the powerful freedman of the emperor Claudius, proposed a law to meet this problem. Known as the *senatusconsultum Claudianum* ("Claudian decree of the Senate"), the law was probably intended to benefit especially the imperial household, whose male slaves frequently married free women [see Weaver 1972, 162–8; 1986, 150–4; for the *s.c. Claudianum* in late antiquity, see Part II.B.4.].

Tacitus, *Annales* XII.53 (written early 2nd c.)

Among the things which he (Claudius) referred to the senators (was a proposal) about the punishment of women who were joined with slaves. It was decided that, if the (slave's) master was ignorant (of the union), they would for that reason fall into slavery, but if he had consented, they would be considered his freedwomen. To Pallas, who Caesar (Claudius) had disclosed was the originator of this proposal, the consul designate Barea Soranus decreed the insignia of praetorian rank and fifteen million sesterces.... [the rest of the passage is omitted here]

145

Gaius, *Institutes* I.84: For observe that as a result of the *s.c. Claudianum*, a Roman citizen woman who joins with someone else's slave when his master is willing was able to remain free herself on the basis of this agreement, but to give birth to slaves. For that which was agreed between her and that slave's master is ordered to be ratified on the basis of the Senate's decree. But afterwards the deified Hadrian, moved by the policy's inequity and the law's inelegance, restored the rule of the law of nations:[16] that when the woman herself remains free, she gives birth to a free child.

> After Hadrian's modification of the original law, a free woman cohabiting with a slave without his master's permission became the master's slave, as did her children. If she had permission, she was reduced to the status of a freedwoman of her partner's master, but her children remained free.
>
> Around the beginning of the fourth century, the *Sent. Pauli* set forth a number of different scenarios in which a free woman would be affected by the law [Evans Grubbs 1993, 136–7]:

Sent. Pauli II.xxi^a (selections)

2 A daughter under her father's power (*filiafamilias*), if she has joined herself to someone else's slave without her father's knowledge or against his wishes, keeps her own (freeborn) status even after warning, since the parents' status cannot become worse by the children's act.[17]

10 If a daughter under her father's power has, at her father's command, entered into *contubernium* with someone else's slave against his master's will, she does become a slave, since parents are able to make their children's status worse.

12 If a woman who mistakenly thought she was a slave, and therefore entered into a *contubernium* with someone else's slave, has continued in the same *contubernium* after learning that she is free, she does become a slave.

13 If a *patrona* (former mistress) has joined herself to her freedman's slave, it has been decided that she not become a slave even after the warning.

16 If a mother has joined herself to her son's slave, the *s.c. Claudianum* does not remove the respectful reverence due to a mother, even in a shameful matter, by the example of the woman who has joined herself to her freedman's slave.[18]

18 A daughter in her father's power, if she has persevered in *contubernium* with a slave after her father's death, becomes a slave, consistent with the policy of the *s.c. Claudianum*.

3 Unions between women and their freedmen

In general, under the Empire marriage between freeborn people and former slaves (*libertini*, feminine *libertinae*) was legal; only members of senatorial families were forbidden to marry former slaves [see II.B.4 below].

Marriage between a former master (*patronus*) and his *liberta* was not uncommon, and funerary epitaphs record many such marriages. (There were those, however, who considered concubinage between a patron and his freedwoman to be more appropriate than marriage: see

Part I.B.5 below.) In fact, manumission "for the sake of marriage" (*matrimonii causa*) was a valid reason to free a slave under the legally-required age of thirty.[19] (Moreover, a woman freed in order to marry her master could not divorce him against his will: see Chapter 4, Part I.D.)

On the other hand, it was felt that marriage between a *female* patron (*patrona*) and her former slave (*libertus*) was inappropriate [Evans Grubbs 1993]. This was believed (by members of the elite, including the jurists and emperors commenting on such relationships) to be fitting only in the case of a woman who had been freed from slavery first and was freeing her former partner in slavery, a situation suggested also in funerary epitaphs [Flory 1984]:

D.40.2.14.1 (Marcian): There are those who think that even women can manumit "for the sake of marriage," but only if, by chance, her own fellow slave has been bequeathed to her for this reason.

D.23.2.62.1 (Papinian): A woman is joined to the freedman of her (former) husband or patron improperly.

D.23.2.13 (Ulpian): If a *patrona* is of such low birth (*ignobilis*) that even marriage with her own freedman is honorable for her, it (the marriage) ought not to be prohibited by the office of the judge holding a hearing on this matter.

Ulpian's statement (D.23.2.13, above) implies that *patrona–libertus* marriages where the woman was not herself of slave birth or low status were now considered illegal and subject to prosecution.[20] A rescript of Septimius Severus and Caracalla to a woman named Valeria bears this out:

Cod. Just. 5.4.3, 14 November, 196
Emperors Severus and Antoninus (Caracalla) to Valeria:
You will be able to lay charges against a freedman who dared to marry his patroness, or the daughter, wife, granddaughter, or great-granddaughter of his patron, with the appropriate judge. He will give a sentence in accordance with the *mores* of my reign, which have rightly considered such unions to be odious. The Ides of November in the second consulship of Dexter and the consulship of Priscus.

It is not clear what the legal grounds for such a prosecution would be. As a woman, Valeria could not herself bring a charge of *stuprum* or adultery; indeed, she could not undertake a prosecution except in cases involving her or her immediate family [see Chapter 1, Part V].

The *Sent. Pauli*, dating from the late third or early fourth century, gives the penalty for the freedman who "dared" to marry his former mistress:

***Sent. Pauli* II.xix.9:** It has been decided that a freedman, who has aspired to marriage with his *patrona* or with the wife or daughter of his patron, is to be suppressed by the penalty of the mines or the public works, depending on the rank of the person.[21]

Despite the legal restrictions on *patrona–libertus* marriages, funerary epitaphs indicate that they did take place [Evans Grubbs 1993, 130–1].

Some women may have hoped to avoid the law's consequences by not marrying their freedman, but living in *contubernium* with a slave. Christian writers of the early third century suggest that women of high status (presumably from senatorial families), who would lose their rank if they married someone of lower status, chose to cohabit with slaves or freedman instead.[22] A particularly egregious case of a free woman living in a monogamous relationship with her slave is known from a rescript of the emperors Diocletian and Maximian:

Cod. Just. 7.20.1, 18 June, 290

Emperors Diocletian and Maximian Augusti to Theodora:

You declare that your mother's slave both defiled his own mistress by illicit sexual relations (*stuprum*) and wished to cover up the stain of this shameful union by colluding, before the appropriate judicial authority, in a claim of pretended free birth and the cover of a (claim of) false captivity. Nor, you claim, did your mother actually free him, but she attempted to bring him into the condition of a freeborn person by a lie based purely on her own wish. It is thus clear that he is a slave, since he does not appear to have been made freeborn under the terms of the rescript of the deified Antoninus Pius concerning captivity – which you claim did not occur – nor did his claim of your consent have the power to confer the right of free birth. Posted on the fourteenth day before the Kalends of July in the consulship of Diocletian and Maximian.

Theodora claimed that her mother and her mother's slave had lived in an illicit sexual relationship (*stuprum*), which they had attempted to disguise by pretending that the slave had been born free, captured by barbarians, been redeemed from captivity by Theodora's mother, and then had gone through the process of reclaiming the right of free birth (*ingenuitas*) that he had supposedly lost in captivity. Now, it appears, her mother is dead, and Theodora wants the slave "husband" punished. A sexual relationship between a free woman and her slave was punishable as *stuprum* (if she were not married) or adultery (if she were), and, as we have seen, even marriage between a woman and her freedman was also subject to penalty. Theodora's mother and her slave had therefore (according to Theodora; we do not know if her accusation was true) colluded in a spurious claim of free birth for the slave – which was also punishable, if discovered [Evans Grubbs 1993, 137–40]. Under the legal circumstances, it was the only way Theodora's mother and her lover could hope to have their relationship considered marriage by those who did not know his true origins.

4 Unions between senators and former slaves

Augustus' *lex Julia de maritandis ordinibus* (Julian law on the Marrying of the Social Orders) forbade the marriage of a senator or his child or grandchild with a freedperson. The same restrictions applied to senatorial unions with others of low-degree: those who were public entertainers, or who were marked with legal infamy (*infamia*). Freeborn men who were not of senatorial rank could legally marry freedwomen other than prostitutes, procuresses or condemned adulteresses [McGinn 1998, 91–104; see Chapter 2, Part I.B].

The ramifications of the *lex Julia* elicited considerable juristic discussion. Several jurists, particularly Ulpian and Paulus, devoted entire books to the Augustan legislation, from which a number of the excerpts below and in Part I.B.5 (on concubines) were taken.[23]

D.23.2.44 pr. (Paulus): The Julian law decrees thus:
"Whoever is a senator, or whoever is or will be his son, or a grandson from a son, or a great-grandson born from a son, shall not knowingly or deceitfully have as fiancée or wife a freedwoman or a woman who herself or whose mother or father leads or has led a career on the stage. Nor shall the daughter of a senator, nor a granddaughter born from a son nor a great-granddaughter born from a grandson born from a son, knowingly and deceitfully be a fiancée or wife to a freedman or to a man who himself or whose father or mother leads or has led a career on the stage, nor shall any of those men deceitfully and knowingly have her as a fiancée or a wife."
D.23.2.23 (Celsus): The Papian Law decrees that all freeborn men except senators and their children are permitted to have a freedwoman as wife.

If a senator did want to live with a freedwoman as a wife, the marriage would not be in compliance with the Augustan marriage laws and therefore the partners would be subject to the penalties on their right to inherit [see Chapter 2, Part I.B]. That meant that they could not inherit from each other, or receive a legacy from anyone beyond the sixth degree of kinship:

Rules of Ulpian 16.2: Sometimes (husband and wife) receive nothing by inheritance from each other, that is, if they have contracted marriage against the Julian and Papian–Poppaean law. For instance, if anyone has married a woman with legal infamy, or if a senator has married a freedwoman.
D.23.2.44.6 (Paulus): If afterwards (that is, after she has already married a senator) the father or mother of a freeborn wife begins to lead a career on the stage, it is most unjust for him to have to dismiss her, since marriage was honorably contracted and perhaps children have already been born. 7: Of course, if she herself begins to lead a career on the stage, she must by all means be dismissed.
D.23.2.27 (Ulpian): If a member of the senatorial order has a freedwoman as a wife, though in the meantime (that is, while he is a senator) she is not a wife, however she is in such a situation that, if he should lose his rank, she shall begin to be his wife.

It was possible for senators, who of course had much more influence than ordinary citizens, to circumvent this law with imperial permission:

D.23.2.31 (Ulpian): If a senator has been permitted by the emperor's indulgence to have a freedwoman as a legitimate wife, she is able to be a legitimate wife.

Sometimes even senators might not know the legal status of their partner, as appears to have been the case with a senator who had been deceived into "marriage" with a freedwoman. Such a case came before the emperor Antoninus Pius (reigned 138–61):

D.23.2.58 (Marcian): It was stated in a rescript by the deified (Antoninus) Pius, that if a freedwoman has deceived a senator as if she were freeborn and has married him, a legal action should be given against her on the model of the Praetor's Edict, since she has no gain from a dowry which does not exist.

Since there could be no dowry in non-marital unions [cf. Cod. Just. 5.18.3 in Part I.B.1], a freedwoman who had brought what she considered dowry to a union with a senator could not get it back if the marriage ended, as a legally married wife could.

Augustus' general prohibition against marriage between members of the senatorial order and former slaves was strengthened in the second century by a ruling of Marcus Aurelius. This ruling said that marriage between a woman of senatorial status and a freedman was null and void, that is, it had none of the effects of legal marriage. Prior to this time, it appears that a marriage in contravention of the Augustan laws was evidently *iniustum matrimonium*, and still had some of the legal effects of marriage.[24] Marriage between a high-ranking woman and a low-ranking man was especially offensive to elite Roman sensibilities, because it ran counter to the assumption that the husband was the superior partner [Evans Grubbs 1993].

D.23.2.16 pr. (Paulus): A speech of the deified Marcus decrees that, if a senator's daughter has married a freedman, it is not marriage; and a decree of the Senate followed (the emperor's decision).

Even if her father was ejected from the senatorial order, she retained her rank, and so still could not marry a freedman:

D.23.2.34.3 (Papinian): Her father's fall from rank does not make the daughter of a senator who has married a freedman a (legal) wife. For rank (*dignitas*) that has been acquired should not be taken away from children on account of their father's crime.

Only if she lowered herself in society by engaging in a dishonorable profession (prostitution or acting) would she lose her rank and no longer be subject to the Augustan restrictions on marriage with former slaves:

D.23.2.47 (Paulus): A senator's daughter who has earned money with her body or has led a stage career or has been condemned in a public trial, can marry a freedman with impunity. For honorable rank is not preserved for one who has led herself into such shame.

5 Concubinatus *(concubinage)*

Concubinatus, usually translated as "concubinage," was a non-marital relationship that in Roman society served as an alternative to legitimate marriage. A Roman man would have a concubine instead of a wife, not in addition to a wife (though he might have mistresses, or casual sexual relationships with his slaves). *Concubinatus* was not illegal, but did not carry the legal rights of marriages: a concubine's children were not legitimate, and were not automatically the heirs of their father, as children born in legal marriage were. Normally the *concubina* was of a lower status than her man (there is no Latin word to describe the male partner in *concubinatus*), usually a freedwoman, though freeborn women of humble birth might be concubines [Rawson 1974; Treggiari 1981a].

The Augustan restrictions on marriage between men of senatorial status and freedwomen meant that a senator (or his son or grandson) who wished to have a monogamous relationship with a freedwoman had to live with her in *concubinatus* rather than marriage. Thus it has been said that Augustus' laws "indirectly encouraged the rise of respectable concubinage as an institution recognized in its own right" [McGinn 1991, 338]. This in turn led to juristic discussion of the status of concubines, especially regarding who could be a concubine without both partners risking prosecution for illicit sex (*stuprum*) under Augustus' adultery statute [see Chapter 2, Part I.B. on the adultery law].

It was sometimes difficult to tell if a woman was a wife or a concubine, but her status relative to that of her partner, and the way he treated her, were indicators. Concubines were generally of lower social status than wives. And if it appeared that the couple's intention was that she be a concubine rather than a wife, then presumably she was [Treggiari 1981a, 63]:

D.25.7.4 (Paulus): It is necessary (for a woman) to be considered a concubine solely on the basis of intention.

D.32.49.4 (Ulpian): Moreover, it matters little, whether someone leaves as a legacy to a wife or a concubine those things which were bought and provided for her sake. For of course there is no difference at all (between wife and concubine) except in rank (*dignitas*).

Thus the woman's status, relative to her partner's, could be an indication of which of the two she was intended to be [Treggiari 1981a, 63–4]. Former prostitutes, for instance, were more appropriately concubines:

D.23.2.24 (Modestinus): In regard to sexual intercourse with a free woman, marriage, not concubinage, ought to be understood, if she has not been a prostitute.[25]

D.25.7.3 pr. (Marcian): Both someone else's freedwoman and a freeborn woman can be held in concubinage, and especially a woman who was of low birth or has been a prostitute.[26]

If the woman was of appropriate status to be a concubine and was not married to someone else, the relationship was not adulterous:

D.25.7.3.1 (Marcian): Nor is adultery committed by a man through having a concubine. For because concubinage has taken its name through the laws, it is outside the penalty of the law, as Marcellus also wrote in the seventh book of his digests.

Most concubines were freedwomen rather than freeborn [Rawson 1974; Treggiari 1981a, 64–71]. A man might have his own freedwoman as a concubine rather than a wife (though,

151

unless he was of senatorial status, he could marry her; see Part I.B.4). Such a *liberta*-concubine was granted respect almost equal to that of a legally married wife of respectable standing:

D.23.2.41 (Marcellus): Dishonorable conduct is understood also in those women, who used to live shamefully and were prostitutes, even if not openly. And if any woman handed herself over into concubinage with someone other than her patron (former master), I say that she did not have the honor of a *materfamilias*.[27]

Indeed, Ulpian thought it was more socially appropriate for a freedwoman to be the concubine of her patron than his wife, unless he were himself of humble status [see Treggiari 1981a, 72]:

D.25.7.1 pr. (Ulpian): Will a woman who is in concubinage be able to leave her patron if he is unwilling, and to give herself to another either in marriage or in concubinage? I, at least, judge that the right of marriage (*conubium*) should be taken away from a concubine if she deserts her unwilling patron, since certainly it is more honorable for a patron to have his own freedwoman as concubine than as a *materfamilias*.

Just as a freedwoman married to her patron could not divorce him and marry someone else without his consent [see Chapter 4, Part I.D], so Ulpian believed that a freedwoman concubine should not take another partner without her patron's permission. He also thought that a man could bring charges against his *liberta*-concubine for adultery, though not as a husband but as a third party (*extraneus*):

D.48.5.14 pr. (Ulpian): If it was not a wife (caught) in adultery, but a concubine, he will not be able to accuse her with a husband's right, since she was not a wife. However, he will not be prevented from instituting an accusation by the right of a third party, if only she is a woman who did not lose the name of matron in giving herself in concubinage, as for instance, she who was the concubine of her patron.

Ulpian applied the same rules to concubinage as to marriage in other respects also, for instance in regard to the age when a girl could be a concubine [see Chapter 2, Part I.C.1 for age at marriage]:

D.25.7.1.4 (Ulpian): Clearly it is possible to have a concubine of any age whatsoever, unless she is under twelve years old.

Moreover, Ulpian thought that prohibitions on marriage with former in-laws should be applied to concubinage as well as marriage [cf. Gaius, *Institutes* I.63 and D.23.2.12.1 (Ulpian), in Part I.A.1]. The same sentiment appears in a rescript of Alexander Severus, below.

D.25.7.1.3 (Ulpian): If a woman was in concubinage to her patron, then began to be the concubine of his son or grandson, or vice versa, I do not think she behaves properly, since a union of this kind is almost wicked, and therefore a wicked act of this sort ought to be prohibited.

Cod. Just. 5.4.4, 11 April, 228

Emperor Alexander Augusti to Perpetuus:

Children are not able to take as wives the concubines of their parents, since they appear to be committing an act that is not at all pious (*religiosa*) or commendable. Those who have acted contrary to this are committing the crime of *stuprum* (illicit sex). The third day before the Ides of April in the consulship of Modestus and Probus.

In unions not recognized as legal marriage (*iustum matrimonium*), the usual rule against gifts between spouses [Chapter 2, Part I.E] did not apply. Thus a concubine, unlike a wife, could receive gifts from her partner. But if, as sometimes happened, a man later married the woman who had been his concubine, any gifts made after the union became marriage would be invalid. The point at which *concubinatus* became *matrimonium* could be difficult to pinpoint; again, the couple's intent and behavior toward each other would be the basis for judging [Treggiari 1991a, 51]:

D.39.5.31 pr. (Papinian): It is fitting that gifts given to a concubine are not able to be revoked, nor does what previously was legally valid become invalid, if marriage was later contracted between the same persons. However, I replied that we must carefully examine whether marital honor and sentiment already preceded (the giving of the gift) for some time previously, after comparing the persons involved and considering their way of life together. For marriage tablets do not make a marriage.[28]

The anomaly that a legitimate wife could not receive a gift from her husband during marriage, but someone in a non-marital relationship could, disturbed Ulpian:

D.24.1.32.28 (Ulpian): But if a senator has become betrothed to a freed-woman or a guardian to his ward or any other of those who are prohibited to join in marriage, and he has married her, would the gift be valid as if it were made during betrothal? And I should think indeed that these betrothals are to be condemned and that those gifts which are made, as if by unworthy people, are seized and claimed for the imperial treasury.

D.24.1.3.1 (Ulpian): Let us see between which people gifts have been prohibited. And indeed if a marriage stands according to custom and law, the gift will not be valid. But if some impediment should intervene, so that it not be marriage at all, the gift will be valid. Therefore if the daughter of a senator has married a freedman contrary to the decree of the Senate, or a provincial woman has married the man who governs her province or who gains (office) there, against the rules, the gift will be valid, since the marriage is not.[29] But it is not right for those gifts to be valid, nor should the situation of those who are transgressing be better. However, the deified

(Septimius) Severus ruled the opposite way in the case of the freedwoman of the senator Pontius Paulinus, because she was not considered with the disposition of a wife, but rather of a concubine.

Septimius Severus had decided that Pontius Paulinus had considered his freedwoman as a concubine, not a wife (as a senator he was prohibited from marrying her under the Augustan legislation, see I.B.4). Thus she could receive gifts from him. Ulpian does not like the decision, but his may have been a minority opinion [cf. Treggiari 1981a, 75].[30]

Papinian mentions another case, also decided by Septimius Severus, involving a man of senatorial status and his freeborn concubine (whom he could have married, since she was not a freedwoman; presumably she was of very humble status). He had named his illegitimate daughter by his concubine as a co-heir, and questions arose about the validity of her claim. Apparently the emperors (Septimius Severus and Caracalla) allowed Rufina to inherit despite her illegitimate status, though it is not clear exactly what their decision was. Some people evidently thought the relationship of Cassianus and Rufina was *stuprum* rather than *concubinatus*, and wished to deny the daughter's claim [see Rawson 1986a, 178–9; McGinn 1991, 354–7].

D.34.9.16.1 (Papinian): Since it has been agreed that (a charge of) *stuprum* is not incurred in the case of a woman who allows herself to be the concubine of someone other than her patron, an action will not be denied in regard to what was left in the will of the man who had (such a) concubine.[31] Our best and greatest emperors made this judgment regarding the will of Cocceius Cassianus, a man of senatorial status, who had loved and esteemed Rufina, a freeborn woman, with full honor. Her daughter, whom Cassianus had called his foster-daughter (*alumna*) in his will and had appointed as co-heir with his granddaughter, appeared to have been illegitimate.

C Other prohibitions

Several other types of unions were not considered valid marriage under Roman law, and in some cases were subject to penalty.

1 Unions between citizens and non-citizens

Before 212, another important status distinction was between Roman citizens and non-citizens. Roman citizens (including ex-slaves who had been formally manumitted by Roman citizens and thereby gained the citizenship themselves) had *conubium* (the right of legal marriage) with other Roman citizens. In general, they did not have the same right with non-Roman citizens (called peregrines), though there were some non-Roman citizens (for instance, Latins) who had been granted the right of marriage with citizens. Also, grants of citizenship to provincials who had served in the Roman army included the right to marry a Roman citizen, and the attendant consequences of *iustum matrimonium*, in particular the father's *potestas* over his children [on *patria potestas*, see Chapter 1, Part II.A].

Rules of Ulpian 5.4: Roman citizens have the right of marriage with Roman citizens; moreover, (they have the right of marriage) even with peregrines, if it has been allowed.

Gaius, *Institutes* I.56: Moreover, Roman citizens are understood to have contracted legitimate marriage and to have children born from it in their power, if they have married Roman citizen women or Latin or peregrine women with whom they have the right of marriage. For it happens that, because the right of marriage results in children following their father's status, not only do they (the children) become Roman citizens, but they are also in their father's power. **57:** Therefore imperial constitutions customarily grant also to certain veterans the right of marriage with those Latin or peregrine women whom they have first taken as wives after their release from service. And those who are born from this marriage become both Roman citizens and in their father's power.

***Rules of Ulpian* 5.8:** If there is the right of marriage between (the couple), the children always follow the father (i.e., have their father's status). If there is no right of marriage, they enter upon their mother's status. The exception is that a child who is born from a peregrine man and a Roman citizen woman is a peregrine, since the Minician law orders that one born from either a father or mother peregrine follows the status of the parent whose status is lower.[32] **9:** From a Roman citizen male and a Latin woman, a Latin is born, and from a free man and a slave woman, a slave is born, since, because there is no right of marriage in these cases, the offspring follow their mother (i.e., have her status).

In unions between partners of different citizen status who did not have *conubium*, as in other unions which Roman law did not consider legitimate marriage (e.g., between free people and slaves), any children born took the status of their mother, not their father as in legitimate marriage. Consequently, such children would not fall under their father's *potestas*.

From the extensive discussion Gaius devotes to it, it appears that ignorance of citizen identity was quite common, and (mainly in the provinces) Roman citizens might unwittingly marry a non-citizen. Unless the partners had *conubium*, the children of such unions would not be Roman citizens or fall under their father's *potestas* (since *patria potestas* was a feature of Roman marriage only). It was so possible to make a mistake in determining one's citizenship or the citizenship of one's spouse that the Roman Senate passed legislation on the matter:[33]

Gaius, *Institutes* I.67: If a Roman citizen man has married a Latin or peregrine wife through ignorance, because he believed that she was a Roman citizen, and has begotten a son, this (son) is not in his power, because he is not even a Roman citizen, but either a Latin or peregrine. That is, his status was that of his mother, since a person does not achieve his father's status other than if his mother and father have the right of marriage together. But by a decree of the Senate it is permitted to prove a case of error, and so the wife also and the son arrive at Roman citizenship, and from that time the son begins to be in his father's power ... **68:** Likewise, if a Roman citizen woman has married a peregrine man through error, as if he were a Roman citizen, it is permitted to her to prove a case of error, and so also her son and her husband arrive at Roman citizenship, and equally the son begins to be in his father's power.... **72:** We should understand whatever we have said to be

155

the case regarding a son to apply likewise regarding a daughter.... **75:** ... However, if no error has occurred, but they joined together knowing their own status, the defect in this marriage is not emended by any event.... **87:** In those cases, however, in which a child follows his mother's status and not his father's, it is more than obvious that he is not in his father's power, even if he is a Roman citizen....

Other marriage prohibitions arose because the social relationship between partners might have enabled the husband to have undue power over his wife or her property.

2 *Marriage between* tutor *and* pupilla

A law banning marriage between a fatherless minor girl (*pupilla*) and her guardian (*tutor* or *curator*) or his son was enacted during the joint reign of Marcus Aurelius and his son Commodus (177–180). Exception was made only if the girl's father had explicitly stated before his death that he wanted the marriage. The reason for the ban was to prevent a conflict of interest: "so that female wards not be defrauded of their family property by those who are compelled to render acounts of the guardianship to them, after the guardianship has ended" [D.23.2.64.1, Callistratus below]. [On guardianship, see Chapter 1, Part II.C.]

D.23.1.15 (Modestinus): A *tutor* is not able to marry his *pupilla* himself nor to join her to his son in marriage. You should know, moreover, that what we discuss in regard to marriage pertains also to betrothal.

D.23.2.66 (Paulus): It is not (legal) marriage, if a *tutor* or *curator* marries his own *pupilla* or marries her to his son before she has turned twenty-six, if she was not betrothed (to him) by her father or intended (for him) by (the father's) will. If this is done, each party suffers legal infamy and is subject to legal penalty, according to the rank of the *pupilla*.

D.48.5.7 (Marcian): If someone marries his own *pupilla* contrary to the Senate's decree, this is not marriage, and the *tutor* or *curator* who married a woman under twenty-six who was not betrothed by her father or designated or named (as such) in his will can be accused of adultery.

D.30.128 (Marcian): If a *tutor* has married his *pupilla* contrary to the decree of the Senate, she indeed is able to take under his will, but he himself is not able to (take under her will). And deservedly so: for they do wrong, who contract prohibited marriages and they should be punished deservedly. But fault is not able to be imputed to the woman, who was deceived by her *tutor*.

D.23.2.59 (Paulus): A grandson is understood also in the decree of the Senate, which forbids a *tutor* to marry his *pupilla* or to place her in marriage to his son.

D.23.2.64 (Callistratus): The Senate decided that a freedman, who was likewise the *tutor* of a *pupilla*, should be relegated (exiled without loss of citizenship or property), because she was given in marriage to the *tutor* himself or with his son.

3 Marriage between imperial officials and locals

Roman government officials or military officials were also prohibited from marrying women in the province in which they served:

D.23.2.38 (Paulus): If anyone administers an office in a province, he is not able to marry a woman who originated or is living there. However, he is not forbidden to become betrothed to her, of course so that, if after he has laid down his office the woman should prefer not to contract the marriage, she may do this as long as she has returned the marriage pledges (*arrhae*) which she had accepted.[34] 1: A man is able to marry a fiancée of long standing (i.e., one to whom he was betrothed before he took office) in the province where he administers some office, and the dowry that is given does not become forfeit to the imperial fisc. 2: A man who administers an office in a province is not forbidden from placing his own daughters in marriage in that province and from constituting a dowry.

In both this case and the ban on *tutor–pupilla* marriage, the prohibition was based on the possibility that the guardian or the provincial official, being in a position of authority and responsibility over the person or the property of the *pupilla* or provincial respectively, would abuse his power:

D.23.2.63 (Papinian): The prefect of a cohort or the prefect of cavalry or a tribune has married a wife of that province in which he carried out his office, contrary to the prohibition: it will not be (legal) marriage. This case should be compared to that of a female ward, since the concern for (his) power (over her) has forbidden it. But it is debatable whether, if indeed the maiden has married him, what was left to her by will should not be taken away from her. However, by the example of a ward married to her tutor, the woman is able to obtain what has been left to her. However, it is necessary that the money given as dowry be returned to the woman's heir.

D.34.9.2.1 (Marcian): Likewise if anyone has, against his orders, married a woman from the province in which he carries out some office, the deified (Septimius) Severus and Antoninus (Caracalla) wrote in a rescript that he is not able to keep what he acquired from his wife's will, just as if a *tutor* had led his *pupilla* (as wife) into his own home contrary to the decree of that most magnificent order (the Senate). Therefore, in both cases, though he has entered upon the inheritance, having been instituted sole heir, it becomes an occasion for the fisc (imperial treasury) to step in. For he is deprived of the inheritance as an unworthy person.

Relationships between Roman officials and women in the provinces in which they were serving were not totally prohibited, only legal marriage [on concubines, see Part II.B.5]:

D.25.7.5 (Paulus): A man can have a concubine in the province in which he holds an administrative position.

Moreover, the relationship could become legitimate marriage later, as we see in this rescript (response) from the emperor Gordian to a petition from a woman Valeria, who was perhaps concerned about the status of her own marriage and offspring. The ruling of Paulus (the jurist) to which Gordian refers is found at D.23.2.65.1.

Cod. Just. 5.4.6, 20 August, 239
Emperor Gordian Augustus to Valeria:

Though marriage was contracted in the province with the woman's consent against the mandates of former emperors, however, after the office has been laid down, if she still persists in the same desire (to be married), the marriage will become legally valid. And therefore, the response of that most sagacious man Paulus declares that children born and brought up afterwards from legal marriage (*iustum matrimonium*) are legitimate. The twelfth day before the Kalends of September in the consulship of Gordian Augustus and Aviola.

4 Marriage of soldiers while in service

Another rule, apparently made by Augustus,[35] forbade soldiers to be married while in service (high-ranking officers could marry, as long as their wives were not provincials; see I.C.3 above). This applied both to those in the legions, who already had Roman citizenship before enlisting, and to the auxiliaries, who comprised non-citizens (peregrines). Soldiers might form liaisons with women in the provinces where they were serving, but these were not legal marriages and their children were not legitimate [Gardner 1986a, 33–5; Youtie 1975]. Once the soldier had completed his term of service, the woman he was living with could become his legal wife, and children born after that time would come under his power (see below). But if he died while still a soldier, any dowry that the woman had given to him could not be reclaimed, and children born during that time were illegitimate and could not inherit from him on intestacy. We know from the records of court cases in Egypt that this could cause great hardship and distress for both the soldiers and their families [Anagnostou-Cañas 1984, 343–5; Youtie 1975; see Campbell 1994, 154–6 for translation of M.Chr. 372].

Hadrian (reigned 117–138) ameliorated the situation somewhat for the illegitimate children by enabling them to inherit from their fathers by intestate succession as cognates (though any legitimate children that the father might have would have precedence), and by the time of Marcus Aurelius (161–180), a soldier could name his illegitimate children and their mother as heirs in his will [Campbell 1994, 157–8]. However, it seems that it was not until the reign of Septimius Severus (193–211) that soldiers were allowed to be married while still in service [Campbell 1978].[36]

Upon completion of his term of service (twenty years for legionaries, twenty-five years for auxiliaries), a soldier received certain privileges, including Roman citizenship (for non-citizens), the right of marriage (*conubium*) with the woman with whom he had been living in a non-legal union, and citizenship for his partner and children by her. Children born before his discharge evidently received citizenship, but apparently did not come under their father's *potestas*, whereas those children born after the union became legal did [Campbell 1984,

439–45; cf. Dixon 1992, 55–8]. Under Antoninus Pius (reigned 138–161), this benefit was partly rescinded in the case of auxiliaries: though they continued to receive citizenship and *conubium* with the woman of their choice, and citizenship for their children born after discharge, any children they had had in a non-legal union while still in service did not receive citizenship [Campbell 1984, 444].

Gaius, *Institutes* I.57: Whence also to certain veterans imperial constitutions customarily concede the right of marriage (*conubium*) with those Latin or peregrine women whom they first took as wives after their discharge. And those who are born from this marriage become both Roman citizens and under the power of their parents.[37]

Auxiliaries, sailors, and members of the prestigious Praetorian Guard and the Urban Cohorts received certificates of discharge recounting these privileges, and many of these certificates, called *diplomata* from the fact that they were in the form of two sheets of bronze fastened together to make a diptych, have survived. Legionaries generally did not receive *diplomata* upon leaving the army, but probably did receive the privileges of *conubium* and citizenship for their partners and children. In 140, the privilege of citizenship for the non-citizen partner and children born during service was abolished for auxiliaries, though not for legionaries [Campbell 1984, 439–45; 1994, 193–202; Wells 1997].

This *diploma* is from the first sheet of a bronze diptych found in the Roman province of Moesia Superior, now in the Belgrade museum. The names of seven witnesses would have been written on the second sheet of the *diploma*, which is not extant.[38]

ILS 9055, 29 June, 120

Emperor Caesar Trajan Hadrian Augustus, son of the deified Trajan Parthicus, grandson of the deified Nerva, chief priest (*pontifex maximus*), in the fourth year of his tribunician power, consul for the third time, gave to the infantry whose names are written below, who served in the cohort first Flavian Bessians, which is in Macedonia under Octavius Antoninus, who have been released with an honorable discharge after completing twenty-five years of service: citizenship to them, their children and their descendants, and the right of marriage (*conubium*) with the wives which they had at the time when they were given citizenship; or, if any of them were unmarried, (the right of marriage) with those whom they married afterwards, as long as each man has only one wife.[39] On the third day before the Kalends of July in the consulship of C. Publicius Marcellus and L. Rutilius Propinquus.

Of the cohort first Flavian Bessians, of which A. Aelius Sollemnianus is in command, from the infantry: to M. Antonius Timus, son of Timus, of Hierapolis, and to his wife Tioroturma daughter of Dotochas of Tricornum (?), and to his son Secundus, and to his daughter Marcellina.

Recorded and authenticated from the bronze tablet which has been affixed at Rome on the wall behind the temple of the deified Augustus at (the statue of?)[40] Minerva.

5 Marriage to two women simultaneously

Finally, it should be said that it was impossible in Roman law for a man to have a marital relationship with two women at the same time, without divorcing one woman to marry another [Gardner 1986a, 91–3]:

Cod. Just. 5.5.2, 11 December, 285
Emperors Diocletian and Maximian Augusti to Sebastiana:

It is allowed to no one who is under Roman authority to be able to have two wives openly, since even in the Praetor's Edict men of this sort have been branded with legal infamy (*infamia*). The appropriate judge will not allow this matter to go unpunished. Posted on the third day before the Ides of December in the consulship of the Augustus Diocletian for the second time and of Aristobulus.

Sebastiana may have been one of the "wives" of a bigamous man, who was concerned about the status of her marriage. Another woman, Theodora, wrote to the emperors Valerian and Gallienus after discovering that she had "married" a man who already had a wife. She feared that she might be liable for adultery charges and wondered whether she could still claim the betrothal gifts he had promised her. The emperors' rather lengthy reply was divided in two by the compilers of the *Code of Justinian*:

Cod. Just. 9.9.18, 15 May, 258
Emperors Valerian and Gallienus Augusti and the Caesar to Theodora:

Without a doubt legal infamy attends the man who had two wives at the same time, for in this matter it is not the effect of the law – since our citizens are forbidden to contract multiple marriages – but the intention that is considered. (1) Moreover, the accusation of *stuprum* also will be formally brought by a legally authorized accuser against the man who asked for your hand in marriage, pretending that he was unmarried, when he had left another *materfamilias* in the province. But you are free from this charge, because you believed that you were a wife. (2) Certainly you will request from the governor of the province that all your possessions, which you lament were taken by him under the pretense of marriage, be restored to you by immediate requisition. But those things, which he promised he would give you as his fiancée, how can you effectively reclaim them as if you were (legally) a fiancée? Received at Antioch on the Ides of May in the consulship of Tuscus and Bassus.

Cod. Just. 5.3.5 (address omitted):
You cannot effectively reclaim those things which the man who asked for your hand in marriage promised he would give you as his fiancée, pretending that he was unmarried when he had left another *materfamilias* at home, since you were not a fiancée because he had a wife established at home. (date omitted)

As a bigamist, the man who "married" Theodora will suffer *infamia*, which would entail certain legal disabilities such as not being able to represent others in court [Gardner 1993,

160

110–18]. More seriously, he could be prosecuted for *stuprum*, illicit sex with a respectable woman, which carried severe criminal penalties under the Augustan adultery law [see Chapter 2, Part I.B]. Theodora, as she had considered herself a married woman, was not liable for *stuprum*, and could reclaim what she had given her spurious husband, but could not claim any betrothal gifts promised (though evidently not already given) to her.

The other "wife" of Theodora's "husband" is described as a *materfamilias* [see Chapter 1, Part I.B], indicating that, like Theodora, she was a respectable woman and his relationship with her could therefore be construed as marriage. The man had been able to deceive Theodora into marrying him because his first wife was back in his home province, and there would be no easy way for Theodora to check on his past. One wonders how she had eventually learned of the other wife's existence.

In 393, the emperor Theodosius explicitly prohibited polygamy, in the context of a ban on "Jewish" marriage customs [see Part II.D].

II Prohibited and non-marital unions in late antiquity

Late Roman law, like classical law, denied legal validity to some unions. As with classical law, most of these prohibitions were based on close kinship or on great disparity in the status of the partners. In late antiquity, however, the number of prohibitions increased, in regard both to kinship and status. And penalties for those disobeying prohibitions based on status are much harsher in the late period, with corporal punishment and even death replacing what had been mostly financial penalties – or simply lack of legal recognition – for non-marital unions in the earlier Empire.

A *Prohibitions based on kinship*

A law of 342 banned all uncle–niece marriage, thereby implicitly revoking the first-century senatorial decree which had allowed marriage between a woman and her father's brother [see Chapter 3, Part I.A.2]. The law was specifically addressed to residents of Phoenicia (modern Lebanon), and was enacted in Antioch (in ancient Syria, now in southern Turkey), which was an imperial seat. This region had a tradition of close-kin marriage, which emperors sought to suppress: about 50 years earlier, Diocletian and Maximian had enacted a long edict from Damascus (also in Phoenicia) strongly condemning them [in Part I.A.5]. The "capital penalty" in the fourth century could be death or exile. Whether such punishments were actually applied in cases of incestuous marriage in this period is unknown; both legal and non-legal sources suggest that it was not difficult for those with influence to obtain an imperial dispensation for close-kin marriages [see selection from Ambrose, below, and Cod. Theod. 3.10.1 in II.C]. The penalty in the following law was mitigated somewhat by Cod. Theod. 3.12.3 [below].

Cod. Theod. 3.12.1, 31 March, 342

Emperors Constantius and Constans Augusti to the Phoenician Provincials:

If anyone has believed – abominably – that the daughter of a brother or a sister should be made a wife, or has flown into her embrace not as a paternal or maternal uncle, he shall be held by the penalty of a capital sentence.

Given at Antioch on the day before the Kalends of April in the third consulship of Constantius and the second consulship of Constans Augusti.[41]

Classical law had prohibited the marriage of a man with his former mother-in-law or daughter-in law [Gaius, *Institutes* I.63, Part I.A.1], but it is only in late Roman law that unions between former siblings-in-law are banned. The provisions of the following law were repeated in later laws of the emperors Theodosius I [Cod. Just. 5.5.5, dated 393] , Theodosius II [Cod. Theod. 3.12.4, 412], and Zeno [Cod. Just. 5.5.8, 475; see below]. Similar prohibitions are found in the rulings of fourth-century church councils, and the imperial laws were probably influenced by Christianity. [42]

Cod. Theod. 3.12.2, 30 April, 355

Emperors Constantius and Constans[43] Augusti and Julian Caesar to Volusianus, praetorian prefect:

Though the ancients believed that it was legal to take a brother's wife after the brother's marriage had been dissolved, (and) even legal after a wife's death or divorce to contract marriage with her sister, everyone should abstain from marriage of this sort nor should they think that legitimate children are able to be created from this association. For it is agreed that those who will be born are illegitimate (*spurii*).

Given at Rome on the day before the Kalends of May in the consulship of Arbitio and Lollianus.

The emperor Theodosius I (reigned 379–395) banned marriage between first cousins. His law is no longer extant, but is referred to in contemporary non-legal sources [*Epitome de Caesaribus* 48.10; and see Ambrose and Augustine below] and in the following laws, enacted after his death.

The first law [Cod. Theod. 3.12.3], enacted only a year after Theodosius' death, mitigates the apparently extremely harsh provisions of the original law (confiscation of goods and exile), while still refusing legitimacy to incestuous marriages and their offspring. Another law nine years later [Cod. Just. 5.4.19] rescinds the ban on cousin marriage altogether. Though in the names of both the sons of Theodosius, Honorius who ruled the western Empire and Arcadius who ruled in the east, these laws are both of Arcadius, as the places of promulgation (Constantinople and Nicaea, both cities of the eastern Empire) and addressee (Eutychianus, praetorian prefect in the east) show. In the western Empire, marriage between cousins continued to be illegal, but a law of 409 suggests that imperial indulgences allowing such marriages were regularly granted [see Cod. Theod. 3.10.1, 409, in Part II.C].

Cod. Theod. 3.12.3, 8 December, 396

Emperors Arcadius and Honorius Augusti to Eutychianus, praetorian prefect:

The imperial opinion remains concerning those who were absolved or punished in any way after the law which was formerly enacted. If anyone after this has polluted himself with incestuous (marriage) of his own cousin, or of the daughter of either his sister or his brother, or finally, of his (brother's) wife, whose marriage has been prohibited and condemned,[44] he shall indeed be free from the penalty designated by the (previous) law, that is, of fires and proscription; he shall even have his own property for as long as he lives. But he shall be believed to have neither a wife nor children born from her, he shall certainly neither give while alive nor bequeath when dead anything to those mentioned above, not even through an intermediary. The dowry, if by chance according to custom it has been either given or stated or

162

promised, shall, according to the ancient law, yield to the advantage of our fisc.

He shall bequeath nothing by his will to unrelated parties, but whether (he has died) testate or intestate, those persons shall succeed to him rightfully and by the laws, who by chance have been born from a legal and legitimate marriage. That is, from descendants: son, daughter, grandson, granddaughter, great-grandson, great-granddaughter; from ascendants: father, mother, grandfather, grandmother; laterally: brother, sister, paternal uncle, paternal aunt. [In a sentence here omitted, the law goes on to say that if those who are allowed to inherit have advised or helped in making the incestuous marriage, they may not succeed, but are passed over in favor of the next eligible heir.]

Of course, that which we decree concerning men also is to be observed concerning women who have stained themselves by associations of the aforementioned kinds. But if none of the people mentioned before are living, the opportunity lies open for the fisc. If by chance any already in the past – that is, before the promulgation of this law – have been somehow able to lie hidden, stained by the illicit crimes of the marriages mentioned above, we order that the bond and status of this law pertains (to them).

Given at Constantinople on the sixth day before the Ides of December in the fourth consulship of Arcadius and third consulship of Honorius Augusti.

Cod. Just. 5.4.19, 11 June, 405

Emperors Arcadius and Honorius Augusti to Eutychianus, praetorian prefect:

By the salubrious nature of this law, license has been granted for celebrating marriages between cousins, so that now that the authority of the old law has been revoked and the fomenting of slanders has been extinguished, marriage between cousins is to be considered legitimate, whether (the participants) have been born from two brothers or from two sisters or from a brother and a sister. And from this marriage legitimate (children) are produced and considered to be heirs to their own fathers.

Given at Nicaea on the third day before the Ides of June in the second consulship of Stilicho and the consulship of Anthemius.

The actual frequency of close-kin marriage in the Roman Empire has been debated [Shaw and Saller 1984, Goody 1983]. Evidence from the fourth and fifth centuries suggests that late Roman senatorial aristocrats considered marriage with relatives, either by blood or marriage, to be an appropriate way of keeping estates and inheritances within the family, but it is not usually possible to determine how closely related were the aristocrats who actually married [Evans Grubbs 1995, 153].

Marriage between the offspring of siblings does seem to have caused some discomfort in the Roman west. In the early 390s Ambrose, bishop of Milan, wrote to the senator Paternus, who had served as proconsul of Africa under Theodosius I, protesting a marriage which Paternus was arranging between his son Cynegius and his granddaughter (from his daughter by another wife).[45] Marriage between a man and his sister's daughter had always been illegal under Roman law [Part I.A.2], but this did not seem to worry Paternus, who was apparently confident of getting imperial permission for the match. Ambrose, on the other hand, was alarmed at the proposed marriage, and invokes both divine and imperial law in his arguments.

Another letter of Ambrose [*Epistle* 59 (84)], written to Cynegius, reveals that the son was not particularly happy about his proposed marriage but was acceding to it out a sense of filial duty (*pietas*). It may be, however, that despite Ambrose's protests, the marriage took place.[46]

Ambrose, *Epistle* 58 (60)

(1) I have read the greeting of Paternus, my comrade, but the matter about which you consult me is not at all paternal: that you wish to join your granddaughter from your daughter to your son – a proposal worthy of you neither as grandfather or as father. And so consider what you have consulted about. For in regard to everything which we wish to do, let us first examine the name of the deed and then we will determine whether it is worthy of praise or vituperation. ...

(2) ... You are preparing to join your own son and your granddaughter from your daughter, that is, (you are preparing) that he receive the daughter of his own sister, though he was born from a mother different from his mother-in-law. Examine the piety (*religio*) of the names. For indeed he is called her uncle, and she his niece. ... You will be called grandfather and father-in-law alike, and she also will be named granddaughter and daughter-in-law by a different name. ...

(3) ... For what is there that can be doubted, when divine law even prohibits paternal cousins, who are associated in the fourth degree, to join in marriage? But this (marriage) is the third degree, which seems to have been removed from conjugal joining even in civil law. ...

[Ambrose gives scriptural and moral arguments against the marriage, here omitted.]

(8) But if divine matters pass you by, at least the precepts of the emperors, from whom you have received the most splendid honor, ought by no means to bypass you. For the emperor Theodosius has also forbidden that paternal and maternal cousins come together among themselves in the name of marriage, and he has ordained a very severe penalty, if anyone should have dared to defile the bonds of brotherly duty....

(9) But you say that (the law) has been relaxed for some people; however, this does not prejudice the law. That which is not decreed in common, only benefits the person for whom it seems to have been relaxed with a very different sort of envy. Moreover, though we read in the Old Testament that someone called his own sister "wife," it is unheard-of that anyone should receive his own niece as wife and call her "spouse." ...

(11) Therefore it is necessary for you to depart from this intention, which even if it were permitted, still would not propagate your own family. For our son owes grandchildren to you, (and) our very dear granddaughter also owes great-grandchildren to you. Farewell (to you) with all of yours.

At the end of his letter, Ambrose reminded Paternus that marrying close relations to each other would restrict the extension of family bonds. In book 16 of his massive work *City of*

God, written in the early fifth century, Augustine of Hippo gives much the same rationale against kin marriage, especially between cousins.[47] Though in early (Old Testament) times, Augustine says, patriarchs practiced close-kin marriage because of the lack of available partners outside the family, now men are able to extend their range of relationships and influence far beyond their kin. Moreover, according to Augustine, though cousin marriage had only recently been restricted by law, it had never been a popular option. In addition to practical considerations (the desirability of extending family ties), it went against modesty and family feeling for the same person to be both a blood relation and a sexual partner (Ambrose had made much the same point in his letter to Paternus).

Augustine, *City of God* XV.16

... Moreover, who would doubt that the marriages even of cousins have more honorably been prohibited at this time, not only according to those reasons we have argued, so that on account of the multiplying of relationships one person would not have two bonds of kinship when two (people) could have them and the number of kin could be increased, but also because there is in some way or other a certain natural and laudable quality of human shame (*verecundia*). So that, from her to whom the reason of kinship owes reverend honor, it nevertheless restrains the lust about which we see even wifely modesty blush, though it results in children.

Both Ambrose and Augustine lived in the Latin-speaking milieu of the Roman west, where marriage between close kin had always been frowned upon in law and custom [Part I.A]. If Augustine is right, Romans had never favored cousin marriage, and it is worth noting that though the western emperor Honorius showed himself willing to grant indulgences to (presumably influential) citizens who wished to marry against the law [Cod. Theod. 3.10.1 in Part II.C], he did not actually repeal his father Theodosius' law, whereas his brother Arcadius in the east did [Cod. Just. 5.4.19, above]. In the medieval west, limits on close-kin marriage became ever stricter, particularly under the direction of the Christian Church [Goody 1983].

Many of the peoples of the eastern half of the Empire, however, had traditionally practiced marriage unions between kin, including between uncle and niece and even siblings (or half-siblings). Though the imposition of Roman marriage law on provincials after 212 seems to have largely eliminated brother–sister marriage in Egypt, it is clear from later Roman laws that close-kin marriage continued in some places. Both Diocletian in 295 [Part I.A.5] and Constantius in 342 [Cod. Theod. 3.12.1, above] had directed legislation to Near Eastern provinces. In the mid-fifth century, Theodoret, bishop of Cyrrhus in northern Syria, heard that in the nearby city of Zeugma, marriages between uncle and niece and between cousins were taking place. In a strongly worded letter to the magistrates of Zeugma, Theodoret made the same arguments against such unions as had Ambrose fifty years earlier.[48] Legislation of the sixth-century emperors Justinian and Justin indicates that close-kin marriage, evidently including sibling and even father–daughter unions, was still practiced in parts of the eastern Empire near to the Persian Empire [Lee 1988]. Cousin marriage was, however, officially allowed by Justinian in his *Institutes* [I.10.4] of 533.

A law of the eastern Empire dated 475 bans the marriage of a man to his deceased brother's wife. This practice, known as "levirate marriage," was an ancient Jewish custom [see *Deuteronomy* 25.5–10], but seems to have been practiced rarely by Jews in the period after the First Jewish Revolt and destruction of the Temple [Ilan 1995, 152–7]. Along with marriage to a former wife's sister, marriage to a brother's wife had already been prohibited in 355 [Cod. Theod. 3.12.2, above]. The law of 475, however, refers only to a brother's marrying the still-virgin wife of his deceased brother, which is called a practice of "the Egyptians."

Cod. Just. 5.5.8, 1 September, 475

Emperor Zeno[49] Augustus to Epinicus, praetorian prefect:

Certain of the Egyptians have joined the wives of their dead brothers to themselves in marriage, because they (the wives) are said to have remained virgins after their (husbands') death, evidently thinking – because it was pleasing to certain founders of the laws – that marriage does not really appear to have been contracted since they had not come together carnally; and marriages celebrated at that time have been confirmed. However, we ordain by the present law that if any marriages of this type have been contracted, their contractors and those born from them are subject to the tenor of the ancient laws, nor do they (the marriages) appear to have been confirmed or confirmable by the example of the Egyptians, concerning whom we spoke above.

Given at Constantinople on the Kalends of September in the year after the consulship of the younger Leo.

B Prohibitions based on status

In addition to marriage prohibitions based on kinship, late Roman emperors expanded the category of prohibitions based on status, and decreed harsher penalties for those who entered into prohibited unions.

1 Expansion of the Augustan prohibitions

The Augustan legislation against marriages between members of the senatorial class and former slaves [Part II.B.4] was expanded to include members of provincial and municipal aristocracies, and the category of women who were prohibited from marrying such men was likewise expanded [Evans Grubbs 1995, 283–94; McGinn 1999]. A late law of Constantine set forth his new rules:[50]

Cod. Theod. 4.6.3, 21 July, 336

Emperor Constantine Augustus to Gregorius (praetorian prefect):

It is decided that senators or *perfectissimi*,[51] or those in the cites whom the duumvirate or the office of quinquennal or the distinctions of the office of flamen or a provincial priesthood adorn,[52] are to undergo the stain of *infamia* and become peregrines under Roman laws,[53] if, either by their own judgment or by the right of a rescript from us, they have wished to consider among the number of (their) legitimate children those who have been begotten from:

a slavewoman or the daughter of a slave woman or his freedwoman or (the daughter) of his freedwoman, whether one made a Roman citizen or a Latin,[54] or an actress or the daughter (of an actress), or a tavern-keeper or the daughter of a tavern-keeper, or a humble or despicable woman (*vel humili vel abiecta*) or the daughter of a pimp or a gladiator or a woman who has been in

166

charge of publicly sold merchandise. So that, whatever their father has given to such children, whether he has called them legitimate or natural,[55] is to be taken back in its entirety and given to his legitimate offspring[56] or to his brother or sister or father or mother.

But whatever of any kind has been given to such a wife[57] or has been conferred upon her by bill of sale, this also we order to be taken back and returned.[58] If anything that is to be returned to those to whom we have ordered or to our fisc[59] is sought or is said to have been entrusted (to such women), we order that the women themselves, by whose poisons the minds of the ruined men have been infected, (be subjected) to tortures. And so if anything has been given through the man himself who is said to be the father or through another or through a fraudulently substituted person[60] or has been bought by him or by another or in the name of the (illegitimate children) themselves, it is immediately to be taken back and returned to those to whom we have ordered, or, if they do not exist, it is to be claimed by the power of the imperial fisc. But if, though they exist and are present[61] they were not willing to act, prevented by an agreement or an oath, the fisc shall enter upon the whole without delay.

For those who are silent or are lying, a time limit of two months shall be set to defend themselves from the fisc. If within this time they have not either withdrawn (the property from the illegitimate children) or appealed to the provincial governor in regard to withdrawing (the property), our fisc shall taken possession of whatever an impure generosity bestowed on such children or wives, seeking out with severe torture the things given or entrusted, under a fourfold penalty.[62]

Moreover, the son of Licinnianus, who has been captured while fleeing, is to be bound with fetters and condemned to the service of the weaving mills at Carthage.[63]

Read out at Carthage on the [twelfth] day before the Kalends of August in the consulship of Nepotianus and Facundus.[64]

The list of women whom senators and provincial and local notables are forbidden to marry includes not only freedwomen and actresses, who had been legally ineligible for marriage with senators and their descendants under the Augustan laws [see Part I.B.4] but also slaves, who had never under Roman law been able to contract legal marriage [Part I.B.1]. Prostitutes, who under classical law could not marry any freeborn man (including, of course, senators), are not explicitly mentioned in Cod. Theod. 4.6.3, but presumably are among those in the "humble and despicable" category. The other women mentioned would have been of very low status; gladiators and pimps were legally classified with prostitutes as subject to infamy (*infamia*), and tavern-keepers were subject to other legal disabilities in late Roman law (female tavern-keepers were equated with prostitutes in a law of Constantine on adultery prosecutions).[65] Constantine was not only extending the category of high-status men for whom lowborn women were ineligible as legal wives, but also extending the category of women whose birth or occupation rendered them ineligible [McGinn 1999].

Moreover, women in the prohibited group who did receive something from high-ranking men, or whose children by those men received something, were threatened with torture. Torture would in general only be appropriate to people of slave or very low status, and is here (as normally in Roman law) used as a means of extracting information. Note the characterization of the women as "infecting" with "poisons" the minds of noble men – who consider them their wives and their children legitimate. It is also interesting that the law foresees the possibility that legitimate members of the men's families may try to deceive the law by not coming forward or even by helping the illegitimate children to claim their legacies or gifts. It appears that many subjects, even those of high rank, did not agree with the emperor's attitude toward unions of those of different status. This may be due at least in part to the fact that many of the new senators and office-holders, especially in the eastern Empire, were themselves of relatively humble origins [Evans Grubbs 1995, 287–9].

Over the following century emperors, in both the eastern and western halves of the Empire, continued to enact legislation on the inheritance rights of illegitimate children born from the unions prohibited by Constantine in 336. A law of the western emperor Valentinian I allowed illegitimate children or their mother to inherit up to one-fourth of their father's estate if there were no legitimate heirs, or one-twelfth if there were [Cod. Theod. 4.6.4, 371]. This was a substantial improvement on Constantine's law, which had prohibited him from leaving anything under the threat of severe penalties. But the policy on illegitimate children continued to fluctuate, with western emperors taking a more severe attitude and eastern emperors generally adhering to Valentinian's ruling.[66] That men of sufficient importance were able to evade the laws and make their illegitimate children heirs is shown by the case of the famous teacher of rhetoric, Libanius of Antioch [Evans Grubbs 1995, 300–1; Arjava 1996, 213–17].

The legislative fluctuation suggests that the laws caused concern and confusion and that emperors had to clarify the situation of illegitimate children repeatedly (often in response to a law from the other half of the Empire). We know from a law of the eastern emperor Marcian (reigned 450–457) that another aspect of Constantine's law caused confusion: who exactly were the "humble and despicable" (*vel humilis vel abiecta*) women mentioned in the law?[67] Marcian's law was intended to clarify the status of such a woman. His law reveals an interesting mixture of ideas about the blamelessness of poverty (no doubt influenced by Christian teachings) and very traditional, pre-Christian attitudes about the importance of free birth (*ingenuitas*), which was still considered the mark of a morally upright and socially acceptable person. The preamble to his law suggests that actual cases had come to court involving men of rank wishing to marry freeborn but poor women.

Novel 4 of Marcian, 4 April, 454

Emperors Valentinian and Marcian Augusti to Palladius, praetorian prefect:
The most sacred laws, which restrict the lives of all, ought to be understood by all, so that everyone, once their (the laws') precepts have been learned more clearly, shall decline forbidden things and follow those which are permitted. But if, indeed, anything rather obscure has by chance been put in these same laws, it is necessary that it be made manifest by imperial interpretation, so that the ambiguity of every sanction is removed and the alternating lawsuits of litigants cannot divert uncertainties in the law to their own side, and also lawyers in such affairs and judges of tribunals, following an open pronouncement of the laws, do not toss about among uncertain rulings with inconclusive and wavering opinions.... (1) Your Magnificence, always eager to hold to the correct path of justice in concluding all lawsuits, has consulted Our Clemency regarding that part of the Constantinian law, in which some ambiguity appears to exist. For when he decreed that it was not permitted to a senator, a *perfectissimus*, a duovir, a

municipal flamen, or a provincial priest to have as wife a slave woman, ...
[The law repeats the list of women in Cod. Theod. 4.6.3, omitted here]

... he added to the forbidden and prohibited persons also a "humble and despicable" (*humilem abiectamque*) person. Your Highness observed that great doubt arose subsequently in legal judgments concerning marriage about whether these words also ought to refer to poor, freeborn women and (whether) the rule of the law excludes them from marriage with senators.

May this wickedness be far removed from our times, that it should be believed that poverty has been given as a dishonor to anyone, since often moderate resources have prepared much glory for many, and a rather small property rating has been a testimony to self-control! Who would think that Constantine of renowned memory, when he forbade senators to contaminate their marriage couches with the dregs of polluted women, had put the gifts of fortune above natural good qualities and had put riches, which the vicissitudes of chance are as able to remove as to give, above free birth, which cannot be taken away once it has been inborn?

(2) But that man, who most loved the honorable and was a most holy censor of character, judged those women to be "humble and despicable" persons and considered them unworthy of marriage with senators, whom either the shameful stain of birth or a life given over to disgraceful occupations has polluted with sordid marks of dishonor and has infected either through the turpitude of origin or the indecency of profession. Therefore, removing all the doubt which had been thrown into the minds of certain people, ... we judge that a "humble and despicable" woman is not at all to be understood as she who, though poor, has nevertheless been born from freeborn parents. But we decree that senators and those endowed with certain exalted ranks are permitted to join to themselves in marriage women born from freeborn parents, though poor, and that there is no distinction among freeborn women on the basis of wealth or more opulent fortune.

(3) But we think that "humble and despicable" persons are only those women, who, specified and expressly stated, were not allowed by the aforementioned law to be joined in marriage with senators, that is:
[the list of women in Cod. Theod. 4.6.3 is here repeated, with the exception of "humble and despicable"]

... Which we believe beyond a doubt that Constantine of divine memory himself intended in that law which he promulgated and therefore he forbade marriages of this kind, lest senators be joined, not so much in the marriages as in the vices of these women whom we have enumerated.

(4) Also, whatever other things have been laid down in sacred constitutions by Constantine of renowned memory or by other divine emperors after him concerning natural children and their mothers, and also about freeborn concubines and about those who came together in marriage after a wife's death,[68] we order to be preserved inviolably. Moreover (they should be preserved) so that those laws which have been passed later should precede in

authority laws promulgated earlier and whichever of them is later in time should be more valid in law, dearest and most loving parent Palladius.

(5) Therefore, your illustrious and magnificent authority shall see to it that this law of Our Serenity, which will endure perpetually in every age, comes to the notice of all, after edicts have been posted in the customary way.

Given at Constantinople on the day before the Nones of April in the consulship of Aetius and Studius, vv. cc.[69]

2 Concubines

Constantine's law of 336 [Cod. Theod. 4.6.3, above] not only forbade marriage between men of rank and the women enumerated in the law, but also penalized those men who lived in concubinage with such women, if they tried to benefit their concubines or (more usually) their illegitimate children. In classical law gifts to a concubine were valid (whereas those to a wife were not, which disturbed the jurist Ulpian; see Part I.B.5), and a man could leave bequests to his concubine and illegitimate children in his will. As we have seen above, Constantine's regulations concerning the inheritance rights of illegitimate children of high-ranking men were modified by later emperors, who allowed such children to receive at least part of their father's property.

We know of two other Constantinian laws on concubines, neither preserved in the *Theodosian Code* though possibly they were part of the now-missing Cod. Theod. 4.6.1 and 2 [Evans Grubbs 1995, 294–300]. One is known only from a single sentence in the *Code of Justinian*:

Cod. Just. 5.26.1, 14 June, 326

Emperor Constantine Augustus to the People:

No one shall be granted liberty to keep a concubine in his home while he is married.

Posted on the eighteenth day before the Kalends of July in the seventh consulship of Constantine and the consulship of the Caesar.

A similar statement appears in the *Sent. Pauli*, probably redacted at about the same time.[70] Both represent the classical Roman legal position: *concubinatus* was an alternative, not a supplement, to *iustum matrimonium* [Treggiari 1981a, 177–8]. Not all inhabitants of the Empire would necessarily have adopted the Roman view, however, so a restatement in law may have seemed necessary.[71] Cod. Just. 5.26.1 does appear to leave the door open for a married man to keep a concubine somewhere besides his home. Opinions vary as to whether Constantine intended to prohibit married men from having concubines altogether [Beaucamp 1990, 172–5].

The other Constantinian ruling on concubines, mentioned by Marcian [Novel 4.4, above], was revived in a law of the eastern emperor Zeno:

Cod. Just. 5.27.5, 20 February, 477

Emperor Zeno Augustus to Sebastianus, praetorian prefect:

We renew the most sacred constitution of the divine Constantine, who fortified the Roman Empire by the venerable faith of the Christians, concerning freeborn concubines being taken as wives, and indeed (about) their children also born from the same women either before or after marriage being considered legitimate. (And) we order that those men who before this law have begotten children of either sex in chosen concubinage with free-born women, with no marriage intervening, who of course do not have a wife (*uxor*), and have no legitimate offspring begotten from legal marriage, if they wished to take as wives those women who had previously been their concubines, they are able to contract legitimate marriage with freeborn women of this kind, as it was said (in Constantine's law). As well, the children of both sexes born in the earlier concubinage from the same women, as soon as marriage with their mothers has been celebrated, can become their (the men's) own and be in their legal power, along with those, who afterwards have been begotten from the same marriage, or by themselves, if no other is later born. And, if their fathers are willing, they can also inherit in full by will or seek their paternal inheritance from an intestate (father) ... [72]

It is striking that the emphasis in Zeno's law, and presumably in Constantine's also, is on freeborn (*ingenuae*) concubines, those of good enough birth that they would be expected to enter marriage rather than *concubinatus*. Freedwomen concubines (who were much more usual; see Part I.B.5) and their offspring are *not* covered by the law. Though Zeno's opening sentence implies that Constantine's law was motivated by Christian concerns, it was in fact a very explicit expression of traditional Roman prejudices about the moral and social value of free birth. It was also the first mention in Roman law of retroactive legitimation of illegitimate children [see Evans Grubbs 1995, 297, with references there].

In late antiquity, the most common kind of concubinage was apparently that of a young man, not yet ready to make a socially acceptable marriage, with a woman of lower status. The young Augustine, whose father was apparently a town councillor (decurion or *curialis*), is the most famous example [Arjava 1996, 205–10; Evans Grubbs 1995, 300–1]. In his *Confessions*, written at Carthage in the final years of the fourth century, Augustine, now bishop of Hippo, looked back on his life two decades earlier.[73] As a young man, he had begun a monogamous relationship with a woman with whom he lived for almost fifteen years and by whom he had a son, Adeodatus (meaning "given by God"). We know nothing of his concubine apart from what he tells us in the *Confessions*; he never even mentions her name (probably out of consideration for her reputation). Given the fact that she was a concubine rather than a wife, and that Augustine did not consider marrying her, we can assume that she was of much lower status than he was, perhaps a former slave, or one of the "humble and despicable" women condemned by Constantine in his law of 336.

Augustine, *Confessions* IV.2 and VI.15

Confessions IV.2: ... In those years I had one woman, not one known in that marriage (*coniugium*) which is called legitimate, but one whom a wandering ardor, bereft of good sense, had sought out – only one, however, to whose bed I remained faithful. In regard to whom, I could experience by my own example what a distance there is between the moderation of the conjugal agreement, which would have been entered into for the sake of begetting children, and the pact of lustful love, where offspring are born even against one's wish – though once born, they compel themselves to be cherished.

171

As Augustine progressed on the career track which would probably have led him to the imperial administration had he not turned to the church instead, he began to feel the need to make a legal marriage that would bring him wealth and social advantages. His mother, Monnica, was the driving force behind his marriage arrangements, since Augustine's father had died many years earlier [Shaw 1987a, 34]. A betrothal agreement was made, but Augustine's fiancée was still two years below the legal age of marriage (which was twelve, as in classical law). Augustine (who was around thirty at this time) dismissed his concubine of many years, but found he could not remain celibate until his fiancée reached marriageable age:

Confessions **VI.15:**   Meanwhile my sins were being multiplied, and since she with whom I had been accustomed to sleep had been torn from my side as an impediment to marriage, my heart had been cut and wounded where it was clinging, and was drawing blood. And she had returned to Africa, vowing to you[74] that she would not know another man, and my natural son born from her had been left with me. But I, unhappy and not imitating the woman, (but) impatient of the delay, as I was going to receive the one whom I sought after a two year period, since I was not a lover of marriage but a slave of lust, I procured another woman, not, of course, a wife, in order that the disease of my soul might be, so to speak, supported and prolonged, either unimpaired or strengthened, by a convoy of enduring habit in the uxorial kingdom. Nor was that wound of mine, which had been made by the cutting off of my former (relationship), cured, but after very fierce burning and grieving, it putrefied, and it hurt, as if colder, but more desperate.

Augustine's decision to reject his concubine, the mother of his son, for an arranged marriage with a girl one-third his age, caused him not only pain at the loss of a sexual partner, but shame at his own selfish and sinful behavior. A few years after he wrote the *Confessions*, he referred obliquely to his concubine in his treatise, *On the Good of Marriage (de bono coniugali)*.[75]

Augustine, *On the Good of Marriage* V

It is often also asked, when a male and female – he not being a husband nor she being the wife of another man – are joined with each other, not for the sake of begetting children, but for the sake only of sleeping together on account of lack of self-control, by that in-between sort of fidelity, so that he does not do this with another woman nor she with another man – whether this should be called marriage (*nuptiae*). And indeed it is able perhaps not absurdly to be called marriage (*conubium*), if it (the union) has been agreeable to them up to the death of one of them, and though they were not joined for this reason, nevertheless they have not avoided the begetting of offspring, in such a way that either they did not want children to be born to them or they even took action by some evil deed so that they were not born.

But if either one or the other of these things is lacking, I do not see how we can call this marriage. And indeed if the man has taken some woman for himself for a time, until he should find another woman (who is) worthy because of her rank or her resources, whom he can take as a partner, he is an adulterer in his mind, not with the woman whom he wishes to find, but with that woman with whom he is sleeping in such a way that he does not have marital union (*maritale consortium*) with her. Wherefore also she herself (is an adulterer), if knowing this[76] she willingly has intercourse shamefully with a man with whom she does not have a wifely bond. But if she remains faithful to his bed and, when he has taken a wife, she herself does not think of marrying and she prepares to restrain herself from such activity henceforth, I, indeed, would not perhaps dare easily to call her an adulterer. But who would say that she does not sin, when she knows that she has intercourse with a man, whose wife she is not? ...

For Augustine, as for Roman law [see Chapter 2, Part I.A], both marital intent and the intention of having children are essential for marriage, though a life-long union which accepts children even if they were not originally desired can "not absurdly" be considered marriage. But whereas in Roman law (increasingly so in late antiquity), the status of both partners was an important factor in whether or not a union could be considered marriage, for the mature bishop Augustine it is not. The man who puts away a low-status concubine in order to marry a woman of rank and wealth is an adulterer "in his mind" – though not in law, as Augustine well knew.

3 Free men and slave women

Constantine's law prohibiting marriage between men of high status and low-status women [Cod. Theod. 4.6.3, above] included slaves among the women prohibited. Relationships between slave and free had never been valid under Roman law, but late antique lawmakers felt this had to be stated explicitly. Evidently many inhabitants of the Empire, even those of high status, either did not know that marriage with a slave was impossible, or did not care.

Another law of Constantine was aimed at town councillors (decurions, called *curiales* in late Roman law) who abandoned their positions to live on another landowner's estate and cohabit with one of his slaves. The law was enacted at Aquileia in north Italy.[77] The underlying issue is the abdication of his municipal responsibilities by the *curialis*, a topic frequently addressed in late Roman law [Evans Grubbs 1995, 278–80].

Cod. Theod. 12.1.6, 1 July, 318
Emperor Constantine Augustus to Patroclus:

Though it seems unworthy for men who do not possess any rank to descend to sordid marriages (*conubia*) with slave women, it is nevertheless not at all prohibited by the laws. But marriage (*conubium*) with servile persons is not possible and from a union (*contubernium*) of this type slaves are born.[78] Therefore we order that decurions are not to flee, led by lust, to the laps of very powerful houses. For if a decurion secretly, without the knowledge of overseers or stewards,[79] has been joined to someone else's slave, we order that the woman be driven into the mines by a judge's sentence, and that the decurion himself be deported to an island. His movable property and urban slaves are to be confiscated,[80] but his estates and rural slaves are to be handed over to the city whose *curialis* he has been, if he has been freed from paternal power and has no children or parents or even relatives, who are called to succeed him according to the rule of the laws....[81]

Late Roman emperors also reiterated the classical rule that children of slavewomen were slaves, even if their father were their mother's master. Constantine denied that children of a master by his slave could claim their liberty, even if they had lived in de facto freedom for many years:[82]

Cod. Theod. 4.8.7, 28 February, 331

... For it is necessary by common law (*ius commune*) that a child follow its mother's condition, so that, even if a slave woman should ascend the bed of her master, she shall bring forth to her master the offspring not of free people, but of slaves.

The legal situation of a man's illegitimate children by his slavewoman seems to have become confused with the situation of freeborn children from other illegal unions, such as those between men of rank and the women listed in Constantine's law of 336 (which had included both slave and free women). This is suggested by a western law of Valentinian III, which describes the children of both types of unions as "natural:"

Cod. Theod. 4.6.7, date missing (426/7)

Emperors Theodosius (II) and Valentinian (III) Augusti to Bassus, praetorian prefect:

We order that the name of "natural" (children) be imposed on those who were brought forth into the light by a legal joining without honorable celebration of matrimony. However, it is clear from law itself that slaves are born from the womb of a slavewoman, though by force of nature it is not possible to take away the name of "natural" (children) even from them [there is a lacuna in the manuscript] ... Clearly, if natural (children) have been born from a slavewoman and are not manumitted by their master, they are counted among the slaves of the estate ...[83]

Valentinian's requirement that a marriage have external signs of validity (either a celebration or a written document) is new in Roman law, which had never before required documentation [Chapter 2, Part I.A]. In another part of (probably) the same law, Valentinian made an exception for soldiers, to whom he permitted "the free capacity of contracting marriage with freeborn women without any solemnities of marriage."[84] The need for external evidence of a marriage was rejected by the eastern emperor Theodosius II in 428 [Cod. Theod. 3.7.3, Chapter 2, Part II.C].[85]

Late Roman laws on the unions of free men and slave women were not simply abstract statements with little basis in actual conditions; there are many references to such non-marital unions in contemporary non-legal sources. Ambrose, bishop of Milan, addressed members of his congregation who were preparing for baptism and warned them that though they were to imitate the Old Testament patriarch Abraham in his faithfulness to God, they should not imitate his having a child by his slavewoman, Hagar.[86]

Ambrose stresses that such children cannot be legitimate heirs:

174

Ambrose, *On Abraham* 1.3.19 (excerpt)

Therefore let men learn not to despise (legitimate) marriages, or to join to themselves women who are not their equals, in order that they not bring up children of the sort that they cannot have as heirs. So that, if they are not moved by any consideration of decency (*pudor*), they may be eager for a worthy marriage at least by the thought of passing on their inheritance.

The Christian writer Jerome, around the year 400, described men whose poverty supposedly prevented them from marrying.[87] He notes, however, that it was possible to obtain an imperial rescript granting otherwise ineligible women the right to marry, if a man was willing to pay for it:

Jerome, *Epistle* 69.5 (excerpt)

We see many men decline the burden of wives on account of excessive poverty, and have their own slavegirls instead of wives, and raise up children conceived from them. If by chance they have become rich and have earned the *stola*[88] for them (their wives) from the Emperor, let them without delay submit their neck to the Apostle[89] and be forced, unwilling, to receive them in the ranks of wives.

Jerome's statement was occasioned by a dispute that had arisen in the church: should a man who had been married and widowed before his baptism, then married again after baptism, become a bishop, or would this go against the apostolic rule [1 Timothy 3] that a church leader should be the husband of only one woman? Some thought that any previous marriage, even before baptism, would disqualify a man from becoming a cleric, but that a non-marital relationship with a concubine would not, and Jerome derided the hypocrisy of this attitude.[90]

About half a century later, Pope Leo received an inquiry from Rusticus, bishop of Narbonne, on a related issue.[91] Should a cleric give his daughter in marriage to a man who did not have a legally married wife, but did have a relationship with a woman by whom he had had children? Like lawgivers of the western Empire, the Pope saw the difference between marriage and concubinage as determined by the status of the woman and by the presence of external proof that the relationship was marriage, and like Ambrose, he stressed heirship as the identifying feature of legitimate children:

Leo the Great, *Epistle* 167.4–5 (excerpt)

(4) Not every woman joined to a man is the man's wife, because not every son is his father's heir. Moreover, the legal contracts of marriage are between freeborn people and equals; the Lord decided this very thing long before the beginning of Roman law existed.... Therefore if a cleric of any place has given his daughter in marriage to a man having a concubine, it should not be received as if he gave her to a married man – unless by chance that woman, having been made freeborn[92] and legally dowered, should appear to have been made honorable by a publicly celebrated marriage ceremony.

(5) Since a married woman is one thing, a concubine is another, to throw out a slavegirl from one's bed and receive a wife of undisputed free birth is not a duplication of marriage, but the advance of honor (*honestas*).

175

Leo's conception of marriage as a public celebration between social equals which produces legitimate heirs, in contrast to the non-marital union of a man with a slaveborn woman, probably drew on fifth-century Roman law, particularly the law of Valentinian III [Cod. Theod. 4.6.7, above] and perhaps also the recently enacted law of Majorian [Novel 6.9, in Chapter 2, Part II.C].[93] Despite Augustine's emphasis on life-long monogamous intent as the defining characteristic of marriage, ecclesiastical and secular authorities both found it easier to evaluate a union by the legal status of its partners.

4 Free women and slave men

All of the above laws involve free men who had quasi-marital relationships with slave or lowborn women. What about free women who wished to "marry" slave men? Such a situation was much more shocking to the Roman elite than that of a man who lived with a lowborn woman, for it went against traditional ideas of sexual and social hierarchy [Evans Grubbs 1993].

In the earlier Empire, the *senatusconsultum Claudianum* had regulated the status of free women who lived with someone else's slave [Part I.B.2], and this continued to be the case in the fourth century. According to a law of 314:

Cod. Theod. 4.12.1, 1 April, 314

Emperor Constantine[94] Augustus to Probus:

If any free women have suffered violence either at the hands of slaves or anyone else and have been joined against their will to men of servile status, they shall obtain vindication with suitable severity of the laws. (1) However, if any woman should be forgetful of her own honor (*honestas*), she shall lose her liberty and her children shall be slaves of the master of that man to whom she joined herself in *contubernium*. It is necessary that this law be observed for the past also.

Posted on the Kalends of April in the consulship of Volusianus and Annianus.

This law correctly uses the term *contubernium* to describe such a free–slave relationship. Note the idea that a free woman who would cohabit with a slave has forgotten the obligations of her reputation and status.

Several years later, a law of Constantine ameliorated the condition of women who lived with "fiscal" (imperially owned) slaves, but did not affect women cohabiting with the slaves of private (non-imperial) owners:

Cod. Theod. 4.12.3, 31 January, 320

Emperor Constantine Augustus to the People:

Since ancient law compels freeborn women joined in *contubernium* with fiscal slaves to a boiling-down of their birth-status,[95] with no pardon granted on the basis of ignorance or age, it is decided that the bonds of such unions are to be avoided. But if a freeborn woman, either in ignorance or even willingly, has come together with a fiscal slave, (it is decided) that she suffer no loss of her freeborn status. However, the offspring, who are born from a fiscal slave father and a freeborn mother, are to hold the middle lost, so that they, as children of slave men and illegitimate (*spurii*) children of free women, shall be Latins who, though they are released from the fate of slavery, nevertheless will be bound by a patron's privilege.[96]

[The rest of the law, omitted here, says it does not apply to women who live with slaves belonging to municipalities.]

Given at Serdica on the second day before the Kalends of February in the seventh consulship of Constantine Augustus and the consulship of Constantius.[97]

Five other laws are found under the title *ad senatusconsultum Claudianum* in the *Theodosian Code*, four of which deal with the requirement that a woman cohabiting with another's slave was to be officially "warned" three times before she could be enslaved.[98] The fifth law is of interest for the moral judgment it passes on a free woman who chooses to "marry" a slave:

Cod. Theod. 4.12.6, 4 April, 366(?)
Emperors Valentinian, Valens, and Gratian Augusti to Secundus, praetorian prefect:

If desire has more value to a lustful woman than liberty, she has become a slavewoman not by war, not by payment, but by marriage (*conubium*), so that her children shall lie under the yoke of slavery. For it is clear that she, who regretted being free, wanted to be a slavewoman.

Given at Trier[99] on the day before the Nones of April in the consulship of Gratian, *n.p.*[100] and Dagalaifus.

Another law of the same period, found not in the *Theodosian Code* but in a private collection of laws called the "Consultation of a certain ancient Jurist" (*Consultatio Veteris Cuiusdam Iurisconsulti*),[101] suggests that some freeborn women may have "married" slave men when below twenty-five (the age of majority) and then tried to regain their freedom later:

Consultatio Vet. CuiusD.Iurisc. IX.7, 19 July, 365
Emperors Valentinian and Valens Augusti to Felix, *consularis* of Macedonia:

(Among other matters and at the place)[102] If formerly freeborn (*ingenuae*) women have submitted themselves to servile *contubernia*, and now, scorning the master of (their) younger age,[103] try to flee the yoke of slavery, your Gravity shall impose the necessity of undergoing slavery on those who did not flee a servile status immediately at the very beginning of the union.

Given at Milan on the fourteenth day before the Kalends of August in the consulship of the emperors themselves.[104]

By the reign of Valens and Valentinian, the sanctions of the *s.c. Claudianum* were being applied to free women who married fiscal slaves working in the imperial weaving mills and mints.[105] Clearly the law still had the same practical purpose as it did when it was introduced in the mid-first century: to ensure a supply of imperial slaves by requiring that the illegitimate children of imperial slaves and free women followed their father's status rather than their mother's, contrary to the usual rule [Part I.B.2]. But late Roman law frames the situation in moral terms: freeborn women who enter quasi-marital unions with slaves are led to do so by lust and disregard for their honor, and so deserve condemnation.

Classical Roman law and society had also frowned upon women who freed their slaves in order to marry them [Part I.B.3]. And a woman of respectable status who had a sexual relationship with a slave without freeing and marrying him could have been prosecuted under the Augustan law on adultery and illicit sex (*stuprum*).[106] But not until the fourth century did Roman law explicitly address the situation of a free woman who lived in a quasi-marital union with her own slave [see Evans Grubbs 1993; 1995, 273–7]:

Cod. Theod. 9.9.1, 29 May, 326 or 329
Emperor Constantine Augustus to the People:

If any woman is discovered to have dealings in secret with (her) slave, she shall undergo a capital penalty,[107] and the worthless scoundrel[108] is to be handed over to the flames. All shall have the opportunity to denounce the public crime, all shall have the power to announce it to the authorities, even a slave shall have the licence to bring information, who will be given liberty once the crime is proven – though a penalty threatens for a false accusation.

(1) A woman married (*nupta*) before this law shall be separated from such a union and, deprived not only of her home, but even of the community of the province, she shall lament the absence of her exiled lover.[109]

(2) Also the children, whom she had from this union, shall remain in bare freedom, stripped of all marks of rank, nor will they receive anything from the woman's property, either through themselves or through an intermediary under any title of her will.

(3) But intestate succession to the woman's property shall be granted to her children, if they are legitimate,[110] or to her next-of-kin and cognates, or to that person whom the judgment of the law admits, so that also anything which that man, who was once her lover, and the children conceived from him appear by some chance to have held in their own possession, is to be joined with the woman's property and claimed by the afore-mentioned heirs.

(4) All these things should be observed in this way even if the woman or her beloved died before (this) law, since even one author of this offense incurs judgment.

(5) But if both parties have already died, we spare the offspring, so that they not be weighed down by the crimes of their deceased parents. They shall be (acknowledged as) her children, they shall be preferred to (her) brothers,[111] and to her next-of-kin and cognates; they shall be heirs to the remaining inheritance.

(6) Those who commit this crime after (this) law we punish with death. Moreover, those who, having been separated according to the law, have secretly come together again renewing the forbidden union, will undergo a similar penalty, convicted on the evidence of slaves or the office of the *speculator*[112] or even the information of their next-of-kin.

Given at Serdica on the fourth day before the Kalends of June in the seventh consulship of Constantine Augustus and the consulship of Constantius Caesar.[113]

Whereas Constantine's law on the unions of high-ranking men with lowborn women unleashed a spate of imperial legislation on the subject for decades to come, there are no further references to the subject of Cod. Theod. 9.9.1 for almost 150 years. It may not have been enforced, and there may have been few women of status and wealth who wanted to "marry" their own slaves. But in 468, the western emperor Anthemius (reigned 467–72) received a petition from an otherwise unknown woman named Julia, who evidently feared that her marriage to her freedman violated Constantine's law. It is very unlikely that Julia would have approached the emperor spontaneously about the status of her marriage; its validity must have been questioned, and she may have been appealing a charge already brought against her.

Novel 1 of Anthemius, 21 February, 468
Emperors Leo and Anthemius to Lupercianus, praetorian prefect:

[The opening sentences, omitted here, stress the need for the emperor to guide his subjects well, in order to have a flourishing and tranquil state.]

... A certain Julia pours our her prayers at our altars, adding that marriage has befallen her with a man who indeed was a slave of her household, but who deserved liberty because of the nobleness of his character, and she begs our divine majesty that she not be harmed by the fact that the venerable law of Constantine, with the strictest rigor, does not allow a mistress to be inflamed by the embraces of her own slaves. Indeed, she thinks that in her own case it is unfitting to deliberate about those things decided concerning unions with slaves, since she herself did not marry a slave, but a freedman. In particular, (she says) that her own marriage cannot come into blame, because it is clear [that no law has been made] about prohibiting associations (*consortia*) with freedmen, [for] whatever no law has previously forbidden is nevertheless considered [no evil].[114]

(1) Therefore Our Serenity has found a double cause for deciding upon cases of this kind, so that confirmation not be taken away from those who are in doubt about (a union) undertaken, as it were, in error, and so that what has been determined satisfactorily and honorably be preserved from now on without any ambiguity. Therefore, first we decree by this edict, that marriages (*matrimonia*), if similar marriages (*coniugia*) are proven to have been begun up to the second consulship of Our Divinity, shall not lack legal validity, but may rejoice also that this munificence of our authority has looked favorably on their own security. Thus, if there are any women who, because of the nobility of their birth, perhaps fear anything from an association (*consortium*) of this sort, they may throw away the empty weight of their unreasonable fear, nor shall they be afraid that they have done illicitly, as it were, what no laws up to now clearly forbade. They appear thus to have contracted legitimate marriage (*iustae nuptiae*) with their freedman so that the children born and to be born from them shall undergo no inquiry about the union of their parents at any time, but shall receive the inheritance of

their mother and father by the custom of the laws. Also, those between whom a society of this sort has been contracted shall themselves not lose the liberty of making a will among themselves or of succeeding to each other according to the form of the law, nor shall they, because of their marriage, be thought to differ in any way from others about whom the decrees of the law prescribed nothing before this sanction of Our Divinity ... [the last sentence is here omitted]

(2) Therefore, wishing to increase the public honor, from this consulship of Our Clemency onward, we forbid mistresses and patronesses to have the ability to enter marriages with their freedmen, in order that the famous nobility of outstanding families not become worthless by the foulness of an unworthy association and not lose, by the contracting of a most vile bond, that which it perhaps obtained by the splendor of senatorial excellence, or a family conspicuous only by the bare brightness of freeborn liberty be diminished by a rather shameless embrace in regard to a woman. Undoubtedly this will be with the proviso that, whatever the divine Constantine decided with his venerable law about associations with slaves, shall be preserved with eternal firmness.

(3) But about those women, who henceforth have entered into vows with their own freedmen, we decree that it shall be maintained by a law that will endure forever that this forbidden union obtain not even the name of marriage, but those execrably aspiring to illicit associations shall be struck by confiscation of all their property and perpetual deportation. Those who are born from an association of this sort shall be deprived not only of the rights, but even the name, of children,[115] and shall also be properly assigned to a servile status, so that our fisc shall claim ownership over them.

[The final sentences of the law, omitted here, reconfirm earlier laws about men's unions with slaves and freedwomen and their "natural" children (see I.B.1–3 above) and ask Lupercianus to make sure the law is publicized so that all will know its contents.]

Given at Rome on the tenth day before the Kalends of March in the consulship of our lord Anthemius. Received at Rome on the Ides of March in the same consulship.

Anthemius' law thus relieved Julia (and any other women in similar unions) of anxiety about the legitimacy of her marriage and children, while at the same time it confirmed and indeed went beyond the letter of Constantine's law, by declaring that in the future marriages between patronesses and their freedmen would be just as illegal as those between mistresses and slaves. The enslavement of the children of such a couple, who will become the property of the imperial treasury, is a new touch; even Constantine had not gone that far.

In the sixth century, the Byzantine emperor Justinian enacted a series of laws improving the position of illegitimate children, so that they could inherit in the absence of any legitimate heirs [Arjava 1996, 216–17; Beaucamp 1990, 199–201; Evans Grubbs 1995, 282–3].[116] Justinian also repealed the *senatusconsultum Claudianum* [Cod. Just. 7.24.1 and Justinian *Institutes* 7.24.1].[117] The union of a free woman with her own slave continued to be punished, however, as shown by the inclusion of an abridged version of Constantine's law in Justinian's *Code* [Cod. Just. 9.11.1].

C Forced marriages

It is clear from the laws on consent to marriage that late Roman emperors considered the agreement of the *paterfamilias* to be essential in making a legitimate marriage. Thus in addition to reiterating the necessity of paternal consent for a valid marriage pact, they also banned unions that were achieved by force or extortion on the part of the prospective husband.

A law of Constantine was enacted against a "marriage strategy" directly opposed to marriages arranged by the *paterfamilias* and betrothal pacts between families – marriage by abduction (*raptus*), also known as bride theft [Evans Grubbs 1989; 1995, 183–93]. Constantine's law harshly punished not only the abductor himself, but also the abducted girl, if she did not resist, and even her parents, if they later acquiesced in the marriage. Like Cod. Theod. 3.5.12 of 422 [Chapter 2, Part II.B], this law assumes that a young woman does not really know what is good for her, and if allowed to have her own choice, will make a foolish decision against her own best interests.

Cod. Theod. 9.24.1, 1 April, 326

Emperor Constantine Augustus to the People:

If someone who has not previously made any agreement with a girl's parents should seize her (when she is) unwilling or if he should lead her away (when she is) willing – hoping for protection from the response of one whom, on account of the frivolity and fickleness of her sex and judgment, our ancestors completely excluded from making legal complaints and from giving testimony and from all judicial matters[118] – the girl's response shall be of no use to him according to the ancient law, but rather the girl herself shall be made guilty by association in the crime.

(1) And since often the watchfulness of parents is frustrated by the stories and wicked persuasions of nurses, this punishment shall first of all threaten them (the nurses), whose service is proven to have been hateful and whose talk is proven to have been bought: the opening of their mouth and throat, which brought forth destructive encouragements, shall be closed by the swallowing of molten lead.

(2) And if voluntary assent is revealed in the virgin, she shall be struck with the same severity as her abductor. Nor shall impunity be offered to those girls who are abducted against their will, since they too could have kept themselves at home till their marriage day and, if the doors were broken down by the abductor's audacity, they could have sought help from the neighbors with all their efforts. But we impose a lighter penalty on these girls, and order that only legal succession to their parents is to be denied them. (3) Moreover, if the abductor who has been proven guilty without guilt should wish to appeal, he shall certainly not be heard.

(4) But if any slave should bring forth into public the fact that the crime of abduction (*raptus*) has been neglected by deception or disregarded by an agreement,[119] he shall be rewarded with Latin status, or if he already has Latin status, he shall become a Roman citizen.[120] The parents, for whom vengeance was especially a concern, if they displayed forbearance and repressed their sorrow,[121] shall be struck with deportation. (5) We order that partners and accomplices of the abductor also be subjected to the same

punishment without regard to sex; and if among these attendants anyone of servile status should be caught, we order that person to be burned without regard to sex.

Given at Aquileia on the Kalends of April in the consulship of Constantine Augustus for the sixth time and of Constantius Caesar.[122]

Constantine's law has shocked many modern commentators, particularly since it calls for the victim to suffer the same penalty as her abductor, if she did not actively try to prevent the abduction. What this penalty actually was is not specified in the law as it is preserved in the *Theodosian Code*. Presumably it was death, perhaps a particularly shameful form of the death penalty, such as being thrown to the beasts in the arena. This seemed too harsh to later emperors, and a law of Constantine's son Constantius [Cod. Theod. 9.24.2, 349] reduces the sentence to the "capital penalty" – death by decapitation rather than something more painful and humiliating (the penalties for slave accomplices remained the same). However, it is doubtful whether even this "milder" punishment was inflicted by judges to whom abduction cases were brought – when, indeed, such cases were actually brought to court. More often they would have been handled privately, which is what the law wants to prevent. A third law [Cod. Theod. 9.24.3, 374] urges that a case be brought as soon as abduction has occurred, and puts a statute of limitation of five years on prosecution, after which time no one can make an accusation or question the legitimacy of the marriage or the children born from it.[123]

Abduction was not the only means of forcing a marriage against the will of a young woman or her family. A law of 380 attacks a more subtle method of forcing the hand of a *paterfamilias*: pressure brought to bear by powerful officials. Late antique emperors were anxious to repress abuses of power by office-holders [Harries 1999, esp. 153–71], and the following law of Theodosius I penalizes officials who use their authority to force alliance with local families. Marriage between an imperial official (especially the provincial governor) and a woman in the province in which he held office had been forbidden already in the earlier Empire [Part I.C.3]. Betrothal agreements, however, were not prohibited, and marriage could take place as soon as the official laid down his office. The following passage is part of a longer law, other parts of which also dealt with abuses of power by provincial governors and with penalties for breaking betrothals [see Chapter 2, Part II.C].[124]

Cod. Theod. 3.11.1, 17 June, 380

Emperors Gratian, Valentinian (II), and Theodosius Augusti to Neoterius, praetorian prefect:

If anyone endowed with ordinary or any kind of power should use the occasion of his power in regard to contracting marriage when the (women) themselves or their relatives[125] are unwilling, whether they are *pupillae*[126] or virgins or widows in their fathers' home or widows who are legally independent, or finally of any kind whatever, and is revealed to exhibit or have exhibited his favor in a threatening manner to those whose interests are being considered here[127] when they are unwilling, we decree that he is liable to a fine of ten pounds of gold, and, when he has left office, we forbid him to usurp the rank which he has reached.[128] To be sure, (we punish him) with such a penalty so that, if he has been unwilling to obey the sanction of our law in regard to claiming that honor which he has used badly, he shall not be allowed ever for two years continuously to live in that province in which he usurped this (honor) for himself.

182

(1) Since, however, we understand that certain homes or certain relatives must be additionally fortified against hidden malice, we order that whatever man or woman has been assailed by hidden promises or threats by the official[129] for a marriage to which they scorn to give consent, (then) immediately after filing an official complaint, they along with their house and that of their family, shall cease to belong to his jurisdiction; the defenders of each city and the public servants of the same official shall take care of this. And indeed, if this will be a matter of the wickedness of an ordinary official, all the business of this household and all its affairs, either civil or criminal, shall be in the competency of his vicar[130] for as long as the same man will be in office. But if, however, the vicar or someone of similar authority shall attempt violence in contracting a marriage of this sort, in turn the ordinary official shall be the intermediary. But if both will be suspected, protection of such homes shall belong especially to the illustrious (praetorian) prefecture, for as long as the same man shall be in office.

Given at Thessalonica on the fifteenth day before the Kalends of July in the fifth consulship of Gratian Augustus and the first consulship of Theodosius Augustus.[131]

Despite general laws against extorting marriages by violence or social presssure, it was still possible for influential citizens (especially senators and imperial office-holders) to receive special permission from the emperor for unions which would otherwise be invalid, as the remarks of Ambrose [Part II.A] and Jerome [Part II.B.3] reveal. (This was the case in the earlier imperial period also; cf. D.23.2.31.4 in Part I.B for imperial indulgence granted to senators for marriage with a freedwoman.) To prevent abuse of imperial generosity, a western law of 409 explicitly prohibited the seeking of imperial indulgence for forbidden marriages and denied all validity to indulgences which were thus given. Exception was made for cousin marriage, which was still illegal in the western Empire [Part II.A], and for requests for imperial help in recovering *arrhae sponsaliciae* when a betrothal had been broken [Chapter 2, Part II.C].

Cod. Theod. 3.10.1, 23(?) January, 409

Emperors Honorius and Theodosius (II) Augusti to Theodorus, praetorian prefect:

Certain people, neglecting the rule of ancient law, think that a marriage – which they understand they do not deserve – should be requested from us by creeping up with their entreaties, pretending that they have the girl's consent. For this reason we prohibit such a kind of betrothal by the decision of the present law. Therefore, if anyone has obtained a marriage by surreptitious entreaties contrary to this decision, he shall not doubt that he will undergo the loss of his property and the penalty of deportation and that, having lost the right of legal marriage which he obtained by forbidden usurpation, he shall not have legally recognized children by this means, nor has he ever earned the efficacious accomplishment of a pardon, by the favor of a requested indulgence or the emperor's special decision.[132] Those whom the law of our father of triumphal memory did not forbid to supplicate for the union of cousins, that is, the fourth degree of relationship, on the model of imperial indulgences are excepted (from this law). Also excepted are those who desire to fulfill the betrothal made by parents concerning the marriage of their daughters, or who ask that betrothal gifts, that is, those given in the name of *arrhae*, be returned to them with the quadruple penalty according to the decision of the laws. To be sure, we prohibit that marriages be sought by supplication from us which should fittingly be requested either from the permission of the parents or from the adult girls or women themselves. On the other hand, if a lawsuit should arise when a marriage which had previously been promised has (later) been refused, we do not prohibit that we be consulted according to law.

Given at Ravenna on the tenth day before the Kalends of February[133] in the eighth consulship of our lord Honorius and the third consulship of our lord Theodosius.[134]

D *Other prohibitions*

Late Roman law also introduced new prohibitions based on religion and ethnicity. A law of Valentinian I prohibited marriage between provincials (who would be Roman citizens) and "barbarians," presumably members of non-citizen peoples either outside or within the boundaries of the Empire. It is likely that this law originated as an imperial response to a revolt by a Moorish chieftain, Firmus, in the North African province of Mauretania in the early 370s, which was eventually put down by Count Theodosius, the Master of Horse (*magister equitum*), the official to whom the law is addressed [Sivan 1996]. Its inclusion in the *Theodosian Code* sixty-five years later gave it a general application that it did not have originally. The law does not seem ever to have been actively enforced.

Cod. Theod. 3.14.1, 28 May, 370 or 373
Emperors Valentinian and Valens Augusti to Theodosius, Master of Horse:

No provincial, whatever his rank or location, may have marriage with a barbarian wife, nor shall a provincial woman be joined to any of the barbarians.[135] But if anything suspicious or harmful is revealed in those connections by marriage between provincials and barbarians which have (already) existed from marriages of this sort, it shall be expiated by a capital penalty.

Given on the fifth day before the Kalends of June in the consulship of Valentinian and Valens Augusti.[136]

A law of Theodosius I prohibited marriage between Jews and Christians, and called for criminal charges to be laid against such mixed marriages "after the manner of adultery." Both Jews and Christians disapproved of marriages between their adherents and members of other religious groups, but this law marks the first appearance in imperial legislation of such a marriage ban.[137] Its enactment was a result of Christian influences, perhaps on the part of Ambrose, the powerful bishop of Milan, or of the law's recipient, Cynegius, a pious Christian. [Linder 1987, 178–81; Sivan 1997]

Theodosius' law appears twice in the *Theodosian Code*, once in the title "On Marriages" (Cod. Theod. 3.7, *de nuptiis*), and again in the title "on the Julian law of Adultery" (Cod.

Theod. 9.7, *ad legem Juliam de adulteriis*). But unlike adultery accusations, which under late Roman law could be brought against a woman only by her husband or male relatives,[138] charges against a Jewish–Christian couple could be brought by any (male) member of the public.

Cod. Theod. 3.7.2 (= Cod. Theod. 9.7.5), 14 March, 388

Emperors Valentinian (II), Theodosius (I) and Arcadius Augusti to Cynegius, praetorian prefect:

No Jew may receive a Christian woman in marriage (*matrimonium*), nor may a Christian man obtain marriage (*coniugium*) with a Jewish woman. For if anyone has committed anything of this sort, he shall receive a criminal charge for this offense after the manner of adultery, with freedom for bringing an accusation opened up even to the voices of the public.

Given at Thessalonika on the day before the Ides of March in the second consulship of Theodosius Augustus and the consulship of Cynegius, *v. c.*[139]

Theodosius I also issued a law condemning Jewish marriage custom (*mos*) and law, which specifically mentioned polygamy. The possibility of a man's having more than one wife is found in rabbinical sources (dating to the imperial period), but the actual frequency of polygamy among Jews in the Empire is debated [Ilan 1995, 85–8].[140] However, Theodosius evidently thought Jewish polygamy was enough of a live issue to merit legislation prohibiting it. He may also have been thinking of other ancient Jewish marriage customs, such as the preference for close-kin marriage, particularly uncle–niece [Ilan 1995, 75–8], or levirate marriage, the marriage of a man to his deceased wife's sister. These practices had already been banned in laws of Constantius [Cod. Theod. 3.12.1 and 2] and were to be again forbidden in 396 [Cod. Theod. 3.12.3] and 475 [Cod. Just. 5.5.8, all in Part II.A].

Cod. Just. 1.9.7, 30 December, 393

Emperors Valentinian,[141] Theodosius (I) and Arcadius Augusti to Infantius, Count of the east:

No one of the Jews will maintain his own custom in marital unions, nor shall he obtain a marriage according to his own law, nor shall he enter into different marriages at one time.

Given at Constantinople on the third day before the Kalends of January in the third consulship of Theodosius Augustus and the consulship of Abundantius.

Finally, another law of the same period called for the confiscation of any kind of gifts made between partners in prohibited unions, while making exceptions for those who married illegally because they were deceived or were too young to realize what they were doing. This is apparently a law of the young western emperor Valentinian II, but it may well have been influenced by the older and more forceful Theodosius, with whom Valentinian had sought refuge in Constantinople between 387–389.[142] It is addressed to the *comes rerum privatarum* (Count of the Privy Purse), because its purpose is to ensure that gifts exchanged in illegal marriages end up in the imperial treasury.

Cod. Just. 5.5.4, 23 February, 392(?)
Emperors Valentinian (II), Theodosius, and Arcadius Augusti to Andromachus, Count of the Privy Purse (*comitem rerum privatarum*):

Whoever has by chance contracted marriage against the precepts of the laws or against the mandates and constitutions of the emperors, shall acquire nothing from that marriage, whether it was donated before marriage or afterwards given in any way. And we decree that all that which has proceeded from the liberality of one (partner) towards the other is to be vindicated by the imperial fisc as having been taken away from an unworthy man or woman.

(1) Women as well as men, who either were deceived by a most bitter error – not by an affected or pretended (error) nor from a contemptible cause – or have fallen because of the slipperiness of age, are excepted.[143]

(2) However, it has been decided that these are thus removed from the snares of our law only if, either once their error has been discovered or when they have arrived at adult years, they have broken off a union of this sort without any delay.

Given on the seventh day before the Kalends of March.[144]

4

DIVORCE AND ITS
CONSEQUENCES

I Divorce in classical law

Classical Rome had a very liberal divorce policy (as did Greco-Roman Egypt; see Part III). By the first century B.C.E., women who were not married with *manus* [see Chapter 1, Part II.B.] had the right to divorce their husbands unilaterally, and eventually the same right was enjoyed by women married with *manus*. Husbands had been able to divorce their wives unilaterally, particularly for adultery or other misbehavior, from a very early period [Treggiari 1991a, 441–6, 459]. Whether unilateral or by mutual agreement, divorce was an accepted fact of Roman life, and was subject to very few restrictions until the fourth century C.E. How frequent divorce actually was, and what percentage of divorces was initiated by wives rather than husbands, are unanswerable questions. Indeed, there is little information on Roman divorce apart from the legal sources, except for literature which focuses on the Roman elite in the late Republic and early Empire [Treggiari 1991b].

The title in the *Digest* on "Divorce and Repudiatons" (D.24.2, with eleven entries) is very short, especially compared to the title on marriage (D.23.2, with sixty-eight entries). Most of the legal sources we have for the first three centuries come to us filtered through the compilations made in the sixth century under the Christian emperor Justinian (the *Digest* and the *Code of Justinian*) which omitted passages that no longer had relevance or legal validity. By Justinian's day, there were considerable restrictions on the right of either partner, especially the wife, to divorce unilaterally, and on the right to remarry someone else. Thus we can assume that divorce was much more frequently discussed by the classical jurists than the Justinianic corpus suggests.[1]

A Definition and causes of divorce

D.24.2.1 (Paulus): Marriage is broken by divorce, death, captivity or another kind of slavery affecting one of the two partners.

D.50.16.101.1 (Modestinus): It is said that there is "divorce" (*divortium*) between man and wife, but "*repudium*" seems to be sent to a fiancée. This refers not absurdly also to the person of a wife.

D.50.16.191 (Paulus): Between "divorce" and "*repudium*" there is this difference, that even a future marriage (i.e. a betrothal) can be repudiated. However, a fiancée is not properly said to have divorced, because it has been called "divorce" from the fact that those who separate go off into diverging directions.

D.24.2.2 (Gaius): Moreover, it has been called "divorce" either from the diverging of minds or because those who are separating go off into diverging directions. 1: However, in repudiations, that is, in renunciation, these words have been established: "Have your own things for yourself;" likewise these words: "Attend to your own affairs." 2: In splitting up betrothals also, it has been decided that a renunciation ought to occur, in which event these words have been established: "I do not employ a marriage match with you." 3: But it makes no difference at all if the renunciation is made in the presence of the person (being repudiated) or in his (or her) absence through someone who is in his power or (through someone) in whose power he or she is.

D.24.2.3 (Paulus): A divorce is not real unless it occurs with the intention of forming a permanent separation. And so whatever is either done or said in the heat of anger, is not settled unless it has become apparent by perseverance that it was a definite decision. Therefore, if, after a *repudium* was sent in anger, a wife returned in a brief time, she does not appear to have divorced.[2]

Pre-nuptial agreements not to divorce had no legal validity:

Cod. Just. 8.38.2, 3 February, 223

Emperor Alexander Augustus to Menophilus:

From ancient times it has been determined that marriages are unrestricted. Therefore it is agreed that pacts not to permit divorce are not valid, and stipulations by which penalties were imposed on the person who had effected a divorce are considered invalid. Posted on the third day before the Nones of February in the second consulship of Maximus and the consulship of Aelianus.

Whereas gifts between spouses were not valid, it was possible for spouses who divorced amicably to give each other gifts. The jurists mention several reasons why couples might agree to divorce on good terms:

D.24.1.60.1 (Hermogenian): Gifts made "on account of divorce" have been allowed between husband and wife. For often it happens, that on account of the priesthood or even sterility,

D.24.1.61 (Gaius): or old age or ill health or military service, a marriage could not be conveniently maintained;

D.24.1.62 pr. (Hermogenian): And therefore the marriage is dissolved "with a good grace" (*bona gratia*).

The husband who commemorated his wife of many years in the long inscription known as the *Laudatio Turiae* recalled that she had suggested a divorce because of their inability to have children. He hotly rejected her offer, declaring that he would rather live childless with her than have children by any other woman. After all, she had saved his life during the civil wars and had kept faith with him throughout the political and social upheavals of the second triumvirate. We may wonder why a husband would talk about such an intimate matter in a public funeral oration for his wife, and record it on stone for posterity. He may have felt that it was necessary to provide a public defense of his non-compliance with the recently enacted legislation of Augustus on marriage and child-bearing [Chapter 2, Part I.B].[3.] The passage is indeed a remarkable testament to the Roman ideal of the harmonious, lifelong marriage; at another point in his speech the husband declares: "Rare are such long-lasting marriages, ended by death, not broken by divorce; for it happened that ours lasted for forty years without offense" [I.27–8]. This husband's clear privileging of the marriage relationship over having children, even in the face of social and legal pressure to produce heirs, helps to explain why Augustus' marriage legislation ultimately failed.

Laudatio Turiae II.31–47, late 1st c. B.C.E.

31: Distrusting your fertility and grieving about my childlessness, (afraid) that by being married to you I was giving up hope of having children and would be unhappy for that reason, you spoke openly about divorce. (You said) that you would hand over our empty home to another woman's fertility, with no other intention except that, with our well-known marital harmony, you yourself would seek out and procure for me a worthy and suitable marriage match, and you would promise to consider my future children as held in common with you and as if they were yours. Nor would you make a separation of our property, which up to then had been held by us in common, but it would continue to be under my authority and, if I wished, under your stewardship. You would have nothing divided, nothing separated, and you would thereafter exhibit to me the offices and sense of duty (*pietas*) of a sister and a mother-in-law.

40: I must confess that I became so inflamed, I almost went out of my mind; I was so horrified at your efforts that I scarcely regained control. For the possibility of a divorce between us to be considered before the law (*lex*) had been spoken by fate – that you were able to conceive in your mind some situation whereby you would cease to be my wife while I was still alive, when you had remained most faithful to me when I was an exile almost from life! 44: What desire or need of having children would be so important to me, that I would for that reason cast off my faithfulness and exchange sure things for unsure? – But why should I say more? [You remained my wife] with me; for I was not able to yield to you without my own dishonor and our mutual unhappiness.

B Sending a notice of divorce

Though formulas of repudiation like those given in the passages above are known from legal and literary sources, they were not essential to effect a unilateral divorce. Nor was a written notice of divorce (*repudium*) necessary. Augustus' legislation said that in order for a unilateral divorce to be fully valid, the divorcing spouse had to repudiate the other in front of witnesses, as the following extract from Paulus' commentaries on the Augustan adultery law states [Treggiari 1991a, 453–7]:

D.24.2.9 (Paulus): No divorce is valid unless seven (male) Roman citizens who have reached puberty have been summoned, other than the freedman of the person who will be making the divorce.

Publicly attested divorce was especially important for a husband divorcing his wife for adultery, because a husband who did not divorce an obviously adulterous wife could be charged with pimping (*lenocinium*) [see McGinn 1998, 171–94]. Moreover, many people would want to give clear evidence of intent to divorce, so that they could remarry without fear of appearing bigamous, and (in the case of women) so they could bring an action for return of the dowry. Failure to repudiate a partner publicly might cast doubt on the validity of the divorce, and could have legal repercussions:[4]

D.24.1.35 (Ulpian): If a divorce has not been made according to legal observance, gifts given after such a divorce have been made ineffective, since the marriage does not appear to have been dissolved.

In one of his books on Augustus' adultery law, Papinian remarks that the emperor Hadrian punished a man for adultery with another man's wife, because he had taken her home before she was divorced from her husband. Evidently the woman was not similarly punished:

D.24.2.8 (Papinian): The deified Hadrian relegated for three years a man who had led someone else's wife to his own home (in marriage) while she was on a journey and had only then sent a *repudium* to her husband.

On the other hand, if one spouse unilaterally repudiated the other in the proper way, it was not necessary that the repudiated spouse be aware of this:

Cod. Just. 5.17.6, 15 December, 294
Emperors Diocletian and Maximian and the Caesars to Phoebus:
Though a notice of divorce has not been handed over or made known to the husband, the marriage is dissolved. Given at Nicomedia on the eighteenth day before the Kalends of January in the consulship of the Caesars.

Ulpian, citing the Hadrianic jurist Julian, presents a case where a wife would be unaware that she was being divorced:

D.24.2.4 (Ulpian): Julian, in his eighteenth book of the Digests, asks whether a madwoman is able to send a *repudium* or to be repudiated. And he writes that a madwoman is able to be repudiated, since she is considered in the position of one who is ignorant. However, she is neither able to send a *repudium* herself, on account of her madness, nor through her curator; but her father is able to send a message (of divorce).[5]

By the same token, a wife could repudiate a husband who was mad – unless she was a freedwoman married to her former master [see Part I.D].

Sometimes, even when a notice of divorce was sent, the divorce might not be finalized. This excerpt is from the first book of Papinian's commentary on the adultery law (whether or not someone was known to be divorced would be relevant to the question of liability for prosecution under the adultery law):

D.24.2.7 (Papinian): If the person who gave a notice of divorce to be handed over (to the other spouse) came to regret it, and the notice of divorce was handed over in ignorance of this change of mind, the marriage ought to be said to endure – unless, upon learning of the change of mind, the person who received the notice wanted to dissolve the marriage himself. For in that case the marriage is dissolved by the person who received the notice.

C Return of dowry after divorce

If a marriage ended by divorce, the wife or her father could bring an action for return of dowry. If the divorce were due to the woman's fault or at her (or her father's) instigation, or there were children, the husband would be entitled to withholdings of part of the dowry, known as *retentiones*:

***Rules of Ulpian* 6.9:** Withholdings are made from the dowry [either on account of children] or on account of morals (*mores*) or on account of expenses or on account of things given or on account of things removed. **10:** A withholding is made on account of children if the divorce has been made by the woman's fault, or that of her father if she is in his power. For in that case, a sixth (of the whole dowry) is withheld in the name of each individual child, however, not more than three-sixths (altogether).... **12:** Indeed, a sixth is withheld on the grounds of more serious moral defects, however, an eighth for lighter ones. More serious moral defects are only adulterous acts; the rest are lighter.[6]

If the wife's *paterfamilias* were still alive, the dowry would be returned to him, but only if she was willing:

D.24.3.2 (Ulpian): When the marriage has been dissolved, the dowry is paid to the woman.... This (is the case) if the woman is legally independent. **1:** But if she is under paternal power and the dowry came from him, the dowry is his and his daughter's; and then the father is not able to get back the dowry, either through himself or through a legal agent, except at his daughter's wish....**2:** But when the father brings an action concerning the dowry, do we accept "his daughter's wish" (to mean) that she consents or, on the other hand, that she does not object? And there is a rescript from the emperor Antoninus (Caracalla) that a daughter appears to give her consent to her father, unless she clearly objects....[7]

Sometimes the dowry might be returned to the wife even when her father was still alive. Even if she were under paternal power and owned no property of her own, she might have contributed the dowry from her *peculium*, the allowance that Roman fathers gave their children to administer during the father's lifetime:

D.23.3.24 (Pomponius): If a daughter under her father's power who is about to marry gave a dowry to her husband from the *peculium* whose management she has, then, when her *peculium* was in the same position, there was a divorce, the dowry is paid to her correctly, just as (it would be) by any debtor on a *peculium*.

The peculiar position of dowry is illustrated by the following rescript of Diocletian and Maximian to a father who wanted to repossess money he had given his daughter. If he had given it as dowry, he could not get it back while the marriage was intact, since it belonged to the husband. If he tried to force his daughter to divorce (see Part I.E), her husband would return the dowry, but it would not go to the father unless his daughter were willing. This presumably acted as a check on fathers breaking up their children's marriages for mercenary reasons.[8] On the other hand, he could take back any money other than dowry (i.e., her *peculium*, the allowance often given by a *paterfamilias* to children under his control) that he had given a daughter under his power. This may be one reason why unlike the situation in some other societies, dowry did not make up the major portion of a Roman daughter's paternal inheritance.

Cod. Just. 5.18.7, 9 February, 294
Emperors Diocletian and Maximian and the Caesars to Erotius:
You are not at all prevented from taking away the money of a daughter who is under your power. But if you gave (the money) as dowry on her behalf, you are not able to get it back during the marriage even if she agrees. Moreover, if the marriage has been dissolved, you are not able to get (the dowry) back if she is unwilling. Subscribed at Sirmium[9] on the fifth day before the Ides of February in the consulship of the Caesars.

D Freedwomen and divorce

Marriage between a man and his former slave was not forbidden except to members of senatorial families [Chapter 3, Part I.B.4], and seems to have been quite common. A man's manumission of his slavewoman for the purpose of marriage did not have to meet the age requirements of the *lex Aelia Sentia*.[10] Thus the emperors Diocletian and Maximian replied to a petitioner, who may have been a man who wished to marry his freedwoman:

Cod. Just. 5.4.15, 292–305
Emperors Diocletian and Maximian Augusti and the Caesars to Titianus:
It is not forbidden for a manumittor to take his own freedwoman as wife, as long as she is not among those persons who are especially prohibited, and it is quite certain that legitimate children are born to their father from this marriage. [not dated, but between 292–305]

The freedwoman had to agree to the marriage (but in such cases it must have been rather difficult to refuse):

D.23.2.28 (Marcian): A patron is not able to marry an unwilling freed-woman.

Because marriage to her patron elevated a freedwoman to the level of a respectably married woman, he could not demand the services (*operae*) normally expected of ex-slaves by their patrons [see Gardner 1993, 20–32 on *operae*]. The emperor Alexander Severus had to tell one such patron:

Cod. Just. 6.3.9, 20 February, 225
Emperor Alexander (Severus) Augustus to Laetorius:

You have increased the rank (*dignitas*) of your freedwoman by marrying her, and therefore she should not be forced to offer services to you, since you can be content by the benefit of the law, because she cannot legally marry someone else if you are unwilling.

Given on the tenth day before the Kalends of March in the consulship of Fuscus and Dexter.

Alexander's reply refers to a significant restriction on freedwomen, introduced by Augustus in his marriage legislation [see Chapter 2, Part I.B]: though a freedwoman wife apparently could leave her patron husband, she could not make a valid marriage with someone else. Her marital status was in a sort of limbo.[11] The following passage and the other excerpts from Ulpian below [D.23.2.45.4, 5 and 6] are from his commentaries on the Augustan laws:

D.24.2.11 pr. (Ulpian): In regard to what the (Augustan) law says: "A freedwoman who has married her patron is not to have the power of effecting a divorce," this does not appear to have made the divorce invalid, because it is usual to dissolve marriage by civil law. Therefore we are not able to say that the marriage still exists, since there has been a separation. And so (the jurist) Julian writes that she does not have a legal action for return of dowry. Therefore quite rightly, as long as her patron wants her to be his wife, she does not have the right of marriage (*conubium*) with anyone else. For since the maker of the law understood that the marriage was as it were broken by the freedwoman's act, he took away from her the right of marriage with another. Therefore whomever she has married, she will not be considered as a married woman. Julian, indeed, thinks further that she is not able to live as the concubine of another (man other than her) patron. 1: The law says: "As long as the patron wants her to be his wife." And it is necessary both that he want her to be his wife and that he continue to be her patron; if therefore he should cease to be her patron or to want her (as wife), the law's authority has ended.[12]
D.23.2.51 pr. (Licinnius Rufinus): A slavewoman manumitted "for the sake of marriage" is not able to be married by anyone other than the man by whom she was manumitted, unless her patron has renounced marriage with her.

Cod. Just. 5.5.1, 222–235
Emperor Alexander Augustus to Amphigenes:
Your freedwoman, who is also your wife, if she has left you when you were unwilling, does not have the right of marriage (*conubium*) with another, if you still want to have her as your wife.

As with consent to marriage [see Chapter 2, Part I.C.3], so with divorce there was some legal debate as to what constituted consent or lack of consent on the part of a patron husband. What if the patron was no longer in his right mind, or did not even know about the divorce? Clearly, he could not consent to a divorce, and so the freedwoman was unable to make another legal marriage (cf. D.24.2.4 in Part I.B for divorce from a madman).

D.23.2.45.5 (Ulpian): Finally, the (Augustan) law says "her patron being unwilling:" we ought to accept as "unwilling" he who does not consent to the divorce. Therefore, by divorcing a madman, she has not released herself from the necessity of the law, nor (does she) if she has divorced a man when he did not know (that she was divorcing him). For he is more correctly said to be "unwilling" than he who has refused.

More questions arose in the case where the patron was a captive outside the Empire. Normally, Roman marriages were considered dissolved if one party was in captivity.[13] To the jurist Julian and his adherents, the freedwoman wife would be an exception to this rule. But Ulpian regretfully disagreed:

D.23.2.45.6 (Ulpian):   If it is proposed that a patron was captured by the enemy, I am afraid that in marrying she is able to have *conubium* (with someone else), in the same way that she would have it if he were dead. And those who approve the opinion of Julian would say that she does not have *conubium*. For Julian thinks that a man's marriage to his freedwoman lasts even in captivity, on account of the reverence (owed by her) for her patron. Certainly if her patron has been led into some other form of slavery, I have no doubt that the marriage would be dissolved.

In some cases, a freedwoman could marry against her patron's will; for instance, if she had refused to marry her patron in the first place, or if the patron was not the woman's former master, but had freed her at the request of her deceased master:

D.23.2.45.4 (Ulpian): This chapter (of the Augustan marriage legislation) pertains only to the married freedwoman; it does not pertain to the one who is engaged. And therefore if a freedwoman fiancée has sent a message (of repudiation) to her unwilling patron, she has the right of marriage with another.
D.24.2.10 (Modestinus): A freedwoman whom her patron has married is not able to divorce him if he is unwilling, unless she was manumitted by means of a *fideicommissum*.[14] For in that case she is able to, though she becomes his freedwoman.

Augustus' law was anxious to preserve the rights of the patron, who (as Alexander Severus remarked in his rescript to Laetorius, above) had honored his former slave and increased her *dignitas* by marrying her. How did freedwomen feel about this restriction on their freedom to divorce? We have no testimonies from freedwomen themselves, but an unusual inscription suggests that at least one freedwoman felt less grateful to her former master than he expected. A funerary altar erected in Rome in the latter half of the first century by Junius Euphrosynus (whose name suggests strongly that he himself was a freedman) and his wife Junia Acte commemorated the death of their nine-year-old daughter, Junia Procula. It is typical of many such funerary monuments for children by their parents, expressing grief and a hope that the deceased one will rest peacefully. But at some later point, Junius Euphrosynus had another text carved on the back of the altar – a curse, calling on the spirit of the dead Procula as witness of her mother's perfidy. (Acte's name was also erased from the inscription on the front of the altar commemorating her daughter.)[15]

CIL VI.20905 (rear) *c*.80 C.E.

Here the eternal marks of infamy[16] have been written for Acte the freedwoman, the poisoner, faithless and deceitful, hard-hearted. (I bring) a nail and a rope of broom so that she may bind her own neck, and burning pitch to consume her evil heart. Manumitted free of charge, she cheated her patron, following an adulterer, and she stole away his servants – a slavegirl and a boy – while her patron was lying in bed, so that he pined away, an old man left alone and despoiled....[17]

Junius Euphrosynus' freedwoman could not legally divorce him and marry another, but she could still leave him to live with an "adulterer." In such cases, the hope of divine intervention by the spirits of the dead promised more relief to the abandoned husband than the law.

E *Divorce and* patria potestas

The Roman concept of paternal power also played a role in the circumstances and consequences of divorce.

1 *A father's right to break up his child's marriage*

The legal sources make it clear that for a union to be considered *iustum matrimonium*, the consent of the *paterfamilias* of both bride and groom was essential [see Chapter 2, Part I.C]. Was it also necessary that couples who wished to divorce have the permission of their respective fathers? There is no direct statement of this in extant classical Roman law, but on the analogy of consent to marriage, it is probable that a *paterfamilias* had to at least give tacit consent to the divorce of a child in his paternal power – that is, he had not to object.[18] For most men, the question of their father's consent would not arise, since their father was likely to have died even before they married, and even if he were still alive at the time of marriage, he probably would not have lived many years after [cf. Saller 1994, 121]. Women, who married on average ten years younger than men, would be more likely to have a living *paterfamilias* at the time of marriage. However, women whose father had arranged their marriage when they were in their teens might well find themselves legally independent before they turned thirty. They could use their independence to free themselves from an unhappy marriage. (Women under *tutela mulierum* would not need their *tutor's* permission to divorce, but only if they wished to constitute a dowry for a second marriage after divorce; see Chapter 1, Part III.A.)

A young woman with a living *paterfamilias* could probably not divorce if her father objected, but there is nothing in the legal sources about fathers actually trying to prevent their daughter from divorcing [Treggiari 1991a, 445–6]. If a divorced woman were returning to her natal home, she would no doubt need her father's permission. And a father would certainly have an interest in seeing that his daughter's husband returned her dowry after divorce:

Cod. Just. 5.4.7, 29 October, 240
Emperor Gordian to Aper:

If, as you assert, the marriage was broken up after a complaint concerning her husband reported to you by your daughter, nor did she return to him with your consent, the union is not at all legal, since it is no longer according to the will of the father in whose power she is. And therefore, as long as your daughter does not regret (her decision to divorce), you will not be prevented from asking for her dowry back. Posted on the fourth day before the Kalends of November in the consulship of Sabinus and Venustus

On the other hand, until the mid-second century, fathers did have the right to force their children under *patria potestas* to divorce their spouses. The sources attribute the mitigation of this paternal prerogative to either Antoninus Pius (138–161) or Marcus Aurelius (161–180). There may have been more than one ruling by different emperors responding to individual petitions. Even this restraint on *patria potestas* was tempered by the proviso that if he had good reason the father could still break up his child's marriage.

Sent. Pauli V.vi.15: The deified (Antoninus) Pius forbade that a harmonious marriage be broken up by a father, and likewise that a freedman's (marriage) be broken up by a patron, or (the marriage of) a son or daughter be broken up by relatives (*parentes*), unless by chance there is an investigation, when it ought to be more useful to delay.

D.43.30.1.5 (Ulpian): If someone wants to take away his daughter, who has been married to me, or desires that she be shown to him, must an exception be given against the injunction,[19] if by chance the father wants to dissolve a harmonious marriage, perhaps one even supported by children? And certainly we follow the law, that really harmonious marriages are not to be disturbed by the legal right of paternal power. However, (the law) should be employed in such a way that the father be persuaded not to exercise his paternal power in a harsh way.

Frag. Vat. 116: A father sent a *repudium* to his son-in-law against his daughter's wish; I ask whether he can get back the dowry (which was) provided from his own resources. Paulus replied that indeed the marriage seems to have been justly dissolved by the very act (of sending the *repudium*), but that it is not permitted for a father to take his daughter away from her husband against her will, nor for him to be able to get back the dowry unless his daughter consents.

This rather puzzling ruling recalls the paradoxical attitude toward consent to marriage: all parties ought to consent, but lack of active opposition can be taken to imply consent. Perhaps the divorce was valid after the *repudium* was sent, but the father could not forcibly separate his daughter from her husband, nor could he get her dowry back [Buckland 1963, 117; Treggiari 1991a, 460–1]. The outcome would depend on the daughter's personal decision either to return to her husband or agree to the divorce, as is clear from the following imperial replies to petitions, dated more than a century after the Antonine ruling:

Cod. Just. 3.28.18, 14 February, 286

Emperors Diocletian and Maximian to Faustina:

Since you say that you did not violate the observance of *pietas*, but that you were unwilling to break up the marital union which you had been allotted, and for that reason your father, offended and angry, slipped into the disgrace of disinheritance, you will not be prohibited from bringing a complaint of "undutiful will."[20] Posted at Nicomedia[21] on the sixteenth day before the Kalends of March in the second consulship of Maximus and the consulship of Aquilinus.

Cod. Just. 5.17.5, 27 August, 294

Emperors Diocletian and Maximian and the Caesars to Scyrion:

Our father, that most pious Emperor, the deified Marcus (Aurelius), decided that when a daughter under paternal power was a wife living in harmony with her husband, her father's objecting – if he gave his consent to the union in the beginning – was not to be considered valid, unless the father did this when some great and just reason came up. (1) On the other hand, no constitution of law declares that she should return to her husband if she is unwilling. (2) But a father does not have any choice over the divorce of a daughter he has emancipated from paternal power. Given at Nicomedia on the fifth day before the Kalends of September in the consulship of the Caesars.

Cod. Just. 5.4.11, 284–292

Emperors Diocletian and Maximian to Alexander:

If your wife is being held by her relatives against her will, our friend the governor of your province, after you have approached him for help, and following the woman's own wish, when she has been produced in public, will relieve your desire.

Sometimes even mothers tried to force their children's divorce, though such a power had never been granted to them:

Cod. Just. 3.28.20, 5 January, 294

Emperors Diocletian and Maximian and the Caesars to Sabinianus:

A daughter who has been left an orphan by her father, who is living in concord with the husband she married when her mother was willing, does not offer just cause for offense after the same mother's change of mind (about the marriage), nor is she lawfully compelled to be married or unmarried at the momentary whims of her mother. Given at Sirmium on the Nones of January in the consulship of the Caesars.

Cod. Just. 5.17.4, 29 December, 294

Emperors Diocletian and Maximian and the Caesars to Piso:

A mother does not have the power to bring about her daughter's divorce. Given at Sirmium on the fourth day before the Kalends of January in the consulship of the Caesars.

The conflicts we find in the legal sources center around a father's right to break up his daughter's marriage; nothing is said about the marriages of *sons* under paternal power. We do hear of one famous case in which a *stepfather* forced his wife's son to divorce, but since it involved the imperial family, the circumstances were unusual.[22] Augustus ordered Tiberius, his adopted son (son of Augustus' wife Livia by her first marriage) to divorce his wife Vipsania (Agrippina) in order to marry Augustus' daughter Julia (who had previously been married to Marcus Agrippa, Vipsania's father, and was thus the widow of Tiberius' father-in-law):

Suetonius, *Tiberius* 7

(Tiberius) married Agrippina, born from Marcus Agrippa, the grand-daughter of Caecilius Atticus, a Roman *eques*,[23] to whom Cicero's letters were sent. But after he had begotten a son, Drusus, from her, he was forced to dismiss her, though she was well-suited to him and was again pregnant, and immediately to marry Julia, Augustus' daughter – not without great anguish of spirit, since he was possessed by intimacy and affection for Agrippina, and also disapproved of Julia's character, as he had perceived that she desired him even during her previous marriage (to Agrippa), which indeed was quite generally believed. But he grieved that he had driven Agrippina off even after the divorce, and when he saw her face to face just once, he followed her with eager and moist eyes, so much so that precautions were taken that she never again come into his sight.

The case of Tiberius shows that adult children might regret very much being made to divorce (and see Cod. Just. 5.4.11 to Alexander, who claimed his wife was forced to divorce against her will). In Roman Egypt, fathers also exercised their right to bring about their daughter's divorce under local Greco-Egyptian (not Roman) law. Some daughters resisted this, as we know from a long papyrus of the late second century detailing the complaint of one daughter, Dionysia, against her father Chaeremon, which quotes earlier court cases involving similar situations [P.Oxy. II.237; see Rowlandson 1998, 183–8].

2 Children after divorce

In our society, conflicts over the custody of children after divorce are frequent. In Roman law, the situation seems simpler: children born in legitimate marriage came under their father's power, and if the marriage broke up, they remained under his control. A woman who divorced her husband ran the risk of never seeing her children again, and this probably served as a greater deterrent for women contemplating divorce than any legal restrictions would have. It was recognized, however, that sometimes children were better off living with their mother, if the father were a disreputable character:

D.43.30.3.5 (Ulpian): Even if a father should prove completely that a son is in his power, however, after a hearing has been held, the mother will have preference in keeping him, and that is contained in certain oral decisions of the deified (Antoninus) Pius. For a mother has obtained (custody) on account of the father's wickedness, so that the son remained with her (though) without diminution of paternal power.

Antoninus Pius' decision was confirmed in rescripts of Marcus Aurelius and Septimius Severus [D.43.30.1.3]. Note that though a mother might have physical custody of the child, the father did not lose *patria potestas*.

Parents who divorced on amicable terms might make arrangements to share custody, or for the mother to keep very young children with her, but such arrangements were outside the usual scope of the law [Daube 1966]. Local and provincial officials, and even emperors, might be asked to intervene in custody disputes. The emperors Diocletian and Maximian replied to a woman who was probably involved in such a case:

Cod. Just. 5.24.1, 14 June, 294

Emperors Diocletian and Maximian and the Caesars to Caelestina:
There is no legal provision, in any constitution of ours or of our divine parents,[24] that a division of children be made between the parents on the basis of sex. However, the appropriate judge will decide whether the children ought to stay and be cared for at the father's home or at the mother's after a marriage has been broken up. Subscribed on the sixteenth day before the Kalends of July at Beroea in the consulship of the Caesars.

Diocletian replied to this petition when he was at Beroea (modern Aleppo) in Syria. It is possible that Caelestina, who was probably from the Middle East, was referring to a local custom of dividing custody of children by sex, a practice unfamiliar to the imperial chancellery [Yaron 1964, 296–8].

Fathers had financial responsibility for the children born to them in legitimate marriage, even if the children lived with their mother after divorce. Thus if there were children, a man could retain part of his ex-wife's dowry, if the divorce had been due to her fault or at her instigation. But if the children were living with their mother, a divorced father might be reluctant to contribute financially, as so often is the case today. A woman Tatiana went so far as to petition the emperor to force her ex-husband to pay child support:

Cod. Just. 5.25.3, 16 February, 162

Emperors Marcus Aurelius and Lucius Verus to Tatiana:
If you have proven to the appropriate judge that the child whom you say you bore to Claudius is his son, he will order him (Claudius) to provide support to him (the child) according to his means. The same man will

decide whether (the child) ought to be brought up in his (Claudius') household. Posted at Rome on the fourteenth day before the Kalends of March in the consulship of Rusticus and Aquilinus.

Here it appears that Claudius was denying paternity. Probably Tatiana and Claudius had been married, and Tatiana's child had been born during the marriage or shortly after the divorce. The situation of children born within a few months of divorce was so problematic that in the early second century,[25] the Senate passed a decree, the *senatusconsultum Plancianum*, to regulate cases where an ex-wife claimed to be pregnant by her former husband:

D.25.3.1 pr. (Ulpian): The decree of the Senate which was made about the recognizing of children, comprises two cases: one concerning men who recognize (sc. paternity), the other concerning women who substitute false offspring. 1: Therefore it permits a woman or the parent in whose power she is, or the person to whom a mandate has been given by them, if she should believe herself pregnant, to make an official announcement within the thirty days reckoned after the divorce to the (ex-)husband himself or to the parent in whose power he is, or to make an official announcement to his home, if she does not have access to any of them[26] ... 3: ... It is now the husband's (right) either to send observers or to make an official announcement to her, that she is not pregnant by him. Moreover, it is permitted either for the husband himself to do this or for someone else acting in his name. 4: However, the husband shall have this punishment, that, unless he has either sent observers or, on the other hand, has announced that she is not pregnant by him, he shall be forced to recognize the offspring. And, if he has not recognized (the offspring), he will be forced to in court (*extra ordinem*).

The "observers" (*custodes*) were to keep an eye on the woman to be sure she was indeed pregnant and gave birth to a live child.

D.25.3.1.6 (Ulpian): But if the husband voluntarily offers observers and she does not allow them, or if the woman has not made an announcement, or if she has in fact made an announcement, but has not allowed observers (chosen) by the decision of a judge, the husband or his parent is free not to recognize the offspring. 7: If a woman has not announced that she is pregnant within the thirty-day period, if she afterwards announces it, she ought to be heard, after the case has been investigated. 8: But indeed, even if she has omitted an announcement altogether, (the jurist) Julian says that this does not at all harm the offspring which is born.

The procedure described in the Senate's decree was very similar to one called for by the Praetor's Edict for a widow who claimed to be pregnant by her deceased husband. The aim was to ensure that a child who really was the offspring of a man in legitimate marriage be recognized as his heir even if the marriage had ended. Widows in such a situation had not only to notify their former in-laws that they were pregnant, but also had the actual birth monitored under high-security conditions [D.25.4.1.10–15; Chapter 5, Part III.A]. Though this was not usually required of divorced women, in one case it was:

D.25.4.1 pr. (Ulpian): In the times of the deified brothers (Marcus Aurelius and Lucius Verus), when it had happened that a husband said that his wife was pregnant, but the wife denied it, they (the emperors) sent a rescript to the urban praetor, Valerius Priscianus, in these words: "Rutilius Severus appears to desire a new thing, to place an observer over his wife, who had divorced him and claims that she is not pregnant. And so no one will wonder, if we also suggest a new plan and remedy. Therefore if he persists in this demand, it is most suitable that the home of a very respectable woman be chosen, into which Domitia shall go, and there three midwives of proven skill and trust-worthiness, who have been chosen by you, shall inspect her. And if indeed either all or two should announce that she appears pregnant, then the woman will be persuaded that she therefore allow an observer as if she herself had desired this. But if she has not given birth, her husband should know that it is a matter of ill-will (*invidia*) and of his reputation, and that he shall not undeservedly appear to have seized on this as some sort of insult to the woman. If, moreover, either all or most (of the midwives) have announced that she is not pregnant, there will be no reason for observing her."

Domitia had divorced Rutilius Severus, who evidently suspected her of concealing the fact that she was pregnant by him. This is thus the opposite situation from that envisaged by the *s.c. Plancianum*, which concerned cases where a divorced woman claimed to be pregnant and her ex-husband might want to deny paternity. In both situations, as well as the case of a widow claiming to be pregnant by her deceased husband, Roman officials and lawyers thought the appropriate solution was a physical examination and close observation of the allegedly pregnant woman! When the existence of a man's heir was in question, his former wife did not have a right to privacy.

That ex-husbands had reason to be suspicious is suggested by other cases known from the *Digest*, where divorced women did conceal their pregnancies:

D.22.3.29.1 (Scaevola): A pregnant woman who had been divorced (*repudiata*), having given birth to a son, declared him as illegitimate in the records in her (ex-) husband's absence. It was asked whether he were in his father's power and whether, after the mother had died without a will, he could accept an inheritance from his mother at his (the father's) command, and whether the declaration made by his mother when angry should not be prejudicial (to the son). (Scaevola) replied, that there would still be a place for the truth.

D.40.4.29 (Scaevola): (A man) had repudiated his pregnant wife and married another. The former wife, after giving birth, exposed[27] her son. He was rescued and brought up by another, and was called by his father's name. Throughout his father's life it was unknown to the father as much as to the mother, that he (the child) was among the living. When the father died and his will was read out, in which the son was neither disinherited nor instituted heir, the son, recognized by his mother and his paternal grand-mother, obtained inheritance from his father as if he were a legitimate heir succeeding upon intestacy.

Disgruntled ex-wives might even go so far as to abort their former husband's child. This happened in a case that was brought to Septimius Severus and Caracalla, evidently by the ex-husband. The emperors' ruling is referred to at least twice in the *Digest* [cf. also D.48.8.8 (Ulpian)], though only in D.48.19.39 do we learn that the woman was divorced from her husband:

D. 47.11.4 (Marcian): The deified Severus and Antoninus wrote in a rescript that she who intentionally aborted ought to be sent into temporary exile by the governor. For it can appear shameful for her to have defrauded her husband of children with impunity.

D.48.19.39 (Tryphoninus): ... But also if anyone, because she was pregnant, applied violence to her own womb after a divorce, so that she would not bear a child to her estranged husband, it has been stated in a rescript by our best of emperors that she is to be punished by temporary exile.

The woman was not punished for having procured an abortion, which was not *per se* against the law. Though Roman law did consider a fetus as "among human affairs" for some legal purposes [see D.1.5.7 (Paulus)], it was the prerogative of the *paterfamilias* of the yet unborn child to determine whether it would be reared and acknowledged (see Chapter 1, Part II.A on the father's "right of life and death"). In this case, since the child had been conceived in legitimate marriage, the father had the right to decide its fate, and the ex-wife, by having an abortion without his consent, was thought to deserve a serious penalty.[28]

II Divorce in late Roman law

Classical Roman law gave both women and men the right to repudiate their spouse unilaterally [for exceptions to this, see Parts I.D and I.E.1]. A divorced woman could bring an action to get back her dowry in full; part of the dowry might be retained by the husband if the divorce were due to the wife's fault (or at her or her father's instigation) or if there were children from the marriage [see Part I.C]. By contrast, late Roman emperors imposed restrictions on divorce in cases where one partner wanted to repudiate the other unilaterally (divorce by mutual consent was not restricted until the sixth century, and then only for a short period of time).

Extant laws against unilateral divorce begin with Constantine, and have often been attributed to Christian influence – understandably, since Christian condemnations of divorce go back to the Gospels and were frequently reiterated. But the harsh provisions of Constantine's law – which is much harder on wives who wish to divorce than on husbands – are not in keeping with the generally egalitarian attitude taken by early Christian church leaders, though popular Christian attitudes may have differed [Evans Grubbs 1995, 242–53]. Recent scholarship on late Roman divorce law is more skeptical about the extent of Christian influence on imperial legislation [Arjava 1988; Bagnall 1987; Evans Grubbs 1995].

Constantine's law dates from late in his reign and is addressed to his praetorian prefect, Ablabius, a known Christian who was said to have risen from humble origins in the Greek east. The law itself contains a number of words and expressions not usually found in Roman law (classical or late antique), suggesting that the person who drafted the law (possibly Ablabius himself) did not have legal training.[29]

Cod. Theod. 3.16.1, 331

Emperor Constantine Augustus to Ablabius, praetorian prefect:

It is pleasing that a woman not be permitted to send a notice of divorce to her husband because of her own depraved desires, for some carefully contrived cause, such as his being a drunkard or gambler or womanizer.[30] However, neither should husbands be permitted to divorce their own wives for just any reason whatsoever. But in the sending of a notice of divorce by a woman these crimes only are to be looked into: if she has proven that her husband is a murderer or a preparer of poisons or a disturber of tombs, so that only then, after being praised,[31] she shall receive back her entire dowry. For if she has sent a notice of divorce to her husband for any reason other than these three crimes, she should leave it (the dowry), down to a hairpin,[32] in her husband's home, and in return for such great confidence in herself, should be deported to an island.

Also in the case of men, if they send a notice of divorce, it is fitting that these three crimes be inquired into: if they wanted to repudiate an adulteress or a preparer of poisons or a go-between.[33] For if he has ejected a woman who is free of these crimes, he ought to restore the entire dowry and not marry another woman. But if he does, the former wife will be given the opportunity to invade his home and to transfer to herself all the dowry of the second wife, in return for the injury brought against her.

Given ... in the consulship of Bassus and Ablabius.[34]

The penalties for a woman who divorces her husband for any reason other than those allowed by the law are even harsher than the penalties for adultery under Augustus' adultery law of 18 B.C.E. [see Chapter 2, Part II]. The Augustan law had decreed relegation (a milder form of exile than deportation)[35] and confiscation of part of the adulterer's property (for a woman, half her dowry and a third of her other property; for a man, half his property). Late Roman law saw unilateral divorce by a wife as tantamount to an admission of unchaste behavior, indicating that she desired to marry someone else (this comes out clearly in post-Constantinian divorce laws, which mandate a waiting period for remarriage to ensure that the divorcée was repudiating her husband for other reasons; see below). Constantine's divorce law codifies the Roman double standard that said a woman's sexual misbehavior was considered much more serious an offense than a man's. Adultery was, in Roman legal terms, a woman's crime, defined as extramarital sex by or with a married woman. A married man would only be committing adultery if his lover were someone else's wife – and under Constantine's law, that would not be sufficient reason for his wife to divorce him.

Note that though divorces made against the law are penalized, they are not invalidated: the husband who unjustly repudiates his wife can still remarry (so his divorce was valid), but his ex-wife can take revenge by seizing the new wife's dowry – which would only indirectly punish her ex-husband, but which would have more serious consequences for the second wife!

After Constantine's legislation there are no extant laws on divorce in the *Theodosian Code* for almost another century,[36] but this is probably due to the fragmentary state of preservation of the *Code*. References in fourth and early fifth-century Christian writers imply that

Constantine's law of 331 was not being enforced and had evidently been repealed [Arjava 1988, 7–13]. It appears that the emperor Julian (reigned 360–363), Constantine's nephew who apostasized from Christianity and embraced paganism, abolished his uncle's penalties for women who repudiated their husbands.[37] His law is not extant, but a passage in the Christian writer known as "Ambrosiaster" refers to it:[38]

Ambrosiaster, *Liber Quaest. Vet. et Novi Test.* 115.12

... Before the edict of Julian, women were unable to dismiss (that is, divorce) their husbands. But once they had received the power, they began to do what previously they could not do: for they began wantonly to dismiss their own husbands, on a daily basis....

Ambrosiaster reveals the same misogynism as Constantine's law, but there may be some truth to his assertion: women trapped in unhappy marriages may have taken advantage of the return to freedom of divorce under Julian, as has happened in other periods when divorce restrictions have been lifted [Evans Grubbs 1995, 233]. Disapproval of women who divorce can be found in many works of earlier Latin literature, and is probably indicative of Roman popular attitudes, Christian and pagan [Arjava 1988].

The next extant law on divorce is from the fifth-century west, an enactment of the emperor Honorius and his colleague and brother-in-law Constantius. This law reinstitutes the Constantinian penalties for totally unjustified divorce by a wife or a husband, but reduces the penalty for divorce when the other spouse has "middling" faults to loss of dowry and pre-nuptial gift, and denial (for a woman) or delay (for a man) of the right to remarry.

Cod. Theod. 3.16.2, 10 March, 421

Emperors Honorius, Theodosius, and Constantius Augusti to Palladius, praetorian prefect:

A woman who has separated (from her husband) by presenting a *repudium* given by her, if she has proved no causes for her own divorce, having lost the gifts which she had received as a fiancée, shall also be deprived of her dowry and given over to the penalty of deportation. We deny to her not only the bond of a second husband, but also the right of return from exile.[39] But if a woman, struggling against marriage, has proved clearly vices and middling faults (on the part of her husband), she will lose her dowry and is to refund the (pre-nuptial) gift to her husband, certainly never to be joined in marriage with anyone again. And so that she not stain her widowhood with the shamelessness of illicit sex,[40] we offer to the repudiated husband the right to accuse her by law. It remains that, if a woman who has left (her husband) has proven serious causes and knowledge implicated in great crimes (on her husband's part), she shall gain possession of her dowry and shall also obtain the betrothal gift, and she shall receive the power of remarrying five years from the day of divorce. For then she will appear to have done this from abomination of her husband rather than desire for another man.

(1) Certainly, if the husband has first brought about the divorce and has brought a serious criminal charge against the woman, he shall accuse her and

pursue her by law and having obtained his vengeance he shall possess her dowry and shall receive back his generosity (i.e., the pre-nuptial gift) and shall obtain the free choice of marrying another woman soon. But if it is a fault of character, not of crimes, he shall receive back his gift, relinquish the dowry, (and) marry another wife after two years. But if he has preferred to split up the marriage solely because of disagreement and the repudiated woman is weighed down by no vices or sins, the husband shall lose both the pre-nuptial gift and the dowry, and in perpetual celibacy he shall endure the penalty for insolent divorce from grievous solitude, and to the woman the power of marriage has been conceded after the end of a year.[41] (2) However, we order that the provisions of the ancient law concerning withholdings from the dowry on account of children be preserved.[42]

Given at Ravenna on the sixth day before the Ides of March in the consulship of Eustathius and Agricola.[43]

The western law of 421 was not promulgated in the eastern Empire, which by this time had its own separate consistory.[44] But in 438, when the *Theodosian Code* was published and subsequently accepted in both halves of the Empire, Cod. Theod. 3.16.2 was the most recently enacted law on divorce to be found in the *Code*, and so became effective for both east and west. But the eastern emperor, Theodosius II, found the law of Honorius and Constantius too harsh, and in the following year he enacted his own, less stringent law. Unlike the laws in the *Theodosian Code*, this law has been preserved in full.

Theodosius' law upholds classical doctrine that the consent of both parties is the only requirement for valid marriage [cf. Chapter 2, Part I.A.2; Cod. Theod. 3.7.3 in Chapter 2, Part II.C]. But it makes dissolving a marriage more difficult by requiring the issuing of a *repudium*, a (presumably written) notice of divorce [Evans Grubbs 1995, 235; Wolff 1950, 294–5]. In making divorce somewhat less easy to obtain, the law invokes *favor liberorum*, the benefit of the law that should be given to children. This is the first extant mention of children in late Roman divorce law, though it is possible that the original, unabridged versions of the *Theodosian Code* laws did refer to children.

Novel 12 of Theodosius II, 10 July, 439

Emperors Theodosius (II) and Valentinian (III) Augusti to Florentius, praetorian prefect:

We order that legal marriages are able to be contracted by consent, (but) once contracted are not able to be dissolved except if a *repudium* has been sent. For indeed the favor that should be shown to children (*favor liberorum*) demands that the dissolution of marriage ought to be rather difficult.

(1) But in sending a *repudium* and inquiring into the fault for the divorce, it is harsh to go beyond the guidance of the ancient laws. Therefore, having repealed the constitutions which order that now the husband, now the woman be repressed by the most severe penalties after a marriage has been dissolved, by this constitution we propose to revoke the blame for a *repudium* and the punishments for faults (and to return) to the ancient laws and the responses of jurisprudents, Florentius, dearest and most beloved parent.[45] And so your splendid and magnificent authority shall order that these

205

things, which have been most providently decided, be made known by means of posted edicts.

Given at Constantinople on the sixth day before the Ides of July in the seventeenth consulship of Theodosius Augustus and the consulship of Festus, *v.c.*[46]

In 448, Theodosius II sent to the western emperor, Valentinian III (son of Constantius and Galla Placidia), the laws that had been enacted in the eastern Empire since the publication of the *Theodosian Code* ten years earlier. It appears that Valentinian was not pleased with Theodosius' divorce law of 439, for in 452 he enacted his own rule, reinstating the earlier legislation of Honorius and Constantius [Cod. Theod. 3.16.2]. The following excerpt was part of a much longer law [Novel 35, see Chapter 2, Part II.C for another excerpt], on a number of matters, including pre-nuptial gifts, dowry, and the property passed on to children from their mother (*bona materna*).

Novel 35.11 of Valentinian III, 15 April, 452

(11) Regarding the bond of reverence for marriages themselves, however, so that (marriages) not be abandoned rashly and indiscriminately, the new law, which had allowed marriages to be dissolved solely on the basis of an opposing desire, has been rejected. Those things which were decreed by our divine father Constantius will be preserved unimpaired.

Ten years after *his* law returning to the classical rules of divorce [Novel 12, above], Theodosius II changed his mind and reinstated some restrictions on divorce. He issued a second, very long divorce law, detailing the circumstances under which a wife or husband could obtain a justified (and therefore unpenalized) divorce. In cases where a wife or husband can show serious criminal activity or abuse on the part of the other spouse, then he or she can divorce without penalty and remarry (in the woman's case, after an interval of a year). Unjustified divorce will result in the loss of the dowry and the pre-nuptial gift. The lists of justified causes reveal not only some of the less attractive aspects of marital relationships in late antiquity (and at other time periods), but also the imperial ideology regarding gender relations: freeborn women ought not to be whipped, husbands should not shame their wives by having extra-marital relationships in their own homes, and well-behaved wives ought not to attend popular entertainments without their husband's permission or spend the night away from home.

Though this law is found in the *Code of Justinian* in the names of both emperors, it was never received in the west and is a law of Theodosius II only.

Cod. Just. 5.17.8, 9 January, 449

Emperors Theodosius (II) and Valentinian (III) Augusti to Hormisdas, praetorian prefect:

[The beginning is the same as first two sentences of Novel 12.]

(1) Moreover, by this most salubrious law we define more clearly the causes for a *repudium*. For just as, by a just limit we prohibit marriages to be dissolved without just cause, so do we wish that a man or woman oppressed by adverse necessity be freed by aid that, though unfortunate, is nevertheless necessary.

(2) If, therefore, (a woman) has discovered that her husband is an adulterer or a murderer or a poisoner or certainly is plotting something against our reign or has been condemned for the crime of forgery, or is an overturner of tombs, or is taking something away from sacred temples, or is a bandit or a harborer of bandits or a cattle-stealer or a kidnapper or has intercourse with unchaste women in his own home in contempt of her while she herself is looking on – a thing which particularly exasperates chaste women – or if she has proven that he is plotting against her own life with poison or the sword or some other similar way, or is afflicting her with whippings – which are inappropriate for freeborn women – then we permit her to make use of necessary freedom by the aid of a *repudium* and to prove the causes of her divorce by law.

(3) The husband, also, shall be closed in by an equal limit, nor will he be permitted to repudiate his own spouse without clearly defined causes, nor shall he drive her out in any way unless he has discovered that she is an adulterer, or a poisoner or murderer or kidnapper or overturner of tombs or taking something from the sacred temples or a protectress of bandits or is eager for entertainments with unrelated men without his knowledge or against his will, or, of course, is spending the night away from home if he is unwilling without just and probable cause, or unless she is enjoying herself in circus or theatrical games or spectacles in the arena in the very places where they are customarily celebrated when he forbids her to, or unless she is plotting against him with poison or the sword or some other similar way, or is knowledgeable about those plotting something against our reign, or is involved in the crime of forgery, or he has proven that she is applying audacious hands to him. For then we permit to him the necessary ability to divorce and to prove the causes of divorce by law.

(4) If the man or woman have not observed these (rules), they shall be struck with the avenging penalty of this most providential law. For if a woman has attempted to send a *repudium* in contempt of the law, she shall lose her own dowry and the pre-nuptial gift nor shall she have the power of marrying again within a five-year period. For it is right that she lack the right of marriage in the meantime, in that she has shown herself unworthy. (4a) But if she has married before this, she herself will indeed be infamous, but we do not want it to be called marriage. Moreover, we even grant the liberty of proving this to the one who wants. (4b) But if she has proven that the cause was maintained,[47] then we decree that she can recover her dowry and have the pre-nuptial gift with profit or claim it by law and we allow her the ability to remarry after a year, so that no one have doubts about the offspring.[48]

(5) We decree by this just decision that the man also, if he has proven that the woman was attempting forbidden things, can keep for himself or claim from his wife the dowry as well as the pre-nuptial gift, and, if he

wishes, can immediately remarry. But if he wanted to renounce his own wife otherwise, he shall give back the dowry and shall lose the pre-nuptial gift.

(6) Of course, if a charge of adultery or treason is brought, the male or female slaves over puberty, of the husband as well as of the wife, are to be submitted to torture for the purpose of examining the reason for the *repudium*, in order that the truth may either be more easily dug up or more clearly uncovered, however, (only) if other proofs are lacking[49] ... [the rest of this passage is omitted here]

(7) But if a *repudium* has been sent when there is a son or sons, a daughter or daughters extant, we decree that everything acquired from the marriage is to be preserved for the son or sons, daughter or daughters after the death of the person receiving it; that is, if the father rashly sent a *repudium*, the pre-nuptial gift is to be preserved by the mother, (or) if the mother (sent a *repudium*), the dowry itself is to be given up to the same son/s or daughter/s when the father dies. Of course the choice is to be preserved for the father or mother in designating their children as heirs (in their will), if they should wish to designate as heir one son or one daughter or all or to make a gift to one from among them....

Given on the fifth day before the Ides of January in the consulship of Protogenes and Asterius.

The laws say much about the imperial attitude toward divorce (suggesting a somewhat more restrictive view in the western Empire than the east), but they do not tell us anything about actual practice. Did the threat of legal penalties deter women in unhappy marriages from seeking a divorce? Papyri from late Roman Egypt suggest that imperial law did not make much difference to what people actually did, at least in that province [Bagnall 1987; see Part III.A below]. Unfortunately, our evidence for "real life," as opposed to legal prescriptions, is very scanty for anywhere outside Egypt. Christian leaders generally opposed divorce except in the case of a wife's adultery, but their writings suggest that many in their congregations did not agree [see Evans Grubbs 1995, 242- 53].

We do hear of one case of divorce in fourth-century Rome, from the Christian writer Jerome in a letter after the death of his good friend Fabiola.[50] Fabiola was descended from an ancient Roman senatorial family, and was apparently a baptized Christian at the time her divorce occurred. Jerome's letter was written in 399, but the divorce had taken place many years before, when Fabiola had been quite young. It may even have pre-dated the relaxation of Constantine's law by the emperor Julian (see the passage from Ambrosiaster above), or perhaps Fabiola was one of the women criticized by Ambrosiaster who rushed to repudiate her husband after Julian's edict.

Jerome felt the need to excuse Fabiola's actions, which were contrary to Christian teachings, and aroused considerable criticism from Christians. According to him, she had good reason to end her marriage, for it was well-known that her husband was sexually dissolute. (However, his behavior would not have met the criteria for unilateral divorce as set forth in Constantine's law of 331, or for divorce and remarriage as required by Honorius and Constantius' law of 421.) But to Christians, the fact that Fabiola had remarried while her first husband was still alive, apparently quite soon after her divorce, was even more shocking than her repudiation of her husband. Christian condemnation of divorce and of remarriage after divorce goes back to the New Testament, and was one of the few issues of sexual morality on which Jesus himself actually taught [see Evans Grubbs 1995, 242–53]. Moreover, it appears

208

that by this time divorce among the Roman aristocracy (Christian or pagan) was extremely rare.[51]

Jerome, *Epistle* 77.3

And immediately, in the beginning, a certain rock, as it were, and a tempest of detractors oppose me, because she undertook a second marriage and abandoned her first. I will not praise the woman after she was transformed unless I have absolved her after she was accused.

Her former husband is said to have had such great vices that not even a harlot or a lowly slave could bear them. If I wanted to describe them, I would destroy the fortitude of a woman, who preferred to undergo the blame for divorce rather than bring ill repute on a part of her own body and to reveal his character stains. I will reveal only this, which is enough for a modest Christian woman. The Lord commanded that a wife ought not to be put away, except for fornication, and, if she was put away, she ought to remain unmarried.[52] Whatever is ordered for men, this fittingly applies to women. For an adulterous wife should not be put away and an adulterous husband retained. If he who is joined to a prostitute becomes one body (with her),[53] then also she who is joined to an impure whoremonger is made one body with him.

The laws of the emperors are one thing, the laws of Christ, another; Papinian taught one thing, our Paul another.[54] Among them (pagans) the reins of shame are relaxed for men and their lust is let loose hither and thither through brothels and slave girls; only *stuprum* and adultery are condemned – as if the sin were that of status, not lust. Among us, what is not permitted to women, is equally not permitted to men and the same servitude is decreed by an equal condition. Therefore she put away, as they say, a depraved man; she put away a man who was guilty of this crime and that; she put away a – I almost said that which his wife alone did not reveal when the neighbors were shouting it from the rooftops.

But if the charge is made that, having repudiated her husband, she did not remain unmarried, I will readily admit the fault, while, however, I maintain the necessity. For it is better, the apostle says, to marry than to burn.[55] She was a young woman, she was not able to preserve her widowhood. She saw another law in her own limbs fighting against the law of her mind,[56] and she saw herself being dragged, a captive in chains, to sexual intercourse. She thought it better to confess her own weakness and to submit to the shade of a wretched marriage rather than practice prostitution under the renown of being a one-man woman. The same apostle wants young widows to marry, to bear children, to give no occasion for the purpose of reproach. And immediately he explains why he wants this: for already certain women have gone behind Satan.[57] Therefore also Fabia (sic), because she had persuaded herself and thought that her husband had been lawfully divorced by her – nor did she know the force of the gospel, in which every pretext for remarrying is cut off for women while their husbands are still alive – while she avoided many wounds of the devil, she heedlessly received one wound.

It is odd to find Jerome, who is known as a staunch proponent of Christian virginity and critic of female sexuality, excusing a woman's remarrying because she had uncontrollable sexual needs. Elsewhere he denied the possibility of remarriage after divorce for any reason at all.[58] No doubt the fact that Fabiola did finally perform a spectacular public penance some years later (after her second husband died) – and the fact that she was a good friend of his – made up for her earlier behavior in Jerome's eyes. Fabiola ended her days as a devout Christian and generous benefactor of the church.

Jerome contrasted the norms of Roman law and society, which applied a double standard and always judged women's sexual misbehavior more harshly than men's, with Christian ideology, which held men and women to the same sexual standard. The Christian writer put his finger on the difference between the Roman legal definition of adultery and the Christian one. The law on adultery and *stuprum* was based on the marital and legal status of the parties involved: adultery was extramarital sex by or with a married woman; *stuprum* (which included adultery) was sex by or with a woman of respectable status (unmarried, married, widowed or divorced). A married man's sexual activities with slaves, prostitutes, or other women of low status were not, in legal terms, adultery, and he could not be prosecuted.[59] Moreover, under Augustus' law, adultery (in the Roman legal sense) was subject to criminal penalties, and in late antiquity, such penalties could even include death [Evans Grubbs 1995, 216–21]. All of the late Roman laws allow a man to divorce his wife for adultery, but only in the law of Theodosius II [Cod. Just. 5.17.8] is a husband's adultery considered appropriate grounds for unilateral divorce by a wife. And even there, the classical definition of "adultery" still holds – a husband's affairs with slaves or prostitutes would not present a valid reason for divorce.

On the other hand, Christian writers, particularly in the west, condemned promiscuous husbands equally with promiscuous wives, as Jerome does. But many Christian pastoral leaders, despite recognizing a single sexual standard in theory, still treated the sexual sins of women more harshly than those of men in practice.[60] Theodosius II's law of 449, with its careful paralleling of the causes for which wives and husbands may seek a divorce, comes close to the (theoretical) "Christian" position; even there, however, the law does not really demand an "equal condition" for men and women, but upholds a higher standard of behavior for women. More of the valid causes for divorce of a wife by a husband concern moral misconduct, whereas the valid causes for divorcing a husband center on his criminal behavior and violence toward his wife and others [Beaucamp 1990, 174].

Valentinian's law of 452 is the last extant divorce law before 476, but the sixth-century Byzantine Empire saw extensive legislation enacted, particularly by Justinian.[61] It continued to be an issue on which Christian church, official law, and popular practice diverged, often sharply.

III Divorce in Egypt and the Near East

The frequency of divorce in Roman imperial society cannot be ascertained, and may have varied widely according to region and social class. As with marriage, the documentary evidence for divorce comes almost entirely from Egypt, but two divorce agreements from Dura Europos are also known.

A *Divorce documents from Roman Egypt*

Census documents from Roman Egypt suggest that divorce was not uncommon [Bagnall-

Frier 1994, 123–4], and further evidence for divorce in Egypt is found in divorce agreements and other documents relevant to the break-up of a marriage. As with marriage, neither written documentation nor notification of authorities was necessary to legalize a divorce. However (again, as with marriage), property was often involved, in particular the wife's dowry, which she was entitled to reclaim upon divorce (unless it was stated otherwise in the marriage contract). Moreover, both spouses would want to be free to marry another person, and to be sure that they would not later be liable to legal charges related to their former union. The following documents range in date from the late first century B.C.E. to the late fourth century C.E.[62]

1 A synkhoresis *from Alexandria*

The archive of Protarchos, which preserved eight marriage contracts from Alexandria during the reign of Augustus [see Chapter 2, Part III.A.1], also offers three documents relating to divorce. The following agreement (a *synkhoresis*, as are the marriage contracts from the archive) was drawn up in 13 B.C.E., after four years of marriage.[63] Its wording and format are virtually identical to another divorce document from the archive [BGU IV.1104]. Both are divorces by mutual consent. (The third document [BGU IV.1105] is the complaint of an abused wife against her husband, asking Protarchos to help her obtain a divorce.)

The wife in this agreement has been identified as a Jew on the basis of her father's name, Sambathion, which at this date was a name used only by Jews; possibly the husband was also.[64] However, the terms of the divorce are not in keeping with either early Jewish law of the Torah or the later rabbinical writings. In Jewish law, a wife could not divorce her husband, though she could ask a tribunal to force him to divorce her.[65] This divorce, by mutual consent, is no different from the divorce agreements of contemporaraneous non-Jewish Greeks in Egypt, and reflects the cosmopolitan Hellenistic environment of Alexandria and the Mediterranean [Modrzejewski 1961, 1995]. Like the marriage contracts between Jews written in Greek from Judaea and Arabia [Chapter 2, Part III.B], it raises questions about the influence of Greco-Roman practices on Jews in the Near East.

BGU IV.1102, 13 B.C.E.

To Protarchos, from Apollonia daughter of Sambathion with her *kyrios*, her mother's brother Herakleides son of Herakleides, and from Hermogenes, son of Hermogenes from the deme of Archegetes (?).[66] Apollonia and Hermogenes acknowledge that they have separated from each other from the union which they had established according to an agreement (*synkhoresis*) through the same court in the thirteenth (year) of Caesar (Augustus) in Pharmouthi.[67] And Apollonia (agrees) that she has also received back from Hermogenes by hand from his house what he received from her parents, Sambathion and Irene, as dowry, on her behalf according to the agreement, sixty (drachmas) of silver.[68]

(They agree) that their marriage agreement is invalid from now on, and that neither Apollonia nor any one else on her behalf will take legal action against Hermogenes concerning a demand for the dowry, and that they both (will not take legal action) against each other either about their marriage or anything else at all up to the present day, from which day also it is permitted to Apollonia (to marry) another man and for Hermogenes (to marry) another woman, both of them being not liable (to prosecution). And that the one trangressing (the agreement) will be liable to the prescribed penalty.

In the seventh year of Caesar (Augustus), 14 Phamenoth.[69]

2 A wife's complaint

The divorce agreements surviving on papyri primarily deal with disposition of spousal property (especially the wife's dowry) and release of both partners from legal liability in the future. They do not usually reveal the reasons for the break-up of the marriage. Other types of documents can be more helpful in that regard, particularly petitions to local authorities filed by one of the spouses against the other. A number of such complaints have survived, some from aggrieved wives, some from husbands. Few people, no matter how troubled their marriage, would go so far as to request legal action against their spouse. In most cases, divorce would be a family matter, for which there might be no documentation (apart from perhaps a receipt for the return of dowry). The petitions to officials illustrate the most dysfunctional type of marriage, often where one spouse has abandoned the other and spent or absconded with the other's property. Abuse is mentioned only by women; men complain only of abandonment and removal of property [Arnaoutoglou 1994; Rupprecht 1998].

In the following petition from Oxyrhynchus, the wife Syra complains of physical abuse and abandonment by her husband Sarapion. They had earlier been married by *synkhoresis* (cf. BGU IV.1050, the *synkhoresis* between the Alexandrian couple translated in Chapter 2, Part III.A.1). Here, as in BGU IV.1050, it appears that the husband had agreed to repay his wife's dowry plus a 50 per cent penalty if he did not honor his obligations to her. Note that Syra claims that Sarapion, being poverty-stricken, had actually moved into her parents' home with her; cf. Chapter 2, Part III.A.6 for such an arrangement as part of a marriage contract in the fourth century [P.Ross. Georg. III.28].[70]

P.Oxy. II.281, 20–50 C.E.

To Herakleides, priest and archidikastes and in charge of the circuit-judges and other courts, from Syra the daughter of Theon. I lived in marriage with Sarapion, giving him a dowry according to an agreement (*synkhoresis*) for the amount of 200 drachmas of silver. And indeed, I received him into my parents' home, since he was completely impoverished, and I conducted myself without reproach in everything. But Sarapion, having disposed of my dowry for whatever purpose he wished, did not leave off mistreating me and insulting me and laying his hands on me, and after he rendered me in need of the necessities (of life), he finally left me, when I had become impoverished. Therefore I request you to order him to be brought before you, in order that he may be arrested and forced to pay back my dowry to me plus fifty percent. I retain and [will retain] (my right of legal action) in regard to other matters [I have against him].

3 A divorce agreement from Tebtunis

The parties to this divorce agreement are the wife Thenstotoetis (also spelled Thenstouetis), her father Heron (who is also her *kyrios*), her husband Lysas, and a certain Sosas, who represents Lysas. Interestingly, Lysas is a former slave (of a woman Herakleia, not of Thensotoetis or her father). The couple had married only three years earlier (when the bride was about thirteen). The dowry and the *parapherna* are returned to the wife's father, and she is free to marry again. All parties except Heron are illiterate, so Lysas and Sosas have a "subscriber" (*hypographeus*) sign for them, and Heron signs for his daughter. The divorce agreement, like the earlier marriage contract, was drawn up and registered in the *grapheion* (record-office) of Tebtunis.[71]

P.Lips. 27, 123 C.E.

In the seventh year of the Emperor Caesar Trajan Hadrian Augustus, 21 Phamenoth, in Tebtunis of the Polemon division of the Arsinoite nome. Thenstotoetis, about sixteen years old, without distinguishing marks, with her *kyrios* her father Heron son of Neilos about forty-four years old, with a scar on the little finger of his left hand, and the same Heron, and the one who was the husband of Thenstotoetis, Lysas the freedman of Herakleia the daughter of Lysimachos, about twenty-two years old, with a scar on his right cheek, and Sosas, son of Areotos, about fifty-four years old, with a scar on his right shin – these four acknowledge to each other that Thenstotoetis and Lysas have jointly annulled their marriage with each other, which was established by them (and) completed by virtue of a written agreement (*homologia*) of marriage through the same record-office in the fifth year of our lord Hadrian Caesar, ... [day missing] Hathur, and they have also presented this [agreement] for the purpose of having it annulled and invalidated.

And (they acknowledge) that Heron has back from Sosas the three hundred drachmas of silver (given) through the dowry agreement and all the *parapherna*. And that it is possible for each [of them] to dispose of [his own] things as he or she chooses, and (it is possible) for Thenstotetis to join herself in marriage again, to [whatever] man she wishes, not [being] open to accusation from Lysas. And that they will not bring charges against each other [about] any aspect of the things connected with the marriage nor about any matter in general up to the present day. [Subscriber] Marepsemis son of Pakebkis, [about] forty-eight years old with a scar on his nose.

[written in a second hand] Lysas, freedman of Herakleia, [and] Sosas son of Areotos ... that they have jointly annulled the marriage with Thenstouetis (sic), and that they will not bring charges against each other in general. Marepsemis son of Pakebkis[72] wrote on their behalf since they do not know letters.

[in a third hand] Thenstotoetis with her *kyrios* her father Heron – I have annulled the marriage and I have back the dowry. Heron – I wrote on her behalf because she does not know letters.

[in a fourth hand] I have signed it.

4 A grave-digger's divorce

This divorce agreement (which calls itself an *apozuge*) from the early fourth century from the Great Oasis was made by the gravedigger Soulis (also called Soul) and his wife Senpsais. The separation is said to be due to an evil spirit (*daimon*), which conveniently avoids assigning blame. The daimon who causes couples to split up appears in later divorce documents also [see Bagnall 1987, 55–6; cf. Rupprecht 1998, 69]. This document also contains one of the earliest references to *hedna*, gifts given by the husband, which become a regular feature of late antique marriages [see Chapter 2, Part II.C]. The beginning and end of the document are lost.[73]

P.Grenf. II.76, 305–306 C.E.

... Soulis, grave-digger of the toparchy of Kusis, to Senpsais, daughter of Psais, her mother being Tees, gravedigger from the same (toparchy), greetings.

Since it has happened by means of some evil demon (*daimon*) that we have separated from each other (in regard to) our common marriage, therefore I, the afore-mentioned Soul, acknowledge that I know that I have been paid back in full all the things bestowed on her by [me in any way whatever], (and) that I am sending her away [and] will [not] bring charges later about either the marriage [or] about the *hedna*, but it will be possible for her to go away and to marry whenever she wishes. And (I), the afore-mentioned Senpsais, (acknowledge) that I have been paid back in full from him, the afore-mentioned Soul, all the things given [to him][74] for the dowry together with other ... of my utensils and in any other way whatever. And (we acknowledge) that we will not bring charges later against each other henceforth about any matter whatsoever in general, [written] or unwritten, because of the divorce being final.

This deed of divorce, having been written in duplicate with signatures, shall be [valid] and secure as if [put] in a public record-office, and having been asked, [I have] agreed.

[The fragmentary ending gives the regnal years of the emperors Constantius and Maximian, indicating a date of 305/306.]

5 A late fourth-century divorce agreement

Two other divorce agreements survive from the late third–early fourth century [P.Oxy. XLIII.3139 and P.Oxy. XXXVI.2770]. But for the next two centuries, from the reign of Constantine up to that of Justinian, only one divorce deed is extant. This is in line with the survival rate for marriage contracts during this period [see Chapter 2, Part III.A]. The following document (which calls itself a *perilysis*, a "cancellation" or "release") is a declaration from a woman, Aurelia Allous, to her husband, Aurelius Elias, agreeing that their marriage has ended, that she has no further claim on him and that he can remarry.[75] As with Soulis and Senpsais [P.Grenf. II.76, above], an evil daimon is blamed for breaking up their marriage. Note that here the wife is accompanied by her mother as *synestos* [see Chapter 1, Part III.E].

Divorce agreements from the early fourth century, and later ones from the sixth century, explicitly state two copies were made. In two cases from the sixth century, both copies have survived, one copy being addressed to the wife from the husband, the other to the husband from the wife [P.Cair. Masp. II.67153 and 67253, dated 568; P.Lond. V.1713 and P.Flor. I.93, dated 569]. Though this agreement of 391 does not mention two copies, it is likely that there was also a declaration from Elias to Allous, stating that he had no further claim on her and that she was free to remarry [Beaucamp 1992, 142]. Like the divorce documents from the early fourth century, this one records a divorce by mutual consent, which was unaffected by contemporary legal restrictions on divorce. (Of course, the reality behind the document may have been different, but it was in the interest of both partners to agree to the divorce rather than risk future legal problems.)

P.Stras. III.142, 391 C.E.

In the consulship of Tatianus the most illustrious prefect of the sacred prefecture and of the most illustrious Flavius Symmachus, 18 Phaophi of the fifth indiction.[76] Aurelia Allous daughter of Onnophrios, with her mother Aurelia Apina assisting (*synestos*), from the village Nestou of the Arsinoite nome, to Aurelius Elias son of Ariston from the village Onnito(n) of the same nome:

Whereas I, Allous, have lived with you, Elias, in marriage for some time, (however) it seemed best, due to a wicked daimon (which) came upon our marriage with each other, to depart, having been set free. In regard to this, I, Allous, acknowledge that I have no argument with you, Elias, about our marriage or any other debt, written or unwritten, demand, complaint, (or) official inquiry, once and for all, simply (and) completely. And (I acknowledge) that you, Elias, have the power to enter another marriage, with you being blameless regarding this. And there will be ... a document of divorce (*perilysis*) and having been asked, I acknowledged (that it was so).

I, Aurelia Allous, the one mentioned above, with her mother Apia assisting, delivered (this document). [the rest is fragmentary]

[on the back of the papyrus] *Perilysis* of Allous, daughter of Onnophrios.

Despite the paucity of divorce agreements from the fourth and fifth centuries, it is clear that marriages continued to break up, often by one spouse (usually the husband) simply abandoning the other. We learn of such break-ups from petitions sent by abandoned spouses to local officials, of which a number have survived.[77] In these documents, the petitioner asks not for a reconciliation or return of the partner who deserted, but rather the return of the dowry or other belongings which the abandoning spouse had taken.

6 A mother's complaint against her son-in-law

The following petition was submitted to a *syndikos*[78] from the mother of an abandoned wife, Aurelia Ptolema. Ptolema had earlier given her daughter in marriage, presumably after the death of the girl's father Diogenes [cf. P.Oxy. X.1273 in Chapter 2, Part III.A.4]. Unfortunately, the petition is very fragmentary, but it appears that the daughter's husband, Theon, has abandoned the marriage for good (having taken his bedding and left town) and is asking Aurelia Ptolema for the return of the pre-nuptial gifts which he had given (the *hedna*, on which see P.Grenf. II.76 above and Chapter 2, Part II.C). There is no mention in the extant part of the petition of the dowry which Arilla would have brought to the marriage; perhaps Theon had already returned the dowry, and now wanted the *hedna* in return, or perhaps Ptolema demanded the return of the dowry in a missing part of the petition.

It is not clear that Theon is responsible for the marriage's demise; it is possible that Arilla returned to her mother, taking her baby and the *hedna* with her, and that Theon only moved out after his wife's desertion. In a petition of 362 from Hermopolis [P.Cairo Preis. 2], Aurelius Serenus Pinoution claimed that his wife's mother, after telling him that her daughter had a daimon,[79] had given her to another man while Pinoution was away, and in the same town a year later, another husband claimed that his wife had waited until he was absent and had then left him, taking with her the *hedna* and some important books of his [P.Lond. V.1651]. The mother's role in these cases, and in P.Oxy. LIV.3770 below, is worth noting. In other petitions of the period, it is either the wife's father [P.Panop. 28] or the abandoned wife herself [PSI I.41; PSI IX.1075; P.Oxy. VI.903; P.Oxy. L.3581] who makes the complaint.

Note how Aurelia Ptolema asserts that Theon "despised her weakness." Claims that men had taken advantage of their unprotected and "weak" condition are made by other female petitioners (particularly widows) of the late third and early fourth century; it was evidently a useful rhetorical strategy, though may well reflect social reality, where women would have depended on husbands or fathers to defend them against other males [cf. P.Oxy. XXXIV.2713 (297) and P.Oxy. I.71 (303) in Chapter 1, Part IV.C.2; P.Sakaon 36 (c.280) in Chapter 5, Part II.B.4].[80]

P.Oxy. LIV.3770, 334 C.E.

To Aurelius Julianus, syndikos of the city of the Oxyrhynchites.

From Aurelia Ptolema, daughter of Dionysios, from the same city.

I gave our daughter Arilla, daughter of Diogenes ... to a husband, a certain Theon, for the purpose of marriage ... from whom he also had a male son whom she nursed for a year and a half.[81] And he has not furnished support to the child nor to his own wife. But already he has even been in foreign parts for a long time, having taken his bedding.... And having left my daughter in widowhood, he even tries to demand back from me the *hedna* which he provided, despising my weakness. Therefore, not being able to bear the man's lack of conscience, I am handing in this petition, asking that if he remains in the same stubbornness and ... the laws ... support of his son and wife ... not even wanting to give sustenance ... that she is estranged from her husband.

In the consulship of Flavius Optatus the patrician and of Anicius Paulinus, most splendid men, 30 Phamenoth.[82]

[in another hand] I, Aurelia Ptolema, have handed in (this petition).

As we have seen [Part II above], late Roman law imposed significant restrictions on the right of wives (and, to a lesser extent, husbands) to repudiate their spouses unilaterally. Did the new legal restrictions have any impact on the divorce rate, or on the ability of women to end an unhappy marriage? Egypt is the only area of the Empire where evidence for actual practice survives to any extent, so it is natural to look to the papyri for evidence of the influence of law on lived reality. But it is impossible to find direct references to the law in either the divorce agreements or the complaints against spouses of the fourth and fifth centuries. The lack of divorce agreements might be thought to signify a decline in divorce, but the numbers of papyri documents of all types decline in this period, so no conclusions can be drawn [see further Bagnall 1987].

In one petition by a wife against her chronically unfaithful and abusive husband, we are told that she had sent him a *repudium*, "through the *tabellarius* of the city, according to imperial law" [P.Oxy. L.3581]. His response was not to invoke imperial legislation against unilateral divorce, but to break into the house and assault her. Unfortunately this petition is not dated, so we do not know to what law the petitioner refers (she may mean only "the law" in a general sense).[83] Possibly she is thinking of Theodosius II's law of 439, which abolished earlier restrictions and returned (albeit for only ten years) to the pre-Constantinian legal situation [Novel 12 of Theodosius II, dated 439; see Part II above]. But another wife's petition also says that she sent a *repudium*, and it is dated 390, long before Theodosius' law; we do not even know what law on divorce was in effect in Egypt at that period.[84] The husband's response was the same: he broke into the house and beat her mercilessly; breaking her hand and blackening her eyes [P.Lips. 39]. Violent husbands like these were unlikely to care about what the law did or did not allow them to do. If restrictions on divorce had any effect at all on people's behavior, it may have been to make husbands more abusive (in the knowledge that their wives could not easily divorce them[85]) and to make both wives and husbands more likely to end a bad marriage by simple abandonment, rather than by seeking a divorce through the courts [Evans Grubbs 1995, 239–42].

B A divorce from Dura Europos

Two deeds of divorce, both written in Greek, survive from Dura Europos on the Euphrates (in addition to a marriage contract, for which see Chapter 2, Part III.C). One dates to 204, eight years before the emperor Caracalla's grant of universal Roman citizenship, and records a divorce between two non-citizens, Nabusamaus and his wife Acozzis [P.Dura 31]. Acozzis had been married before and had an (evidently adult) son from her previous marriage, who signed the document on her behalf. The couple, who had been married in an unwritten marriage,[86] give each other the right to remarry and declare they will not bring any claims against each other in the future, promising to pay a monetary penalty if they do.[87]

The second divorce agreement, translated below, was written in 254 and is the last dated document found at Dura before the city's destruction by the Persians only a few years later [Millar 1993, 162]. As a Roman army outpost, Dura of course had a large military population; the husband in this divorce was a soldier (as was the husband in P.Dura 30, the marriage contract). Like P.Dura 31, and like the marriage contract P.Dura 30, this was a "double document" with an inner text that had been folded over and fastened shut, and an outer text (cf. on P.Dura 30 in Chapter 2, Part III.C). The papyrus was then folded over and over again, and consequently there are many small holes which have destroyed much of the writing. Thus the text is incomplete, but the gist of the document, which calls itself an *apostasion* ("divorce") is clear.[88]

P.Dura 32 (outer text only), 254 C.E.

[first hand] In the consulship of our lords the Emperors Augusti Valerian for the second time and Gallienus, on the day before the Kalends of May ... of the 565th year, in the sacred and inviolate and autonomous *colonia* of the Europans of Seleukos Nikator.[89]

Julius Antiochus, a soldier of the vexillation here [of the Fourth Legion] Scythica [Valeriana] Galliena, of the century of Alexander, and Aurelia Amimma ... a citizen of Dura, his [wife] ... [the following line cannot be read] ... and that they have been released from their common life with each other, and they [now] acknowledge to each other, on the one side Antiochus to Amimma (acknowledges) that he has handed over all the things [which] he held in possession from her, from small to large ... of her common life with Antiochus and that he concedes to her (the right) to join herself to [another] man and that he does not [bring charges] nor [will] he bring charges against Amimma, neither about (anything) written or unwritten, nor [about] anything else, [simply] (and) completely in any way.

... [And] likewise also Amimma ... [to Antiochus] that she does not bring charges nor will she bring charges but that she has received in full from him all the things which [Antiochus] held in possession [and] that she does not bring charges (?) ... will bring charges now, neither about (anything) written or unwritten nor [about anything else], simply (and) completely in any way. But if not ... of them has laid claim and [has prevailed], (we acknowledge) that the claim or accusation is invalid and (the person who made it) will pay in addition, without argument [or legal judgment] to the other a fine of 1000 denarii of silver and [an equal amount] to the most sacred treasury [and] this divorce is also thus valid ... as if there had been a guaranteed and acknowledged pledge. And it also has a copy.

[another hand] I, Julius Antiochus, soldier, as written above, acknowledge that he has made the divorce according to the things written above ...

[another hand] I, Aurelius Valentinus son of Antoninus, a citizen of Dura, having been requested, wrote on behalf of Amimma ... who is illiterate (and) who acknowledges that she has made the divorce ...

[On the other side are the signatures of four witnesses.]

5

WIDOWS AND
THEIR CHILDREN

Given ancient life expectancy and the fact that most wives were younger than their husbands, the marriages of many women in the Roman Empire were ended by their husband's death rather than by divorce. It was common, at least in the Roman world, for widows still of child-bearing age to remarry, and this tendency was reinforced by the Augustan marriage legislation, which mandated remarriage of widows within two years. In the classical period remarriage was without stigma for both elite Roman women and those further down the social scale (who were more likely to have financial pressures to remarry as well). This was not necessarily the case elsewhere in the Empire; evidence from census returns in Roman Egypt indicates that widowed women were unlikely to remarry after the age of thirty or thirty-five (whereas widowed men were).[1]

Often, however, remarried widows would have children from their first marriage, and this could cause complications. Legally, children born in legitimate marriage belonged to their father's family, and were his heirs if he died intestate (without a will), as they would normally be if he had left a will. Their mother, on the other hand, would belong to *her* father's family, unless she had come under her first husband's *manus* upon marriage, which rarely happened in the imperial period [see Chapter 1, Part II.B]. She would inherit from her father when he died, but would inherit from her husband only if he specifically left her something in his will. (Roman law always looked with suspicion on the transfer of property between spouses; see Chapter 2, Parts I.E and II.A.) Nor would she be likely to inherit from any of her children who predeceased her. If their *paterfamilias* were still alive, anything they had accumulated would legally be his; if they were no longer under paternal power when they died, their prop-erty would go to their closest agnate relatives (those in their father's line).[2] Moreover, until late in the second century, a woman's own children were not her heirs upon intestacy unless she had no agnate kin. And in order to make a will, a woman needed the permission of her *tutor mulierum* [Chapter 1, Part III.A] and had to go through the archaic legal ritual of self-sale *(coemptio fiduciaria)*.[3] When a mother did leave her property to her children by will, if they were still under paternal power, the property would automatically go to their *paterfa-milias* (probably her husband). He would have to be trusted to pass on the *bona materna* to them, perhaps when they reached adulthood, perhaps upon his death.[4]

The second century saw improvements in the right of mothers and children to inherit from each other. Under Hadrian, a decree of the Senate (the *senatusconsultum Tertullianum*) enabled mothers who had the *ius liberorum* to inherit from children who predeceased them.[5] Another senatorial decree of Hadrian's reign gave women the right to make a will without undergoing *coemptio* [Gaius, *Institutes* I.115a and II.112]. And in 178, the Senate passed the *senatusconsultum Orphitianum*, giving a woman's children (both legitimate and illegitimate) first claim to inherit from her upon intestacy. This expressed in law what had long been the feeling of many Romans, namely that children should be their mother's heirs [Dixon 1988, 51–60; Arjava 1996, 105–6; Gardner 1998, 228–33].

Young children would probably still live with their mother after their father's death. Boys under fourteen and girls under twelve who had lost their *paterfamilias* would have a guardian (*tutor impuberum*) appointed for them; by the third century this would be followed by a *curator* until they reached the legal age of twenty-five. Under classical law, a woman could not serve as guardian, even of her own children, though papyrological evidence shows that in the Greek East, many mothers did exercise the functions of guardian. Conflicts could arise between mothers and their children's guardian.

There might also be conflict between children and stepfathers. A woman's husband would not serve as legal guardian of her children by a previous marriage; that role would probably be played by a male relative of their deceased father, an uncle if possible. One issue that might arise in such a situation was the fate of the mother's own property (which she would have acquired by inheritance from her natal family, and perhaps also from her first husband by his will). Though a woman's children were not her intestate heirs, there was a widespread feeling, even before the second century, that they were entitled to *bona materna* (maternal property), and that they had more right to such property than her second husband [Dixon 1988, 50–1].

Late Roman law continued the trend toward legal recognition of mother–child inheritance rights already seen in second-century legislation. Much late imperial legislation is devoted to *bona materna*. The father's right over *bona materna* was modified, so that he had only the usufruct (lifetime use and possession, but not outright ownership or the right to sell or give away) of property his children had received from their mother's side.[6] Constantine extended the *s.c. Tertullianum* by allowing mothers without the *ius liberorum* to inherit one-third of a deceased child's estate even when there were paternal uncles.[7] And Theodosius I officially granted widowed mothers who vowed not to remarry the legal right to serve as their child's guardian.

I Remarriage in Roman law

According to the marriage legislation of the emperor Augustus, widows were to remarry within two (or three) years of their husband's death (and divorcées within eighteen months of divorce).[8] Those who did not were not in compliance with the law and therefore could not inherit from people not related to them in the sixth degree [Chapter 2, Part I.B]. In 320, Constantine abolished the Augustan penalties on the unmarried and childless, thus removing the legal pressure on widows to remarry [Chapter 2, Part II.B]. Late Roman law reinforced sanctions against remarriage within a short period of time, and restricted the rights of remarried mothers over any property they had inherited from their husbands.

A Legally imposed delays on remarriage

Though Augustus' legislation enjoined widows to remarry, earlier policy penalized those who remarried too soon. Numa, the second king of Rome, was said to have ruled that widows who remarried before the end of a ten-month mourning period for their husband were to sacrifice a pregnant cow [Plutarch, *Numa* 12; Humbert 1972, 113–14]. The Praetor's Edict decreed a penalty of legal infamy (*infamia*) against a woman (or her *paterfamilias*, if he had given her in marriage) who had remarried within ten months of her husband's death.[9] Originally, the rationale behind the mourning period was religious: the widow should honor her dead husband and early remarriage would offend the spirits (*Manes*) of the dead man [Humbert 1972, 116–19]. By the late Republic, however, another justification for a ten-month delay had developed: the need to avoid *turbatio sanguinis* ("confusion of blood"), that is, uncertainty about the paternity of any child conceived in a second marriage [Humbert 1972, 119–31; Gardner 1986a, 50–4; Beaucamp 1990, 211–14; Treggiari 1991a, 493–5]. Ten months was considered the normal duration of pregnancy in antiquity [Hanson 1987], so a child born to a woman within ten months of her husband's death would be assumed to have been conceived from him.

In the sixth book of his commentary on the Praetor's Edict, Ulpian cites the opinions of two earlier jurists, Pomponius and Neratius, for what was evidently a problematic (but no doubt fairly common) situation:

D.3.2.11 (Ulpian): However, mourning for children or parents is not an impediment to marriage.[10] 1: Though a husband may be such that by the custom of our ancestors he ought not to be mourned, it is not possible for her to be given in marriage within the legal time limit. For the praetor has referred to this time, in which a husband is to be mourned; he is accustomed to be mourned on account of confusion of blood. 2: Pomponius thinks that a woman who has given birth within the legal time limit is able to give herself in marriage immediately, which indeed I believe (also). 3: However, enemies or those condemned for treason are not accustomed to be mourned, as Neratius says, nor those who hanged themselves, nor those who laid hands on themselves not from weariness of life, but from a bad conscience. (But) accordingly, if anyone after the death of a husband of this sort has given herself in marriage, she will be marked with legal infamy. 4: "He who took her in marriage" is also marked with infamy, but (only) if he did it knowingly. For ignorance of the law is not excused, but ignorance of the facts is. A man is excused if he married her by the order of the person whose power he is in, and he himself, who allowed him to marry, is marked with infamy, in each case correctly. For even the one who obeyed is worthy of pardon and the one who allowed him to marry is worthy of ignominy.

The fact that a woman is not expected to mourn a husband who was a traitor or who committed suicide out of shame, but is still punished with *infamia* if she remarries within ten months of his death, and that she could remarry immediately upon giving birth to a child (presumed to be that of her deceased husband) within the ten-month period, suggest that by Ulpian's day the ban on remarriage within ten months was based on concerns about the paternity of unborn offspring rather than religious reasons.[11] (On the other hand, divorcées were not subject to any legally opposed delay in remarrying, and in fact were required under the Augustan legislation to remarry within a shorter period of time than were widows.)

D.3.2.9 (Paulus): Men are not compelled to mourn for their wives. There is no mourning for a fiancé.
D.3.2.10 (Paulus): It is customary for a woman to receive permission from the emperor to marry within the legal time limit. 1: It does not harm the woman who is mourning her husband to have become engaged within the time limit.

But though women could receive imperial permission to remarry within the ten-month period, some emperors upheld the ancient ban. Gordian sent this reply to a woman who had petitioned him:

Cod. Just. 2.11.15, 15 June, 239

Emperor Gordian Augustus to Sulpicia:

By the decree of the most splendid order, when women's grief has lessened, their more mournful dress and the other distinctive marks of this sort are given up. It is still not permitted to contract marriage within the time in which it is customary to mourn a husband, since even if she has pursued another marriage within this time, she as well as the man who knowingly took her to wife, even if he is a soldier, contracts the stain of shame, according to the Perpetual (Praetor's) Edict. Posted on the seventeenth day before the Kalends of July in the consulship of Gordian Augustus and Aviola.

The date of the decree of the Senate ("the most splendid order") to which the rescript refers is not known [Talbert 1984, 456], but may not be much earlier than 239. It had eliminated the need for a woman to wear widow's weeds, but had not changed the ban on remarriage laid down in the Praetor's Edict. The "stain of shame" (*labes pudoris*) is the penalty of legal infamy.

Almost a century and a half after Gordian's ruling, Theodosius I enacted new regulations regarding the mourning period. The following excerpt is part of a longer law, one of several Theodosian laws that discourage remarriage in order to safeguard the property rights of a widow's children. Another part of the law (not translated here) said that a widow who remarried too soon not only incurred *infamia*, but also could not receive anything by legacy, inheritance, *fideicommissum* (trust), or gift in contemplation of death, nor could she give more than a third of her property as dowry to her second husband or leave him more than a third in her will.[12]

Cod. Just. 6.56.4, 18 December, 380

Emperors Gratian, Valentinian (II), and Theodosius Augusti to Eutropius, praetorian prefect:

If any woman, by the hastiness of her nuptials, has not at all displayed religious respect (*religio*) for a former husband by whom she does not have sons or daughters, indeed she shall, by the very well-known law, be infamous, unless the imperial generosity should remit a stain of this sort.

(1) But if, however, she has sons or daughters and has asked for imperial indulgence, we allow the abolition of *infamia* and the repeal of the remaining penalties, if she has given half of the property which she had at the time of her marriage to her son or daughter, or sons or daughters, which she had conceived from her former husband, after, of course, all formalities of donation have been completely accomplished and not even the usufruct has been retained. (2) If indeed, she has given half to two sons or daughters or more, and one (son) or one (daughter) has died intestate from a fatal lot, or another (male) or another (female) from them, we wish (the property) to belong always to the surviving brothers or sisters.

(3) But if, however, all females or all males have died intestate, consolation for her harsh fortune shall return anew to the mother, in such a way that she shall again assume this half which she had given to her sons or daughters, after

the sons or daughters have died intestate, specially from the inheritance of her last (surviving) son or daughter.[13]

Posted on the fifteenth day before the Kalends of January in the fifth consulship of Gratian Augustus and the consulship of Theodosius Augustus.[14]

The reference to the lack of "religious respect" for her first husband displayed by a woman who remarries too soon suggests that in late antiquity, religious considerations regain importance as a reason for legally mandated delays on remarriage, as in early Roman law, whereas classical law had placed more emphasis on avoidance of *turbatio sanguinis* [Humbert 1972, 379–87]. A year later, Theodosius I enacted another law, which increased by two months the mandatory delay before a widow could remarry and removed all possibility of imperial indulgence for women who did not observe the delay:

Cod. Theod. 3.8.1, 30 May, 381

Emperors Gratian, Valentinian (II), and Theodosius Augusti to Eutropius, praetorian prefect:

If any woman, having lost her husband, has hastened to wed another within the space of a year – for we add a small amount of time to be observed after the ten months, though we think even this itself is very little – branded with marks of digrace, she shall be deprived of both the honor and the right of a more honorable noble person, and she shall lose everything, which she had obtained from the property of her former husband or by right of betrothal gifts or by the will of her deceased husband. And she shall know that she should hope for no help from our generosity or special decision.[15] Given at Constantinople on the third day before the Kalends of June in the consulship of Eucherius and Syagrius.

By abolishing the possibility of imperial pardon for hasty remarriage, Theodosius also effectively abrogated the other part of his law of 380, which had stipulated that in order to receive pardon, women had to give half of all their property to children by their first marriage. Therefore, in 382, he enacted a new law about the fate of property a widow had received from her first husband if she later remarried [Cod. Theod. 3.82., below in Part I.B].

In late antiquity, remarriage of a woman after divorce was also subject to an imperially mandated waiting period, whereas in classical law divorced women could remarry as soon as they wished (this did, however, lead to questions of paternity: see Chapter 4, Part I.E.2 on the *s.c. Plancianum*). A western divorce law of 421 imposed a one-year moratorium on remarriage on women who had been unjustifiably divorced by their husbands [Cod. Theod. 3.16.2, in Chapter 4, Part II], as did an eastern law of 449, which explicitly stated that the purpose of the delay was to prevent "doubts about the offspring" [Cod. Just. 5.17.8, Chapter 4, Part II].

B Remarriage and inheritance

The two laws of Theodosius I penalizing women who married before the end of the mandated waiting period suggest disapproval on the part of the imperial government toward widows with children who remarry at all. Indeed, imperial disapproval of remarried mothers appears in a number of late Roman laws, particularly those of Theodosius I. Concern for the inheritance and the welfare of a woman's children by her first husband is the primary motivation, though Christian disapproval of remarriage may also have influenced the Theodosian legislation [Humbert 1972, 375–94, but cf. Arjava 1996, 167–77].

The discouragement of remarriage found in late Roman laws contrasts sharply with the earlier Augustan legislation mandating marriage for Roman women between the ages of twenty and fifty, and Roman men between twenty-five and sixty [see Chapter 2, Part I.B]. However, Augustus' requirement that widows remarry within two years of their husband's death itself ran counter to popular Roman attitudes toward remarriage. The law conflicted with the ancient Roman ideal of the *univira* ("one-man woman"), the woman who married only once, and evidently there were some Roman women who resisted both social and legal pressures to remarry [Treggiari 1991a, 216–18 and 233–6]. Funerary epitaphs praised the *univira*, and bereaved spouses declared that they would not remarry, since marital bonds survived beyond the grave [Humbert 1972, 59–75]. But economic as well as legal constraints led many women to remarry, including those with children from their first marriage.

There was a strong feeling in Roman society that property which a wife had inherited from her husband ought to go to the children she had by him, and not be passed on to the husband or children of a second marriage, and concomitantly, fear that a remarried mother would favor her new husband over her children from her first marriage. Ultimately, in the fourth century, these concerns were embodied in legislation insisting that widowed mothers who planned to remarry hand over everything they had received from their first husband to their children by him. But long before this practice became law, it was a moral obligation [Dixon 1988, 47–51], and non-legal writers express admiration for mothers who made proper provision for their children by a first marriage, and condemn those who failed to do so.

The moralist Valerius Maximus, writing under Tiberius, devoted a chapter of his *Memorable Deeds and Sayings* to "wills which were rescinded" (VII.7), and included a will made by a woman who, according to the author, had remarried at an advanced age simply to spite her children by her first marriage, by leaving her estate to her elderly husband. Such a marriage went against the spirit of the emperor Augustus' recently enacted marriage legislation, which promoted marriage "for the sake of producing children." The *s.c. Calvisianum*, a decree of the Senate passed at some point after Augustus' original legislation, even declared that marriage of a man under sixty to a woman over fifty was *impar* ("unequal"), and said that the couple did not have the right to receive legacies or inheritances and that after the wife's death, her dowry would be confiscated [*Rules of Ulpian* 16.4; Treggiari 1991a, 78]. The date of the *senatusconsultum* is uncertain, but was probably not much later than the time when Valerius Maximus was writing [see Talbert 1984, 451].

Valerius Maximus VII.7.4, written *c*.30 C.E.

Also, Septicia, mother of the Trachali of Ariminum, angry at her children, as an insult to them married Publicius, quite an old man, though she was already unable to bear him children, (and) even passed them both over in her will. Approached by them, the deified Augustus rejected both the woman's marriage and her final judgment. For he ordered her children to have their maternal inheritance, (and) he forbade her husband to retain her dowry, since their marriage had not occurred "for the sake of procreating children." If Equity itself were judging about this matter, could it pronounce more justly or with more seriousness? You scorn those whom you bore, you marry (when you are) sterile, you malevolently upset the proper order of a will, nor do you blush to hand over your entire patrimony to a man to whose already corpse-like body you submitted your own withered old age. Therefore while you are conducting yourself in this way, you were blasted by a heavenly thunderbolt all the way to hell.

On the other hand, one son, the child of his mother's first marriage, praised her for her even-handed treatment of her children by both husbands. He described dutiful behavior of his mother, Murdia, in a funerary oration from around the time of Augustus, which was preserved on stone:[16]

CIL VI.10230 (ILS 8394), early 1st c. C.E.

[the beginning of the inscription is lost]

... She made all her sons her heirs equally, having given her daughter her share as a legacy;[17] her maternal love is apparent in her affection for her children (and) her equal distribution of portions. She bequeathed a certain sum of money to her (second) husband, so that his right to her dowry was augmented by the honor of her judgment. Recalling the memory of my father and consulting that and her own sense of loyalty (*fides*), she made a valuation of her property, and in addition in her will left me a legacy of certain properties to be taken out of the estate.[18] (She did this) not with the intention of preferring me to my (step)brothers out of some disrespect to them, but mindful of my father's generosity, she decided that what she had taken from my patrimony by her (first) husband's judgment ought to be returned to me, so that those things, preserved by her use of them, might be restored to my ownership.

Therefore she was consistent in this, with the result that, having been given by her parents to worthy men, she maintained her marriages by obedience (and) upright behavior, as a wife she became more pleasing by her merits, was held more dear by her sense of loyalty, remained more adorned by her good judgment, (and) was praised after her decease by the consensus of the citizens, since her distribution of shares (in her will) observed a pleasing and loyal spirit toward her husbands, equal treatment toward her children, (and) justice in the truth.

[The rest of the inscription, not translated here, praises Murdia for her behavior toward both husbands and her children, and for possessing the traditional female virtues of modesty, chastity (*pudicitia*), and wool-working.]

Murdia had taken care to pass on to the son of her first marriage those properties she had received from her first husband. She did this voluntarily, though perhaps exhorted to do so by her first husband in his will (in the late Empire, the same practice was to be enjoined upon widows by law). Another remarried mother who provided for her sons by her first marriage, both in her will and earlier, was Pudentilla, the wealthy widow of the North African town of Oea (now Tripoli in Libya) who married the rhetor and novelist Apuleius in the mid-second century. We know of Pudentilla's financial and family affairs from a very biased source, Apuleius himself, who faced charges in court that he had enticed Pudentilla into marriage by magical means.[19]

According to Apuleius, Pudentilla's older son Pontianus had begged Apuleius to marry his mother, to save her from less amenable suitors and from ill health caused by a long period of celibacy (she had been a widow for fourteen years, until both her sons had reached puberty).[20] But after Pontianus himself married, he changed his mind, and opposed the match he had previously proposed. Pontianus then died (Apuleius was initially charged with his murder, but the accusation was later dropped), but his younger brother, Pudens (then a teenager, though over fourteen), brought charges of magic against Apuleius. Pudens was supported by Pudentilla's former in-laws, who had wanted her to marry a brother of her deceased husband,[21] and by Pontianus' former father-in-law, with whom Pudens was living and whose daughter (his brother's widow) he was intended to marry.[22]

The result was an ugly family squabble in court, pitting Apuleius against his stepson Pudens, in which both sides said a number of unflattering things about Pudentilla (who presumably was not present at the trial). The trial was held before the governor of Africa Proconsularis, Claudius Maximus, at the town of Sabratha [Bradley 1997]. Apuleius was anxious to dispel his image as a "wicked stepfather" who had married for money and persuaded his wife to neglect the interests of her children by her first marriage. This image appears in later Roman law, and reflects popular opinion in earlier Roman society also [Dixon 1997, 162–3]. According to Apuleius, when Pudentilla's older son Pontianus had received a letter from his mother saying that she was considering remarriage, he had rushed home in fear that his expectations of Pudentilla's wealth would be ruined by a stepfather [*Apol.* 71, in Chapter 2, Part I.E.2]. Apuleius noted the relatively small size of Pudentilla's dowry [*Apol.* 92, in Chapter 2, Part I.D.2] and that she had needed the authorization of her *tutor mulierum* to make financial outlays [*Apol.* 101, Chapter 1, Part III.B]. He also claimed that Pudentilla had married on condition that if she and Apuleius did not have children (she was at least forty), her dowry would go to her sons by her first marriage [*Apol.* 91, Chapter 2, Part I.D.3]. He even cited provisions of her will to demonstrate that he had urged her to make her son Pudens her heir:

Apuleius, *Apologia* 99–100, 158/9 C.E.

(99) [the first sentence is omitted here] For – something I very nearly forgot – very recently when Pudentilla was writing her will, in great ill-health after the death of her son Pontianus, for a long time I struggled against her, so that she would not disinherit him (Pudens) because of his many conspicuous insults, his many affronts. I begged her to destroy the very harsh clause (in her will), already completely written – as god is my witness! Finally, I threatened that I would divorce her unless I was granted my request; (I begged) that she grant me this favor, that she win over a wicked son by kindness, that she free me from all suspicion and envy. I did not desist until she did it. [a few sentences are omitted] I, a stepfather, fought with an irate mother on behalf of his wicked stepson, just as a father (would fight) against a stepmother on behalf of his excellent son, nor was that enough, unless I, with excessive fairness, restrained the ample generosity of my good wife towards myself.

(100) You, hand over to her hostile son the will already made by a mother, as I, whom those men call a robber, preceded every single word with entreaties! Order those tablets to be broken open, Maximus: you will find that the son is heir, that I have been left some small legacy for the sake of respect, in order that, if anything human had happened to her after the manner of mortals, I would have the good name of husband in my wife's will. Take that will of your mother, this indeed "undutiful" will – for what is not undutiful (about a will) in which she disinherited a most obedient husband, and made a most hostile son her heir?[23] But no, not a son, but rather the hope of Aemilianus and the son-in-law of Rufinus, rather that drunken club, your hangers-on. Take it, I say, o best of sons, and having put

aside for a while your mother's love letters,[24] read her will instead. You will find here, indeed quite soon after the beginning, (the words): "Sicinius Pudens, my son, is to be my heir." I confess, whoever has read it will think it insane. [A few sentences are omitted] Therefore, open it, I beg you, good lad, open the will: you will thus more easily prove your mother's insanity.

Sometimes a husband would leave his wife a legacy on condition that she not remarry after his death. Such a condition went against the intent of the Augustan marriage legislation, which in fact enjoined widows to remarry within two years of their husband's death or become ineligible to receive legacies from those outside the sixth degree of relationship. Jurists sought to reconcile the need to promote marriage and child-bearing, as set forth in Augustus' laws, with the desire to obey the testator's wishes whenever possible [Humbert 1972, 160–70]. Thus a blanket condition that a woman could only receive a legacy if she did not (re)marry was invalid, but conditions that she not marry certain individuals were valid [D.35.1.63 pr. (Gaius)]. And a husband could specify that his widow receive a legacy if she did not remarry while the children were still little, as it was understood that his concern was for the well-being of the children. The following is from a commentary on the Augustan marriage laws:

D.35.1.62.2 (Terentius Clemens): When a man has left his wife something "if she does not marry away from the children" in successive years, what is the law's view? Julian replies that the woman is able to marry and to take the legacy. But if it had been written thus: "if she does not marry away from the children under puberty," the law would not apply, since care for the children rather than widowhood would be imposed.

But though there was some popular sentiment against a widowed mother's remarrying, the only evidence for disapproval of remarriage on the part of Roman lawmakers before the fourth century is a rescript of Alexander Severus to a certain Dionysodorus, a guardian (*tutor*) of fatherless children who had petitioned the emperor regarding the rearing of his wards (*pupilli*):

Cod. Just. 5.49.1, 7 February, 223
Emperor Alexander Augustus to Dionysodorus:
The upbringing of your *pupilli* should be entrusted to no one more than their mother, if she has not introduced a stepfather to them. (1) However, when doubt has arisen between her and relatives and the tutor concerning this matter, the governor of the province, when approached, will assess where the boy ought to be brought up, having investigated both the character and the association of the persons in question. (2) But if, however, he has made an assessment about where he ought to be brought up, he (the boy?) will have to do what the governor has ordered. Posted on the seventh day before the Ides of February in the second consulship of Maximus and the consulship of Aelianus.

Dionysodorus was involved in a dispute with his wards' mother and her relatives (*cognati*) over where the children should live. It is not clear whether the mother had actually

227

remarried, or whether remarriage is mentioned hypothetically, as the one situation where it would be better for children from a first marriage to live elsewhere. Some scholars have suspected that the words "if she has not introduced a stepfather to them" are a Justinianic interpolation, but others accept their authenticity.[25] In any case, this was a private rescript without general application, expressing what was probably a widespread view that stepfathers could pose a danger to children from a former marriage, but not imposing a universal policy.

Distrust of stepfathers appears also in a law of Constantine. The law as a whole [Cod. Just. 5.37.22] attacked what the emperor saw as the predatory practices of the guardians (tutors and curators) of fatherless children under twenty-five. Constantine extended a law of 195, which had forbidden guardians to sell or mortgage the rural or suburban estates of their wards, to include any items of value on urban properties owned by the ward as well.[26] But he was concerned not only with the malfeasance of guardians, for one sentence of the law is aimed at mothers:

Cod. Just. 5.37.22.5, 15 March, 326 or 329

For the law has looked out for the interests of minors not only against guardians, but also against immoderate and intemperate women, who often surrender to their new husbands not only their children's property, but even their life.[27]

This law reflects a traditional Roman fear that remarried mothers would favor their new spouse over their children by their deceased husband, and that a stepfather would not have the best interests of his stepchildren at heart. Some mothers themselves took on the guardianship of their fatherless children, though classical Roman law did not approve [see Part II below], and Constantine's law may have been particularly directed at them.[28]

Several years later, Constantine enacted another law, aimed this time at widowed fathers who remarried [Cod. Theod. 8.18.3, 334]. If children by a first marriage were still under their father's paternal power (as they would be unless he had emancipated them; see Chapter 1, Part II), then any property they had inherited from their deceased mother (*bona materna*) would legally belong to their *paterfamilias*. He was expected to pass it on to them, but not legally compelled to under classical law. Earlier legislation of Constantine had allowed a father only the usufruct (use and possession, but not actual ownership) of *bona materna*, which he was required to hand over to his children if he emancipated them.[29] In his law of 334, however, Constantine deprived fathers who remarried of even the usufruct of *bona materna* [see Humbert 1972, 401–5; Arjava 1996, 102–3]:

Cod. Theod. 8.18.3, 30 March, 334

Emperor Constantine to Severus, Count of Spain:

It has become known that certain fathers, deprived of the bond of their original marriage, rush to the destruction of their children beyond the pity of blood ties and then, having taken up other marriages, claim for themselves a greater role in their children's property. Since they appear to have retained the usufruct in this property, they are confident that they can usurp and subvert it, so that through this (means) no opportunity either of possessing or of bringing suit (over it) is given to those who have remained in orphanhood. Therefore we have decided that no father should think, after he has later taken up marriage, that he ought to claim the right to these things which were from a prior marriage except in the function of guardian, until the minors appear to be of proven age. Moreover, our moderation orders everything to be preserved and restored to them (the children).

Posted at Constantinople on the third day before the Kalends of April in the consulship of Optatus and Paulinus.

Constantine's approach presages the later policies of Theodosius I, who deprived remarried mothers of even the usufruct of property they received from their first husband and required them to hand it on immediately to the children of their first marriage [see Cod. Just. 6.56.4 in Part I.A, and Cod. Theod. 3.8.2 and Cod. Just. 5.10.1, below]. Ultimately, however, Constantine's law was rescinded in 468 by the eastern emperor Leo [Cod. Just. 6.60.4, below].

Disapproval of the remarriage of a woman with children appears also in legislation of Constantius, Constantine's son, regarding a mother's right to revoke half of the amount of gifts she had made to a child who later became "undutiful" (*impius*). The overriding concern in these laws is the preservation of property left by the deceased parent, which, in the law's opinion, should go to the children of the first marriage and not fall into the hands of either a step-parent or children by a second marriage.

Cod. Theod. 8.13.1 (excerpts), 20 September, 349

Emperors Constantius and Constans Augusti to Philippus, praetorian prefect:

Mothers, if they are confident that they are able to prove that their children are undutiful, may approach the courts publicly. (1) Moreover, we ordain that a mother be received and heard, who is freeborn, free, or freed,[30] by whom the rights of Roman citizenship have of course been obtained, just as they were able to bring a complaint under ancient law, and likewise sons or daughters who were freeborn, freed or Roman citizens with an equal status. (2) We set aside the woman who has married into the bond of a second marriage, and we ordain only to women of one marriage the ability to revoke gifts in proportion to one-half. [a sentence is omitted]

[Paragraphs 3–5 are omitted]

(6) Therefore, we think that we have prescribed enough, even silently, about other women, either of another status or of an abnormal vileness or despicable modesty.[31] For who is there who would think anything should be granted to these women, when we wish none of these privileges to be granted even to those who have lawfully contracted marriage, albeit a second marriage?

Given on the twelfth day before the Kalends of October in the consulship of Limenius and Catullinus.[32]

The emperor whose laws reveal the greatest hostility to remarriage by a woman with children from a former marriage is certainly Theodosius I, whose legislation reinforcing and extending the mandated period of delay before a widow could remarry has already been seen [Part I.A above]. In 380, he had decreed that if a widow remarried before the end of the mandated period of delay, she could obtain imperial pardon if she gave half of her property to any children by her first marriage [Cod. Just. 6.56.4, at Part I.A]. The next year he removed the possibility of pardon from widows remarrying within a year of their husband's death [Cod. Theod. 3.8.1, at Part I.A]. In 382, he enacted the following law, demanding that a widowed mother who remarried was to leave all the property she had received from her first husband to the children of her first marriage, retaining only the possession of it during her lifetime:

Cod. Theod. 3.8.2, 17 December, 382

Emperors Gratian, Valentinian (II), and Theodosius Augusti to Florus, praetorian prefect:

Women, who have moved on to second marriages and have children brought up from a former marriage, are to transmit whatever they received from the resources of their former husbands by right of betrothal gifts, also, whatever (they received) from the formalities of marriage, or whatever they obtained from their husbands' property from gifts made in contemplation of death or directly by right of will or under title of trust or legacy[33] or as the reward of any generous liberality whatsoever, to the children which they had from the preceding marriage. Or (they may transmit this property) to whichever they like of their children, to whom the mother has believed the judgment of her own generosity should be directed in contemplation of his merits, just so long as we judge them most worthy of such a succession. Nor shall these same women assume or have the power of alienating anything from the same resources to whatever unrelated person they like or successors brought up from the joining of their second marriage: only the possibility of possession till the end of her life, not indeed the possibility of alienating has been granted (to them). For if anything from these things has been transferred by the possessor to anyone whatever, it will be restored to the account balance of the maternal resources, in order that the properties arrive undiminished and undamaged to those whom we have established as heirs.

[The next two paragraphs, not translated here, say that if a woman has no surviving sons but only daughters, she has the right to succeed to any of her children who die,[34] but only to possess what she has inherited in her lifetime; at her death it must go to any surviving children of her first marriage. If there are no surviving children from her first marriage, she may fully own what she has received by inheritance (or by any other means) and may leave it to anyone she wishes.]

(4) We wish for husbands to be admonished by a similar example both of family feeling (*pietas*) and law. Though we do not bind them as if by a chain of a rather severely imposed sanction, however we restrain them by the law of religious respect (*religio*), so that they should know that what is enjoined upon mothers by the necessity of the proposed rule is more readily expected from them (the fathers) by the consideration of justice; so that, if thus necessity has urged, that which, for the present, it is fitting to hope for and expect should not have to be demanded from them (later) by the reinforcement of a sanction in regard to their case also.

Given at Constantinople on the sixteenth day before the Kalends of January in the consulship of Antonius and Syagrius.[35]

230

The final sentence of Theodosius' law urges that fathers also leave what they had inherited from their deceased wife to their children by her, and hints that if they do not do so voluntarily, they may eventually be forced to by law. This in fact turned out to be the case: in 439, Theodosius II, grandson of the first Theodosius, decreed that what had previously been "urged" upon men by his grandfather was now demanded by law [Novel 14.2 of Theodosius II, in Chapter 2, Part II.C].

In yet another law ten years later, Theodosius went even further, depriving remarried mothers of even the lifetime use (usufruct) of all the property they had received from their first marriage, which they were to give to the children of their first marriage as soon as they remarried. Exception was made for pre-nuptial gifts, of which they could continue to have the usufruct. Theodosius also alludes to the possibility, allowed by his law of 390, that a widow who declared she would not remarry could undertake the guardianship of her children rather than have a tutor appointed [Cod. Theod. 3.17.4; see Part II.A.3]. Clearly if she later did remarry, she would have to restore what she had received from her first husband:

Cod. Just. 5.10.1, 15 March, 392

Emperors Valentinian (II), Theodosius and Arcadius Augusti to Tatian, praetorian prefect:

If a husband when dying has left the usufruct of his property to his wife, and she has entered into second marriage and union, she shall lose the usufruct which she obtained from her previous husband, and shall restore it to her children quickly, from the day on which she married. (1) But if the weakness of infancy still holds the children from her previous marriage and the aid of a tutor does not protect (them), and through an opportunity of this sort the mother has usurped that which had been left, she shall bring the accounts into clarity and shall restore everything, when it is legitimately demanded, along with the appropriate profits.

(2) These things are in regard to the usufruct, which a husband, establishing his final wish, has left to the wife from his own property. But in regard to the usufruct of property given before marriage, we ordain that those things which earlier constitutions decreed are to be maintained.

Given on the Ides of March in the second consulship of Arcadius Augustus and the consulship of Rufinus.

Laws of Theodosius' sons repeated that the usufruct of pre-nuptial gifts was retained by the remarried mother, unlike other property she had received from her first husband (Cod. Theod. 3.9.1, dated 398, of the eastern emperor Arcadius; Cod. Theod. 3.8.3, dated 412, of the western emperor Honorius).

In the following law, Valentinian III, grandson of Theodosius I and emperor in the West from 423 to 455, deprived remarried mothers of the full benefit of the *senatusconsultum Tertullianum*. This second-century enactment had enabled women with the *ius liberorum* to inherit from their children, a right extended by Constantine to cover mothers without the *ius liberorum* also [see chapter introduction]. Valentinian's law allowed a mother who remarried only the usufruct of the property a deceased child had received from its father (though she could still fully inherit the property the child had received from others). This excerpt was part of a very long law dealing with various aspects of inheritance and the sources of law.[36] The law as a whole explicitly applied the same provisions regarding succession to a deceased child to both mothers and fathers.[37] Another excerpt says that a father who has introduced a stepmother into his home may have only the usufruct of property his deceased children obtained from *bona materna*, but full possession of whatever they received from outside sources [Cod. Theod. 8.18.10].

Cod. Theod. 5.1.8, 7 November, 426

Emperors Theodosius (II) and Valentinian (III) Augusti to Albinus, prefect of the city (of Rome):

(After other matters). A mother who has the *ius liberorum*[38] and, after her son or daughter has died without children, succeeds along with their sister, shall be held by an equal example of the paternal lot, so that, if she has not altered her first marriage bed with a second embrace, she shall acquire everything left by her child's death with full rights. But if she has chosen the marriage of another husband, she shall possess with similar firmness the things obtained for the son or daughter from outside (the paternal inheritance), but by contemplation of what is humane, she shall possess only the usufruct of the patrimony of the deceased, and shall transmit the ownership to the deceased's brothers. But if a son or daughter who dies has left children, in any case they shall succeed to their mother or father by the law itself. We think without a doubt that this should be observed also in the case of great-grandchildren. (And other matters).

Given at Ravenna on the seventh day before the Ides of November in the consulship of our lords the Augusti Theodosius for the twelfth time and Valentinian for the second time.[39]

The late Roman laws, eastern and western, are all concerned about the consequences of remarriage by a widowed mother (or father) for the children of the first marriage.[40] Widows *without* children, as long as they observed a twelve-month delay before remarrying, were unaffected. Apparently, however, even childless widows were avoiding remarriage, influenced by legal, social and religious factors [cf. Barnish 1988, 45]. The lifting of the Augustan penalties on the childless by Constantine had removed legal compulsion to remarry, and church fathers encouraged even young widows to see their husband's death as a release from the burdens of marriage and an opportunity to turn to a life of devout widowhood, a state second only to virginity in holiness.[41] Not all approved of childless women refusing remarriage, however, and in 458 the western emperor Majorian attacked what he saw as the self-indulgent and uncivic behavior of young widows. The following excerpts are part of Majorian's long Novel 6, of which other selections are found elsewhere in this book [Chapter 2, Parts II.B and C].

Majorian was apparently concerned about the decline of the Roman population, perhaps because of the increasing presence of non-Roman "barbarians" in large parts of the western Empire. In his law, he also strongly condemned legacy-hunters (*captatores*), non-relatives who paid court to wealthy childless people in the hope of benefiting from their wills. The greedy *captator* is an ancient topos in Latin literature, and it is difficult to know to what extent it corresponds to actual social practice in the late Empire.[42] It should be noted, however, that Majorian's claim that childless widows were being taken advantage of by Christian clergy ("the pretended religion of importunate persons") and other non-kin finds support in fourth-century laws and literature. In 371, Valentinian I had decreed that widows below the legal age of twenty-five required their father's consent to remarry, even if they had been freed from paternal power. According to Valentinian, some widows (presumably wealthy ones) had become the target of intense marriage brokering and even bribery by aspiring suitors [Cod. Theod. 3.7.1; see Chapter 2, Part II.B]. The historian Ammianus Marcellinus, denouncing what he saw as the decadence of the Roman aristocracy of his day, mentions the cultivation of childless persons by fortune-hunters and also criticizes unmarried women (not necessarily widows) so old enough that, if they had married, they could already have had three children, who instead gad about with artificially curled hair and dance till they drop [Amm. Marc. XIV.20–2]. Ammianus' contemporary, the Christian writer Jerome, provides a similar description of socializing widows who parade in public preceded by their eunuchs and patronize Christian clergy, who are eager for their money [*Epistle* 22.16]. Both Ammianus and Jerome were playing on ancient satirical themes, best exemplified by Juvenal's long denunciation of women in his sixth *Satire*, but there was probably some truth to their portrayals. Jerome himself was not above such patronage; indeed his close friendships with celibate Christian aristocratic women, in particular the wealthy widow Paula, led to his eventually having to leave Rome in the face of scandal and possible legal action [see Evans Grubbs 2001].

The clergy, in particular, came in for criticism, since they encouraged women to refuse marriage or remarriage and turn their devotion (and their wealth) to spiritual rather than family matters [see selection from Ambrose in Chapter 2, Part II.B]. Valentinian I, in a law addressed to Damasus, the bishop of Rome, and read aloud in the churches of Rome in 370, attacked "ecclesiastics" who preyed on widows and fatherless female minors (*pupillae*) in the hopes of gaining benefits either by gift or in the women's will [Cod. Theod. 16.2.20]. Twenty years later, Theodosius I ruled that women could become Christian deaconesses only at the age of sixty, when they had had children to whom they were to give all of their worldly possessions [Cod. Theod. 16.2.27, 21 June, 390]. Like the widowed mothers in the laws above, deaconesses were to have only the usufruct of their property, so that they would not be vulnerable to ecclesiastical legacy-hunters (who were to be sent into exile if they were discovered to have extorted a bequest from a dying deaconess). However, Theodosius quickly rescinded his law, which had been intended only for the eastern half of the Empire, as the western church did not have an office of deaconess [Cod. Theod. 16.2.28, 23 August, 390].

By the mid-fifth century, female monasticism was widespread, and donations to the church from aristocratic female benefactors, often widows, had become frequent. Three years before Majorian's law, the eastern emperor Marcian had declared (in response to a particular legal case involving a wealthy woman who had made a priest her heir) that religious women could leave as much as they liked to churches, clerics or monastics, or the poor [Marcian Novel 5, 455]. Majorian's law attempted to regulate both the nubility and the wealth of young women, virgins and widows, whose fecundity he feared would be lost to Rome if they entered a monastic life too early. At the beginning of the law [in Chapter 2, Part II.B], he had condemned the practice of parents consigning their daughters to a life of virginity, and had decreed that women could not become consecrated virgins until they had reached the age of forty, by which time their child-bearing years would be over. In the following excerpt, which echoes Ammianus' and Jerome's depiction of frivolous women, he sets a similar rule for young widows.

Novel 6.5–8 of Majorian, 26 October, 458

(5) Of course, we are moved by the obstinacy of widows, who having raised no offspring, condemn their own fecundity and the restoration of their family and have refused the repetition of marriage. They do not choose the solitary life so that they may serve chastity (*pudicitia*) from the love of religion, but from the misfortune of their own childlessness, they choose the vain display of power, seeking out lascivious liberty of living, for which either the pretended religion of importunate persons or the admiration of the clever legacy-hunter applauds them to every license. Calling them back to the path of a more honorable life by an ancient arrangement, we decree by

this ever-lasting law that a woman bereaved by her husband's death, (if she is) less than forty years old, as long as she is able to procreate children because of her age, is to marry within a period of five years. For that reason we bestow a grace period of the current five years, so that through the space of a legitimate time of mourning, having put aside her grief, she may have the power of choosing more honorable marriage. But if indeed, she has condemned a worldly life and completely hates the marriage torches, persisting in widowhood when the five-year period, as has been mentioned, has been completed, immediately she shall divide her own properties with her full brothers or sisters and their children or her parents or relatives, through whom the origin of the family is restored, or, if by chance these (relatives) are lacking, her patrimony shall be shared with the imperial fisc. She is to know that within the five-year period of that time which we have assigned for mourning and deliberation, she shall alienate nothing from the afore-mentioned six-twelfths, which Our Serenity has decreed is to profit her parents or relatives, (but) content only with the usufruct of living, she will then be able to prove that she has rejected second marriage by the zeal for chastity, since she has been generous toward her relatives.

(6) But the rule is different for those women, who rejoicing in offspring they have raised, for that reason do not move to a second marriage, in order to preserve the affectionate memory of their deceased husband with solicitous sense of duty (*pietas*) in rearing and enriching their children. We release them from the condition of the pronouncement related above, and they have received the freedom of (re)marrying, if they have preferred this, in such a way that they look out for the children brought up from their former marriage – if however the party consisting of the children has wished this – and have provided a guarantor who promises with a clear guarantee that the entire body of their betrothal largesse will be safe. (7) Of course, to mothers of continuous widowhood we open up their power of choice to such a degree that they either furnish their children, who have been placed in the lap of their indulgence, with gifts in proportion to merit while they (the mothers) are still alive, or make them heirs by their final will.

(8) Of course, we abolish that part of the divine constitution by which it had been permitted to mothers that they have the free ability of conferring the greatest portion of the sum of their betrothal largesse on one child, if they wished.[43] In regard to which we order that children succeed without partiality, if indeed that gift is rightly numbered among the paternal property, which the husband brought to his wife at the time of marriage. But if an external heir and layer of traps has stealthily crept up on the mother, against the scruples of blood tie and the rule of family feeling (*pietas*), whatever has been given by her or left or alienated and transferred with impious intent – without there being just reasons for disinheritance, which undoubtedly the one who seems to be preferred to the children will have to prove – all that will be claimed by those same children.

Majorian's demand that childless widows remarry within five years was out of keeping with contemporary sentiment, as well as unenforceable. His successor in the west, Severus, repealed almost all of Majorian's long Novel 6. Severus ruled that whether or not she remarried, a mother had only the usufruct of her betrothal gifts, which were to be retained for her children. He did agree with Majorian that mothers were not to favor some of their children over others in bestowing their pre-nuptial gift. Mothers who chose to remarry did not have to provide a guarantee that the pre-nuptial property would remain safe, since, Severus said, such a requirement was difficult to enforce and the children already had sufficient legal means available to them to claim the pre-nuptial gifts [Severus, Novel 1, enacted at Rome, 20 February, 463].

In the east, the emperor Leo (reigned 457–474) also enacted legislation on remarriage. A law of 468 says that whether or not he remarried, a man had a right to the lifetime use (usufruct) of *bona materna*, property left by his first wife to their children. This overturned the law of Constantine that had penalized fathers who remarried [Cod. Theod. 8.18.3, see above].

Cod. Just. 6.60.4, 1 September, 468

Emperor Leo Augustus to Callicrates, praetorian prefect for Illyricum:

Cutting back all ambiguous confusion, we ordain by this clear and succinct law concerning the usufruct of maternal properties that there is no difference if a father has wished to remain in the former marriage, from which he had children, or has introduced a stepmother to his children. The laws which were enacted concerning *bona materna* have their own validity. (1) Therefore fathers, even if they have moved on to a second marriage, without a doubt ought to have the usufruct of maternal properties. Nor can any improper objection or accusation against the fathers lie open to the children or anyone acting on their behalf. Given on the Kalends of September in the second consulship of Anthemius Augustus.

Four years later, Leo restricted the amount that the spouse of a remarried parent (mother or father) could receive, so that no child of the prior marriage would receive less than the step-parent:

Cod. Just. 5.9.6 pr.-2, 27 February, 472

Emperors Leo and Anthemius Augusti to Erythrius, praetorian prefect:

By this edict that will endure forever we ordain that, if a father or mother has moved on to vows of a second or third or further repeated marriage, when there are children born from the previous marriage, it shall not be allowed to leave more to the stepmother or stepfather, by will, even without writing, or by codicils, or by right of inheritance or legacy, or by title of trust, or to confer, in the name of dowry or pre-nuptial gift or by a gift made in contemplation of death, nor by gifts drawn up between living spouses (which, though they are forbidden by civil law when the marriage is intact, however are accustomed to be confirmed for certain reasons upon the death of the giver[44]) than to a son or daughter, if any has survived. (1) But if there are more children, with each having equal shares, it shall not at all be allowed that more be transferred to their stepfather or stepmother than what has come to each one of them. (2) But if, however, the above-mentioned possessions have gone over to the same children in unequal portions, then also it shall not be permitted for the testator to leave or to give or to confer under title of dowry or pre-nuptial gift more to their stepmother or stepfather than the son or daughter has to whom the lesser portion has been left or given by last will. So also, the fourth part, which is owed to children by the laws, shall in no way be diminished except for those causes which rule out complaints of "undutiful will."[45]

[The rest of the law is not translated here]

II Widows and the guardianship of fatherless children

From a very early period, Roman law had recognized that pre-adolescent children whose *paterfamilias* was dead were vulnerable to deceit and manipulation by those with designs on their property. Originally, the law's concern was simply to protect the property left to such children by their fathers, in the interest of the agnates, the father's relatives. Thus arose the institution of guardianship of an underage ward (*tutela pupilli*). But by the beginning of the imperial period it was generally felt that guardians should be concerned with the welfare as well as the property of their wards [Saller 1994, 181–203; Schulz 1951, 162–79]. This does not mean that *tutores* would live with their *pupilli*; mothers (if they were still alive) were usually the ones responsible for the rearing of their children and their physical welfare.

The guardian of a child who had not yet reached adolescence (legally speaking, fourteen for boys and twelve for girls) was called a *tutor*. He might be appointed by the *paterfamilias* in his will; this was a *tutor testamentarius*. If the *paterfamilias* had not named a *tutor*, the role would usually be assumed by the nearest male relative on the father's side (agnate), called a *tutor legitimus*. However, maternal as well as paternal relatives could be guardians; the choice would depend on the family's circumstances [Gardner 1998, 241–7].

A Mothers and tutela *(guardianship) in Roman law*

1 The obligation to request a guardian

If the mother of a minor child were still alive, she would probably undertake the care and upbringing of the child herself, but in classical law she was not supposed to serve as his official *tutor* [see Part II.A.3 below], and she was required by Roman law to see that a male guardian was appointed. In the absence of a *tutor testamentarius* or *tutor legitimus*, application was supposed to be made (probably by the child's mother or other relatives) to an official, asking him to appoint a suitable guardian. At Rome, the urban praetor was responsible for appointing guardians [Gaius, *Institutes* I.185]; in the provinces, appointment would be made by the governor or his legate, or by a local magistrate [D.26.5.1 and 3 (Ulpian); cf. D.38.17.2.23 below]. Sometimes the town council (variously called the *ordo* or *curia* or, in Greek, *boule*) was involved, as at Petra in the province of Arabia, where the Jewish woman Babatha brought suit against her son's guardians [P.Yadin 12; Cotton 1993; Part II.B below]. Mothers were not legally capable of making the appointment themselves, as they did not have paternal power [Beaucamp 1990, 314].[46]

If she did not ask for a guardian to be appointed, a mother would forfeit the right to inherit from her child granted to women with the *ius liberorum* by the *s.c. Tertullianum* enacted under Hadrian.[47] A treatise by the jurist Modestinus on those who can be excused from the duty of serving as a minor's guardian (which was regarded as burdensome) cites a letter (*epistula*) of the emperor Septimius Severus (reigned 193–211) to this effect. (Modestinus' treatise was written in Greek, and the *Digest* excerpt is in Greek, except for the quote from Severus' letter, which is cited in the original Latin.)

D.26.6.2.2 (Modestinus): The things said about a mother are shown in an *epistula* of Severus, as the words have been appended below: "The deified Severus to Cuspius Rufinus: I wish it to be clear to all that I direct my whole consideration to coming to the aid of fatherless minors (*pupilli*), since it pertains to the public welfare. And therefore, a mother who has either not requested suitable guardians for her children, or has not immediately made known the names of others when the first ones (she requested) have been excused or rejected, shall not have the right of claiming the property of children who die intestate."

D.38.17.2.28 (Ulpian): Moreover, she is punished for not requesting (a tutor) for her sons, and undoubtedly for her daughters. What about for her grandchildren? Similarly, she is punished for not requesting.

This applied to mothers with Roman citizenship both in Rome and in the provinces. Exceptions might be made if the fatherless child had not inherited any property that needed protection, or if the mother were very young:

D.38.17.2.23 (Ulpian): [the beginning of the passage is omitted here.] But from whom does she "not request"? Indeed, the constitution (of Septimius Severus) says from the praetor (of Rome): but I think the law has application even in the provinces, even if she does not request (a guardian) from municipal officials, since the necessity of giving (guardians) is associated also with municipal magistrates.

D.38.17.2.26 (Ulpian): But if she does not request (a tutor) for completely destitute children, she ought to be pardoned.

D.38.17.2.45 (Ulpian): I think that also, if a mother has not requested a tutor for one who will not be able to discharge his debts, she should be pardoned. For she took thought for his interests, so that he would be less troubled (by creditors taking legal proceedings against him) as someone who was without a defense.

Cod. Just. 2.34.2, 3 March, 294

Emperors Diocletian and Maximian and the Caesars to Procula:

Though it is agreed that no one is excused by reason of age in the case of delicts,[48] however, it is not at all fitting that a mother who erred due to the slipperiness of her age and did not request a tutor for her children be denied to succeed to them, since this only applies in the case of mothers who are of the age of majority.[49] The fifth day before the Nones of March in the consulship of the Caesars.

Sometimes mothers did request a guardian, only to find that circumstances beyond their control prevented him from serving. They had to take steps to have another guardian appointed immediately or risk losing their right to succeed to a deceased child. The following replies to petitions suggest problems that could arise in what would appear to be a simple procedure:

Cod. Just. 5.31.3, 12 July, 215
Emperor Antoninus (Caracalla) Augustus to Atalanta:

Make application from the relevant official for another suitable guardian to be given to your children from the same province in place of the guardian who died or was sent into perpetual exile. He (the official) will see to their advantage according to his own duty. Posted on the fourth day before the Ides of July in the second consulship of Laetus and the consulship of Cerealis.

Cod. Just. 5.31.8, 11 March, 291
Emperors Diocletian and Maximian Augusti to Musicus:

Since the careful duty of seeking a guardian is demanded from mothers, random accidents are not regarded as impediments. You declare that the procurator, who had been appointed by a mother for seeking a guardian for a fatherless minor, was killed by bandits and that her petition was delayed by necessity. It is very hard that a mother, in whom, you assert, no moral defect was present, be rejected from succession to the inheritance. Posted on the fifth day before the Ides of March in the consulship of Tiberianus and Dion.

> The mother about whom Musicus wrote to the emperors had appointed a legal representative (procurator) to bring her request for a guardian for her child. The procurator had been murdered by bandits, and the petition was evidently not delivered and approved before the child died. The emperors appear sympathetic, but state the rule firmly. Loss of a child and an inheritance (and a procurator!) at the same time must have been a blow.
>
> If a child's mother did not request a tutor, others might do so:[50]

Cod. Just. 5.31.10, 30 April, 294
Emperors Diocletian and Maximian Augusti and the Caesars to Priscus:

If their mother does not fulfill the duty she owes in requesting guardians for your brother's grandchildren, you are able to make a formal request for guardians. Subscribed at Sirmium on the day before the Kalends of May in the consulship of the Caesars.

Cod. Just. 5.34.6, 30 April, 293
Emperors Diocletian and Maximian Augusti and the Caesars to Leontius:

In regard to the fact that you say their mother was not willing to request tutors for her children, concerning this matter approach the governor of the province, since, if he has determined that she neglected (to do this), even the magistrate himself is not prohibited from giving tutors or from submitting names, so that they can be assigned by the decree itself.[51] Posted on the day before the Kalends of May in the consulship of the Augusti.

Constantine allowed mothers whose children had died after reaching puberty to inherit from them even if they had neglected to appoint a *tutor* when the child was below puberty.[52] There was some legal precedent for this [D.38.17.2.29 (Ulpian); Chiusi 1994, 159–63], and it may already have been the practice [Beaucamp 1990, 317]:

Cod. Just. 6.56.3, 27 July, 318
Emperor Constantine Augustus to Catullinus, proconsul of Africa:

It is certain that mothers, who have lost children[53] past puberty, though they did not request guardians for them when they were minors, ought not at all to be prevented by the objection of "guardian not requested" for the purpose of excluding them from succession to them (their children). Given on the sixth day before the Kalends of August in the fourth consulship of Constantine Augustus and the fourth consulship of Licinius.[54]

A law of the eastern emperor Theodosius II repealed an earlier law that had said that a mother who had not petitioned for a guardian for her minor children was to die intestate – that is, as if she herself had not made a will. This law (said by the early sixth-century Interpretation of Novel 11 to have been in the *Theodosian Code*) is no longer extant, but may have been Cod. Theod. 3.18.2, which is not preserved [Chiusi 1994, 161]. While describing the law he repeals as punishing mothers too harshly, Theodosius II repeated that those who failed to have a guardian appointed for a minor were banned from succession upon the child's death.[55] He also repeated his grandfather's rule that a widow who remarried could not undertake the legal guardianship of her children by her first husband [Cod. Theod. 3.17.4; see Part II.A.3 below].

Novel 11 of Theodosius II, 10 July, 439
Emperors Theodosius and Valentinian Augusti to Florentius, praetorian prefect:

In all things moderation is desired, especially in the laws, through which it is fitting that offenders be corrected according to the nature of their crimes. For that which exceeds the limit of correction is not useful nor should it be observed by judges. Thus, we decree that the constitution, which ordered that mothers, who do not seek legal protection for their *pupilli* or minors[56] or make an inventory of the possessions left (by their deceased children), die (as if) intestate, is to become obsolescent, seeing that it is harsh and punishes mothers with an immoderate penalty.

(1) But in order that we not appear to promise impunity to offenders by cutting back superfluous or inhumane measures, we have decided that the advantages of *pupilli* must be provided for by this most salutary law. And so let those who are called to the succession of a deceased *pupillus* know, that if they have not sought a tutor according to the laws within a year (of the death of the child's father), that all succession to him, whether from intestacy or by the law of substitution, shall be denied to them.

(2) We wish the same to be observed also if the mother, having undertaken the legal guardianship of her children, has aspired to a second marriage against the oath which she offered, before she had another tutor appointed for him and performed what she owed to him from the accounts of a guardianship that had been administered.

(3) But if, contrary to the authority of this law, before she has completed these things, she has believed that she should be joined to a second husband, her husband's goods also shall be held liable by right of security to the accounts of the previous guardianship, Florentius, dearest and most loving parent. (4) And so your illustrious and magnificent authority shall enjoin, by the posting of edicts, that this law, which will endure forever, is observed by all. Given at Constantinople on the sixth day before the Ides of July in the seventeenth consulship of Our Lord Theodosius Augustus and the consulship of Festus, a man of senatorial rank (*v.c.*).[57]

In 479, the eastern emperor Zeno extended the requirement that mothers have tutors appointed for their fatherless children to apply to illegitimate children as well [Cod. Just. 5.31.11].

2 *Guarding the guardians*

A mother was supposed not only to request the appointment of a tutor, but to see that he exercised the guardianship responsibly and honorably. Otherwise she would lose her right to inherit from her children if they died intestate [see Part II.A.1 above]:

D.38.17.2.34 (Ulpian): What if she requested unworthy men, that is, less suitable for guardianship, since she knew that the praetor would not appoint them? But what if the praetor did appoint them, following the mother's request? Indeed, it is the fault of the praetor, but we also punish the mother's plan.

D.38.17.2.42 (Ulpian): What if she did not compel them (the tutors) to be involved in the guardianship? And since we desire a complete duty from the mother, she ought to take care of these things also, lest they stand in her way in regard to the inheritance.

In general, women were legally incapable of bring an action on behalf of others [Chapter 1, Part V.A.1], but exception was made when the guardians of an underage relative were believed to be fraudulent or untrustworthy. A legal action against untrustworthy guardians (*crimen suspecti tutoris* or *de suspectis tutoribus*) could be brought during the period of guardianship, with the purpose of removing the tutor from responsibility, and (if actual fraud rather than incompetence or negligence could be shown) penalizing him with the legal brand of *infamia*. If the guardianship had already ended, an action on the conduct of the guardianship (*actio tutelae*) could be brought, the penalty for which was also *infamia* [Buckland 1963, 160–5]. The possibility of legal action, and the apparent frequency of cases against negligent or fraudulent guardians, no doubt served to keep *tutores* honest and cautious, and to deter some from undertaking the guardianship [Saller 1994, 198–200].

In the case of *actio tutelae*, the most suitable person to bring charges would be the former ward, now of an age to act legally for himself or herself. But the action *de suspectis tutoribus* was open to any woman who could claim to be motivated by the sense of duty (*pietas*) to kin, though she should not violate her "sense of shame" [see Chapter 1, Part IV.B] by being over-bold or aggressive. The following is from Ulpian's commentary on the Praetor's Edict:

D.26.10.1.6 (Ulpian): It is fitting to see who can bring charges against untrustworthy guardians; and it should be known that this action is, as it were, a public action, that is, it lies open to all. 7: But indeed, even women are allowed (to prosecute untrustworthy guardians), but only those women, who come to this course of action led by the sense of duty owed to kin, as for instance, a mother. A nurse also and a grandmother can bring charges. Even a sister can, for there is a rescript of the deified (Septimius) Severus regarding a sister. And if there is any other woman, whose well-considered sense of duty (*pietas*) the praetor has understood (to be that) of a woman who does not go beyond her sense of shame (*verecundia*) for her sex, but, induced by her sense of duty, is not able to keep to herself the injury done to the minor, he will allow her to bring an accusation.

Cod. Just. 5.43.1, 13 August, 212

Emperor Antoninus (Caracalla) Augustus to Domitia:

You can make an accusation of "untrustworthy guardian" against your freedman and the guardian of your son, if you think that he is administering his (the son's) property in a fraudulent manner, only if his term of duty (as guardian) has not ended with the puberty of his ward. For if he has legally ceased to be guardian, he must be brought to trial in a judgment on the guardianship. Posted on the Ides of August in the consulship of the two Aspers.

Cod. Just. 5.43.3, 13 January, 229

Emperor Alexander (Severus) Augustus to Fortunata:

The governor of the province will force the guardians of your children to acknowledge their duty of administration in every way, after more severe remedies have been applied. But if they persevere in the same obstinate disobedience, you are not prevented from bringing an accusation of "untrustworthy guardians," so that others may be sought in their place. Posted on the Ides of January in the third consulship of Alexander Augustus and the consulship of Dio.

On the other hand, mothers were not positively required to bring charges against guardians, as this was really a "man's job:"

D.26.6.4.4 (Tryphoninus): She who did not bring a charge of untrustworthy guardian, does not incur a penalty either by the words or the opinion of the constitution,[58] because it is the characteristic of a masculine mind to judge and evaluate deeds of this sort and a mother is able to be ignorant even

241

of (a guardian's) crimes, and it is enough for her to have requested such a guardian as appeared suitable when an investigation was made by the praetor. And therefore also her judgment is not sufficient for choosing guardians, but an investigation is made, even if she has in her will given guardians to her own children especially for their own property.

Moreover, maternal vigilance did not extend to bringing criminal charges of forgery against their children's legal adversaries [cf. Cod. Just. 9.22.19 in Chapter 1, Part V.A]. Defending their wards' property and business affairs was in fact the duty of tutors and (for those above puberty) curators, as Alexander Severus reminded one mother:

Cod. Just. 9.1.5, 1 October, 222
Emperor Alexander (Severus) Augustus to Marcellina:
By a decree of the Senate it has not been permitted for a woman to prosecute someone under the Cornelian law (on forgery), unless the matter pertains to her. Therefore, since your sons have tutors and curators, they ought to deliberate whether they should make the accusation that the documents, on account of which you say your sons' enemy has prevailed, are forgeries. Posted on the Kalends of October in the consulship of Alexander Augustus.

Sometimes exception was made if a mother acted out of her sense of duty (*pietas*) to appeal a judgment already made against her child:

D.49.5.1 (Ulpian): But also when a mother (who) perceived that her son's property was destroyed by a court judgment has appealed, it should be attributed to *pietas* that she also ought to be heard. And if she has preferred to take charge of preparing a lawsuit, she does not appear to intercede,[59] though she is not able to defend (the case) from the beginning.

3 Mothers as guardians

In classical Roman law, women, even mothers, were not supposed to be tutors. But a number of legal passages indicate that many mothers did undertake the administration of their children's property, and effectively served as guardian [see Chiusi 1994]. Emperors had to inform some mothers that taking on the official responsibility of their child's guardianship was too much for the "weakness" of their sex [cf. Chapter 1, Part IV.C]:

Cod. Just. 5.35.1 and 5.31.6, 20 September, 224
The Emperor Alexander (Severus) Augustus to Otacilia:
(5.35.1) Administering a guardianship is a man's burden, and such a duty is beyond the sex of feminine weakness.
(5.31.6) A mother's sense of duty (*pietas*) is able to instruct you which

tutors you ought to request for your son, but also to observe that nothing contrary to what is necessary is done concerning the boy's affairs. However, the necessity of requesting curators has not been imposed on mothers, since those who have reached puberty but are less than twenty-five ought to request curators for themselves, if their affairs require it. Posted on the tenth day before the Kalends of October in the consulship of Julianus and Crispinus.[60]

Cod. Just. 2.12.18, 21 January, 294
The Emperors Diocletian and Maximian Augusti and the Caesars to Dionysia:
It is generally agreed that undertaking someone else's defense is a man's duty and beyond the womanly sex. Therefore, if your son is a fatherless minor (*pupillus*), request a tutor for him. Subscribed (by the emperor) on the twelfth day before the Kalends of February at Sirmium in the consulship of the Caesars.

Two passages in the *Digest*, attributed to second-century jurists, suggest that it was possible for a mother to receive the right to serve as her child's guardian by imperial grant. (Both passages may have been subject to later interpolation, however.[61])

D.26.1.16 pr. (Gaius): Guardianship is generally a masculine duty.
D.26.1.18 (Neratius): Women are not able to be given as guardians, since this is an obligation of males, unless they make a special request from the emperor for the guardianship of their children.

Sometimes, however, a husband would state in his will that he wished his wife to be their children's guardian after his death. This may particularly have been the case in provinces where there was a custom of widowed mothers serving as their children's guardians [see Part II.B below]. In the following passage, Papinian's emphasis on "our laws" (*leges nostrae*) implies that those making such appointments were provincials who had recently acquired Roman citizenship and were continuing to use their native laws and customs:

D.26.2.26 pr. (Papinian): In our law, the guardianship of children held in common is entrusted to the mother in the father's will without effect. Nor, if the governor of the province had made a mistake through inexperience, and has decided that the father's wish is to be followed, shall his successor correctly follow his (predecessor's) ruling, which our laws do not accept.

Not only were some husbands in the provinces appointing their wives guardians because they did not realize it had no effect in Roman law, but some governors were also unaware of the law and were ratifying the appointment.
Papinian, who was executed by Caracalla in 212, must have written this passage before the *Constitutio Antoniniana* granted Roman citizenship to all provincials. But the number of passages that refer to a husband's entrusting of the administration of his children's property to their mother suggests that this was a phenomenon known in Italy as well as in the provinces:

D.38.17.2.25 (Ulpian): What if the father had prohibited that a tutor be requested, since he wanted their (the children's) property to be administered through the mother? She will fall under the penalty[62] if she does not request (a guardian) or administer the guardianship legitimately.

D.26.7.5.8 (Ulpian): Papinian writes the following in the fifth book of his *Responses*: A father entrusted the guardianship of his children to be carried on by their mother's counsel, and he released the guardians (from responsibillity) for that reason. Therefore the duty of the guardians will be no less diminished, but it will be suitable for good men to admit the mother's counsel in a beneficial way, though neither the guardian's release nor the father's wish, or the mother's intercession, shall infringe upon the duty of the guardian.

> In the following case, the husband had actually made his wife heir rather than their son, and she had assumed full responsibility for the inheritance, passing it on to the son when he reached an age old enough not to have a tutor. Because he legally did not own any property while underage, but only acquired it upon reaching puberty, his mother could be exempted from the requirement that she have a tutor appointed for him [on which see II.A.1], so the penalty decreed by Septimius Severus for mothers who failed to have tutors appointed did not apply [Chiusi 1994, 161–3, and cf. D.38.17.2.26 in II.A].

D.38.17.2.46 (Ulpian): And if by chance someone made his wife, the mother of their son held in common, heir, and asked that, having waived security (against loss) she restore the inheritance to their son when he reached puberty, and the mother did not request tutors, it ought to be said that the constitution (of Septimius Severus) does not apply, since she followed the father's wish and did not request tutors for a son who had nothing. But if she did not waive security against loss, the opposite will be true, since indeed on account of this he ought to have tutors. [the rest of the passage is omitted here]

> In the case below, a mother took full responsibility for her daughter's inheritance (Scaevola does not say whether the father had requested this in his will) and, like the mother in the previous passage, had handed over the property to her daughter when she reached maturity. The mother's administration of her daughter's financial affairs does not appear to have been questioned by the bankers with whom she dealt. It was only because the daughter later complained that she had not received the money herself, that the question of responsibility arose:[63]

D.46.3.88 (Scaevola): A mother administered the business affairs of her daughter, heir to her father who died intestate, and gave items to be sold through the bankers, and this very fact was written in the account-book. The bankers paid the entire proceeds of the sale (to the mother) and for almost nine years after the payment, whatever had to be done, the mother did in the name of the *pupilla* and arranged for her marriage to a husband

and handed her property over to her. It was inquired, whether the girl has an action against the bankers, when she herself did not stipulate for the price of the items which were given for sale, but her mother did. He replied that if the question were whether the bankers were legally released by this payment, he responded that they were legally released. (Claudius): For this question pending from the jurisdiction underlies (the decision): whether they seem in good faith to have paid the prices for the items which they knew belonged to the *pupilla*, to the mother, who did not have the right of administration. And therefore, if they knew this, they are not released, to be sure, if the mother should not be able to discharge her debts.

There were certain things a mother could not do legally [see Gardner 1998, 249–50; cf. Cod. Just. 9.1.5 and D.49.5.1 in Part II.A.2]:

D.3.5.30.6 (Papinian): Though a mother may administer her son's business affairs according to the father's wish, trusting in her sense of family duty (*pietas*), however, she will not have the right of appointing an advocate for the sake of lawsuits at her own risk, because she herself does not correctly act in her son's name nor can she alienate his property or release one who is a debtor to the youth by accepting money.

A mother who did administer her child's affairs instead of having a guardian appointed would herself be responsible for any mismanagement that might occur, and would need to produce her child's financial accounts when the child passed the age of guardianship:

Cod. Just. 5.45.1, (no day given) 259
Emperors Valerian and Gallienus Augusti to Marcellus:
Even women, if they have administered a pupil's affairs in place of a tutor, are bound to render an account. Posted in the consulship of Aemilianus and Bassus.

However, appointed guardians who then relinquished their authority to their wards' mother were still considered responsible. A tutor would want to get some sort of security from the mother to guarantee that she herself would be financially liable for any mismanagement. Two tutors found themselves in an awkward situation when their former pupils became unhappy with the way their affairs had been managed:[64]

Cod. Just. 5.46.2, 12 July, 246
Emperors Philip Augustus and Philip Caesar to Asclepiades and Menander:
You assert that certain of your pupils' affairs were administered by their mother and likewise by their paternal grandfather, and that security from loss was promised to you in their names. If this is so and the same pupils, having reached legal age, prefer to go to law not against their own mother and grandfather, but against you, not undeservedly will you desire security

245

from the loss to be offered by those whom you claim previously undertook the administration at their own risk. Posted on the fourth day before the Ides of July in the consulship of Praesens and Albinus.

A mother who gave security that she would be responsible could not later claim the protection of the *s.c. Velleianum* [see Chapter 1, Part IV.D] on the grounds that she had been interceding on behalf of someone else:

Sent. Pauli II.xi.2: A mother, who promised an indemnity on behalf of the tutors of her children, does not come under the benefit of the Senate's decree.

D.16.1.8.1 (Ulpian): If a mother has intervened as guarantor before her son's tutors, so that they do not sell his estates, and has promised an indemnity to them, Papinian in his ninth book of *Questions* does not think that she has interceded. For (he says) she did not take on another's obligation either old or new, but she made this obligation her own.

But if she had not provided surety or a guarantor, she could claim the protection of the Senate's decree and avoid liability for any losses:

Cod. Just. 4.29.6, 10 March, 228
Emperor Alexander (Severus) Augustus to Torquatus:
   If a mother, when she was administering her own children's patrimony, promised security to their tutors and offered a guarantor or gave pledges, neither she nor the guarantor offered by her nor her pledged property are helped by the aid of the Senate's decree, since in a certain way she appears to have administered her own business.
   (1) But if, however, when the tutor was willing to excuse himself, she interposed herself, promising an indemnity to him, she is by no means prohibited from using the aid of the Senate's decree. (2) But if indeed, she requested tutors and undertook the risk of her own accord, in so far as she is held (liable), she is protected by the law's authority. Posted on the sixth day before the Ides of October in the consulship of Modestus and Probus.

A mother who undertook administrative duties properly belonging to a tutor could be prosecuted for "unauthorized administration" (*negotia gesta*) or "unauthorized guardianship" (*pro tutore negotia gesta*):

Sent. Pauli I.iv.4: A mother, who intervened in the affairs of her own children, will be held liable to the children themselves and to the tutors for "unauthorized administration."

But if she requested the appointment of guardians who turned out to be fraudulent, she was not legally liable for the damage, nor was she expected to provide surety for guardians who had been appointed at her request. In such cases "womanly weakness" could be an advantage:

Cod. Just. 5.46.1, 13 March, 234

Emperor Alexander (Severus) to Bruttia:

The magistrates gave the guardians which you requested at their own risk, rather than you, contrary to the condition of your sex, being bound by this obligation for anyone else because you asked for guardians to be given to your children at your risk. Posted on the third day before the Ides of March in the second consulship of Maximus and the consulship of Urbanus.

In the fourth century, imperial law allowed mothers to serve as guardians to their own children, provided they declared that they would not remarry and thereby subject their children to the hostile machinations of a stepfather. The first extant law to this effect is that of Theodosius I, who legislated extensively on the remarriage of widows [cf. Part I above]. But the book of the *Theodosian Code* which preserves this law has not come down to us in its original state, and it is possible that there was earlier legislation allowing widows to serve as their children's guardian, and that Theodosius' innovation was the restriction of this right to mothers who did not remarry [Arjava 1996, 91–2; cf. Chiusi 1994, 192–3; Gardner 1986a, 150–1]. On the other hand, in stressing that mothers do not have to serve as guardians, and that they can do so only if there is no *tutor legitimus*, the law appears to be explicating a new policy [Beaucamp 1990, 325–30].

The weakening and ultimate disappearance of the guardianship of women may have made the idea of a woman serving as a tutor herself more acceptable [Chiusi 1994, 191]. Note, however, that mothers can undertake the guardianship only if there is no *tutor legitimus* available – that is, no male relative on the father's side such as a paternal uncle (who would be the most suitable tutor) – or if existing guardians have been excused or disqualified through misconduct or ill health.[65]

Cod. Theod. 3.17.4, 21 January, 390

Emperors Valentinian (II), Theodosius (I) and Arcadius Augusti to Tatian, praetorian prefect:

Mothers who request the guardianship of administering business affairs for their children after the loss of their husbands, are to avow in the public records that they will not enter a second marriage, before the confirmation of such a duty can come to them legally.[66] (1) Certainly no woman is forced in a choice of this sort, but she is to proceed freely by will into the conditions which we have set forth. For if they prefer to choose other marriages, they ought not to administer their children's guardianship.

(2) But so that after the guardianship has been legally undertaken, incursion upon it may not be easy for them, we order that first the property of the man who aspired to the marriage of the woman carrying out the guardianship is to come under obligation and be held liable to the accounts of the little ones, so that nothing is lost by carelessness, nothing lost by fraud.

(3) We add the following to this: that a woman, if she is above legal age, shall have the right of requesting the guardianship only when a *tutor legitimus* has been lacking or is excused by privilege from the guardianship, or is removed by the character of "untrustworthy" or is discovered to be not even suitable for administering his own properties on account of the ill health of his mind or body.

(4) But if women have fled from guardianship and have preferred marriage, and there is not any *legitimus* able to be called for reasonable causes, then only the urban prefect, illustrious man, with the approval of the praetor who is in charge of bestowing guardianships, or the judges who restore laws to the provinces will order defenders from another order to be given to the minors by means of investigation.

Given at Milan on the twelfth day before the Kalends of February in the fourth consulship of Valentinian Augustus and the consulship of Neoterius.[67]

B Mothers and guardians in the Greek East

The prescriptions of classical Roman law, which said that mothers could not officially serve as guardians, do not reflect the situation all over the Empire (and indeed, may not reflect the de facto situation even in Rome and the most Romanized parts of the Empire). In Egypt and parts of the Greek east, mothers were able to serve as guardians of their minor children, particularly if they had been named as such in their husband's will. Not all widowed mothers were guardians, however; many requested local authorities to have a guardian appointed for their children, and some "assisted" in the guardianship along with male guardians.

1 Appointment of guardians

In Roman Egypt, the guardian of a fatherless minor was called an *epitropos*, the Greek equivalent of Latin *tutor*. The papyri suggest that in Roman Egypt several different officials might be asked to appoint *epitropoi*. A number of such requests have been preserved, submitted by the children's mother or other relatives, and there was evidently a standard procedure for such appointments [Lewis 1970; Taubenschlag 1955, 157–70; cf. P.Oxy. VI.888].

The Egyptian papyri also indicate the growing importance of the *curator* [Taubenschlag 1955, 178–81; cf. Chapter 1, Parts II.C and III.E]. From the third century on, fatherless children above puberty but below the legal age of twenty-five were expected to have their *epitropos/tutor* replaced by a curator, who would play a less active role than a *tutor*, but was still important for the administration of their estates. In 287, the prefect (governor) of Egypt issued an edict calling for the appointment of guardians for all minor orphans (that is, fatherless children) who did not have them. He declared this was necessary since "now many of the affairs of orphans relating to guardians meet delay because there are not *epitropoi* or *kouratores* for orphans" [P.Oxy. VI.888]. The mention of *curatores* (transliterated directly from Latin, as there was no Greek equivalent) indicates this was to refer to fatherless children below the legal age of twenty-five, not just those below puberty. However, it was not the mother's job to have a *curator* appointed for her children who had reached puberty. According to a rescript of Alexander Severus, this was something they could do for themselves [Cod. Just. 5.31.6; see Part II.A.3 above].

In the following petition of the early third century, the widow Demarion, acting with her father as *kyrios* [see Chapter 1, Part III.C], asks a local official to have a guardian appointed for her son and daughter:[68]

P.Oxy. XXXIV.2709, 206 C.E.

To Androsthenes also called Rufus, strategos of the Oxyrhynchite (nome), from Demarion daughter of Apion son of Dorion, her mother being Helen, from the city of Oxyrhynchus, with her *kyrios*, her father Apion son of Dorion, whose mother was Kleuparous, from the same city.

My husband, Dionysios also called Sarapion, son of Apollonios, his mother being Sinthonis, from the same city, died on the past second[69] (day) intestate with minor heirs, his children by me, Hermes and Herais. Therefore, having handed in the petition, I ask that you command the *grammateus* of the city to appoint a guardian for the minors so that nothing will be lost to them. Year 14 of the Emperors Caesars Lucius Septimius Severus Pius Pertinax Arabicus Adiabenicus Parthicus Maximus and Marcus Aurelius Antoninus Pius Augusti [[and Publius Septimius Geta]]. 24 Mecheir.[70]

[2nd hand] I, Demarion, daughter of Apion, have handed in (the petition). I, Apion son of Dorion, have been registered as *kyrios* of my daughter, and I have written on her behalf because she does not know letters.

Demarion had to request a guardian for her children because her husband had died without making a will, and had left no instructions as to who should serve as guardian. Often fathers named a guardian for their young children in their will, as in the following papyrus dated 276.[71] Aurelius Hermogenes, a prominent town councilor of Oxyrhynchus, apportioned his considerable property among his five children, three of whom were still underage. For them he appointed an *epitropos*: in the boys' case, until they came of age; in the girl's case, until she married (at which point her husband would presumably become her *kyrios*). However, Hermogenes states explicitly that his wife is to be *epakolouthousa*, "concurring" in the guardianship, and that his nephew was also to assist the guardian in any way necessary. This appointment of a widowed mother as a sort of assistant to the official guardian, called an *epakolouthetria*, seems to have been a way of reconciling Roman law with a local custom of mothers serving as guardians [Modrzejewski 1970, 361; Montevecchi 1981, 113; see further Part II.B.3 below].

All involved are Roman citizens, as this was more than sixty years after the Edict of Caracalla. The will was written in Greek, but follows a Roman legal format. The final sentence states when the will was opened (after Hermogenes' death), indicating that this papyrus was a copy made afterwards.

P.Oxy. VI.907, 276 C.E.

Aurelius Hermogenes, also called Eudaimon, *exegetes*, member of the *boule* [and prytanis[72] of the illustrious] and most illustrious [city of the Oxyrhynchites, dictated this will] in Greek letters according to the concession (of Roman law):[73]

The Aurelii Hermeinos and Horeion and Herakleides and Ptolemais and Didyme, my five sweetest children [from my ... wedded wife], Aurelia Isidora also called Prisca, a *matrona stolata*,[74] ... by the condition attached below in regard to which each [... shall be my heirs, and the rest] shall all be disinherited, and they shall enter on the inheritance from me in regard to the things left to each [whenever they determine and are able to give testimony] that they themselves are my heirs, and they shall be responsible for giving, doing (and) providing all these things [which have been written in this will of mine], and I entrust this to their good faith.

[The three sons jointly receive one vineyard with its appurtenances; the two daughters jointly receive another vineyard with appurtenances; one son gets another piece of land and a slave; one daughter, already married, is bequeathed her dowry and a slave; the other daughter receives some property and a slave; and the three brothers and unmarried daughter receive four slaves among them.]

To Aurelia Isidora, also called Prisca, my wedded [wife ...] who has conducted herself fittingly in respect to our marriage, I leave with full property rights those (arouras)[75] which I have jointly near the [same ... .around ...] all the arouras of grainland previously mortgaged to her by me for the purpose of the ... dowry which was brought to me by her.

I make Aurelius Demetrios, son of Dionysotheon, *epitropos* of my three above-mentioned underage children, Horeion and Herakleides and Didyme, until the males [come of age and the female] marries a husband, with [my afore-mentioned wife] Isidora also called Prisca concurring (*epakolouthousa*) in all the things relating to the guardianship, and therefore, I do not want a magistrate or anyone acting in place of a magistrate or anyone else to get involved[76] ... For I enjoin upon the piety also of my nephew Didymos to help Demetrios in these things if ever he [asks] him ...

[Bequests to friends follow, and his sons are enjoined to provide a dowry of four silver talents to Didyme, the unmarried daughter.]

7 Pauni of (year) 1 of Emperor Caesar Marcus Claudius Tacitus Pius Felix Augustus. I, Aurelius Hermogenes, also called Eudaimon, have made the will in regard to the things attached above. It was opened in Epeiph of the same (year) 1.[77]

2 A mother brings suit against her son's guardians

In Roman law, mothers could not be guardians themselves and were supposed to see that guardians were appointed for their underage fatherless children, but they did have the responsibility to see that their children were not cheated or misused by their guardians. An action against untrustworthy guardians could be brought during the period of guardianship by anyone, including female relatives, who alleged fraud or misbehavior on the part of a ward's *tutores*, and third-century rescripts to concerned mothers [Part II.A.2] indicate that some women contemplated bringing such an action.[78] We know of such a case from the Roman province of Arabia, formerly the kingdom of Nabatea. Documents relating to this case are among the papers of the Jewish woman Babatha, which were discovered in a cave on the Dead Sea [see Chapter 2, Part III.B].

Nabatea had been an independent kingdom for centuries until in 106 it was subsumed into the Roman Empire under the emperor Trajan (reigned 98–117). One of the most surprising things revealed by the Babatha archive is the extent to which Roman administrative and legal apparatus had already become entrenched in the new province of Arabia, only two decades after its formation. Even more fascinating is the fact that a provincial woman (not even a Roman citizen), in a culture where women were certainly not encouraged to undertake legal action, had enough self-confidence – and enough knowledge of Roman law– to use the Romal legal system to sue her son's guardians. Another woman whose name appears in the Babatha archive (as a legal opponent of Babatha) is the mysterious Julia Crispina, a Roman citizen evidently of very high status who had much local influence (see further below). Other documents in the archive include marriage agreements [Chapter 2, Part

III.B] and papers relating to the marital and financial affairs of Babatha and of her step-daughter, the daughter of her second husband.

In Jewish law mothers could serve as their children's guardians if appointed by the father [Cotton 1993, 98]. However, Babatha was not the guardian of her son by her first marriage, Jesus (Joshua). Jesus had two male guardians, who had been appointed by the town council (*boule*) of Petra, a metropolis of the province of Arabia. But Babatha was not happy with the arrangement, and in 124, she went to court against her son's guardians, alleging that they were not giving him a maintenance allowance (out of his own estate) in keeping with the lifestyle he deserved. Interestingly, though neither Babatha nor her opponents were Roman citizens and Arabia had been a province less than two decades, she chose to go through the Roman legal system and use the provincial governor's court. This suggests that the Roman legal system, whatever its flaws, was seen as an attractive alternative to local law by some provincials, including women.

Several papyri in the Babatha dossier are concerned with Babatha's lawsuit. The first (P.Yadin 12, not translated here) is an extract from minutes of a meeting of the boule of Petra in 124, giving the names of the two guardians appointed by the boule for Jesus, Abdobdas son of Illouthas, a Nabatean and John Eglas,[79] a Jew like Babatha and her son. Evidently Babatha had copied the exact names of the men she wished to sue from a register of appointed guardians posted at Petra [Cotton 1993, 95]. The second (P.Yadin 13, not translated here and unfortunately very fragmentary) was a copy of the petition which Babatha submitted later in the same year to the governor of Arabia, Julius Julianus, alleging that Abdobdas and John, who had been appointed four months earlier, were not giving Jesus the amount of money he needed, but only two denarii a month. (This appears to have been sufficiently generous in comparison to maintenance allowances for wards in Roman Egypt: see Lewis 1993, 30.) Presumably Babatha submitted the petition in order to get the governor's signature (*subscriptio*), which would enable her to bring a summons against her opponents (cf. the petition of Bathsabbatha in Chapter 1, Part V.C). There is no *subscriptio* in the dossier (P.Yadin 13 is Babatha's own copy of her petition, not the original which she gave to the governor's office). However, we can assume that one was received, since P.Yadin 14 (below), is the actual summons to John son of Eglas, demanding that he appear before the governor's court [Cotton 1993, 106].

In addition to the documents below, three papyri with blank legal forms for bringing an action on the conduct of the guardianship (*actio tutelae*) were found [P.Yadin 28–30], evidently for possible use against the guardians. However, since an *actio tutelae* could only be brought after a guardianship had ended, Babatha did not use the forms [Cotton 1993, 105; cf. Part II.A.2].

As with official documents in Roman Egypt and elsewhere in the Middle East, the language used is Greek. However, several of the witnesses to these legal documents signed in local languages, either Nabatean or Aramaic. Babatha herself, like most women in the Roman Empire, was illiterate, and so had someone sign on her behalf.[80]

Babatha's summons to John Eglas was (like most of the documents in the Babatha archive) a double document, written twice on the same papyrus, with one copy written above the other [see Chapter 2, Part III.B].[81] It is not clear why only John Eglas is summoned, and not her son's other guardian, Abdobdas (also spelled Abdoobdas) son of Illouthas (also spelled Ellouthas). Perhaps he had come to an arrangement with Babatha outside of court [cf. Lewis 1989, 54].

Like Roman women, who needed a *tutor mulierum* unless they had the right of three children, and like women in Roman Egypt, who needed a *kyrios* for undertaking certain transactions, Babatha presents her summons through her guardian, her second husband, Judah son of Khthousion. (In documents from Judaea and Arabia, a woman's guardian is called an *epitropos*, the same word used to describe guardians of minors; see Chapter 1, Part III.C).

251

P.Yadin 14 (outer text), 11(?)[82] October,125

In the ninth year of Emperor Trajan Hadrian Caesar Augustus, in the second consulship of Marcus Valerius Asiaticus and the consulship of Titius Aquileius, on the fourth day before the Ides of October, of the twentieth year according to the numbering of the province of Arabia, the twenty-fourth of the month Hyperberetaios called Thesrei, in Maoza around Zoara. Babatha, daughter of Simon son of Menahem, in the presence of the witnesses concerned, through her guardian for this affair Judah son of Khthousion, summoned John son of Joseph Eglas, one of the guardians appointed by the *boule* of the Petreans for her son Jesus, being the orphan of Jesus, saying: "Because of your not having given to my son ... the same orphan from whom ... just as Abdoobdas son of Ellouthas your colleague gave by a receipt, therefore I summon you to attend at the court of the governor Julius Julianus in Petra, the metropolis of Arabia, until we are heard in the tribunal in Petra on the second day of the month Dios or at his next assizes in Petra[83] ...

The witnesses concerned: John son of Makoutha

Shammu'a son of Menahem

Joseph son of Ananias

... son of Libanos

[possibly traces of 2–3 lines in Aramaic]

I have written.

[On the back of the document the witnesses signed, the first in Nabatean, the second in Aramaic, the third in Greek, and the fourth in Aramaic; the fifth signature is not readable.]

The next document, P.Yadin 15, bears the same date as P.Yadin 14. Like P.Yadin 14, this was a double document with inner and outer texts.[84] It is Babatha's deposition in court in which she detailed her charges that the allowance given her son by his guardians was inadequate, and that if it was not increased, her statement was to serve as evidence in a case of *suspecti tutoris*, on charges that the guardians were profiteering from the funds intended for her son's maintenance. Babatha also notes that she had earlier offered to take on the distribution of the allowance herself, pledging her own property as security, but her offer had evidently not been taken up.[85] Again, Babatha acts through her guardian (and husband), though presumably she was present in court.

P.Yadin 15 (outer text), 11(?) October, 125

In the ninth year of Emperor Trajan Hadrian Caesar Augustus, in the second consulship of Marcus Valerius Asiaticus and the consulship of Titius Aquileius, on the fourth day before the Ides of October, of the twentieth year according to the numbering of the province of Arabia, the twenty-fourth of the month Hyperberetaios called Thesrei, in Maoza around Zoara. In the presence of the witnesses concerned, Babatha daughter of Simon son of Menahem produced evidence against John son of Joseph Eglas and Abdoobdas son of Ellouthas, guardians of Jesus son of Jesus, her orphan son, having been appointed guardians for the same orphan by the *boule* of the Petreans, with the same guardians being present, saying:

"Because of your not having given to my son, the orphan ... maintenance (*trophia*) according to the value of the interest on his money and his other properties, and especially according to a lifestyle which ... , and (because of your) not furnishing him with the interest of the money except one half-denarius per one hundred denarii, I, having properties sufficient for the money which you have of the orphan's, therefore I have previously borne witness that, if it seems good to you, you give to me the money on security ... concerning a pledge of my properties, with me furnishing the interest on the money of one and a half denarii per hundred denarii. Whence my son might be splendidly maintained, giving thanks for the most blessed times of the governorship of the governor Julius Julianus, in the presence of whom I, Babatha, have summoned the afore-mentioned John, one of the guardians of the orphan, concerning the refusal of rendering of maintenance. If not, this will be a statement on oath for the purpose of supporting documentation of (your) profiting from the money of the orphan if giving ..."

Babatha has presented evidence as written above through her guardian for the matter, Judah Kthousion, who, being present, signed.

[second hand] Babatha, daughter of Simon, I have presented evidence against John son of Eglas and Abdoobdas of Ellouthas, guardians of Jesus, my orphan son, through my guardian Judah Kathousion (sic), in accordance with the conditions written above. I, Eleazar son of Eleazar, have written on her behalf, having been asked to because of her not knowing letters.

[first hand] And seven witnesses were present.

[At the bottom Judah son of Khthousion signed his name in Aramaic, and Abdoobdas son of Ellouthas, signed in Nabatean for himself and his fellow guardian, John Eglas. John's son, Joseph, also signed for him in Aramaic.]

[in Greek] The one who wrote this was Theenas son of Simon, the scribe.[86]

[On the back were the signatures of the seven witnesses; the first three names are lost.]

We do not have a record of the governor's decision, but the final document below, P.Yadin 27, is a receipt from Babatha to Simon, described as the "hunchback," the son of John Eglas, who seems to have taken over the guardianship of Jesus from his father John. In the receipt, Babatha acknowledges that she had received from Simon six denarii for a three-month period for Jesus' maintenance. This is two denarii a month, the same amount which eight years earlier she had claimed was inadequate. Perhaps the governor had ordered the original sum be doubled, with each guardian disbursing two denarii a month, and Babatha had also received two denarii from Abdobdas [Chiusi 1994, 185]. Or perhaps she had lost her case, and Jesus had continued to receive two denarii a month [cf. Lewis 1989, 116]. Possibly she had been making up the difference with her own funds, or had been able to take over the distribution of some of the allowance herself, as she had offered years before. The document is in Greek with the exception of Babatha's statement in Aramaic, which is then translated into Greek. This is the latest dated document in the Babatha papers found in the Dead Sea cave.[87]

P.Yadin 27, 19 August, 132

In the consulship of Gaius Serrius Augoreinus and Ploutius Trebius Sergianus, on the fourteenth day before the Kalends of September, of the twenty-seventh year according to the numbering of the new province of Arabia, on the first of the month Gorpiaios, in Maoza in the surrounding area of the Zoorans. Babatha daughter of Simon, with her guardian Babeli son of Manaemos (Menahem) being present and writing on her behalf, both of them from the same Maoza, to Simon hunchback son of John Eglas of the same Maoza, greetings.

Since you have been appointed as the second guardian ... by the *boule* of the Petreans for my orphan son Jesus son of Jesus, I have received from you for the account of maintenance and garments for the same Jesus my son, six denarii of silver from the first of the month of Panemos of the same twenty-seventh year up to the thirtieth of Gorpiaios, three completed months.

[Second hand, in Aramaic, Babatha acknowledges having received the six silver denarii for maintenance and clothing; her guardian writes for her.]

[first hand] Translation of Babatha daughter of Simon: I have received from Simon hunchback son of John, guardian of my son Jesus, for the account of maintenance and his garments, six denarii of silver from the first of the month of Panemos up to the thirtieth of Gorpiaios of the twenty-seventh year, which are three complete months. Through her guardian, Babeli son of Manaemos.

I, Germanus son of Judah, wrote this.

The dispute over her son's maintenance was not the only legal matter concerning the property of underage wards in which Babatha was involved. In 131, she was summoned to court by another woman, Julia Crispina, who claimed that Babatha was holding by force lands belonging to the orphans of Jesus son of Khthousion, the deceased brother of Babatha's second husband Judah (who was also dead by this time). Babatha issued a countersummons to Julia Crispina denying the charge [P.Yadin 25]. In this and in an earlier document [P.Yadin 20, dated 130], Julia Crispina is described as the *episkopos*, "overseer" of the orphans of Jesus son of Khthousion, along with a man, Besas son of Jesus, who is called an *epitropos*. (Besas did not take part in the summons issued by Julia Crispina in P.Yadin 25, because he was ill.) Julia Crispina obviously exercises some sort of guardianship over the orphans, though she does not seem to be related to them,[88] and it is noteworthy that she is not called an *epitropos*, the term usually used in Greek for the guardian of minors. Her name indicates she was a Roman citizen, and she seems to have been a woman of status and wealth.[89] She is not said to be acting through a guardian; perhaps she had the *ius liberorum* [Cotton 1993, 97; Chapter 1, Part III.D.] Her role in the guardianship is evidently analogous to that of the *epakalouthetria* of third-century documents from Eygpt [Lewis 1993, 31–3; see Part II.B.3 below].

3 Mothers as guardians

Evidence for mothers acting as the guardians of their fatherless children can be found in both Roman Egypt and the Greek cities of Asia Minor. In both places the custom goes back to the period before Roman rule. From Egypt, a petition dated 142 B.C.E. refers to a mother *prostatis* ("protector") who evidently served as guardian of her fatherless son.[90] By the mid-first century, the term *epitropos* is being used to describe a mother-guardian. In a petition of the mid-first century B.C.E. to the Hellenistic rulers of Egypt, Cleopatra and Berenike, a widow claims that she was appointed *epitropos anenlogistos* ("guardian without audit") of her daughter in her husband's will, meaning that she did not have to submit an account of the guardianship after it ended [see Wegener 1947]. A marriage contract of 127 from the city of Oxyrhynchus specifies that if the husband dies first and there are children, the wife or her nearest relation is to be joint *epitropos* along with a relative to be appointed by the husband (presumably in his will) from his side of the family. If he does not appoint someone else, she is to be sole *epitropos*, "with no one being able to eject her from the guardianship or a part (of it) [P.Oxy. III.496, at lines 10–13], and two other marriage contracts from the same city say that if the husband dies first, the wife is to be joint guardian with another appointed male.[91] In all cases, these are Greco-Egyptian women who are not Roman citizens, to whom the Roman legal restriction on mothers as guardians did not apply [Montevecchi 1981]. On the other hand, the will of the soldier Antonius Silvanus, who was a Roman citizen, calls for an arrangement in keeping with Roman law. His son (whose age is not given, but who is evidently still a child) is to be heir, but the boy's mother, Antonia Thermutha (whose name indicates she is also a Roman citizen), is to "preserve" the inheritance until the boy's *tutela* ends; she is not guardian herself.[92]

Of course, mothers who did serve as guardians might not always have the best interests of their children at heart. So at least claims a young man, Didymos, in a petition from Oxyrhynchos dated 123.[93] Didymos complains that his *epitropos* mother has defrauded him of his rightful property and has not paid his maintenance allowance for three months. Even before this petition, Didymos (or someone acting in his interest), had taken steps to have another guardian appointed for him.

P.Oxy. VI.898, 123 C.E.

To Hermodoros, royal scribe also acting for the strategos,[94] from Didymos son of Dionysios, also called Phatres, from the city of Oxyrhynchus:

My mother, Matrina, daughter of Herakles also called Matres, being my *epitropos* and wronging me in many ways, still deceives me, and she has made me go down into the Oasis and cause to be written up for Dioskoros, husband of her freedwoman, who is her intimate, a ... of one and a half silver talents and to mortgage whatever possessions I have in the Oasis, after receiving a decree of indemnification from Dioskoros. And when I came up to Oxyrhynchus along with Dioskoros, she lay in wait until she could ask me for the decree of indemnification.[95] And having gained possession of it and being conscious that she has snatched away many of my possessions, she does not want to confess (this) before asking me for a receipt for the guardianship, thinking that by this she is able to escape what she has done. And yet Philonikos the strategos, according to the minutes of proceedings, has decided to have another guardian appointed for me, since he does not trust either her or me, on account of my youth. And besides these things, she has not furnished me with my allowance for three months now, oppressing me in every way so that I cannot bring legal proceedings against her. Because of all these things, I have handed in the petition by necessity and ask that you have it registered and handle it as seems best to you. Year 7 of the Emperor Caesar Trajan Hadrian Augustus, 29 Pauni.

Mothers who served as the guardians of their underage children are also known from the Greek cities of the eastern Mediterraenan. Three inscriptions from Asia Minor, dating from the late third–early second century B.C.E.) record mothers as *epitropoi*. As in Egypt, this practice continued after the Roman takeover, at least to the late first century C.E.[96]

The following inscription from Xanthos in Lycia (on the southern coast of Turkey)[97] records the thanks of one such son, a provincial notable to his mother, Senbreidase, who (in contrast to Didymos' mother Matrina in the petiton above) exercised her guardianship in a satisfactory way.[98] The son's private dedication was engraved on the architrave of a building in the sanctuary of Leto (Letoon) beside another inscription honoring Senbreidase from the citizens of Xanthos.[99] A third inscription on a statue base that once held a bronze statue of Senbreidase, also erected by the Xanthians, commemorates her for her "modest behavior" (*sophrosyne*) and "greatness of mind" (*megalophrosyne*). All testify to the esteem in which she was held, not only by her son but by her city [Balland 1981, 250–6]. The date is unknown, but is from the late first century B.C.E. or early first century C.E.

Fouilles de Xanthos VII.81, late 1st c. B.C.E.–early 1st c. C.E.

Kleon, son of Kleon the son of Apollonides, the Xanthian, serving in the government in all the cities around Lycia, (set this up) for Senbreidase, daughter of Kleon, the Xanthian, his own mother, who exercised the guardianship (*epitropeusasan*) well and justly and was honored by the city of the Xanthians with second honors[100] because of her good will and affection.

Another inscription erected near Attaleia, also in Lycia and Pamphylia, under the reign of Domitian (81–96 C.E.), records that a certain Timotheus son of Menneos, acting through his *epitropos* mother, Killa daughter of Moos, restored a tower that had previously been erected by his grandmother while she was priestess of Demeter. Thus a wealthy widow's guardianship of her underage son had consequences not only for him and his family, but for their city, which relied upon the benefactions of its leading citizens, male and female, for maintaining civic and social structures.[101]

However, references to mothers as *epitropoi* disappear around 130 C.E., perhaps as a result of influence from Roman law [Montevecchi 1981, 113–15]. Instead, some widowed mothers in Egyptian papyri are described as "concurring" in the guardianship of their children, rather than actually serving as guardian themselves. One example has already been noted, Aurelia Isidora, whose husband Aurelius Hermogenes specified in his will that she was to be *epakolouthousa* [Part II B.1; see Lewis 1993, 31–3 for other examples].

Another third-century papyrus from Oxyrhynchus, a contract for the sale of acacia trees, shows how a "concurring" mother would assist her children's guardian in selling property belonging to the minors. The document begins: "Aurelius Ptollion son of Ptollion from the city of Oxyrhynchus, *epitropos* of the underage children of Apollonius also called Didymus son of Onesas, and the mother of the underage children, and the concurring party (*epakolouthetria*), Aurelia Eudaimonis daughter of Antinoos also called Hermes, acting without a *kyrios* according to the customs of the Romans by the right of children, to the Aurelii Serenus son of Aurelius Ammonios, former exegete of the city of the Oxyrhynchites and to Serenus son of Serenus also using (the name) Theonates, whose mother is Taamiusis and to Soterichos Didymos from the same city, greetings...."[102] In addition to being *epakolouthetria*, the mother Aurelia Eudaimonis was able to act without a guardian herself by virtue of the *ius liberorum* [see Chapter 1, Part III.D]. Not only mothers could be named as *epakolouthetria*: in 172/3, in the Arsinoite nome, a veteran (and Roman citizen) named two male *epitropoi* for his daughter in his will, with her grandmother as *epakolouthetria*.[103]

A papyrus dated 219 gives a variation of the term *epakolouthetria*. Aurelius Hierax, the *epitropos* of two fatherless minors, acting with the children's mother, Nicarus, gives an account of receipts and expenditures made from the children's funds during the previous year. The word used to describe Nicarus' function is unclear, but it seems to be *parakolouthetria*.[104]

In the late third century we again find women acting as guardians of underage children, but now the term used is *kedestria*, evidently the female equivalent of *kedemon*, a blanket term in Greek for "guardian" covering both *tutor* (*epitropos*) and *curator*. A fragmentary petition of the late third or early fourth century refers to a woman, Apollonia, exercising the guardianship (*kedemonia*) of the children of her deceased sister, along with another sibling, either male or female (the second name is lost) [Beaucamp 1992, 172–9]. The most notable example of a mother-*kedestria* is Aurelia Artemis, the widow from Theadelphia who vehemently defended her sons' interests after their father's death [see Part B.4 below].

Interestingly, there are no explicit references to widowed mothers as guardians of their children in papyri after the early fourth century, even though the practice of the mother-*tutor* was recognized in Roman law under Theodosius I [see Part II.A above]. Yet it can be shown that widowed mothers were acting as guardians in the late Roman period, even when there were male relatives available, and that they exercised authority over their fatherless children. This is one aspect of the legal and social independence of widows in late Roman Egypt, compared to married women, whose husbands took over the role of a *kyrios* [Beaucamp 1992, 179–91; see Chapter 1, Part III.E].

A widowed mother's guardianship of her children in late antiquity thus continues a practice of mothers acting as guardians which, as we have seen, predated Roman rule and went on even in the third century, when mothers were not supposed to serve as guardians under Roman law. The rescripts of Alexander Severus to Otacilia [Cod. Just. 5.35.1 and 5.31.6, in Part II.A] and Diocletian and Maximian to Dionysia [Cod. Just. 2.12.18, in Part II.A], informing them that women are not to undertake the guardianship of their children, may well have been directed to women in eastern provinces, like Egypt or Lycia and Pamphylia, where such guardianship was customary. Roman law was aware that some husbands were appointing their wives guardian in their will, and that some governors were even approving such a move [D.26.2.26 pr., in Part II.A]. We do not have evidence of actual practice for Italy or the western provinces to match the documentary sources of the east. It is possible that in the west too, particularly below the elite, widowed mothers were acting as their children's guardians without interference from the authorities. Eventually Roman law recognized the practice, though not until the end of the fourth century.

4 A guardian mother defends her children's interests

Mothers, whether or not they served as their children's guardians, could be tireless defenders of their financial and legal interests. We have already seen how Babatha attempted to force her son's guardians to increase the allowance they were giving him from his inheritance. Another mother who went to court on behalf of her children was Aurelia Artemis, a widow from a village near the city of Theadelphia in the Arsinoite nome in Egypt. Three papyri, dating from the early 280s, feature Aurelia Artemis as litigant or petitioner on behalf of her underage children. Only in the last one does she style herself her children's *kedestria* (though that document actually contains two petitions, in both of which she uses the term), but she is clearly acting in that capacity in all three. Aurelia Artemis' troubles apparently began after the death of her husband, when a local notable who had a grudge against her husband invaded her home. Later she had a falling-out with her husband's sister over taxes the sister owed on her share of the inheritance from Artemis' husband's father.

In a petition of the late third century, Aurelia Artemis writes to the prefect that Syrion, a *dekaprotos* (a local tax-collecting official), took advantage of her husband's death and seized his livestock, literally over his dead body.[105] Though she does not say so directly, it is possible that Syrion may have claimed that her husband had cheated the Treasury and that he (Syrion) was merely appropriating what rightfully belonged to the Treasury. Aurelia Artemis repeatedly mentions her widowed state and her responsibility for her children, now fatherless, whom she describes as "infant" (*nepioi*), though this may be an exaggeration (in the court records [P.Sakaon 31], and in her later petitions [P.Sakaon 37], they are described only as *aphelikes*, "underage"[106]). The stress on her widowhood is intended to evoke pity and support from the prefect, like the claims of "womanly weakness" by other female petitioners in the papyri (see Chapter 1, Part IV.C.2, esp. P.Oxy. I.71 for another widow's petition).

The prefect's reply (subscription), at the end of the petition, tells her to approach the *epistrategos*, the official one step below the prefect.

P.Sakaon 36 (P.Ryl. II.114) *c*.280

To Hadrianus Sallustius the most eminent governor, from Aurelia Artemis, daughter of Paesios, from the village Thraso of the Arsinoite nome:

Perceiving your love of moderation,[107] my lord governor, and your care for all, especially for women and widows, I approach you, thinking myself worthy to receive aid from you. The matter is like this:

Syrion, having become a *dekaprotos* from the same village, Thraso, persuaded my husband, Kaet by name, to shepherd his flocks – who unjustly took off with my afore-mentioned husband's goats and sheep to the number of sixty. And as long as my afore-mentioned husband was alive, each man reaped his own profits, my husband his own and the afore-mentioned (Syrion) his own. But when my afore-mentioned husband went the way of men, Syrion burst in, exploiting his local power, even wishing to snatch away the property of my infant children from my husband's very bed and with his body lying there. And when I tried to take back our property and to cover up (the body of) my husband, he sent me away with threats, and up till today he happens to have hold of our flocks.

Therefore I ask you, lord, to send help to me by your command, in order that I might get back the property of my infant children and of myself, a widow, and that I might be able to comply with my tax assessment readily. For my afore-mentioned husband was not caught out regarding property belonging to the Treasury, but it is in the nature of the afore-mentioned Syrion always to despoil me, a widow with infant children – so that having taken the grain of my deceased husband through his assistant [name missing], he did not give a receipt for the payments in kind that were due – in order that I might get back my own property by your benevolent decision, lord and benefactor of all, and might be able to stay together with my infant children in my own home and always be able to acknowledge my thanks to your fortune. Farewell.

[in a 2nd hand] ... 9 [month missing]. With a view to what is advantageous to the revenues, ... [name missing] the excellent *epistrategos* will judge the matter according to what is most just.

Sheet 69, Roll 1.[108]

Aurelia Artemis duly went with her complaint to the *epistrategos*, who ordered Syrion to appear in court to answer the charges. But Syrion, evidently a man of considerable influence in the community, flouted the summons of *epistrategos* and kept the livestock. In this record of a court proceeding, the advocate speaking for Aurelia Artemis and her children again asks that Syrion be made to appear in court and give back the stolen animals.[109] According to the procurator (an imperial official representing the interests of the state Treasury[110]), Syrion was away on important state business, and unable to attend. Consequently the *epistrategos* refuses to take action for the time being.

Note that Aurelia Artemis does not speak in court, which would have been considered unseemly [cf. Chapter 1, Part V], but is represented by an advocate, Isidorus. She does not appear to have a *kyrios*; in documents dated twenty-five years later recording her purchase of two houses [P.Sakaon 59–60], she is said to have the *ius liberorum*, so presumably she did already in 280 (but cf. Chapter 1, Part III.E. on widows acting without a *kyrios* in late antiquity). The suit apparently was brought in the name of her minor children, who were the direct victims of Syrion's theft of their inheritance. As a woman, Aurelia Artemis could not act legally on behalf of others, though as we have seen, exceptions were made for mothers acting on behalf of their fatherless children.[111]

P.Sakaon 31 (P.Thead.15), 280/1

Year 6 of our lord Marcus Aurelius Probus Augustus, in the Arsinoite nome, before the tribunal.

Isidoros, one of the advocates, said: Artemis [...][112] two months ago is petitioning, and her underage children are appearing in your court. They are appearing in court upon the order of the most eminent governor, who remanded the matter to you, in order that you might prevent an act of violence. We have often cited this act of violence in your official minutes. For Syrion, after the death of the children's father, greedily eyeing the animals left to them by their father – for he happened to be a shepherd – seized sixty of them in number. And you, displeased at this, ordered the same Syrion to present the shepherds with whom the children's father was herding flocks, both Aunes and his brother, in order that, there not being any dispute, he might restore the flocks to the children. But look at what Syrion is doing: he is opposing the orders given by you and by the governor. And therefore even now we call upon you to order once and again that he be brought here and give back to the children what he seized.

The procurator said: Since Syrion has been dispatched for the purpose of necessary business regarding the Treasury, just as soon as he has returned he will answer the charges brought against him.

Isidorus, one of the advocates, said: And if he should flee from justice?

Aurelius Herakleides, the most excellent *epistrategos*, said: When I have been petitioned, I will give a decision.

We do not know if Aurelia Artemis was ever able to recover her children's property from Syrion. But another document from several years later shows that she was still active on their behalf, this time in a dispute with her sister-in-law Aurelia Annous, her children's paternal aunt, over inheritance taxes that Aurelia Artemis claimed she had paid on Aurelia Annous' behalf. This document consists of two petitions, the first a cover letter to the local official, the nome *strategos*, enclosing a copy of a petition sent earlier to the governor of Egypt.[113] The governor had added his subscription to that petition, approving it, thus enabling Aurelia Artemis to go back to the *strategos* and request that he force her sister-in-law to pay what she owed. Both petitions are in the name of Aurelia Artemis' children, but in both she states clearly that they are acting through her as guardian (*kedestria*). Again, we do not know the outcome of this dispute.

P.Sakaon 37 (P.Thead. 18), January/February 284

To ... former (?) *hypomnematographos*,[114] strategos of the Arsinoite nome, from the Aurelii ... and Keletes, both underage children of Kaet, through their *kedestria* mother, Aurelia Artemis, daughter of Paesios, from the village Thraso of the Arsinoite nome.

I have attached below and deliver to you, best of *hypomnematographoi*, the copy of the petition which I handed in to the most eminent governor, Pomponius Ianuarianus, along with a copy of the subscription which I obtained from his Magnificence. I ask that you send a copy of it through one of your attendants to the woman accused by me, Aurelia Annous, in order that she can know and not plead ignorance as an excuse ... from bringing in the public payments according to the two-thirds share that falls to her. Farewell. It is as follows:

To the prefect of Egypt, from the Aurelii ... and Keletes, both underage children of Kaet, through me, their mother, Aurelia Artemis, daughter of Paesios, from the village Thraso of the Arsinoite nome. I offer to you a most just and lawful petition concerning my underage children, my lord governor, begging ... my underage children. The matter is like this: Their grandfather on their father's side, from the village Thraso, ... inspection concerning public land around the afore-mentioned village Thraso for which dues ... And then when Sotikes died, with his children as heirs – I mean the afore-mentioned father of the children, Kaet ... and Isidorus and Annous – and then also it was necessary for Annous herself to present herself at the most sacred Treasury in order to pay together in common ... of my children of needy age, she does (not) want to give the public payments falling to her share. And I, being annoyed and ... by the *dekaprotoi* in the district, I render the payments on her behalf, so that I run the risk of abandoning my own ... with my children. Therefore I flee to your feet, begging and pleading on behalf of my underage children, so that you might order the strategos of the nome,[115] or whomever your Magnificence approves, to force Annous to fulfill and render the accounts for the land, since she has received her paternal inheritance. For thus, having received aid, we will be able to acknowledge the greatest thanks to you for everything. Farewell. Of the second year, 5 Hathyr. Demand for the dues ... to the *strategos*.

Sheet 38 of Roll 1.[116]

[2nd hand] We, the Aurelii ... and Keletes, being underage, have handed this in through our mother. I, Aurelius Didymos, son of Ammonios, wrote on their behalf.

[1st hand] In the second year of our lords Carinus and Numerianus Augusti, ... Mecheir.[117]

III Pregnant widows

Guardianship (*tutela*) was a legal institution developed to protect children whose *paterfamilias* had died before they were of an age to manage their own property (property which, presumably, they had inherited from him). Normally, such children would have been born during their father's lifetime and within a legitimate marriage, and would have been recognized by their father as his legal heirs before he died. But what of children who, though conceived within legitimate marriage, had not been born until after their father had died? In such a situation, not inherited property was at stake, but also questions of paternity and legitimacy, upon which the transfer of paternal property depended.

Children conceived in a legitimate marriage were their father's heirs if he died intestate. An unborn child had to be explicitly disinherited in their father's will [Thomas 1986, 214]. If the father had left a will but had not included a posthumous child (called a *postumus*), presumably because he had not been aware of his wife's pregnancy, proof of the child's existence would break the will [see D.40.4.29 in Chapter 4, Part I.E.2]. In the eyes of property-conscious Romans, it was essential to ensure both the paternity and the survival of such children yet to be born. As with the divorcée who claimed to be pregnant by her ex-husband [Chapter 4, Part I.E.2], attention centered on the widow who had become pregnant before her husband's death but who did not give birth until afterwards.

A Surveillance of pregnant widows

As we saw, widows were supposed to observe a "mourning period" of ten months after their husband's death before they could legally remarry [Part I.A]. A child born to the widow during this time was assumed to have been conceived from her husband before he died. Since a posthumous child conceived during marriage would have the right to inherit from his deceased father, it was vital that everyone, especially the father's other heirs, recognize the child as the true and legitimate son of his father. Five titles of the *Digest* [D.25.4–6 and 37.9–10] are devoted to determining whether a woman really was pregnant, to securing the unborn child's inheritance claim and to ensuring that the child, both before and after birth, was taken care of until any challenges to its claim could be resolved, and to punishing women who falsely claimed they were pregnant.

A section of the Praetor's Edict, "On examining the womb and the guarding of the offspring"[118] sets out an elaborate procedure to be followed when a widow claimed after her husband's death that she was carrying his child. Since the deceased husband himself was not able to state whether or not he recognized the child, the widow's pregnancy had to be closely monitored and birth had to take place under extreme high security precautions, lest an attempt be made to smuggle in a "supposititious" (substitute) child. The law (and perhaps many in-laws of widows) supposed that a woman might claim that she had borne the supposititious child herself, in order to obtain the property of her deceased husband in the name of his alleged child. The following passages are all from Ulpian's commentaries on the Praetor's Edict:

D.25.4.1.10 (Ulpian): About examining the womb and guarding the offspring the Praetor says the following:

If a woman says that she is pregnant after her husband has died, she should take care to announce this twice within a month to those to whom this matter pertains or to their representative (*procurator*), so that they, if they wish, can send those who will examine her womb. Moreover, up to five free women are to be sent and these are all to examine together, as long as none of them, while she examines, touches the stomach if the woman is unwilling. The woman shall give birth in the house of a very respectable (*honestissima*) woman, whom I will determine.

Thirty days before she thinks that she will give birth, the woman is to announce (this) to those to whom this matter pertains or to their representatives, so that they, if they wish, can send those who are to guard the womb. There should be no more than one entrance to whatever room the woman will give birth in; if there are, they are to be obstructed on both sides by boards. Before the entrance of this room three free men and three free women are to stand guard along with two companions each. As often as the woman goes into that room or into any other room or to the bath, the guards, if they wish, are to stand look-out in front and to search[119] those who have entered. The guards, who have been placed in front of the room, if they wish, are to search all who have entered either the room or the house. When the woman begins to give birth, she will announce this to those to whom this matter pertains or their representatives, so that they can send those in whose presence she is to give birth. Up to five free women are to be sent, so that in addition to two midwives, there shall be no more than ten free women in that room, and no more than six slavewomen. All the women who are within are to be searched in that room, lest any be pregnant. Let there be three lights, no less, there, of course because shadows are more suitable for substituting (a baby). Whatever is born is to be shown to those to whom this matter pertains or to their representatives, if they wish to examine it.

It (the child) is to be raised at the home of the person whom the parent has ordered.[120] However, if the parent ordered nothing or the person, at whose home (the parent) wished it to be raised, will not accept the responsibility, I will decide at whose home it is to be raised after holding a hearing. The person at whose home it is being raised is to show that which is born, when he (or she) wishes, twice a month up to (the age) of three months, once a month from that time until it is (the age) of six months, every other month from six months until it becomes a year old, and once every six months from a year old until it is able to speak.

If someone is not allowed to examine the womb or to guard or be present at the birth, or if something has been done so that these things do not happen as has been dealt with above, having held a hearing, I will not give possession to the one who has been born. Or if it has not been permitted to examine that which has been born, as was decreed above, if it is shown to me that there is just cause, I will not give to that person those legal actions which I promise that I will give to those to whom possession of property (*bonorum possessio*) has been given according to my edict.

D.25.4.1.12 (Ulpian): Therefore, it is necessary that the woman announce (her pregnancy) to those, certainly, in whose interest it is that she not give birth to offspring, those who would have either the entire inheritance or part of it either upon intestacy or by will.

D.25.4.1.14 (Ulpian): Moreover, it is necessary that she announce (her pregnancy) to those whom the next hope of succession touches; as, for instance, the heir instituted in the first grade (not, indeed, the substituted heir)[121] and, if the *paterfamilias* died intestate, the one who holds the first place upon intestacy. But if several people are to succeed together, it must be announced to all.

These would be members of her deceased husband's family, who would inherit from him if he died childless or without a will. They would have a considerable interest in whether or not she was actually pregnant (hence the need to examine her) and in whether she actually gave birth to a live baby or had another baby smuggled in (hence the room with only one entrance and the physical search of all who entered it), and in whether that child actually survived and was not replaced by a substitute (hence the inspection of the child at regular intervals until it could speak). For a widow whose pregnancy was contested, birth was a very public and intrusive event [Gardner 1984]. There could be as many as eight people (three men and three women, plus two companions each) guarding the room where she gave birth, and as many as eighteen (ten free women, two midwives, and six slavewomen) in the room itself during the birth! This doubling of midwives and attendants was meant to assure both sides that their interests were being represented [Hanson 1994, 176]. How often such an elaborate procedure was actually followed is not known, but we know of a case in second-century Egypt [see Part III.C], and a case at Rome where a man claimed his ex-wife was pregnant and demanded that she undergo a similar examination [D.25.4.1 pr., in Chapter 4, Part I.E.2]. However, if her husband's family accepted the widow's claim (which was probably usually the case), there would be no need for a physical examination or for monitoring the birth.

Women could be excused for not following the prescribed procedure if this was due to ignorance (cf. Chapter 1, Part IV.A on *imperitia* as an excuse) or to differences in local custom:

D.25.4.2.1 (Julian): But sometimes the Praetor ought to relax this (rule), if it has happened not through the woman's malice, but through her inexperience, that the womb was not inspected or the birth observed.

D.25.4.1.15 (Ulpian): However, as to what the Praetor says, that after holding a hearing he will not grant possession or will deny legal actions, this pertains to the case where something of those matters which the Praetor wished to be observed has been omitted, so that it not be to the disadvantage of the offspring. For what a situation it would be for possession of property (*bonorum possessio*) to be denied to the offspring, if any of those things, which the Praetor decreed were to be observed leniently, has not been done. But the custom (*mos*) of the region must be taken into consideration, and the womb and the offspring and the infant ought to be observed according to it.

The legal presumption behind the edict *de inspiciendo ventre* is the same as that behind the *senatusconsultum Plancianum*, concerning pregnant divorced women [Chapter 4, Part I.E.2]: the claim of a widow or divorcée to be pregnant by her former husband might be disputed by the ex-husband himself (in the case of a divorcée) or by his family (in the case of a widow). Which came first, the procedure for pregnant widows (*de inspiciendo ventre*) or for pregnant divorcées (the *s.c. Plancianum*)? The edict *de inspiciendo ventre* is known from juristic commentaries to have been included in the Praetor's Edict, which was given final form under Hadrian (reigned 117–138). The Senate probably passed its decree on pregnant divorcées under Trajan (98–117), the reign prior to Hadrian's. However, the edict *de inspiciendo ventre* probably went back much earlier than the reign of Hadrian, at least to the late Republic.[122] Roman law had dealt with the question of the paternity of a child born to a widow much earlier than that; already in the Twelve Tables (450 B.C.E), we find the rule that a child born within ten months of the death of his father is his heir [D. 38.16.3.9–11 (Ulpian)]. A passage in a Roman comedy, the *Andria* of Terence, performed in 166 B.C., mentions the presence of free women (*liberae*) at a birth where the paternity of the child is questioned.[123] Sanctions against widows who remarried less than ten months after their husband's death go back to very early Rome, and though such rules were originally religious in nature, they also served the practical purpose of ensuring that a child born within the ten-month period had been conceived by the woman's husband [see Part I.A above]. Both the penalizing of a widow who remarried too soon and the monitoring of a widow who declared her pregnancy were intended to assure the paternity of a child born after her husband's death, and to protect his inheritance.

B Inheritance rights and the supposititious child

Roman law wanted to be sure that paternal property went to the proper heir. The inheritance rights of an unborn child and potential heir had to be protected, and so agnates (relatives on the father's side) who would have inherited if the deceased had been childless had to wait until the child was born:

D.38.16.3.9 (Ulpian): Certainly even in the law of the Twelve Tables he who was in the womb is admitted to the legitimate succession, if he has been born. Therefore it is customary to keep waiting agnates who come after him (in succession), to whom he is preferred, if he has been born. Therefore also he has a share with those who are of the same degree (of relation to the deceased), as for instance, (when) there is a brother and the unborn child, or one son born to a paternal uncle and one who is in the womb.

D.5.4.3 (Paulus): The ancients provided for the free unborn child[124] in such a way that they preserved for it all legal rights intact until the time of birth. Thus it appears in the law of successsion, where those who come after what is in the womb in regard to degree of agnation are not admitted (to the inheritance), as long as it is uncertain whether it can be born. Where, however, others are of the same degree as the unborn child, they (jurists) therefore asked what portion ought to be in suspension then, since they could not know how many were able to be born. Therefore indeed so many varied and incredible things about a matter of this sort are believed that they are counted among fables.

[Paulus continues with several stories of amazing multiple births in Greece and Egypt. Jurists decided that three was the maximum number that could be born at one time except in very unusual cases, and so no more than three portions of the inheritance would be held back until the woman gave birth.]

D.37.9.1 pr. (Ulpian): Just as the Praetor had a care for those children who are already among human affairs, so also he has not neglected even those who have not yet been born, on account of their expectation of being born. For he has protected their interests also in this part of the edict, in which he put the unborn child into possession instead of (granting) possession of property contrary to the will,[125] 1: It is necessary that the woman be pregnant in every case, nor does it suffice that she says she is pregnant. Therefore the granting of possession of property does not hold, unless she truly was pregnant both at the time of (her husband's) death and at the time when she asks to be put into possession.

A curator was to be appointed, at the woman's request, for both the unborn child and its property; sometimes a curator was appointed only for the child [D.37.9.17 (Ulpian)]. The curator authorized deductions from the inheritance for the maintenance of the pregnant woman "in proportion to the means of the deceased and also in proportion to the status of the woman" [D.37.9.19 (Ulpian)].[126]

D.37.9.27 (Ulpian): Moreover, the unborn child ought to be in possession until she either gives birth or has a miscarriage or it is certain that she is not pregnant. 28: And if she consumed (part of the inheritance) knowing and aware that she was not pregnant, Labeo says that she has consumed it at her own expense.

If a woman fraudulently claimed to be pregnant and went to court to obtain *bonorum possessio* in the name of her unborn child, she could be charged with *calumnia* (bringing of false charges or vexatious prosecution), which resulted in legal infamy (*infamia*) [cf. the widow who remarried within ten months of her husband's death; Part I.A]. However, women who were honestly mistaken as to their pregnancy were not penalized. Of course, it would be difficult to prove that a woman who claimed to be pregnant was deliberately bringing a fraudulent claim. Physical examination might determine whether or not she was pregnant, but could not prove that she had intentionally deceived by a false claim.

D.25.6.1 (Ulpian): If there is an inquiry concerning possession in the name of the unborn child (*venter*) and, when the heir brings an accusation, the woman has sworn that she is pregnant, the oath should be observed, nor will the woman be held, as if she came into possession for the sake of *calumnia*, nor should force be used on her after swearing. If, however, she has given birth, the truth shall be inquired into, whether she was pregnant from him (her husband). For an oath made between others neither benefits nor harms another, and therefore it will not harm the offspring. 1: And this edict arises from the same cause as the one above: for inasmuch as it is easy for (an action) concerning possession of property to be given to a woman in the name of her unborn child, so the praetor ought not to leave her *calumnia* unpunished. 2: However, she who wanted to come into possession knowing and aware that she was not pregnant, seems to have come into possession through *calumnia*.

D.3.2.15 (Ulpian): She is penalized with *infamia* who came into possession in the name of her unborn child (*venter*), while she declared that she was pregnant,

D.3.2.16 (Paulus): when she was not pregnant or had conceived from another (than her husband):

D.3.2.17 (Ulpian): For she who deceived the Praetor ought to be punished. But she is penalized with *infamia*, when she does this of her own power.

D.3.2.18 (Gaius): She who was deceived by a false opinion (that she was pregnant), cannot appear to have come into possession through *calumnia*.

D.3.2.19 (Ulpian): Moreover, no one is branded with *infamia* other than the woman about whom it has been judged that she had come into possession for the sake of *calumnia*. And that also will be observed in the case of the father, who for the sake of *calumnia* allowed a daughter whom he had in his legal power to come into possession in the name of her unborn child.

What if those who otherwise stood to inherit continued to claim, even after the child's birth, that it was not the legitimate heir? Under the Carbonian Edict, the child would still have possession of the disputed inheritance until he or she reached puberty (fourteen for boys, twelve for girls), at which time the question of ownership would be resolved in court. During the period when the inheritance was still in dispute, the child could draw maintenance from the estate [D.37.10; Buckland 1963, 726].

Challenges to the child's claim to inherit might be made on the grounds that he or she was "supposititious" (from Latin *suppositus*, "substituted"), that is, that someone else's baby had been brought in just after or during the birth itself, either to substitute for a stillborn infant or to conceal the fact that the woman was not pregnant. This fell under the *lex Cornelia de falsis* (Cornelian law on forgery), evidently by analogy with forged wills) and carried a criminal penalty [Robinson 1995, 37].

D.34.9.16 pr. (Papinian): A father had in "second tablets" named co-heirs and made his brother's sons substitute heirs for his son who was below puberty,[127] and after the boy's death the substitute heirs, the sons of the brother, had brought charges of "substituted offspring" against his mother, in order that they might obtain their uncle's property as legitimate heirs.[128]

A petitioner, rather ostentatiously named "Legitimus," believed that his aunt had perpetrated a fraud on the family in the same way; presumably he was next in line as heir if the child could be proved to be a *suppositus*:

Cod. Just. 9.22.10, 21 September, 285
Emperors Diocletian and Maximian Augusti to Legitimus:

Since you are stirring up a criminal charge of "substituted offspring" against the wife of your paternal uncle, bring an accusation and prove it before the governor of the province. Posted on the eleventh day before the Kalends of October in the second consulship of Diocletian Augustus and the consulship of Aristobulus.

It was the possibility of substitution which had prompted the security precautions called for in the edict *de inspiciendo ventre* [Part III.A above]. How often such a substitution actually occurred is not known; legal references may reflect the anxieties of a society obsessed with questions of legitimacy and property (and distrustful of women) rather than actual frequency. The charge that a woman had had a baby smuggled in goes back to Greek comedy [Hanson 1994, 78–80] and appears also in the Roman playwright Terence [*Andria*, lines 514–15; cf. Part III.A above].

Among the Roman elite, charges that a woman had fraudulently claimed to have borne a child could have a political motivation. In the reign of Tiberius, Aemilia Lepida, descendant of an illustrious republican family, was charged with *falsum* for having pretended to have had a child by her former husband (from whom she was divorced), a "rich and childless" man. Accusations of adultery, poisoning, and consulting astrologers regarding the imperial house were thrown in. Amidst the protests and laments of other senatorial women, she was convicted by the Senate and banished from Roman territories (*interdictio aquae et ignis*, "prohibition from fire and water"), though her property was not confiscated [Tacitus, *Annales* III.22–23; see Talbert 1984, 467].

A law of 393 indicates that the Carbonian Edict, and controversies over the status and inheritance rights of a posthumous child, continued into late antiquity:

Cod. Theod. 4.3.1, 28 Sept., 393

Emperors Valentinianus, Theodosius, and Arcadius Augusti[129] to Rufinius, praetorian prefect:

The Carbonian Edict is deployed in regard to legitimate persons from an undoubted marriage, when the offspring has been guarded and the legitimate succession has been proven, so that certainly the new heir, placed in possession until the age of puberty, may in some instances enjoy the possessions of others without disturbance.

Given at Constantinople on the fourth day before the Kalends of October in the third consulship of Theodosius Augustus and the consulship of Abundantius.[130]

C Pregnant widows in the papyri

Interest in pregnant widows is not confined to Roman legal texts, as we can see from the papyri. Financial considerations, such as the expenses of bearing and rearing a fatherless child and inheritance rights, were obviously a real concern.[131] Marriage contracts might make provision for a wife's pregnancy at the time of divorce [cf. P.Oxy. X.1273 in Chapter 2, Part III.A.4], and other documents involve arrangements in the case of a father's death before his child is born.

The archive of Protarchos, an official at Alexandria during the reign of Augustus with whom documents in the form of a *synkhoresis* were registered [cf. Chapter 2, Part III.A.1 and Chapter 4, Part III.A.1], contains an agreement between a pregnant widow and her mother-in-law.[132] The agreement gives Dionysarion, the widow, the right to "expose" her newborn child, that is, to abandon it.[133] If Dionysarion's husband were alive, he would have the right to decide whether it should be exposed or raised, and it was to be expected that his family would have an interest in whether or not his child was reared [see Part III.A above]. Here Hermione, the husband's mother, relinquishes any interest in the fate of the unborn child. For her part, Dionysarion agrees not to ask for childbirth expenses or make any other financial claims on Hermione, who has already returned Dionysarion's dowry to her. Evidently Hermione was her son's heir and had control of his property; these are not Roman citizens, and did not follow Roman inheritance law. The couple apparently had been married less than two years; probably this was Dionysarion's first pregnancy, and there are no other children to provide for.

BGU IV.1104, 8 B.C.E.

To Protarchos, from Dionysarion daughter of Protarchos with her *kyrios*, her brother Protarchos, and from Hermione daughter of Hermias, a citizen woman (of Alexandria) with her *kyrios*, Hermias, the son of her brother Hermias.

Dionysarion acknowledges that the agreement which the deceased son of the same Hermione, Hermias son of Hermias, brought through the same tribunal, through the same Hermione as surety, in the Year 21 of Caesar, Phaophi[134] is invalid (and) that Dionysarion has gotten back from Hermione, for the sake of her deceased husband, by hand from the house the dowry which she brought to Hermias through Hermione as surety, clothes worth two hundred forty silver drachmas and earrings and a finger-ring ... and a hundred silver drachmas. (And she acknowledges) that the agreement ... is invalid with all the things declared by it, and that neither Dionysarion nor another on her behalf will take legal proceedings against Hermione either with a view to the things left by the deceased Hermias nor concerning the dowry or their marriage or concerning anything else in general, written or unwritten, from the time before up to the present day. And since also Dionysarion is pregnant, (she acknowledges) that she will not take legal proceedings concerning the childbirth on account of being compliant concerning these things and that it is possible for her ... to expose her own baby and to be joined in wedlock with another man, and apart from the things agreed being valid (she acknowledges) that if she transgresses (the agreement) she is liable both for damages and for the penalty which has been determined. We ask (that this document be registered)....

Year 22 of Caesar, Pachon.[135]

The papyri also provide interesting evidence that the elaborate procedure *de inspiciendo ventre*, as set out in the Praetor's Edict [Part III.A above], was indeed followed in second-century Egypt. A widow named Petronilla, who was a Roman citizen and therefore was expected to follow Roman law, petitioned the *iuridicus* of Egypt for a guardian for her young son Lucius Herennius, child of her deceased husband Herennius Valens [P.Gen. II.103, dated 147]. Prior to her child's birth, she had gone to a woman recommended by the *iuridicus*, presumably a "very respectable" woman like those called for in the Praetor's Edict, and the woman had had Petronilla inspected by a midwife, who had confirmed the pregnancy. But Petronilla had not been able to give birth at the woman's house, though she had promised that she would keep Petronilla under observation until the birth had taken place. In her petition to the *iuridicus*, Petronilla stresses that her inability to follow procedure to the letter was not her fault, and that she deserves the benefit of the law.[136] According to the jurist Ulpian, failure to follow the Praetor's procedure in all respects because of the "rusticity" of the people involved should not prejudice the rights of the unborn child, and "the custom of the region should be taken into consideration" [D.25.4.1.15; at Part III.A above], so Petronilla could have expected some leniency.

Another fragmentary papyrus relating to the same case appears to be a petition to the prefect (governor) of Egypt from Petronilla, appealing for help [P.Gen. II.104]. Evidently Petronilla's in-laws were not satisfied with the inspection procedures (which they had probably demanded) during Petronilla's pregnancy and childbirth, and were now charging that her son Lucius Herennius was illegitimate, as a suppositious child. If they could prove this to be the case, Petronilla's child would not only lose his inheritance rights and his right to Petronilla's husband's name, but Petronilla herself might be liable for *calumnia* for having falsely claimed to have her dead husband's child [see Part III.B]. Interestingly, it appears that those challenging Petronilla's claim were her husband's relatives on his mother's side, who as cognates would have had less chance of succeeding to him than would his relations on his father's side, who would have been first in line if he had died without legitimate offspring. Perhaps there were no agnates surviving.[137]

We do not know how Petronilla's case turned out. Another case from Egypt, twenty-seven years earlier than that of Petronilla, also involved a widowed spouse accused of substituting a baby, allegedly to replace a deceased legitimate child [P.Fam.Tebt. 20, dated 120–121]. In that case, however, the accused spouse was the husband, Herakleides, who claimed that the child he had raised had been born to his wife Apia before her death. On the other hand, his mother-in-law and her relatives said that Apia's baby had died and Herakleides had reared another in its place (perhaps having picked up an infant who had been exposed at birth; cf. BGU IV.1104 above). Apparently Herakleides was claiming his deceased wife's property on behalf of the child he claimed was hers, and her relatives contested his right to it. Then the child being reared by Herakleides (whether or not born from his wife) also died. At that point the two sides came to an agreement, in which Apia's relatives agreed to drop all charges against Herakleides, and he in turn agreed not to make any claim on them for Apia's property.[138]

SUMMATION

The condition of women:
rights and restrictions

The third-century legal writer Papinian declared, "In many parts of our law the condition of women is below that of men." [D.1.5.9] A catalog of the rights women had in Roman law, and the restrictions to which they were subject, bears out his statement:

1. In order to undertake many types of legal or business activities, a woman required the formal authorization of her *tutor*. [Chapter 1, Part III]
2. A woman could own property, but she could not alienate certain types of property without her *tutor*'s authorization. [Chapter 1, Part III]
3. A woman could contract a debt for herself, but she could not act as financial surety for the debt of another person. [Chapter 1, Part IV.D]
4. A woman could seek redress from local and imperial officials, in person or by sending a petition. She could go to court on her own behalf to pursue offenses against herself or members of her family. She could also appear as a witness in court in a case brought by someone else. But she could not represent others in court as an advocate, nor could she go to court on behalf of someone who was not a member of her family (even then, it was assumed that she would only pursue an offense against a family member if there were no male in the family available to do so). [Chapter 1, Part V]
5. A woman could loan money at interest to individuals, but she could not be a professional banker. [Chapter 1, Part VI.B]
6. A woman could express her support for political candidates, but she could not vote for them herself, nor could she hold public office at any level (except for some priesthoods). A wealthy woman was expected to use her wealth for civic obligations and expenditures, but was not expected to perform civic duties if they involved actual physical activity. [Chapter 1, Parts VI.B and C]
7. A woman needed the consent of her *paterfamilias* in order to make a valid marriage. Her consent to a marriage arranged by her father was likewise

required, but unless she had valid reasons to object to a match, her consent was assumed. [Chapter 2]

8   In classical law, a woman could divorce her husband unilaterally (with her *paterfamilias'* consent), but might forfeit part of her dowry. [Chapter 4]

9   Upon her husband's death, a woman was responsible for appointing a guardian (*tutor*) for her underage children (unless he had done so in his will), but until late antiquity, she could not herself serve as *tutor* to her children. [Chapter 5, Part II]

10 A woman could inherit in her own right, and female children had equal inheritance rights with male children under intestate succession. A woman could make a will, but only with her *tutor's* authorization, and until Hadrian's reign, in order to make a valid will she had to go through the process of a mock sale of herself (*coemptio*). Until the second century, her own children did not have intestate succession rights to her. [Chapter 5, Part I]

Essentially, Roman law drew a distinction between actions a woman might undertake on her own behalf (which were allowed, though often subject to a *tutor's* authorization), and actions she might undertake on behalf of another (which were generally not allowed). There was an aversion to women appearing in a prominent and professional role in public – holding office, speaking in court as an advocate, being a banker, etc. Certain public roles and responsibilities were considered "men's business" and inappropriate for women. This attitude toward different gender roles was deeply ingrained in ancient culture, even when it was known that individual women (and men) did not always abide by their societally assigned roles.

NOTES

INTRODUCTION: HISTORICAL AND LEGAL BACKGROUND

1 See Honoré 1994 and Watson 1974a on the essentially classical nature of the law of late third-century imperial rescripts. Different scholars take somewhat different chronological boundaries, depending on their perspectives: Gardner 1986a covers the period through the reign of Diocletian (284–305), whereas Crook 1967 ends with the emperor Caracalla's grant of universal citizenship in 212. Most scholars writing on "classical" law stop somewhere in between, at 235 (the end of the Severan dynasty).

2 The *Digest* was edited by Th. Mommsen with P. Krueger in *Corpus Iuris Civilis I. Institutiones et Digesta* (Berlin: Weidmann, 1868). A four-volume translation, *The Digest of Justinian*, with English facing the Latin text of Mommsen, was edited by Alan Watson, with contributions from many Roman legal scholars (Philadelphia: University of Pennsylvania Press, 1985). There is now a revised English translation (without the facing Latin text) in two volumes (Philadelphia: University of Pennsylvania Press, 1998). For the sources of Roman law, especially of the classical period, see Crook 1967; Johnston 1999; Kunkel 1973; Nicholas 1962, 14–45, and Robinson 1997.

3 For reasons of space, I omit the titles of the works of the jurists being cited, and include only the name of the jurist. Watson's translation (see n.2) includes the titles of the original work from which the *Digest* excerpt was taken.

4 There have been several English translations of Gaius' *Institutes*; the most accessible is probably the one by Professors W.M. Gordon and O. Robinson, which provides facing Latin text: *The Institutes of Gaius* (Ithaca: Cornell University Press, 1988).

5 No complete English translation has been made of any of these works, whose Latin texts are found in the second volume of *Fontes Iuris Romani Antejustiniani* (*FIRA*), edited by Professor Johannes Baviera and published in Florence in 1968 (2nd edn.). See Robinson 1997, 62–6 on pre-Justinianic compilations. It should be noted that though citations from the *Sententiae Pauli* and *Rules of Ulpian* appear in this book as "classical," in some respects they appear to reflect Constantinian law.

6 Found in *Corpus Iuris Civilis ii. Codex Iustinianus*, edited by P. Krueger (Zurich: Weidmann, 14th edn., 1967). There is no reliable English translation of the entire *Code*.

NOTES

7 On pre-Constantinian rescripts, see Corcoran 1996; Honoré 1994; Williams 1974. Much material on rescripts is found also in Millar 1977.

8 On *leges generales*, see Harries 1999, esp. 20–1. On the government of the Roman Empire at this period, see Jones 1964.

9 See Honoré 1998 on the legislative split between the east and west.

10 Edited by Th. Mommsen and P. Meyer as *Theodosiani Libri XVI cum Constitutionibus Sirmondianis et Leges Novellae ad Theodosianum Pertinentes* (Berlin: Weidmann, 1904). A reliable translation of the *Theodosian Code* and the post-Theodosian novellae, including an excellent glossary and index, is Clyde Pharr, *The Theodosian Code* (Princeton: Princeton University Press, 1952).

11 On the language and purpose of the *Theodosian Code*, see Harries 1999; Honoré 1998; and the essays in *The Theodosian Code*, edited by J. Harries and I. Wood (London and Ithaca: Duckworth and Cornell University Press, 1993).

12 See Jones 1964 for a survey of these developments.

13 For examples of pre-Christian moral fervor, see Diocletian's edict on close-kin marriages (Chapter 3, Part I.A.5); and Cod. Just. 5.4.3 (ibid., I.B.3) and 5.4.4 (ibid., I.B.5). All involve unions considered socially and morally abhorrent by emperors.

14 On the historical importance of the *Code*, see Honoré 1998; for Constantine's legislation on marriage, much of which was repealed or modified by later emperors, see Evans Grubbs 1995.

15 G. Alföldy, *The Social History of Rome*, trans. D. Braund and F. Pollock (Baltimore: Johns Hopkins University Press, rev. edn., 1988), esp. 146. See also Garnsey and Saller 1987, esp. 107–25, and Jones 1964 for the later period.

16 The fundamental work on Roman citizenship is. A.N. Sherwin-White, *The Roman Citizenship* (Oxford: Clarendon Press, 2nd edn., 1973). Note, however, that citizenship continued to be important in private law, especially in regard to marriage and manumission: see Gardner 1993, 186–91.

17 The most complete exposition of this in English is still Garnsey 1970.

18 See Chapter 1, Part VI.A; Talbert 1984; Hopkins 1983.

19 Talbert 1984, 39–98; cf. Duncan-Jones 1982, 17–32 on the finances of one senator, Pliny the Younger.

20 See Chapter 2, Part I.B and Chapter 3, Part I.B on the Augustan legislation. Public performance: see B. Levick, "The *Senatus Consultum* from Larinum," *JRS* 73 (1983), 97–115.

21 See Jones 1964, 523–62; Matthews 1975. Evans Grubbs 1995, 21–3 gives brief exposition of Constantine's reforms, with further references there.

22 See Chapter 3, Part II.B; Evans Grubbs 1995, 261–316; McGinn 1999.

23 Cf. Hopkins 1983, 120–75; Talbert 1984, 76–80. The equestrian order as such disappears in the late Empire; see n.21 for references.

24 Comum, the hometown of Pliny the Younger, required decurions to have a net worth of 100,000 sesterces (Pliny, *Epistles* I.19).

25 On beneficence by municipal aristocracies, see Chapter 1, Part VI.C.

26 See P. Garnsey, "Aspects of the Decline of the Urban Aristocracy in the Empire," in *Cities, Peasants and Food in Classical Antiquity*, ed. W. Scheidel (Cambridge: Cambridge University Press, 1998), 3–27 (orig. pub. 1974).

27 Chapter 1, Part VI. See Boatwright 1991; van Bremen 1983 and 1996; Forbis 1990; Kajava 1990; MacMullen 1980 and 1986; Marshall, "Roman Women in

the Provinces," *Ancient Society* 6 (1975), 109–27; Nicols 1989; Raepset-Charlier 1981 and 1993; Rogers 1992.

28 See Garnsey and Saller 1987 and Duncan-Jones 1982 on land-holding and the Roman economy.

29 For exceptions, see Chapter 3, Parts I.B.2 and II.B.4 on the *senatusconsultum Claudianum*, Part I.C.1 on the Minician law.

30 See Bradley 1994, 31–56; W. Scheidel, "Quantifying the Sources of Slaves in the Early Roman Empire," *JRS* 87 (1997), 156–69; W.V. Harris, "Demography, Geography, and the Sources of Roman Slaves," *JRS* 89 (1999), 62–75.

31 See Harris 1994.

32 See R. MacMullen, "Late Roman Slavery," *Historia* 36 (1987), 359–82; C.R. Whittaker, "Circe's Pigs: From Slavery to Serfdom in the Later Roman World," in *Classical Slavery*, ed. M.I. Finley (London, 1987), 88–122.

33 Bradley 1984, 47–80; Flory 1978; Rawson 1966; cf. Chapter 3, Part I.B.1. For female slaves, see Treggiari 1979.

34 On manumission, see Bradley 1984, 81–112; 1994, 154–65.

35 Gaius, *Institutes* I.42–6; Gardner 1993, 40–1. Those with between 101 and 500 slaves could free one-fifth; those with over 500 (very rare) could free no more than 100. Those with only one or two slaves were not subject to restriction.

36 Gaius, *Institutes* I.13–32a, 37–41, 47, 65, 68–9; Gardner 1993, 39–44.

37 See Chapter 3, Parts I.B and II.B; Evans Grubbs 1993.

38 On Junian Latins, see Weaver 1990 and 1997.

39 On penalties, see Garnsey 1970, 103–52; Millar 1984.

40 On torture of slaves in legal proceedings, see Bradley 1994, 165–73.

41 See Chapter 1 and Summation.

1 THE STATUS OF WOMEN IN ROMAN LAW

1 The sixteenth title (section) of Book 50 of the *Digest* is entitled *De Verborum Significatione* ("on the Meaning of Words"). In it, the Justinianic compilers culled definitions of terms from various passages in classical writers, taking them out of their larger context (see Introduction, n.3). Many of the definitions translated here from D.50.16 are from Ulpian's commentary on the Praetor's Edict (on which see n.75 below), where they would have explained the usage of the words in question as they related to the praetor's rulings.

2 A patron was the former owner of a manumitted slave. Patrons still retained certain rights over their former property; see Gardner 1993, 20–51.

3 For the beginning of this passage, see D.50.16.195 pr. above. I translate only parts of this extensive passage; here and elsewhere in translations of legal sources … indicates where I have deleted sentences or clauses.

4 The Twelve Tables is the earliest written compilation of Roman law, dating to 451/450 B.C.E.; see Crawford 1996, vol. II. Agnates are relatives in the male line: father and paternal grandfather, siblings and the children of brothers.

5 Here *materfamilias* is used as the female equivalent of *paterfamilias* (though with the unmentioned difference, obvious to Romans, that a *materfamilias* never had *potestas* over others). See Saller 1999, 194, and cf. Part I.B above for other meanings of *materfamilias*.

6 Despite the famous statement of Cato the Elder (quoted by Aulus Gellius, *Noctes Atticae* 10.23.2–5) that a husband who caught his wife in adultery could kill her with impunity, there is no evidence that such a right was approved in Roman law. However, husbands who killed wives in flagrante received lenient treatment. See Treggiari 1991a, 268–75.

7 There is evidence for *manus*-marriage in the long inscription known as the *Laudatio Turiae* (see n.128 below), dating from the reign of Augustus. "Turia's" father is said to have married his (second?) wife by *coemptio*, by which she would come under his *manus*, and "Turia's" sister also married with *manus*. "Turia" herself may have come under her husband's *manus*: he says that she handed over her property to him to administer, and if she had come under his legal control, her property would have also (see Chapter 2, n.13). The Flavian Municipal Law (*c.*80 C.E.) also refers to *manus*; see Part III.A.1.

8 For another archaic use of *coemptio* ("mock sale") still evidently employed in the second century, see Gaius' account of how a woman could change her *tutor mulierum* (Part III.A; *Institutes* I.115). For *mancipatio*, see Glossary.

9 The *senatusconsultum Gaetulicianum*, known only from a papyrus fragment (P.Berol.11753), closed a loophole in the Augustan marriage laws used by childless couples, whereby the wife entered the husband's *manus* and so inherited from him as a daughter when he died (rather than receiving only one-tenth, as under the Augustan law; see Chapter 2, Part I.B). The date of this decree of the Senate is not known; scholars often put it in the early third century, but David Noy argues for the first century, when other loopholes to the Augustan laws were being closed; see his "The *Senatusconsultum Gaetulicianum*: *Manus* and Inheritance," *Tijdschrift voor Rechtsgeshiedenis* 56 (1988), 299–304.

10 The extent of emancipation in the third century is debated: Watson 1974a notes the number of rescripts on the subject, but cf. Gardner 1993, 71–2. On emancipation, see Gardner 1998, 6–113 and for late antiquity, Arjava 1998.

11 Whether the tutor forbidden to marry his ward was a *tutor impuberum* or *tutor mulierum*, or both, is debatable. Most scholars assume it was a *tutor mulierum*, or conflate the two. Given the second-century date of the ban on *tutor–pupilla* marriage [Chapter 3, Part I.C], when *tutela mulierum* was in decline, the ban was probably aimed at *tutores impuberum*, not *mulierum*.

12 See further Part III.C. A wax tablet from the Italian town of Herculaneum also apparently refers to the granting of tutors by the Julian and Titian law; see Part III.B. The Atilian law, which applied to women in Rome, was enacted at the end of the third century B.C.E.; see Modrzejewksi 1974, 273.

13 Statutory (*legitima*) courts are defined by Gaius (*Institutes* IV.104) as courts "in the city of Rome or within the first milestone of the city of Rome, between (those who are) all Roman citizens under one judge." See Marshall 1989, 37.

14 In the rescript, Domitian says that whereas indulgence for marriages not according to Roman law has been given before, this will no longer be the case. See J.-L. Mourgues, "The So-called Letter of Domitian at the end of the *Lex Irnitana*," *JRS* 77 (1987), 78–87.

15 By the *lex Aelia Sentia* of 4 C.E., manumissions of slaves by owners younger than twenty years of age were not fully valid unless approved by an advisory board (*consilium*) of five senators and five equestrians (see Introduction, Part II). Under

the *lex Irnitana*, the *consilium* is made up of a quorum of town councilors rather than senators or equestrians, who were no doubt in very short supply in Irni.

16 "... *quo ne a iusto tutore abeat*" meaning that appointments of tutors by the duovir would only be valid if there were no existing *tutor legitimus* (that is, the closest male agnate relative; see Introduction to this section). Claudius abolished the *tutor legitimus* for women (before the date of this law), but *pupilli* continued to be subject to a *tutor legitimus* unless another tutor had been appointed by their *paterfamilias* in his will. Presumably this provision of the *lex Irnitana* refers only to *pupilli* and to freedwomen and emancipated daughters, who did still have a *tutor legitimus*. Cf. n.37 and n.40 below.

17 Calatoria Themis was giving bail for her appearance in the case involving the woman "who calls herself Petronia Justa," who Calatoria Themis was claiming was her freedwoman (whereas Justa claimed she had been born after her mother had been freed by Calatoria and her husband). See Weaver 1991; 1997, 68–72; Crook 1967, 48–50.

18 The text for this and the following two inscriptions is from *Corpus Inscriptionum Latinarum* (hereafter CIL), ed. Th. Mommsen, vol. 6.

19 Filiation in Latin inscriptions is the identification of the person named as the son or daughter of someone, as here Furfania Saturnina is the "daughter of Lucius" (Lucii f. – *Lucii filia*). Slaves did not legally have a father; therefore former slaves could not have filiation. They could have Roman citizenship and use the three names (*tria nomina*) of Roman male citizens, as M(arcus) Valerius Hesychus, the freedman of Furfania's husband, M(arcus) Valerius Ismarus, does. Hesychus took his patron's *praenomen* (Marcus) and *nomen* (Valerius).

20 A(ulus) Manneius Celsus must be Furfania Saturnina's son by another husband, not M. Valerius Ismarus, since he has a different *nomen*, Manneius. The same seems to be the case for the son of Ostoria Acte in CIL VI.7468 below.

21 A *verna*, or "home-born slave," was particularly cherished since he or she was assumed to be more loyal than slaves acquired from outside the household.

22 This inscription is also found in H. Dessau, ed., *Inscriptiones Latinae Selectae* (hereafter ILS) 7313, and in *FIRA* III, no. 93.

23 The text used is Hunink 1997. The speech was presumably re-worked later for wider publication; see Harrison 2000, 42.

24 *Res mancipi* usually included urban or rural land in Italy but not elsewhere (Gardner 1986a, 18). Some *coloniae* in the provinces had the *ius Italicum* ("Italic right") and so could be considered Italian land; in Africa Proconsularis, these included (by the third century) Carthage, Utica, and Leptis Magna [D.50.15.8.11 (Paulus)]; see Arjava 1996, 113 n.4. Pudentilla's purchase was probably in Africa rather than Italy, so would have been in one of those cities.

25 Claudius Maximus, the governor of Africa Proconsularis, before whom Apuleius was being tried. See Bradley 1997, 215–17.

26 This would then be an example of Roman law being followed (presumably after 212), rather than a native custom. It may be that before the adoption of Roman law, women in this area did not have guardians. For the Euphrates documents, see Feissel and Gascou 1989 and at Part V.C below. P.Euphr.15 was published by Feissel and Gascou in *Journal des Savants* 2000, 157–208 at 189–92.

27 Originally published in *The Oxyrhynchus Papyri* I, ed. B.P. Grenfell and A.S. Hunt (1898). For later readings and corrections to the text, see BL I, 312, BL III,129, and BL VIII, 231. I am using the text in Pestman 1994, 216–18.

28 There is some uncertainty over the year. The original editors read it as Year 20 of Septimius Severus and his sons (expressed by the Greek letter *kappa*), which would be 211. But a more recent reading suggested the possibility of Year 12 (the Greek letters *iota beta*) instead, which would be 203. See P.Oxy. XLVII.3346, at n.1; BL VIII, 231; and Pestman 1994, 282.

29 Tabesammon's mother was a citizen (*aste*) of one of the four Greek cities (*poleis*) of Egypt at this time: Alexandria, Naukratis, Ptolemais, or Antinoopolis (founded by Hadrian in 130). See Delia 1991, 13–21.

30 Another request for a *kyrios* (P.Ryl. II.120, dated 167), states that the petitioner has paid nine and a half obols, presumably the "established tax."

31 The double brackets [[ ]] indicate that the name of Geta, Septimius Severus' younger son, was deleted later, as it was from all official documents after Geta's murder by his brother Caracalla in 212. See Pestman 1994, 37, for illustration. Phaophi is the Egyptian month corresponding to 28 September–27 October.

32 Thus the format is similar to that found on the fragmentary wax tablets from Herculaneum (on which see Part III.B and n.12 above). See Arangio-Ruiz 1956; Modrzejewski 1974, 287–91.

33 On literacy in the Roman world, see W.V. Harris, *Ancient Literacy*, (Cambridge, MA: Harvard University Press, 1989); literates were only a small percentage of the entire population, and women were far less likely to be literate than men. On illiteracy in Roman Egypt, see Hanson 1991; on women and literacy in Egypt, see Sheridan 1998.

34 Originally published in *The Oxyrhynchus Papyri* XII, ed. Grenfell and Hunt (1916); re-edited by Modrzejewski 1974, 269–70 (cf. BL VII and BL X). I am using the text in *Chartae Latinae Antiquiores*, XLVI, ed. A. Bruckner and R. Marichal (Zurich: URS Graf Verlag, 1995), no. 1361 (pp. 4–5), which reproduces the text of Modrzejewski and also includes a photograph. Brackets indicate words missing from the text but restored by the editors on the basis of other examples.

35 The reference to the Senate's decree here, missing from the extant text (which is lacunose on the right side), was suggested by Modrzejewski 1974. Just what this decree of the Senate was has been a matter of debate; it appears that at some point the Senate had enacted a law regulating the appointment of women's guardians in the provinces. See Modrzejewski 1974.

36 The petition was pasted as the 94th sheet in the first roll of petitions kept in the prefect's office. The Egyptian month Pachon runs from 26 April–25 May.

37 This appears to mean that the prefect's approval is contingent on Aurelia Arsinoe not already having a *tutor legitimus*, who could not be replaced; this would be the case only if she were a freedwoman or a daughter freed from paternal power (Part III.A), but it was apparently a standard phrase on all such responses. See n.16 above.

38 Description and a diagram are found in the tablet's original publication by B.P. Grenfell, "A Latin–Greek Diptych of A.D. 198," *Bodleian Quarterly Record* 11

(1919), 258–62, republished as SB III.6223. I am using the text of Arangio-Ruiz found in *FIRA* III.25, 68–9). This and another Latin wax tablet dated between 126–132 recording the grant of a guardian are also in CPL, ed. R. Cavenaile (Wiesbaden, 1958), as nos. 202 and 200 respectively; cf. Modrzejewski 1974, 264–72, who also gives the texts of two fragmentary wax tablets from Herculaneum recording assignment of a tutor.

39 C. Terentius Sarapammon's role here has been debated. Arangio-Ruiz suggested that he was Mevia's current tutor, who was requesting that another take his place. But see A. Bruckner and R. Marichal in *Chartae Latinae Antiquiores* IV (Olten and Lausanne: URS Graf Verlag, 1967), 47–8 on Ch.Lat.Ant. 247, dated 223, in which the same man appears: he is evidently a *nomikos*, a lawyer, who brings legal requests (*postulare*) on behalf of others.

40 For this phrase, see n.16 above on *lex Irnitana*, chapter 29 (Part III.A), and cf. n.37 on a similar phrase (in Greek) at the end of P.Oxy. XII.1466.

41 The meaning of these initials, found in other Latin documentary papyri, is uncertain; perhaps "about this matter from the same copy two tablets have been sealed" (*de ea re eodem exemplo binae tabulae signatae sunt*; Arangio-Ruiz's conjecture; see his n.2 to *FIRA* III.25) or "transcribed and authenticated from two copies of the tablet written above" (*descriptum et recognitum ex exemplis binis tabulae supra scriptae*; Mitteis' conjecture; see Modrzejewski 1974, 268).

42 Thot is the Egyptian month corresponding to 27 August–27 September.

43 According to *Sent. Pauli* IV.ix.9, a woman has the *ius liberorum* if she has had three children at any time, but this is in regard to her inheritance rights from deceased children under the *s.c. Tertullianum*. The rules varied depending on what privilege was sought; see Parkin 1992, 116–19. Arjava 1996, 77–80 and 114–15 believes that all children ever born counted and thus that few adult women apart from freedwomen were subject to *tutela*.

44 Under the *lex Aelia Sentia* of 4 C.E., manumission of a slave under thirty was not completely valid; those freed would be Junian Latins, as would those freed by owners under twenty (see n.15 above; and Introduction, Part II). There were exceptions: e.g., manumission of a slavewoman under thirty for the purpose of marriage to her manumittor was valid (cf. Chapter 3, Part I.B.3).

45 P.Euphr. 15 (see n.26 above). It was evidently a "double document" (cf. on SB III.6223 in Part III.C), leaving a blank space for the inside text, which indicates that the act itself was never completed.

46 Originally published in *The Oxyrhynchus Papyri* XII (1916), ed. Grenfell and Hunt. I use the text in Pestman 1994, 243–5, which includes some revisions to the original (see BL VIII, 246). See also G.H.R. Horsley, *New Documents Illustrating Early Christianity*, vol. 2 (Sydney: Macquarie University, 1982), 29–31. The beginning of the petition is lost; words in brackets have been restored.

47 According to Pestman 1994, 245, this means the prefect will not bother to check the veracity of Thaisous' claim, but will keep her petition on file; only if someone challenges her right to the *ius liberorum* will he look into the matter.

48 The month Epeiph runs from 25 June–24 July. The precise day is not clear; the original editors read the 21st, but cf. BL VIII, 246: the letters are not clear.

49 This text is also found at *FIRA* III.95 (pp. 302–3) with Arangio-Ruiz's notes.

50 *Mancipatio* fell out of use before the sixth century, and so is omitted from the Justinianic corpus. The amount of one sestertius seems to be purely symbolic (cf. CIL VI.10231, where the same amount is given); it was well below the actual cost of funerary monuments: Duncan-Jones 1982, 127–31.

51 The Latin word is *fictor*, defined by the *Oxford Latin Dictionary* (p. 696) as "An attendant of a priest, who kneaded the *liba*" (sacrificial cakes).

52 The inscription uses the abbreviation c.v. (*clarissimi viri*) to indicate that the priests are of senatorial status.

53 The syntax is confused; "yielded to vacant possession" is a conflation of two legal expressions (see Mommsen's note ad loc. in CIL VI and Arangio-Ruiz in *FIRA* III, p. 302). As the property being donated has a tomb on it, the recipient is permitted not only ordinary access (the "rustic praedial servitudes," see Part III.B on CIL VI.7468), but also to use the land for burial and rites of the dead.

54 For "feeding" of the dead (pouring liquids through a hole in the grave), see Toynbee 1971, 51–2; Hopkins 1983, 233–4. The word used, *vescor*, could also refer to the commemorative feasting of family members at the grave.

55 *Locus datus decreto decurionum*, "place given by a decree of the decurions" (Keppie 1991, 138). This indicates that the town council had paid for the placing of the inscription (perhaps on a monument, as was often the case).

56 Persicus was presumably born before his father's manumission and therefore took his mother's *nomen*, as he was freeborn but illegitimate: cf. Cod. Just. 5.18.3 in Chapter 3, Part I.B on a similar situation.

57 Persicus must have been manumitted by someone below the age of twenty, and under the *lex Aelia Sentia* such a manumission had to be approved by a *consilium*; see n.15 above. The *consilium* that approved Persicus' manumission was presided over by Domitian in 73, eight years before he became emperor. It is not clear who his manumittor was, perhaps the same Cornelius who manumitted his wife. Though he was free when he set up the inscription, Persicus gives only his slave name, not his citizen *nomen*.

58 The Latin is *custodiolam Peladiana* (sic). The *Oxford Latin Dictionary* says *custodiola* ("little guard-house") can in everyday speech mean "tomb," but this inscription is the only source cited, which begs the question. "Peladiana" seems to refer to a location in Rome (a misspelling of "Palatana"?) where the tomb was located.

59 Many epitaphs prescribe a penalty for those who disturb the tomb: see Toynbee 1971, 75–7. It is not clear what *preteriti mei* means here; *preteriti* can refer to those passed over in a will (i.e., those who would normally be heirs), but that would not fit syntactically with the sentence, unless it is intended to be genitive plural (*preteritorum meorum*), "if anyone of those I passed over in my will has broken the law ..."

60 Claudia Antonia Tatiane and the man she calls her brother, Aemilius Aristeides, both have good Roman *nomina*, but not the same *nomen*. If they are brother and sister, it must be by different fathers (cf. n.20 above). Van Bremen 1996, 227, suggests that here "brother" "may be simply a form of respect."

61 Greek text in *Supplementum Epigraphicum Graecum* IV (1929–30). See also van Bremen 1996, 227. Words within square brackets are lost from the inscription and have been restored; ... indicates missing words.

62 Text used is *Inscriptiones Latinae Christianae Veteres* (*ILCV*), ed. E. Diehl (Berlin, 1925–31).

63 A person's *forum* was his or her legal residence (*domicilium*; see Part VI.A below). The emperors here state the general rule that lawsuits were tried in the *forum* of the defendant, not of the plaintiff; see Crook 1967, 75.

64 A *procurator* was usually an aid in business or administrative affairs rather than a legal representative (Marshall 1989, 37), but here the *procurator* seems to be an advocate in court, on which see Crook 1995. Cf. D.50.17.2 in Part VI.B.

65 On praedial urban servitudes, see Introduction to CIL VI.10231 in Part III.B.

66 But note that in a woman's will dated 264 from Hermopolis (P.Princ. II.38), the testator has both a *kyrios* (her husband) and a curator; see Arjava 1996, 120 n.23 and 144 n.83; and Rowlandson 1998, 197–8 for a translation.

67 As suggested by older scholarship; cf. L. Mitteis, *Reichsrecht und Volksrecht in den östlichen Provinzen des römischen Kaiserreichs* (1891), 217–21 and 549; R. Taubenschlag, *Vormundschaftsrechtliche Studien: Beiträge zur geschichte des römischen und griechischen Vormundschaftsrechts* (Berlin, 1913), 69–86.

68 Late laws on *ius liberorum*: Cod. Theod. 8.16.1 (320) and 8.17.1–4 (396–412) (in Chapter 2, Part II.A); Cod. Theod. 5.1.1, 2, 7 and 8 (319–426) (see Chapter 5, Introduction and Part I.B); Cod. Theod. 13.5.7 (334); Novel 21.1 of Valentinian III (446); Cod. Just. 8.58.2 (528). See Beaucamp 1992, 260–2; Arjava 1996, 79–80.

69 *Rusticitas*, that is, a lack of sophistication.

70 In other words, a woman can use ignorance of the law as an excuse unless she has committed a *delict* (an act of wrong-doing that fell under private law). Crook 1986b, 91, n.9 says this passage is post-classical (i.e., not Paulus) but Paulus expresses similar qualifications on the question of giving women additional aid or leniency in legal matters in the other passages cited here; cf. D.22.6.8 (Papinian). See further Beaucamp 1990, 81–7 for cases where women could (and could) not rely on the benefit of ignorance of the law.

71 *Bonorum possessio* is possession by succeeding to a deceased person's property. The Perpetual Edict is the Praetor's Edict, on which see n.75 below.

72 This sentence is also found at Cod. Just. 1.18.11. The rest of Cod. Theod. 3.5.3 (not found in Cod. Just.), omitted here, concerns minor women in the process of divorce whose husbands had not publicly registered their pre-nuptial gifts.

73 Though the *Code* gives the names of both emperors, the place of issue and the addressee indicate that this is a law of the western emperor Honorius. Interestingly, the version in Justinian's *Code* (Cod. Just. 2.21.8) omits the word "women" and mentions only minors, implying a less lenient attitude on the part of the Justinianic compilers (Beaucamp 1990, 88). On the other hand, the western *Interpretatio* of Cod. Theod. 2.16.3 (dating to the later fifth or early sixth century) stresses that the law was made *pro fragilitate sexus*, because women have overlooked many things "through ignorance;" see Gaudemet 1959, 214.

74 This was originally part of a longer law; see Cod. Just. 5.1.5 in Chapter 2, Part II.C.

75 In the Republic and early Empire, the urban praetor, who was responsible for maintaining justice in Rome, published an edict at the beginning of his term in office stating what legal remedies he would make available for particular situations. The praetorship was a one-year appointment, and praetors tended to take over the edict published by their predecessor, making additions or changes as they saw fit. By the early Empire few additions were being made, and Hadrian

(117–138) asked the jurist Julian to put the Praetor's Edict into its final form. It is also called the "Perpetual Edict" (cf. n.71) because it was issued for the praetor's entire term in office rather than one specific occasion. See Johnston 1999, 3–4; Nicholas 1962, 21–3; and especially Watson 1974b, 31–62.

76 The final sentence of Cod. Just. 2.12.21, omitted here, reads: "But if he has received a mandate, though he is a husband, he ought to perform only that which the assigned procuratorship (i.e., the mandate to act as legal agent) has ordered." This is not from Constantine's original law, but was added by Justinian's compilers, who took it from a law of Theodosius I (Cod. Theod. 2.12.4, 393). See Beaucamp 1990, 138, n.37; Arjava 1996, 144. The principle that a woman's husband can act for her without a mandate is found in classical law: D.46.73.3 (Ulpian); Arjava 1996, 244.

77 Valerius Maximus II.1.5a claims that in early Rome, matronly honor was afforded the protection of *verecundia*, so that not even the garment (*stola*) of a respectable woman could be touched when she was being summoned to court; see Gardner 1993, 105. On *materfamilias*, see Part I.B.

78 This law is also found at Cod. Just. 1.48.1 with slight changes. The principle that no one (male or female) should be dragged from his/her home appears also in earlier law: D.2.4.18 (Gaius) and 21 (Paulus); Arjava 1996, 244.

79 This is an excerpt from a much longer law, also at Cod. Just. 2.44.2 (in part). Though the manuscript date is 321 (the second consulship of Crispus and Constantine Caesar), it must be a mistake for 324 (the third consulship of the Caesars): see Mommsen's note ad loc. and Seeck 1919, 61–2.

80 This law is also found at Cod. Just. 9.4.3.

81 See Dixon 1984, 356–7; Marshall 1989, 52–3. Cicero's remark that "our ancestors wished all women to be in the power of tutors on account of the weakness of their judgment" (*Pro Murena* XII.27) is often cited by scholars as a classic example, though Cicero probably did not mean it very seriously.

82 Also at Cod. Just. 10.32.44. See Beaucamp 1990, 29–31, on curial service as a male privilege/burden and cf. the Introduction, Part II and Part VI.C below.

83 Cod. Theod. 9.21.1 (319) though only the penalties according to status are given in the law. Cod. Theod. 9.21.4 (329) extends special indulgence to widows and fatherless minors whose lands are near the operating quarters of counterfeiters.

84 The Falcidian law of 40 B.C.E. said that one-fourth of an estate fell to the heir(s), even if the testator had bequeathed more than that amount in legacies to non-heirs. If a child had been left less than one-fourth by a parent (or than his or her share of the one-fourth, if there was more than one child), he or she could bring a "complaint of undutiful will" (*querela inofficiosi testamenti*) and, if successful, would get the requisite fourth. (See also Chapter 5, n.23 and n.45.) The Falcidian fourth is here referred to as the portion given to an "ungrateful" daughter, that is, a daughter who received only the minimum amount required by law (though in this case the mother could not leave more to her daughter even had she wanted to do so).

85 This is an excerpt from a much longer law, found also at Cod. Just. 9.8.5 (with some changes in wording). Though the *Codes* attribute the law to both emperors, it was actually a law of the eastern emperor Arcadius, as shown by the place of promulgation (Ancyra is the modern Ankara, in Turkey) and the addressee, who was praetorian prefect in the east.

86 See the remarks in Rowlandson 1998, 354, and discussion by A.L. Connolly in *New Documents Illustrating Early Christianity*, vol. 4 (Sydney: Macquarie University, 1987), 131–3.

87 Originally published in *The Oxyrhynchus Papyri* II, ed. B.P. Grenfell and A.S. Hunt (1899), reprinted in Hunt and Edgar, *Select Papyri* no. 60. See also BL VIII, 234; Rowlandson 1998, 178–9.

88 See n.29 above. She must have been a citizen of Alexandria, since her *kyrios* and grandson are both citizens of Alexandrian demes (below, n.90).

89 "Neos Sebastos" ("New Augustus") is the Egyptian month Hathyr (October 28–November 26). The day of the month was for some reason left blank.

90 Corrected from "Leneian" in the original publication; see BL VIII, 234. Demes were the divisions of Greek cities in Egypt (as in Attica in Greece): see Delia 1991, 49–70. All the parties to this agreement held Alexandrian citizenship, which carried prestige and privileges.

91 Indicates the agreement was made before a public notary (*agoranomos*).

92 Text used is *The Oxyrhynchus Papyri* XXXIV, ed. L. Ingrams, P. Kingston, P.J. Parsons, and J.R. Rea (1968), 101–3, with corrections from BL VI, 111 and BL VIII, 261 as noted. See also Rowlandson 1998, 94–5.

93 Other petitions from women against uncle guardians, from the same period as P.Oxy. XXXIV.2713, are: P.Oxy. XVII.2133 (late 3rd c.); P.Mich.XV.723 (4th c.); P.Cair.Isid. 63 (296), 64 (*c*.298), and 77 (320). For another complaint against a guardian (brought by the minor's mother), see Chapter 5, Part II.B.

94 See BL VIII, 111, citing a correction by H.C. Youtie in P.Oxy. XXXVI (1970), 95.

95 She died. For this reading, see P.Oxy. XXXVI, 95, a correction by J.R. Rea.

96 See BL VIII, 111 and P.Oxy. XXXVI, 95 for corrections to the original edition.

97 The Greek word is *oikopedon*, which denotes a building-site, with or without buildings on it. See G. Husson,*OIKIA: Le vocabulaire de la maison privée en Égypte d'après les papyrus grecs* (Paris: Sorbonne, 1983), 210; BL VIII, 261.

98 Originally published in *The Oxyrhynchus Papyri* I, 133–4; cf. also BL I, 314. This is the second of three petitions to the same prefect on the same papyrus, of which the third is entirely lost. Unreadable words are represented by ...

99 See BL I, 314 for this reading.

100 She seeks the prefect's subscription, the notation in his own hand at the bottom of the petition which indicated that he had read it and was directing her to a local official for redress. Cf. the petitions of Aurelia Artemis, about twenty years earlier, who also sought the prefect's subscription so that she could go to the *epistrategos*: see Chapter 5, Part II.B.4.

101 This is the suggestion of Crook 1986b, 89–91. For a different interpretation, see Dixon 1984, 363–9; cf. Gardner 1993, 97–100.

102 Dixon 1984, 363–7, who believes that the desire to protect a woman's dotal property from her husband, rather than "womanly weakness," prompted the Senate's decree. Beaucamp 1990, 68–71 thinks it was intended as a protective measure, but for the jurists, protection was closely linked to women's weakness.

103 See Part VI.C below on women and civic responsibilities.

104 That is, the judges who are hearing a claim for recovery of a debt brought by the creditors of those on whose behalf a woman provided guarantees.

105 That is, and not their generosity to family members.

106 See Gardner 1998, 238 on this rescript. I have translated *prudentes viri* as "legal experts," believing that it refers to *prudentes iuris*, jurisprudents.

107 Other parts of the law are at CTh 4.3.1, 4.8.9, and 11.30.52. Though the heading names all three reigning emperors, it was really an enactment of the senior emperor, Theodosius I, father of Arcadius and Honorius. See Arjava 1996, 239–40 on the *s.c. Velleianum* in late antique and early medieval law.

108 14 March, 200; Apokrimata 1–5 were posted on that day; 6–9 were posted the next day (15 March); 10–13 on the day after (16 March). Phamenoth is the Egyptian month corresponding to 25 February–26 March.

109 P.Col VI.123, first published in Westerman and Schiller 1954 (translation and some commentary by Westerman; legal commentary by Schiller). New examination of the papyrus significantly changed the readings; see H.C. Youtie's corrections in Schiller and H.C. Youtie, "Second Thoughts on the Columbia *Apokrimata* (P.Col. 123)," *Chronique d'Égypte* 60 (1955), 327–45 and BL IV.17–21. I use the revised text in Oliver 1989, 451–8. The papyrus itself was found in the Fayum, not Alexandria.

110 Schiller (in Westerman and Schiller 1954, 38–49) considered them *subscriptiones*, that is, rescripts to individual, non-official recipients similar to those found in the Cod. Just., as does Williams 1974. Lewis 1978, 269–70 defines *apokrimata* as "… pronouncements, oral or written, made by the emperors in the exercise of their judicial function," and equates the Greek term *apokrima* with the Latin *responsum* rather than *subscriptio*. Turpin 1981, 145–60, argues that *apokrimata* are to be equated with *decreta*, oral decisions, given by the emperors in person to the recipients on the days mentioned in the papyrus; this seems to me to be the most likely explanation. Another papyrus, P.Amh. II. 63, also contains one of the *apokrimata* in P.Col.VI.123, indicating that those other than the recipients were interested in the rulings, perhaps professional advocates or officials who wanted precedents for future cases.

111 This too is a matter of dispute. Schiller (in Westerman and Schiller 1954, 47) believed the *apokrimata* were Greek translations of Latin originals; on the other hand, Westerman (ibid., 11–12) saw no reason to think so. Lewis 1978, 262 believed they were originally in Latin; but Oliver 1989, 456 thinks they were more likely to have been in Greek originally.

112 C.B. Welles suggested [Ma]thalge (BL IV, 19); adopted by Oliver 1989.

113 Assuming that the *apokrimata* are *decreta* recording actual court hearings before the emperors (see n.110). If they are rescripts, [Ma]thalge, probably not a resident of Alexandria, would have sent her son there to deliver her petition and bring back the answer.

114 *Postulare*, that is, to request the praetor or another magistrate to appoint a judge to hear one's case (in civil law), or to accept an accusation (in criminal law). See Crook 1995, 159–60; McGinn 1998, 45–8; and Arjava 1996, 235–6.

115 A third group could not *postulare* on behalf of others except for close relatives (including in-laws) and patrons or patronesses and their children [D.3.1.1.7–11]. These included those subject to legal infamy (see n.122) such as actors, pimps,

and those convicted of crimes such as armed robbery, *iniuria* (cf. n.119), fraud or theft, and others; see McGinn 1998, 46–8.

116 *Verecundia stolae.* On *verecundia*, see Part IV.B. The *stola* was the traditional garment of the respectable married woman.

117 *Calumnia* was "vexatious prosecution" or bringing a false charge, punishable under the *lex Remnia* of the late Republic. Dropping a prosecution that one had already begun without having obtained an official annulment (*abolitio*) was also punishable under the *senatusconsultum Turpillianum* of 61 C.E. See Robinson 1995, 99–103, and cf. below at n.120.

118 A *popularis actio* was one "which protects the law of the people" [D.47.23.1 (Paulus)], which could be brought by any (male adult) member of the public; see Crook 1967, 74–5.

119 *Iniuria* ("outrage" or "insult") included not only physical assault, but defamation and harm to one's reputation; see Robinson 1995, 49–51. Cf. D.47.10.18.2 in Part V.B.1 below.

120 Note that if a woman did bring a prosecution when she was not allowed to and subsequently dropped it, she would not be liable under the *s.c. Turpillianum* (on which see n.117 above): D.48.16.1.10 (Marcian).

121 A *iudicium publicum* was a trial by jury, specifically one held before one of the permanent jury-courts (*quaestiones perpetuae*) established in the late Republic or under Augustus for certain offenses including forgery, murder, violence, treason and adultery (under Augustus' adultery law, the *lex Julia*; see Chapter 2, Part I.B). See D.48.1.1 (Macer); Crook 1967, 69–73. By the early third century, the standing-courts had all ceased operating (Garnsey 1967), but even in late antiquity the offenses which had been tried in the jury-courts were still referred to as *iudicia publica*, and the restrictions on who could bring an accusation continued to apply (Beaucamp 1990, 41–5).

122 Those marked with legal *infamia*, who were subject to certain legal disabilities; see Gardner 1993, 110–54 and McGinn 1997, 44–69.

123 The emperor wrote underneath the petition *Subscripsi* ("I have written underneath" or "I have subscribed"). See Honoré 1994, 45 and Introduction, Part I.A. Cf. the prefect's subscription to petitions at n.100 above.

124 However, women could inform on themselves, if they had inherited illegally – and then they could keep half of the illegal legacy.

125 *Cognitoria opera.* A *cognitor* represented someone legally: see Crook 1995, 158; McGinn 1998, 48–51. The word translated "affair" (*res*) can also mean "property."

126 *Vidua*, which can mean a widow or divorcée, or even a woman who has never married (*virgo*); see D.50.16.242.3 (Javolenus) in Part I.B above.

127 The *lex Fabia* on kidnapping, which probably fell under the *iudicia publica*; see Robinson 1995, 32–5. In the mid-third century, since the permanent jury-courts were no longer in operation (see n.121), the accused were subject to trial before a judge (*cognitio extraordinaria*), in this case, the governor.

128 The text used is Wistrand 1976; the inscription is also found at ILS 8393. For "Turia" see further Chapter 2, Parts I.D.2 and I.E.2.

129 An interdict was an injunction granted by the praetor: see Johnston 1999, 118–19.

130 The beginning of D.48.12.3, omitted here, actually calls the emperors "Antoninus and Verus," which would be Marcus Aurelius and Lucius Verus

rather than Septimius Severus and his son Antoninus (Caracalla), but the similarity in names would account for the confusion. This passage was taken from Papirius Justus' first book "on imperial constitutions" (*de constitutiones*), the first collection of imperial rescripts known to us (Kunkel 1973, 129–30).

131 The petitions are edited (with French translation) by Feissel and Gascou 1995, whose text I use. On the documents from the Middle Euphrates, see Feissel and Gascou 1989; Bowersock 1991; and Millar 1993, 452–81.

132 Feissel and Gascou 1995, 111 remark that both Bathsabbatha's name and that of her mother suggest Jewish connections, but her brother's name does not.

133 Feissel and Gascou 1995, 116–17. They compare D.47.2.73 (Modestinus), for another woman composing a petition (*libelli*) to give to the centurion (in the *Digest* case, however, the woman never actually handed in the petition, though it was later read aloud in court, evidently after being stolen).

134 Bathsabbatha identifies herself by her mother's name rather than, as was usual, her father's. This implies that she was illegitimate; the editors suggest (111–112) that her father may have been in the Roman army (which had a considerable presence in the region), since soldiers were not allowed to marry legally until at least the reign of Septimius Severus (see Chapter 3, Part I.C).

135 The Greek word used, *eleutheroumai*, means "be freed" but Bathsabbatha evidently is referring to her recovery of a corpse rather than a living person (Feissel and Gascou 1995, 110).

136 This is the centurion's subscription, which gives Bathsabbatha the authorization she needs to pursue her accusation. The editors note that there is no closing salutation or signature by Bathsabbatha (the petition was written by a professional scribe with a practiced hand). Either it was at the bottom of the papyrus, which is broken off, or the papyrus we have was a duplicate, which was also certified by the centurion (Feissel and Gascou 1995, 107).

137 There were two stages in a criminal trial: the *actio prima*, followed by an adjournment, then the *actio secunda*, and then the verdict: Crook 1995, 132–4. It is puzzling that Maesia was acquitted after only one *actio*; but see Marshall 1990b, 51–2.

138 Possibly women no longer had the right to appear as witnesses in the fourth and fifth centuries, or so Constantine asserted in 326 (in Cod. Theod. 9.24.1; see Chapter 3, Part II.C). But this may be in regard to witnessing contracts rather than appearing in court; see Arjava 1996, 235–7.

139 The emperor Augustus' law on adultery; see Chapter 2, Part I.B. (This passage is from the second book of Paulus' commentaries *de adulteriis*.) Prostitutes were also prohibited from giving testimony in cases concerning the Julian law on violence: D.22.5.3.5 (Callistratus), and very likely in other cases as well: see McGinn 1998, 61–4.

140 That is, she could not be a witness to a will made by someone else. Women did have the right to make wills, but needed their tutor's consent; see Part III.A.

141 The statements in the life of the emperor Heliogabalus (*Historia Augusta, Hel.* 4.1–2 and 15.6), that the emperor had his mother and grandmother invited into the Senate, would (if true) commemorate exceptional incidents: see Chastagnol 1979, 3–5; Talbert 1984, 162.

142 See Arjava 1991 on Greek titles, which were less defined than in the west.

143 Chastagnol 1979 suggests that Caracalla was responsible; Raepsaet-Charlier 1981 argues for Marcus Aurelius.

144 The same law (with the addressee called Martinianus) is found also at Cod. Just. 10.40.9 and at Cod. Theod. 2.1.7, which omits the second sentence.

145 An *as* is a small unit of Roman money; Septicia will be paying 6 per cent a year.

146 Septicia opens her declaration with the verb *philotimoumai*, which literally means "I am desirous of honor." The word is frequently used in inscriptions praising benefactors who have given generously to their cities, presumably for the purpose of being honored by them.

147 *Pace* van Bremen 1996, 234–5, the word *filii* could include female as well as male children: see D.50.16.84 and 116, in Part I.A. Perhaps the reason the Boule wanted to take administration of the contest away from Septicia's children was because they *were* daughters, not sons. On *iniuria*, see n.119 above.

148 The first two inscriptions, in Greek, are from H.W. Pleket's collection of inscriptions illustrating the social history of the Greek cities of the Aegean and Asia Minor (Pleket 1969). The texts are also found in *Inscriptiones Graecae*, XII.5, ed. F. Hiller von Gaetringen (1909).

149 The wife's property would still be kept separate from that of her husband, however: see Chapter II, Part I.E. A wife's property could not be distrained upon to pay for her husband's *munera*: Cod. Just. 4.12.3 (293).

150 See Cod. Just. 10.69.1 (Gordian) for the policy that a man who has five living children is excused from personal *munera*.

151 Though this law and the following (Cod. Theod. 13.5.12) are given in the names of both reigning emperors, the addressees (Olybrius was prefect of the city of Rome; Demetrianus the prefect of the grain supply of Africa, a western province) indicate that they are laws of the western emperor Valentinian.

152 The grammar of the law is very obscure; the word translated "since" is *quando*, but the writer appears to mean *quoniam*, otherwise the law does not make sense. I follow Mommsen and Pharr in accepting the meaning "since."

153 The "gifts" are those given to the people in return for the honor of the praetor-ship. "Full age" means the legal age of twenty-five; "adult" is someone above puberty (fourteen for boys, twelve for girls) but below twenty-five.

154 The "glebal tax" was a tax on senators in proportion to their property. The word with asterisks is unclear; perhaps "Carbonarian" or "*cardinarium*."

155 Here one's *forum* is where one has obligations (*munera*). *Navicularii* who try to get out of their responsibilities are to be stopped even after illegally receiving imperial permission to "transfer their forum."

156 The "noble boy" (abbreviated "n.p." for *nobilis puer*) is the future emperor Valentinian II, the son of Valentinian I.

2 MARRIAGE IN ROMAN LAW AND SOCIETY

1 This passage, from the *Digest*'s section on "definitions" (see Chapter 1, n.1), is also found at D.35.1.15, where the context concerns a legacy to be given to the wife as soon as she has married. These and the following passages have been suspected of being interpolated: see Wolff 1950, 26–7.

2 On *affectio maritalis*, see Treggiari 1991a, 54–57. Even if the phrase is a later interpolation, the idea is classical.

3 The jurist Cinna wrote during the late Republic. Note that in this passage it is the wife who is said to be absent, rather than the husband as in D.23.2.5. Thus the text has often been emended, but Lewis 1986 argues that this is unnecessary. Cf. Watson 1967, 25–7; Donahue 1979, 7–13. On required mourning for a husband, see Chapter 5, Part I.A.

4 See Gardner 1986b; 1993, 179–91 on the use of proofs in legal matters. In the classical period, written documentation is not privileged over the oral evidence of respectable witnesses. The phrase in D.20.1.4 , "if there is (unwritten) evidence to prove it," may be a later interpolation: Gardner 1993, 181–2. Written documents deposited in the public records become more important in the late Empire, however; see Harries 1999, 70–6.

5 The phrase "for the sake of producing children" (*liberorum procreandorum causa*) is also found in Latin marriage contracts from Egypt (see Part III) and evidently was used in Augustus' marriage law (Part I.B): Treggiari 1991a, 8, n.37.

6 Marriage between a woman *over* fifty (and therefore past child-bearing age) and a man under sixty (and therefore still enjoined to procreate under the law) was similarly penalized by a decree of the Senate of unknown (but later) date (the *s.c. Calvisianum*): *Rules of Ulpian* 16.4; Treggiari 1991a, 78.

7 See Chapter 3, Part I.B.4 for prohibition of marriages between senators and freedwomen. It is not clear why there would be more males than females among the "well-born" (which may mean simply "freeborn"), and it is unlikely that Dio had any statistical information to back up his assertion.

8 The Voconian Law of 169 B.C.E. said that women in the top property class could not be heirs. (Dio is incorrect in saying that women could not inherit property worth more than 100,000 sesterces.) Augustus allowed a woman to be heir to her husband (even if she was in the top property class) *if* they had had a certain number of children surviving to a certain age (one child beyond puberty, two beyond age three, three beyond the ninth day of birth), or if they were younger or older than the ages at which the Augustan law required them to be married, or were related within the sixth degree. (A husband could be heir to his wife in the same circumstances.) See *Rules of Ulpian* 16.1; and Treggiari 1991a, 69–71. If they did not meet these qualifications, spouses could inherit only one-tenth of each other's property.

9 From the requirement that widows remarry soon after their husband's death. According to *Rules of Ulpian* 14, the *lex Julia* said widows had to remarry within a year and the *lex Papia–Poppaea* had extended that to two years. Suetonius says the later law allowed three years.

10 Son of Livia's son Drusus, and adopted son of Tiberius. Germanicus and his wife Agrippina had nine children, of whom six survived past infancy.

11 Treggiari 1991a, 174 (cf. 1982, 42) believes such a union would be considered *iniustum matrimonium*: the partners would not have *conubium* (the legal right of marriage with each other) but the relationship would still have some of the consequences of marriages. Corbett 1930, 62 thinks the union was null.

12 Note that there is some disagreement about the meaning of this passage: cf. Treggiari 1991a, 174 n.99; Arjava 1996, 40. The *Sententiae Pauli* were written on the cusp of the late Roman period, and do not always represent classical law.

13 For a case where the mother of a fatherless *pupilla* not only administered her daughter's affairs, but even gave her in marriage, see Chapter 5, Part II.A.3.

14 An even more complicated question was whether the children of a father who had gone mad could marry without his permission. According to a law of Justinian (Cod. Just. 5.4.25), some jurists thought that a madman's *daughter* could marry, but his son could not. See Gardner 1993, 174–6 for an explanation.

15 See also Chapter 1, Part V.B.2 on "Turia." The text is fragmentary; ... indicate where I have omitted sentences.

16 The Latin text used is the Loeb Classical Library edition of *Pliny: Letters and Panegyrics*, vol. 1, ed. Betty Radice (Cambridge, MA: Harvard University Press, 1969).

17 See Chapter 1, Part IV.C for the concept of "womanly weakness" (which lies behind Pliny's statement). On the other hand, in this letter and the next, Pliny refers to the *pudor* ("modest demeanor") and *verecundia* ("sense of shame") of men, terms which are often used to describe feminine modesty (see Chapter 1, Part IV.B). For Pliny they are equally admirable in males.

18 Apparently this means that part (or all?) of what Calvina's father had given her as dowry was actually money he owed to Pliny, so it came, so to speak, from Pliny's account. See A.N. Sherwin-White, *The Letters of Pliny: A Historical and Social Commentary* (Oxford: Clarendon Press, 1966), 149, who considers the letter, with its blunt discussion of Calvina's father's debts and of Pliny's own generosity, "a remarkable document of Roman lack of delicacy."

19 On *munera*, see Chapter 1, Part VI.C.

20 *Senatusconsultum de Cn. Pisone Patre* lines 100–6. For discussion of this passage see David Potter, "Senatus consultum de Cn. Pisone," *Journal of Roman Archaeology* 11 (1998), 437–57, at 447. Potter points out that one million sesterces was probably equivalent to a year's income on Piso's estate, the standard proportion for a dowry in an elite Roman family (Saller 1994, 216–17, and cf. Pudentilla's dowry, Part I.D.2). However, he errs in saying that Roman fathers often left daughters "nothing beyond the money for the dowry" in their wills; see Saller 1994, 210–21.) On a daughter's *peculium*, see Saller 1994, 218–20.

21 If a man served as a magistrate, he would be obliged to pay for games as part of his official duties (*munera*); see n.19 above.

22 Quintus Mucius Scaevola (consul 95 B.C.E., died 82 B.C.E.) was one of the earliest jurists whose work is cited in the *Digest* (Nicholas 1962, 40; Robinson 1997, 43–4). The legal presumption that what a woman owned came from her husband unless otherwise proven is known as the *praesumptio Muciana*.

23 Wistrand 1976, 39–40 and Treggiari 1991a, 377, suggest that "Turia's" husband may have also been her guardian. Horsfall 1983, 92 suggests that they had a *manus*-marriage (as did "Turia's" sister and her husband and her father and his wife). *Manus*-marriage was uncommon by the later first century B.C.E. (see Chapter 1, Part II.B), but is possible in this case. In *manus*-marriage, the wife's property would have become her husband's, and she would have been his heir along with any children he had.

24 This excerpt also appears in Cod. Just. 8.57.1, except for paragraph (2). It was originally part of a longer edict on inheritance and debt, parts of which are found elsewhere in the *Codes*. Serdica is now Sofia, Bulgaria.

25 See Part I.B and Chapter 1, Part III.D on the *ius liberorum*. Cod. Theod. 8.17.1, a law of the eastern emperor Arcadius dated 396, allowed couples to petition for

the *ius liberorum* at any time and age, since "the despair of (having) children alone shall be enough for the wretched to seek aid."

26 Found at Cod. Just. 8.57.2 and 8.58.1 respectively. Another part of the same law, not in the *Theodosian Code*, is found at Cod. Just. 1.19.6. Though in the names of both reigning emperors, this was actually a law of Theodosius II only. Isidorus was prefect of Constantinople.

27 *Vir clarissimus*, a man of senatorial rank. See Chapter 1, Part VI.A.

28 Cod. Theod. 5.1.9, given at Constantinople 21 February, 428. This law repeals an earlier law, otherwise unknown, that had apparently allowed spouses to be each other's heirs without a will, even when there were living kin of the deceased spouse. Cod. Theod. 5.1.9 also refers to the ancient skepticism about the motives of spouses toward each other, as did Constantine's law of 320.

29 Valentinian, Novel 21.1; see Arjava 1996, 126–7. It appears from the law that Leonius' right to inherit in full from his wife was being challenged, probably by her relatives. They may have received the *ius liberorum* before the publication of the *Theodosian Code* in the west seven years earlier. In classical law, joint wills were not valid (Schulz 1951, 206).

30 See Arjava 1996, 133–56 for a discussion of married women's property and the financial relationship between husband and wife in late antiquity.

31 In early Roman law, betrothal had been actionable, but this was no longer the case by the first century B.C.E. See Corbett 1930, 8–16.

32 The "Interpretation" of Cod. 3.5.5 applied the sanctions affecting those who betrothed a woman to a civilian as well as a soldier, but this dates to the late fifth or early sixth century and cannot be taken as evidence of the intent of the original law.

33 Cod. Theod. 3.5.4 is also found at Cod. Just. 5.1.2 (with the addition of "while living in the same province" after "within two years"); 3.5.5 is not in Cod. Just.; see Beaucamp 1990, 254–5. Marcianopolis is in Bulgaria.

34 But note that Cod. Theod. 3.7.1 explicitly involves widows. Humbert 1972, 373–7 thinks Cod. Theod. 3.7.1 was intended to discourage widows from remarrying and thus belongs to a series of fourth and fifth century laws that placed restrictions on widows who remarried, which he thinks are due to Christian influence (see Chapter 5, Part I.B). However, Cod. Just. 5.4.20 (the second law) says nothing about widows, but both laws refer to women under twenty-five who have been emancipated from paternal power.

35 See D. 45.1.134 pr. (Paulus) for the classical view of this situation.

36 That is, if the widow should die.

37 This law is found also at Cod. Just. 5.4.18. Despite the attribution in the *Codes* to all three reigning emperors, it is a law of Valentinian alone.

38 That is, under *patria potestas*. Such circumlocution is typical of late Roman laws.

39 *Verecundia*, on which see Chapter 1, Part IV.B.

40 The date is lost. The law is perhaps part of the same legislation as Cod. Theod. 3.10.1 (on which see Chapter 3, Part II.C). Though in the name of both emperors, it is a law of Honorius only.

41 *Defensor*, i.e. a *tutor* or *curator*.

42 This is part of a longer law (as the phrases "after other matters" and "and other matters" indicate), also including Cod. Theod. 3.13.3 (on dowry; in part II.C below) and Cod. Just. 5.9.4 (on *bona materna*, on which see Chapter 5, Part I.B).

43 Also at Cod. Just. 5.1.4. Though in the names of both reigning emperors, it is a law of Honorius only, as it was enacted at Ravenna, seat of the western emperor at this time.

44 For laws on Christian celibate women, see Clark 1993, 50–6; Arjava 1996, 157–67; Evans Grubbs 2001.

45 Greek text is from *Grégoire de Nysse: Vie de Sainte Macrine*, ed. P. Maraval (Paris: *Sources Chrétiennes* 178, 1971). See Maraval 35–67 for discussion.

46 Latin text is from *Patrologia Latina* 16, col. 203–6. See N.B. McLynn, *Ambrose of Milan* (Berkeley: University of California Press, 1994), esp. 53–6 and 60–8.

47 The Latin word is *parentes*, which can mean "parents" or "relatives" more generally; see D.50.16.51 (Gaius), in Chapter 1, Part I.B. It is clear from the passage, however, that Ambrose is talking about young women whose fathers are dead (and who therefore are not bound by the decision of a *paterfamilias*).

48 The relative who had asked whether her father would have approved.

49 On the western Empire in this period, see J. Harries, *Sidonius Apollinaris and the Fall of Rome* (Oxford: Clarendon Press, 1994), esp. 82–102 on Majorian.

50 An earlier law, Cod. Theod. 16.2.27 (Theodosius, I, 390) had said that women could not become deaconesses until they were at least sixty, invoking 1 Timothy 5:9, which had said that no one under sixty was to be enrolled in the order of widows. The law was rescinded soon afterwards: see Chapter 5, Part I.B and Evans Grubbs 2001. On the other hand, Majorian's age limit applied to all consecrated virgins, not just deaconesses (who were unknown in the western church). Theodosius' law was concerned with safeguarding the property of wealthy Christian women for their families, whereas Majorian was concerned with promoting child-bearing, and so allowed consecration only after women had passed the age at which they could be expected to have children. His age limit is in line with ecclesiastical rulings: in 451, Council of Chalcedon (Canon 15) had said deaconesses could not be ordained until the age of forty; in 380, the Council of Saragossa (Canon 8) had said holy virgins were not to be veiled before forty.

51 The most exhaustive treatment of pre-nuptial gifts and *arrhae sponsaliciae* is L. Anné, *Les Rites des fiançailles et la donation pour cause de mariage dans le Bas-Empire* (Louvain, 1941). For a succinct treatment, see Arjava 1996, 52–62; for Constantine's legislation, see Evans Grubbs 1995, 156–83.

52 This law is found at Cod. Just. 5.3.15, with some changes. Two dates are preserved: that of the law's enactment and of its publication (posting) in Rome.

53 Also at Cod. Just. 5.3.16. Hispalis is the modern Seville. Again, dates of both issue and posting have been preserved.

54 Though in the name of all reigning emperors, this is a law of Theodosius, emperor of the eastern half of the Empire, as indicated by the place of promulgation (now Thessaloniki in northern Greece).

55 Other parts of the same original law are found at Cod. Just. 5.1.3 (= the missing Cod. Theod. 3.5.10); Cod. Theod. 3.6.1; 3.11.1; 4.19.1; 6.10.1; 9.27.2; 9.42.8–9; Cod. Just. 6.23.16. Not all of these have to do with betrothal, but they do involve issues of family wealth (e.g. inheritance). Note that Cod. Theod. 3.5.11 is not found in Cod. Just., since the quadruple penalty was abolished by the eastern emperor Leo in 472 (Cod. Just. 5.1.5, below).

56 Cod. Theod. 3.5.10 (now lost, but also at Cod. Just. 5.1.3).

57 Originally part of the same law as Cod. Theod. 3.5.12 (see n.42 above) and Cod. Just. 5.9.4. A briefer version is found at Cod. Just. 5.18.11.
58 On the classicizing tendencies of the eastern Empire, see Honoré 1998.
59 The eastern origin of this law is clear, since it was issued at Constantinople.
60 This law is found also at Cod. Just. 5.4.22, and is part of the same legislation as Cod. Theod. 4.6.8 (on which see Chapter 3, Part II.B.1, n.66).
61 This refers to Cod. Theod. 3.8.2 (382) and Cod. Just. 5.10.1 (392), laws of Theodosius II's grandfather Theodosius I, which said that if a widow remarried, she had to pass on to the children of her first marriage anything she had received from her first husband. Theodosius I had *recommended* that when a widower remarried, he pass on whatever he had received from his first wife to the children of his first marriage (Cod. Theod. 3.8.2; see Chapter 5, Part I.B). In his law, Theodosius II gives legal force to his grandfather's recommendation, making remarried men subject to the same rules as women.
62 Under classical divorce law, revived by Theodosius II two months before this law (his Novel 12 in Chapter 4, Part II), a husband was able to retain part of his ex-wife's dowry if the divorce had occurred through the fault of the wife. In this law, Theodosius II allows a husband to get back all of his pre-nuptial gift, even if it had been absorbed in his wife's dowry, if the divorce was due to her fault.
63 The earlier legislation referred to is Cod. Theod. 8.19.1 (Honorius, 426); cf. also Cod. Theod. 8.18.1–3 (Constantine; see Chapter 5, Part I.B) which had deprived fathers with *patria potestas* of the right to sell or give away their children's maternal inheritance. Under classical law, everything children under paternal power received or owned, including anything left to them by their mother, legally belonged to their father, and was considered *peculium*. Theodosius II applies the provisions of the earlier laws to pre-nuptial gifts or dowry received by a married person still under paternal power: it is to go to *their* children, not to their *paterfamilias*.
64 *Vir clarissimus*, see n.27 above. An abbreviated version of this law is found at Cod. Just. 5.9.3. Its place of issue, Constantinople, indicates it is a law of Theodosius II, despite its attribution to Valentinian III also.
65 Though in the name of both emperors, this is a law of Theodosius II alone (Hormisdas was praetorian prefect of the east) and reflects the legal approach of his consistory (cf. n.58 above).
66 Presumably meaning Albinus, serving his second stint as praetorian prefect. So I interpret the reference in the law's preface to men "recalled" to the imperial court.
67 See Barnish 1988 on the western senatorial aristocracy at this time, with some interesting speculations on the impact of imperial laws on dowry, *donatio ante nuptias*, and remarriage.
68 Addressed to the praetorian prefect Firminus and enacted at Rome on 15 April, 452. For the provisions on divorce, see Chapter 4, Part II. This law is not in the *Code of Justinian*.
69 Her *pudor*, on which see Chapter 1, Part IV.B. A husband's gifts were regarded as made in return for his wife's sexual chastity. See Evans Grubbs 1995, 177, 181, 195; Cod. Theod. 9.42.1 (Constantine, 321), and for an earlier period, Pliny, *Epistles* I.14.
70 The "dear and devout names" are those of the deceased husband's parents.

71 In other words, the deceased wife's relatives usually get half of her dowry back if there are no children, but the husband ought to keep any part of the dowry which was originally his pre-nuptial gift and was converted into dowry upon marriage (see Novel 14 of Theodosius II, above, for this practice). The emperor wants to ensure that the widowed husband can give an adequate gift to his second wife should he wish to remarry.

72 In other words, the bride's parents demand a huge pre-nuptial gift, and then refund it to the couple in the form of the bride's dowry. Novel 14.3 of Theodosius II (above) had said that this commonly happened in the east; clearly Majorian did not think it should in his territories.

73 Other excerpts from Leo's original law are found at: Cod. Just. 1.18.13 (translated in Chapter 1, Part IV.A); Cod. Just. 5.30.3 (on which see Chapter 1, Part III.E, at Cod. Theod. 3.17.2); Cod. Just. 5.6.8, which says that marriage between a girl and a man who has usurped the function of a guardian but is not really her guardian is legal (cf. Chapter 3, Part I.C.2); and Cod. Just. 1.4.16, which is the same as paragraphs 3, 4, and the beginning of 5 of Cod. Just. 5.1.5.

74 The "indulgence of age" (*venia aetatis*), which could be granted by request to women at age eighteen, enabled a woman under twenty-five to conduct her affairs as an adult. See Cod. 2.17.1 (translated in part in Chapter 1, Part IV.B).

75 Beaucamp 1990, 254–5 compares this law to Cod. Theod. 3.5.5 of Constantine (in Part II.B) and Cod. Theod. 3.5.11 of Theodosius I (above). She notes that whereas in the earlier laws, the guardian's responsibility for making the betrothal (and hence his liability if it is broken) is as great as that of the *paterfamilias*, in Leo's law the guardian plays only a subsidiary role, as one "through whom" the woman may have made the betrothal. Her mother, on the other hand, is considered as responsible as her father (or grandfather or great-grandfather) and penalized accordingly.

76 In other words, if *arrhae* had been given for a prohibited marriage (see Chapter 3, Part II), then presumably the whole transaction is void and no penalty applies. But if the marriage was allowed by law, then breaking the betrothal entails a penalty. The next paragraph gives an exception to this rule.

77 The rest of the law, not translated here, applies the exceptions given in paragraph (3) to men also, abolishes the quadruple penalty known from the legislation of Theodosius I (e.g., Cod. Theod. 3.5.11, above), and says that no stipulations other than those made in the law are valid: "since the power of contracting marriages ought to be free."

78 There is an up-to-date list of all known marriage contracts from Egypt and the Near East by Instone Brewer at www.Instone.Brewer.com, with links to texts available on-line. Note also an unpublished contract dated to the third century, apparently from Bostra in the province of Arabia: see H.M. Cotton, W.E.H. Cockle and F.G.B. Millar, "The Papyrology of the Roman Near East: A Survey," *JRS* 85 (1995), 214–35 at 223.

79 See Rowlandson 1998, 156–60 for examples.

80 See Rowlandson 1996, 317–19 for contents of dowries from Oxyrhynchus.

81 For example, P.Ryl. II.154 (66 C.E.); BGU IV.1045 (154). See Wolff 1939. The practical differences between "unwritten" and "written" marriages are not very clear; one difference seems to be that the father of a daughter born in an unwritten marriage could force her to divorce against her wishes (cf. Chapter 4, Part I.E).

82 The *Gnomon of the Idiologos* is a list of rules for application by Roman officials in Egypt. Many of the rules go back to Augustus, though the *Gnomon* as found in the papyri dates to the second century. Among the rules are many relating to marriage and inheritance, from which it is clear that Roman marriage law, including the ban on incestuous marriages, was applied to Roman citizens. See Rowlandson 1998, 175–7 for partial translation.

83 Much has been written on sibling marriage in Roman Egypt. See Hopkins 1980; Lewis 1983, 43–4 and 69–73; and recently, W. Scheidel, "Incest Revisited: Three Notes on the Demography of Sibling Marriage in Roman Egypt," *BASP* 32 (1995), 143–56, and *Measuring Sex, Age and Death in the Roman Empire: Explorations in Ancient Demography* (Ann Arbor: Journal of Roman Archaeology Supplementary Series 21, 1996), 9–51.

84 See O. Montevecchi, "Endogamia e cittadinanza romana in Egitto," in Montevecchi 1998, 251–8 (orig. pub. 1979); Chapter 3, Parts I.A.5 and II.A.

85 BGU I.183 (M.Chr.313), dated 85 C.E.; see Hopkins 1980, 322–3. It was not uncommon to combine marriage agreements with property settlements on the bride: Rowlandson 1996, 162–4. In this case, the mother divides her property among all her surviving children (and the children of a deceased child).

86 Discussion of marriage contracts in Roman Egypt in Wolff 1939; Modrzejewski 1993 (1981); Katzoff 1995a; and Rupprecht 1998. For lists of marriage contracts from Egypt, see most recently Brewer (above, n.78); earlier lists in Montevecchi 1936, 4–6, updated in Montevecchi 1988, 203–5.

87 Yiftach 1997, 178 defines *synkhoresis* as "an address to a governmental authority, in this case municipal jurisdiction, informing it of the accomplishment of a transaction." The documents from the Protarchos archive are the only known marriage contracts drawn up in the form of a *synkhoresis*. Other documents from the Protarchos archive can be found at Chapter 4, Part III.A (BGU IV.1102) and Chapter 5, Part III.C (BGU IV.1104).

88 The others are BGU IV.1051, 1052 (also in Hunt and Edgar, *Select Papyri* no. 3); 1098–1101; and P.Berol. 25423, in W. Brashear, "An Alexandrian Marriage Contract," in *Classical Studies in Honor of David Sohlberg*, ed. R. Katzoff, with Y. Petroff and D. Schaps (Ramat Gan: Bar-Ilan University Press, 1996), 367–84.

89 Originally published in W. Schubart, ed., *Aegyptische Urkunden aus den Königlichen Museen zu Berlin. Griechische Urkunden* IV (Berlin, 1912, rpt. on microfiche from Scholars Press). See BL I, 92 for revised readings. I use the text as found in Pestman 1994, 100–2. According to Pestman, traces of a date can be read at the end of the document.

90 In Roman Egypt, the drachma was a silver-alloy coin (which became more and more debased in the later Empire), and the standard unit of currency. It was equivalent to a Roman sestertius; four drachmas (a tetradrachm) was equivalent to the Roman denarius.

91 This is the so-called "moral" or "good behavior" clause, stating the expected proper behavior for each spouse, and the penalty a spouse who fails to behave accordingly will undergo. In the Roman period, the stated expectations become less explicit than in the Ptolemaic contracts. See especially Rupprecht 1998.

92 The meaning of this clause is debated. The *hierothytai* were a board of priests, and Wolff 1939, 34–47 suggests that a marriage that was also filed with the *hierothytai* was "more solemn," and desirable for establishing the eligibility of the couple's

offspring for privileges in Alexandrian society (cf. Delia 1991, 55 n.25). Recently, however, another *synkhoresis* from the Protarchos archive has been published (P.Berol. 25423, see n.88 above). In that document the couple add, after the clause about filing a contract with the *hierothytai*, provisions for their property in the event that one of them should die. It appears the contract filed with the *hierothytai* also contained those provisions. The second document then serves the purpose of a will (though it is not a will itself); see Yiftach 1997.

93 See Boak 1926, with his revised interpretation in P.Mich. II, pp. 29–33 (on P.Mich.II.121.recto II.i, another alimentary contract).

94 Text used is *Papyri from Tebtunis Part I* (P.Mich. II), ed. A.E.R Boak (Ann Arbor: University of Michigan Press, 1933), pp. 45–50. The names of the wife's father and mother's father are not certain.

95 This is the explanation of A. Bruckner and R. Marichal in *Chartae Latinae Antiquiores* (Ch.Lat.Ant.) IV (Olten and Lausanne: URS Graf Verlag, 1967), no. 249, pp. 49–53, whose text I am using. On the other hand, H.A. Sanders, in his publication of P.Mich. VII.434 (*Latin Papyri in the University of Michigan Collection*, Ann Arbor, 1947, 21–7; original publication in *TAPA* 69 [1938], 104–16), explained the text as in the form of a papyrus "diploma," analogous to a wax tablet diptych (for which see Chapter 1, Part III.C on SB III.6223), of four pages, with the text written once on the outer (first and fourth) pages and again on the inner (second and third) pages, with the inner sewn shut to protect the text; Sanders' explanation was accepted by C.H. Roberts and E.G. Turner, editors of P.Ryl. IV.612 (*Catalogue of the Greek and Latin Papyri in the John Rylands Library Manchester IV*, 1952). Given the fact that papyrus was used rather than a wax tablet, it seems to me more likely that this was a "double document" of the type found in the Cave of Letters (Part III.B) and elsewhere in the east rather than a four-leaf papyrus on the model of a wax tablet.

96 I am using the text in Ch.Lat.Ant. IV.249 (see note above). The combined text of P.Mich. VII.434 and P.Ryl. IV.612 is also published in *Corpus Papyrorum Latinarum* (= CPL), ed. R. Cavenaile (Wiesbaden, 1958), nos. 208–9, pp. 313–17, with a few different readings. (The text in *FIRA* III.17 is based only on P.Mich. VII.434 and therefore superseded by *Ch.Lat.Ant.* and CPL.) Because both inner and outer texts are fragmentary, I draw on both for my translation; thus brackets indicate restorations only when words are missing from *both* inner and outer texts. Words that cannot be restored are indicated by "…"

97 But see BL IX, 160: he may be [L. Ignatius]s Nomissianus, not. [C.. Antistiu]s.

98 *C. Antistiu}s Nomissianus filiam suam virginem {Zenarion e lege Iuli}a quae de maritandis ordinibus lat{a est liberorum procreando}rum causa in matrimonio eam collo{cavit* (P.Mich. VII.434). The word *eam* (her) is readable only in P.Mich. VII.434; it appears to be the object of *collocavit*, but this is redundant since *filiam suam virginem Zenarion* has already been expressed as object. Sanders in P.Mich. VII.434, suggests reading *eram* (meaning "mistress of a household") but *era* is an unusual word and it is perhaps better to see *eam* as an example of grammatical infelicity on the part of the composer of the text, as do the editors of *Ch.Lat.Ant.* IV.249.

99 The Augustan marriage law of 18 B.C.E., on which see Part I.B. The last

letters of "procreating" (*ndorum*) are visible in P.Ryl. IV.612, so the restoration is almost certain. Cf. Cod. Just. 5.4.9 in Part I.A.

100 Iugera are the Latin equivalent of the Greek arouras, a unit of land equivalent to 0.68 of an acre. Katoikic land was a special category of private land; see Rowlandson 1996, 41–8.

101 The meaning of this word (*cottatia*) is unknown, but apparently it refers to some sort of jewelry. The words "silver bracelets" are barely discernible.

102 The meaning of *heratianon* is unknown. It may be a type of clothing, or possibly a statuette of the goddess Hera, like the statuette of Aphrodite (see below). The word evidently comes from Greek, like many of the words in this ostensibly Latin document; see Sanders' note ad loc. in P.Mich. VII.434, p. 25.

103 A statuette of Venus/Aphrodite. Such bronze statuettes appear as part of the *parapherna* in eight other marriage contracts (usually of quite wealthy metroplitan dwellers) and are known from other types of documents too. Their purpose was presumably to ensure sexual success and fertility. See F. Burkhalter, "Les statuettes en bronze d'Aphrodite en Égypte Romaine d'après les documents papyrologiques," *Revue Archéologique* 1 (1990), 51–60.

104 Greek text found in *The Oxyrhynchus Papyri* X, ed. B.P. Grenfell and A.S. Hunt (1914), 207–10; also in Hunt and Edgar, *Select Papyri* vol. I, no. 5.

105 A dalmatic, a tunic with wide full sleeves, was an item of women's clothing that came into fashion in the later Empire. See Walker and Bierbrier 1997, 161–2 and 178–9 for illustrations. A "dalmatic cape" (*delmatikomaphorte*) may be a dalmatic tunic with a hood or cloak attached.

106 A chiton was a tunic, a standard item of both men's and women's clothing. This tunic is described as *monachon*, "made out of a single piece of cloth" (BL IX, 184; citing L. Casson, *The Periplus Maris Erythraei*, 248). See Rowlandson 1998, 313–16 for women's clothing often found in dowry lists; Walker and Bierbrier have many illustrations of both clothing and jewelry.

107 Compare this with Roman legal procedures in the event of divorce when the wife is pregnant, for which see Chapter 4, Part I.E.2.

108 The Egyptian month corresponding to 26 January–24 February. The emperors are Valerian and Gallienus, the year is 260.

109 Greek text in *The Oxyrhynchus Papyri* XLIX, ed. A. Bulow-Jacobsen and J.E.G. Whitehorne (Cambridge, 1982).

110 See Modrzejewski 1993 (1981), 57–60 on self-*ekdosis* (he did not know of P.Oxy. XLIX.3500, which was published in 1982). Cf. H.A. Rupprecht, review of P.Oxy. XLIX in *ZSSR,RA* 101 (1984), 349 (cited in BL VIII, 271).

111 Rupprecht (cited n.110 above) suggests that the dowry may have been the subject of another document drawn up later.

112 That is, both also embalmers.

113 Though the total number of extant papyri also drops in the third, fourth, and fifth centuries, the decline in the number of marriage contracts is even greater. (It does pick up again in the sixth century; see Beaucamp 1992, 106–16.) There are also two fragments of possible marriage contracts from the fifth century, SB XII.11075 and BGU XIII.2328. I owe this information to A. Arjava.

114 The name is somewhat garbled. The phrase immediately before "according to ... law" is missing except for the last word "for the sake of;" the editor plausibly

NOTES

supplies "the procreation of legitimate children" in the lacuna. Cf. the Latin
contract (Part III.A.3 above), which uses the same terminology, evidently taken
from the law itself. See n.99 above.

115 Text in *Einige Wiener Papyri*, ed. E. Boswinkel (Leiden, 1942). The date is 304,
not 305 as in P.Vind.Bosw.: see Bagnall, Cameron, Schwartz and Worp 1987,
143.

116 Cf. P.Oxy. II.281 in Chapter 4, Part III.A.2 for a similar situation three
centuries earlier. As far as I know, this earlier papyrus has not been mentioned
in connection with P.Ross. Georg. III.28, which is usually said to be the
earliest attestation of such an arrangement.

117 *Papyri Russicher und Georgischer Sammlungen III. Spätrömische und byzantinische
Texte,* ed. Gregor Zereteli and P. Jernstedt (Tiflis, 1930), 114–21. The date is
358: Bagnall, Cameron, Schwartz and Worp 1987, 69 and 251; BL IX, 226.

118 "In late 313 or early 314, yet another form of chronological reckoning appears,
the indiction. The indiction cycle contained fifteen years and was counted from
312; a new cycle thus began in 327, 342, and so on, and the same year number
would recur at intervals of fifteen years. A document dated only by indiction
number, therefore, while perfectly clear in its original context, cannot be given
an exact date now except by other information such as prosopography"
(Bagnall 1993, 328).

119 Evidently these items were accidentally left out of the enumeration of the
wedding-gift and are added here. The phrase "But indeed, also ..." (*ou men
alla*) must have been taken down just as it was spoken.

120 The Greek word is *strophe*. See editor's note at P.Ross.Georg. p. 120. Asep's
abandonment of Apia is seen as a betrayal not so much of her as of her father!

121 P.Strass. III.131, published in *Papyrus Grecs de la Bibliothèque Nationale et
Universitaire de Strasbourg*, ed. P. Collomp *et al.* (Paris, 1948), 6–7; republished
as 8013 in SB V (Heidelberg, 1934). See also BL III, 232; BL V, 130–1; and
BL X, 254.

122 P.Jand.Inv.Nr. 507, dated 489/90, now published as SB XVIII.13886 (ed. H.-
A. Rupprecht, Wiesbaden, 1993). The couple agree they have come together
in marriage, and the duties of each are apparently set out, with the husband
promising to support and clothe his wife, and the wife declaring that she will
love her husband and work with him to maintain their common home.

123 See *La Ketouba de Cologne: Un contrat de mariage juif à Antinoopolis*, ed. C. Sirat,
P. Cauderlier, M. Dukan, and M.A. Friedman, with French translation.

124 For a list of Jewish marriage contracts (Greek and Aramaic), see Cotton 1994.
Translation of P.Mur. 20 and 21 (both in Aramaic) and P.Mur. 115 and 116
(both in Greek) in Archer 1990, 291–7. The other Greek contracts are P.Yadin
37 (also from the Cave of Letters), translated in Lewis 1989, 131–2; and
X.Hev/Se Gr. 2, first published (with translation) in Cotton 1994, final publication in Cotton and Yardeni 1997. The other Aramaic contracts are P.Yadin
10 (see n.130 below) and the fragmentary X.Hev/Se 11 (also in Cotton and
Yardeni 1997).

125 See discussion of "Jewish Law and Society" in Cotton and Yardeni 1997,
153–6.

126 On Babatha and the province of Arabia, see Millar 1993, 20–1, 92–9, and
414–28, G.W. Bowersock, *Roman Arabia* (Cambridge, MA: Harvard

University Press, 1983), 76–89. Lewis 1989 is the publication of the archive's Greek papyri, reviewed by Bowersock 1991. The archive is also sometimes referred to as "P.Babatha."

127 I follow the Greek text in Lewis 1989, 76–82. Original publication in Lewis, Katzoff, and Greenfield 1987. See also BL IX, 376 and BL X, 286. There is an excellent illustration in Lewis 1989, Plate 18. Words in brackets [ ] indicate words missing in the papyri, but restored on the basis of the inner text. Words in parentheses ( ) are supplied by me for explanatory purposes.

128 *Pace* Katzoff in Lewis, Katzoff, and Greenfield 1987, 237. Cimber is a *cognomen*, not a *nomen*, and is not an indicator of citizen status.

129 By Wasserstein, "A Marriage Contract from the Province of Arabia Nova: Notes on Papyrus Yadin 18," *Jewish Quarterly Review* LXXX (1989), 93–130. Katzoff responded to Wasserstein's criticisms in "Papyrus Yadin 18 Again: A Rejoinder," *Jewish Quarterly Review* LXXXII (1991), 171–6; cf. N. Lewis, "The World of P.Yadin," *BASP* 28 (1991), 35–41. See also J. Geiger, "A Note on P.Yadin 18," *ZPE* 93 (1992), 67–8.

130 P.Yadin 10, published in the *Israeli Exploration Journal* 44 (1994), 75–101.

131 Cf. the Latin marriage contract in Part A for the groom's contribution. See Part II.C for pre-nuptial gifts in Roman law. For *hedna* in later documents from Egypt, see P.Grenf. II.76 and P.Oxy. LIV.3770 in Chapter 4, Part III. For the groom's contribution here as a Jewish practice, see Katzoff at Lewis, Katzoff and Greenfield, 1987, 242; cf. R. Katzoff, "*Donatio ante nuptias* and Jewish Dowry Additions," in N. Lewis, ed., *Yale Classical Studies vol. XXVIII: Papyrology* (Cambridge: Cambridge University Press, 1985).

132 Greek "*helleniko nomo.*" The meaning of this phrase has been much discussed. See Lewis, Katzoff, and Greenfield 1987, 240–2 and n.129 above.

133 Judah will buy back the contract. This has parallels in Aramaic documents from the Judaean desert: see Katzoff in Lewis, Katzoff, and Greenfield 1987, 242–3.

134 Cf. BGU IV.1050 and P.Oxy. X.1273 in Part A above for this clause.

135 This is a *stipulatio* clause, denoting that the contractants were asked formally if they agreed with what had been stated, and they then orally stipulated that they did. It reflects Roman law. This is the earliest extant example of a *stipulatio* clause in a Greek document; it becomes common only in the third century (cf. P.Oxy X.1273 and P.Ross.Georg. III.28 in Part A above). See Katzoff in Lewis, Katzoff, and Greenfield 1987, 236–7.

136 In Greek, *liblarios*. The same Theenas son of Simon appears as *liblarios* in P.Yadin 15 and 17, and a certain Germanos is *liblarios* in P.Yadin 20–2. Lewis 1989, 64 (note on P.Yadin 15.18) says this is the Greek transliteration of Latin *librarius* (a scribe or copyist). But Bowersock 1991, 339 (cited in BL X, 286), argues for a Greek version of Latin *libellarius*, someone who wrote *libelli* (petitions). Given the context, *librarius* seems to me preferable.

137 See F. Cumont, ed., *Fouilles de Doura-Europos (1922–1923): Texte* (Paris, 1926), 344–7 and 416–19. I am grateful to Simon Corcoran for this reference.

138 This doesn't quite add up. 175 plus 565 comes to 740, not 750.

139 Text used is Welles, Fink, and Gilliam 1959, 156–8; cf. BL VI, 34. In the translation ... marks where words or letters are missing; words in brackets are missing but have been supplied by the editor.

140 *Agathe Tyche*, "Good Luck" or "Good Fortune." This appears also at the beginning of marriage contracts from Egypt (Welles, Fink, and Gilliam 1959, 155 n.13); cf. P.Oxy. X.1273 in Part A above.

141 *Parapheromen{en.* See BL VI, 34 for supplement of [*proika*], which only appears in the extant text in relation to the groom's contribution. Because of the fragmentary state of the text, it is impossible to be sure if the 565 denarii of silver are supposed to be the total of the items listed (which appear to come to 510 denarii) plus a small amount of cash, or if the 565 denarii are in addition to the material items. I am assuming the latter. The clothing items listed would then be *parapherna*, rather than *proix*.

142 These were apparently men who verified the value of the items listed to the satisfaction of both parties. See n.28 in Welles, Fink, and Gilliam 1959, 159.

3 PROHIBITED AND NON-LEGAL UNIONS

1 Romans counted kinship by degrees based on how many acts of generation were required to produce the relationship. A person was related to his parents and to his children by one degree, to his siblings and grandchildren by two degrees, to his grandparents, aunts/uncles and nieces/nephews by three, to his cousins and great-uncles/aunts by four, and to his second cousins by six. See Goody 1983, 136–8 and D.38.10, summarized in Justinian, *Institutes* III.6.

2 … indicate sentences omitted in this translation.

3 The word used is *sobrinarum*, which usually means "second cousins," as opposed to *consobrini/ae*, "first cousins." See Goody 1983, 50–2.

4 In Suetonius' account (*Deified Claudius* 26.3) a freedman and a *primipilaris* (chief centurion) are said to have taken advantage of Claudius' encouragement of uncle–niece marriages.

5 *Mosaicarum et Romanarum Legum Collatio* VI.4, in *FIRA* II, 558–60. On the *Collatio* generally, see Corcoran 1996, 11 and Robinson 1997, 65. On this edict, see Corcoran 1996, 173–4 and Evans Grubbs 1995, 99–101.

6 Barnes 1982, 54 and 62–3.

7 December 30, 295, eight months after the date of the edict.

8 Cod. Just. 5.4.17 includes a very abbreviated version of this edict, which omits everything except paragraph 5 (on the female relatives a man was prohibited from marrying) but adds the prohibition on marrying a brother's daughter (which was not reintroduced until 342; see Part II.A).

9 Corcoran 2000, 13. On penalties and rank, see Introduction, Part II.

10 On the case of Petronia Justa, see Gardner 1986b; Weaver 1991; 1997, 69–71; Gardner and Wiedemann 1991, 163–4 has translations of several of the tablets.

11 Fully legal manumission entailed meeting the requirements of the *lex Aelia Sentia* of 4 C.E., on which see Introduction, Part II and Weaver 1990; 1991; 1997.

12 The *peculium* was a fund given to slaves (male and female) by their owners. Slaves sometimes used their *peculium* (perhaps supplemented by other earnings) to purchase their freedom, but since the *peculium* legally belonged to the owner, he or she could reclaim the *peculium* upon manumission – in which case it could not be converted into dowry.

13 The word for "married" here is *duxisti*, which normally is used of the man marrying (literally, "leading") the woman. *Nubere* is the verb used of a woman marrying. Perhaps the status disparity, with the woman in the superior position, has influenced the lawgiver's choice of words. See Donahue 1979, 20.

14 Eros was a common slave name, and this, combined with his apparent lack of a *nomen* (family name, indicating free status), might have tipped Hostilia off as to his slave identity. See Evans Grubbs 1993 on free women and slaves.

15 If a free man cohabited with someone else's slave, her master might resent this and could prosecute him under the *lex Aquilia* for damage done to his slave property, or bring an action for *iniuria* (outrage): see Watson 1987, 54–64.

16 For the "law of nations," see Gaius, *Institutes* I.82 in Part I.B.1 above.

17 That is, her parents' status will be decreased by having a slave daughter. This would change after her father's death: cf. *Sent. Pauli* II.xxi^a.(18).

18 As in *Sent. Pauli* II.xxi^a(13). In both cases, the woman's relationship to her partner's owner (*patrona* or mother) is such that it would be shameful for her to become his slave, so the law does not apply.

19 Under the *lex Aelia Sentia*, on which see Introduction, Part II.

20 See Evans Grubbs 1993, 129 on the relationship of this rescript (probably written by Papinian while secretary for petitions) to the passage by Ulpian.

21 Apparently the rank (*dignitas*) of the *patrona*. Both these penalties are used for *humiliores* in this period; see Introduction, Part II. Condemnation to public works (*opus publicum*) was less severe and degrading than the mines (Millar 1984). This may mean that if the *patrona* were of high rank, the freedman's offense would be considered worse than if she were herself of humble origins; therefore, he would get the more severe penalty, the mines. But it is not clear.

22 See J. Gaudemet, "La Décision de Callixte en matière de mariage," in Gaudemet 1980 (article orig. pub. 1955); Evans Grubbs 1993, 132–4.

23 D.23.2.44, D.23.2.44.6, D.23.2.27, D.23.2.31, and D.23.2.47, all placed by the compilers in the *Digest* title on marriage, were taken from books on the *lex Julia et Papia* by either Ulpian or Paulus. In Part II.B.5, D.25.7.1, 4, and 3 (found in the very short *Digest* title "On concubines") were all originally from Ulpian's books on the Augustan marriage laws, and D.48.5.14 pr. was from his work "On adulteries," commenting on the Augustan adultery law. The jurists Gaius, Marcellus, and Terentius Clemens also wrote commentaries on the Augustan legislation.

24 I am following Treggiari 1991a, 49–51. There is some disagreement among scholars about the meaning of *iniustum matrimonium* and the status of unions between those of senatorial rank and freedpeople before Marcus Aurelius.

25 See McGinn 1991, 362–9 on this passage.

26 The rest of this passage, which says that if a man wishes to have a freeborn respectable woman as a concubine, he must openly profess this in front of witnesses or risk a charge of *stuprum* (illicit sexual relations), is generally thought to be interpolated (Treggiari 1981a, 72–3, but see McGinn 1991, 359–62). Ulpian (D.25.7.1.1) also thought that only women of such low reputation as to be immune from adultery charges could be concubines, but this was a minority opinion: see Treggiari 1981b, 72–5; cf. Wolff 1939, 94–7.

27 See McGinn 1991, 351–2 on this passage. He points out that giving the *liberta*-concubine standing equivalent to a married woman meant that the relationship could not be liable under the adultery law – but any other sexual relationship the concubine had could be. For the meaning of *materfamilias*, see Chapter 1, Part I.B.

28 See D.20.1.4 in Chapter 2, Part I.A.2 for this idea.

29 For the ban on senator–freedwoman marriage, see Part I.B.4; for the ban on marriage between an imperial official and a local woman, see Part I.C.3.

30 Thus some scholars (e.g. Wolff 1950, 305) have thought the sentence where Ulpian expresses his opinion ("But it is not right …") must have been interpolated. But cf. n.26 above.

31 See McGinn 1991, 354–5 for this translation.

32 On the Minician law, see D. Cherry, "The Minician Law: Marriage and the Roman Citizenship," *Phoenix* 44 (1990), 24–66; cf. Gardner 1997, 38–9.

33 See Gardner 1997, 51–2 on this passage. I am omitting a number of sentences; omitted sentences are signified by "…"

34 The reference to *arrhae* is interpolated: Corbett 1930, 8 and 18. On the use of *arrhae* for the purpose of marriage in late antiquity, see Chapter 2, Part II.C.

35 See Wells 1998, who dates the rule to 13 B.C.E. (and therefore not part of the Augustan marriage legislation discussed in Chapter 2, Part I.B) and shows how it fits with other Augustan legislation on the military.

36 Cf. P.Dura 30, a soldier's marriage contract dated 232, in Chapter 2, Part III.C, and P.Dura 32, attesting a soldier's divorce in 254, in Chapter 4, Part III.B. By the reign of Constantine, the soldier's right to marry was assumed in law: see Cod. Theod. 3.5.5, dated 332, in Chapter 2, Part II.B.

37 See Campbell 1984, 441–2 on this passage. He thinks it implies that there were some veterans whose children, though born while they were in service, also came under their *potestas*. Presumably these were the most privileged military, the Praetorian Guard and Urban Cohorts.

38 Latin text is from *Inscriptiones Latinae Selectae*, ed. Dessau. See ILS 9052–9 and Campbell 1994, 195–201 for other examples.

39 This restriction to only one wife per veteran is not otiose; some soldiers may well have formed more than one liaison during their decades of service (Wells 1998, 189–90). Cf. the famous will of the veteran Gaius Longinus Castor (BGU I.326 = *FIRA* III.50; translations in Campbell 1994, 228–9 and Rowlandson 1998, 188–90), who evidently preferred to have two slavewomen as concubines rather than make the choice of marrying only one of them: see J. Keenan, "The Will of Gaius Longinus Castor," *BASP* 31 (1994), 101–7.

40 As suggested by Campbell 1994, 197 (his translation of ILS 9054).

41 Actually a law of Constantius only, as the place of issue (Antioch, in Syria) shows. At this time Constantius was ruling the eastern half of the Empire, Constans the west. This law is not in the *Code of Justinian*.

42 See Goody 1983, 40 and 60–2. Cf. Canon 61 of the Council of Elvira (probably held in the first decade of the fourth century); Canon 2 of the Council of Neocaesarea (held between 314 and 325); also Basil of Caesarea, Canon 23 (*Epistle* 199, written 375) and Canon 78 (*Epistle* 217, written 375). Another letter of Basil (*Epistle* 160, written 373 or 374) sharply criticizes a presbyter of Antioch who had permitted a

man to marry his wife's sister after her death. Basil gives religious arguments against such marriage, but does not mention imperial law.

43 Constans is erroneously named; he had been killed in 350, and Constantius was sole emperor. "Julian Caesar" is the future emperor (reigned 361–363). This law is not in the *Code of Justinian*.

44 ... *uxorisve eius postremo, cuius vetitum damnatumque coniugium est* ... This appears to be a reference to Cod. Theod. 3.12.2 (above), forbidding marriage to a sibling's former spouse, but the Latin is somewhat obscure.

45 Text used is *Corpus Scriptorum Ecclesiasticorum Latinorum* (*CSEL*) 82.2, ed. M. Zelzer (Vienna, 1990), where the letter to Paternus is no. 58. In the older *Patrologia Latina* edition it is number 60. I am translating only excerpts, not the entire letter; ... indicate that sentences have been omitted.

46 So suggests Matthews 1975, 143–4 (cf. also 110–11).

47 Latin text used is that of B. Dombart as revised by A. Kalb, originally published in the Teubner series (Leipzig, fourth edition, 1928–9), as found in the Loeb vol. 4 (Cambridge, MA: Harvard University Press, 1966) at p.508. I am translating only a short excerpt. A complete translation by Philip Levine is found in the Loeb volume.

48 Theodoret, *Epistle* VIII, in *Theodoret de Cyr: Correspondence I*, ed. Yvan Azéma (Sources Chrétiennes vol. 40, Paris, 1955), 78–81. See Clark 1993, 43–4. Like Ambrose, Theodoret assumes that his correspondents are expecting imperial dispensation for their illegal marriages.

49 Though this law appears in the *Code of Justinian* in the name of the eastern emperor Zeno, at the time the law was enacted he was in flight from Constantinople because of a revolt by Basiliscus, brother of Zeno's mother-in-law Verina, wife of the previous emperor Leo (see Jones 1964, 224–5). This is apparently a law of Basiliscus (see Krueger's note at Cod. Just. 5.5.8). The *Code of Justinian* does contain two other laws against incestuous marriage from Zeno's troubled reign (474–491): Cod. 5.8.2 and 5.5.9, both of which are particularly concerned with uncle–niece marriage (Cod. Just. 5.5.9 also mentions marriage with a brother's former wife).

50 Cod. Theod. 4.6.3, the law translated here, was originally the third law under the title "On natural children and their mothers" (*de naturalibus filiis et matribus eorum*). The first is now lost (for its possible citation by later emperors, see Evans Grubbs 1995, 296–7). Of the second, only the final sentences remain (translated in Evans Grubbs 1995, 284). Like the final sentence of Cod. Theod. 4.6.3, the second law had a postscript dealing with the case of the "son of Liciniannus," on whom see n.63 below.

51 The number of senators was greatly expanded under Constantine and later emperors (especially after the creation of a second Senate in Constantinople). *Perfectissimi* held high equestrian rank, and were eligible for many posts within the late Roman administration, including some governorships. See Jones 1964, 525–30.

52 *Duumviri* and *quinquennales* were the chief magistrates of municipalities. *Flamines* held local (pagan) priesthoods, and provincial priests (*sacerdotes provinicae*) were responsible for maintenance of the imperial cult (still extant under Christian emperors). See Jones 1964, 724–5 and 763–4.

53 *Infamia* (legal infamy) was frequently used as a penalty in the fourth and fifth centuries, and differed somewhat from the classical *infamia*. It primarily entailed exclusion from public office and honors. See A.H. J. Greenidge, *Infamia: Its Place in Roman Public and Private Law* (Oxford, 1894), 144–70. Peregrine status would entail losing Roman citizenship and the privileges that accompanied it, including the right to make a will. For men of rank both these penalties would have been significant: they would be reduced to the low status of the women they had wished to marry (Evans Grubbs 1995, 291–2).

54 The word for freedwoman is *liberta*, implying (at least in classical Latin) one's own former slavewoman, not just a former slavewoman in general (who would be called a *libertina*). On (Junian) Latin status, see Introduction, Part II and cf. below at n.96 and n.120.

55 *Naturalis*, that is, illegitimate.

56 That is, other children he had by a legal wife.

57 The word translated "wife" here and below is *uxor*, which is usually used to describe a legitimate wife. In this case, such women are not considered wives by law, but they are by the men who have "married" and had children by them.

58 That is, to the man or his legitimate kin, or to the imperial fisc (treasury) if he is dead and has no legitimate kin.

59 The imperial treasury, which confiscated illegal legacies.

60 Perhaps someone who claims to be the man's legitimate child, and then hands the property over to the illegitimate children or their mother.

61 Adopting the translation of McGinn 1999, 58.

62 That is, when the property is recovered from the children or "wives" (after torture, presumably), they (or those who have colluded on their behalf?) shall be forced to repay four times the original amount.

63 The identity of this "son of Licinnianus" is unclear. He may have been an (otherwise unattested) illegitimate son of Constantine's former co-emperor, Licinius (defeated by Constantine in 324), or he could have been the illegitimate son of a local Carthaginian notable, whose case was covered by the law (and perhaps even prompted its passage). See Evans Grubbs 1995, 285–6. On the penalty, see Millar 1984, 144–5.

64 Found (with slight changes) at Cod. Just. 5.27.1.

65 Cod. Theod. 9.7.1 (326), on which see Evans Grubbs 1995, 205–8. For other laws regarding tavern-keepers, see ibid., 290. For the women in Cod. Theod. 4.6.3 as "analogues" for prostitutes in late antiquity, see McGinn 1997; 1999.

66 In 397, the western emperor Honorius reverted to Constantine's policy (Cod. Theod. 4.6.5), but a law of Honorius' brother Arcadius (Cod. Theod. 4.6.6) restored Valentinian I's ruling for the eastern half of the Empire. Then a western law of Valentinian III reduced the amount left to illegitimate children to one-eighth, apparently whether or not there were other heirs (4.6.7; see Part II.B.3 below; Beaucamp 1990, 198). In a law of 428 (Cod. Theod. 4.6.8), the eastern emperor Theodosius II returned to Valentinian I's policy, which became valid throughout the Empire upon the *Code*'s publication in 438. In later laws (not received in the west), Theodosius allowed illegitimate children to inherit in full from their fathers, provided they became decurions (town councilors) if male, or married decurions if female (Evans Grubbs 1995, 302–4). At least one law under Cod. Theod. 4.6 appears to be missing; see A. Arjava, "Ein verschollenes

Gesetz des Codex Theodosianus über uneheliche Kinder (CTh 4,6,7a)," *ZSSR.RA* 115 (1998), 414–18.

67 See McGinn 1997, 78–86 for discussion of *vel humilis vel abiecta*.

68 On this (now lost) law of Constantine, see Part II.B.2 below.

69 *vv.cc.* = *viri clarissimi* (men of senatorial status). The first two sentences of this law are found (with an additional phrase) at Cod. Just. 1.14.9. There is an abbreviated version of paragraphs (2) and (3) at Cod. Just. 5.5.7. A few, non-essential phrases have been omitted in the translation.

70 "A man is not able to have a concubine at the time that he has a wife. Therefore, a concubine is distinguished from a wife by choice alone" (*Sent. Pauli* II.xx.1). It is not clear whether this passage pre-dates or post-dates the Constantinian law; they are roughly contemporary.

71 See Evans Grubbs 1995, 298–300. Seventy-five years later, Augustine, bishop of the north African city of Hippo, had to tell his congregation they could not have both a wife and a concubine: *Sermo* 224.3 in *Patrologia Latina* 38, col. 1094–5; on which see Shaw 1987b, 16; cf. *Sermo* 392.2 in *Patrologia Latina* 39, col. 1710, and see Part II.B.2 for Augustine on concubines. (But note that Augustine's congregation seems to have considered slavewomen who were sexually exploited by their masters to be "concubines," whereas under the Roman legal definition such relationships, while certainly not illegal, were not really *concubinatus*.)

72 The rest of the law, here omitted, says that disposition of pre-nuptial gifts and dowry are covered by the same policy, and that the offer of retroactive legitimation is good only for those who marry their concubines now.

73 Latin text used is that of P. Knoll, originally published in 1909 in the Teubner series, as found in the Loeb vol. 1 of the *Confessions* (Cambridge, MA: Harvard University Press, 1912) at pp.148–50 and 324–5.

74 "You" is God; the *Confessions* are addressed to God throughout.

75 Latin text used is *CSEL* 41 (Vienna, 1900), ed. J. Zycha, at pp. 193–4.

76 That is, knowing that he does not have marital intent toward her and will eventually dismiss her and marry another.

77 The law's manuscript date is 319, but Seeck 1919, 56 re-dates to 318. It is also at Cod. Just. 5.5.3 (with some changes). The addressee, Patroclus, is unknown.

78 The law first inaccurately uses the term *conubia*, meaning legal marriages, to describe the free–slave relationship, but then correctly calls it *contubernium* (see Part I.B). Cf. the use of *uxor* in Cod. Theod. 4.6.3 and *nupta* in Cod. Theod. 9.9.1, both meaning "wife," to describe non-marital relationships.

79 That is, employees of the "very powerful house" to which he has fled.

80 By the imperial treasury, whereas rural properties go to his town or heirs. In Justinian's version (Cod. Just. 5.5.3), his city gets all his property.

81 The rest of the law, omitted here, dealt with penalties for the landowner to whom the *curialis* fled and his overseers and stewards, if they knew about the relationship. See Evans Grubbs 1995, 278–9 for translation and discussion.

82 Addressed to Junius Bassus, praetorian prefect, Not found in Cod. Just. Only part of the law is translated here; see Evans Grubbs 1995, 280–2 for the rest.

83 The rest of the law, omitted here, said that "natural" children who were born from a free mother (whether freed or freeborn), could inherit up to one-eighth of

their father's estate. Though in the names of both reigning emperors, it was a law of Valentinian III only. It is not in the *Code of Justinian.*

84 Cod. Just. 5.4.21, also to Bassus, undated (not in the *Theodosian* Code). The identity of recipient and similarity of subject matter make it likely that these were part of the same law originally.

85 The sixth-century emperor Justinian required that the highest classes have written evidence of a marriage: Arjava 1996, 206. This may have been because, after many of the prohibitions on marriage between those of different status had been abolished or mitigated (see below), it was considered more important to have external documentation that a couple intended marriage rather than concubinage. See Wolff 1939, 91–2 and 98–9.

86 Latin text is found in *CSEL* 32, Part 1, ed. C. Schenkl (Vienna, 1897).

87 Latin text is found in *CSEL* 54, ed. I. Hilberg (Vienna, 1909) at p. 688.

88 The *stola* was the dress of the respectable Roman matron, which distinguished her from prostitutes and disreputable women; see McGinn 1998, 154–5. An imperial rescript, by granting the man the right to marry legally an otherwise ineligible woman, would have thereby granted her respectability.

89 Paul, 1 Corinthians 7 ("better to marry than to burn").

90 See J.N.D. Kelly, *Jerome: His Life, Writings, and Controversies* (New York: Harper & Row, 1975), 213–14 for the background. Among Jerome's targets on this issue was Ambrose, whom Jerome detested.

91 Leo, *Epistle* 167.4–5, written 458 or 459. Text in *Patrologia Latina* 54, at col. 1204–5. An English translation of the whole letter by E. Hunt is found in *Pope St. Leo the Great: Letters* (Fathers of the Church vol. 34: New York, 1957), 289–97. See Crouzel 1971, 304–12; Evans Grubbs 1995, 315–16.

92 This refers to an official procedure by which a person who had been held in slavery would be legally recognized as not only free, but freeborn, and granted *ingenuitas.* Cf. Cod. Theod. 4.8.5 and 6 for legislation regarding claims for freedom and free birth.

93 D. Hughes, "From Brideprice to Dowry in Mediterranean Europe," in *The Marriage Bargain: Women and Dowries in European History,* ed. M.A. Kaplan (New York and Binghamton: Herrington Park Press, 1985), 13–58, suggests that Majorian's law requiring dowry for a legal marriage influenced his contemporary Pope Leo. But Leo does not explicitly mention dowry as a necessary accompaniment of marriage. It seems more likely that if Leo was influenced by a Roman law, it was Cod. Theod. 4.6.7 of Valentinian III, denying legitimacy to children born "without honorable celebration of matrimony," see above.

94 This law has been attributed to both Constantine and to Licinius, his co-ruler and rival in the east. It is better to take it as a law of Constantine, one of many he enacted on mixed-status relationships: see Evans Grubbs 1995, 264–5.

95 *Decoctio natalium,* a unique expression. See Evans Grubbs 1995, 266.

96 They would be Junian Latins. Cf. n.54 above and n.120 below.

97 This is part of a much longer law dealing with matters of inheritance and debt, which was divided up and put under different titles by the *Code's* compilers. Cod. Theod. 8.16.1, repealing the Augustan penalties on celibacy (Chapter 2, Part II.A), is part of the same law. See Evans Grubbs 1995, 119–20.

98 Cod. Theod. 4.12.2 of Constantine, dated 317, required three warnings in the presence of seven Roman citizens (the law itself is lost but the "Interpretation,"

dating to the late fifth–early sixth century, supplies the content). Cod. Theod. 4.12.4 (Constantine, 331) rescinded the need for three warnings, but 4.12.5 (Julian, 362) reinstated it. Cod. Theod. 4.12.7 (Arcadius, 398) again required three warnings before a woman could be enslaved. This must have caused some confusion. See Evans Grubbs 1995, 265–9; cf. Beaucamp 1990, 185–7.

99 Secundus, the addressee of the law, was praetorian prefect of the east, and so would not receive a law enacted at Trier in the west. Seeck 1919, 109 suggests the place-name Thyatira (in Asia Minor) was corrupted in the manuscripts to the more famous Trier. This is then a law of the eastern emperor Valens.

100 *n.p.* = *nobilis puer* ("noble boy"). Gratian, the son of Valentinian by his first marriage, was not designated emperor until 367, after the apparent date of this law, so ascription to him as "Augustus" in the law's heading is apparently incorrect. He was seven years old at the time of this law.

101 Text of the *Consultatio Veteris Cuiusdam Iurisconsulti* is found in *FIRA* II, pp. 593–613. It evidently dates to the fifth century (Robinson 1997, 65–6).

102 The words "among after matters and at the (same) place" (*inter cetera et ad locum*) indicate that this was excerpted from a longer law.

103 "... *et nunc contemnentes dominum minoris aetatis servitutis iugum conantur effugere* ..." Possibly it is the *dominus* (master) who is a minor (as A. Arjava has suggested to me) rather than the woman. Cf. Cod. Just. 5.5.4 (Part II.D) for leniency toward those who contracted illegal unions in their youth.

104 This was a law of the western emperor Valentinian, brother of Valens (note that it was issued from Milan, the seat of imperial government in the west at this time). This is then a western counterpart to Cod. Theod. 4.12.6.

105 Cod. Theod. 10.20.3, dated 365; Cod. Theod. 10.20.10, dated 380; but cf. Cod. Theod. 12.1.179, which says it is "confirming the authority of the *s.c. Claudianum*" and orders that children born from freeborn mothers of curial families are to serve as *curiales* in their mother's municipality.

106 Cf. Cod. Just. 7.20.1 in Part I.B.3 for this situation. A married woman who had sexual relations with someone other than her husband could be prosecuted for adultery. Unmarried women (virgins, widows, or divorcées) who engaged in sexual relations could be prosecuted for *stuprum*. The penalties for both were severe, involving exile and confiscation of property and in late antiquity, sometimes even the death penalty. See Evans Grubbs 1995, 201–21.

107 The capital penalty would be either death or exile with confiscation of property (in other words, the penalty for *stuprum*; see n.106 above).

108 That is, the slave. The word used, *verbero*, is very rare in Roman law, but found in early Latin literature. See Evans Grubbs 1993, 145–7 on the unusual language of this law.

109 *Nupta* means married woman, but according to the law this cannot be a legal marriage. Cf. the use of *uxor* (wife) in Cod. Theod. 4.6.3 and *conubium* in Cod. Theod. 12.1.6 above. The word for "lover," *amatus* (more literally, "beloved"), is a literary, not legal, term (cf. n.108 above).

110 That is, if they are her children from another, legal marriage (cf. the mention of legitimate children in Cod. Theod. 4.6.3, Part II.B.1).

111 In Roman inheritance law, a woman's intestate heirs would be her agnate relatives (those on her father's side), first of all her brothers. Not until 178 C.E. could a woman's own children (legitimate and illegitimate) inherit from her

upon intestacy; see Gardner 1986a, 198–200 and Chapter 5, Introduction. Here the illegitimate children by the slave man are still preferred to her agnates, if she and her lover are both dead. The translation in Evans Grubbs 1995, 273, says "*their* brothers," the Latin text does not have a possessive pronoun, but the sense must be "her." Surely illegitimate children would not be preferred to their own, legitimate brothers.

112 An official in the civil service. For encouragement of slave informers, cf. Cod. Theod. 9.24.1 on abduction marriage in Part II.C.

113 The law's date is uncertain; the manuscript date is 326, but Seeck 1919, 64, re-dated it to 329. See Evans Grubbs 1995, 51–2 on problems with dating Constantinian legislation. An abridged version appears at Cod. Just. 9.11.1.

114 There are lacunae in the manuscripts. I use Mommsen's suggested reconstruction. I have also omitted the last sentence of paragraph (1).

115 The word translated as "children" is *liberi*, which can also mean "free people." The lawmaker probably intended a play on words.

116 The restrictions on marriage between men of rank and low-status women were removed [Justinian Novel 117.6; see Beaucamp 1990, 208]. On the other hand, the union of a decurion with another landowner's slave was preserved among the marriage prohibitions in the *Code of Justinian* [Cod. Just. 5.5.3]

117 However, other fourth-century laws that called for the enslavement of free women married to imperial workers were retained: Cod. Theod. 10.2.3 is at Cod. Just. 11.8.3, and Cod. Theod. 10.20.11 is at Cod. Just. 11.8.7 (cf. n.105 above). See Beaucamp 1990, 194–5.

118 Constantine is mistaken, at least as far as classical law goes: women's testimony was always accepted, and women could also bring legal actions in matters concerning themselves or their family. See Chapter 1, Part V.

119 That is, between the abductor and the girl's parents.

120 Latin status at this period was a sort of halfway-state between slavery and full Roman citizenship. See Part II.B.4, n.96.

121 That is, if they accepted the abduction marriage and did not bring the abductor to court. The Latin word is *parentes*, which could mean "relatives" more generally; see Chapter 2, Part II.B, n.47 and n.125 below.

122 Not in the *Code of Justinian* (cf. Cod. Just. 7.13.3 for one sentence), because Justinian substantially modified the law on *raptus*; see Evans Grubbs 1989, 77–9. Aquileia is in Italy, on the north Adriatic coast.

123 Imperial law starting with Constantius also repressed the abduction of Christian women who had dedicated themselves to God: see Evans Grubbs 2001.

124 This law appears also at Cod. Just. 5.7.1, with some changes. Other parts of the law are probably Cod. Theod. 3.6.1, and 8.15.6; probably also Cod. Theod. 3.5.10–11 on return of *arrhae* after a broken betrothal (Chapter 2, Part II.C). Cod. Theod. 3.6.1 says that *arrhae* do not have to be returned if the betrothal was the result of pressure from a provincial official.

125 The Latin word is *parentes*; see n.121 above.

126 Fatherless women under a guardian; see Chapter 1, Part II.C.

127 I follow the translation of Pharr 1952, 73 of the Latin *quorum utilitas agitur*, referring to the women who are being coerced into marriage.

128 The Cod. Just. version adds "though he will not have achieved the prohibited marriage," implying that the union was not *iustum matrimonium*. See Gaudemet 1949 (1980), 85–6.

129 The Latin word, *iudex,* which literally means "judge," is used in later Roman law to designate an imperial official with judicial powers – more specifically, the governor of a province.

130 The *vicarius* was an imperial official in charge of a diocese, a group of provinces. In the administrative hierarchy, he ranked below the praetorian prefect (the highest administrative official apart from the emperor himself) and above a provincial governor. See Jones 1964, 373–5. The Christian church adopted this imperial terminology for its own (later) vicars and dioceses.

131 Though in the name of all three reigning emperors, the place of issue (in northern Greece) indicates that this is a law of Theodosius.

132 *Adnotatio*, a document attached to a rescript particularly in cases where a decision was being made contrary to the usual policy, in which the emperor might give his reasons for making an exception. See Corcoran 1996, 57–8.

133 There is a problem with the day, since Theodorus was no longer praetorian prefect on January 23. The law was probably issued earlier in January.

134 Though in the names of both eastern and western emperors, Cod. Theod. 3.10.1 is a law of the western emperor Honorius, as the place of issue (Ravenna, by this time the seat of the western emperor) indicates. This law appears with some changes (e.g., no mention of cousin marriage) at Cod. Just. 5.8.1. Cod. Just. 5.4.20 on consent to marriage (see Chapter 2, Part II.B) may be part of the law too.

135 The law first uses the word *barbara* to describe the barbarian wife, but then switches to the term *gentiles* at the end of the first sentence and in the second sentence.

136 Though in the name of both reigning emperors, the addressee of the law, Count Theodosius (a western official, father of the future emperor Theodosius I), and the circumstances in which it was probably enacted (a revolt in the western province of Mauretania; see Sivan 1996) indicate it is a law of Valentinian. The date is unclear; it could belong to any of the years in which the emperors held the consulship jointly. The law is not in the Cod. Just.

137 Sivan 1997, 91–5, discusses another law, Cod. Theod. 16.8.6 (339), which she believes is an earlier ban on Jewish–Christian marriage, but which really concerns Christian women employees in imperial weaving factories who were abandoning their jobs at the instigation of Jewish men, and were also perhaps converting to Judaism (it was originally part of the same law as Cod.Theod. 16.9.2, against the purchase of Christian slaves by Jews). Though such defections might also involve sexual relationships, the law is not about Jewish–Christian marriage per se. See Evans Grubbs 2001; Linder 1987, 144–51.

138 Under Augustus' adultery law, a woman's husband and father had first priority in bringing adultery charges, but if neither did so within sixty days of the act of adultery, then the opportunity to prosecute was thrown open to any citizen male (women did not have the right to bring adultery charges). Constantine changed this in a law of 326 (Cod. Theod. 9.7.2), by limiting the right to

bring a prosecution against a woman to her husband or male relatives (men who committed adultery with married women could still be prosecuted by unrelated parties, however). See Evans Grubbs 1995, 208–14.

139 *v.c.* = *vir clarissimus*, a man of senatorial rank. Though in the names of all three reigning emperors, the law's place of issue (Thessalonika, in northern Greece) and its addressee (Cynegius was praetorian prefect of the east) indicate that this is a law of Theodosius. It is found also at Cod. Just.1.9.6.

140 A passage in a papyrus from the "Babatha archive" (P.Yadin 26, lines 13–14) has been taken by some scholars to mean that Babatha's husband had two wives simultaneously: see Lewis 1989, 22–4. But this interpretation has been questioned, and it may mean only that both women were married to the same man at different times: see Katzoff 1995b. In any case, the Babatha archive involves a Jewish community 250 years earlier than the date of this law.

141 Valentinian II died in May 392, so the *Code's* ascription to him is erroneous; it should be Honorius (Linder 1987, 191). In any case, the place of promulgation shows this is a law of Theodosius, the senior emperor (and father of both Arcadius and Honorius). This law is not found in the *Theodosian Code*.

142 For the events of these years, see Honoré 1998, 179–87; Chapter 5, n.14.

143 Cf. *Consultatio Veteris Cuiusdam Iurisconsulti* IX.7 in Part II.B.4 above, which apparently forbade free women who had contracted *contubernia* with slaves when they were minors to leave the relationship.

144 No consulship is given, so this law cannot be assigned to a particular year; it dates from between August 25, 383, when Valentinian acceded to the throne and May 15, 392, when he died. Seeck 1919, 127, dates it to 392, connecting it with Cod. Just. 5.10.1, on widows who remarry, though that law is dated 15 March, 392 and is addressed to Tatian, Theodosius' praetorian prefect in the east (see Chapter 5, Part I.B). Gaudemet 1949 [1980], 86 dates it to 387–93 and says it is not possible to know to which emperor to attribute it. But Honoré 1998, 186 dates the law to 389 or 392 and attributes it to Valentinian II. He identifies Andromachus, here Count of the Privy Purse, with the praetorian prefect of Gaul in 401.

4 DIVORCE AND ITS CONSEQUENCES

1 In addition to D.24.2, other passages in the *Digest* relevant to divorce are found in D.23.2 (the title on marriage), D.24.1 (on gifts between spouses); D.43.30 (on exhibiting of children, in regard to a father's right to break up his child's marriage; see Part I.E.1); D.25.3 (on acknowledgment of children born to pregnant divorcées; see Part I.E.2); and D.50.16 (definitions of terms). The *Digest* excerpts come from a range of juristic writings, particularly (as noted below) commentaries on the Praetor's Edict or on Augustus' marriage laws.

2 The last two sentences of this passage, which is from one of Paulus' books on the Praetor's Edict, are repeated at D.50.17.48.

3 See Horsfall 1983, 92–4. Under the Augustan legislation, the couple's failure to have children would mean the husband could inherit only 10 per cent of his wife's estate; see Chapter 2, Part I.B. The date of "Turia's" death is not known; she may have died before 18 B.C.E. when the Augustan law was passed.

NOTES

4 An extreme case of ambiguity surrounding the ending of a marriage is that of the emperor Claudius' wife Messalina, who celebrated a very public wedding to Gaius Silius without actually divorcing Claudius (Tacitus, *Annales* XI.27–30). Claudius' advisors assume he is divorced, but there was no evidence of it apart from Messalina's new "marriage;" see Gardner 1986a, 85; Treggiari 1991a, 458.

5 For an elaborate juristic working-out of the possible scenarios for a madwoman wife, see Ulpian at D.24.3.22.7–10, with Gardner 1993, 176–7.

6 See Treggiari 1991a, 350–3. The passage continues (*Rules of Ulpian* 6.13) that if the *husband* has moral defects, he has to return the dowry immediately (for serious defects) or within six months (for "lighter" ones). As Treggiari (1991a, 52) remarks, "... the immorality threshold was higher for husbands ..."

7 In this passage ... indicate that I have omitted phrases in my translation. Cf. the question of a daughter's consent to marriage – in the absence of outright rejection "consent" was assumed: see D.23.1.12 in Chapter 2, Part I.C.3.

8 Ulpian, at D.24.3.22.5–6, even suggests that a daughter would be so unwilling for her father to get her dowry back that she would go into hiding or "oppose her father modestly (*verecunde*) through her absence."

9 The emperor's reply was written below (subscribed) the petition, and would then have been posted in a public place in Sirmium (in Serbia), which was the site of an imperial residence in the late third and early fourth centuries.

10 On the *lex Aelia Sentia*, see Introduction, Part II, "Roman social structure and the legal system." Female slaveowners were not similarly encouraged to marry *their* former slaves: see Chapter 3, Part I.B.3.

11 See Gardner 1986a, 86–7; cf. D.38.11.1.1 (Ulpian). From the extant juristic commentary, this appears to have been the case whether or not she was freed explicitly for the purpose of marriage. Compare the situation in late Roman law of women who unjustly repudiated their husbands, who were forbidden to remarry ever or within a five-year period: see Part II and Wolff 1950.

12 Much of this passage (and much of D.24.2.11.2, following it), which are from the third book of Ulpian's commentaries on the Augustan marriage laws, has in the past been suspected of post-classical interpolation. See Wolff 1950.

13 Those captured by the enemy became slaves, and therefore had no right of marriage. Captives who returned to Roman territory regained their former position by the right of *postliminium*, but their marriage was not automatically resumed unless their former spouse consented. The marriage of a freedwoman to her patron was an exception to this. See Buckland 1908, 291–8.

14 A *fideicommissum* was a trust made by the deceased. If someone had been bequeathed a slavewoman by means of a *fideicommissum* to manumit her, he would have the rights of patron over her, but did not have the right to keep her in marriage against her will as her original owner would have had.

15 See D. Kleiner, *Roman Imperial Funerary Altars with Portraits* (Rome, 1987), #23 for the altar and inscriptions.

16 The Latin word is *stigmata*, which can refer also to branding or tattooing (of a criminal or a runaway slave). For curses in antiquity, see J.G. Gager, *Curse Tablets and Binding Spells from the Ancient World* (Oxford and New York: Oxford University Press, 1992, esp. 175–99). For further discussion of this inscription, see Evans Grubbs, 2002.

17 The final line of the inscription, omitted here, is difficult to read. Henzen in CIL VI.20905 read it as "and the same marks of infamy to Hymnus, those who followed Zosimus." Hymnus was presumably the slave whom Acte took with her when she ran away from Euphrosynus.

18 Modern scholars are not in complete agreement about the situation of adult children under paternal power who wished to divorce. Corbett 1930, 242–3 thought that both a son and a daughter *in potestate* could divorce without their *paterfamilias'* consent, but Gardner 1986a, 11 and 86, disagrees; and cf. Gardner 1993, 177 and 229, n.51. For a more nuanced interpretation, see Treggiari 1991a, 445–6, who notes that "[a]t the very least, [the legal texts] show ... that people could regard daughters in power as agents in their own divorces."

19 This refers to the praetor's interdict, given to a man who demands that someone under his *potestas* be produced: see D.43.30 pr.-1. This passage is from Book 71 of Ulpian's commentaries on the Praetor's Edict.

20 Legitimate children who were left out of their father's will had the right to bring an action challenging the will on the grounds that their father had been "undutiful" (*inofficiosus*): see Chapter 1, n.84 and Chapter 5, n.23. The phrase "slipped into the disgrace of disinheritance" (*ad exheredationis notam prolapsum*) implies that Faustina's father "fell down" in his duty to her.

21 Nicomedia, where Diocletian's imperial residence was located, is in north-western Turkey (modern Izmit). On the "posting" of laws, see the Introduction, Part I.A.

22 Tiberius was not at that time actually under Augustus' *patria potestas*, so Augustus did not have any legal right to interfere in his marriage. But it would have been difficult for Tiberius to refuse, given the political situation. Some years later, in 4 C.E., Augustus adopted Tiberius, which did give him *patria potestas* over Tiberius. By then Tiberius and Julia were divorced, Julia having been banished by her father in 2 B.C.E. for sexual misconduct. Augustus himself sent the *repudium* to Julia in Tiberius' name (Suetonius, *Tiberius* 11).

23 A member of the equestrian order, on which see Introduction, Part II.

24 That is, earlier emperors. Diocletian's staff had checked to see if there were previous imperial decisions relevant to Caelestina's case.

25 The date of the *s.c. Plancianum* is not known. Talbert 1984 attributes it to the reign of Hadrian (his *senatusconsultum* #85, 445), but a Trajanic date is also possible. Its relationship to the section of the Praetor's Edict which called for inspection of a widow who claimed to be pregnant by her deceased husband is not clear. I believe that the Senate's decree on pregnant divorcées was passed under Trajan, but was influenced by the much earlier policy on pregnant widows found in the Praetor's Edict. See further Chapter 5, Part III.A. Note that this and the following passages from Ulpian (D.25.3.1.6 and 25.4.1 pr.) are from his books of commentaries on the Praetor's Edict.

26 I have omitted a few sentences, indicated by "..."

27 That is, she abandoned the newborn infant, a not uncommon practice in antiquity: see Harris 1994. Cf. BGU IV.1104 in Chapter 5, Part III.C, involving the possibility of exposure of a newborn by a pregnant widow; such cases suggest that exposure was most likely in situations where the marriage was ended by the husband's death or by divorce.

28 See Gardner 1986a, 158–9, on this case. Gardner states that the fetus was not considered a human being, and therefore aborting it was not illegal. The real issue in the case cited by the jurists was the right of the *paterfamilias* to determine the fate of the child, not the question of the fetus' own status.

29 See Evans Grubbs 1995, 257–9, drawing on E. Volterra and M. Sargenti.

30 *Muliercularius*, an example of non-legal terminology.

31 That is, she will be praised for having revealed her husband's crimes.

32 *Ad acuculam capitis*, another example of non-legal colloquial language.

33 *Conciliatrix*, that is, a procuress (another example of non-legal language).

34 The day of issuing is missing. This law is not found in the *Code of Justinian*, which adopted the milder divorce regulations of Theodosius II (see below).

35 Unlike *deportatio*, the more severe form of exile, *relegatio* did not involve loss of citizenship or the right to make a will: Garnsey 1970, 111–17. The wife who divorces her husband in this law is sentenced to *deportatio*; the adulterous wife in Augustus' law was sentenced to *relegatio*. (By this period, the adulterous wife might even be sentenced to death: Evans Grubbs 1995, 216–21.)

36 Cod. Just. 5.17.7, a law of 337 (not extant in the *Theodosian Code*), sets forth a more lenient policy for wives of soldiers who have not heard from their husbands for at least five years: they can get a divorce and receive back their dowry, and they may remarry. The law is attributed to Constantine but was apparently enacted after his death: see Evans Grubbs 1995, 232, and Barnes 1982, 87 n.172 on who was responsible for issuing this law.

37 Cod. Theod. 3.13.2 (363), a law of Julian, refers to the *retentiones* (withholdings) made from a divorced wife's dowry because of fault on her part or the presence of children (Part I.C). This may have been part of Julian's divorce law, the rest of which is lost.

38 The work is the *Liber Quaestionum Veteris et Novi Testamenti* ("Book of Questions on the Old and New Testament"), question 115, chapter 12, in *Corpus Scriptorum Ecclesiasticorum Latinorum* 50, ed. A. Souter (Vienna, 1908), 322. On Ambrosiaster, see W.G. Rusch, *The Later Latin Fathers* (London: Duckworth, 1977), 65–7 and D.G. Hunter, "The Paradise of Patriarchy: Ambrosiaster on Woman as (Not) God's Image," *Journal of Theological Studies* 43 (1992).

39 *Postliminium*, the right to return from exile (or captivity outside the Empire) and resume one's position and rights as a Roman citizen. See n.13.

40 *Stuprum*, which denoted illicit sex, including adultery (sex between a married woman and someone other than her husband) and sex with or by an unmarried woman (virgin, widow, or divorcée) of respectable status. According to this law, a man whose wife had divorced him for only "middling faults" could prosecute her for *stuprum* if she remarried after the divorce.

41 The one-year waiting period for remarriage is the same as that imposed on widows in 381 by Theodosius I (Cod. Theod. 3.8.1) See further Chapter 5, Part I.A on legally imposed delays on remarriage of widows. Only in late law is such a delay imposed on divorced women, but it was no doubt due to the same concern about paternity, as well as about female propriety. See Beaucamp 1990, 227–9.

42 On withholdings (*retentiones*) from the dowry, see Part I.C. and n.37 above.

43 Though the law appears in the name of the eastern emperor, Theodosius II, as well as the western emperors Honorius and Constantius, the fact that it was issued from Ravenna, the imperial seat in the west since 402, indicates that it is

a law of Honorius and Constantius only. Constantius (III) was married to Honorius' sister, Galla Placidia, and was co-emperor for a few months in 421; see Matthews 1975, 377–9. Cod. Just. 9.9.34 is an abridged version of this law.

44 See Honoré 1998 on the development of different consistories (and legal approaches) in the two halves of the Empire in the fifth century.

45 In another law two months later (Novel 14.4, in Chapter 2, Part II.C), Theodosius said that if a marriage "has been dissolved by *repudium* by the woman's fault," the husband was to get back all of the pre-nuptial gifts he had given her, even if they had been converted into dowry. Since the fate of pre-nuptial gifts after divorce had not been regulated in classical law, it was necessary for Theodosius II to add this provision to his otherwise "classical" divorce law. See Chapter 2, Part II.C on pre-nuptial gifts.

46 *Vir clarissimus*, of senatorial status; see Chapter 1, Part VI.A. The first sentence of this law is repeated at the beginning of Cod. Just. 5.17.8 of 449.

47 *Intentata*, apparently meaning that she is able to show justification for the divorce.

48 Any child born in that interval will be assumed to have been conceived from her first husband; see n.41 above.

49 It was routine practice to subject slaves to torture in order to obtain their testimony, on the assumption that they would not otherwise tell the truth: see Bradley 1994, 165–70. Though normally slaves could not testify against their owners, the Augustan adultery law allowed the torture of the slaves belonging to a man or woman accused of adultery (but not of *stuprum*): D.48.18.17 pr. (Papinian); D.48.5.28.6 (Ulpian); Cod. Just. 9.41.1 (196); 9.9.3 (213); Cod. Theod. 9.7.4 (385). Treason was so serious a crime that slaves could even bring an accusation against their owner, something they were generally forbidden to do; thus they could also be tortured to extract evidence of their owner's treason. See further O. Robinson, "Slaves and the Criminal Law," *ZSSR.RA* 98 (1981), 213–54. In late antiquity, liability to torture was extended to include lowborn free people as well as slaves; see Harries 1999, 118–34. Cf. also Cod. Theod. 4.6.3 (336) in Chapter 3, Part II.B.1.

50 The Latin text is in *Corpus Scriptorum Ecclesiasticorum Latinorum* (*CSEL*), vol. 55, part II, ed. I. Hilberg (Vienna, 1912), 37–49 (translated passage is at pp. 38–40). A translation of the entire Epistle 77 can be found in *St. Jerome: Select Letters*, trans. F.A. Wright (Cambridge, MA: Loeb Classical Library, 1933), 309–37.

51 See Barnish 1988, 145, who finds that Fabiola is the only attested divorce in *Prosopography of the Later Roman Empire* vols. I and II. This does not mean that divorce was uncommon in other segments of society, however.

52 Matthew 5:31–32 says a man may only divorce his wife for her adultery, and if she remarries, she and her second husband are committing adultery (cf. Matthew 19:9). The other Gospels which cite this teaching of Jesus (Mark 10:2–12; Luke 16:18) do not mention the exception for adultery, but condemn all divorce and remarriage after divorce, as does Paul in 1 Corinthians 7:10 (cf. Romans 7:2–3). See Evans Grubbs 1995, 243–4.

53 Paul, 1 Corinthians 6:16.

54 The view of the famous jurist Papinian (early third century) is contrasted with that of the apostle Paul, whose views on marriage are found in his first letter to the Corinthians.

55 Paul, 1 Corinthians 7:8–9.

56 Cf. Paul, Romans 7:22–3.

57 1 Timothy 5:14–15.

58 Jerome's views on the superiority of virginity over marriage are most forcefully expressed in his treatise *Against Jovinian*; cf. also his *Epistle* 22 to the young virgin Eustochium. Several years before he wrote his eulogy of Fabiola, Jerome had condemned the remarriage of a woman who had left her dissolute husband, as long as her husband was still alive: see *Epistle* 55.4. For Jerome's views on divorce see Crouzel 1971, 284–303.

59 This attitude was codified in a law of Constantine (Cod. Theod. 9.7.1, 326) that defined the type of woman who could be accused of adultery (as being respectable enough to have to meet the law's sexual standards): female tavern-owners were liable to prosecution for adultery, but the women who served wine to customers were not, and therefore a man could have sex with them with impunity. See Evans Grubbs 1995, 205–8; McGinn 1997, 89–94.

60 See Clark 1993, 38–41; Evans Grubbs 1995, 242–53. Crouzel 1971 collects and discusses the relevant passages on divorce from Christian writers (Latin and Greek), in French translation.

61 On post-476 legislation, see Beaucamp 1990, 174–7; cf. 221–38; Rabello 1981, 87–9; Arjava 1996, 181–3.

62 For an up-to-date list of divorce documents from Egypt and the Near East, see Instone Brewer at www.Instone.Brewer.com. Older lists are in Montevecchi 1936, 20 and 1988, 206. I have also consulted the relevant volumes of the *Berichtigungsliste der griechischen Papyruskunden aus Aegypten* (BL) for revised readings and references in later publications.

63 Originally edited by W. Schubart and published in *Aegyptische Urkunden aus den Königlichen Museen zu Berlin, Griechische Urkunden* IV (Berlin, 1912). I use the Greek text in *Corpus Papyrorum Judaicarum*, vol. II, ed. V.A. Tcherikover and A. Fuks (Cambridge, MA: Harvard University Press, 1960), 10–12 (= CPJ II.144).

64 See Tcherikover and Fuks (see n.63), 1–5; Modrzejewski 1961 and 1995. However, this interpretation has been disputed: see Rabello 1981, 97. Tcherikover and Fuks (n.7 at CPJ II.144) suggest it may have been a "mixed marriage" between a Jewish woman and a non-Jew, since the husband Hermogenes may have belonged to a deme and thus had Alexandrian citizenship, which Jews in Alexandria generally did not (see Delia 1991, 26–7). But see n.66 below.

65 For Jewish divorce rules in this period, see Rabello 1981 and D.J. Brewer, "Jewish Women Divorcing their Husbands in Early Judaism: The Background to Papyrus P.Şe'elim 13," *Harvard Theological Review* 92 (1999), 349–57. No Jewish divorce documents in Greek have been found in Judaea or Arabia (unlike marriage contracts in Greek; see Chapter 2, Part III.B). P.Mur. 19, a deed of divorce in Aramaic, is translated in Archer 1990, 297. There has been much controversy over an Aramaic document from the Judaean desert (P.Şe'elim 13), which has been variously described as a receipt for return of *ketubah* and renunciation of further claims by the wife to her husband (who was divorcing her), or a divorce declaration by the wife herself, which would be against Jewish law. For the latter interpretation, see T. Ilan, "Notes and Observations on a Newly Published Divorce Bill from the Judaean Desert," *Harvard Theological Review*

(*HTR*) 89.2 (1996), 195–202; her arguments are challenged by A. Schremer in *HTR* 91 (1998), 193–202, and accepted with some modification by Brewer 1999. The final publication of P.Ṣe'elim 13 (Cotton and Yardeni 1997) tentatively calls it a "Waiver of Claims?"

66 For Alexandrian demes, cf. Chapter 1, n.90 on P.Oxy. II.261. The reading here is controversial. Schubart, the original editor, read *Archegetou* but was unsure; his reading has been confirmed as "fairly certain" (Delia 1991, 59). Tcherikover and Fuks suggested *Archistrateiou*, but that is problematic. See BL IV, 7; BL VI, 15, and BL X, 19; cf. Delia 1991, 59–60. Recently, Modrzejewski 1995, 312–13 has suggested *archeg(ou)*, referring to a term found in literary and epigraphical Jewish sources to mean "leader" (of a synagogue or of the Jewish community). In that case, Hermogenes would not belong to a deme, and his identity as a Jew would be more probable (cf. n.64 above).

67 17 B.C.E. The Egyptian month Pharmouthi runs from 27 March to 25 April.

68 Tcherikover and Fuks note ad loc. that this dowry is rather modest; cf. P.Oxy. II.281 below with a dowry of 200 drachmas of silver.

69 10 March, 13 B.C.E. The month Phamenoth runs from 25 February to 26 March.

70 Published in *The Oxyrhynchus Papyri* II, ed. B.P. Grenfell and A.S. Hunt (Oxford, 1899); also found at Mitteis and Wilcken 1912 (MChr. 66).

71 Originally published in *Griechische Urkunden der Papyrussammlung zu Leipzig*, ed. L. Mitteis (Leipzig, 1906), reprinted in Mitteis and Wilcken 1912 (MChr. 293). See BL III, 91; BL IV, 42; BL V, 48, BL VII, 79; and BL VIII, 170 for corrections and new readings, incorporated in the revised text of Pestman 1994, 110–11, which I am using. Brackets [ ] indicate where text is lost but has been restored; ... indicate missing words.

72 Marepsemis son of Pakebkis appears in several other papyri as *hypographeus* (subscriber) to documents drawn up at the Tebtunis *grapheion*. See H.C. Youtie, "Hypographeis and Witnesses of 2nd Century Tebtunis," *ZPE* 19 (1975), 191–201, esp. 199–201 (who also gives a revised text of lines 31–7).

73 Greek text found in *New Classical Fragments and other Greek and Latin Papyri*, ed. B.P. Grenfell and A.S. Hunt (Oxford, 1897), 119–21; also in Hunt and Edgar 1932, 26–9 (= *Select Papyri* no. 8); Mitteis and Wilcken 1912 (MChr. 295).

74 Supplying *autoi* (masculine dative) with Hunt and Edgar and Mitteis, rather than *autei* (feminine dative) with Grenfell and Hunt.

75 Originally published in *Papyrus Grecs de la Bibliothèque Nationale et Universitaire de Strasbourg*, ed. P. Collomp *et al.* (Paris, 1948), 19–20; republished as SB V.8024. My translation incorporates additions from BL V, 132; cf. also corrections in *Papyrus Grecs de la Bibliothèque Nationale et Universitaire de Strasbourg*, ed. J. Schwartz (Strasbourg, 1963), 185.

76 On indictions, see Chapter 2, n.118. In this papyrus, the consuls Tatian and Symmachus provide the exact year. Phaophi is the Egyptian month running from 28 September to 27 October.

77 Other petitions from or on behalf of the wife are: P.Panop. 28 (329), from the wife's father against her husband; P.Oxy. VI.903 (4th/5th c.), translated in Rowlandson 1998, 207–8; P.Oxy. L.3581 (4th/5th c.), trans. in Rowlandson 1998, 209–10; P.Lips. 39 (390); PSI I.41 (4th c.); PSI IX.1075 (458); cf P.Lips. 41 (later 4th c.), a lawyer's notes on behalf of the wife. From the husband:

P.Cair.Preis. 2 (362); P.Lond. V.1651 (363). See Bagnall 1987; Beaucamp 1992, 146–56; Evans Grubbs 1995, 239–42. Cf. P.Oxy. II.281 above for a petition from an earlier period.

78 The Greek term for the *defensor civitatis*, at this time a local official concerned with cases involving property: Bagnall 1993, 165; R. Frakes, "The Office of the *Defensor Civitatis*," *Classical Journal* 89 (1994), 337–48.

79 Daimons were seemingly quite active in fomenting marital discord in late antiquity; cf. P.Grenf. II.76 and P.Stras. III.142 above. In P.Cair.Preis. 2, however, the daimon may signify epilepsy; see Beaucamp 1992, 92.

80 Text edited by R.A. Coles in *The Oxyrhynchus Papyri* LIV (1987), 200–1. The text is fragmentary; ... indicates where the Greek cannot be read.

81 An interesting detail, intended to show that Arilla, unlike the boy's father, was providing support for the child. Not all mothers breast-fed their babies and Arilla could have hired a wet-nurse: see Dixon 1988, 120–9; cf. Rowlandson 1998, 275–6 for a translation of one from the Protarchos archive (BGU IV.1058).

82 The date is 26 March, 334. *Lamprotatoi* (most splendid) is the equivalent of Latin *viri clarissimi* (*v.c.*), indicating men of senatorial status.

83 The *tabellarius* was evidently a sort of private notary; see editor's note at P.Oxy. L.3581. For speculation about what law is being referred to, see ibid. and Bagnall 1987, 43.

84 P.Lips. 39, in Mitteis and Wilcken 1912, 141 (M.Chr. 127). After the emperor Julian apparently rescinded Constantine's law in the early 360s, it is not clear what the legal situation was, especially in the east. There may well have been legislation that does not survive. See Arjava 1988 and 1996, 177–83.

85 Constantine's law (Cod. Theod. 3.16.1, [331]) ruled out legal divorce due to a husband's violence; he would have to be a murderer, poisoner-magician, or tomb-robber for a wife to repudiate him legally and get back her dowry. Honorius' law (Cod. Theod. 3.16.2, [421]), which was not promulgated in the eastern provinces, would probably have classified wife-beating among the "middling faults" that allowed divorce but penalized the wife by loss of dowry and pre-nuptial gift, and refused her the right to marry again. Theodosius II's law of 449 (Cod. Just. 5.17.8) allowed a wife to divorce if her husband was "afflicting her with whippings." Cf. the bishop Basil of Caesarea on wife-beating: wives should bear with the blows and stay in the marriage (Epistle 188, canon 9; Evans Grubbs 1995, 251). Augustine's mother Monnica avoided beatings by skillful handling of a bad-tempered husband, but her friends did not fare so well (*Confessions* 9.9.19; Arjava 1996, 130–2; Shaw 1987b, 31–2).

86 See Chapter 2, Part III.A at n.81. This document from Dura shows that the custom of unwritten marriage was not unique to Roman Egypt.

87 See Welles, Fink, and Gilliam 1959, 160–6 for text and translation of P.Dura 31. They suggest Nabusamaus and Acozzis may have been paternal cousins, as they both have a grandfather named Abissaeus.

88 For the Greek text and discussion, see Welles, Fink, and Gilliam 1959, 166–9. In my translation, ... signify places where the writing has been destroyed; words in brackets [ ] indicate restorations by the editors of words no longer readable; words in parentheses ( ) are my explanatory additions.

89 The date is 30 April, 254. The year is reckoned from the original founding of Dura by the Seleucids in the fourth century B.C.E. The city's title is evidence that by the mid-third century it had gained the prestigious rank of Roman *colonia*; see Welles, Fink, and Gilliam 1959, 166–7. The day may perhaps be 29 April: see BL VIII, 118, citing P.J. Sijpesteijn in *ZPE* 33 (1979), 235, n.29.

5 WIDOWS AND THEIR CHILDREN

1 For Egypt, see Bagnall and Frier 1994, 126–7 and 153–5; Hanson 2000. For the assumption that remarriage was usual, see esp. Humbert 1972; cf. Parkin 1992, 132–3, n.196. Saller's (1994, 43–69) computer simulations of Roman demographics also assume remarriage was usual (though he admits the census data from Egypt show otherwise). Widows and "orphans" (usually children whose father was dead but mother still living) are the subject of an exhaustive study by J.-U. Krause, *Witwen und Waisen im römischen Reich* (4 vols, Stuttgart 1994–5). See the review article, "Widows, Orphans, and Social History" by T.A.J. McGinn in *Journal of Roman Archaeology* 12 (1999), 617–32.

2 Under the praetorian scheme of inheritance, priority in succession to a deceased male child not under *patria potestas* would be given to his own children (if he had any), then to other "legitimate heirs," including agnates. Priority in succession to a female child would follow the same order, except, of course, that their own children would not have priority, but would be considered part of their husband's family. Mothers, as cognates, would only inherit in the absence of agnates. Under the older, civil law scheme of succession, a mother could not inherit at all. See Gardner 1998, 15–24 on succession under the civil law and the praetorian rules.

3 See Gardner 1986a, 164–9 on women making wills. Other times when a woman might undergo *coemptio* would be in order to change her *tutor mulierum* (Gaius *Institutes* I.115; see Chapter 1, Part III.A) or to enter a marriage with *manus* (Gaius, *Institutes* I.109–113; see Chapter 1, Part II.B).

4 She could make her children heirs on condition that their father emancipated them, or leave them a legacy or *fideicommissum* (trust) to take effect upon their father's death. For one such case, see J. Gardner, "Another Family and an Inheritance: Claudius Brasidas and his Ex-wife's Will," *Liverpool Classical Monthly* 12.4 (1987), 52–4.

5 On the *ius liberorum*, see Chapter 1, Part III.D. Under the *s.c. Tertullianum*, a mother with the *ius lib.* inherited as a "legitimate heir" rather than a cognate, though even there she ranked behind other relatives. See Gardner 1998, 228–9.

6 Most of the laws on *bona materna* are not translated here, but see Cod. Theod. 8.18.3 and Cod. Just. 6.60.4 in Part I.B below, and cf. the regulations regarding the fate of dowry and pre-nuptial gifts in Cod. Theod. 3.13.3 (422) and Novel 14 of Theodosius (439), translated in Chapter 2, Part II.C, and Cod. Just. 5.17.8 (449) in Chapter 4, Part II. On *bona materna* in late antiquity, see Humbert 1972, 397–401; Arjava 1996, 98–105; Evans Grubbs 1995, 115–18.

7 Cod. Theod. 5.1.1 (317–19). However, even if the mother did have the *ius liberorum*, the deceased child's paternal uncles and their children and grandchildren would still get one-third of the inheritance collectively. Cod. Theod. 5.1.2 of Valens (368 or 369) added that the deceased's brothers (natural or adopted)

would be preferred to their mother, unless they had been emancipated (Constantine's law probably intended this too). Cod. Theod. 5.1.7 of Valentinian III allowed emancipated brothers the same one-third as paternal uncles. See Cod. Theod. 5.1.8 in Part I.B for another modification.

8 The original law of 18 B.C.E., the *lex Julia de maritandis ordinibus*, had allowed only a year's delay in remarrying for widows, and six months for divorcées, but this was changed by the later *lex Papia*: see *Rules of Ulpian* 14; Treggiari 1991a, 73–4. See further Chapter 2, Part I.B, at n.9.

9 *Infamia* involved restrictions on the right to represent others in court (which women could not do anyway) or to appoint representatives to act for them, or to act as witnesses; see Gardner 1993, 110–28; cf. Gardner 1986a, 46. On the Praetor's Edict, see Chapter 1, Part IV.B, n.75.

10 On mourning, see Treggiari 1991a, 493–4. The *Sent. Pauli* I.xxi.13 say that parents and children over six are to be mourned for a year, husbands for ten months and relatives within the eighth degree for eight months.

11 But cf. D.23.2.6 in Chapter 2, Part I.A.2: even a bride married in absentia whose husband dies returning from dinner must mourn him. This was written in the late Republic, about 250 years before Ulpian.

12 Cod. Just. 5.9.1, same addressee and date. The opening sentence is the same as in Cod. Just. 6.56.4. Neither excerpt is extant in the *Theodosian Code*. See Beaucamp 1990, 214–18.

13 In other words, as each of her children dies, his or her portion goes to the surviving siblings; only when the last child has died intestate does the mother get back the half of her property that she had given them when she married.

14 Though the Codes give the law in the names of all reigning emperors, Eutropius was the praetorian prefect of the east, ruled by Theodosius I, who was older and more active a legislator than the western emperors Gratian and Valentinian II. Thus this was a law of Theodosius I, as was the following law (Cod. Theod. 3.8.1) and Cod. Theod. 3.8.2 in Part I.B below, also enacted at Constantinople, Theodosius' seat. Gratian and Valentinian II were both sons of Valentinian I (reigned in the west, 364–75), by different wives. Gratian (named Augustus as a boy in 367) was killed in 383 by the forces of Magnus Maximus, who was later condemned and killed by Theodosius as a usurper. Valentinian II (named emperor at the age of four after Valentinian I's death in 375) was also overthrown by a usurper in 387, but was eventually restored by Theodosius, and died in 392, probably by suicide. Theodosius was made emperor in the east in 378 after the death of Valentinian I's brother, Valens, at the battle of Adrianople, so technically he was the least senior of the three. But due to his age and personality, he was definitely the dominant force in legislation from 378 on. See Honoré 1998 on legislation of this period.

15 *Adnotatio*, on which see Chapter 3, n.132.

16 This is the *Laudatio Murdiae* ("Eulogy of Murdia"). I am using the Latin text as in Dessau, ILS 8394. Part of the inscription is also found at *FIRA* III.70. For a translation of the entire inscription, see Gardner and Wiedemann 1991, 132–3.

17 Rather than making her a co-heir along with her brothers, Murdia gave her daughter her share as a legacy. See Champlin 1991, 116; Dixon 1988, 56–7.

18 Murdia gave him a *praelegatum*, on which see Buckland 1963, 352–3.

19 See Fantham 1995; Bradley 1997; Dixon 1997, 162–4; Hunink 1997 and 1998; and Harrison 2000, 39–88 for recent discussion. The text used is Hunink 1997. See Chapter 1, Part III.B and Chapter 2, Parts I.D.2 and 3, and I.E.2 for the *Apologia*.

20 For the idea that enforced celibacy of young widows was injurious to their health, see Hanson 2000, 149–50.

21 She had in fact been betrothed to her husband's brother, and marriage tablets (*tabulae nuptiales*) had been drawn up, but when her father-in-law died she broke the engagement to his son: *Apologia* 68.

22 Fantham 1995, 223, suggests there may have been a local custom of widows marrying their husband's brother; cf. the banning of such "levirate" marriage in late Roman law: Cod. Theod. 3.12.2 (355) and Cod. Just. 5.5.8 (470), in Chapter 3, Part II.A.

23 An "undutiful will" (*inofficiosum testamentum*) was one in which the testator over-looked or gave less than expected to those he or she should have included according to legal and social norms, particularly children, parents, and siblings. Those who had been so slighted could bring a *querela inofficiosi testamenti* ("complaint of undutiful will"), and the will could be broken (see Chapter 1, n.84). Cases in which children of first marriages brought complaints when their parent favored a second spouse in his or her will were particularly common. See Gardner 1986a, 183–90. Pudens evidently thought Pudentilla's will would favor Apuleius at his expense.

24 Apuleius is referring to a letter (in Greek) written by Pudentilla to her elder son, Pontianus, in which she had jokingly alluded to the claim of Apuleius' detractors that he was a magician and had bewitched her. The prosecution, erroneously describing this as a "love letter," had read out carefully selected passages of the letter out of context in an attempt to show that Pudentilla was not in her right mind. Apuleius put the passages in context and reproached Pudens for destroying his mother's privacy by making her letter public. See *Apologia* 79–84 and Hunink's notes ad loc.

25 Humbert 1972, 298–9 believes the passage is interpolated; Beaucamp 1990, 313 accepts it as genuine. The rescript as a whole is badly composed: the opening sentence uses the plural *pupilli*, but paragraphs (1) and (2) refer to only one boy (*puer*).

26 This was a law of Septimius Severus, referred to in a number of legal sources; see esp. D.27.9 and Cod. Just. 5.71; Talbert 1984, 449, #134. On *tutores* and *curatores*, see Chapter 1, Parts II.C and III.E and Part II below.

27 This is an excerpt from a long edict "to the People" enacted at Sirmium (now in Kosovo, Yugoslavia). Other parts of the law are at Cod. Just. 2.16.1 and 5.72.4 and the fragmentary Cod. Theod. 3.30.3. Seeck 1919, re-dated it to 329. For a list of Constantine's laws on guardians, see Evans Grubbs 1995, 346–7.

28 Humbert 1972, 405–9, thinks that this law deprived remarried mothers of their right to *raise* the children of their first marriage, rather than of any control over their property. I do not think the text as we have it supports this.

29 Cod. Theod. 8.18.1 (315) and 8.18.2 (318 or 319). The children were in turn expected to offer their father one-third of the *bona materna*. On *bona materna*, see above at n.6.

30 The Latin words are *ingenuam, liberam, libertam, libertinam*. An *ingenua* would have born free; a *libera* could be freeborn or a former slave who had been freed.

Liberta and *libertina* both denote a freedwoman; *liberta* is used of a freedwoman in relation to her former master (patron), *libertina* means "freedwoman" generally. Pharr 1952, 215 translates *libertina* as "daughter of a freedwoman." In the Justinianic version (Cod. Just. 8.55.7), this first sentence is omitted, and the emphasis is solely on remarried mothers.

31 The Latin is *portentosae vilitatis abiectaeque pudicitiae*, presumably meaning prostitutes or women of promiscuous lifestyle. Cf. Chapter 3, Part II.B for laws forbidding marriage with high-ranking men to "humble or despicable" women.

32 Though in the names of both surviving sons of Constantine, this is a law of Constantius, at that time ruling in the eastern Empire. Other parts of the same law are found at Cod. Theod. 8.13.2 and 3.13.1. The law's provisions were repeated in another law of Constantius, Cod. Theod. 8.13.4, enacted in 358 and addressed to the urban prefect of Rome (thus clearly extending the same policy to the west as had already been in effect in the east.) Cod. Theod. 8.13.1 is found at Cod. Just. 8.55.7, with the change that mothers who do not remarry can revoke their entire gift, not just one-half.

33 Gifts "in anticipation of death" (*donationes mortis causa*), trusts (*fideicommissa*), and legacies were all ways of transferring property after death by will or codicil. See Nicholas 1962, 264–70.

34 Under the *s.c. Tertullianum*, on which see Introduction to this chapter and Part II.A.1 below. She can inherit only half of a deceased child's property; presumably any surviving daughters get the other half. If there are sons surviving, they have priority over their mother, and she does not inherit.

35 Though the law as recorded in the Codes is in the names of all three emperors, its promulgation at Constantinople indicates that, like Cod. Just. 6.56.4 and Cod. Theod. 3.8.1 in Part I.A above, this is a law of Theodosius I; see n.14 above. It was, however, received in the west as well.

36 The words "After other matters" at the beginning and "And other matters" at the end indicate that this is an excerpt.

37 See Honoré 1998, 249–51. The same law also included the so-called "law of citations" (Cod. Theod. 1.4.3) detailing which classical jurists were to be considered authoritative by fifth-century judges. Other parts of the law are: Cod. Just. 1.14.2 and 3; 1.19.7 and 1.22.5, all on the definition and validity of different types of legal enactment; Cod. Theod. 4.1.1 (father has right of succession to deceased child without the need for a decree, just as mother does); 8.18.9 (father or grandfather with *patria potestas* has usufruct of *bona materna*) and 10 and 8.19.1 (in no case does a father gain ownership of *bona materna*); and Cod. Just. 6.30.18 (child's succession rights). All of the excerpts from the law of 426 except Cod. Theod. 5.1.8 are addressed "to the Senate" (or "to the Senate of Rome") in the Codes, but it is part of the same law, directed toward the senatorial class of Rome and hence a law of Valentinian III (then ruling from Ravenna), despite co-attribution to the eastern emperor Theodosius II.

38 In 410, a law of the eastern emperor, Theodosius II, had granted the *ius liberorum* to all (Cod. Theod. 8.17.3; see Chapter 2, Part II.A), but this did not affect the western Empire until the publication of the *Theodosian Code* in 438.

39 Found at Cod. Just. 6.56.1 + 6.55.11; see Beaucamp 1990, 233.

40 Cod. Theod. 3.8.1 of Theodosius I (Part I.A), which extended the mandated

delay in remarrying to one year, presumably applied to all widows, but all the other laws involve widows with children only.

41 On patristic exhortations to widows, see Humbert 1972, 327–40; and J.N. Bremmer, "Pauper or Patroness: The Widow in the Early Christian Church," in *Between Poverty and the Pyre: Moments in the History of Widowhood*, ed. J.N. Bremmer and L. van den Bosch, (London and New York: Routledge, 1995), 31–57.

42 Champlin 1991, 87–102 tends to see the *captator* as more of a literary topos than a social reality, but the convergence of literary and legal evidence in late antiquity suggests that there was a basis for concern. The final paragraph of Majorian's novel denounces all legacy hunters, and says if an 'extraneous' person does inherit, he must give one-third of the inheritance to the fisc.

43 This refers to Cod. Theod. 3.8.2 (382), of Theodosius I, above.

44 See Chapter 2, Part I.E on gifts between living spouses.

45 Under the *lex Falcidia*, children, as heirs, were entitled to at least one-fourth of the inheritance, and if they did not receive it, could bring a claim of "undutiful will." See n.23 above; Chapter 1, n.84; Chapter 4, n.20.

46 A mother could appoint a tutor for her children in her will only if she had made them her heirs. However, governors were accustomed to confirm such testamentary appointments whether or not the children were their mother's heirs: see D.26.3.2 pr. (Neratius) and Cod. Just. 5.28.4 (Alexander Severus, 224).

47 See chapter Introduction. Gardner 1998, 247–8 notes that mothers with the *ius liberorum* had little chance of being their child's heir anyway, since siblings would succeed over their mother. Septimius Severus' ruling, which denied even succession as a cognate to mothers who failed to have a guardian appointed, would have been more of an impetus.

48 A delict was an act of wrong-doing that fell under private law, as opposed to a *crimen* that fell under public (criminal) law. Failing to request a tutor was not a delict (or a crime).

49 That is, under twenty-five. For the "slipperiness of age" (*aetatis lubricum*) as an excuse from liability, cf. Cod. Just. 5.5.4 in Chapter 3, Part II.D.

50 Another rescript of Alexander Severus says that a paternal aunt can also request a guardian (Cod. Just. 5.31.4, dated 223).

51 This rescript is to be joined with Cod. Just. 5.71.12, which indicates that Leontius wanted to recover a debt owed to him by a minor by having the governor issue a decree allowing the minor's rural property to be sold to pay the debt. It is possible that the child's mother intentionally did not have a tutor appointed to avoid legal proceedings against him; cf. D.38.17.2.45 above.

52 This apparently applied to mothers with and without the *ius liberorum*; see Cod. Theod. 5.1.1, cited at n.7.

53 The word translated as "children" is *filios*, which can include daughters as well as sons: see Chapter 1, Part I.A.

54 Ms. date 315; re-dated by Seeck 1919, 166 to 318.

55 Including mothers, but also grandparents, who were also obliged to have guardians appointed in accordance with the laws; see D.38.17.2.28 above and Cod. Theod. 3.18.1 (Constantius, 357).

56 This implies that at the time of Theodosius' law, mothers were supposed to see to the appointment not only of tutors for their children below puberty (*pupilli*) but also curators for minors, i.e. those above puberty but under twenty-five. Cf.

Cod. Just. 5.31.6 (Part II.A.3 below) for the earlier policy. Justinian restored the old policy that mothers were not responsible for the appointment of curators: Beaucamp 1990, 319.

57 Excerpts from this law are found at Cod. Just. 6.58.10, 6.56.6, and 8.14.6. The place of enactment and the addressee (Florentius was praetorian prefect in the east) indicate that this is a law of Theodosius II.

58 That is, Septimius Severus' ruling that a mother must ask for a guardian to be appointed or lose her right to inherit under the *s.c. Tertullianum*.

59 On "interceding," see Chapter 1, Part IV.D. This passage is from Book 29 of Ulpian's commentaries on the Praetor's Edict.

60 Cf. n.56 above. Though preserved separately, Cod. Just. 5.35.1 and 5.31.6 were part of the same rescript, as they have the same addressee and date.

61 Arjava 1996, 89–90; cf. Gardner 1986a, 150–1; and Beaucamp 1990, 327–8, who notes that Cod. Just. 9.41.2 (a rescript of Septimius Severus and Caracalla dated 204) says that slaves should not be heard (in court) against their masters' tutors or mother, unless it is an accusation concerning the guardianship; she believes this implies that mothers could also be tutors.

62 Decreed by Septimius Severus for mothers who did not request tutors; see Part II.A.1 above.

63 See Chiusi 1994, 167–70 on this passage. "Scaevola" is Q. Cervidius Scaevola, writing in the mid–late second century, not Q. Mucius Scaevola, the Republican jurist. "Claudius" is Claudius Tryphoninus, a jurist of the early third century.

64 In another case, where the mother had given an indemnity to the tutor and had since died, her son was told that he had to bring an action against the tutor rather than the mother's heirs (Cod. Just. 5.51.9, 293). Presumably the tutor could claim in his defense that he had been released from liability. See Chiusi 1994, 166–7; Gardner 1998, 250–1.

65 This law was confirmed in the east by Theodosius' grandson, Theodosius II (Novel 11, Part II.A.1 above). Justinian extended Theodosius' law to allow mothers of illegitimate children to serve as their tutors, if their father had not made other provisions in his will, and also enabled grandmothers to undertake the guardianship: Beaucamp 1990, 331.

66 The Justinianic version (Cod. Just. 5.35.2) adds *sacramento praestito* after "avow," specifying that the mother is to make a solemn oath. An oath is also mentioned in Theodosius II's law of 439 (Novel 11.2). See Beaucamp 1990, 333–4.

67 This is a law of Theodosius I, who was in the west at Milan from summer 388 to mid-391. See Honoré 1998, 58–9, who identifies the quaestor who drafted this law as Nicomachus Flavianus, defender of traditional Roman "pagan" religion.

68 Published in *The Oxyrhynchus Papyri* XXXIV, ed. L. Ingrams, P. Kingston, P.J. Parsons, and J.R. Rea (London, 1968), 94–7; see also BL VI, 111 and VIII, 261.

69 For this reading, see H.C. Youtie in *ZPE* 4 (1969), 39; cited in BL VI, 111.

70 The date is 18 February, 206: see BL VIII, 261. The name of Geta, son of Septimius Severus, was deleted after his murder by his brother Caracalla in 212; cf. Chapter 1, n.31.

71 Originally published in *The Oxyrhynchus Papyri* VI, ed. B.P. Grenfell and A.S. Hunt (London, 1906), 247–53, republished in Mitteis and Wilcken 1912 as MChr. 317 and by V. Arangio-Ruiz in *FIRA* III.51, 153–9. I am using the text in Migliardi Zingale (2nd edn., 1991), 84–7. See also BL I, 329 and III, 133 for

restorations to the lacunae in the text. The papyrus is not completely preserved, with the last part of each line missing; in my translation, words between brackets [ ] have been restored where the text is missing; ... indicate missing words. I am not translating the entire will, but only the parts that relate to guardianship and the mother's role.

72 The *exegetes* was a municipal official (see P.Oxy. I.56 in Chapter 1, Part III.C) in Roman Egypt; the prytanis was the head of the town council (*boule*). Note that prytanis is not extant in the text but has been supplied; another suggestion for the lacuna was *enarchos prytanis* (see BL I, 329), "the prytanis in office," but that has not been generally adopted.

73 This refers to Alexander Severus' concession that wills written in Greek were valid under Roman law; see the note of the editors of P.Oxy. VI.907 ad loc.

74 The Latin term *matrona stolata* is here transliterated into Greek. It is a title of respect for women (referring to the *stola* traditionally worn by the respectable Roman matron) and indicates high status; see B. Holtheide, "Matrona Stolata–Femina Stolata," ZPE 38 (1980), 127–31.

75 An aroura was a measurement of land, about 0.68 of an acre.

76 See Chiusi 1994, 177 on this clause. She suggests it is similar to the provision in a marriage contract of 127 (P.Oxy. III.496; see Part II.B.3 below) that says no one is to eject the mother from the guardianship.

77 The Egyptian month Pauni runs from 26 May to 24 June; Epeiph runs from 25 June to 24 July. Hermogenes died less than two months after making this will.

78 There are also many accusations against guardians known from the Egyptian papyri, where the accuser is not the ward's mother, but the ward himself (or herself); for instance, P.Oxy. XXXIV.2713 in Chapter 1, Part IV.C.2.

79 The name "Eglas" is from Égaltein, the Aramaic name for Zoar, the district in which the village of Maoza is located; it is evidently not John's patronymic (Bowersock 1991, 340–1, cited in BL X, 286).

80 All the documents are published in Lewis 1989. For discussion of the case, see Chiusi 1994, 178–91 Cotton 1994 and Lemosse 1968.

81 I translate only the outer text, as in Lewis 1989, 55. The papyrus is very fragmentary (see Plate 8 in Lewis 1989). Rather than mark with brackets all words missing from the papyrus which have been restored, I adopt Lewis' restorations; ... indicate where the papyrus cannot be read or restored. The inner text is of use in restoring the outer text, as is the text of P.Yadin 15, which was written directly after P.Yadin 14.

82 There is a discrepancy in the day according to the Roman calendar (the fourth day before the Ides of October = 12 October) and the Greek (Macedonian) calendar (24 Hyperberataios = 11 October); see Lewis 1989, 57 note ad loc., who thinks 11 October is more likely. Thesrei is the Jewish month.

83 During his year in office, a governor would travel to various cities in his province, hear cases and receive petitions; these assizes are known in Latin as his *conventus* or in Greek (as here), *parousia*.

84 The translation here is from the outer text in Lewis, 1989, 58–60 (cf. Plate 10) with a few restorations based on the inner text when it was better preserved.

85 Cf. the practice of mothers giving security to tutors, as seen in the rescripts Cod. Just. 4.29.6 pr. and 5.46.2 in Part II.A.3 above. See Chiusi 1994, 189–90.

86 Greek *liblarios*. See Chapter 2, Part III.B, n.136.

87 Greek text in Lewis 1989, 116–17 with Plate 36. See also BL IX, 376 for correction of a typographical error in line 15.

88 But see J.R. Rea in *The Oxyrhynchus Papyri* LVIII (London, 1991) at P.Oxy. LVIII.3921: he thinks Julia Crispina was the orphans' mother.

89 In "Julia Crispina, Daughter of Berenicianus, A Herodian Princess in the Babatha Archive: A Case Study in Historical Identification," *Jewish Quarterly Review* LXXXII (1992), 361–81, Tal Ilan suggested that Julia Crispina was the granddaughter of Berenike, the Jewish princess who was for a time the mistress of the emperor Titus. Berenike is known to have named her son Berenikianus, and Julia Crispina is said to be the "daughter of Bernikianus" (sic) in P.Yadin 25. A Julia Crispina is also known from BGU I.53 to have been the absentee landowner of two houses in the village of Euhemeria in the Arsinoite nome in Egypt, and has been identified with the Julia Crispina of P.Yadin 20 and 25; see Lewis 1989, 111, n.2 and Ilan, op. cit., 368–9.

90 P.Med.Bar. 1, published in Montevecchi 1981 (= Montevecchi 1998, 273–85), republished as SB XVI.12720; translation in Rowlandson 1998, 167–8.

91 Marriage contract of 127: P.Oxy. III.496, at lines 10–13. Other contracts: P.Oxy. III.497 (early second century) and P.Oxy. II.265 (81–95 C.E.), where it is added that if the appointed guardian dies, the wife is to be sole guardian.

92 *FIRA* III.47, also in CPL 221 and Migliardi Zingale 1988, 22–6; translation in Campbell 1994, 158–9. A wax tablet polyptych in Latin, dated 142. As Campbell notes, Antonia Thermutha is called the boy's mother, not Silvanus' wife. As a soldier in the second century, he could not legally marry, but he could make his illegitimate child heir in his will; see Chapter 3, Part I.C.4.

93 Text used is *The Oxyrhynchus Papyri* VI, ed. B.P Grenfell and A.S. Hunt (London, 1908), 221–2.

94 For the "royal scribe" (*basilikos grammateus*) also acting for the strategos (a nome official), cf. P.Oxy. I.56 (211 C.E.) in Chapter 1, Part III.C.

95 See editors' note ad loc. Matrina wanted Didymus to absolve her from all responsibility for mismanagement of the guardianship.

96 Van Bremen 1996, 228–30. A third-century B.C.E. inscription from the Aegean also mentions a woman as *prostatis*, perhaps in a quasi-guardian function as in Ptolemaic Egypt: see O. Montevecchi, "Ancora su Prostates-Prostatis," in Montevecchi 1998, 287–90 (orig. pub. 1989).

97 Though Lycia did not become a Roman province until the reign of Claudius (41–54 C.E.), after the date of this inscription, it had come into the Roman sphere of influence earlier.

98 The Greek text of the inscription is found in Balland 1981, 251; see also *New Documents Illustrating Early Christianity* vol. 6, ed. S.R. Llewellyn with R.A. Kearsley (Sydney: Macquarie University, 1992), 24.

99 Balland restored the inscription from the Xanthians (VII.80) to show that Senbreidase's husband had been her first cousin; such intermarriage among leading families was not at all uncommon in the cities of Asia Minor in the early Empire: Balland 1981, 253–4; cf. van Bremen 1996, 229 and 258.

100 "Second" in relation to the honors accorded her by the Xanthians on the accompanying inscription; cf. Balland 1981, 252–3.

101 *Supplementum Epigraphicum Graecum* (*SEG*) VI.672 (1932). On the honoring of women benefactors, see Chapter 1, Part VI.C.

102 P.Oxy. VI.909, lines 1–13, dated 225. Originally published by Grenfell and Hunt in 1908 (n.93 above), republished in Hunt and Edgar, *Select Papyri* no. 35.

103 SB V.7558; also in *FIRA* III.30 and *Select Papyri* no. 260. See also BL III, 189; IV, 80; VII, 195 and the revised text by H.C. Youtie, "P.Mich.Inv. 2922 = Sammelbuch V.7558," *ZPE* 13 (1974), 241–8. This is actually a request for release from the guardianship by one of the two men appointed *epitropoi*.

104 P.Oxy. LVIII.3921, ed. J.R. Rea (cited at n.88 above); cf. Lewis 1993, 31–3.

105 I use the Greek text in Parássoglou 1978 (on which see the review by R. Bagnall, *BASP* 17 [1980], 97–104). The papyrus is broken off at the left side, so a number of words are lost but have been restored. I do not bracket the restorations in my translation, since there are so many and most are uncontroversial (but see BL VI, 123, VII, 176; VIII, 300, IX, 230). P.Sakaon 36 was first published as P.Ryl. II.114 (ed. J. de M. Johnson, V. Martin, and A.S. Hunt, Manchester, 1915), and is also in Hunt and Edgar 1932–4, vol. II, no. 293.

106 The age denoted by *aphelix* ("underage") in the later third century is unclear. Earlier it was synonymous with Latin *impubes*, denoting a boy under fourteen or a girl under twelve. At least some of the children must be under fourteen; otherwise it would be absurd for her to call them *nepioi* (but cf. Beaucamp 1992, 173–4; one son may have been almost twenty-five!).

107 In Greek, *to metrophiles*. The meaning of this word has been debated. Parássoglou 1978, 86 translates it as "love of equity;" P.J. Parsons prefers "your love of humble people" (in *Journal of Egyptian Archaeology* 71 [1985], 210, cited in BL VIII, 300); M. Blume says "ton amour de la mesure" (in *Egitto e storia antica dall' ellenismo all'età araba* [Bologna, 1989], 279–81, cited BL IX, 230). In any case, it is meant to be flattering and to stress the prefect's probity.

108 This is the prefect's subscription to the petition, which was then pasted as the 69th sheet in a roll of petitions to be kept in the prefect's office.

109 P.Sakaon 31 was first published in Jouguet 1911 as P.Thead. 15, and is also in *Select Papyri* II, no.262; cf. BL I, 430. I follow the Greek text in Parássoglou 1978, 68–71. (Note that Crook 1995, 101–2 uses Jouguet's text of P.Thead. 15).

110 The Greek translation of the Latin procurator is *epitropos*, but here it means an imperial official; cf. Crook 1995, 101 n.182.

111 See Part II.A and Chapter 1, Part V.B. Beaucamp 1992, 21–8 discusses cases where women in late antique Egypt go to court; cf. also her Annexe III (pp. 389–93) of women in the papyri who appear in court. In all cases women are acting either in their own interests and/or those of close family members; in no case do women represent others apart from their children or minor relatives. (Thus the evidence of the papyri and the strictures of Roman law actually coincide: see Chapter 1, Parts V.A and B.) Aurelia Artemis is unusual in acting on behalf of others [Beaucamp 1992, 24], but of course they are her own children, whose father is dead (and her own interests are also involved).

112 A word cannot be read here; proposed readings include "having appeared" (as in Hunt and Edgar 1932–4) or "being dead" (cf. app. crit. in Parássoglou 1978; Crook 1995, 101), which cannot be the case, since Aurelia Artemis was still alive more than twenty years later.

113 P.Sakaon 37 was first published in Jouguet 1911 as P.Thead. 18. It is quite fragmentary, and there are many restorations. I follow the text in Parássoglou 1978, 87–90, except where noted. See also BL I, 430; V, 148; VII, 176; VIII, 300.

114 The functions of the *hypomnematographos* ("recorder"?) are unclear. Here he is evidently acting as strategos: see Jouguet 1911, 113–14.

115 Or, "so that you might order the strategos by means of your sacred subscription": see G. Foti Talamanca, *Ricerche sul processo nell'Egitto greco-romano* II.1 (Milan: Giuffre, 1979), 137 n.238 (cited at BL VIII, 300).

116 This is the notation made by the prefect's office; see n.108 above. Hathyr runs from 28 October to 26 November (of the year 283).

117 See BL V, 148 and VII, 176. Mecheir runs from 26 January to 24 February (284). The day is missing.

118 *De inspiciendo ventre custodiendoque partu.* The Latin word *venter* can mean "stomach," "womb," or "the unborn child." See Thomas 1986, 211–14. My translation varies according to what sounds more appropriate in English.

119 *Excutio* can mean either "drive out" or "search." "Search" is preferable here.

120 The Latin word *parens* can mean father or mother, or even some other relative; see D.50.16.51 (Gaius) in Chapter 1, Part I.B. Here it evidently refers to the child's deceased father, who might have made provision in his will for children yet to be born. This passage suggests that a fatherless child might live with someone other than its mother; see Gardner 1984, 133.

121 The heir "instituted in the first grade" would be the person named in the will as heir. The testator could also name a "substitute" heir to inherit if for some reason the heir in the first grade could not inherit (perhaps because he or she had died since the making of the will) or refused the inheritance.

122 Watson 1974b, 31–62 points out that though it is very difficult to know when individual edicts were first introduced into the Praetor's Edict, an *edictum de inspiciendo ventre*, dealing with the inspection of pregnant women, was known already to the republican jurist Sulpicius Rufus (died 43 B.C.E.). On the date of the *s.c. Plancianum*, see Chapter 4, n.25.

123 *Andria*, lines 770–1. This was in response to a claim that a baby had been smuggled in during the alleged birth (see Part III.B below).

124 *Liber venter.* Here *venter* clearly means "unborn offspring" (cf. n.118). *Liber* can mean either "child" or "free;" here the the latter is more likely.

125 On *bonorum possessio contra tabulas*, see Buckland 1963, 382 ff.; Schulz 1951, 270–4.

126 The following passages (D.37.9.27; D.25.6.1; D.3.2.15–19) are all from juristic commentaries on the Praetor's Edict.

127 On "pupillary substitution" (naming a substitute heir for a child who was a *pupillus*, that is, below puberty) and "second tablets," see Schulz 1951, 263.

128 In the following sentence (not translated here), Papinian says that he replied (i.e, to the person who had consulted him) that if the deceased's nephews lost the case, they should not inherit even as substitute heirs.

129 The emperors were actually Theodosius I and his sons Arcadius, and Honorius. This is a law of Theodosius I.

130 This was part of a longer law, other excerpts from which are at Cod. Theod. 2.12.5 (see Chapter 1, Part IV.E); Cod. Theod. 4.8.9.; and Cod. Theod. 11.30.50. Cod. Theod. 4.3.1 is found also in Cod. Just. 6.17.2.

131 For pregnant women in the papyri, see S. Adam "La femme enceinte dans les papyrus," *Anagennesis. A Papyrological Journal* 3 (1983), 9–19; and Montevecchi 1998, 259–64 (orig. pub. 1979).

132 The text used is W. Schubart, ed., *Aegyptische Urkunden aus den königlichen Museen zu Berlin: Griechische Urkunden Band IV* (Berlin, 1912). Lacunae in the papyrus are indicated by …

133 On infant exposure, see Harris 1994; cf. D.40.4.29 in Chapter 4, Part I.E.2 for a pregnant divorcée who exposed her child.

134 Year 21 of Augustus' reign, 10 B.C.E. The Egyptian month Phaophi runs from 28 September to 27 October. The agreement is their marriage contract, now made null and void.

135 8 B.C.E. The month Pachon runs from 26 April to 25 May. In the Roman period, the Egyptian year began at the end of August, so this is eighteen months after Dionysarion and her husband made the marriage agreement.

136 P.Gen. II.103–4 are published in *Les Papyrus de Genève, Part II*, ed. C. Wehrli (Geneva, 1986), 76–80; for corrections see Wehrli in *ZPE* 67 (1987), 117–18; BL VIII, 13; IX, 91. For a translation see Rowlandson 1998, 289–91; discussion ibid. and in Hanson 2000, 138–9; cf. Gardner 1984.

137 P.Gen. II.104 mentions Antonioi, Diogenes and at least one other, "on the female side." Gardner 1984, 133 notes that if Petronilla's mother-in-law had the *ius liberorum*, she would have been able to succeed to her son under the recently enacted *s.c. Tertullianum* (see chapter Introduction) if he had no legitimate children and no brothers.

138 Published in *A Family Archive from Tebtunis (P.Fam.Tebt.)*, ed. B.A. van Gronigen (Leiden, 1950), 70–5. Translation in Rowlandson 1998, 180–1.

BIBLIOGRAPHY

Anagnostou-Cañas, B. (1984) "La femme devant la justice provinciale dans l'Egypte romaine," *RHDFE* 62, 337–60.

Arangio-Ruiz, V. (1956) "Due Nuove Tavolette di Ercolano relative alla Nomina di Tutori Muliebri," in *Studi in onore di Pietro de Francisci vol. 1*, Milan: Giuffrè, 3–17.

Archer, L. (1990) *Her Price is Beyond Rubies: The Jewish Woman in Greco-Roman Palestine*, Sheffield: JSOT Press.

Arjava, A. (1988) "Divorce in Later Roman Law," *Arctos* 22, 5–21.

—— (1991) "Zum Gebrauch der griechischen Rangprädikate des Senatorenstandes in den Papyri und Inschriften," *Tyche* 6, 17–35.

—— (1996) *Women and Law in Late Antiquity*, Oxford: Clarendon Press.

—— (1997) "The Guardianship of Women in Roman Egypt," in B. Kramer, W. Luppe, H. Maehler, and G. Poethke (eds.), *Akten des 21. Internationalen Papyrologenkongresses Berlin I*, Stuttgart and Leipzig: Teubner, 25–30.

—— (1998) "Paternal Power in Late Antiquity," *JRS* 88, 147–65.

Arnaoutoglou, I. (1994) "Marital Disputes in Greco-Roman Egypt," *Journal of Juristic Papyri* 25, 11–28.

Bagnall, R. (1987) "Church, State and Divorce in Late Roman Egypt," in Robert E. Somervile and Karl-Ludwig Selig (eds.), *Florilegium Columbianum: Essays in Honor of Paul Oskar Kristeller*, New York, 41–61.

—— (1993) *Egypt in Late Antiquity*, Princeton: Princeton University Press.

Bagnall, R., Cameron, A., Schwartz, S.R., and Worp, K.A. (1987) *Consuls of the Later Roman Empire*, Atlanta: Scholars Press.

Bagnall, R. and Frier, B.W. (1994) *The Demography of Roman Egypt*, Cambridge: Cambridge University Press.

Balland, A. (1981) *Fouilles de Xanthos VII. Inscriptions d'époque impériale du Létôon*, Paris.

Barnes, T.D. (1982) *The New Empire of Diocletian and Constantine*, Cambridge, MA: Harvard University Press.

Barnish, S.J.B. (1988) "Transformation and Survival in the Western Senatorial Aristocracy, c. A.D. 400–700," *PBSR* 56, 120–55.

Beaucamp, J. (1976) "Le Vocabulaire de la faiblesse feminine dans les textes juridiques romains du IIIe au VIe siècle," *RHDFE* 54, 485–508.

—— (1990) *Le statut de la femme à Byzance (4e–7e siècle). I. Le droit impérial*, Paris: de Boccard.

—— (1992) *Le statut de la femme à Byzance (4e–7e siècle). II. Les pratiques sociales*, Paris: de Boccard.

Boak, A. (1926) "Alimentary Contracts from Tebtunis," *Journal of Egyptian Archaeology* 12, 100–9.

Boatwright, M.T. (1991) "Plancia Magna of Perge: Women's Roles and Status in Roman Asia Minor," in S. Pomeroy (ed.), *Women's History and Ancient History*, Chapel Hill: University of North Carolina Press.

Bowersock, G. (1991) "The Babatha Papyri, Masada, and Rome," *Journal of Roman Archaeology* 4, 336–44.

Bradley, K.R. (1987) *Slaves and Masters in the Roman Empire: A Study in Social Control*, New York and Oxford: Oxford University Press; orig. pub. 1984.

—— (1994) *Slavery and Society at Rome*, Cambridge: Cambridge University Press.

—— (1997) "Law, Magic, and Culture in the *Apologia* of Apuleius," *Phoenix* 51, 203–23.

Bremen, R. van (1983) "Women and Wealth," in A. Cameron and A. Kuhrt (eds.), *Images of Women in Antiquity*, Detroit: Wayne State University Press.

—— (1996) *The Limits of Participation: Women and Civic Life in the Greek East in the Hellenistic and Roman Periods*, Amsterdam: J.C. Gieben.

Brown, P. (1967) *Augustine of Hippo: A Biography*, Berkeley and Los Angeles: University of California Press.

Buckland, W.W. (1908) *The Roman Law of Slavery*, Cambridge: Cambridge University Press; repr. New York: AMS Press, 1969.

—— (1963) *A Textbook of Roman Law from Augustus to Justinian*, Cambridge: Cambridge University Press; 3rd edn. rev. P. Stein.

Campbell, B. (1978) "The Marriage of Soldiers under the Empire," *JRS* 68, 153–66.

—— (1984) *The Emperor and the Roman Army*, Oxford: Clarendon Press.

—— (1994) *The Roman Army, 31 B.C.–A.D. 337: A Sourcebook*, London and New York: Routledge.

Champlin, E. (1991) *Final Judgments: Duty and Emotion in Roman Wills*, Berkeley and Los Angeles: University of California Press.

Chastagnol, A. (1979) "Les femmes dans l'ordre sénatorial: titulature et rang social à Rome," *Revue Historique* 262, 3–28.

—— (1982) "Dioclétien et les 'Clarissimae Feminae,'" in *Studi in onore di Arnaldo Biscardi II*, Milan.

Chiusi, T.J. (1994) "Zur Vormundschaft der Mutter," *ZSSR.RA* 111, 155–96.

Clark, E.G. (1979) *Jerome, Chrysostom, and Friends: Essays and Translations*, New York and Toronto: Edwin Mellen Press.

—— (1981) "Ascetic Renunciation and Feminine Advancement: A Paradox of Late Ancient Christianity," *Anglican Theological Review* 63, 240–57.

Clark, G. (1993) *Women in Late Antiquity: Pagan and Christian Lifestyles*, Oxford: Oxford University Press.

Cloke, G. (1995) *This Female Man of God: Women and Spiritual Power in the Patristic Age, AD 350–450*, London and New York: Routledge.

Corbett, P.E. (1930) *The Roman Law of Marriage*, Oxford: Clarendon Press.

Corcoran, S. (1996) *The Empire of the Tetrarchs: Imperial Pronouncements and Government A.D. 284–324*, Oxford: Clarendon Press.

—— (2000) "The Sins of the Fathers: A Neglected Constitution of Diocletian on Incest," *The Journal of Legal History* 21 (2), 1–34.

Cotton, H. (1993) "The Guardianship of Jesus son of Babatha: Roman and Local Law in the Province of Arabia," *JRS* 83, 94–108.

—— (1994) "A Cancelled Marriage Contract from the Judaean Desert (XHev/Se Gr. 2)," *JRS* 84, 64–86.

—— (1997) "The Guardian (ἐπίτροπος) of a Woman in the Documents from the Judaean Desert," *ZPE* 118, 267–73.

Cotton, H. and Yardeni, A. (1997) *Aramaic, Hebrew and Greek Documentary Texts from Nahal Hever and other Sites (DJD XXVII)*, Oxford: Clarendon Press.

Crawford, M.H. (ed.) (1996) *Roman Statutes*, London: Institute of Classical Studies.

Crook, J. (1967) *Law and Life of Rome*, Ithaca: Cornell University Press.

—— (1986a) "Feminine Inadequacy and the *senatusconsultum Velleianum*," in Rawson 1986a, 83–92.

—— (1986b) "Women in Roman Succession," in Rawson 1986a, 58–82.

—— (1995) *Legal Advocacy in the Roman World*, Ithaca: Cornell University Press.

Crouzel, H. (1971) *L'Église primitive face à divorce*, Paris: Beauchesne.

Daube, D. (1966) "Dividing a Child in Antiquity," *California Law Review* 54, 1630–7.

Delia, D. (1991) *Alexandrian Citizenship during the Roman Principate*, Atlanta: Scholars Press.

Dixon, S. (1984) "*Infirmitas Sexus*: Womanly Weakness in Roman Law," *Tijdschrift voor Rechtsgeschiedenis* 52, 343–71.

—— (1988) *The Roman Mother*, London and Norman: University of Oklahoma Press.

—— (1992) *The Roman Family*, Baltimore: Johns Hopkins University Press.

—— (1997) "Conflict in the Roman Family," in Rawson and Weaver 1997, 149–67.

Donahue, C. (1979) "The Case of the Man Who Fell into the Tiber: The Roman Law of Marriage at the Time of the Glossators," *American Journal of Legal History* 22, 1–53.

Duncan-Jones, R. (1982) *The Economy of the Roman Empire: Quantitative Studies*, Cambridge: Cambridge University Press, 2nd edn.

Dyson, S. (1992) *Community and Society in Roman Italy*, Baltimore: Johns Hopkins University Press.

Evans Grubbs, J.A. (1989) "Abduction Marriage in Antiquity: A Law of Constantine (CTh 9.24.1) and its Social Context," *JRS* 79, 59–83.

—— (1993) "'Marriage More Shameful than Adultery': Slave–Mistress Relationships, 'Mixed Marriages,' and Late Roman Law," *Phoenix*, 125–54.

—— (1995) *Law and Family in Late Antiquity: The Emperor Constantine's Marriage Legislation*, Oxford: Clarendon Press.

—— (2001) "Virgins and Widows, Show-girls and Whores: Late Roman Legislation on Women and Christianity," in R. Mathisen (ed.), *Law, Society, and Authority in Late Antiquity*, Oxford: Oxford University Press, 220–41.

—— (2002) "*Stigmata Aeterna*: A Husband's Curse," in C. Damon, K.S. Myers, and J. Miller (eds.), *Vertis in usum. Studies in Honor of Edward Courtney*, Leipzig: K.G. Saur Verlag, 230–42.

Fantham, E. (1995) "Aemilia Pudentilla: Or The Wealthy Widow's Choice," in R. Hawley and B. Levick (eds.), *Women in Antiquity: New Assessments*, London and New York: Routledge, 220–32.

Feissel, D. and Gascou, J. (1989) "Documents d'archives romains inédits du Moyen Euphrate (IIIe siècle après J.-C.)," *Académie des Inscriptions et Belles-Lettres, Comptes Rendus*, 535–61.

—— (1995) "Documents d'archives romains inédits du Moyen Euphrate (IIIe siècle après J.-C.)," *Journal des Savants*, 65–119.

Flory, M.B. (1978) "Family in *familia*: Kinship and Community in Slavery," *American Journal of Ancient History* 3, 78–95.

—— (1984) "Where Women Precede Men: Factors Influencing the Order of Names in Roman Epitaphs," *Classical Journal* 79 (216–224).

Forbis, E. (1990) "Women's Public Image in Italian Honorary Inscriptions," *American Journal of Philology* 111, 493–512.

Gardner, J.F. (1984) "A Family and an Inheritance: The Problems of the Widow Petronilla," *Liverpool Classical Monthly* 9.9, 132–3.

—— (1986a) *Women in Roman Law and Society*, London: Croom Helm.

—— (1986b) "Proofs of Status in the Roman World," *Bulletin of the Institute of Classical Studies* 33, 1–14.

—— (1993) *Being a Roman Citizen*, London and New York: Routledge.

—— (1995) "Gender-Role Assumptions in Roman Law," *EMC/CV* 39, n.s. 14, 377–400.

—— (1997) "Legal Stumbling-Blocks for Lower-Class Families in Rome," in Rawson and Weaver 1997, 35–53.

—— (1998) *Family and Familia in Roman Law and Life*, Oxford: Clarendon Press.

—— (1999) "Women in Business Life: Some Evidence from Puteoli," in P. Setala and L. Savunen (eds.), *Female Networks and the Public Sphere in Roman Society*, Rome: Acta Instituti Romani Finlandiae vol. XXII, 11–27.

Gardner, J.F. and Wiedemann, T. (1991) *The Roman Household: A Sourcebook*, London and New York: Routledge.

Garnsey, P. (1967) "Adultery Trials and the Survival of the Quaestiones in the Severan Age," *JRS* 57, 56–60.

—— (1970) *Social Status and Legal Privilege in the Roman Empire*, Oxford: Clarendon Press.

Garnsey, P. and Saller, R. (1987) *The Roman Empire: Economy, Society and Culture*, Berkeley: University of California Press.

Gaudemet, J. (1945) "Le mariage en droit romain: *justum matrimonium*," in Gaudemet 1980 (orig. pub. 1949), 309–66.

—— (1959) "Le statut de la femme dans l'Empire romain," in *"La femme": Recueils de la Société Jean Bodin XI*, Brussels, 191–222; reprint in *Études du droit romain*, vol. 3 (1979).

—— (1980) *Sociétés et mariage*, Strasbourg.

Gonzalez, J. (1986) "The Lex Irnitana: A New Copy of the Flavian Municipal Law," *JRS* 76, 147–243.

Goody, J. (1983) *The Development of the Family and Marriage in Europe*, Cambridge: Cambridge University Press.

Gordon, W.M. and Robinson, O.F. (trans.) (1988) *The Institutes of Gaius*, Ithaca: Cornell University Press.

Hanson, A.E. (1987) "The Eight Months' Child and the Etiquette of Birth: Obsit Omen!," *Bulletin of the History of Medicine* 61, 589–602.

—— (1991) "Ancient Illiteracy," in *Literacy in the Roman world*, Ann Arbor: *Journal of Roman Archaeology*, Supplementary Series, no. 3, 159–98.

—— (1994) "A Division of Labor: Roles for Men in Greek and Roman Births," *Thamyris* 1, 157–202.

—— (2000) "Widows too Young in their Widowhood," in D.E.E. Kleiner and S.B. Matheson (eds.), *I, Claudia II: Women in Roman Art and Society*, Austin: University of Texas Press, 149–65.

Harries, J. (1999) *Law and Empire in Late Antiquity*, Cambridge: Cambridge University Press.

Harris, W. (1986) "The Roman Father's Power of Life and Death," in R.S. Bagnall and W.V. Harris (eds.), *Studies in Roman Law in Memory of A. Arthur Schiller*, Leiden: E.J. Brill, 81–95.

—— (1994) "Child-Exposure in the Roman Empire," *JRS* 84, 1–22.

Harrison, S.J. (2000) *Apuleius: A Latin Sophist*, Oxford: Oxford University Press.

Honoré, T. (1994) *Emperors and Lawyers*, Oxford: Clarendon Press, 2nd edn.

—— (1998) *Law in the Crisis of Empire 379–455 A.D.: The Theodosian Dynasty and its Quaestors*, Oxford: Clarendon Press.

Hopkins, K. (1964) "The Age of Roman Girls at Marriage," *Population Studies* 18, 309–27.

—— (1980) "Brother–Sister Marriage in Roman Egypt," *Comparative Studies in Society and History* 22, 303–54.

—— (1983) *Death and Renewal*, Cambridge: Cambridge University Press.

Horsfall, N. (1983) "Some Problems in the 'Laudatio Turiae,'" *Bulletin of the Institute for Classical Studies* 30, 85–98.

Humbert, M. (1972) *Le Remariage à Rome: Étude d'histoire juridique et sociale*, Milan: Giuffrè.

Hunink, V. (ed.) (1997) *Apuleius of Madauros: Pro Se de Magia (Apologia) edited with a Commentary*, Amsterdam: J.C. Gieben.

—— (1998) "The Enigmatic Lady Pudentilla," *American Journal of Philology* 119, 275–91.

Hunt, A.S. and Edgar, C.C. (1932–4) *Select Papyri vols. I and II*, Cambridge, MA: Harvard University Press.

Ilan, T. (1995) *Jewish Women in Greco-Roman Palestine*, Peabody, MA: Hendricks.

Johnston, D. (1999) *Roman Law in Context*, Cambridge: Cambridge University Press.

Jolowicz, H.F. and B. Nicholas (1972) *Historical Introduction to the Study of Roman Law*, Cambridge: Cambridge University Press, 3rd edn.

Jones, A.H.M. (1964) *The Later Roman Empire 284–602*, Oxford: Basil Blackwell; repr. 1986, Baltimore: Johns Hopkins University Press.

Jouguet, P. (1911) *Papyrus de Théadelphie*, Paris: Fontemoing & Cie.

Kajava, M. (1990) "A New City Patroness?," *Tyche* 5, 27–36.

Katzoff, R. (1995a) "Hellenistic Marriage Contracts," in M.J. Geller and H. Maehler (eds) with A.D.E. Lewis, *Legal Documents of the Hellenistic World*, London: Warburg Institute, University of London.

—— (1995b) "Polygamy in P.Yadin?," *ZPE* 109, 128–32.

Keppie, L. (1991) *Understanding Roman Inscriptions*, Baltimore: Johns Hopkins University Press.

Kunkel, W., and J.M. Kelly (trans.) (1973) *An Introduction to Roman Legal and Constitutional History*, Oxford: Clarendon Press, 2nd edn.

Lattimore, R. (1962) *Themes in Greek and Latin Epitaphs*, Urbana: University of Illinois Press.

Lee, A.D. (1988) "Close-Kin Marriage in Late Antique Mesopotamia," *Greek, Roman, and Byzantine Studies* 29, 403–13.

Lemosse, M. (1968) "Le Procès de Babatha," *The Irish Jurist* 3, 363–76.

Lewis, A. (1986) "Digest 23.2.6," in N. MacCormick and P. Birks (eds.), *The Legal Mind: Essays for Tony Honoré*, Oxford: Clarendon Press.

Lewis, N. (1970) "Instructions for Appointing a Guardian," *BASP* 7, 116–18.

—— (1978) "The Imperial Apokrimata," *RIDA* 25, 261–78.

—— (1983) *Life in Egypt under Roman Rule*, Oxford: Oxford University Press.

—— (1989) *The Documents from the Bar Kokhba Period in the Cave of Letters: Greek Papyri*, Jerusalem: Israel Exploration Society.

—— (1993) "Notationes Legentis," *BASP* 30, 27–33.

Lewis, N., Katzoff, R., and Greenfield, J. (1987) "Paprus Yadin 18," *Israeli Exploration Journal* 37, 229–50.

Linder, A. (1987) *The Jews in Roman Imperial Legislation*, Detroit: Wayne State University Press.

Lintott, A. (1993) *Imperium Romanum: Politics and Administration*, London and New York: Routledge.

Looper-Friedman, S. (1987) "The Decline of *Manus*-marriage in Rome," *Tijdschrift voor Rechtsgeschiedenis* 55, 281–96.

McGinn, T.A.J. (1991) "Concubinage and the *Lex Julia* on Adultery," *TAPA* 121, 335–75.

—— (1997) "The Legal Definition of Prostitute in Late Antiquity," *Memoirs of the American Academy in Rome* 42, 73–116.

—— (1998) *Prostitution, Sexuality, and the Law in Ancient Rome*, New York and Oxford: Oxford University Press.

—— (1999) "The Social Policy of Emperor Constantine in *Codex Theodosianus* 4,6,3," *Tijdschrift voor Rechtsgeschiedenis* 67, 57–73.

MacMullen, R. (1980) "Woman in Public in the Roman Empire," *Historia* 29, 208–18; repr. in *Changes in the Roman Empire*, New Haven: Yale University Press, 1990.

—— (1986) "Women's Power in the Principate," *Klio*, 68, 434–43; repr. in *Changes in the Roman Empire*, New Haven, 1990.

Mackie, N. (1990) "Urban munificence and the growth of urban consciousness in Roman Spain," in T. Blaggs and M. Millett (eds.), *The Early Roman Empire in the West*, Oxford: Oxbow Books.

Marshall, A. J. (1989) "Ladies at Law: The Role of Women in the Roman Civil Courts," in C. Deroux (ed.), *Studies in Latin Literature and Roman History V*, Brussels: Latomus.

—— (1990a) "Women on Trial before the Roman Senate," *EMC/CV*, n.s. 34, 333–66.

—— (1990b) "Roman Ladies on Trial: The Case of Maesia of Sentinum," *Phoenix* 44, 46–59.

Matthews, J. (1975) *Western Aristocracies and Imperial Court*, Oxford: Clarendon Press; repr. Oxford, 1990.

Migliardi Zingale, L. (1988) *I Testamenti Romani nei Papiri e nelle Tavolette d'Egitto: Silloge di documenti del I al IV secolo D.C.*, Torino: Giappichelli.

Millar, F. (1977) *The Emperor in the Roman World 31 B.C.–A.D. 337*, Ithaca: Cornell University Press; rev. edn., 1992.

—— (1983) "Empire and City, Augustus to Julian: Obligations, Excuses and Status," *JRS* 73, 76–96.

—— (1984) "Condemnation to Hard Labour in the Roman Empire, from the Julio-Claudians to Constantine," *PBSR* 52, 124–47.

—— (1993) *The Roman Near East 31 B.C. – A.D. 337*, Cambridge, MA: Harvard University Press.

Mitteis, L. and Wilcken, U. (1912) *Grundzüge und Chrestomathie der Papyruskunde II. Juristischer Teil*, Leipzig and Berlin: Teubner.

Modrzejewski, J.M. (1961) "Les Juifs et le droit hellénistique: Divorce et égalité des époux (CPJud. 144)," *Iura* 12, 162–93.

—— (1970) "La règle de droit dans l'Egypte romaine," in D.H. Samuel (ed.), *Proceedings of the Twelfth International Congress of Papyrology*, Toronto: A.M. Hakkert, 317–77.

—— (1974) "À propos de la tutelle dative des femmes dans l'Egypte romaine," in *Akten des XIII Internationalen Papyrologenkongresses*, Munich: Münchener Beiträge zur Papyrusforschung und antiken Rechtsgesichte, 66, 263–92.

—— (1993) "La structure juridique du mariage grec," in *Statut personnel et liens de famille dans les droits de l'Antiquité*, Aldershot: Variorum, 39–71; orig. pub. 1981.

—— (1995) "Jewish Law and Hellenistic Legal Practice in the Light of Greek Papyri from Egypt," in *Collatio Iuris Romani: Études dédiées à Hans Ankum à l'occasion de son 65e anniversaire*, ed. R. Feenstra, A.S. Hartkamop, J.E. Spruit, P.J. Sijpsteijn, and L.C. Winkel, vol. I, Amsterdam: J.C. Gieben, 299–315.

Montevecchi, O. (1936) "Ricerche di sociologia nei documenti dell'Egitto greco-romano. II. I contratti di matrimonio e gli atti di divorzio," *Aegyptus* 16, 3–83.

—— (1981) "Una donna 'prostatis' del figlio minorenne in un papiro del IIa," *Aegyptus* 61, 103–15; repr. in Montevecchi 1998, 273–85.

—— (1988) *La Papirologia*, Milan, 2nd edn..

—— (1998) *Scripta Selecta*, ed. S. Daris., Milan: Universita Cattolica.

Nicols, J. (1989) "*Patrona Civitatis*: Gender and Civic Patronage," in C. Deroux (ed.), *Studies in Latin Literature and Roman History V*, Brussels:

Nicholas, B. (1962) *An Introduction to Roman Law*, Oxford: Clarendon Press.

Noy, D. (1990) "Matchmakers and Marriage-Markets in Antiquity," *EMC/CV* 38, n.s. 9, 375–400.

Oliver, J.H. (ed.) (1989) *Greek Constitutions of Early Roman Emperors from Inscriptions and Papyri*, Philadelphia: American Philosophical Society.

Parásoglou, G.M. (1978) *The Archive of Aurelius Sakaon: Papers of an Egyptian Farmer in the Last Century of Theadelphia*, Bonn: Rudolf Habelt Verlag GmbH.

Parkin, T.G. (1992) *Demography and Roman Society*, Baltimore: Johns Hopkins University Press.

Pestman, P.W. (1994) *The New Papyrological Primer*, Leiden: E.J. Brill, 2nd edn.

Pharr, C. (ed. and trans.) (1952) *The Theodosian Code*, Princeton: Princeton University Press.

Pleket, H.W. (ed.) (1969) *Epigraphica vol II. Texts on the Social History of the Greek World*, Leiden: E.J. Brill.

Purcell, N. (1983) "The *Apparitores*: A Study in Social Mobility," *PBSR* 51, 125–73.

Rabello, A.M. (1981) "Divorce of Jews in the Roman Empire," *Jewish Law Annual* 4, 79–102.

Raepsaet-Charlier, M.-T. (1981) "*Clarissima femina,*" *RIDA* 28, 189–212.

—— (1993) "Nouvelles recherches sur les femmes sénatoriales du Haut-Empire romain," *Klio* 75, 257–71.

Rawson, B. (1966) "Family Life Among the Lower Classes at Rome in the First Two Centuries of the Empire," *Classical Philology* 61, 71–83.

—— (1974) "Roman Concubinage and Other *de facto* Marriages," *TAPA* 104, 279–305.

—— (ed.) (1986a) *The Family in Ancient Rome: New Perspectives*, Ithaca: Cornell University Press.

—— (1986b) "Children in the Roman *Familia,*" in Rawson 1986a, 170–200.

—— (ed.) (1991) *Marriage, Divorce and Children in Ancient Rome*, Oxford: Clarendon Press.

Rawson, B. and Weaver, P. (eds.) (1997) *The Roman Family in Italy: Status, Sentiment, Space*, Oxford: Clarendon Press.

Robinson, O.F. (1995) *The Criminal Law of Ancient Rome*, Baltimore: Johns Hopkins University Press.

—— (1997) *The Sources of Roman Law: Problems and Methods for Ancient Historians*, London and New York: Routledge.

Rogers, Guy (1992) "The Constructions of Women at Ephesos," *ZPE* 90, 215–23.

Rowlandson, J. (1996) *Landowners and Tenants in Roman Egypt*, Oxford: Clarendon Press.

—— (ed.) (1998) *Women and Society in Greek and Roman Egypt: A Sourcebook*, Cambridge: Cambridge University Press.

Rupprecht, H.-A. (1998) "Marriage Contract Regulations and Documentary Practice in the Greek Papyri," *Scripta Classica Israelica* 17, 60–76.

Saller, R.P. (1984) "Roman Dowry and the Devolution of Property in the Principate," *Classical Quarterly* 34, 195–205.

—— (1986) "*Patria potestas* and the Stereotype of the Roman Family," *Continuity and Change* 1, 7–22.

—— (1987) "Men's Age at Marriage and its Consequences in the Roman Family," *Classical Philology*, 82, 21–34.

—— (1994) *Patriarchy, Property and Death in the Roman Family*, Cambridge: Cambridge University Press.

—— (1999) "*Pater Familias, Mater Familias*, and the Gendered Semantics of the Household," *Classical Philology* 94, 182–97.

Schulz, F. (1951) *Classical Roman Law*, Oxford: Clarendon Press.

Seeck, O. (1919) *Regesten der Kaiser und Päpste für die Jahre 311 bis 476 n. Chr.*, Stuttgart: J.B. Metzlersche.

Shackleton-Bailey, D.R. (ed.) (2000) *Valerius Maximus: Memorable Doings and Sayings*, Cambridge, MA: Harvard University Press (Loeb Classical Library).

Shaw, B.D. (1987a) "The Age of Roman Girls at Marriage: Some Reconsiderations," *JRS* 77, 30–46.

—— (1987b) "The Family in Late Antiquity: The Experience of Augustine," *Past and Present* 115, 3–51.

Shaw, B.D. and Saller, R. (1984) "Close-Kin Marriage in Roman Society?," *Man*, n.s. 19, 432–44.

Sheridan, J. (1996) "Women without Guardians: An Updated List," *BASP* 33, 117–31.

—— (1998) "Not at a Loss for Words: The Economic Power of Literate Women in Late Antique Egypt," *TAPA* 128, 189–203.

Sijpesteijn, P.J. (1965) 'Die ΧΩΡΙΣ ΚΥΡΙΟΥ ΧΡΗΜΑΤΙΖΟΥΣΑΙ ΔΙΚΑΙΩ ΤΕΚΝΩΝ in den Papyri,' *Aegyptus* 45, 171–89.

Sirks, B. (1989) "*Munera Publica* and Exemptions (*Vacatio, Excusatio* and *Immunitas*)," *Studies in Roman Law and Legal History in Honour of Ramon d'Abadal I de Vinyals, Annals of the Archive of Ferran Valls I Taberner's Library* 6, 79–111.

Sivan, H. (1996) "Why not Marry a Barbarian? Marital Frontiers in Late Antiquity (the Example of CTh 3.14.1)," in R.W. Mathisen and H. Sivan (eds.), *Shifting Frontiers in Late Antiquity*, Aldershot: Variorum, 136–45.

—— (1997) "Rabbinics and Roman Law: Jewish-Gentile/Christian Marriage in Late Antiquity," *Revue des Études Juives* 156, 59–100.

Spawforth, A.J.S. (1985) "Families at Roman Sparta and Epidauros: Some Prosopographical Notes," *Annual of the British School at Athens* 88, 191–258.

Talbert, R.J.A. (1984) *The Senate of Imperial Rome*, Princeton: Princeton University Press.

Taubenschlag, R. (1955) *The Law of Greco-Roman Egypt in the Light of the Papyri, 332 BC – 640 AD*, Warsaw: Panstowe Wydawnictwo Naukowe, 2nd edn.

—— (1959) "La compétence du *kyrios* dans le droit gréco-égyptien," in *Opera Minora II*, Warsaw: Panstowe Wydawnictwo Naukowe, 353–77.

Thomas, Yan (1986) "Le 'ventre,' Corps maternel, droit paternel," *Le genre humain* 14, 211–36.

—— (1992) "The Division of the Sexes in Roman Law," in P.S. Pantel (ed.), A. Goldhammer (trans.), *A History of Women in the West I. From Ancient Goddesses to Christian Saints*, Cambridge, MA and London: Harvard University Press; orig. pub. in French, 1990, 83–137.

Toynbee, J.M.C. (1971) *Death and Burial in the Roman World*, Ithaca: Cornell University Press; repr. 1996, Baltimore: Johns Hopkins University Press.

Treggiari, S.M. (1979) "Questions on Women Domestics in the Roman West," in *Schiavitù, Manomissione e Classi Dipedenti nel Mondo antico*, Rome: "L'Erma," di Bretschneider, 185–201.

—— (1981a) "*Concubinae*," *PBSR* 49, 59–81.

—— (1981b) "*Contubernales* in *CIL* 6," *Phoenix* 35, 42–69.

—— (1982) "Consent to Roman Marriage: Some Aspects of Law and Reality," *EMC/CV* 26, n.s. 1, 34–44.

—— (1984) "*Digna Condicio*: Betrothals in the Roman Upper Class," *EMC/CV* 28, n.s. 3, 419–51.

—— (1991a) *Roman Marriage: Iusti Coniuges from the Time of Cicero to the Time of Ulpian*, Oxford: Clarendon Press.

—— (1991b) "Divorce Roman Style: How Easy and How Frequent was It?," in Rawson 1991, 31–46.

Turpin, W. (1981) "Apokrimata, Decreta, and the Roman Legal Procedure," *BASP* 18, 145–60.

Walker, S. and Bierbrier, M. (1997) *Ancient Faces: Mummy Portraits from Roman Egypt*, London: British Museum Press.

Wallace-Hadrill, A. (1981) "Family and Inheritance in the Augustan Marriage Laws," *Proceedings of the Cambridge Philological Society*, 207, 58–80.

Watson, A. (1967) *The Law of Persons in the Later Roman Republic*, Oxford; Clarendon Press.

—— (1974a) "The Rescripts of the Emperor Probus," *Tulane Law Review* 48, 1122–8.

—— (1974b) *Law Making in the Late Roman Republic*, Oxford: Clarendon Press.

—— (1987) *Roman Slave Law*, Baltimore: Johns Hopkins University Press.

Weaver, P.R.C. (1972) *Familia Caesaris: A Social Study of the Emperor's Freedmen and Slaves*, Cambridge: Cambridge University Press.

—— (1986) "The Status of Children in Mixed Marriages," in Rawson 1986a, 145–69.

—— (1990) "Where have all the Junian Latins gone? Nomenclature and Status in the Roman Empire," *Chiron* 20, 275–305.

—— (1991) "Children of Freedmen (and Freedwomen)," in Rawson 1991, 166–90.

—— (1997) "Children of Junian Latins," in Rawson and Weaver 1997, 55–72.

Wegener, E.P. (1947) "Petition Concerning the Dowry of a Widow (P.Berl.Inv. 16.277)," *Mnemosyne* 13, 302–16.

Wehrli, C. (1986) *Les Papyrus de Genève, II*, Geneva: Bibliotheque Publique et Universitaire.

Welles, C.B., Fink, R.O., and Gilliam, J.F. (1959) *The Excavations at Dura-Europus, Final Report V. Part 1: The Parchments and Papyri* , New Haven: Yale University Press.

Wells, C.M. (1997) " 'The Daughters of the Regiment': Sisters and Wives in the Roman Army," in W. Groenman-van Waateringe, B.L. van Beek, W.J.H. Willem and S.L. Wynia (eds.), *Proceedings of the XVIth International Congress of Roman Frontier Studies*, Oxford: Oxbow Monographs 91, 571–4.

—— (1998) "Celibate Soldiers: Augustus and the Army," *American Journal of Ancient History* 14 [1989], 180–90.

Westermann, W.L. and Schiller, A.A. (1954) *Apokrimata: Decisions of Septimius Severus on Legal Matters*, New York: Columbia University Press.

Williams, W. (1974) "The *Libellus* Procedure and the Severan Papyri," *JRS* 64, 86–103.

Wistrand, E. (1976) *The So-Called Laudatio Turiae*, Göteburg: Studia Graeca et Latina Gothoburgensia 34.

Wolff, H.J. (1939) *Written and Unwritten Marriages in Hellenistic and Postclassical Roman Law*, Haverford, PA: American Philological Association.

—— (1950) "Doctrinal Trends in Postclassical Roman Marriage Law," *ZSSR.RA* 67, 261–319.

Yaron, R. (1964) "Reichsrecht, Volksrecht and Talmud," *RIDA* s. 3, 11, 281–98.

Yiftach, U. (1997) "The Role of the *Syngraphe* 'compiled through the *Hierothytai*,' " *ZPE* 115, 178–82.

Youtie, H.C. (1975) "Ἀπάτορες: Law vs. Custom in Roman Egypt," in *Le Monde Grec, Hommages à Claire Préaux*, Brussels, 723–40; repr. in *Scriptiunculae Posteriores*, vol. 1, Bonn: Habelt Verlag, 1981, 17–34.

INDEX OF SOURCES

GENERAL INDEX

165, 166, 174, 195, 196; after
divorce 191, 198–202, 205, 308 n.1;
and Augustan legislation 83–7,
103–4; guardianship of 14, 43, 44,
45; illegitimate 4, 41, 115, 119,
138, 139, 142, 144–5, 151, 154,
158, 162, 166–72, 174, 177, 180,
219, 240, 269, 279 n. 57, 321 n.65,
323 n.92; as purpose of marriage 81,
83, 122, 171–3, 188–9, 224; status
of in slave-free unions 143–5, 155,
158, 159, 173, 174, 176–80;
supposititious 261–9; and widowed
mothers 219–69; *see also* exposure;
inheritance; *ius liberorum; patria
potestas; tutela impuberum*
Christians 5–6, 14, 42, 73, 103,
108–10, 119, 130, 133, 141, 148,
162, 163–5, 168, 170–3, 174–6,
184–5, 187, 202–4, 208–10, 224,
232–3, 290 n.50, 300–1 n.42, 301
n.52, 306 n.123, 307 n.137
Cicero 69, 89, 281 n. 81
clarissima femina 7, 54, 72, 73, 75
Claudius 56, 137–8, 143, 145, 298 n.4,
309 n.4; on *tutela mulierum* 24–7, 35,
38, 44, 45, 55
Code of Justinian 3–6, 15, 24, 30, 38, 43,
44, 57, 113, 141, 160, 180, 187,
206, 280 n.73, 281 n.76, 301 n.49,
311 n.34; *see also* Index of sources
coemptio 14, 22, 26, 219, 271, 275
n.7–8, 316 n.3
Commodus 24, 41, 156; *see also* Marcus
Aurelius
concubinatus 92, 114, 150–4, 170–3,
175, 303 n.71, 304 n.85
concubines 27, 139, 150–4, 157–8,
169, 170–3, 175, 193, 299 n.26,
300 n.39, 303 n.70–1
consent: to marriage 83, 88–91, 103,
10–7, 115, 122, 129, 136, 152, 158,
181, 183–4, 192–3, 195, 270–1,
307 n.134, 309 n.7; to divorce 194,
195–8, 205, 271
Constantine 1, 3–4, 6, 14, 42, 44–6,
49, 52, 64, 79, 84, 103–5, 112–13,
129, 167–71, 179–80, 181–2,
202–4, 220, 228–9, 231, 232, 235,
285 n.138, 301 n.51, 302 n.63,
307–8 n.138, 311 n.36, 313 n.59,

315 n.84–5, 317 n.7; *see also* Index of
sources
Constantius II 165, 182, 185, 229, 300
n.41 and 43, 306 n.123, 319 n.332;
see also Index of sources
Constantius III 204–6, 208, 311–12
n.43; *see also* Index of sources
Constitutio Antoniniana see Caracalla,
Edict of
contubernium 13, 30, 138–9, 143–4,
146, 148, 173, 176–7, 303 n.78,
308 n.143
conubium 82, 136, 143, 152, 154–5,
158–9, 172–3, 177, 193–4, 287
n.11, 303 n.78, 305 n.109
curator minorum 23, 44, 45, 50, 90, 91,
105–7, 113, 129, 156, 220, 228,
242–3, 248, 257, 320–1 n.56
curialis see decurions

decurions 7–10, 31, 38, 40, 41, 51–2,
94, 171, 173, 236, 305 n.105, 306
n.116; see also *boule; duoviri*
deportation 173, 180, 181, 183, 203,
204, 311 n.35; *see also* exile
Digest 1–5, 15, 16, 23, 24, 30, 56, 60,
81, 92, 187, 243, 299 n.23, 308 n.1;
see also Index of sources
dikaion teknon 38, 42, 46; *see also* ius
liberorum
Diocletian 3, 4, 6, 14, 79, 140–1; and
Maximian 140, 161, 257; *see also*
Index of sources
divorce 4, 14, 84, 86, 91, 96, 102, 116,
147, 149, 160, 162, 187–218, 219,
223, 226, 267, 271, 280 n. 72, 291
n.62, 292 n.81; in marriage contracts
122–4, 127–30, 134; *see also* children
divorcées 84, 87, 220–1, 261, 264, 305
n.106, 311 n.40–41; *see also*
pregnancy
Domitian 30, 123, 256, 279 n. 57
donatio ante nuptias see gifts, pre-nuptial
dowry 24, 27, 30, 58, 81, 84, 90, 91–8,
101, 105, 109, 114–20, 122–31,
157, 175, 196–7, 224–6, 235–6,
250, 268, 303 n.72, 314 n.68, 316
n.6; after divorce 190–3, 199,
202–8, 211–15, 271, 309 n.6, 311
n.36–7, 312 n.45, 315 n.85; in
illegal unions 139, 144–5, 150, 158,
162–3